Microsoft

W9-AVB-292

Windows Server® 2008

Administrator's Pocket Consultant,
Second Edition

William R. Stanek
Author and Series Editor

PUBLISHED BY
Microsoft Press
A Division of Microsoft Corporation
One Microsoft Way
Redmond, Washington 98052-6399

Library of Congress Control Number: 2009939911

Printed and bound in the United States of America.

1 2 3 4 5 6 7 8 9   QWE   4 3 2 1 0 9

Distributed in Canada by H.B. Fenn and Company Ltd.

A CIP catalogue record for this book is available from the British Library.

Microsoft Press books are available through booksellers and distributors worldwide. For further
information about international editions, contact your local Microsoft Corporation office or contact
Microsoft Press International directly at fax (425) 936-7329. Visit our Web site at www.microsoft.
com/mspress. Send comments to mspinput@microsoft.com.

Acquisitions Editor: Martin DelRe
Developmental Editor: Karen Szall
Project Editor: Rosemary Caperton
Editorial Production: Publishing.com
Technical Reviewer: Bob Hogan; Technical Review services provided by Content Master,
                        a member of CM Group, Ltd.
Cover: Tom Draper Design

Body Part No. X16-38615

Contents

What do you think of this book? We want to hear from you!

Microsoft is interested in hearing your feedback so we can continually improve our
books and learning resources for you. To participate in a brief online survey, please visit:

microsoft.com/learning/booksurvey

Chapter 10 Creating User and Group Accounts   297

What do you think of this book? We want to hear from you!

Microsoft is interested in hearing your feedback so we can continually improve our
books and learning resources for you. To participate in a brief online survey, please visit:

microsoft.com/learning/booksurvey

Acknowledgments

Writing *Windows Server 2008 Administrator's Pocket Consultant* was a lot of fun, and updating the book for Windows Server 2008 Release 2 (R2) was even more so. As I set out to write *Windows Server 2008 Administrator's Pocket Consultant* and then to update the book for this second edition, my goal was to determine what had changed and what new administration options were available. As with any new release of an operating system, and especially with Windows Server 2008 R2, this meant a great deal of research to determine exactly how things work—and a lot of digging into the operating system internals. I was thankful I'd already written several books on Windows 7 and its new features, so I had a starting point of reference for my research, but by no means a complete one.

When you start working with Windows Server 2008 R2, you'll see at once that this operating system is different from previous releases of Windows Server. What won't be readily apparent, however, is just how different Windows Server 2008 R2 is from its predecessors—and that's because many of the most significant changes to the operating system are under the surface. These changes affect the underlying architecture, not just the user interfaces, and these changes were some of the hardest for me to research and write about.

Because Pocket Consultants are meant to be portable and readable—the kind of book you use to solve problems and get the job done wherever you might be—I had to carefully review my research to make sure I focused on the core of Windows Server 2008 R2 administration. The result is the book that you hold in your hand—a book that I hope you'll agree is one of the best practical, portable guides to Windows Server 2008 and Windows Server 2008 R2.

It is gratifying to see techniques that I've used time and again to solve problems put into a printed book so that others might benefit from them. But no man is an island, and this book couldn't have been written without help from some very special people. As I've stated in all my previous books with Microsoft Press, the team at Microsoft Press is top-notch. Throughout the writing process, Karen Szall and Rosemary Caperton were instrumental in helping me stay on track and in getting the tools I needed to write this book. They did a first-rate job managing the editorial process. Thanks also to Martin DelRe for believing in my work and shepherding it through production.

Unfortunately for the writer (but fortunately for readers), writing is only one part of the publishing process. Next came editing and author review. I must say, Microsoft Press has the most thorough editorial and technical review process I've seen anywhere—and I've written a lot of books for many different publishers. Bob Hogan was the technical reviewer for the book, Curtis Philips and John Pierce were the project managers, John was also the copy editor, and Andrea Fox was the proofreader.

I hope I haven't forgotten anyone, but if I have, it was an oversight. *Honest.* ;-)

Introduction

Welcome to *Windows Server 2008 Administrator's Pocket Consultant,* Second Edition. Over the years, I've written about many different server technologies and products, but the one product I like writing about the most is Windows Server. From top to bottom, Windows Server 2008 Release 2 (R2) is substantially different from earlier releases of Windows Server. For starters, many of the core components of Windows Server 2008 R2 are built off the same code base as Windows 7 rather than Windows Vista. This means that you can apply much of what you know about Windows 7 to Windows Server 2008 R2. That's good news, but you still need to learn how Windows Server 2008 R2 is different from previous releases of Windows Server, and while some of these differences are small, others are very important.

Because I've written many top-selling Windows Server books, I was able to bring a unique perspective to this book—the kind of perspective you gain only after working with technologies for many years. Long before there was a product called Windows Server 2008 Release 2, I was working with the beta product. From these early beginnings, the final version of Windows Server 2008 R2 evolved until it became the finished product that is available today.

As you've probably noticed, a great deal of information about Windows Server 2008 R2 is available on the Web and in other printed books. You can find tutorials, reference sites, discussion groups, and more to make using Windows Server 2008 R2 easier. However, the advantage of reading this book is that much of the information you need to learn about Windows Server 2008 R2 is organized in one place and presented in a straightforward and orderly fashion. This book has everything you need to customize Windows Server 2008 R2 installations, master Windows Server 2008 R2 configurations, and maintain Windows Server 2008 R2 servers.

In this book, I teach you how features work, why they work the way they do, and how to customize them to meet your needs. I also offer specific examples of how certain features can meet your needs, and how you can use other features to troubleshoot and resolve issues you might have. In addition, this book provides tips, best practices, and examples of how to optimize Windows Server 2008 R2. This book won't just teach you how to configure Windows Server 2008 R2, it will teach you how to squeeze every last bit of power out of it and make the most from the features and options it includes.

Unlike many other books about administering Windows Server 2008 R2, this book doesn't focus on a specific user level. This isn't a lightweight beginner book. Regardless of whether you are a beginning administrator or a seasoned professional, many of the concepts in this book will be valuable to you, and you can apply them to your Windows Server 2008 R2 installations.

Who Is This Book For?

Windows Server 2008 Administrator's Pocket Consultant, Second Edition covers the Foundation, Standard, Enterprise, Web, Datacenter, and Itanium-based editions of Windows Server 2008 R2. The book is designed for the following readers:

- Current Windows system administrators
- Accomplished users who have some administrator responsibilities
- Administrators upgrading to Windows Server 2008 R2 from previous versions
- Administrators transferring from other platforms

To pack in as much information as possible, I had to assume that you have basic networking skills and a basic understanding of Windows Server. With this in mind, I don't devote entire chapters to explaining Windows Server architecture, Windows Server startup and shutdown, or why you want to use Windows Server. I do, however, cover Windows server configuration, Group Policy, security, auditing, data backup, system recovery, and much more.

I also assume that you are fairly familiar with Windows commands and procedures as well as the Windows user interface. If you need help learning Windows basics, you should read other resources (many of which are available from Microsoft Press).

NOTE This book has been completely updated for Windows Server 2008 R2. If you are using Windows Server 2008 RTM, features and procedures will vary slightly. However, you can still use this book to help you with Windows Server 2008 RTM.

How This Book Is Organized

Rome wasn't built in a day, and this book wasn't intended to be read in a day, in a week, or even in a month. Ideally, you'll read this book at your own pace, a little each day as you work your way through all the features Windows Server 2008 R2 has to offer. This book is organized into 20 chapters. The chapters are arranged in a logical order, taking you from planning and deployment tasks to configuration and maintenance tasks.

Speed and ease of reference are essential parts of this hands-on guide. This book has an expanded table of contents and an extensive index for finding answers to problems quickly. Many other quick reference features have been added to the book as well, including quick step-by-step procedures, lists, tables with fast facts, and extensive cross references.

As with all Pocket Consultants, *Windows Server 2008 Administrator's Pocket Consultant,* Second Edition is designed to be a concise and easy-to-use resource for managing Windows servers. This is the readable resource guide that you'll want on your desktop at all times. The book covers everything you need to perform the core administrative tasks for Windows servers. Because the focus is on giving you maximum value in a pocket-size guide, you don't have to wade through hundreds of pages of extraneous information to find what you're looking for. Instead, you'll find exactly what you need to get the job done, and you'll find it quickly.

In short, the book is designed to be the one resource you turn to whenever you have questions regarding Windows Server administration. To this end, the book zeroes in on daily administration procedures, frequently performed tasks, documented examples, and options that are representative while not necessarily inclusive. One of my goals is to keep the content so concise that the book remains compact and easy to navigate while at the same time ensuring that it is packed with as much information as possible. This means you get a valuable resource guide that can help you quickly and easily perform common tasks, solve problems, and implement advanced Windows technologies.

Conventions Used in This Book

I've used a variety of elements to help keep the text clear and easy to follow. You'll find code terms and listings in monospace type, except when I tell you to actually type a command. In that case, the command appears in **bold** type. When I introduce and define a new term, I put it in *italics*.

> **NOTE** Group Policy now includes both policies and preferences. Under the Computer Configuration and User Configuration nodes, you find two nodes: Policies and Preferences. Settings for general policies are listed under the Policies node. Settings for general preferences are listed under the Preferences node. When referencing settings under the Policies node, I use shortcut references, such as User Configuration\Administrative Templates\Windows Components, or specify that the policies are found in the Administrative Templates for User Configuration under Windows Components. Both references tell you that the policy setting being discussed is under User Configuration rather than Computer Configuration and can be found under Administrative Templates\Windows Components.

Other conventions include the following:

Best Practices To examine the best technique to use when working with advanced configuration and administration concepts

Caution To warn you about potential problems you should look out for

More Info To provide more information on a subject

Note To provide additional details on a particular point that needs emphasis

Real World To provide real-world advice when discussing advanced topics

Security Alert To point out important security issues

Tip To offer helpful hints or additional information

I truly hope you find that *Windows Server 2008 Administrator's Pocket Consultant,* Second Edition provides everything you need to perform the essential administrative tasks on Windows servers as quickly and efficiently as possible. You are welcome to send your thoughts to me at *williamstanek@aol.com* or follow me at *twitter.com/WilliamStanek*. Thank you.

Other Resources

No single magic bullet for learning everything you'll ever need to know about Windows Server 2008 R2 exists. While some books are offered as all-in-one guides, there's simply no way one book can do it all. With this in mind, I hope you use this book as it is intended to be used—as a concise and easy-to-use resource. It covers everything you need to perform core administration tasks for Windows servers, but it is by no means exhaustive.

Your current knowledge will largely determine your success with this or any other Windows resource or book. As you encounter new topics, take the time to practice what you've learned and read about. Seek out further information as necessary to get the practical hands-on know-how and knowledge you need.

I recommend that you regularly visit Microsoft's Web site for Windows Server (*microsoft.com/windowsserver/*) and *support.microsoft.com* to stay current with the latest changes. To help you get the most out of this book, you can visit my corresponding Web site at *williamstanek.com/windows*. This site contains information about Windows Server 2008 R2 and updates to the book.

Support for This Book

Every effort has been made to ensure the accuracy of this book. As corrections or changes are collected, they will be added to a Microsoft Knowledge Base article accessible via the Microsoft Help and Support site. Microsoft Press provides support for books, including instructions for finding Knowledge Base articles, at the following Web site:

http://www.microsoft.com/learning/support/books/

If you have questions regarding the book that are not answered by visiting this site or viewing a Knowledge Base article, send them to Microsoft Press via e-mail to *mspinput@microsoft.com*.

Please note that Microsoft software product support is not offered through these addresses.

We Want to Hear from You

We welcome your feedback about this book. Please share your comments and ideas via the following short survey:

http://www.microsoft.com/learning/booksurvey

Your participation will help Microsoft Press create books that better meet your needs and your standards.

> **NOTE** We hope that you will give us detailed feedback via our survey. If you have questions about our publishing program, upcoming titles, or Microsoft Press in general, we encourage you to interact with us via Twitter at *twitter.com/MicrosoftPress*. For support issues, use only the e-mail address shown above.

CHAPTER 1

Windows Server 2008 R2 Administration Overview

Windows Server 2008 Release 2 (R2) is a powerful, versatile, full-featured server operating system that builds on the enhancements that Microsoft provided in Windows Server 2008. Windows Server 2008 R2 and Windows 7 share a number of common features because they were part of a single development project. These features share a common code base and extend across many areas of the operating systems, including management, security, networking, and storage. You can apply much of what you know about Windows 7 to Windows Server 2008 R2.

This chapter covers getting started with Windows Server 2008 R2 and explores the extent to which the architectural changes affect how you work with and manage Windows Server 2008 R2. Throughout this and the other chapters of this book, you'll also find discussions of the many security changes. These discussions introduce techniques for enhancing all aspects of computer security, including physical security, information security, and network security. Although this book focuses on Windows Server 2008 R2 administration, the tips and techniques it presents can help anyone who supports, develops for, or works with the Windows Server 2008 R2 operating system.

Windows Server 2008 R2 and Windows 7

Like Windows 7, Windows Server 2008 R2 has a revolutionary architecture that uses the following features:

- **Modularization for language independence and disk imaging for hardware independence**   Each component of the operating system is designed as an independent module that you can easily add or remove. This functionality provides the basis for the configuration architecture in Windows Server 2008 R2. Microsoft distributes Windows Server 2008 R2 on media with Windows Imaging Format (WIM) disk images that use compression and single-instance storage to dramatically reduce the size of image files.

- **Preinstallation and preboot environments**   The Windows Preinstallation Environment 3.0 (Windows PE 3.0) replaces MS-DOS as the preinstallation environment and provides a bootable startup environment for installation, deployment, recovery, and troubleshooting. The Windows Preboot Environment provides a startup environment with a boot manager that lets you choose which boot application to run to load the operating system. On systems with multiple operating systems, you access pre–Windows 7 operating systems in the boot environment by using the legacy operating system entry.

- **User account controls and elevation of privileges**   User Account Control (UAC) enhances computer security by ensuring true separation of standard user and administrator user accounts. Through UAC, all applications run using either standard user or administrator user privileges, and you see a security prompt by default whenever you run an application that requires administrator privileges. The way the security prompt works depends on Group Policy settings. Additionally, if you log on using the built-in Administrator account, you typically do not see elevation prompts.

In Windows 7 and Windows Server 2008 R2, features with common code bases have identical management interfaces. In fact, just about every Control Panel utility that is available in Windows Server 2008 R2 is identical to or nearly identical to its Windows 7 counterpart. Of course, exceptions exist in some cases for standard default settings. Because Windows Server 2008 R2 does not use performance ratings, Windows servers do not have Windows Experience Index scores. Because Windows Server 2008 R2 does not use Sleep or related states, Windows servers do not have sleep, hibernate, or resume functionality. Because you typically do not want to use extended power management options on Windows servers, Windows Server 2008 R2 has a limited set of power options. Further, Windows Server 2008 R2 does not include the Windows Aero enhancements (Aero Glass, Flip, 3D Flip, and so on), Windows Sidebar, Windows Gadgets, or other user interface enhancements because Windows Server 2008 R2 is designed to provide optimal performance for server-related tasks and is not designed for extensive personalization of the desktop appearance. That said, you can install the Desktop Experience feature on a Windows server and then enable some Windows 7 features on your server. For more information, see Chapter 2, "Deploying Windows Server 2008 R2."

Because the common features of Windows 7 and Windows Server 2008 R2 have so many similarities, I will not cover changes in the interface from previous operating system releases, discuss how UAC works, and so on. You can find extensive coverage of these features in *Windows 7 Administrator's Pocket Consultant* (Microsoft Press, 2009), which I encourage you to use in conjunction with this book. In addition to its coverage of broad administration tasks, *Windows 7 Administrator's Pocket Consultant* examines how to customize the operating system and Windows environment, configure hardware and network devices, manage user access and global settings, configure laptops and mobile networking, use remote management and remote assistance capabilities, troubleshoot system problems, and much more. This book, on the other hand, zeroes in on directory services administration, data administration, and network administration.

Getting to Know Windows Server 2008 R2

The Windows Server 2008 R2 operating system includes several different editions. Each edition has a specific purpose, as described here:

- **Windows Server 2008 R2 Foundation** This edition is designed to provide a cost-effective, entry-level foundation for small businesses. While this edition does not support Active Directory Federation Services or Hyper-V, it does support all other primary server roles, with some limitations. The Foundation edition can be used to deploy certificate authorities, but it cannot host other related services.

- **Windows Server 2008 R2 Standard** This edition is designed to provide services and resources to other systems on a network. This edition has a rich set of features and configuration options as well as support for all primary server roles, with some limitations. Like the Foundation edition, the Standard edition can be used to deploy certificate authorities, but it cannot host other related services.

- **Windows Server 2008 R2 Enterprise** The Enterprise edition extends the features provided in Windows Server 2008 R2 Standard to provide greater scalability and availability and add support for additional services, such as Failover Clustering and Active Directory Federation Services.

- **Windows Server 2008 R2 Datacenter** This is the most robust Windows server operating system. It has enhanced clustering features and supports very large memory configurations and large numbers of processors.

- **Windows Server 2008 R2 for Itanium-Based Systems** This edition is an enterprise-class platform for hosting business-critical applications and implementing large-scale virtualization solutions. Because this edition is not designed to provide core services, it supports only the Application Server and Web Server (IIS) roles. No other roles are supported at the time of this writing.

- **Windows Web Server 2008 R2**   This is the Web edition of Windows Server 2008 R2. This edition is designed to provide Web services for deploying Web sites and Web-based applications and supports only related features. Specifically, this edition includes the Microsoft .NET Framework, IIS, ASP.NET, Application Server, and network load-balancing roles and features, as well as DNS Server, Windows Server Update Services, and Media Services. However, this edition lacks many other features, including Active Directory, and you need to use the Windows Server Core Installation option to obtain some standard functionality.

NOTE   Windows Server 2008 R2 is Microsoft's first 64-bit-only operating system. In this book, I refer to 64-bit systems designed for the x64 architecture as *64-bit systems* and 64-bit systems designed for Itanium-based systems as *Itanium 64-bit (IA64)* systems. Support for Itanium 64-bit (IA64) processors is no longer standard in Windows operating systems. Microsoft has developed a separate edition of Windows Server 2008 R2 for Itanium-based computers, and this edition is meant to provide specific server functions. As a result, some server roles and features might not be supported for IA64 systems.

Table 1-1 provides a quick reference for additional differences between the various server editions. The table is not meant to be all inclusive. Additionally, it is important to note that all Windows Server 2008 R2 editions support multiple processor cores. For example, although Foundation supports only one discrete-socketed processor (also referred to as a *physical processor*), that one processor could have eight processor cores (also referred to as *logical processors*). With the Datacenter and Itanium-based editions, the maximum number of processor cores supported is 256.

TABLE 1-1 Important Differences Between Windows Server Editions

FEATURE	STAN-DARD	ENTER-PRISE	DATA-CENTER	WEB	ITANIUM	FOUN-DATION
Active Directory Rights Manage-ment Services	Yes	Yes	Yes	No	No	Yes
BranchCache content server	Yes	Yes	Yes	Yes	Yes	Yes
BranchCache hosted server	No	Yes	Yes	No	No	No
Cross-file replication	No	Yes	Yes	No	Yes	No
DirectAccess	Yes	Yes	Yes	No	No	No
Failover cluster nodes	N/A	16	8	N/A	N/A	N/A

FEATURE	STAN-DARD	ENTER-PRISE	DATA-CENTER	WEB	ITANIUM	FOUN-DATION
Fault tolerant memory sync	No	Yes	Yes	No	Yes	No
Hot add memory	No	Yes	Yes	No	Yes	No
Hot add processors	No	No	Yes	No	Yes	No
Hot replace memory	No	No	Yes	No	Yes	No
Hot replace processors	No	No	Yes	No	Yes	No
Hyper-V	Yes	Yes	Yes	No	No	No
IAS connections	50	Unlimited	Unlimited	N/A	2	10
Languages	Standard	Standard	Standard	Standard	Limited	Standard
RAM	32 GB	2 TB	2 TB	32 GB	2 TB	8 GB
Remote Desktop Services Gateway	250	Unlimited	Unlimited	N/A	N/A	50
Retail purchase	Yes	Yes	No	Yes	No	No
Routing and Remote Access (RRAS) connections	250	Unlimited	Unlimited	N/A	N/A	50
Server core	Yes	Yes	Yes	Yes	No	No
Socketed processors	4	8	64	4	64	1
Stand-alone DFS roots	1	Unlimited	Unlimited	N/A	N/A	1
Virtualization images	Host + 1 VM	Host + 4 VM	Unlimited	Guest only	Unlimited	N/A
Volume licensing	Yes	Yes	Yes	Yes	Yes	No
Windows PowerShell	Yes	Yes	Yes	Yes	Yes	Yes
WINS Server	Yes	Yes	Yes	No	No	Yes

Because the various server editions support the same core features and administration tools, you can use the techniques discussed in this book regardless of which Windows Server 2008 R2 edition you're using. Because you can't install Active Directory on the Web edition, you can't make a server running Windows Web Server 2008 R2 a domain controller. A Web server can, however, be part of an Active Directory domain.

When you install a Windows Server 2008 R2 system, you configure the system according to its role on the network, as the following guidelines describe.

- Servers are generally assigned to be part of a workgroup or a domain.

- Workgroups are loose associations of computers in which each individual computer is managed separately.

- Domains are collections of computers that you can manage collectively by means of domain controllers, which are Windows Server 2008 R2 systems that manage access to the network, to the directory database, and to shared resources.

NOTE In this book, *Windows Server 2008 R2* and *Windows Server 2008 R2 family* refer to five products: Windows Server 2008 R2 Foundation, Windows Server 2008 R2 Standard, Windows Server 2008 R2 Enterprise, Windows Server 2008 R2 Datacenter, and Windows Web Server 2008 R2. The various server editions support the same core features and administration tools.

Unlike Windows Server 2008, Windows Server 2008 R2 uses only the simple Start menu (rather than the classic Start menu or the simple Start menu). The simple Start menu allows you to directly access commonly used programs and directly execute common tasks. You can, for example, click Start and then click Computer to access a server's hard drives and devices with removable storage.

With the simple Start menu, you access administrative tools by clicking Start and then clicking Administrative Tools. You access Control Panel by clicking Start and then clicking Control Panel.

Logoff is the default action for Windows Server 2008 R2. This is an important change, allowing you to click Start and then click Logoff. Press the server's physical power button to initiate an orderly shutdown by logging off and then shutting down. If you are using a desktop-class system and the computer has a sleep button, the sleep button is disabled by default. Additionally, servers are configured to turn off the display after 10 minutes of inactivity.

Windows 7 and Windows Server 2008 R2 support the Advanced Configuration and Power Interface (ACPI) 4.0 specification. Windows uses ACPI to control system and device power state transitions, putting devices in and out of full-power (working), low-power, and off states to reduce power consumption.

The power settings for a computer come from the active power plan. You can access power plans in Control Panel by clicking System And Security and then clicking Power Options. Windows Server 2008 R2 includes the Power Configuration (Powercfg.exe) utility for managing power options from the command line. At a command prompt, you can view the configured power plans by typing **powercfg –l**. The active power plan is marked with an asterisk.

The default, active power plan in Windows Server 2008 R2 is called Balanced. The Balanced plan is configured to do the following:

- Never turn off hard disks (as opposed to turning off hard disks after a specified amount of idle time).

- Enable timed events to wake the computer (as opposed to disabling wake on timed events)

- Enable USB selective suspend (as opposed to disabling selective suspend)

- Use moderate power savings for idle PCI Express links (as opposed to maximum power savings being on or off)

- Use active system cooling by increasing the fan speed before slowing processors (as opposed to using passive system cooling to slow the processors before increasing fan speed)

- Use a minimum processor and maximum processor state if supported (as opposed to using a fixed state)

NOTE Power consumption is an important issue, especially as organizations try to become more earth friendly. Saving power also can save your organization money and, in some cases, allow you to install more servers in your data centers. If you install Windows Server 2008 R2 on a laptop—for testing or for your personal desktop, for example—your power settings will be slightly different, and you'll also have settings for when the laptop is running on battery.

Power Management Options

When working with power management, important characteristics to focus on include the following:

- Cooling modes
- Device states
- Processor states

ACPI defines active and passive cooling modes. These cooling modes are inversely related to each other:

- Passive cooling reduces system performance but is quieter because there's less fan noise. With passive cooling, Windows lessens power consumption to reduce the operating temperature of the computer but at the cost of system performance. Here, Windows reduces the processor speed in an attempt to cool the computer before increasing fan speed, which would increase power consumption.

- Active cooling allows maximum system performance. With active cooling, Windows increases power consumption to reduce the temperature of the machine. Here, Windows increases fan speed to cool the computer before attempting to reduce processor speed.

Power policy includes an upper and a lower limit for the processor state, referred to as the *maximum processor state* and the *minimum processor state*, respectively. These states are implemented by making use of a feature of ACPI 3.0 (and later versions) called *processor throttling,* and they determine the range of currently available processor performance states that Windows may use. By setting the maximum and minimum values, you define the bounds for the allowed performance states, or you can use the same value for each to force the system to remain in a specific performance state. Windows reduces power consumption by throttling the processor speed. For example, if the upper bound is 100 percent and the lower bound is 5 percent, Windows can throttle the processor within this range as workloads permit to reduce power consumption. In a computer with a 3 GHz processor, Windows would adjust the operating frequency of the processor between .15 GHz and 3.0 GHz.

Processor throttling and related performance states were introduced with Windows XP and are not new to Windows 7 or Windows Server 2008 R2, but these early implementations were designed for computers with discrete-socketed processors and not for computers with processor cores. As a result, they are not effective in reducing the power consumption of computers with logical processors. Windows 7 and Windows Server 2008 R2 reduce power consumption in computers with multicore processors by leveraging a feature of ACPI 4.0 called *logical processor idling* and by updating processor throttling features to work with processor cores.

Logical processor idling is designed to ensure that Windows uses the fewest number of processor cores for a given workload. Windows accomplishes this by consolidating workloads onto the fewest cores possible and suspending inactive processor cores. As additional processing power is required, Windows activates inactive processor cores. This idling functionality works in conjunction with management of process performance states at the core level.

ACPI defines processor performance states, referred to as *p-states,* and processor idle sleep states, referred to as *c-states.* Processor performance states include P0 (the processor/core uses its maximum performance capability and may consume maximum power), P1 (the processor/core is limited below its maximum and consumes less than maximum power), and Pn (where state *n* is a maximum number that is processor dependent, and the processor/core is at its minimal level and consumes minimal power while remaining in an active state).

Processor idle sleep states include C0 (the processor/core can execute instructions), C1 (the processor/core has the lowest latency and is in a nonexecuting power state), C2 (the processor/core has longer latency to improve power savings over the C1 state), and C3 (the processor/core has the longest latency to improve power savings over the C1 and C2 states).

MORE INFO ACPI 4.0 was finalized in June 2009. Computers manufactured prior to this time will likely not have firmware that is fully compliant, and you will probably need to update the firmware when a compatible revision becomes available. In some cases, and especially with older hardware, you might not be able to update a computer's firmware to make it fully compliant with ACPI 4.0. For example, if you are configuring the power options and you don't have minimum and maximum processor state options, the computer's firmware isn't fully compatible with ACPI 3.0 and likely will not fully support ACPI 4.0 either. Still, you should check the hardware manufacturer's Web site for firmware updates.

Windows switches processors/cores between any p-state and from the C1 state to the C0 state nearly instantaneously (fractions of milliseconds) and tends not to use the deep sleep states, so you don't need to worry about performance impact to throttle or wake up processors/cores. The processors/cores are available when they are needed. That said, the easiest way to limit processor power management is to modify the active power plan and set the minimum and maximum processor states to 100 percent.

Logical processor idling is used to reduce power consumption by removing a logical processor from the operating system's list of nonprocessor-affinitized work. However, because processor-affinitized work reduces the effectiveness of this feature, you'll want to plan carefully prior to configuring processing affinity settings for applications. Windows System Resource Manager allows you to manage processor resources through percent processor usage targets and processor affinity rules. Both techniques reduce the effectiveness of logical processor idling.

Windows saves power by putting processor cores in and out of appropriate p- and c-states. On a computer with four logical processors, Windows may use p-states 0 to 5, where P0 allows 100 percent usage, P1 allows 90 percent usage, P2 allows 80 percent usage, P3 allows 70 percent usage, P4 allows 60 percent usage, and P5 allows 50 percent usage. When the computer is active, logical processor 0 would likely be active with a p-state of 0 to 5, and the other processors would likely be at an appropriate p-state or in a sleep state. Figure 1-1 shows an example. Here, logical processor 1 is running at 90 percent, logical processor 2 is running at 80 percent, logical processor 3 is running at 50 percent, and logical processor 4 is in the sleep state.

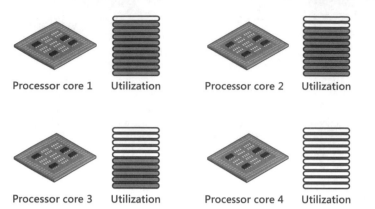

Processor core 1   Utilization   Processor core 2   Utilization

Processor core 3   Utilization   Processor core 4   Utilization

FIGURE 1-1 Understanding processor states

REAL WORLD   ACPI 4.0 defines four global power states. In G0, the working state in which software runs, power consumption is at its highest, and latency is at its lowest. In G1, the sleeping state, in which software doesn't run, latency varies with sleep state, and power consumption is less than the G0 state. In G2 (also referred to as S5 sleep state), the soft off state where the operating system doesn't run, latency is long, and power consumption is very near zero. In G3, the mechanical off state, where the operating system doesn't run, latency is long, and power consumption is zero. There's also a special global state, known as S4 nonvolatile sleep, in which the operating system writes all system context to a file on nonvolatile storage media, allowing system context to be saved and restored.

Within the global sleeping state, G1, are sleep state variations. S1 is a sleeping state where all system context is maintained. S2 is a sleeping state similar to S1 except that the CPU and system cache contexts are lost and control starts from a reset. S3 is a sleeping state where all CPU, cache, and chip set context are lost and hardware maintains memory context and restores some CPU and L2 cache configuration context. S4 is a sleeping state in which it is assumed that the hardware has powered off all devices to reduce power usage to a minimum and only the platform context is maintained. S5 is a sleeping state in which it is assumed that the hardware is in a soft off state where no context is maintained and requires a complete boot when it wakes.

Devices have power states as well. D0, the fully on state, consumes the highest level of power. D1 and D2 are intermediate states that many devices do not use. D3hot is a power-saving state where the device is software enumerable and can optionally preserve device context. D3 is the off state where the device context is lost and the operating system must reinitialize the device to turn it back on.

Networking Tools and Protocols

Like Windows 7, Windows Server 2008 R2 has a suite of networking tools that includes Network Explorer, Network And Sharing Center, Network Map, and Network Diagnostics. Figure 1-2 shows Network And Sharing Center.

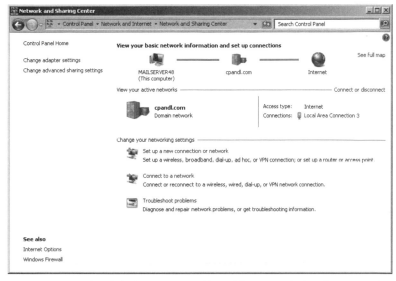

FIGURE 1-2 Network And Sharing Center provides quick access to sharing, discovery, and networking options.

Understanding Networking Options

The sharing and discovery configuration in Network And Sharing Center controls basic network settings. When network discovery settings are turned on and a server is connected to a network, the server can see other network computers and devices and is visible on the network. When sharing settings are turned on or off, the various sharing options are allowed or restricted. As discussed in Chapter 15, "Data Sharing, Security, and Auditing," sharing options include file sharing, public folder sharing, printer sharing, and password-protected sharing.

In Windows 7 and Windows Server 2008 R2, networks are identified as one of the following network types:

- **Domain** A network in which computers are connected to the corporate domain to which they are joined.

- **Work** A private network in which computers are configured as members of a workgroup and are not connected directly to the public Internet.

- **Home** A private network in which computers are configured as members of a homegroup and are not connected directly to the public Internet.

- **Public** A public network in which computers are connected to a network in a public place, such as a coffee shop or an airport, rather than an internal network.

These network types are organized into three categories: home or work, domain, and public. Each network category has an associated network profile. Because a computer saves sharing and firewall settings separately for each network category, you can use different block and allow settings for each network category. When you connect to a network, you see a dialog box that allows you to specify the network category. If you select Private, and the computer determines that it is connected to the corporate domain to which it is joined, the network category is set as Domain Network.

Based on the network category, Windows Server configures settings that turn discovery on or off. The On (enabled) state means that the computer can discover other computers and devices on the network and that other computers on the network can discover the computer. The Off (disabled) state means that the computer cannot discover other computers and devices on the network and that other computers on the network cannot discover the computer.

Using either the Network window or Advanced Sharing Settings in Network And Sharing Center, you can enable discovery and file sharing. However, discovery and file sharing are blocked by default on a public network, which enhances security by preventing computers on the public network from discovering other computers and devices on that network. When discovery and file sharing are disabled, files and printers that you have shared from a computer cannot be accessed from the network. Additionally, some programs might not be able to access the network.

Working with Networking Protocols

To allow a server to access a network, you must install TCP/IP networking and a network adapter. Windows Server 2008 R2 uses TCP/IP as the default wide area network (WAN) protocol. Normally, networking is installed during installation of the operating system. You can also install TCP/IP networking through local area connection properties.

The TCP and IP protocols make it possible for computers to communicate across various networks and the Internet by using network adapters. Like Windows 7, Windows Server 2008 R2 has a dual IP-layer architecture in which both Internet Protocol version 4 (IPv4) and Internet Protocol version 6 (IPv6) are implemented and share common transport and network layers. IPv4 has 32-bit addresses and is the primary version of IP used on most networks, including the Internet. IPv6, on the other hand, has 128-bit addresses and is the next generation version of IP.

REAL WORLD The TCP Chimney Offload feature was introduced with Windows Vista and Windows Server 2008. This feature enables the networking subsystem to offload the processing of a TCP/IP connection from the computer's processors to its network adapter as long as the network adapter supports TCP/IP offload processing. Both TCP/IPv4 connections and TCP/IPv6 connections can be offloaded. For Windows 7 and Windows Server 2008 R2, TCP connections are offloaded by default on 10 gigabits per second (Gbps) network adapters, but they are not offloaded by default on 1 Gbps network adapters. To offload TCP connections on a 1 Gbps network adapter, you must enable TCP offloading by entering the following command at an elevated, administrator command prompt: **netsh int tcp set global chimney=enabled**. You can check the status of TCP offloading by entering **netsh int tcp show global**. While TCP offloading works with Windows Firewall, TCP offloading won't be used with IPSec, Windows virtualization (Hyper-V), network load balancing, or Network Address Translation (NAT) service. To determine whether TCP offloading is working, enter **netstat-t** and check the offload state. The offload state is listed as offloaded or inhost.

Windows also uses receive-side scaling (RSS) and network direct memory access (NetDMA). You can enable or disable RSS by entering **netsh int tcp set global rss=enabled** or **netsh int tcp set global rss=disabled,** respectively. To check the status of RSS, enter **netsh int tcp show global**. You can enable or disable NetDMA by setting a DWord value under the EnableTCPA registry entry to **1** or **0**, respectively. This registry entry is found under HKEY_LOCAL_MACHINE\SYSTEM\ CurrentControlSet\Services\Tcpip\Parameters.

IPv4's 32-bit addresses are commonly expressed as four separate decimal values, such as 127.0.0.1 or 192.168.10.52. The four decimal values are referred to as *octets* because each represents 8 bits of the 32-bit number. With standard unicast IPv4 addresses, a variable part of the IP address represents the network ID and a variable part of the IP address represents the host ID. A host's IPv4 address and the internal machine (MAC) address used by the host's network adapter have no correlation.

IPv6's 128-bit addresses are divided into eight 16-bit blocks delimited by colons. Each 16-bit block is expressed in hexadecimal form, such as FEC0:0:0:02BC:FF:BECB:FE4F:961D. With standard unicast IPv6 addresses, the first 64 bits represent the network ID and the last 64 bits represent the network interface. Because many IPv6 address blocks are set to 0, a contiguous set of 0 blocks can be expressed as "::", a notation referred to as *double-colon notation*. Using double-colon notation, the two 0 blocks in the previous address can be compressed as FEC0::02BC:FF:BECB:FE4F:961D. Three or more 0 blocks would be compressed in the same way. For example, FFE8:0:0:0:0:0:0:1 becomes FFE8::1.

When networking hardware is detected during installation of the operating system, both IPv4 and IPv6 are enabled by default; you don't need to install a separate component to enable support for IPv6. The modified IP architecture in Windows 7 and Windows Server 2008 R2 is referred to as the *Next Generation TCP/IP stack*, and it includes many enhancements that improve the way IPv4 and IPv6 are used.

Domain Controllers, Member Servers, and Domain Services

When you install Windows Server 2008 R2 on a new system, you can configure the server to be a member server, a domain controller, or a stand-alone server. The differences between these types of servers are extremely important. Member servers are part of a domain but don't store directory information. Domain controllers are distinguished from member servers because they store directory information and provide authentication and directory services for the domain. Stand-alone servers aren't part of a domain. Because stand-alone servers have their own user databases, they authenticate logon requests independently.

Working with Active Directory

Windows Server 2008 R2 doesn't designate primary or backup domain controllers. Instead, Windows Server 2008 R2 supports a multimaster replication model. In this model, any domain controller can process directory changes and then replicate those changes to other domain controllers automatically. This differs from the Windows NT single master replication model, in which the primary domain controller stores a master copy and backup controllers store backup copies of the master. In addition, Windows NT distributed only the Security Account Manager (SAM) database, but Windows 2000 and later releases of Windows Server distribute an entire directory of information, called a *data store*. Inside the data store are sets of objects representing user, group, and computer accounts as well as shared resources such as servers, files, and printers.

Domains that use Active Directory are referred to as *Active Directory domains*. This distinguishes them from Windows NT domains. Although Active Directory domains can function with only one domain controller, you can and should configure multiple domain controllers in the domain. This way, if one domain controller fails, you can rely on the other domain controllers to handle authentication and other critical tasks.

Microsoft changed Active Directory in several fundamental ways for the original release of Windows Server 2008. As a result, Microsoft realigned the directory functionality and created a family of related services, including:

- **Active Directory Certificate Services (AD CS)** AD CS provides functions necessary for issuing and revoking digital certificates for users, client computers, and servers. AD CS uses certificate authorities (CAs), which are responsible for confirming the identity of users and computers and then issuing certificates to confirm these identities. Domains have enterprise root CAs, which are the certificate servers at the root of certificate hierarchies for domains and the most trusted certificate servers in the enterprise, and subordinate CAs, which are members of a particular enterprise certificate hierarchy. Workgroups have stand-alone root CAs, which are the certificate servers at the root of nonenterprise certificate hierarchies, and stand-alone subordinate CAs, which are members of a particular nonenterprise certificate hierarchy.

- **Active Directory Domain Services (AD DS)** AD DS provides the essential directory services necessary for establishing a domain, including the data store that stores information about objects on the network and makes that information available to users. AD DS uses domain controllers to manage access to network resources. Once users authenticate themselves by logging on to a domain, their stored credentials can be used to access resources on the network. Because AD DS is the heart of Active Directory and is required for directory-enabled applications and technologies, I typically refer to it simply as Active Directory rather than Active Directory Domain Services or AD DS.

- **Active Directory Federation Services (AD FS)** AD FS complements the authentication and access management features of AD DS by extending them to the World Wide Web. AD FS uses Web agents to provide users with access to internally hosted Web applications and proxies to manage client access. Once AD FS is configured, users can use their digital identities to authenticate themselves over the Web and access internally hosted Web applications with a Web browser such as Internet Explorer.

- **Active Directory Lightweight Directory Services (AD LDS)** AD LDS provides a data store for directory-enabled applications that do not require AD DS and do not need to be deployed on domain controllers. AD LDS does not run as an operating system service and can be used in both domain and workgroup environments. Each application that runs on a server can have its own data store implemented through AD LDS.

- **Active Directory Rights Management Services (AD RMS)** AD RMS provides a layer of protection for an organization's information that can extend beyond the enterprise, allowing e-mail messages, documents, intranet Web pages, and more to be protected from unauthorized access. AD RMS uses a certificate service to issue rights account certificates that identify trusted users, groups, and services; a licensing service that provides authorized users, groups, and services with access to protected information; and a logging service to monitor and maintain the rights management service. Once trust has been established, users with a rights account certificate can assign rights to information. These rights control which users can access the information and what they can do with it. Users with rights account certificates can also access protected content to which they've been granted access. Encryption ensures that access to protected information is controlled both inside and outside the enterprise.

Microsoft introduced additional changes in Windows Server 2008 R2. These changes include a new domain functional level, called *Windows Server 2008 R2 domain functional level*, and a new forest functional level, called *Windows Server 2008 R2 forest functional level*. Other changes include the following:

- **Active Directory Administrative Center**   Provides a task-based approach for managing users, groups, computers, and organizational units. Although similar to Active Directory Users And Computers, this console uses the Active Directory module for Windows PowerShell to manage tasks. It also requires Windows Remote Management (WinRM) and Active Directory Web Services (AD WS) to be properly configured. WinRM provides the capabilities needed to remotely manage computers using Windows PowerShell. AD WS provides a Web services interface for AD DS and AD LDS.

- **Active Directory Recycle Bin**   Stores deleted objects in a recycle bin, allowing administrators to undo accidental deletion of Active Directory objects. Requires Windows Server 2008 R2 forest functional level.

- **Authentication Mechanism Assurance**   Makes it possible to control access to resources based on authentication type and authentication strength. Administrators can assign related values to security identifiers for users, groups, and computers, and these values are added to Kerberos tickets for use by applications.

- **Managed service accounts**   Improves management of service accounts by allowing administrators to create one managed service account for each service that is running on a computer, and then Windows automatically manages the password for the account.

- **Offline domain join**   Makes it possible to provision computer accounts in a domain in advance. This allows administrators to prepare operating system images for mass deployment. Computers are joined to the appropriate domain when they are first started.

Using Read-Only Domain Controllers

Windows Server 2008 and Windows Server 2008 R2 support read-only domain controllers and Restartable Active Directory Domain Services. A read-only domain controller (RODC) is an additional domain controller that hosts a read-only replica of a domain's Active Directory data store. RODCs are ideally suited to the needs of branch offices where a domain controller's physical security cannot be guaranteed. Except for passwords, RODCs store the same objects and attributes as writable domain controllers. These objects and attributes are replicated to RODCs through unidirectional replication from a writable domain controller that acts as a replication partner.

Because RODCs by default do not store passwords or credentials other than for their own computer account and the Kerberos Target (Krbtgt) account, RODCs pull user and computer credentials from a writable domain controller that is running Windows Server 2008 or later. If allowed by a password replication policy that is enforced on the writable domain controller, an RODC retrieves and then caches credentials as necessary until the credentials change. Because only a subset of credentials is stored on an RODC, this limits the number of credentials that can possibly be compromised.

TIP Any domain user can be delegated as a local administrator of an RODC without granting any other rights in the domain. An RODC can act in the role of a global catalog but cannot act in the role of an operations master. Although RODCs can pull information from domain controllers running Windows Server 2003, RODCs can pull updates of the domain partition only from a writable domain controller running Windows Server 2008 or later in the same domain.

Using Restartable Active Directory Domain Services

Restartable Active Directory Domain Services is a feature that allows an administrator to start and stop AD DS. In the Services console, the Active Directory Domain Services service is available on domain controllers, allowing you to easily stop and restart AD DS in the same way as for any other service that is running locally on the server. While AD DS is stopped, you can perform maintenance tasks that would otherwise require restarting the server, such as performing offline defragmentation of the Active Directory database, applying updates to the operating system, or initiating an authoritative restore. While AD DS is stopped on a server, other domain controllers can handle authentication and logon tasks. Cached credentials, smart cards, and biometric logon methods continue to be supported. If no other domain controller is available and none of these logon methods applies, you can still log on to the server using the Directory Services Restore Mode account and password.

All domain controllers running Windows Server 2008 or later support Restartable Active Directory Domain Services—even RODCs. As an administrator, you can start or stop AD DS by using the Domain Controller entry in the Services utility. Because of Restartable Active Directory Domain Services, domain controllers running Windows Server 2008 or later have three possible states:

- **Active Directory Started** Active Directory is started and the domain controller has the same running state as a domain controller running Windows 2000 Server or Windows Server 2003. This allows the domain controller to provide authentication and logon services for a domain.

- **Active Directory Stopped** Active Directory is stopped and the domain controller can no longer provide authentication and logon services for a domain. This mode shares some characteristics of both a member server and a domain controller in Directory Services Restore Mode. As with a member server, the server is joined to the domain. Users can log on interactively using cached credentials, smart cards, and biometric logon methods. Users can also log on over the network by using another domain controller for domain logon. As with Directory Services Restore Mode, the Active Directory database (Ntds.dit) on the local domain controller is offline. This means you can perform offline AD DS operations, such as defragmentation of the database and application of security updates, without having to restart the domain controller.

- **Directory Services Restore Mode**   Active Directory is in restore mode. The domain controller has the same restore state as a domain controller running Windows Server 2003. This mode allows you to perform an authoritative or nonauthoritative restore of the Active Directory database.

When working with AD DS in the Stopped state, you should keep in mind that dependent services are also stopped when you stop AD DS. This means that File Replication Service (FRS), Kerberos Key Distribution Center (KDC), and Intersite Messaging are stopped before Active Directory is stopped, and that even if they are running, these dependent services are restarted when Active Directory restarts. Further, you can restart a domain controller in Directory Services Restore Mode, but you cannot start a domain controller in the Active Directory Stopped state. To get to the Stopped state, you must first start the domain controller normally and then stop AD DS.

Name-Resolution Services

Windows operating systems use name resolution to make it easier to communicate with other computers on a network. Name resolution associates computer names with the numerical IP addresses that are used for network communications. Thus, rather than using long strings of digits, users can access a computer on the network by using a friendly name.

Like Windows Vista and Windows Server 2008, Windows 7 and Windows Server 2008 R2 natively support three name-resolution systems:

- Domain Name System (DNS)
- Windows Internet Name Service (WINS)
- Link-Local Multicast Name Resolution (LLMNR)

The sections that follow examine these services.

Using Domain Name System

DNS is a name-resolution service that resolves computer names to IP addresses. Using DNS, the fully qualified host name computer84.cpandl.com, for example, can be resolved to an IP address, which allows it and other computers to find one another. DNS operates over the TCP/IP protocol stack and can be integrated with WINS, Dynamic Host Configuration Protocol (DHCP), and Active Directory Domain Services. As discussed in Chapter 19, "Running DHCP Clients and Servers," DHCP is used for dynamic IP addressing and TCP/IP configuration.

DNS organizes groups of computers into domains. These domains are organized into a hierarchical structure, which can be defined on an Internet-wide basis for public networks or on an enterprise-wide basis for private networks (also known as *intranets* and *extranets*). The various levels within the hierarchy identify individual computers, organizational domains, and top-level domains. For the fully qualified host name computer84.cpandl.com, *computer84* represents the host name for an individual computer, *cpandl* is the organizational domain, and *com* is the top-level domain.

Top-level domains are at the root of the DNS hierarchy; they are also called *root domains*. These domains are organized geographically, by organization type, and by function. Normal domains, such as cpandl.com, are also referred to as *parent domains*. They're called parent domains because they're the parents of an organizational structure. Parent domains can be divided into subdomains that can be used for groups or departments within an organization.

Subdomains are often referred to as *child domains*. For example, the fully qualified domain name (FQDN) for a computer within a human resources group could be jacob.hr.cpandl.com. Here, *jacob* is the host name, *hr* is the child domain, and *cpandl.com* is the parent domain.

Active Directory domains use DNS to implement their naming structure and hierarchy. Active Directory and DNS are tightly integrated, so much so that you should install DNS on the network before you can install domain controllers using Active Directory. During installation of the first domain controller on an Active Directory network, you're given the opportunity to install DNS automatically if a DNS server can't be found on the network. You are also able to specify whether DNS and Active Directory should be fully integrated. In most cases, you should respond affirmatively to both requests. With full integration, DNS information is stored directly in Active Directory. This allows you to take advantage of Active Directory's capabilities. The difference between partial integration and full integration is very important.

- **Partial integration** With partial integration, the domain uses standard file storage. DNS information is stored in text-based files that end with the .dns extension, and the default location of these files is %SystemRoot%\System32\Dns. Updates to DNS are handled through a single authoritative DNS server. This server is designated as the primary DNS server for the particular domain or an area within a domain called a *zone*. Clients that use dynamic DNS updates through DHCP must be configured to use the primary DNS server in the zone. If they aren't, their DNS information won't be updated. Likewise, dynamic updates through DHCP can't be made if the primary DNS server is offline.

- **Full integration** With full integration, the domain uses directory-integrated storage. DNS information is stored directly in Active Directory and is available through the container for the *dnsZone* object. Because the information is part of Active Directory, any domain controller can access the data and a multimaster approach can be used for dynamic updates through DHCP. This allows any domain controller running the DNS Server service to handle dynamic updates. Furthermore, clients that use dynamic DNS updates through DHCP can use any DNS server within the zone. An added benefit of directory integration is the ability to use directory security to control access to DNS information.

If you look at the way DNS information is replicated throughout the network, you can see more advantages to full integration with Active Directory. With partial integration, DNS information is stored and replicated separately from Active Directory. Having two separate structures reduces the effectiveness of both DNS and Active Directory and makes administration more complex. Because DNS is less efficient than Active Directory at replicating changes, you might also increase network traffic and the amount of time it takes to replicate DNS changes throughout the network.

To enable DNS on the network, you need to configure DNS clients and servers. When you configure DNS clients, you tell the clients the IP addresses of DNS servers on the network. Using these addresses, clients can communicate with DNS servers anywhere on the network, even if the servers are on different subnets.

When the network uses DHCP, you should configure DHCP to work with DNS. To do this, you need to set the DHCP scope options 006 DNS Servers and 015 DNS Domain Name as specified in "Setting Scope Options" in Chapter 19. Additionally, if computers on the network need to be accessible from other Active Directory domains, you need to create records for them in DNS. DNS records are organized into zones; a zone is simply an area within a domain. Configuring a DNS server is explained in "Configuring a Primary DNS Server" in Chapter 20.

When you install the DNS Server service on an RODC, the RODC is able to pull a read-only replica of all application directory partitions that are used by DNS, including ForestDNSZones and DomainDNSZones. Clients can then query the RODC for name resolution as they would query any other DNS server. However, as with directory updates, the DNS server on an RODC does not support direct updates. This means that the RODC does not register name server (NS) resource records for any Active Directory–integrated zone that it hosts. When a client attempts to update its DNS records against an RODC, the server returns a referral to a DNS server that the client can use for the update. The DNS server on the RODC should receive the updated record from the DNS server that receives details about the update using a special replicate-single-object request that runs as a background process.

Windows 7 and Windows Server 2008 R2 add support for DNS Security Extensions (DNSSEC). The DNS client running on these operating systems can send queries that indicate support for DNSSEC, process related records, and determine whether a DNS server has validated records on its behalf. On Windows servers, this allows your DNS servers to securely sign zones and to host DNSSEC-signed zones. It also allows DNS servers to process related records and perform both validation and authentication.

Using Windows Internet Name Service

WINS is a service that resolves computer names to IP addresses. Using WINS, the computer name COMPUTER84, for example, can be resolved to an IP address that enables computers on a Microsoft network to find one another and transfer information. WINS is needed to support pre–Windows 2000 systems and older applications that use NetBIOS over TCP/IP, such as the NET command-line utilities. If you don't have pre–Windows 2000 systems or applications on the network, you don't need to use WINS.

WINS works best in client/server environments in which WINS clients send single-label (host) name queries to WINS servers for name resolution and WINS servers resolve the query and respond. When all your DNS servers are running Windows Server 2008 or later, deploying a Global Names zone creates static, global records with single-label names without relying on WINS. This allows users to access hosts using single-label names rather than FQDNs and removes the dependency on WINS. To transmit WINS queries and other information, computers use NetBIOS. NetBIOS provides an application programming interface (API) that allows computers on a network to communicate. NetBIOS applications rely on WINS or the local LMHOSTS file to resolve computer names to IP addresses. On pre–Windows 2000 networks, WINS is the primary name resolution service available. On Windows 2000 and later networks, DNS is the primary name resolution service, and WINS has a different function. This function is to allow pre–Windows 2000 systems to browse lists of resources on the network and to allow Windows 2000 and later systems to locate NetBIOS resources.

To enable WINS name resolution on a network, you need to configure WINS clients and servers. When you configure WINS clients, you tell the clients the IP addresses for WINS servers on the network. Using the IP addresses, clients can communicate with WINS servers anywhere on the network, even if the servers are on different subnets. WINS clients can also communicate by using a broadcast method through which clients broadcast messages to other computers on the local network segment requesting their IP addresses. Because messages are broadcast, the WINS server isn't used. Any non-WINS clients that support this type of message broadcasting can also use this method to resolve computer names to IP addresses.

When clients communicate with WINS servers, they establish sessions that have the following three key parts:

- **Name registration** During name registration, the client gives the server its computer name and its IP address and asks to be added to the WINS database. If the specified computer name and IP address aren't already in use on the network, the WINS server accepts the request and registers the client in the WINS database.

- **Name renewal** Name registration isn't permanent. Instead, the client can use the name for a specified period known as a *lease*. The client is also given a time period within which the lease must be renewed, which is known as the *renewal interval.* The client must reregister with the WINS server during the renewal interval.

- **Name release** If the client can't renew the lease, the name registration is released, allowing another system on the network to use the computer name, IP address, or both. The names are also released when you shut down a WINS client.

After a client establishes a session with a WINS server, the client can request name-resolution services. The method used to resolve computer names to IP addresses depends on how the network is configured. The following four name-resolution methods are available:

- **B-node (broadcast)** Uses broadcast messages to resolve computer names to IP addresses. Computers that need to resolve a name broadcast a message to every host on the local network, requesting the IP address for a computer name. On a large network with hundreds or thousands of computers, these broadcast messages can use up valuable network bandwidth.

- **P-node (peer-to-peer)** Uses WINS servers to resolve computer names to IP addresses. As explained earlier, client sessions have three parts: name registration, name renewal, and name release. In this mode, when a client needs to resolve a computer name to an IP address, the client sends a query message to the server, and the server responds with an answer.

- **M-node (mixed)** Combines b-node and p-node. With m-node, a WINS client first tries to use b-node for name resolution. If the attempt fails, the client then tries to use p-node. Because b-node is used first, this method has the same problems with network bandwidth usage as b-node.

- **H-node (hybrid)** Also combines b-node and p-node. With h-node, a WINS client first tries to use p-node for peer-to-peer name resolution. If the attempt fails, the client then tries to use broadcast messages with b-node. Because peer-to-peer is the primary method, h-node offers the best performance on most networks. H-node is also the default method for WINS name resolution.

If WINS servers are available on the network, Windows clients use the p-node method for name resolution. If no WINS servers are available on the network, Windows clients use the b-node method for name resolution. Windows computers can also use DNS and the local files LMHOSTS and HOSTS to resolve network names. Working with DNS is covered in detail in Chapter 20, "Optimizing DNS."

When you use DHCP to assign IP addresses dynamically, you should set the name resolution method for DHCP clients. To do this, you need to set DHCP scope options for the 046 WINS/NBT Node Type as specified in "Setting Scope Options" in Chapter 19. The best method to use is h-node. You'll get the best performance and have reduced traffic on the network.

Using Link-Local Multicast Name Resolution

LLMNR fills a need for peer-to-peer name-resolution services for devices with an IPv4 address, an IPv6 address, or both, allowing IPv4 and IPv6 devices on a single subnet without a WINS or DNS server to resolve each other's names—a service that neither WINS nor DNS can fully provide. While WINS can provide both client/ server and peer-to-peer name-resolution services for IPv4, it does not support IPv6 addresses. DNS, on the other hand, supports IPv4 and IPv6 addresses, but it depends on designated servers to provide name-resolution services.

Both Windows 7 and Windows Server 2008 R2 support LLMNR. LLMNR is designed for both IPv4 and IPv6 clients in configurations where other name-resolution systems are not available, such as:

- Home or small office networks

- Ad hoc networks

- Corporate networks where DNS services are not available

LLMNR is designed to complement DNS by enabling name resolution in scenarios in which conventional DNS name resolution is not possible. Although LLMNR can replace the need for WINS in cases where NetBIOS is not required, LLMNR is not a substitute for DNS because it operates only on the local subnet. Because LLMNR traffic is prevented from propagating across routers, it cannot accidentally flood the network.

As with WINS, you use LLMNR to resolve a host name, such as COMPUTER84, to an IP address. By default, LLMNR is enabled on all computers running Windows 7 and Windows Server 2008 R2, and these computers use LLMNR only when all attempts to look up a host name through DNS fail. As a result, name resolution works like the following for Windows 7 and Windows Server 2008 R2:

1. A host computer sends a query to its configured primary DNS server. If the host computer does not receive a response or receives an error, it tries each configured alternate DNS server in turn. If the host has no configured DNS servers or fails to connect to a DNS server without errors, name resolution fails over to LLMNR.

2. The host computer sends a multicast query over User Datagram Protocol (UDP) requesting the IP address for the name being looked up. This query is restricted to the local subnet (also referred to as the *local link*).

3. Each computer on the local link that supports LLMNR and is configured to respond to incoming queries receives the query and compares the name to its own host name. If the host name is not a match, the computer discards the query. If the host name is a match, the computer transmits a unicast message containing its IP address to the originating host.

You can also use LLMNR for reverse mapping. With a reverse mapping, a computer sends a unicast query to a specific IP address, requesting the host name of the target computer. An LLMNR-enabled computer that receives the request sends a unicast reply containing its host name to the originating host.

LLMNR-enabled computers are required to ensure that their names are unique on the local subnet. In most cases, a computer checks for uniqueness when it starts, when it resumes from a suspended state, and when you change its network interface settings. If a computer has not yet determined that its name is unique, it must indicate this condition when responding to a name query.

REAL WORLD By default, LLMNR is automatically enabled on computers running Windows 7 and Windows Server 2008 R2. You can disable LLMNR through registry settings. To disable LLMNR for all network interfaces, create and set the following registry value to 0: HKLM/SYSTEM/CurrentControlSet/Services/Dnscache/Parameters/EnableMulticast.

To disable LLMNR for a specific network interface, create and set the following registry value to 0: HKLM/SYSTEM/CurrentControlSet/Services/Tcpip/Parameters/AdapterGUID/EnableMulticast.

Here, AdapterGUID is the globally unique identifier (GUID) of the network interface adapter for which you want to disable LLMNR. You can enable LLMNR again at any time by setting these registry values to 1. You also can manage LLMNR through Group Policy.

Frequently Used Tools

Many utilities are available for administrating Windows Server 2008 R2 systems. The tools you use the most include the following:

- **Control Panel** A collection of tools for managing system configuration. You can organize Control Panel in different ways according to the view you're using. A view is simply a way of organizing and presenting options. You change the view by using the View By list. Category view is the default view, and it provides access to tools by category, tool, and key tasks. The Large Icons and Small Icons views are alternative views that list each tool separately by name.

- **Graphical administrative tools** The key tools for managing network computers and their resources. You can access these tools by selecting them individually from the Administrative Tools program group.

- **Administrative wizards** Tools designed to automate key administrative tasks. You can access many administrative wizards in Server Manager—the central administration console for Windows Server 2008 R2.

- **Command-line utilities** You can launch most administrative utilities from the command prompt. In addition to these utilities, Windows Server 2008

R2 provides others that are useful for working with Windows Server 2008 R2 systems.

To learn how to use any of the NET command-line tools, type **NET HELP** at a command prompt followed by the command name, such as **NET HELP SHARE**. Windows Server 2008 R2 then provides an overview of how the command is used.

Windows PowerShell 2.0

For additional flexibility in your command-line scripting, you might want to use Windows PowerShell 2.0. Windows PowerShell 2.0 is a full-featured command shell that can use built-in commands called *cmdlets*, built-in programming features, and standard command-line utilities. A command console and a graphical environment are available.

Although the Windows PowerShell console is installed by default, the graphical scripting environment is not. You can install the Windows PowerShell graphical scripting environment by completing the following steps:

1. Click the Server Manager button on the Quick Launch toolbar. Alternatively, click Start, point to Administrative Tools, and then click Server Manager.

2. In Server Manager, select the Features node, and then click Add Features.

3. In the Windows Features dialog box, scroll down, and then select Windows PowerShell Integrated Scripting Environment (ISE).

4. Click Next, and then click Install.

The Windows PowerShell console (Powershell.exe) is a 32-bit or 64-bit environment for working with Windows PowerShell at the command line. On 32-bit versions of Windows, you'll find the 32-bit executable in the %SystemRoot%\System32\WindowsPowerShell\v1.0 directory. On 64-bit versions of Windows, you'll find the 32-bit executable in the %SystemRoot%\SysWow64\WindowsPowerShell\v1.0 directory, and the 64-bit executable in the %SystemRoot%\System32\WindowsPowerShell\v1.0 directory.

You can open the Windows PowerShell console by clicking Start, pointing to All Programs, pointing to Accessories, Windows PowerShell, and then clicking Windows PowerShell. On 64-bit systems, the 64-bit version of PowerShell is started by default. If you want to use the 32-bit PowerShell console on a 64-bit system, you must select the Windows PowerShell (x86) option.

You can start Windows PowerShell from a Windows command shell (Cmd.exe) by entering the following:

```
powershell
```

NOTE The directory path for Windows PowerShell should be in your command path by default. This ensures that you can start Windows PowerShell from a command prompt without first having to change to the related directory.

After starting Windows PowerShell, you can enter the name of a cmdlet at the prompt, and the cmdlet will run in much the same way as a command-line command. You can also execute cmdlets in scripts. Cmdlets are named using verb-noun pairs. The verb tells you what the cmdlet does in general. The noun tells you what specifically the cmdlet works with. For example, the Get-Variable cmdlet gets all Windows PowerShell environment variables and returns their values, or it gets a specifically named environment variable and returns its value. The common verbs associated with cmdlets are as follows:

- **Get-** Queries a specific object or a subset of a type of object, such as a specified performance counter or all performance counters.

- **Set-** Modifies specific settings of an object.

- **Enable-** Enables an option or a feature.

- **Disable-** Disables an option or a feature.

- **New-** Creates a new instance of an item, such as a new event or service.

- **Remove-** Removes an instance of an item, such as an event or event log.

At the Windows PowerShell prompt, you can get a complete list of cmdlets by typing **help *-***. To get help documentation on a specific cmdlet, type **help** followed by the cmdlet name, such as **get-help get-variable**.

All cmdlets also have configurable aliases that act as shortcuts for executing a cmdlet. To list all aliases available, type **get-item –path alias:** at the Windows PowerShell prompt. You can create an alias that invokes any command by using the following syntax:

```
new-item –path alias:AliasName –value:FullCommandPath
```

where *AliasName* is the name of the alias to create, and *FullCommandPath* is the full path to the command to run, such as:

```
new-item –path alias:sm –value:c:\windows\system32\compmgmtlauncher.exe
```

This example creates the alias *sm* for starting Server Manager. To use this alias, you would simply type **sm** and then press Enter when you are working with Windows PowerShell.

Windows Remote Management

The Windows PowerShell remoting features are supported by the WS-Management protocol and the Windows Remote Management (WinRM) service that implements WS-Management in Windows. Computers running Windows 7 and Windows Server 2008 R2 or later include WinRM 2.0 or later. If you want to manage a Windows server from a workstation, you need to be sure that WinRM 2.0 and Windows PowerShell 2.0 are installed and that the server has a WinRM listener enabled.

Enabling and Using WinRM

You can verify the availability of WinRM 2.0 and configure Windows PowerShell for remoting by following these steps:

1. Click Start, and then point to All Programs, Accessories, Windows PowerShell. Start Windows PowerShell as an administrator by right-clicking the Windows PowerShell shortcut and selecting Run As Administrator.

2. The WinRM service is configured for manual startup by default. You must change the startup type to Automatic and start the service on each computer you want to work with. At the Windows PowerShell prompt, you can verify that the WinRM service is running by using the following command:

```
get-service winrm
```

As shown in the following example, the value of the Status property in the output should be Running:

```
Status   Name            DisplayName
------   ----            -----------
Running  WinRM           Windows Remote Management
```

If the service is stopped, enter the following command to start the service and configure it to start automatically in the future:

```
set-service -name winrm -startuptype automatic -status running
```

3. To configure Windows PowerShell for remoting, type the following command:

```
Enable-PSRemoting -force
```

You can only enable remoting when your computer is connected to a domain or a private network. If your computer is connected to a public network, you need to disconnect from the public network and connect to a domain or private network and then repeat this step. If one or more of your computer's connections has the Public Network connection type, but you are actually connected to a domain or private network, you need to change the network connection type in Network And Sharing Center and then repeat this step.

In many cases, you are able to work with remote computers in other domains. However, if the remote computer is not in a trusted domain, the remote computer might not be able to authenticate your credentials. To enable authentication, you need to add the remote computer to the list of trusted hosts for the local computer in WinRM. To do so, type the following:

```
winrm set winrm/config/client '@{TrustedHosts"RemoteComputer"}'
```

where *RemoteComputer* is the name of the remote computer, such as:

```
winrm set winrm/config/client '@{TrustedHosts="CorpServer56"}'
```

When you are working with computers in workgroups or homegroups, you must use HTTPS as the transport or add the remote machine to the TrustedHosts configuration settings. If you cannot connect to a remote host, verify that the service on the remote host is running and is accepting requests by running the following command on the remote host:

```
winrm quickconfig
```

This command analyzes and configures the WinRM service. If the WinRM service is set up correctly, you'll see output similar to the following:

```
WinRM already is set up to receive requests on this machine.
WinRM already is set up for remote management on this machine
```

If the WinRM service is not set up correctly, you see errors and need to respond affirmatively to several prompts that allow you to automatically configure remote management. When this process is complete, WinRM should be set up correctly.

Whenever you use Windows PowerShell remoting features, you must start Windows PowerShell as an administrator by right-clicking the Windows PowerShell shortcut and selecting Run As Administrator. When starting Windows PowerShell from another program, such as the command prompt, you must start that program as an administrator.

Configuring WinRM

When you are working with an elevated, administrator command prompt, you can use the WinRM command-line utility to view and manage the remote management configuration. Type **winrm get winrm/config** to display detailed information about the remote management configuration.

If you examine the configuration listing, you'll notice there is a hierarchy of information. The base of this hierarchy, the Config level, is referenced with the path winrm/config. Then there are sublevels for client, service, and WinRS, referenced as winrm/config/client, winrm/config/service, and winrm/config/winrs. You can change the value of most configuration parameters by using the following command:

```
winrm set ConfigPath @{ParameterName="Value"}
```

where *ConfigPath* is the configuration path, *ParameterName* is the name of the parameter you want to work with, and *Value* sets the value for the parameter, such as:

```
winrm set winrm/config/winrs @{MaxShellsPerUser="10"}
```

Here, you set the MaxShellsPerUser parameter under winrm/config/winrs. This parameter controls the maximum number of connections to a remote computer that can be active per user. (By default, each user can have only five active connections.) Keep in mind that some parameters are read-only and cannot be set in this way.

WinRM requires at least one listener to indicate the transports and IP addresses on which management requests can be accepted. The transport must be HTTP, HTTPS, or both. With HTTP, messages can be encrypted using NTLM or Kerberos encryption. With HTTPS, Secure Sockets Layer (SSL) is used for encryption. You can examine the configured listeners by typing **winrm enumerate winrm/config/ listener**. As Listing 1-1 shows, this command displays the configuration details for configured listeners.

LISTING 1-1 Sample Configuration for Listeners

```
Listener
    Address = *
    Transport = HTTP
    Port = 80
    Hostname
    Enabled = true
    URLPrefix = wsman
    CertificateThumbprint
    ListeningOn = 127.0.0.1, 192.168.1.225
```

By default, your computer is probably configured to listen on any IP address. If so, you won't see any output. To limit WinRM to specific IP addresses, the computer's local loopback address (127.0.0.1) and assigned IPv4 and IPv6 addresses can be explicitly configured for listening. You can configure a computer to listen for requests over HTTP on all configured IP addresses by typing the following:

```
winrm create winrm/config/listener?Address=*+Transport=HTTP
```

You can listen for requests over HTTPS on all IP addresses configured on the computer by typing this:

```
winrm create winrm/config/listener?Address=*+Transport=HTTPS
```

Here, the asterisk (*) indicates all configured IP addresses. Note that the CertificateThumbprint property must be empty to share the SSL configuration with another service.

You can enable or disable a listener for a specific IP address by typing

```
winrm set winrm/config/listener?Address=IP:192.168.1.225+Transport=HTTP
@{Enabled="true"}
```

or

```
winrm set winrm/config/listener?Address=IP:192.168.1.225+Transport=HTTP
@{Enabled="false"}
```

You can enable or disable basic authentication on the client by typing

```
winrm set winrm/config/client/auth @{Basic="true"}
```

or

```
winrm set winrm/config/client/auth @{Basic="false"}
```

You can enable or disable Windows authentication using either NTLM or Kerberos (as appropriate) by typing

```
winrm set winrm/config/client @{TrustedHosts="<local>"}
```

or

```
winrm set winrm/config/client @{TrustedHosts=""}
```

In addition to managing WinRM at the command line, you can manage the service by using Group Policy. As a result, Group Policy settings might override any settings you enter.

Deploying Windows Server 2008 R2

Before you deploy Windows Server 2008 Release 2 (R2), you should carefully plan the server architecture. As part of your implementation planning, you need to look closely at the software configuration that will be used and modify the hardware configuration on a per-server basis to meet related requirements. For additional flexibility in server deployments, you can deploy servers using one of two installation types:

- **Full-server installation** An installation option for all editions of Windows Server 2008 R2 that provides full functionality. You can configure a server to have any allowed combination of roles, role services, and features, and a full user interface is provided for managing the server. This installation option provides the most dynamic solution and is recommended for deployments of Windows Server 2008 R2 in which the server role may change over time.

- **Core-server installation** A minimal installation option for the Standard, Enterprise, and Datacenter editions of Windows Server 2008 R2 that provides a fixed subset of roles. You can configure a server to have a limited set of roles, and a minimal user interface is provided for managing the server. This installation option is ideally suited to situations in which you want to dedicate servers to a specific server role or combination of roles. Because additional functionality is not installed, the overhead caused by other services is reduced, providing more resources for the dedicated role or roles.

You choose the installation type during installation of the operating system. You cannot change the installation type once you've installed a server, so you need to carefully consider which installation option to use before deploying your servers. At times, you may want to dedicate a server to a specific role or combination of roles, and at other times you may want to change a server's role. Therefore, both installation options have a place in the typical enterprise.

Server Roles, Role Services, and Features for Windows Server 2008 R2

Windows Server 2008 R2 has a different configuration architecture than its predecessors. You prepare servers for deployment by installing and configuring the following components:

- **Server roles**   A server role is a related set of software components that allows a server to perform a specific function for users and other computers on a network. A computer can be dedicated to a single role, such as Active Directory Domain Services (AD DS), or provide multiple roles.

- **Role services**   A role service is a software component that provides the functionality for a server role. Each role can have one or more related role services. Some server roles, such as Domain Name Service (DNS) and Dynamic Host Configuration Protocol (DHCP), have a single function, and installing the role installs this function. Other roles, such as Network Policy and Access Services and Active Directory Certificate Services (AD CS), have multiple role services that you can install. With these server roles, you can choose which role services to install.

- **Features**   A feature is a software component that provides additional functionality. Features, such as BitLocker Drive Encryption and Windows Server Backup, are installed and removed separately from roles and role services. A computer can have zero or more features installed depending on its configuration.

You configure roles, role services, and features by using Server Manager, a Microsoft Management Console (MMC). The command-line counterpart to Server Manager is Servermanagercmd.exe.

Some roles, role services, and features are dependent on other roles, role services, and features. As you install roles, role services, and features, Server Manager prompts you to install other roles, role services, or features that are required. Similarly, if you try to remove a required component of an installed role, role service, or feature, Server Manager warns that you cannot remove the component unless you also remove dependent roles, role services, or features.

Because adding or removing roles, role services, and features can change hardware requirements, you should carefully plan any configuration changes and determine how they affect a server's overall performance. Although you typically want to combine complementary roles, doing so increases the workload on the server, so you'll need to optimize the server hardware accordingly. Table 2-1 provides an overview of the primary roles and the related role services that you can deploy on a server running Windows Server 2008 R2.

TABLE 2-1 Primary Roles and Related Role Services for Windows Server 2008 R2

ROLE	DESCRIPTION
Active Directory Certificate Services (AD CS)	Provides functions necessary for issuing and revoking digital certificates for users, client computers, and servers. Includes these role services: Certification Authority, Certification Authority Web Enrollment, Online Responder, Network Device Enrollment Service, Certificate Enrollment Web Service, and Certificate Enrollment Policy Web Service.
Active Directory Domain Services (AD DS)	Provides functions necessary for storing information about users, groups, computers, and other objects on the network and makes this information available to users and computers. AD domain controllers give network users and computers access to permitted resources on the network.
Active Directory Federation Services (AD FS)	Complements the authentication and access management features of AD DS by extending them to the World Wide Web. Includes these role services and subservices: Federation Service, Federation Service Proxy, AD FS Web Agents, Claims-Aware Agent, and Windows Token-Based Agent.
Active Directory Lightweight Directory Services (AD LDS)	Provides a data store for directory-enabled applications that do not require AD DS and do not need to be deployed on domain controllers. Does not include additional role services.
Active Directory Rights Management Services (AD RMS)	Provides controlled access to protected e-mail messages, documents, intranet pages, and other types of files. Includes these role services: Active Directory Rights Management Server and Identity Federation Support.
Application Server	Allows a server to host distributed applications built using ASP.NET, Enterprise Services, and .NET Framework 3.5.1. Includes more than a dozen role services.

ROLE	DESCRIPTION
DHCP Server	DHCP provides centralized control over IP addressing. DHCP servers can assign dynamic IP addresses and essential TCP/IP settings to other computers on a network. Does not include additional role services.
DNS Server	DNS is a name resolution system that resolves computer names to IP addresses. DNS servers are essential for name resolution in Active Directory domains. Does not include additional role services.
Fax Server	Provides centralized control over sending and receiving faxes in the enterprise. A fax server can act as a gateway for faxing and allows you to manage fax resources, such as jobs and reports, and fax devices on the server or on the network. Does not include additional role services.
File Services	Provides essential services for managing files and the way they are made available and replicated on the network. A number of server roles require some type of file service. Includes these role services and subservices: File Server, Distributed File System, DFS Namespace, DFS Replication, File Server Resource Manager, Services for Network File System (NFS), Windows Search Service, Windows Server 2003 File Services, Indexing Service, and BranchCache for Network Files.
Hyper-V	Provides services for creating and managing virtual machines that emulate physical computers. Virtual machines have separate operating system environments from the host server.
Network Policy and Access Services (NPAS)	Provides essential services for managing routing and remote access to networks. Includes these role services: Network Policy Server (NPS), Routing and Remote Access Services (RRAS), Remote Access Service, Routing, Health Registration Authority, and Host Credential Authorization Protocol (HCAP).
Print and Document Services	Provides essential services for managing network printers, network scanners, and related drivers. Includes these role services: Print Server, LPD Service, Internet Printing, and Distributed Scan Server.

ROLE	DESCRIPTION
Remote Desktop Services	Provides services that allow users to run Windows-based applications that are installed on a remote server. When users run an application on a terminal server, the execution and processing occur on the server, and only the data from the application is transmitted over the network. Includes these role services: Remote Desktop Session Host, Remote Desktop Virtualization Host, Remote Desktop Licensing, Remote Desktop Connection Broker, Remote Desktop Gateway, and Remote Desktop Web Access.
Web Server (IIS)	Used to host Web sites and Web-based applications. Web sites hosted on a Web server can have both static content and dynamic content. You can build Web applications hosted on a Web server by using ASP.NET and .NET Framework 3.5.1. When you deploy a Web server, you can manage the server configuration using IIS 7.5 modules and administration tools. Includes several dozen role services.
Windows Deployment Services (WDS)	Provides services for deploying Windows computers in the enterprise. Includes these role services: Deployment Server and Transport Server.
Windows Server Update Services (WSUS)	Provides services for Microsoft Update, allowing you to distribute updates from designated servers.

Table 2-2 provides an overview of the primary features that you can deploy on a server running Windows Server 2008 R2. Unlike in earlier releases of Windows, some important server features are not installed automatically. For example, you must add Windows Server Backup to use the built-in backup and restore features of the operating system.

TABLE 2-2 Primary Features for Windows Server 2008 R2

FEATURE	DESCRIPTION
Background Intelligent Transfer Service (BITS)	Provides intelligent background transfers. When this feature is installed, the server can act as a BITS server that can receive file uploads from clients. This feature isn't necessary for downloads to clients using BITS. Additional subfeatures include BITS IIS Server Extension and BITS Compact Server.
BitLocker Drive Encryption	Provides hardware-based security to protect data through full-volume encryption that prevents disk tampering while the operating system is offline. Computers that have Trusted Platform Module (TPM) can use BitLocker Drive Encryption in Startup Key or TPM-Only mode. Both modes provide early integrity validation.
BranchCache	Provides services needed for BranchCache client and server functionality. Includes HTTP protocol, Hosted Cache, and related services.
Connection Manager Administration Kit (CMAK)	Provides functionality for generating Connection Manager profiles.
Desktop Experience	Provides Windows 7 desktop functionality on the server. Windows 7 features added include Windows Media Player, desktop themes, Video for Windows (AVI support), Windows Defender, Disk Cleanup, Sync Center, Sound Recorder, Character Map, and Snipping Tool. Although these features allow a server to be used like a desktop computer, they can reduce the server's overall performance.
Direct Access Management Console	Allows remote users to securely access internal network file shares, Web sites, and applications without connecting to a virtual private network (VPN).
Failover Clustering	Provides clustering functionality that allows multiple servers to work together to provide high availability for services and applications. Many types of services can be clustered, including file and print services. Messaging and database servers are ideal candidates for clustering.
Group Policy Management	Installs the Group Policy Management Console (GPMC), which provides centralized administration of Group Policy.

FEATURE	DESCRIPTION
Ink and Handwriting Services	Provides support for use of a pen or stylus and handwriting recognition.
Internet Printing Client	Provides functionality that allows clients to use HTTP to connect to printers on Web print servers.
Internet Storage Naming Server (iSNS)	Provides management and server functions for Internet SCSI (iSCSI) devices, allowing the server to process registration requests, deregistration requests, and queries from iSCSI devices.
LPR Port Monitor	Installs the LPR Port Monitor, which allows printing to devices attached to UNIX-based computers.
Message Queuing	Provides management and server functions for distributed message queuing. A group of related subfeatures is available as well.
Multipath I/O (MPIO)	Provides functionality necessary for using multiple data paths to a storage device.
.NET Framework 3.5.1	Provides APIs for application development. Additional subfeatures include .NET Framework 3.5.1 Features and Windows Communication Foundation (WCF) Activation Components.
Network Load Balancing (NLB)	NLB provides failover support and load balancing for IP-based applications and services by distributing incoming application requests among a group of participating servers. Web servers are ideal candidates for load balancing.
Peer Name Resolution Protocol (PNRP)	Provides Link-Local Multicast Name Resolution (LLMNR) functionality that allows peer-to-peer name-resolution services. When you install this feature, applications running on the server can use LLMNR to register and resolve names.
Quality Windows Audio Video Experience	A networking platform for audio video (AV) streaming applications on IP home networks.
Remote Assistance	Allows a remote user to connect to the server to provide or receive Remote Assistance.
Remote Differential Compression	Provides support for differential compression by determining which parts of a file have changed and replicating only the changes.

FEATURE	DESCRIPTION
Remote Server Administration Tools (RSAT)	Installs role-management and feature-management tools that can be used for remote administration of other Windows Server 2008 R2 systems. Options for individual tools are provided, or you can install tools by top-level category or subcategory.
Remote Procedure Call (RPC) over HTTP Proxy	Installs a proxy for relaying RPC messages from client applications to the server over HTTP. RPC over HTTP is an alternative to having clients access the server over a VPN connection.
Simple TCP/IP Services	Installs additional TCP/IP services, including Character Generator, Daytime, Discard, Echo, and Quote of the Day.
Simple Mail Transfer Protocol (SMTP) Server	SMTP is a network protocol for controlling the transfer and routing of e-mail messages. When this feature is installed, the server can act as a basic SMTP server. For a full-featured solution, you need to install a messaging server, such as Microsoft Exchange Server.
Simple Network Management Protocol (SNMP) Services	SNMP is a protocol used to simplify management of TCP/IP networks. You can use SNMP for centralized network management if your network has SNMP-compliant devices. You can also use SNMP for network monitoring via network management software.
Storage Manager for SANs	Installs the Storage Manager for SANs console. This console provides a central management interface for storage area network (SAN) devices. You can view storage subsystems, create and manage logical unit numbers (LUNs), and manage iSCSI target devices. The SAN device must support Virtual Disk Services (VDS).
Subsystem for UNIX-Based Applications (SUA)	Provides functionality for running UNIX-based programs. You can download additional management utilities from the Microsoft Web site.
Telnet Client	Allows a computer to connect to a remote Telnet server and run applications on that server.
Telnet Server	Hosts the remote sessions for Telnet clients. When Telnet Server is running on a computer, users can connect to the server with a Telnet client from a remote computer.
Windows Biometric Framework	Provides functionality required for using fingerprint devices.

FEATURE	DESCRIPTION
Windows Internal Database	Installs SQL Server 2005 Embedded Edition. This allows the server to use relational databases with Windows roles and features that require an internal database, such as AD RMS, UDDI Services, WSUS, Windows SharePoint Services, and Windows System Resource Manager.
Windows PowerShell Integrated Scripting Environment	Installs the graphical tool for Windows PowerShell, which can be used instead of or in addition to the PowerShell command-line tool.
Windows Process Activation Service	Provides support for distributed, Web-based applications that use HTTP and non-HTTP protocols.
Windows Server Backup Features	Allows you to back up and restore the operating system, system state, and any data stored on a server.
Windows System Resource Manager (WSRM)	Allows you to manage resource usage on a per-processor basis.
Windows TIFF IFilter	Focuses on text-based documents, which means that searching is more successful for documents that contain clearly identifiable text (for example, black text on a white background.
WinRM IIS Extension	Provides an Internet Information Services (IIS)–based hosting model. WinRM IIS Extension can be enabled at either the Web site or virtual directory level.
WINS Server	A name-resolution service that resolves computer names to IP addresses. Installing this feature allows the computer to act as a WINS server.
Wireless LAN Service	Allows the server to use wireless networking connections and profiles.
XPS Viewer	A program you can use to view, search, set permissions for, and digitally sign XPS documents.

Full-Server and Core-Server Installations of Windows Server 2008 R2

With a full-server installation, you have a complete working version of Windows Server 2008 R2 that you can deploy with any permitted combination of roles, role services, and features. With a core-server installation, you have a minimal installation of Windows Server 2008 R2 that supports a limited set of roles and role combinations. The supported roles include AD CS, AD DS, AD LDS, DHCP Server, DNS Server, File Services, Hyper-V, Media Services, Print Services, and Web Server (IIS). In its current implementation, a core-server installation is not a platform for running server applications. Additionally, with the Standard edition, file services are limited to one stand-alone DFS root on core-server installations.

While both types of installations use the same licensing rules and can be managed remotely using any available and permitted remote administration technique, full-server and core-server installations are completely different when it comes to local console administration. With a full-server installation, you're provided with a user interface that includes a full desktop environment for local console management of the server. With a core-server installation, you get a user interface that includes a limited desktop environment for local console management of the server. This minimal interface includes the following:

- Windows Logon screen for logging on and logging off
- Notepad (Notepad.exe) for editing files
- Registry Editor (Regedit.exe) for managing the registry
- Task Manager (Taskmgr.exe) for managing tasks and starting new tasks
- Command prompt (Cmd.exe) for administration using the command line
- PowerShell prompt for administration using Windows PowerShell
- File Signature Verification tool (Sigverif.exe) for verifying digital signatures of system files
- System information (Msinfo32.exe) for getting system information
- Windows Installer (Msiexec.exe) for managing Windows Installer
- Date And Time control panel (Timedate.cpl) for viewing or setting the date, time, and time zone.
- Region And Language control panel (Intl.cpl) for viewing or setting regional and language options, including formats and the keyboard layout.
- Server Configuration utility (Sconfig), which provides a text-based menu system for managing a server's configuration.

When you start a server with a core-server installation, you can use the Windows Logon screen to log on just as you do with a full-server installation. In a domain, the standard restrictions apply for logging on to servers, and anyone with appropriate user rights and logon permissions can log on to the server. On servers that are not acting as domain controllers and for servers in workgroup environments, you can use the NET USER command to add users and the NET LOCALGROUP command to add users to local groups for the purposes of logging on locally.

After you log on to a core-server installation, you have a limited desktop environment with an administrator command prompt. You can use this command prompt for administration of the server. If you accidentally close the command prompt, you can open a new command prompt by following these steps:

1. Press Ctrl+Shift+Esc to display Task Manager.

2. On the File menu, click New Task.

3. In the Create New Task dialog box, type **cmd** in the Open field, and then click OK.

You can use this technique to open additional Command Prompt windows as well. Although you can work with Notepad and Regedit by typing **notepad.exe** or **regedit.exe** instead of **cmd**, you can also start Notepad and Regedit directly from a command prompt by entering **notepad.exe** or **regedit.exe** as appropriate.

The Server Configuration utility (Sconfig) provides a text-based menu system that makes it easy to do the following:

- Configure domain or workgroup membership

- Change a server's name

- Add a local Administrator account

- Configure remote management features

- Configure Windows Update settings

- Download and install Windows updates

- Enable or disable Remote Desktop

- Configure network settings for TCP/IP

- Configure the date and time

- Log off, restart, or shut down

REAL WORLD You can use Sconfig to install Windows PowerShell by following these steps:

1. At the command prompt, type **sconfig**.

2. At the menu prompt, enter **4**, and then enter **2**.

3. When the installation process is complete, you are prompted to restart the computer. Click Yes.

Once you've installed Windows PowerShell, you can access the PowerShell prompt by entering **powershell** at the command prompt. However, rather than running PowerShell within a command prompt, you might want to open a separate Power-Shell window, which you can do by pressing Ctrl+Shift+Esc to display Task Manager. In Task Manager, click New Task on the File menu. Type **powershell** in the Open field, and then click OK.

When you are logged on, you can display the Windows Logon screen at any time by pressing Ctrl+Alt+Delete. In a core-server installation, the Windows Logon screen has the same options as with a full-server installation, allowing you to lock the computer, switch users, log off, change a password, or start Task Manager. At the command prompt, you have all the standard commands and command-line utilities available for managing the server. However, commands, utilities, and programs run only if all of their dependencies are available in the core-server installation.

Although a core-server installation supports a limited set of roles and role services, you can install most features. Windows Server 2008 R2 also supports the .NET Framework, Windows PowerShell 2.0, and Windows Remote Management (WinRM) 2.0. This support allows you to perform local and remote administration using PowerShell. You also can use Remote Desktop Services to manage a core-server installation remotely. Some of the common tasks you may want to perform when you are logged on locally are summarized in Table 2-3.

TABLE 2-3 Helpful Commands and Utilities for Managing Core-Server Installations

COMMAND	TASK
Cscript Scregedit.wsf	Configure the operating system. Use the /cli parameter to list available configuration areas.
Diskraid.exe	Configure software RAID.
ipconfig /all	List information about the computer's IP address configuration.
Netdom RenameComputer	Set the server's name.
Netdom Join	Join the server to a domain.
Netsh	Provides multiple contexts for managing the configuration of networking components. Type **netsh interface ipv4** to configure IPv4 settings. Type **netsh interface ipv6** to configure IPv6 settings.
Oclist.exe	List roles, role services, and features.
Ocsetup.exe	Add or remove roles, role services, and features.
Pnputil.exe	Install or update hardware device drivers.
Sc query type=driver	List installed device drivers.
Serverweroptin.exe	Configure Windows Error Reporting.
Slmgr –ato	Windows Software Licensing Management tool used to activate the operating system. Runs Cscript slmgr.vbs –ato.
Slmgr –ipk	Install or replace the product key. Runs Cscript slmgr.vbs –ipk.

COMMAND	TASK
SystemInfo	List the system configuration details.
Wecutil.exe	Create and manage subscriptions to forwarded events.
Wevtutil.exe	View and search event logs.
Winrm quickconfig	Configures the server to accept WS-Management requests from other computers. Runs Cscript winrm.vbs quickconfig. Enter without the Quickconfig parameter to see other options.
Wmic datafile where name="FullFilePath" get version	List a file's version.
Wmic nicconfig index=9 call enabledhcp	Set the computer to use dynamic IP addressing rather than static IP addressing.
Wmic nicconfig index=9 call enablestatic("IPAddress"), ("SubnetMask")	Set a computer's static IP address and network mask.
Wmic nicconfig index=9 call setgateways("GatewayIPAddress")	Set or change the default gateway.
Wmic product get name /value	List installed Microsoft Installer (MSI) applications by name.
Wmic product where name="Name" call uninstall	Uninstall an MSI application.
Wmic qfe list	List installed updates and hotfixes.
Wusa.exe PatchName.msu /quiet	Apply an update or hotfix to the operating system.

Installing Windows Server 2008 R2

You can install Windows Server 2008 R2 on new hardware or as an upgrade. When you install Windows Server 2008 R2 on a computer with an existing operating system, you can perform a clean installation or an upgrade. With a clean installation, the Windows Server 2008 R2 Setup program replaces the original operating system on the computer, and all user or application settings are lost. With an upgrade, the Windows Server 2008 R2 Setup program performs a clean installation of the operating system and then migrates user settings, documents, and applications from the earlier version of Windows.

Windows Server 2008 R2 only supports 64-bit architecture. You can install the operating system only on computers with 64-bit processors. To install the operating system on Itanium 64-bit processors, you must use Windows Server 2008 R2 for Itanium-Based Systems.

Before you install Windows Server 2008 R2, you should be sure that your computer meets the minimum requirements of the edition you plan to use. Microsoft provides both minimum requirements and recommended requirements. If your computer doesn't meet the minimum requirements, you will not be able to install Windows Server 2008 R2. If your computer doesn't meet the recommended requirements, you will experience performance issues.

Windows Server 2008 R2 requires at least 10 GB of disk space for installation of the base operating system. Microsoft recommends that a computer running Windows Server 2008 R2 have 40 GB or more of available disk space. Additional disk space is required for paging and dump files as well as for the features, roles, and role services that you install. For optimal performance, you should have at least 10 percent of free space on a server's disks at all times.

When you install Windows Server 2008 R2, the Setup program automatically makes recovery options available on your server as an advanced boot option. In addition to a command line for troubleshooting, these tools include the following:

- **System Image Recovery** Performs a full recovery of the computer using a system image created previously. If other troubleshooting techniques fail to restore the computer and you have a system image for recovery, you can use this feature to restore the computer from the backup image.

- **Windows Memory Diagnostics** Performs diagnostics on the computer's memory. If memory hardware errors are causing startup or other problems with the computer, you can use this tool to identify the problem.

As an administrator, you can use these tools to recover computers. If a remote user can't start Windows, you can boot the server with the Repair option and initiate recovery.

Performing a Clean Installation

Before you start an installation, you need to consider whether you want to manage the computer's drives and partitions during the setup process. If you want to use the advanced drive setup options that Setup provides for creating and formatting partitions, you need to boot the computer using the distribution media. If you don't use the distribution media, these options won't be available, and you'll only be able to manage disk partitions at a command prompt using the DiskPart utility.

You can perform a clean installation of Windows Server 2008 R2 by following these steps:

1. Start the Setup program by using one of the following techniques:
   - For a new installation, turn on the computer with the Windows Server 2008 R2 distribution media in the computer's DVD-ROM drive, and then

press any key when prompted to start Setup from your media. If you are not prompted to boot from the DVD-ROM drive, you need to change the computer's firmware settings to allow this.

- For a clean installation over an existing installation, you can boot from the distribution media, or you can start the computer and log on using an account with administrator privileges. When you insert the Windows Server 2008 R2 distribution media into the computer's DVD-ROM drive, Setup should start automatically. If Setup doesn't start automatically, use Windows Explorer to access the distribution media and then double-click Setup.exe.

2. If you started the computer using the distribution media, choose your language, time and currency format, and keyboard layout when prompted. Only one keyboard layout is available during installation. If your keyboard language and the language edition of Windows Server 2008 R2 you are installing are different, you might see unexpected characters as you type. Be sure that you select the correct keyboard language to avoid this. When you are ready to continue with the installation, click Next.

3. On the next Setup page, click Install Now to start the installation. If you are starting the installation from an existing operating system and are connected to a network or the Internet, choose whether to get updates during the installation. Click either Go Online To Get The Latest Updates For Installation or Do Not Get The Latest Updates For Installation.

4. With volume and enterprise licensed editions of Windows Server 2008 R2, you might not need to provide a product key during installation. With retail editions, however, you need to enter a product key when prompted. Click Next to continue. The Activate Windows When I'm Online check box is selected by default to ensure that you are prompted to activate the operating system the next time you connect to the Internet.

NOTE You must activate Windows Server 2008 R2 after installation. If you don't activate Windows Server 2008 R2 in the allotted time, you see an error stating "Your activation period has expired" or that you have a "Non-genuine version of Windows Server 2008 R2 installed." Windows Server 2008 R2 will then run with reduced functionality. You need to activate and validate Windows Server 2008 R2 as necessary to regain full functionality.

5. On the Select The Operating System You Want To Install page, options are provided for full-server and core-server installations. Make the appropriate selection, and then click Next.

6. The license terms for Windows Server 2008 R2 have changed from previous releases of Windows. After you review the license terms, click I Accept The License Terms, and then click Next.

7. On the Which Type Of Installation Do You Want page, select the type of installation you want Setup to perform. Since you are performing a clean

installation to replace an existing installation or configure a new computer, select Custom (Advanced) as the installation type. If you started Setup from the boot prompt rather than from Windows itself, the Upgrade option is disabled. To upgrade rather than perform a clean install, you need to restart the computer and boot the currently installed operating system. After you log on, you then need to start the installation.

8. On the Where Do You Want To Install Windows page, select the disk or disk and partition on which you want to install the operating system. There are two versions of the Where Do You Want To Install Windows page, so you need to keep the following in mind:

   - When a computer has a single hard disk with a single partition encompassing the whole disk or a single area of unallocated space, the whole disk partition is selected by default, and you can click Next to choose this as the install location and continue. With a disk that is completely unallocated, you may want to create the necessary partition before installing the operating system, as discussed in "Creating, Formatting, Deleting, and Extending Disk Partitions During Installation" later in this chapter.

   - When a computer has multiple disks or a single disk with multiple partitions, you need to select an existing partition to use for installing the operating system or create a partition. You can create and manage partitions as discussed in "Creating, Formatting, Deleting, and Extending Disk Partitions During Installation" later in this chapter.

   - If a disk has not been initialized for use or if the firmware of the computer does not support starting the operating system from the selected disk, you need to initialize it by creating one or more partitions on the disk. You cannot select or format a hard disk partition that uses FAT or FAT32 or has other incompatible settings. To work around this issue, you may want to convert the partition to NTFS. When working with this page, you can access a command prompt to perform any necessary preinstallation tasks. See "Creating, Formatting, Deleting, and Extending Disk Partitions During Installation" later in this chapter.

9. If the partition you select contains a previous Windows installation, Setup provides a prompt stating that existing user and application settings will be moved to a folder named Windows.old and that you must copy these settings to the new installation to use them. Click OK.

10. Click Next. Setup starts the installation of the operating system. During this procedure, Setup copies the full disk image of Windows Server 2008 R2 to the location you selected and then expands it. Afterward, Setup installs features based on the computer's configuration and the hardware it detects. This process requires several automatic restarts. When Setup finishes the installation, the operating system will be loaded, and you can perform initial configuration tasks such as setting the administrator password and server name.

REAL WORLD Servers running core installations of Windows Server are configured to use DHCP by default. As long as the server has a network card and a connected network cable, a Server Core installation should be able to connect to your organization's DHCP servers and obtain the correct network settings. You can configure the server by using Sconfig, which provides menu options for configuring domain/workgroup membership, the computer name, remote management, Windows Update, Remote Desktop, network settings, date and time, log off, restart, and shutdown.

Alternatively, you can configure the server by using individual commands. If you want to use a static IP address, use Netsh to apply the settings you want. Once networking is configured correctly, use **Slmgr –ipk** to set the product key and **Slmgr –ato** to activate Windows. Enter **timedate.cpl** to set the server's date and time. If you want to enable remote management using the WS-Management protocol, enter **winrm quickconfig**.

Next, you'll probably want to set the name of the computer. To view the default computer name, enter **echo %computername%**. To rename the computer, use **Netdom RenameComputer** with the following syntax: **netdom renamecomputer** *currentname* **/newname:***newname,* where *currentname* is the current name of the computer and *newname* is the name you want to assign. An example is **netdom renamecomputer win-k4m6bnovlhe /newname:server18**. You'll need to restart the computer, and you can do this by entering **shutdown /r**.

When the computer restarts, you can join it to a domain by using Netdom Join. For the syntax, enter **netdom join /?**.

Performing an Upgrade Installation

Although Windows Server 2008 R2 provides an upgrade option during installation, an upgrade with Windows Server 2008 R2 isn't what you think it is. With an upgrade, the Windows Server 2008 R2 Setup program performs a clean installation of the operating system and then migrates user settings, documents, and applications from the earlier version of Windows.

During the migration portion of the upgrade, Setup moves folders and files from the previous installation to a folder named Windows.old. As a result, the previous installation will no longer run. Settings are migrated because Windows Server 2008 R2 doesn't store user and application information in the same way as earlier versions of Windows do.

NOTE You cannot perform an upgrade installation of Windows Server 2008 R2 on a computer with a 32-bit operating system, even if the computer has 64-bit processors. You need to migrate the services being provided by the computer to other servers and then perform a clean installation. The Windows Server Migration tools might be able to help you migrate your server. These tools are available on computers running Windows Server 2008 R2.

You can perform an upgrade installation of Windows Server 2008 R2 by following these steps:

1. Start the computer and log on using an account with administrator privileges. When you insert the Windows Server 2008 R2 distribution media into the computer's DVD-ROM drive, Setup should start automatically. If Setup doesn't start automatically, use Windows Explorer to access the distribution media and then double-click Setup.exe.

2. Because you are upgrading an existing operating system, you are not prompted to choose your language, time and currency format, or keyboard layout. Only one keyboard layout is available during installation. If your keyboard language and the language of the edition of Windows Server 2008 R2 you are installing are different, you might see unexpected characters as you type.

3. On the next Setup page, choose Install Now to start the installation. Next, choose whether to get updates during the installation. Click either Go Online To Get The Latest Updates For Installation (Recommended) or Do Not Get The Latest Updates For Installation.

4. With volume and enterprise licensed editions of Windows Server 2008 R2, you might not need to provide a product key during installation of the operating system. With retail editions, however, you are prompted to enter a product key. Click Next to continue. The Automatically Activate Windows When I'm Online check box is selected by default to ensure that you are prompted to activate the operating system the next time you connect to the Internet.

5. On the Select The Operating System You Want To Install page, options are provided for full-server and core-server installations. Make the appropriate selection, and then click Next.

6. The license terms for Windows Server 2008 R2 have changed from previous releases of Windows. After you review the license terms, click I Accept The License Terms, and then click Next.

7. On the Which Type Of Installation Do You Want page, you need to select the type of installation you want Setup to perform. Because you are performing a clean installation over an existing installation, select Upgrade. If you started Setup from the boot prompt rather than from Windows itself, the Upgrade option is disabled. To upgrade rather than perform a clean install, you need to restart the computer and boot the currently installed operating system. After you log on, you can start the installation.

8. Setup will then start the installation. Because you are upgrading the operating system, you do not need to choose an installation location. During this process, Setup copies the full disk image of Windows Server 2008 R2 to the system disk. Afterward, Setup installs features based on the computer's configuration and the hardware it detects. When Setup finishes the installation,

the operating system will be loaded, and you can perform initial configuration tasks such as setting the administrator password and server name.

Performing Additional Administration Tasks During Installation

Sometimes you might forget to perform a preinstallation task prior to starting the installation. Rather than restarting the operating system, you can access a command prompt from Setup or use advanced drive options to perform the necessary administrative tasks.

Using the Command Line During Installation

When you access a command prompt from Setup, you access the MINWINPC (mini Windows PC) environment used by Setup to install the operating system. During installation, on the Where Do You Want To Install Windows page, you can access a command prompt by pressing Shift+F10. As Table 2-4 shows, the mini Windows PC environment gives you access to many of the same command-line tools that are available in a standard installation of Windows Server 2008 R2.

TABLE 2-4 Command-Line Utilities in the Mini Windows PC Environment

COMMAND	DESCRIPTION
ARP	Displays and modifies the IP-to-physical address translation tables used by the Address Resolution Protocol (ARP).
ASSOC	Displays and modifies file extension associations.
ATTRIB	Displays and changes file attributes.
CALL	Calls a script or script label as a procedure.
CD/CHDIR	Displays the name of or changes the current directory.
CHKDSK	Checks a disk for errors and displays a report.
CHKNTFS	Displays the status of volumes. Sets or excludes volumes from automatic system checking when the computer is started.
CHOICE	Creates a list from which users can select one of several choices in a batch script.
CLS	Clears the console window.
CMD	Starts a new instance of the Windows command shell.
COLOR	Sets the colors of the command-shell window.
CONVERT	Converts FAT volumes to NTFS.

COMMAND	DESCRIPTION
COPY	Copies or combines files.
DATE	Displays or sets the system date.
DEL	Deletes one or more files.
DIR	Displays a list of files and subdirectories within a directory.
DISKPART	Invokes a text-mode command interpreter so that you can manage disks, partitions, and volumes using a separate command prompt and commands that are internal to DISKPART.
DISM	Services and manages Windows images.
DOSKEY	Edits command lines, recalls Windows commands, and creates macros.
ECHO	Displays messages or turns command echoing on or off.
ENDLOCAL	Ends localization of environment changes in a batch file.
ERASE	Deletes one or more files.
EXIT	Exits the command interpreter.
EXPAND	Uncompresses files.
FIND	Searches for a text string in files.
FOR	Runs a specified command for each file in a set of files.
FORMAT	Formats a floppy disk or hard drive.
FTP	Transfers files.
FTYPE	Displays or modifies file types used in file extension associations.
GOTO	Directs the Windows command interpreter to a labeled line in a script.
HOSTNAME	Prints the computer's name.
IF	Performs conditional processing in batch programs.
IPCONFIG	Displays TCP/IP configuration.
LABEL	Creates, changes, or deletes the volume label of a disk.
MD/MKDIR	Creates a directory or subdirectory.
MORE	Displays output one screen at a time.
MOUNTVOL	Manages a volume mount point.

COMMAND	DESCRIPTION
MOVE	Moves files from one directory to another directory on the same drive.
NBTSTAT	Displays the status of NetBIOS.
NET ACCOUNTS	Manages user account and password policies.
NET COMPUTER	Adds or removes computers from a domain.
NET CONFIG SERVER	Displays or modifies configuration of a server service.
NET CONFIG WORKSTATION	Displays or modifies configuration of a workstation service.
NET CONTINUE	Resumes a paused service.
NET FILE	Displays or manages open files on a server.
NET GROUP	Displays or manages global groups.
NET LOCALGROUP	Displays or manages local group accounts.
NET NAME	Displays or modifies recipients for messenger service messages.
NET PAUSE	Suspends a service.
NET PRINT	Displays or manages print jobs and shared queues.
NET SEND	Sends a messenger service message.
NET SESSION	Lists or disconnects sessions.
NET SHARE	Displays or manages shared printers and directories.
NET START	Lists or starts network services.
NET STATISTICS	Displays workstation and server statistics.
NET STOP	Stops services.
NET TIME	Displays or synchronizes network time.
NET USE	Displays or manages remote connections.
NET USER	Displays or manages local user accounts.
NET VIEW	Displays network resources or computers.
NETSH	Invokes a separate command prompt that allows you to manage the configuration of various network services on local and remote computers.
NETSTAT	Displays the status of network connections.
PATH	Displays or sets a search path for executable files in the current command window.

COMMAND	DESCRIPTION
PATHPING	Traces routes and provides packet loss information.
PAUSE	Suspends processing of a script and waits for keyboard input.
PING	Determines whether a network connection can be established.
POPD	Changes to the directory stored by PUSHD.
PRINT	Prints a text file.
PROMPT	Modifies the Windows command prompt.
PUSHD	Saves the current directory and then changes to a new directory.
RD/RMDIR	Removes a directory.
RECOVER	Recovers readable information from a bad or defective disk.
REG ADD	Adds a new subkey or entry to the registry.
REG COMPARE	Compares registry subkeys or entries.
REG COPY	Copies a registry entry to a specified key path on a local or remote system.
REG DELETE	Deletes a subkey or entries from the registry.
REG QUERY	Lists the entries under a key and the names of subkeys (if any).
REG RESTORE	Writes saved subkeys and entries back to the registry.
REG SAVE	Saves a copy of specified subkeys, entries, and values to a file.
REGSVR32	Registers and unregisters DLLs.
REM	Adds comments to scripts.
REN	Renames a file.
ROUTE	Manages network routing tables.
SET	Displays or modifies Windows environment variables. Also used to evaluate numeric expressions at the command line.
SETLOCAL	Begins localization of environment changes in a batch file.
SFC	Scans and verifies protected system files.

COMMAND	DESCRIPTION
SHIFT	Shifts the position of replaceable parameters in scripts.
START	Starts a new command-shell window to run a specified program or command.
SUBST	Maps a path to a drive letter.
TIME	Displays or sets the system time.
TITLE	Sets the title for the command-shell window.
TRACERT	Displays the path between computers.
TYPE	Displays the contents of a text file.
VER	Displays the Windows version.
VERIFY	Tells Windows whether to verify that your files are written correctly to a disk.
VOL	Displays a disk volume label and serial number.

Forcing Disk Partition Removal During Installation

During installation, you may be unable to select the hard disk you want to use. This issue can arise if the hard disk partition contains an invalid byte offset value. To resolve this issue, you need to remove the partitions on the hard disk (which destroys all associated data) and then create the necessary partition using the advanced options in the Setup program. During installation, on the Where Do You Want To Install Windows page, you can remove unrecognized hard disk partitions by following these steps:

1. Press Shift+F10 to open a command prompt.
2. At the command prompt, type **diskpart**. This starts the DiskPart utility.
3. To view a list of disks on the computer, type **list disk**.
4. Select a disk by typing **select disk *DiskNumber***, where *DiskNumber* is the number of the disk you want to work with.
5. To permanently remove the partitions on the selected disk, type **clean**.
6. When the cleaning process is finished, type **exit** to exit the DiskPart utility.
7. Type **exit** to exit the command prompt.
8. In the Install Windows dialog box, click the back arrow button to return to the previous window.
9. On the Which Type Of Installation Do You Want page, click Custom (Advanced) to start a custom install.

10. On the Where Do You Want To Install Windows page, click the disk you pre-
    viously cleaned to select it as the installation partition. As necessary, click the
    Disk Options link to display the Delete, Format, New, and Extend partition
    configuration options.

11. Click New. In the Size box, set the size of the partition in megabytes, and
    then click Apply.

Loading Disk Device Drivers During Installation

During installation, on the Where Do You Want To Install Windows page, you can
use the Load Drivers option to load the device drivers for a hard disk drive or a hard
disk controller. Typically, you use this option when a disk drive that you want to use
for installing the operating system isn't available for selection because the device
drivers aren't available.

To load the device drivers and make the hard disk available, follow these steps:

1. During installation, on the Where Do You Want To Install Windows page,
   click Load Drivers.

2. When prompted, insert the installation media into a floppy disk, CD, DVD,
   or USB flash drive, and then click OK. Setup then searches the computer's
   removable media drives for the device drivers.

   a. If Setup finds multiple device drivers, select the driver to install, and then
      click Next.

   b. If Setup doesn't find the device driver, click Browse to use the Browse For
      Folder dialog box to select the device driver to load, click OK, and then
      click Next.

You can click the Rescan button to have Setup rescan the computer's removable
media drives for the device drivers. If you are unable to install a device driver successfully, click the back arrow button in the upper-left corner of the Install Windows
dialog box to go back to the previous page.

Creating, Formatting, Deleting, and Extending Disk Partitions During Installation

When you are performing a clean installation and have started the computer from
the distribution media, the Where Do You Want To Install Windows page has additional options. You can display these options by clicking Drive Options (Advanced).
These additional options are used as follows:

- **New**   Creates a partition. You must then format the partition.

- **Format**   Formats a new partition so that you can use it for installing the
  operating system.

- **Delete**   Deletes a partition that is no longer wanted.

- **Extend**   Extends a partition to increase its size.

The sections that follow discuss how to use each of these options. If these options aren't available, you can still work with the computer's disks. On the Where Do You Want To Install Windows page, press Shift+F10 to open a command prompt. At the command prompt, type **diskpart** to start the DiskPart utility.

CREATING DISK PARTITIONS DURING INSTALLATION

Creating a partition allows you to set the partition's size. Because you can create new partitions only in areas of unallocated space on a disk, you may need to delete existing partitions to be able to create a partition of the size you want. Once you've created a partition, you can format the partition so that you can use it to install a file system. If you don't format a partition, you can still use it for installing the operating system. In this case, Setup formats the partition when you continue installing the operating system.

You can create a new partition by following these steps:

1. During installation, on the Where Do You Want To Install Windows page, click Drive Options (Advanced) to display the advanced options for working with drives.

2. Click the disk on which you want to create the partition, and then click New.

3. In the Size box, set the size of the partition in megabytes, and then click Apply to have Setup create a partition on the selected disk.

After you create a partition, you need to format the partition to continue with the installation.

FORMATTING DISK PARTITIONS DURING INSTALLATION

Formatting a partition creates a file system on the partition. When formatting is complete, you have a formatted partition on which you can install the operating system. Keep in mind that formatting a partition destroys all data on the partition. You should format existing partitions (rather than ones you've just created) only when you want to remove an existing partition and all its contents so that you can start the installation from a freshly formatted partition.

You can format a partition by following these steps:

1. During installation, on the Where Do You Want To Install Windows page, click Drive Options (Advanced) to display the advanced options for working with drives.

2. Click the partition that you want to format.

3. Click Format. When prompted to confirm that you want to format the partition, click OK. Setup then formats the partition.

DELETING DISK PARTITIONS DURING INSTALLATION

Deleting a partition removes a partition that you no longer want or need. When Setup finishes deleting the partition, the disk space previously allocated to the partition becomes unallocated space on the disk. Deleting the partition destroys all data on the partition. Typically, you need to delete a partition only when it is in the wrong format or when you want to combine areas of free space on a disk.

You can delete a partition by following these steps:

1. During installation, on the Where Do You Want To Install Windows page, click Drive Options (Advanced) to display the advanced options for working with drives.

2. Click the partition you want to delete.

3. Click Delete. When prompted to confirm that you want to delete the partition, click OK. Setup then deletes the partition.

EXTENDING DISK PARTITIONS DURING INSTALLATION

Windows Server 2008 R2 requires at least 10 GB of disk space for installation, and at least 40 GB of available disk space is recommended. If an existing partition is too small, you won't be able to use it to install the operating system. To resolve this, you can extend a partition to increase its size by using areas of unallocated space on the current disk. You can extend a partition with an existing file system only if it is formatted with NTFS 5.2 or later. New partitions created in Setup can be extended as well, provided that the disk on which you create the partition has unallocated space.

You can extend a partition by following these steps:

1. During installation, on the Where Do You Want To Install Windows page, click Drive Options (Advanced) to display the advanced options for working with drives.

2. Click the partition you want to extend.

3. Click Extend. In the Size box, set the size of the partition in megabytes, and then click Apply to extend the selected partition.

4. When prompted to confirm that you want to extend the partition, click OK. Setup then extends the partition.

Managing Roles, Role Services, and Features

When you want to manage server configurations, you'll primarily use Server Manager to manage roles, role services, and features. Not only can you use Server Manager to add or remove roles, role services, and features, but you can also use Server Manager to view the configuration details and status for these software components.

REAL WORLD Server Manager's command-line counterpart is the ServerManager module for Windows PowerShell. Generally, this module is not imported into Windows PowerShell by default, so you need to import the module before you can use the cmdlets it provides. You import the Server Manager module by entering **Import-Module ServerManager** at the Windows PowerShell prompt. Once the module is imported, you can use it with the currently running instance of Windows PowerShell. The next time you start Windows PowerShell, you need to import the module again if you want to use its features.

At a Windows PowerShell prompt, you can obtain a detailed list of a server's current state with regard to roles, role services, and features by typing **get-windowsfeature**. Each installed role, role service, and feature is highlighted and marked as such, and a management naming component in brackets follows the display name of each role, role service, and feature. By using Add-WindowsFeature or Remove-Windows-Feature followed by the management name, you can install or uninstall a role, role service, or feature. For example, you can install Network Load Balancing by entering **add-windowsfeature nlb**. You can add **–includeallsubfeature** when installing components to add all subordinate role services or features.

Viewing Configured Roles and Role Services

In Server Manager, when you select Roles in the left pane, you see a list of roles that you installed. As Figure 2-1 shows, the main view of the Roles node displays a Roles Summary entry that lists the number and names of installed roles. In the case of error-related events for a particular server role, Server Manager displays a warning icon to the left of the role name.

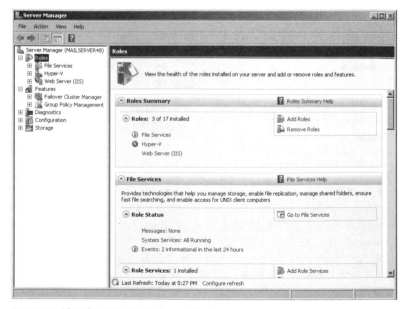

FIGURE 2-1 View the status details for installed roles.

In the Roles pane, the name of the role is a clickable link that displays related role details. The role details provide the following information:

- Summary information about the status of related system services. If applicable, Server Manager lists the number of related services that are running or stopped, such as "System Services: 6 Running, 2 Stopped."

- Summary information about events the related services and components have generated in the last 24 hours, including details about whether any errors have occurred, such as "Events: 2 error(s), 8 warning(s), 14 informational in the last 24 hours."

- Summary information about the role services installed, including the number of role services installed and the status (Installed or Not Installed) of each individual role service that you can use with the role.

TIP By default, Server Manager refreshes details every 2 minutes. You can refresh the details manually by clicking Refresh on the Action menu. If you want to set a different default refresh interval, click Configure Refresh at the bottom of the main pane, use the options provided to set a new refresh interval, and then click OK.

In Server Manager, if you click a role under Roles Summary, Server Manager displays expanded summary details about the events and services for the related role. Server Manager lists all events in the last 24 hours. If you click an event and then click View Event Properties, you can get detailed information about the event. Additionally, Server Manager provides details regarding the system services used by the role and the services' status. You can manage a service by clicking it and then clicking the related Stop, Start, or Restart options provided. In many cases, if a service isn't running as you think it should, you can use the Restart option to resolve the issue by stopping and then starting the service. See Chapter 4, "Monitoring Processes, Services, and Events," for detailed information about working with events and system services.

Adding or Removing Roles on Servers

When you select Roles in Server Manager, the Roles pane provides details about the current roles that are installed. In the Roles Summary section, you'll find options for adding and removing roles.

You can add a server role by following these steps:

1. Start Server Manager by clicking the Server Manager icon on the Quick Launch toolbar or by clicking Start, Administrative Tools, Server Manager.

2. In Server Manager, select Roles in the left pane, and then click Add Roles in the Roles pane. This starts the Add Roles Wizard. If the wizard displays the Before You Begin page, read the introductory text, and then click Next. You can avoid seeing the Before You Begin page the next time you start this

wizard by selecting the Skip This Page By Default check box before clicking Next.

3. On the Select Server Roles page, select the role or roles to install. If additional features are required to install a role, you'll see the Add Features Required For dialog box. Click Add Required Features to close the dialog box and add the required features to the server installation. Click Next twice to continue.

NOTE Some roles cannot be added at the same time as other roles. You have to install each role separately. Other roles cannot be combined with existing roles, and you'll see warning prompts about this. Adding the Active Directory Domain Services role does not configure the server as a domain controller. To configure the server as a domain controller, you must run Dcpromo.exe as discussed in Chapter 7, "Using Active Directory." Additionally, if you plan to have a domain controller also act as a DNS server, Microsoft recommends that you install the Active Directory Domain Services role and then use Dcpromo to configure the server as a DNS server and domain controller. A server running a core-server installation can act as a domain controller and can also hold any of the flexible single-master operations (FSMO) roles for Active Directory.

4. For each of the roles you are adding, you'll see a series of related pages that let you configure the associated role services as well as any other required details. When selecting or clearing role services, consider the following before you click Next to continue:

   - If you select a role service with additional required features, a dialog box is displayed listing the additional required role services and features. After you review the required roles, click the Add Required Role Services button to accept the additions and close the dialog box. If you click Cancel instead, Setup will clear the feature you previously selected.

   - If you try to remove a role service that is required based on a previously installed role service, you'll see a warning prompt about dependent services that Setup must also remove. In most cases, you can click Cancel to preserve the previous selection. If you click the Remove Dependent Role Services button, Setup will also remove the previously selected dependent services, which could cause the server to not function as expected.

5. On the Confirm Installation Selections page, click the Print, E-Mail, Or Save This Information link to generate an installation report and display it in Internet Explorer. You can then use standard Internet Explorer features to print or save the report. After you review the installation options and save them as necessary, click Install to begin the installation process.

6. When Setup finishes installing the server with the features you selected, you'll see the Installation Results page. Review the installation details to ensure that all phases of the installation were completed successfully. If any

portion of the installation failed, note the reason for the failure, and then use the following troubleshooting techniques:

a. Click the Print, E-Mail, Or Save This Information link to create or update the installation report and display it in Internet Explorer.

b. Scroll down to the bottom of the installation report in Internet Explorer, and then click Full Log (Troubleshooting Only) to display the Server Manager log in Notepad.

c. In Notepad, press Ctrl+F, enter the current date in the appropriate format for your language settings (such as 2009-08-30), and then click Find Next. Notepad moves through the log to the first Setup entry from the current date.

d. Review the Server Manager entries for installation problems and take corrective actions as appropriate.

You can remove a server role by following these steps:

1. Start Server Manager by clicking the Server Manager icon on the Quick Launch toolbar or by clicking Start, Administrative Tools, Server Manager.

2. In Server Manager, select Roles in the left pane, and then click Remove Roles in the Roles pane. This starts the Remove Roles Wizard. If Setup displays the Before You Begin page, read the introductory text, and then click Next. You can avoid seeing the Before You Begin page the next time you start this wizard by selecting the Skip This Page By Default check box before clicking Next.

3. On the Remove Server Roles page, clear the check box for the role you want to remove, and then click Next. If you try to remove a role that another role depends on, a warning prompt appears stating that you cannot remove the role unless you remove the other role as well. If you click the Remove Dependent Role button, Setup will remove both roles.

4. On the Confirm Removal Selections page, review the related role services that Setup will remove based on your previous selections, and then click Remove.

5. When Setup finishes modifying the server configuration, you'll see the Removal Results page. Review the modification details to ensure that all phases of the removal process were completed successfully. If any portion of the removal process failed, note the reason for the failure and then use the troubleshooting techniques outlined in the previous procedure to help resolve the problem.

Viewing and Modifying Role Services on Servers

In Server Manager, you can view the role services configured for a role by selecting Roles in the left pane and then scrolling down to the Roles Services section for the role that you want to work with. In the details section, you'll find a list of role services that you can install as well as their current status (Installed or Not Installed).

You can manage role services for servers using the Add Role Services and Remove Role Services options provided for the related role details entry. Some roles, however, do not have individual role services that you can manage in this way. With these roles, you can only modify the server role or remove the role.

You can add role services by following these steps:

1. Start Server Manager by clicking the Server Manager icon on the Quick Launch toolbar or by clicking Start, Administrative Tools, Server Manager.

2. In Server Manager, select Roles in the left pane and then scroll down until you see the Role Services section for the role you want to manage. In the details section for the role, click Add Role Services. This starts the Add Role Services Wizard.

3. On the Select Role Services page, Setup displays the currently installed role services as unavailable so that you cannot select them. To add a role service, select it from the role services list. When you have finished selecting role services to add, click Next, and then click Install.

You can remove role services by following these steps:

1. Start Server Manager by clicking the Server Manager icon on the Quick Launch toolbar or by clicking Start, Administrative Tools, Server Manager.

2. In Server Manager, select Roles in the left pane, and then scroll down until you see the Role Services section for the role you want to manage. In the details section for the role, click Remove Role Services. This starts the Remove Role Services Wizard.

3. On the Select Role Services page, the currently installed role services are selected. To remove a role service, clear the related check box. If you try to remove a role service that another role service depends on, you'll see a warning prompt stating that you cannot remove the role service unless you also remove the other role service. If you click the Remove Dependent Role Service button, Setup will remove both role services.

4. When you have finished selecting role services to remove, click Next, and then click Remove.

Adding or Removing Features in Windows Server 2008 R2

In earlier versions of Windows, you use the Add/Remove Windows Components option of the Add Or Remove Programs utility to add or remove operating system components. In Windows Server 2008 R2, you configure operating system components as Windows features that you can turn on or off rather than add or remove.

You can add server features by following these steps:

1. Start Server Manager by clicking the Server Manager icon on the Quick Launch toolbar or by clicking Start, Administrative Tools, Server Manager.

2. In Server Manager, select Features in the left pane and then click Add Features in the Features pane. This starts the Add Features Wizard. If the wizard

displays the Before You Begin page, read the introductory text and then click Next. You can avoid seeing the Before You Begin page the next time you start this wizard by selecting the Skip This Page By Default check box before clicking Next.

3. On the Select Features page, select the feature or features to install. If additional features are required to install a feature you selected, you'll see the Add Features Required For dialog box. Click Add Required Features to close the dialog box and add the required features to the server installation.

4. When you have finished selecting features to add, click Next, and then click Install.

You can remove server features by following these steps:

1. Start Server Manager by clicking the Server Manager icon on the Quick Launch toolbar or by clicking Start, Administrative Tools, Server Manager.

2. In Server Manager, select Features in the left pane, and then click Remove Features in the Features pane. This starts the Remove Features Wizard. If the wizard displays the Before You Begin page, read the introductory text, and then click Next. You can avoid seeing the Before You Begin page the next time you start this wizard by selecting the Skip This Page By Default check box before clicking Next.

3. On the Select Features page, the currently installed features are selected. To remove a feature, clear the related check box. If you try to remove a feature that another feature depends on, you'll see a warning prompt stating that you cannot remove the feature unless you also remove the other feature. If you click the Remove Dependent Feature button, Setup will remove both features.

4. When you are finished selecting features to remove, click Next, and then click Remove.

Deploying Virtualized Servers

Hyper-V is a virtual machine technology that allows multiple guest operating systems to run concurrently on one computer and provide separate applications and services to client computers. The Hyper-V feature can be installed only on servers with processors that implement hardware-assisted virtualization and hardware data execution protection. The Windows hypervisor acts as the virtual machine engine, providing the necessary layer of software for installing guest operating systems.

Virtualization can offer performance improvements, reduce the number of servers, and reduce the total cost of ownership (TCO). AMD Virtualization (AMD-V) technology is included in second and later generation AMD Opteron processors as well as other next generation AMD processors. Third generation AMD Opteron processors feature Rapid Virtualization Indexing (RVI) to accelerate the performance of virtualized applications. Intel Virtualization Technology (Intel VT) is included in

Intel Xeon 3000, 5000, and 7000 sequence processors; Intel Itanium 2 processors; and next generation Intel processors with the Intel vPro label.

NOTE Hyper-V is a technology in flux. Older processors with virtualization might have different features from newer processors, and these differences can present special challenges when you are migrating from one hardware platform to another.

Windows Server 2008 R2 supports many new virtualization features, including live migration and dynamic virtual machine storage. Live migration allows you to transparently move running virtual machines from one node of a failover cluster to another node in the same cluster. Dynamic virtual machine storage allows you to add or remove virtual hard disks and physical disks while a virtual machine is running.

Windows Server 2008 R2 adds support for up to 64 physical processor cores on servers using Hyper-V and also supports second-level address translation (SLAT) as implemented by Intel and AMD processors. SLAT adds a second level of paging below the architectural paging tables in the server's processors. This improves performance by providing an indirection layer from virtual machine memory access to physical memory access. On Intel-based processors, this feature is called extended page tables (EPT), and on AMD-based processors, this feature is called nested page tables (NPT).

Although Hyper-V is similar to Virtual PC and Virtual Server technology, you cannot install Hyper-V on a computer that has Virtual PC or Virtual Server installed. If you are familiar with Virtual PC or Virtual Server technology, you'll find that working with Hyper-V is similar.

Virtual machines require virtual networks to communicate with other computers. When you install Hyper-V, you can create one virtual network for each adapter available. After installing Hyper-V, you can create and manage virtual networks by using Virtual Network Manager. Microsoft recommends that you reserve one network adapter for remote access to the server. You do this by not designating the adapter for use with a virtual network.

You can install Hyper-V on a server with a virtualization-enabled processor by completing these steps:

1. In Server Manager, select Roles in the left pane, and then click Add Roles. This starts the Add Roles Wizard.

2. On the Select Server Roles page, select Hyper-V, and then click Next twice.

3. On the Create Virtual Networks page, shown in Figure 2-2, select a network adapter on which to create a virtual network so that virtual machines can communicate with other computers.

4. Click Next, and then click Install.

5. After Hyper-V is installed, click Close. When prompted to restart the server, click Yes. You must restart the server to complete the installation.

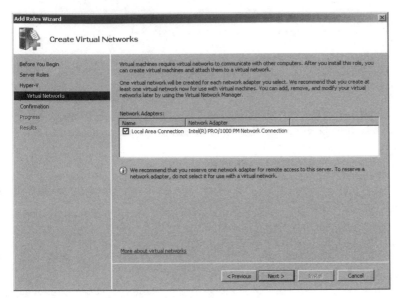

FIGURE 2-2 Select the network adapter to use for virtual networking.

You create and manage virtual machines using Hyper-V Manager, shown in Figure 2-3. Start Hyper-V Manager by clicking Start, Administrative Tools, Hyper-V Manager.

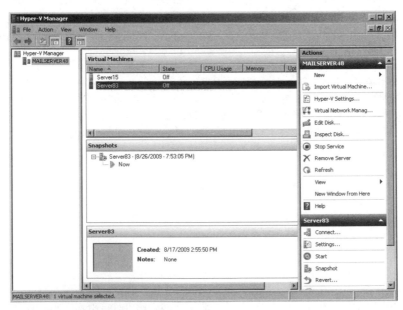

FIGURE 2-3 Use Hyper-V Manager to install and manage virtual machines.

Installing Hyper-V on a server establishes the server as a virtualization server. Each virtual machine you install on the server must be assigned resources to use and then be configured. The number of virtual machines you can run on any individual server depends on the server's hardware configuration and workload. During setup, you specify the amount of memory available to a virtual machine. Although you can change that memory allocation, the amount of memory actively allocated to a virtual machine cannot be used in other ways.

To install and configure a virtual machine, complete the following steps:

1. Start Hyper-V Manager by clicking Start, Administrative Tools, Hyper-V Manager.

2. In Hyper-V Manager, right-click the server node in the left pane, point to New, and then select Virtual Machine. This starts the New Virtual Machine Wizard.

3. Click Next. In the Name text box, enter a name for the virtual machine, such as AppServer02.

4. By default, the virtual machine data is stored on the system disk. To select a different location, select the Store The Virtual Machine In A Different Location check box, click Browse, and then use the Select Folder dialog box to select a save location.

5. Click Next. On the Assign Memory page, specify the amount of memory to allocate to the virtual machine. In most cases, you should reserve at least the minimum amount of memory recommended for the operating system you plan to install.

6. Click Next. On the Configure Networking page, use the Connection list to select a network adapter to use. Each new virtual machine includes a network adapter, and you can configure the adapter to use an available virtual network for communicating with other computers.

7. Click Next. On the Connect Virtual Hard Disk page, use the options provided to name and create a virtual hard disk for the virtual machine. Each virtual machine requires a virtual hard disk so that you can install an operating system and required applications.

8. Click Next. On the Installation Options page, select Install An Operating System From A Boot CD/DVD-ROM. If you have physical distribution media, insert the distribution media, and then specify the CD/DVD drive to use. If you want to install from an .iso image, select Image File, click Browse, and then use the Open dialog box to select the image file to use.

9. Click Next, and then click Finish.

10. In Hyper-V Manager, right-click the name of the virtual machine, and then click Connect.

11. In the Virtual Machine Connection window, click Start. After the virtual machine is initialized, the operating system installation should start

automatically. Continue with the operating system installation as you normally would.

When the installation is complete, log on to the virtual machine and configure it as you would any other server. From then on, you manage the virtual machine much as you would any other computer, except that you can externally control its state, available resources, and hardware devices using Hyper-V Manager. Additionally, when it comes to backups, several approaches are available:

- Back up the host server and all virtual machine data
- Back up the host server and only the configuration data for virtual machines
- Log on to virtual machines and perform normal backups as you would with any other server
- Use Hyper-V manager to create point-in-time snapshots of virtual machines

Ideally, you should use a combination of these approaches to ensure that your host server and virtual machines are protected. In some cases, you may want to back up the host server and configuration data and then log on to each virtual machine and use normal backups. Other times, you may want to back up the host machine and all virtual machine data. You will likely want to supplement your backup strategy by creating point-in-time snapshots of virtual machines.

CHAPTER 3

Managing Servers Running Windows Server 2008 R2

S ervers are the heart of any Windows network. One of your primary responsibilities as an administrator is to manage these resources. Windows Server 2008 Release 2 (R2) comes with several integrated management tools, including the Initial Configuration Tasks console for initially setting up a server and Server Manager for handling core system administration tasks. Although the Initial Configuration Tasks console is a handy tool for quick setup, Server Manager provides similar setup options, includes the functions of the Computer Management console, and has options for managing roles, features, and related settings. You can use Server Manager to perform a wide range of general administration tasks, including:

- Managing server setup and configuration
- Managing user sessions and connections to servers
- Managing file, directory, and share usage
- Setting administrative alerts
- Managing applications and network services
- Configuring hardware devices
- Viewing and configuring disk drives and removable storage devices

Server Manager is great for general system administration, but you also need a tool that gives you fine control over system environment settings and properties.

This is where the System utility comes into the picture. You can use this utility to do the following:

- Change a computer's name
- Configure application performance, virtual memory, and registry settings
- Manage system and user environment variables
- Set system startup and recovery options

Performing Initial Configuration Tasks

The Initial Configuration Tasks console, shown in Figure 3-1, can help you quickly set up a new server. Windows Server 2008 R2 automatically starts this console after you complete the installation of the operating system. If you do not want the console to start each time you log on, select the Do Not Show This Window At Logon check box in the lower-left corner of the console window. If you close the console and want to reopen it, or if you configured the console so that it doesn't start automatically, you can start the console by clicking Start, typing **oobe** in the Search box, and then pressing Enter.

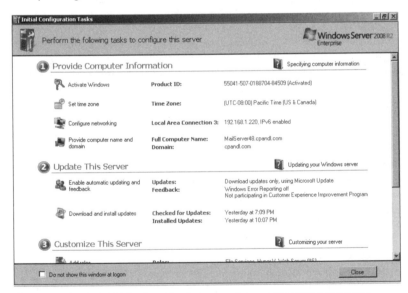

FIGURE 3-1 Use the Initial Configuration Tasks console to quickly set up a new server.

> **REAL WORLD** When you are working with Server Core installations, you can use Sconfig to configure domain and workgroup membership, the computer's name, remote management, Windows Update, Remote Desktop, network settings, and the date and time. You also can use Sconfig to log off, restart, and shut down the server. To start Sconfig, simply enter **sconfig** at the command prompt. You can then choose menu options and follow the prompts to configure the server.

You can use the Initial Configuration Tasks console to perform the following tasks:

- **Activate Windows** Use this option to enter a product key and activate the operating system over the Internet.

- **Set Time Zone** Use this option to display the Date And Time dialog box. You can then configure the server's time zone by clicking Change Time Zone, selecting the appropriate time zone, and then clicking OK twice. You can also display the Date And Time dialog box by right-clicking the clock on the taskbar and then selecting Adjust Date/Time. Although all servers are configured to synchronize time automatically with an Internet time server, the time synchronization process does not change a computer's time zone.

- **Configure Networking** Use this option to display the Network Connections console. You can then configure network connections by double-clicking the connection you want to work with and then clicking Properties to open the Properties dialog box. By default, servers are configured to use dynamic addressing for both IPv4 and IPv6. You can also display the Network Connections console by clicking Manage Network Connections under Tasks in Network And Sharing Center.

- **Provide Computer Name And Domain** Use this option to display the System Properties dialog box with the Computer Name tab selected. You can then change a computer's name and domain information by clicking Change, providing the computer name and domain information, and then clicking OK. By default, servers are assigned a randomly generated name and are configured as part of a workgroup called WORKGROUP. In the Small Icons or Large Icons view of Control Panel, you can display the System Properties dialog box with the Computer Name tab selected by double-clicking System and then clicking Change Settings under Computer Name, Domain, And Workgroup Settings.

- **Enable Automatic Updating And Feedback** Use this option to enable Windows automatic updating and feedback. By default, servers are not configured for automatic updating but are configured to provide automatic feedback. This means error reports are sent to Microsoft through the Windows Error Reporting feature and that anonymous usage information is sent to Microsoft through the Customer Experience Improvement Program. Microsoft recommends that you enable both these features to ensure that servers receive updates and to help improve future releases of the Windows operating system.

- **Download And Install Updates** Use this option to display the Windows Update utility in Control Panel, which you can then use to enable automatic updating (if Windows Update is disabled) or to check for updates (if Windows Update is enabled). By default, Windows Update is not enabled. In the Small Icons or Large Icons view of Control Panel, you can display Windows Update by selecting the Windows Update option.

- **Add Roles** Use this option to start the Add Roles Wizard, which you can then use to install roles on the server. By default, servers have no configured roles. In Server Manager, options for adding or removing roles are provided when you select Roles.

- **Add Features** Use this option to start the Add Features Wizard, which you can then use to install features on the server. By default, servers have no configured features. In Server Manager, options for adding or removing features are provided when you select Features.

- **Enable Remote Desktop** Use this option to display the System Properties dialog box with the Remote tab selected. You can then configure Remote Desktop by selecting the configuration option you want to use and clicking OK. By default, no remote connections to a server are allowed. In the Small Icons or Large Icons view of Control Panel, you can display the System Properties dialog box with the Remote tab selected by double-clicking System and then clicking Remote Settings in the left pane.

- **Configure Windows Firewall** Use this option to display the Windows Firewall utility. You can then configure Windows Firewall by clicking Change Settings. Use the Windows Firewall Settings dialog box to set the configuration. By default, Windows Firewall is enabled. In the Small Icons or Large Icons view of Control Panel, you can display Windows Firewall by double-clicking the Windows Firewall option.

NOTE I've provided this summary of options as an introduction and quick reference. I'll discuss the related configuration tasks and technologies in more detail throughout this and other chapters in the book.

Managing Your Servers

The Server Manager console is designed to handle core system administration tasks. You'll spend a lot of time working with this tool, and you should get to know every detail. Start the Server Manager console with either of the following techniques:

- Choose Start, click Administrative Tools, and then click Server Manager.

- Click Server Manager on the Quick Launch toolbar.

As Figure 3-2 shows, the main window in Server Manager has a two-pane view similar to Computer Management. You use the console tree in the left pane for navigation and tool selection. In the left pane, the primary nodes are divided into five broad categories:

- **Roles** Provides an overview of the status of the roles installed on a server as well as options for managing the roles. For each installed role, you'll find a node that you can select to view a detailed status of the role, which includes events generated in the last 24 hours, the installed/not installed status of related role services, and resource links. Expand a role's node to display related management tools.

- **Features** Provides an overview of the status of the features installed on the server as well as options for managing features. Features that you add—such as Windows Server Backup—are included in Server Manager.

- **Diagnostics** Provides access to general-purpose tools for managing services and devices, monitoring performance, and viewing events.

- **Configuration** Provides access to general-purpose configuration tools.

- **Storage** Provides access to drive management tools.

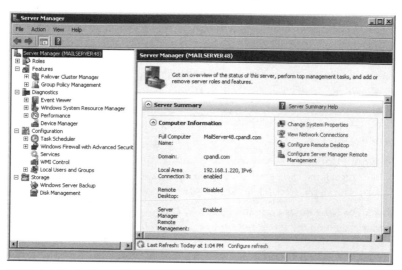

FIGURE 3-2 Use the Server Manager console to manage a server's configuration.

The right pane is the details pane. When you select the top-level Server Manager node in the left pane, you get an overview of the server's configuration in the right pane. Under Server Summary, the Computer Information section lists the computer name, workgroup or domain name, local administrator account name, network configuration, and product ID. You'll also find the following options:

- **Change System Properties** Use this option to display the System Properties dialog box, which you can use to configure general system properties.

- **View Network Connections** Use this option to display the Network Connections console, which you can use to configure network connections by double-clicking the connection you want to work with and then clicking Properties to open the Properties dialog box.

- **Configure Remote Desktop** Use this option to display the System Properties dialog box with the Remote tab selected. Use this tab to configure Remote Desktop by selecting configuration options and then clicking OK.

- **Configure Server Manager Remote Management**   Use this option to enable or disable remote management of the server using Server Manager and other Microsoft Management Consoles (MMCs). In many environments, you need to perform other procedures to fully enable remote management. See "Managing Your Servers Remotely" later in this chapter for more information.

NOTE   Because these and other summary options available in Server Manager are similar to those in the Initial Configuration Tasks console, I have provided a brief summary only. I'll discuss the related configuration tasks and technologies in more detail throughout this and other chapters in the book.

Under Server Summary, the Security Information section lists the state of Windows Firewall, the Windows Update configuration, the last time updates were checked for and installed, and the status of Internet Explorer Enhanced Security Configuration (IE ESC). You'll also find the following options:

- **Go To Windows Firewall**   Use this option to access Windows Firewall With Advanced Security, which you can use to configure advanced security settings for Windows Firewall by specifying inbound, outbound, and connection security rules.

- **Configure Updates**   Use this option to display the Windows Update utility in Control Panel. You can then enable automatic updating (if Windows Update is disabled) or check for updates (if Windows Update is enabled).

- **Check For New Roles**   Use this option to check whether new roles have been installed on the server since the last refresh or restart of Server Manager.

- **Run Security Configuration Wizard**   Use this option to start the Security Configuration Wizard, which you can use to create, edit, apply, or roll back security policies. Security policies are one way of configuring a broad spectrum of security settings. You can also use security templates to configure server security. To combine the benefits of both security policies and security templates, you can include a security template in a security policy file.

- **Configure IE ESC**   Use this option to enable or disable Internet Explorer Enhanced Security Configuration (IE ESC). If you click the link for this option, you can turn this feature on or off for administrators, users, or both. IE ESC is a security feature that reduces the exposure of a server to potential attacks by raising the default security levels in Internet Explorer security zones and changing default Internet Explorer settings. By default, IE ESC is enabled for both administrators and users.

REAL WORLD   In most cases, you should enable IE ESC on a server for both users and administrators. However, enabling IE ESC reduces the functionality of Internet Explorer. When IE ESC is enabled, security zones are configured as follows: the Internet zone is set to Medium-High, the Trusted Sites zone is set to Medium, the Local

Intranet zone is set to Medium-Low, and the Restricted zone is set to High. When IE ESC is enabled, the following Internet settings are changed: the Enhanced Security Configuration dialog box is on, third-party browser extensions are off, sounds in Web pages are off, animations in Web pages are off, signature checking for down-loaded programs is on, server certificate revocation is on, encrypted pages are not saved, temporary Internet files are deleted when the browser is closed, warnings for secure and nonsecure mode changes are on, and memory protection is on.

The Roles Summary section lists the roles installed on the server. In this section, you'll also find the following options:

- **Go To Roles**   Selects the Roles node in Server Manager, which provides a summary and details about each installed role.

- **Add Roles**   Starts the Add Roles Wizard, which you can use to install roles on the server.

- **Remove Roles**   Starts the Remove Roles Wizard, which you can use to unin-stall roles on the server.

The Features Summary section lists the features installed on the server. In this section, you'll also find the following options:

- **Add Features**   Starts the Add Features Wizard, which you can use to install features on the server.

- **Remove Features**   Starts the Remove Features Wizard, which you can use to uninstall features on the server.

The Resources And Support section lists the current settings for the Customer Experience Improvement Program and Windows Error Reporting (WER). In addition to feedback and Web site links, you'll find the following options:

- **Participate In CEIP**   Use this option to change the participation settings for the Customer Experience Improvement Program (CEIP). Participation in CEIP allows Microsoft to collect information about the way you use the server. Microsoft collects this data to help improve future releases of Windows. No data collected as part of CEIP personally identifies you or your company. If you elect to participate, you can also provide information about the number of servers and desktop computers in your organization, as well as your orga-nization's general industry. If you opt out of CEIP by turning this feature off, you miss the opportunity to help improve Windows.

- **Turn On Windows Error Reporting**   Use this option to change the par-ticipation settings for WER. In most cases, you'll want to enable WER for at least the first 60 days following installation of the operating system. With WER enabled, your server sends descriptions of problems to Microsoft, and Windows notifies you of possible solutions to those problems. You can view problem reports and possible solutions using Action Center. To open Action Center, click the Action Center icon in the notification area of the taskbar, and then select Open Action Center.

Managing Your Servers Remotely

You can use Server Manager and other Microsoft Management Consoles (MMCs) to perform some management tasks on remote computers, as long as the computers are in the same domain or you are working in a workgroup and have added the remote computers in a domain as trusted hosts. You can connect to servers running either full or core installations. On the computer you want to use for managing remote computers, you must be running Windows Server 2008 R2 or Windows 7 and have the Remote Server Administration Tools (RSAT) installed.

Remote management uses Windows PowerShell and depends on Windows Remote Management (WinRM) being properly configured, as discussed in Chapter 1, "Windows Server 2008 R2 Administration Overview." You must be a member of the Administrators group on computers that you want to manage by using Server Manager. For remote connections in a workgroup-to-workgroup or workgroup-to-domain configuration, you should be logged on using the built-in Administrator account or configure the LocalAccountTokenFilterPolicy registry key to allow remote access from your computer. To set this key, enter the following command at an elevated, administrator command prompt:

```
reg add HKLM\SOFTWARE\Microsoft\Windows\CurrentVersion\Policies\System /v
LocalAccountTokenFilterPolicy /t REG_DWORD /d 1 /f
```

Before you configure a server for remote management through Server Manager, MMCs, or both, you must enable several Group Policy settings that control Windows Firewall exceptions. You can do this by modifying Group Policy settings that apply to the server you want to manage as discussed in this procedure:

1. Open the Local Group Policy Editor by clicking Start, typing **gpedit.msc** in the Search box, and then pressing Enter. Or open the appropriate Group Policy object for editing using the Group Policy Management Console.

2. In the left pane, expand Computer Configuration, Administrative Templates, Windows Components, Windows Remote Management (WinRM), and then select WinRM Service.

3. In the details pane, double-click Allow Automatic Configuration Of Listeners. Select Enabled, and then click OK. In the left pane, expand Windows Settings, Security Settings, Windows Firewall With Advanced Security, and then Windows Firewall With Advanced Security—Local Group Policy Object.

4. Right-click Inbound Rules, and then click New Rule. In the New Inbound Rule Wizard, on the Rule Type page, select Predefined. On the Predefined menu, select Remote Event Log Management. Click Next. On the Predefined Rules page, click Next to accept the new rules. On the Action page, select Allow The Connection, and then click Finish. Allow The Connection is the default selection. Repeat this process to create inbound rules for Remote Service Management and Windows Firewall Remote Management.

5. Close the Group Policy editor.

You also can enable remote management via Server Manager and other MMCs, and by entering **configure-SMRemoting.ps1 –force –enable** at an elevated, administrator Windows PowerShell prompt. This configures remote management settings and enables exceptions for the following firewall rules: Remote Service Management (NP-In), Remote Service Management (RPC), Remote Service Management (RPC-EPMAP), Remote Event Log Management (NP-In), Remote Event Log Management (RPC), Remote Event Log Management (RPC-EPMAP), Windows Firewall Remote Management (RPC), and Windows Firewall Remote Management (RPC-EPMAP). You can verify that these exceptions are enabled by using Windows Firewall With Advanced Security.

You can configure remote management on a Server Core installation of Windows Server 2008 R2 by following these steps:

1. Start the Server Configuration utility by entering **sconfig**.

2. If Windows PowerShell isn't enabled, you should enable it. At the main menu prompt, enter **4** to access the Configure Remote Management menu, and then enter **2** to enable Windows PowerShell. After Windows PowerShell is installed, you need to restart the computer. Click Yes when prompted to restart. After the computer restarts, start the Server Configuration utility by entering **sconfig**.

3. At the main menu prompt, enter **4** to access the Configure Remote Management menu, and then do one or more of the following as appropriate for the configuration you want:

   a. Enter **1** to allow MMC remote management. After remote management is configured, click OK.

   b. Enter **3** to enable Server Manager remote management. After remote management and Windows PowerShell are configured, click OK.

   c. If you want to check the Windows Firewall settings, enter **4**. To return to the main menu, enter **5**. On the main menu, you can exit by entering **13**.

Using Server Manager, you can connect to and manage a remote computer by completing these steps:

1. Open Server Manager. In the left pane, right-click Server Manager, and then click Connect To Another Computer.

2. In the Connect To Another Computer dialog box, enter the host name, fully qualified domain name, or IP address of the remote server that is running Windows Server 2008 R2. Click OK.

After you connect to a remote computer, the Server Manager console shows the name of the remote computer. Server Manager always resolves IP addresses to fully qualified domain names.

You can work with a remote computer using an interactive remote Windows PowerShell session. To do this, open an elevated, administrator Windows PowerShell prompt. Type **enter-pssession** *ComputerName* **–credential** *UserName*, where *ComputerName* is the name of the remote computer and *UserName* is the name of a user who is a member of the Administrators group on the remote computer or in the domain of which the remote computer is a member. When prompted to enter the authorized user's password, type the password, and then press Enter. You can now enter commands in the session as you would if you were using Windows PowerShell locally. To exit the session, enter **exit-pssession**.

The following example enters an interactive remote session with Server85 using the credentials of Williams:

```
enter-pssession server85 -credential williams
```

Managing System Properties

You use the System console to view system information and perform basic configuration tasks. To access the System console, double-click System in Control Panel. As Figure 3-3 shows, the System console is divided into four basic areas that provide links for performing common tasks and a system overview:

- **Windows Edition** Shows the operating system edition and version and lists any service packs that you've applied.

- **System** Lists the processor, memory, and type of operating system installed on the computer. The type of operating system is listed as 32-bit or 64-bit.

- **Computer Name, Domain, And Workgroup Settings** Provides the computer name, description, domain, and workgroup details. If you want to change any of this information, click Change Settings, and then click Change in the System Properties dialog box.

- **Windows Activation** Shows whether you have activated the operating system and the product key. If Windows Server 2008 R2 isn't activated yet, click the link provided to start the activation process, and then follow the prompts. If you want to change the product key, click Change Product Key, and then provide the new product key.

When you're working in the System console, links in the left pane provide quick access to key support tools, including the following:

- Device Manager

- Remote Settings

- Advanced System Settings

Although volume-licensed versions of Windows Server 2008 R2 might not require activation or product keys, retail versions of Windows Server 2008 R2 require both activation and product keys. If Windows Server 2008 R2 has not been activated, you can activate the operating system by selecting Activate Windows Now under Windows Activation. You can also activate windows by entering **slmgr –ato** at a command prompt.

FIGURE 3-3 Use the System console to view and manage system properties.

Unlike in earlier versions of Windows, you can change the product key provided during installation of Windows Server 2008 R2 to stay in compliance with your licensing plan. To change the product key, follow these steps:

1. Click System in Control Panel.

2. In the System window, under Windows Activation, click Change Product Key.

3. In the Windows Activation window, type the product key.

4. When you click Next, the product key is validated. You then need to reactivate the operating system.

You can also enter a product key using Slmgr. At a command prompt, type **slmgr –ipk** followed by the product key you want to use, and then press Enter.

Within the System console, you can access the System Properties dialog box and use this dialog box to manage system properties. Click Change Settings under Computer Name, Domain, And Workgroup Settings. The following sections examine key areas of the operating system that you can configure using the System Properties dialog box.

The Computer Name Tab

You can display and modify the computer's network identification on the Computer Name tab of the System Properties dialog box. The Computer Name tab displays the full computer name of the system and the domain membership. The full computer name is essentially the Domain Name System (DNS) name of the computer, which also identifies the computer's place within the Active Directory hierarchy. If a computer is a domain controller or a certificate authority, you can change the computer name only after removing the related role from the computer.

You can join a computer to a domain or workgroup by following these steps:

1. On the Computer Name tab of the System Properties dialog box, click Change. This displays the Computer Name/Domain Changes dialog box.

2. To put the computer in a workgroup, select the Workgroup option, and then type the name of the workgroup to join.

3. To join the computer to a domain, select the Domain option, type the name of the domain to join, and then click OK.

4. If you've changed the computer's domain membership, you'll see a Windows Security prompt. Enter the name and password of an account with permission to add the computer to the specified domain or to remove the computer from a previously specified domain, and then click OK.

5. When prompted that your computer has joined the workgroup or domain you specified, click OK.

6. You'll see a prompt stating that you need to restart the computer. Click OK.

7. Click Close, and then click Restart Now to restart the computer.

To change the name of a computer, follow these steps:

1. On the Computer Name tab of the System Properties dialog box, click Change. This displays the Computer Name/Domain Changes dialog box.

2. In the Computer Name text box, type the new name for the computer.

3. You'll see a prompt stating that you need to restart the computer. Click OK.

4. Click Close, and then click Restart Now to restart the computer.

The Hardware Tab

The System Properties dialog box's Hardware tab provides access to Device Manager and Windows Update Driver Settings. To access the Hardware tab, open the System Properties dialog box, and then click the Hardware tab.

For installed devices, you can configure Windows Server to download driver software and realistic icons for devices. By default, Windows Server does not do this. If you want a computer to check for drivers automatically, click the Device Installation Settings button, and then select either Yes, Do This Automatically or No, Let Me Choose What To Do. If you want to choose what to do, you can specify the following:

- Always install the best driver software from Windows Update

- Install driver software from Windows Update if it is not found on the computer

- Never install driver software from Windows Update.

Click Save Changes, and then click OK to apply your changes.

NOTE Although you can enable or disable system services for specific hardware profiles as part of troubleshooting, the System Configuration utility provides better controls for managing the startup behavior of the operating system. The System Configuration utility is now available on the Administrative Tools menu. You can use it as discussed in Chapter 6, "Configuring Windows 7 Computers," in *Windows 7 Administrator's Pocket Consultant* (Microsoft Press, 2009).

The Advanced Tab

The System utility's Advanced tab controls many of the key features of the Windows operating system, including application performance, virtual memory usage, the user profile, environment variables, and startup and recovery. To access the Advanced tab, open the System Properties dialog box, and then click the Advanced tab.

Setting Windows Performance

Many graphics enhancements were added to the Windows Server 2008 interface and these enhancements are available in R2 as well. These enhancements include many visual effects for menus, toolbars, windows, and the taskbar. You can configure Windows performance by following these steps:

1. Click the Advanced tab in the System Properties dialog box, and then click Settings in the Performance panel to display the Performance Options dialog box.

2. The Visual Effects tab is selected by default. You have the following options for controlling visual effects:

   - **Let Windows Choose What's Best For My Computer** Enables the operating system to choose the performance options based on the hardware configuration. For a newer computer, this option will probably have the same effect as choosing the Adjust For Best Appearance option. The key distinction, however, is that this option is chosen by Windows based on the available hardware and its performance capabilities.

   - **Adjust For Best Appearance** When you optimize Windows for best appearance, you enable all visual effects for all graphical interfaces. Menus and the taskbar use transitions and shadows. Screen fonts have smooth edges. List boxes have smooth scrolling. Folders use Web views and more.

   - **Adjust For Best Performance** When you optimize Windows for best performance, you turn off the resource-intensive visual effects, such as slide transitions and smooth edges for fonts, while maintaining a basic set of visual effects.

   - **Custom** You can customize the visual effects by selecting or clearing the visual effects options in the Performance Options dialog box. If you clear all options, Windows does not use visual effects.

3. Click Apply when you have finished changing visual effects. Click OK twice to close the open dialog boxes.

Setting Application Performance

Application performance is related to processor scheduling caching options that you set for the Windows Server 2008 R2 system. Processor scheduling determines the responsiveness of applications you are running interactively (as opposed to background applications that might be running on the system as services). You control application performance by following these steps:

1. Access the Advanced tab in the System Properties dialog box, and then display the Performance Options dialog box by clicking Settings in the Performance panel.

2. In the Performance Options dialog box, click the Advanced tab.

3. In the Processor Scheduling panel, you have the following options:

   - **Programs**   Use this option to give the active application the best response time and the greatest share of available resources. Generally, you'll want to use this option only on development servers or when you are using Windows Server 2008 R2 as your desktop operating system.

   - **Background Services**   Use this option to give background applications a better response time than the active application. Generally, you'll want to use this option for production servers.

4. Click OK.

Configuring Virtual Memory

With virtual memory, you can use disk space to extend the amount of memory available on a system by using part of the hard disk as part of system memory. This feature of processors using Intel 386 and later writes RAM to disks by using a process called *paging*. With paging, a set amount of RAM, such as 1,024 megabytes (MB), is written to the disk as a paging file. The paging file can be accessed from the disk when needed in place of physical RAM.

An initial paging file is created automatically for the drive containing the operating system. By default, other drives don't have paging files, so you must create these paging files if you want them. When you create a paging file, you set an initial size and a maximum size. Paging files are written to the volume as a file named Pagefile.sys.

REAL WORLD   Windows Server 2008 R2 automatically manages virtual memory much better than its predecessors. Typically, Windows Server 2008 R2 allocates virtual memory in an amount at least as large as the total physical memory installed on the computer. This helps to ensure that paging files don't become fragmented, which can result in poor system performance. If you want to manage virtual memory manually, you can use a fixed virtual memory size in most cases. To do this, set the initial size and the maximum size to the same value. This ensures that the paging file is consistent and can be written to a single contiguous file (if possible, given the amount of space on the volume). In most cases, for computers with 8 GB of RAM or less, I recommend setting the total paging file size so that it's twice the amount of physical RAM on the system. For instance, on a computer with 1,024 MB of RAM, you would ensure that the Total Paging File Size For All Drives setting is at least 2,048 MB. On systems with more than 8 GB of RAM, you should follow the hardware manufacturer's guidelines for configuring the paging file. Typically, this means setting the paging file to be the same size as physical memory.

You can configure virtual memory by following these steps:

1. Access the Advanced tab in the System Properties dialog box, and then display the Performance Options dialog box by clicking Settings in the Performance panel.

2. In the Performance Options dialog box, click the Advanced tab, and then click Change to display the Virtual Memory dialog box, shown in Figure 3-4.

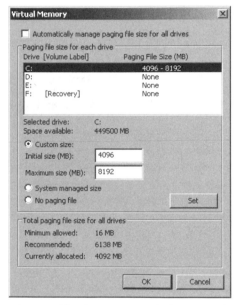

FIGURE 3-4 Virtual memory extends the amount of RAM on a system.

The following information is provided:

- **Paging File Size For Each Drive** Provides information on the currently selected drive and allows you to set its paging file size. Space Available indicates how much space is available on the drive.

- **Drive [Volume Label] and Paging File Size** Shows how virtual memory is currently configured on the system. Each volume is listed with its associated paging file (if any). The paging file range shows the initial and maximum size values set for the paging file.

- **Total Paging File Size For All Drives** Provides a recommended size for virtual RAM on the system and tells you the amount currently allocated. If this is the first time you're configuring virtual RAM, notice that the recommended amount has already been given to the system drive (in most instances).

3. By default, Windows Server 2008 R2 manages the paging file size for all drives. If you want to configure virtual memory manually, clear the Automatically Manage Paging File Size For All Drives check box.

4. In the Drive list, select the volume you want to work with.

5. Select Custom Size, and then enter values in the Initial Size and Maximum Size fields.

6. Click Set to save the changes.

7. Repeat steps 4–6 for each volume you want to configure.

   NOTE The paging file is also used for debugging purposes when a Stop error occurs on the system. If the paging file on the system drive is smaller than the minimum amount required to write the debugging information to the paging file, this feature is disabled. If you want to use debugging, you should set the minimum size to equal the amount of RAM on the system. For example, a system with 1 GB of RAM would need a paging file of 1 GB on the system drive.

8. Click OK. If prompted to overwrite an existing Pagefile.sys file, click Yes.

9. If you updated the settings for a paging file that is currently in use, you'll see a prompt indicating that you need to restart the system for the changes to take effect. Click OK.

10. Click OK twice to close the open dialog boxes. When you close the System utility, you'll see a prompt asking if you want to restart the system. Click Restart.

You can have Windows Server 2008 R2 automatically manage virtual memory by following these steps:

1. Access the Advanced tab in the System Properties dialog box, and then display the Performance Options dialog box by clicking Settings in the Performance panel.

2. Click the Advanced tab, and then click Change to display the Virtual Memory dialog box.

3. Select the Automatically Manage Paging File Size For All Drives check box.

4. Click OK three times to close the open dialog boxes.

   NOTE If you updated the settings for the paging file currently in use, you'll see a prompt indicating that you need to restart the server for the changes to take effect. Click OK. When you close the System Properties dialog box, you'll see a prompt telling you that you need to restart the system for the changes to take effect. On a production server, you should schedule this reboot outside normal business hours.

Configuring Data Execution Prevention

Data Execution Prevention (DEP) is a memory protection technology. DEP tells the computer's processor to mark all memory locations in an application as nonexecutable unless the location explicitly contains executable code. If code is executed from a memory page marked as nonexecutable, the processor can raise an exception and prevent it from executing. This prevents malicious code such as a virus from inserting itself into most areas of memory because only specific areas of memory are marked as having executable code.

NOTE Thirty-two-bit versions of Windows support DEP as implemented by Advanced Micro Devices (AMD) processors that provide the no-execute page-protection (NX) processor feature. Such processors support the related instructions and must be running in Physical Address Extension (PAE) mode. Sixty-four-bit versions of Windows also support the NX processor feature.

USING AND CONFIGURING DEP

You can determine whether a computer supports DEP by using the System utility. If a computer supports DEP, you can also configure it by following these steps:

1. Access the Advanced tab in the System Properties dialog box, and then display the Performance Options dialog box by clicking Settings in the Performance panel.

2. In the Performance Options dialog box, click the Data Execution Prevention tab. The text at the bottom of this tab indicates whether the computer supports execution protection.

3. If a computer supports execution protection and is configured appropriately, you can configure DEP by using the following options:

   - **Turn On DEP For Essential Windows Programs And Services Only** Enables DEP only for operating system services, programs, and components. This is the default and recommended option for computers that support execution protection and are configured appropriately.

   - **Turn On DEP For All Programs Except Those I Select** Configures DEP and allows for exceptions. Select this option, and then click Add to specify programs that should run without execution protection. With this option, execution protection will work for all programs except those you select.

4. Click OK.

If you've turned on DEP and allowed exceptions, you can add or remove a program as an exception by following these steps:

1. Access the Advanced tab in the System Properties dialog box, and then display the Performance Options dialog box by clicking Settings in the Performance panel.

2. In the Performance Options dialog box, click the Data Execution Prevention tab.

3. To add a program as an exception, click Add. Use the Open dialog box to find the executable file for the program you are configuring as an exception, and then click Open.

4. To temporarily disable a program as an exception (this might be necessary for troubleshooting), clear the check box next to the program name.

5. To remove a program as an exception, click the program name, and then click Remove.

6. Click OK to save your settings.

Understanding DEP Compatibility

To be compatible with DEP, applications must be able to mark memory explicitly with Execute permission. Applications that cannot do this will not be compatible with the NX processor feature. If you experience memory-related problems running applications, you should determine which applications are having problems and configure them as exceptions rather than disable execution protection completely. This way you still get the benefits of memory protection and can selectively disable memory protection for programs that aren't running properly with the NX processor feature.

Execution protection is applied to both user-mode and kernel-mode programs. A user-mode execution protection exception results in a STATUS_ACCESS_VIOLATION exception. In most processes, this exception will be an unhandled exception, resulting in termination of the process. This is the behavior you want because most programs violating these rules, such as a virus or worm, will be malicious in nature.

You cannot selectively enable or disable execution protection for kernel-mode device drivers the way you can with applications. Furthermore, on compliant 32-bit systems, execution protection is applied by default to the memory stack. On compliant 64-bit systems, execution protection is applied by default to the memory stack, the paged pool, and the session pool. A kernel-mode execution protection access violation for a device driver results in an ATTEMPTED_EXECUTE_OF_NOEXECUTE_MEMORY exception.

Configuring System and User Environment Variables

Windows uses environment variables to track important strings, such as a path where files are located or the logon domain controller host name. Environment variables defined for use by Windows—called *system environment variables*—are the same no matter who is logged on to a particular computer. Environment variables defined for use by users or programs—called *user environment variables*—are different for each user of a particular computer.

You configure system and user environment variables by means of the Environment Variables dialog box, shown in Figure 3-5. To access this dialog box, open the

System Properties dialog box, click the Advanced tab, and then click Environment Variables.

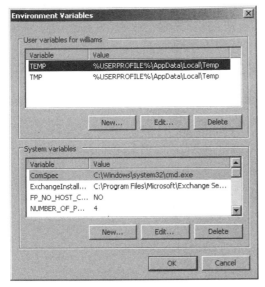

FIGURE 3-5 Configure system and user environment variables in the Environment Variables dialog box.

CREATING AN ENVIRONMENT VARIABLE

You can create an environment variable by following these steps:

1. Click New under User Variables or under System Variables, whichever is appropriate. This opens the New User Variable dialog box or the New System Variable dialog box, respectively.

2. In the Variable Name field, type the variable name. In the Variable Value field, type the variable value.

3. Click OK.

EDITING AN ENVIRONMENT VARIABLE

You can edit an environment variable by following these steps:

1. Select the variable in the User Variables or System Variables list.

2. Click Edit under User Variables or under System Variables, whichever is appropriate. The Edit User Variable dialog box or the Edit System Variable dialog box opens.

3. Type a new value in the Variable Value field, and then click OK.

DELETING AN ENVIRONMENT VARIABLE

To delete an environment variable, select it and click Delete.

> **NOTE** When you create or modify environment variables, most of the variables are valid immediately after they are created or modified. With system variables, some changes take effect after you restart the computer. With user variables, some changes take effect the next time the user logs on to the system.

Configuring System Startup and Recovery

You configure system startup and recovery properties in the Startup And Recovery dialog box, shown in Figure 3-6. To access this dialog box, open the System Properties dialog box, click the Advanced tab, and then click Settings in the Startup And Recovery panel.

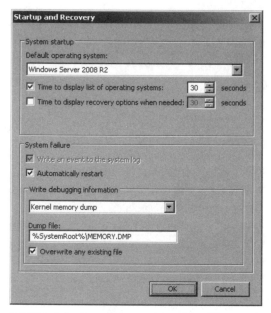

FIGURE 3-6 Configure system startup and recovery procedures in the Startup And Recovery dialog box.

SETTING STARTUP OPTIONS

The System Startup area of the Startup And Recovery dialog box controls system startup. To specify the default operating system for a computer with multiple bootable operating systems, select one of the operating systems listed in the Default Operating System list. These options change the configuration settings used by the Windows Boot Manager.

Upon startup of a computer with multiple bootable operating systems, Windows Server 2008 R2 displays the startup configuration menu for 30 seconds by default. You can change this by performing either of the following actions:

- Boot immediately to the default operating system by clearing the Time To Display List Of Operating Systems check box.

- Display the available options for a specific amount of time by selecting the Time To Display List Of Operating Systems check box and then setting a time delay in seconds.

On most systems, you'll generally want to use a value of 3 to 5 seconds. This is long enough for you to make a selection, yet short enough to expedite the system startup process.

When the system is in a recovery mode and booting, a list of recovery options might be displayed. As you can with the standard startup options, you can configure recovery startup options in one of two ways. You can set the computer to boot immediately using the default recovery option by clearing the Time To Display Recovery Options When Needed check box, or you can display the available options for a specific amount of time by selecting Time To Display Recovery Options When Needed and then setting a time delay in seconds.

SETTING RECOVERY OPTIONS

You control system recovery with the System Failure and Write Debugging Information areas of the Startup And Recovery dialog box. Administrators use recovery options to control precisely what happens when the system encounters a fatal system error (also known as a Stop error). The available options for the System Failure area are as follows:

- **Write An Event To The System Log**   Logs the error in the system log, allowing administrators to review the error later using Event Viewer.

- **Automatically Restart**   Select this option to have the system attempt to reboot when a fatal system error occurs.

NOTE   Configuring automatic reboots isn't always a good thing. Sometimes you might want the system to halt rather than reboot to ensure that the system gets proper attention. Otherwise, you would know that the system rebooted only when you viewed the system logs or if you happened to be in front of the system's monitor when it rebooted.

You use the Write Debugging Information list to choose the type of debugging information that you want to write to a dump file. You can use the dump file to diagnose system failures. The options are as follows:

- **None**   Use this option if you don't want to write debugging information.

- **Small Memory Dump**   Use this option to dump the physical memory segment in which the error occurred. This dump is 256 KB in size.

- **Kernel Memory Dump** Use this option to dump the physical memory area being used by the Windows kernel. The dump file size depends on the size of the Windows kernel.

If you elect to write to a dump file, you must also set a location for it. The default dump locations are %SystemRoot%\Minidump for small memory dumps and %SystemRoot%\Memory.dmp for all other memory dumps. You'll usually want to select Overwrite Any Existing File as well. Selecting this option ensures that any existing dump files are overwritten if a new Stop error occurs.

BEST PRACTICES You can create the dump file only if the system is properly configured. The system drive must have a sufficiently large memory-paging file (as set for virtual memory on the Advanced tab), and the drive the dump file is written to must have sufficient free space. For example, my server has 4 GB of RAM and requires a paging file on the system drive of the same size—4 GB. In establishing a baseline for kernel memory usage, I found that the server uses between 678 and 892 MB of kernel memory. Because the same drive is used for the dump file, the drive must have at least 5 GB of free space to create a dump of debugging information. (That's 4 GB for the paging file and about 1 GB for the dump file.)

The Remote Tab

The Remote tab of the System Properties dialog box controls Remote Assistance invitations and Remote Desktop connections. These options are discussed in Chapter 5, "Automating Administrative Tasks, Policies, and Procedures."

Managing Dynamic-Link Libraries

As an administrator, you might be asked to install or uninstall dynamic-link libraries (DLLs), particularly if you work with IT development teams. The utility you use to work with DLLs is Regsvr32. This utility is run at the command line.

After you open a Command Prompt window, you install or register a DLL by typing **regsvr32** *name*.**dll**. For example:

```
regsvr32 mylibs.dll
```

If necessary, you can uninstall or unregister a DLL by typing **regsvr32 /u** *name*.**dll**. For example:

```
regsvr32 /u mylibs.dll
```

Windows File Protection prevents replacement of protected system files. You can replace only those DLLs installed by the Windows Server 2008 R2 operating system as part of a hotfix, service pack update, Windows update, or Windows upgrade. Windows File Protection is an important part of the Windows Server 2008 R2 security architecture.

CHAPTER 4

Monitoring Processes, Services, and Events

As an administrator, you need to keep an eye on network systems. The status and usage of system resources can change dramatically over time. Services might stop running. File systems might run out of space. Applications might throw exceptions that in turn can cause system problems. Unauthorized users might try to break into the system. The techniques discussed in this chapter can help you identify and resolve these and other system problems.

Managing Applications, Processes, and Performance

Any time you start an application or type a command at the command line, Windows Server 2008 Release 2 (R2) starts one or more processes to handle the related program. Generally, processes that you start in this manner are called *interactive processes*—that is, you start the processes interactively with the keyboard or mouse. If the application or program is active and selected, the interactive process has control over the keyboard and mouse until you switch control by terminating the program or selecting a different one. When a process has control, it's said to be running *in the foreground*.

Processes can also run *in the background*. For processes started by users, this means that programs that aren't currently active can continue to operate, only they generally aren't given the same priority as active processes. You can also configure background processes to run independently of the user logon session;

the operating system usually starts such processes. An example of this type of background process is a scheduled task run by the operating system. The configuration settings for the task tell the system to execute a command at a specified time.

Task Manager

The key tool you use to manage system processes and applications is Task Manager. You can use any of the following techniques to display Task Manager:

- Press Ctrl+Shift+Esc
- Press Ctrl+Alt+Del, and then click Start Task Manager
- Click Start, type **taskmgr** in the Search box, and then press Enter
- Right-click the taskbar, and then click Start Task Manager on the shortcut menu

The following sections cover techniques you use to work with Task Manager.

Managing Applications

The Applications tab in Task Manager (see Figure 4-1) shows the status of programs currently running on the system. You can use the buttons on the bottom of this tab as follows:

- Stop an application by selecting the application and then clicking End Task.
- Switch to an application and make it active by selecting the application and then clicking Switch To.
- Start a new program by clicking New Task and then entering a command to run the application. The New Task button functions the same way as the Start menu's Run utility.

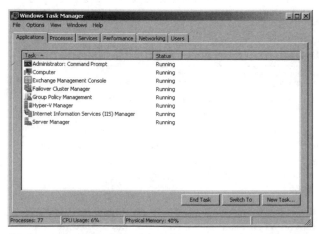

FIGURE 4-1 The Applications tab in Task Manager shows the status of programs currently running on the system.

TIP The Status column tells you whether an application is running normally or has stopped responding. A status of Not Responding indicates that an application might be frozen, and you might want to end the task related to it. However, some applications might not respond to the operating system during certain process-intensive tasks. Because of this, you should be certain the application is really frozen before you end its related task.

Right-clicking an application's listing in Task Manager displays a shortcut menu that you can use to do the following:

- Switch to the application and make it active
- Bring the application to the front of the display
- Minimize and maximize the application
- Tile or cascade the application
- End the application's task
- Create a dump file for debugging the application
- Go to the related process on the Processes tab

NOTE The Go To Process option is very helpful when you're trying to find the primary process for a particular application. Selecting this option highlights the related process on the Processes tab.

Administering Processes

Task Manager's Processes tab is shown in Figure 4-2. This tab provides detailed information about the processes that are running. By default, the Processes tab shows only processes from the currently logged on user. Click Show Processes From All Users to view all processes that are running, including those from the operating system, local services, the interactive user logged on to the local console, and remote users. If you don't want to see processes from remote users, clear the Show Processes From All Users check box.

The fields on the Processes tab provide a lot of information about running processes. You can use this information to determine which processes are over consuming system resources such as CPU time and memory. The fields displayed by default are the following:

- **Image Name** The name of the process or executable running the process.
- **User Name** The name of the user or system service running the process.
- **CPU** The percentage of CPU utilization for the process.
- **Memory (Private Working Set)** The amount of memory the process is currently using.
- **Description** A description of the process.

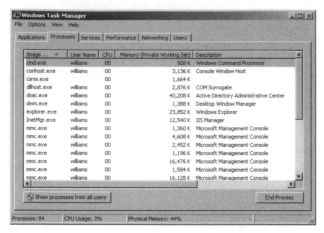

FIGURE 4-2 The Processes tab provides detailed information about running processes.

If you click View and choose Select Columns, you'll see a dialog box that lets you add columns to the Processes tab view. When you're trying to troubleshoot system problems using process information, you might want to add the following columns to the view:

- **Base Priority** Priority determines how much of the system's resources are allocated to a process. To set the priority for a process, right-click the process, choose Set Priority, and then select the new priority from these options: Low, Below Normal, Normal, Above Normal, High, and RealTime. Most processes have a normal priority by default. The highest priority is given to real-time processes.

- **CPU Time** The total amount of CPU cycle time used by a process since it was started. To quickly see the processes that are using the most CPU time, display this column, and then click the column header to sort process entries by CPU time.

- **Handles** The total number of file handles maintained by the process. Use the handle count to gauge how dependent the process is on the file system. Some processes, such as those used by Microsoft Internet Information Services (IIS), have thousands of open file handles. Each file handle requires system memory to be maintained.

- **I/O Reads, I/O Writes** The total number of disk input/output (I/O) reads or writes since the process was started. Together, the number of I/O reads and writes tells you how much disk I/O activity has occurred. If the number of I/O reads and writes is growing disproportionately to actual activity on the server, the process might not be caching files or file caching might not be properly configured. Ideally, file caching will reduce the need for I/O reads and writes.

- **Page Faults** A page fault occurs when a process requests a page in memory and the system can't find it at the requested location. If the requested page is elsewhere in memory, the fault is called a *soft page fault*. If the requested page must be retrieved from disk, the fault is called a *hard page fault*. Most processors can handle large numbers of soft faults. Hard faults, however, can cause significant delays.

- **Paged Pool, Nonpaged Pool** *Paged pool* is an area of system memory for objects that can be written to disk when they aren't used. *Nonpaged pool* is an area of system memory for objects that can't be written to disk. You should note processes that require a large amount of nonpaged pool memory. If there isn't enough free memory on the server, these processes might be the reason for a high level of page faults.

- **Peak Working Set** The highest amount of memory used by the process. The change, or delta, between current memory usage and peak memory usage is important to note as well. Applications that have a high delta between base memory usage and peak memory usage, such as Microsoft SQL Server, might need to be allocated more memory on startup so that they perform better.

- **Process ID (PID)** The numeric identifier for the process.

- **Session ID** The identifier for the session under which the process is running.

- **Threads** The current number of threads that the process is using. Most server applications are multithreaded. Multithreading allows concurrent execution of process requests. Some applications can dynamically control the number of concurrently executing threads to improve application performance. Too many threads, however, can actually reduce performance because the operating system has to switch thread contexts too frequently.

If you examine processes running in Task Manager, you'll notice a process called System Idle Process. You can't set the priority of this process. Unlike processes that track resource usage, System Idle Process tracks the amount of system resources that aren't used. Thus, a 99 in the CPU column of the System Idle Process means that 99 percent of system resources currently aren't being used.

As you examine processes, keep in mind that a single application might start multiple processes. Generally, these processes are dependent on a central process. From this main process, a process tree containing dependent processes is formed. You can find the main process for an application by right-clicking the application on the Applications tab and selecting Go To Process. When you terminate processes, you'll usually want to target the main application process or the application itself rather than dependent processes. This ensures that the application is stopped cleanly.

To stop the main application process and dependent processes, you have several choices:

- Right-click the application on the Applications tab, and then click End Task.
- Right-click the main application process on the Processes tab, and then click End Process.
- Right-click the main or a dependent process on the Processes tab, and then click End Process Tree.

Viewing System Services

Task Manager's Services tab provides an overview of system services. This tab displays services by name, process ID, description, status, and group. As shown in Figure 4-3, multiple services typically run under the same process ID. You can quickly sort services by their process ID by clicking the related column heading. You can click the Status column heading to sort services according to their status, Running or Stopped.

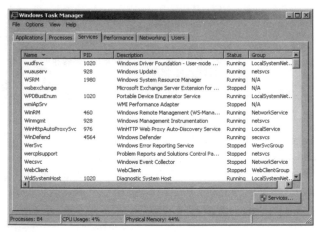

FIGURE 4-3 The Services tab provides a quick overview of the status of system services.

The Group column provides additional options about related identities or service host contexts under which a service runs:

- Services running under an identity with a restriction have the restriction listed in the Group column. For example, a service running under the Local Service identity might be listed as LocalServiceNoNetwork to indicate that the service has no network access, or a service might be listed as Local-SystemNetworkRestricted to indicate that the service has restricted access to the network.
- Services that have Svchost.exe list their associated context for the –k parameter. For example, the RemoteRegistry service runs with the command line

svchost.exe –k regsvc. You'll see an entry of regsvc in the Group column for this service.

Right-clicking a service's listing in Task Manager displays a shortcut menu that allows you to do the following:

- Start a stopped service
- Stop a started service
- Go to the related process on the Processes tab

Viewing and Managing System Performance

The Performance tab in Task Manager provides an overview of CPU and memory usage. As shown in Figure 4-4, the tab displays graphs and statistics. This information gives you a quick check of system resource usage. For more detailed information, use Performance Monitor, as explained later in this chapter.

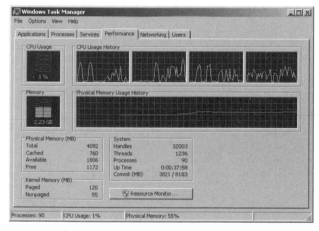

FIGURE 4-4 The Performance tab provides a quick check of system resource usage.

Graphs on the Performance Tab

The graphs on the Performance tab provide the following information:

- **CPU Usage** The percentage of processor resources currently being used.
- **CPU Usage History** A graph of CPU usage plotted over time. The update speed determines how often the graph is updated.
- **Memory** The amount of physical memory currently being used by the system.
- **Physical Memory Usage History** A graph of physical memory usage plotted over time.

NOTE If a system has multiple CPUs, you'll see a graph for each CPU by default. In Figure 4-4, the server has four CPUs, so there are four graphs.

TIP To view a close-up of the CPU graphs, double-click in the Performance tab. Double-clicking again returns you to normal viewing mode. If CPU usage is consistently high, even under average usage conditions, you might want to perform more detailed performance monitoring to determine the cause of the problem. Memory is often a source of performance problems, and you should rule it out before upgrading or adding CPUs. For more details, see "Tuning System Performance" later in this chapter.

Customizing and Updating the Graph Display

To customize or update the graph display, use the following options on the View menu:

- **Update Speed** Allows you to change the speed of graph updating as well as to pause the graph. Updates occur once every 4 seconds for Low, once every 2 seconds for Normal, and twice per second for High.

- **CPU History** On multiprocessor systems, allows you to specify how CPU graphs are displayed. You can, for example, display one CPU in each graph (the default) or multiple CPUs in a single graph.

- **Show Kernel Times** Allows you to display the amount of CPU time used by the operating system kernel. Usage by the kernel is plotted in red (as opposed to green, which is used otherwise).

NOTE Tracking the kernel usage can be handy for troubleshooting. For example, if you are using IIS with output caching in kernel mode, you can get a better understanding of how kernel caching might be affecting CPU usage and overall performance by showing kernel times. Kernel usage tracking isn't enabled by default because it adds to the overhead of monitoring a server in Task Manager.

Beneath the graphs you'll find several lists of statistics. These statistics provide the following information:

- **Physical Memory (MB)** Provides information about the total RAM on the system. Total shows the amount of physical RAM. Cached shows the amount of memory used for system caching. Free shows the RAM not currently being used and available for use. If the server has very little physical memory available, you might need to add memory to the system. In general, you want the available memory to be no less than 5 percent of the total physical memory on the server.

- **Kernel Memory (MB)** Provides information on the memory used by the operating system kernel. Critical portions of kernel memory must operate in RAM and can't be paged to virtual memory. This type of kernel memory is listed as Nonpaged. The rest of kernel memory can be paged to virtual memory and is listed as Paged.

- **System** Provides information about CPU usage. Handles shows the number of I/O handles in use; I/O handles act as tokens that let programs access resources. I/O throughput and disk performance affect a system more than a consistently high number of I/O handles. Threads shows the number of threads in use; threads are the basic units of execution within processes. Processes shows the number of processes in use; processes are running instances of applications or executable files. Up Time shows how long the system has been up since it was last started. Commit (MB) lists the virtual memory currently in use followed by the total amount of virtual memory available. If the current page file usage is consistently within 10 percent of the maximum value (meaning consistent usage of 90 percent or more), you might want to add physical memory, increase the amount of virtual memory, or take both steps.

Viewing and Managing Networking Performance

The Networking tab in Task Manager provides an overview of the network adapters used by the system. You can use the information provided to quickly determine the percent utilization, link speed, and operational status usage of each network adapter configured on a system.

If a system has one network adapter, the summary graph shown in Figure 4-5 details the network traffic on this adapter over time. If a system has multiple network adapters, the graph displays a composite index of all network connections, which represents all network traffic. By default, the graph displays only the network traffic total byte count. You can change this by clicking View, choosing Network Adapter History, and then enabling Bytes Sent, Bytes Received, or both. Bytes Sent are shown in red, Bytes Received in yellow, Bytes Total in green.

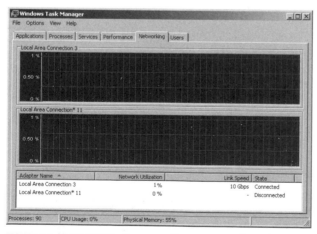

FIGURE 4-5 Networking performance allows you to easily track network activity on the server.

The fields on the Networking tab provide lots of information about network traffic to and from the server. You can use this information to determine how much external traffic a server is experiencing at any time. The following fields are displayed by default:

- **Adapter Name** Name of the network adapter in the Network Connections folder.

- **Network Utilization** Percentage of network usage based on the initial connection speed for the interface. For example, an adapter with an initial link speed of 10 gigabits per second (Gbps) and current traffic of 100 megabits per second (Mbps) is utilized at 1 percent.

- **Link Speed** Connection speed of the interface as determined by the initial connection speed, such as 1 Gbps or 10 Gbps.

- **State** Operational status of network adapters, such as Connected or Disconnected.

REAL WORLD Any time you see usage consistently approaching or exceeding 50 percent of total capacity, you should start monitoring the server more closely, and you might want to consider adding network adapters. Plan any upgrade carefully; a lot more planning is required than you might think. Consider the implications not only for that server but also for the network as a whole. You might also have connectivity problems if you exceed the allotted bandwidth of your service provider—and it can often take months to obtain additional bandwidth for external connections.

If you click View and choose Select Columns, you'll see a dialog box that lets you add columns to the Networking tab's view. When you're trying to troubleshoot networking problems, you might want to add the following columns to the view:

- **Bytes Sent Throughput** Percentage of current connection bandwidth used by traffic sent from the system.

- **Bytes Received Throughput** Percentage of current connection bandwidth used by traffic received by the system.

- **Bytes Throughput** Percentage of current connection bandwidth used for all traffic on the network adapter.

- **Bytes Sent** Cumulative total bytes sent on the connection to date.

- **Bytes Received** Cumulative total bytes received on the connection to date.

- **Bytes** Cumulative total bytes on the connection to date.

Viewing and Managing Remote User Sessions

Remote users can use Terminal Services or Remote Desktop to connect to systems. Terminal Services allow remote terminal connections to systems. Remote Desktop allows you to administer systems remotely, as if you were sitting at the console.

Remote Desktop connections are automatically enabled on Windows Server 2008 R2 installations. One way to view and manage remote desktop connections is to use Task Manager. To do this, start Task Manager, and then click the Users tab, shown in Figure 4-6. The Users tab shows interactive user sessions for both local and remote users.

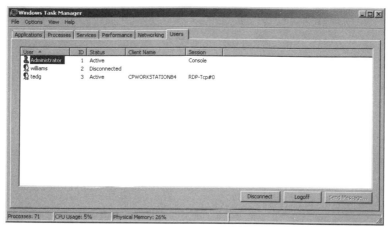

FIGURE 4-6 The Users tab allows you to view and manage user sessions.

Each user connection is listed with user name, session ID, status, originating client computer, and session type. A user logged on to the local system is listed with Console as the session type. Other users have a session type that indicates the connection type and protocol being used, such as RDP-TCP for a connection using the Remote Desktop Protocol (RDP) with TCP as the transport protocol. If you right-click a user session, you have the following options:

- **Connect** Connects the user session if it's inactive.

- **Disconnect** Disconnects the user session, halting all user-started applications without saving application data.

- **Log Off** Logs off the user using the normal logoff process. Application data and system state information are saved as during a normal logoff.

- **Remote Control** Sets the shortcut keys used to end remote control sessions. The default shortcut keys are Ctrl+*.

- **Send Message** Sends a console message to users logged on to remote systems.

Managing System Services

Services provide key functions to workstations and servers. To manage system services, you use the Services node in Server Manager. You can start Server Manager and access the Services node by following these steps:

1. Choose Start, click Administrative Tools, and then click Server Manager. Or click Server Manager on the Quick Launch toolbar.

2. As necessary, connect to the computer you want to manage. In the left pane, right-click the Server Manager node, and then click Connect To Another Computer. Enter the host name, fully qualified domain name, or IP address of the remote server, and then click OK.

SECURITY ALERT The remote server must be running Windows Server 2008 R2 or have the Windows Server Management framework installed. Remote management via Server Manager must be enabled. If there are no Group Policy or other settings blocking remote management, you can enable this feature by logging on to the remote computer and starting Server Manager. In Server Manager, with the Server Manager node selected in the left pane, click Configure Server Manager Remote Management in the details pane. Select Enable Remote Management Of This Server From Other Computers, and then click OK. For more information, see "Managing Your Servers Remotely" in Chapter 3.

3. In the left pane, click the plus sign (+) next to the Configuration node. This expands the node to display its tools.

4. Select the Services node. As shown in Figure 4-7, you should now see a complete list of services installed on the system. By default, this list is organized by service name. The key fields in the Services pane are used as follows:

- **Name** The name of the service. Only services installed on the system are listed here. Double-click an entry to configure its startup options. If a service you need isn't listed, you can install it by installing the related role or feature, as discussed in Chapter 2, "Deploying Windows Server 2008 R2."

- **Description** A short description of the service and its purpose.

- **Status** Whether the status of the service is started, paused, or stopped. (Stopped is indicated by a blank entry.)

- **Startup Type** The startup setting for the service. Automatic services are started at bootup. Users or other services start manual services. Disabled services are turned off and can't be started while they remain disabled.

- **Log On As** The account the service logs on as. The default in most cases is the local system account.

The Services pane has two views: Extended and Standard. To change the view, use the tabs at the bottom of the Services pane. In Extended view, quick links are provided for managing services. Click Start to start a stopped service. Click Restart to stop and then start a service—essentially resetting that service. If you select a service when the Services pane is in Extended view, you'll see a description that details the service's purpose.

NOTE Both the operating system and a user can disable services. Generally, Windows Server 2008 R2 disables a service if a possible conflict with another service exists.

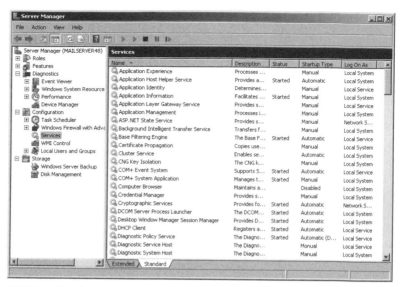

FIGURE 4-7 Use the Services pane to manage services on workstations and servers.

Starting, Stopping, and Pausing Services

As an administrator, you often have to start, stop, or pause Windows Server 2008 R2 services. To start, stop, or pause a service, follow these steps:

1. In Server Manager, click the plus sign (+) next to the Configuration node. This expands the node to display its tools.

2. Select the Services node.

3. Right-click the service you want to manage, and then select Start, Stop, or Pause as appropriate. You can also choose Restart to have Windows stop and then start the service after a brief pause. Additionally, if you pause a service, you can use the Resume option to resume normal operation.

NOTE When services that are set to start automatically fail, the status is listed as blank, and you usually receive notification in a pop-up dialog box. Service failures can also be logged to the system's event logs. In Windows Server 2008 R2, you can configure actions to handle service failure automatically. For example, you can have Windows Server 2008 R2 attempt to restart the service for you. For details, see "Configuring Service Recovery" later in this chapter.

Configuring Service Startup

You can set Windows Server 2008 R2 services to start manually or automatically. You can also turn them off permanently by disabling them. You configure service startup by following these steps:

1. In Server Manager, click the plus sign (+) next to the Configuration node. This expands the node to display its tools.

2. Select the Services node, right-click the service you want to configure, and then choose Properties.

3. On the General tab, use the Startup Type list to choose a startup option from the following choices, as shown in Figure 4-8.

   - **Automatic**   Select Automatic to start services at bootup.

   - **Automatic (Delayed Start)**   Select Automatic (Delayed Start) to delay the start of the service until all nondelayed automatic services have started.

   - **Manual**   Select Manual to allow the services to be started manually.

   - **Disabled**   Select Disabled to turn off the service.

4. Click OK.

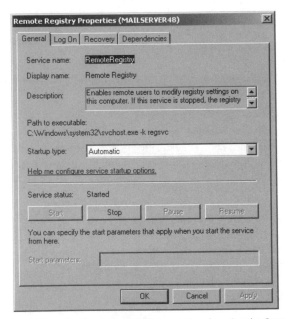

FIGURE 4-8 Configure service startup options by using the General tab's Startup Type list.

REAL WORLD When a server has multiple hardware profiles, you can enable or disable services for a particular profile. Before you disable services permanently, you might want to create a separate hardware profile for testing the server with these services disabled. In this way, you can use the original profile to quickly resume operations using the original service status. The profile doesn't save other service configuration options, however. To enable or disable a service by profile, use the Log On tab of the Service Properties dialog box. Select the profile that you want to work with under Hardware Profile, and then click Enable or Disable as appropriate.

Configuring Service Logon

You can configure Windows Server 2008 R2 services to log on as a system account or as a specific user. To do either, follow these steps:

1. In Server Manager, click the plus sign (+) next to the Configuration node. This expands the node to display its tools.

2. Select the Services node, right-click the service you want to configure, and then choose Properties.

3. Select the Log On tab, shown in Figure 4-9.

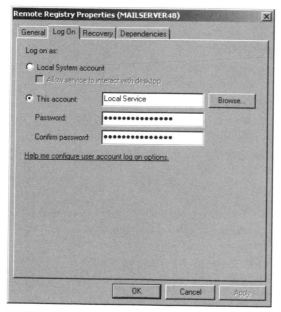

FIGURE 4-9 Use the Log On tab to configure the service logon account.

4. Select Local System Account if you want the service to log on using the system account (the default for most services). If the service provides a user interface that can be manipulated, select Allow Service To Interact With Desktop to allow users to control the service's interface.

5. Select This Account if you want the service to log on using a specific user account. Be sure to type an account name and password in the text boxes provided. Use the Browse button to search for a user account if necessary.

6. Click OK.

SECURITY ALERT You should keep track of any accounts that are used with services. These accounts can be the source of huge security problems if they're not configured properly. Service accounts should have the strictest security settings and as few permissions as possible while allowing the service to perform necessary functions. Typically, accounts used with services don't need many of the permissions you would assign to a normal user account. For example, most service accounts don't need the right to log on locally. Every administrator should know what service accounts are used (so that they can better track the use of these accounts) and should treat the accounts as if they were administrator accounts. This means using secure passwords, carefully monitoring account usage, carefully applying account permissions and privileges, and so on.

Configuring Service Recovery

You can configure Windows Server 2008 R2 services to take specific actions when a service fails. For example, you can attempt to restart the service or run an application. To configure recovery options for a service, follow these steps:

1. In Server Manager, click the plus sign (+) next to the Configuration node. This expands the node to display its tools.

2. Select the Services node, right-click the service you want to configure, and then choose Properties.

3. Click the Recovery tab, shown in Figure 4-10.

NOTE Windows Server 2008 R2 automatically configures recovery for critical system services during installation. In most cases, you'll find that critical services are configured to restart automatically if the service fails. Some extremely critical services, such as DCOM Server Process Launcher and Group Policy Client, are configured to restart the computer if the service fails. You cannot change these settings because they are not available.

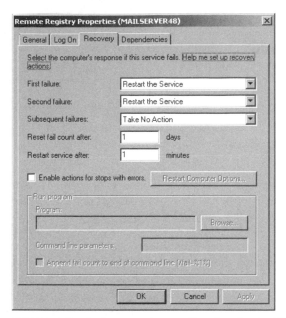

FIGURE 4-10 Use the Recovery tab to specify actions that should be taken in case of service failure.

4. You can now configure recovery options for the first, second, and subsequent recovery attempts. The following options are available:

- **Take No Action** The operating system won't attempt recovery for this failure but might still attempt recovery of previous or subsequent failures.

- **Restart The Service** Stops and then starts the service after a brief pause.

- **Run A Program** Allows you to run a program or a script in case of failure. The script can be a batch program or a Windows script. If you select this option, set the full file path to the program you want to run, and then set any necessary command-line parameters to pass in to the program when it starts.

- **Restart The Computer** Shuts down and then restarts the computer. Before you choose this option, double-check the computer's Startup and Recovery options. You want the system to select defaults quickly and automatically.

BEST PRACTICES When you configure recovery options for critical services, you might want to try to restart the service on the first and second attempts and then reboot the server on the third attempt.

5. Configure other options based on your previously selected recovery options. If you elected to run a program as a recovery option, you need to set options in the Run Program panel. If you elected to restart the service, you need to specify the restart delay. After stopping the service, Windows Server 2008 R2 waits for the specified delay before trying to start the service. In most cases a delay of 1 to 2 minutes should be sufficient.

6. Click OK.

Disabling Unnecessary Services

As an administrator, you need to ensure that servers and the network are secure, and unnecessary services are a potential source of security problems. For example, in many organizations that I've reviewed for security problems, I've found servers running Worldwide Web Publishing Service, Simple Mail Transfer Protocol (SMTP), and File Transfer Protocol (FTP) Publishing Service when these services weren't needed. Unfortunately, these services can make it possible for anonymous users to access servers and can also open the server to attack if not properly configured.

If you find unnecessary services, you have several options. With services installed through roles, role services, or features, you can remove the related role, role service, or feature to remove the unnecessary component and its related services. Or you can simply disable the services that aren't being used. Typically, you'll want to start by disabling services rather than uninstalling components. This way, if you disable a service and another administrator or a user says she can't perform task X anymore, you can enable the related service again if necessary.

To disable a service, follow these steps:

1. In Server Manager, click the plus sign (+) next to the Configuration node. This expands the node to display its tools.

2. Select the Services node, right-click the service you want to configure, and then choose Properties.

3. On the General tab, select Disabled in the Startup Type list.

Disabling a service doesn't stop a running service. It only prevents it from being started the next time the computer is booted, meaning that the security risk still exists. To address this, click Stop on the General tab in the Properties dialog box, and then click OK.

Event Logging and Viewing

Event logs provide historical information that can help you track down system and security problems. The Windows Event Log service controls whether events are tracked on Windows Server 2008 R2 systems. When you start this service, you can track user actions and resource usage events through the event logs. Two general types of log files are used:

- **Windows logs** Logs that the operating system uses to record general system events related to applications, security, setup, and system components.

- **Applications and services logs** Logs that specific applications and services use to record application-specific or service-specific events.

Windows logs you'll see include:

- **Application** This log records events logged by applications, such as the failure of SQL Server to access a database. The default location is %System-Root%\System32\Winevt\Logs\Application.evtx.

- **Forwarded Events** When event forwarding is configured, this log records forwarded events from other servers. The default location is %SystemRoot%\System32\Config\ForwardedEvents.evtx.

- **Security** This log records events you've set for auditing with local or global group policies. The default location is %SystemRoot%\System32\Winevt\Logs\Security.evtx.

  NOTE Any user who needs access to the security log must be granted the user right to Manage Auditing and the Security Log. By default, members of the Administrators group have this user right. To learn how to assign user rights, see "Configuring User Rights Policies" in Chapter 10.

- **Setup** This log records events logged by the operating system or its components during setup and installation. The default location is %System-Root%\System32\Winevt\Logs\Setup.evtx.

- **System** This log records events logged by the operating system or its components, such as the failure of a service to start at bootup. The default location is %SystemRoot%\System32\Winevt\Logs\System.evtx.

SECURITY ALERT As administrators, we tend to monitor the application and system logs the most—but don't forget about the security log. The security log is one of the most important logs, and you should monitor it closely. If the security log on a server doesn't contain events, the likeliest reason is that local auditing hasn't been configured or that domainwide auditing is configured, in which case you should monitor the security logs on domain controllers rather than on member servers.

Applications and services logs you'll see include:

- **DFS Replication** This log records Distributed File System (DFS) replication activities. The default location is %SystemRoot%\System32\Winevt\Logs\DfsReplication.evtx.

- **Directory Service** This log records events logged by Active Directory Domain Service (AD DS) and its related services. The default location is %SystemRoot%\System32\Winevt\Logs\Directory Service.evtx.

- **DNS Server** This log records DNS queries, responses, and other DNS activities. The default location is %SystemRoot%\System32\Winevt\Logs\DNS Server.evtx.

- **File Replication Service** This log records file replication activities on the system. The default location is %SystemRoot%\System32\Winevt\Logs\File Replication Service.evtx.

- **Hardware Events** When hardware subsystem event reporting is configured, this log records hardware events reported to the operating system. The default location is %SystemRoot%\System32\Config\Hardware.evtx.

- **Microsoft\Windows** This provides logs that track events related to specific Windows services and features. Logs are organized by component type and event category. Operational logs track events generated by the standard operations of the related component. In some cases, you'll see supplemental logs for analysis, debugging, and recording administration-related tasks.

- **Windows PowerShell** This log records activities related to the use of Windows PowerShell. The default location is %SystemRoot%\System32\Winevt\Logs\Windows PowerShell.evtx.

Accessing and Using the Event Logs

You access the event logs by following these steps:

1. Open Server Manager. As necessary, connect to the computer you want to manage. In the left pane, right-click the Server Manager node, and then click Connect To Another Computer. Enter the host name, fully qualified domain name, or IP address of the remote server, and then click OK.

2. In the left pane, click the plus sign (+) next to the Diagnostics node. This expands the node to display its tools.

3. Expand the Event Viewer node. You can work with the server's event logs in the following ways:

   - To view all errors and warnings for all logs, expand Custom Views and then select Administrative Events. In the main pane, you should now see a list of all warning and error events for the server.

   - To view all errors and warnings for a specific server role, expand Custom Views, expand Server Roles, and then select the role to view. In the main pane, you should now see a list of all events for the selected role.

- To view events in a specific log, expand the Windows Logs node, the Applications And Services Logs node, or both nodes. Select the log you want to view, such as application or system.

4. Use the information in the Source column to determine which service or process logged a particular event.

As shown in Figure 4-11, entries in the main pane of Event Viewer provide a quick overview of when, where, and how an event occurred. To obtain detailed information on an event, review the details provided on the General tab in the lower portion of the main pane. The event level or keyword precedes the date and time of the event. Event levels include the following:

- **Information** An informational event, which is generally related to a successful action.

- **Audit Success** An event related to the successful execution of an action.

- **Audit Failure** An event related to the failed execution of an action.

- **Warning** A warning. Details for warnings are often useful in preventing future system problems.

- **Error** A noncritical error, such as the failure of a zone transfer request on a DNS server.

- **Critical** A critical error, such as the Cluster service shutting down because a quorum was lost.

NOTE Warnings and errors are the two key types of events that you'll want to examine closely. Whenever these types of events occur and you're unsure of the cause, review the detailed event description.

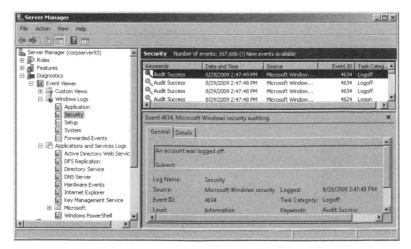

FIGURE 4-11 Event Viewer displays events for the selected log or custom view.

In addition to level, date, and time logged, the summary and detailed event entries provide the following information:

- **Source** The application, service, or component that logged the event.

- **Event ID** Generally, a numeric identifier for the specific event, which could be helpful when searching knowledge bases.

- **Task Category** The category of the event, which is almost always set to None, but is sometimes used to further describe the related action, such as a process or a service.

- **User** The user account that was logged on when the event occurred, if applicable.

- **Computer** The name of the computer on which the event occurred.

- **Description** In the detailed entries, a text description of the event.

- **Data** In the detailed entries, any data or error code output by the event.

Filtering Event Logs

Event Viewer creates several filtered views of the event logs for you automatically. Filtered views are listed under the Custom Views node. When you select the Administrative Events node, you'll see a list of all errors and warnings for all logs. When you expand the Server Roles node and then select a role-specific view, you'll see a list of all events for the selected role.

If you want to create a custom view of your own, you can do so by following these steps:

1. In Server Manager, expand the Diagnostics node and the Event Viewer node.

2. In the left pane, right-click the Custom Views node, and then click Create Custom View. This opens the dialog box shown in Figure 4-12.

3. Use the Logged list to select a time frame for logging events. You can choose to include events from the last hour, last 12 hours, last 24 hours, last 7 days, or last 30 days.

4. Use the Event Level check boxes to specify the level of events to include. Select Verbose to get additional details.

5. You can create a custom view for either a specific set of logs or a specific set of event sources:

   - Use the Event Logs list to select event logs to include. You can select multiple event logs by selecting their check boxes. If you select specific event logs, all other event logs are excluded.

   - Use the Event Sources list to select event sources to include. You can select multiple event sources by selecting their check boxes. If you select specific event sources, all other event sources are excluded.

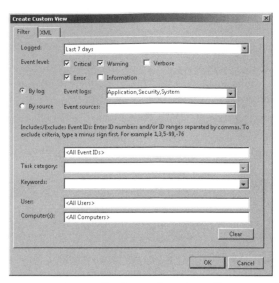

FIGURE 4-12 You can filter logs so that only specific events are displayed.

6. Optionally, use the User and Computer(s) boxes to specify users and computers that should be included. If you do not specify users and computers to include, events generated by all users and computers are included.

7. When you click OK, Windows displays the Save Filter To Custom View dialog box, shown in Figure 4-13.

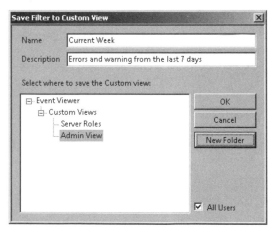

FIGURE 4-13 Save the filtered view.

8. Type a name and description for the custom view.

9. Select where to save the custom view. By default, custom views are saved under the Custom Views node. You can create a new node by clicking New Folder, entering a name for the folder, and then clicking OK.

10. Click OK to close the Save Filter To Custom View dialog box. You should now see a filtered list of events. Review these events carefully and take steps to correct any problems that exist.

If you want to see a particular type of event, you can filter the log by following these steps:

1. In Server Manager, expand the Diagnostics node and the Event Viewer node.

2. Expand Windows Logs or Applications And Services Logs as appropriate for the type of log you want to configure. You should now see a list of event logs.

3. Right-click the log you want to work with, and then click Filter Current Log. This opens a dialog box similar to the one shown earlier in Figure 4-12.

4. Use the Logged list to select the time frame for logging events. You can choose to include events from the last hour, last 12 hours, last 24 hours, last 7 days, or last 30 days.

5. Use the Event Level check boxes to specify the level of events to include. Select Verbose to get additional details.

6. Use the Event Source list to select event sources to include. If you select specific event sources, all other event sources are excluded.

7. Optionally, use the User and Computer(s) boxes to specify users and computers that should be included. If you do not specify users and computers, events generated by all users and computers are included.

8. Click OK. You should now see a filtered list of events. Review these events carefully and take steps to correct any problems that exist. To clear the filter and see all events for the log, click Clear Filter in the Actions pane or on the Action menu.

Setting Event Log Options

Log options allow you to control the size of event logs as well as how logging is handled. By default, event logs are set with a maximum file size. When a log reaches this limit, events are overwritten to prevent the log from exceeding the maximum file size.

To set log options, follow these steps:

1. In Server Manager, expand the Diagnostics node and the Event Viewer node.

2. Expand Windows Logs or Applications And Services Logs as appropriate for the type of log you want to configure. You should now see a list of event logs.

3. Right-click the event log whose properties you want to set, and then click Properties on the shortcut menu. This opens the dialog box shown in Figure 4-14.

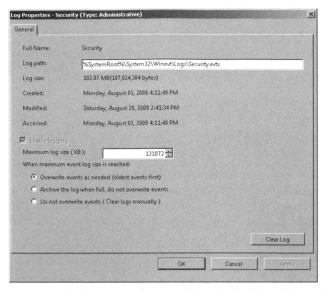

FIGURE 4-14 Configure log settings according to the level of auditing on the system.

4. Type or set a maximum size in kilobytes (KB) in the Maximum Log Size text box. Make sure that the drive containing the operating system has enough free space for the maximum log size you specify. Log files are stored in the %SystemRoot%\System32\Winevt\Logs directory by default.

5. Select an event log–wrapping mode. The following options are available:

   - **Overwrite Events As Needed (Oldest Events First)** Events in the log are overwritten when the maximum file size is reached. Generally, this is the best option on a low-priority system.

   - **Archive The Log When Full, Do Not Overwrite Events** When the maximum file size is reached, Windows archives the events by saving a copy of the current log in the default directory. Windows then creates a new log for storing current events.

   - **Do Not Overwrite Events (Clear Logs Manually)** When the maximum file size is reached, the system generates error messages telling you the event log is full.

6. Click OK when you have finished.

NOTE On critical systems where security and event logging is very important, you should use Archive The Log When Full, Do Not Overwrite Events. When you use this method, you ensure that event history is preserved in archives automatically.

Clearing Event Logs

When an event log is full, you need to clear it. To do that, follow these steps:

1. In Server Manager, expand the Diagnostics node and the Event Viewer node.

2. Expand Windows Logs or Applications And Services Logs as appropriate for the type of log you want to configure. You should now see a list of event logs.

3. Right-click the event log whose properties you want to set, and then click Clear Log on the shortcut menu.

4. Choose Save And Clear to save a copy of the log before clearing it. Choose Clear to continue without saving the log file.

Archiving Event Logs

On key systems such as domain controllers and application servers, you'll want to keep several months' worth of logs. However, it usually isn't practical to set the maximum log size to accommodate this. Instead, you should allow Windows to periodically archive the event logs, or you should manually archive the event logs.

Archive Log Formats

Logs can be archived in four formats:

- Event files (.evtx) format for access in Event Viewer
- Tab-delimited text (.txt) format for access in text editors or word processors or to import into spreadsheets and databases
- Comma-delimited text (.csv) format for importing into spreadsheets or databases
- XML (.xml) format for saving as an XML file

When you export log files to a comma-delimited file, a comma separates each field in the event entry. The event entries look like this:

```
Information,05/18/08 9:43:24 PM,DNS Server,2,None,The DNS server has
started.
Error,05/18/08 9:40:04 PM,DNS Server,4015,None,The DNS server has
encountered a critical error from the Directory Service (DS). The data is
the error code.
```

The format for the entries is as follows:

```
Level,Date and Time,Source,Event ID,Task Category,Description
```

Creating Log Archives

Windows creates log archives automatically when you select the event log–wrapping mode Archive The Log When Full, Do Not Overwrite Events. You can create a log archive manually by following these steps:

1. In Server Manager, expand the Diagnostics node and the Event Viewer node.

2. Expand Windows Logs or Applications And Services Logs as appropriate for the type of log you want to configure. You should now see a list of event logs.

3. Right-click the event log you want to archive, and then click Save All Events As on the shortcut menu.

4. In the Save As dialog box, select a directory and type a log file name.

5. In the Save As Type list, Event Files (*.evtx) is the default file type. Select the log format you want to use, and then choose Save. Note that you might not be able to use the .evtx format to save events from a remote computer to a local folder. In this case, you need to save the events to the local computer in a different file format, such as .xml. Otherwise, save the events in .evtx format on the remote computer.

6. If you plan to view the log on other computers, you may need to include display information. To save display information, select Display Information For These Languages, choose the language in the list provided, and then click OK. Otherwise, just click OK to save the log without display information.

NOTE If you plan to archive logs regularly, you might want to create an archive directory in which you can easily locate the log archives. You should also name the log file so that you can easily determine the log file type and the period of the archive. For example, if you're archiving the system log file for January 2010, you might want to use the file name System Log January 2010.

TIP The best format to use for archiving is the .evtx format. Use this format if you plan to review old logs in Event Viewer. However, if you plan to review logs in other applications, you might need to save the logs in a tab-delimited or comma-delimited format. With the tab-delimited or comma-delimited format, you sometimes need to edit the log file in a text editor for the log to be properly interpreted. If you have saved the log in the .evtx format, you can always save another copy in tab-delimited or comma-delimited format later by doing another Save As after opening the archive in Event Viewer.

Viewing Log Archives

You can view log archives in text format in any text editor or word processor. You should view log archives in the event log format in Event Viewer. You can view log archives in Event Viewer by following these steps:

1. In Server Manager, select and then right-click the Event Viewer node. From the shortcut menu, select Open Saved Log.

2. In the Open Saved Log dialog box, select a directory and a log file name. By default, the Event Logs Files format is selected. This ensures that logs saved

as .evtx, .evt, and .etl are listed. You can also filter the list by selecting a specific file type.

3. Click Open. If you are prompted about converting the log to the new event log format, click Yes.

4. Windows displays the Open Saved Log dialog box. Type a name and description for the saved log.

5. Specify where to save the log. By default, saved logs are listed under Saved Logs. You can create a new node by clicking New Folder, entering a name for the folder, and then clicking OK.

6. Click OK to close the Open Saved Log dialog box. You should now see the contents of the saved log.

TIP To remove the saved log from Event Viewer, click Delete in the Actions pane or on the Action menu. When prompted to confirm, click Yes. The saved log file still exists in its original location.

Monitoring Server Performance and Activity

Monitoring a server isn't something you should do haphazardly. You need to have a clear plan—a set of goals that you hope to achieve. Let's take a look at the reasons you might want to monitor a server and the tools you can use to do this.

Why Monitor Your Server?

Troubleshooting server performance problems is a key reason for monitoring. For example, users might be having problems connecting to the server, and you might want to monitor the server to troubleshoot these problems. Your goal is to track down the problem by using the available monitoring resources and resolve it.

Another common reason for wanting to monitor a server is to improve server performance. You do this by improving disk I/O, reducing CPU usage, and cutting down the network traffic load on the server. Unfortunately, you often need to make trade-offs when it comes to resource usage. For example, as the number of users accessing a server grows, you might not be able to reduce the network traffic load, but you might be able to improve server performance through load balancing or by distributing key data files on separate drives.

Getting Ready to Monitor

Before you start monitoring a server, you might want to establish baseline performance metrics for your server. To do this, you measure server performance at various times and under different load conditions. You can then compare the baseline performance with subsequent performance to determine how the server is performing. Performance metrics that are well above the baseline measurements might indicate areas where the server needs to be optimized or reconfigured.

After you establish baseline metrics, you should formulate a monitoring plan. A comprehensive monitoring plan includes the following steps:

1. Determine which server events should be monitored to help you accomplish your goal.
2. Set filters to reduce the amount of information collected.
3. Configure performance counters to watch resource usage.
4. Log the event data so that it can be analyzed.
5. Analyze the event data to help find solutions to problems.

These procedures are examined later in this chapter. Although you should usually develop a monitoring plan, sometimes you might not want to go through all these steps to monitor your server. For example, you might want to monitor and analyze activity as it happens rather than log and analyze the data later.

The primary tools you use to monitor your servers include:

- **Performance Monitor** Configure counters to watch resource usage over time. Use the usage information to gauge the performance of the server and determine areas that can be optimized.

- **Reliability Monitor** Tracks changes to the system and compares them to changes in system stability. This gives you a graphical representation of the relationship between changes in the system configuration and changes in system stability.

- **Resource Monitor** Provides detailed information about resource usage on the server. The information provided is similar to Task Manager (though more extensive).

- **Event logs** Use information in the event logs to troubleshoot system-wide problems, including those from the operating system and configured applications. The primary logs you work with are the system, security, and application event logs as well as logs for configured server roles.

Using the Monitoring Consoles

Resource Monitor, Reliability Monitor, and Performance Monitor are the tools of choice for performance tuning. You can access Resource Monitor by pressing Ctrl+Alt+Delete, clicking Start Task Manager, and then clicking the Resource Monitor button on the Performance tab. As shown in Figure 4-15, resource usage statistics are broken down into four categories:

- **CPU Usage** The summary details show the current CPU utilization and the maximum CPU frequency (as related to processor idling). If you expand the CPU entry (by clicking the options button), you'll see a list of currently running executables by name, process ID, description, status, number of threads used, current CPU utilization, and average CPU utilization.

- **Disk Usage**   The summary details show the number of kilobytes per second being read from or written to disk and the highest percentage of usage. If you expand the Disk entry below the graph (by clicking the options button), you'll see a list of currently running executables that are performing or have performed I/O operations by name, process ID, file being read or written, average number of bytes being read per second, average number of bytes being written per second, total number of bytes being read and written per second, I/O priority, and the associated disk response time.

- **Network Usage**   The summary details show the current network bandwidth utilization in kilobytes and the percentage of total bandwidth utilization. If you expand the Network entry below the graph (by clicking the options button), you'll see a list of currently running executables that are transferring or have transferred data on the network by name, process ID, server or IP address being contacted, average number of bytes being sent per second, average number of bytes received per second, and total bytes sent or received per second.

- **Memory Usage**   The summary details show the current memory utilization and the number of hard faults occurring per second. If you expand the Memory entry below the graph (by clicking the options button), you'll see a list of currently running executables by name, process ID, hard faults per second, commit memory in KB, working set memory in KB, shareable memory in KB, and private (nonshareable) memory in KB.

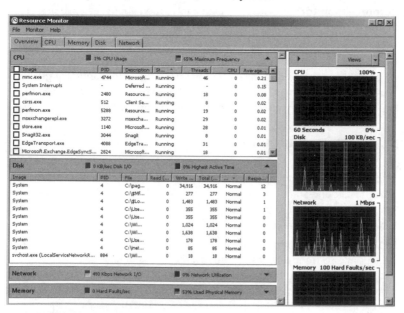

FIGURE 4-15 Review resource usage on the server.

Performance Monitor displays statistics graphically for the set of performance parameters you've selected for display. These performance parameters are referred to as *counters*. When you install certain applications on a system, Performance Monitor might be updated with a set of counters for tracking the server's performance. You can update these counters when you install additional services and add-ons for the application as well.

You can access Performance Monitor in a stand-alone console by clicking Start, pointing to Administrative Tools, and then clicking Performance Monitor. In Server Manager, you can access the tool as a snap-in under the Diagnostics node. Expand the Diagnostics node, then the Performance and Monitoring Tools nodes, and then select Performance Monitor.

As Figure 4-16 shows, Performance Monitor creates a graph depicting the counters you're tracking. The update interval for this graph is set to 1 second by default, but it can be configured with a different value. As you'll see when you work with Performance Monitor, the tracking information is most valuable when you record performance information in a log file so that it can be played back. Also, Performance Monitor is helpful when you configure alerts to send messages when certain events occur.

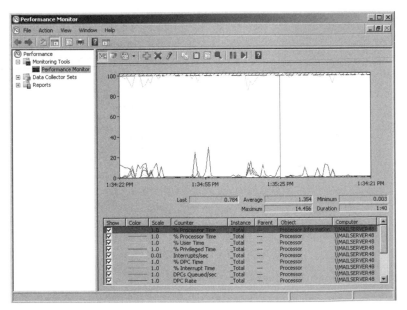

FIGURE 4-16 Review performance measurements for the server.

Windows Server 2008 R2 also includes Reliability Monitor. To access Reliability Monitor, click Start, and then click Control Panel. In Control Panel, click System, and then click Action Center. In Action Center, expand the Maintenance panel, and then click View Reliability History. Alternatively, you can run Reliability Monitor by entering **perfmon /rel** at a command prompt or by entering **Reliability Monitor** in the Search box on the Start menu.

Reliability Monitor tracks changes to the server and compares them to changes in system stability. In this way, you can see a graphical representation of the relationship between changes in the system configuration and changes in system stability. By recording software installation, software removal, application failures, hardware failures, and Windows failures, and key events regarding the configuration of the server, you can see a timeline of changes in both the server and its reliability and then use this information to pinpoint changes that are causing problems with stability. For example, if you see a sudden drop in stability, you can click a data point and then expand the related data set to find the specific event that caused the drop in stability.

Choosing Counters to Monitor

Performance Monitor displays information only for counters you're tracking. Several thousand counters are available, and you'll find counters related to just about every server role you've installed. The easiest way to learn about these counters is to read the explanations available in the Add Counters dialog box. Start Performance Monitor, click Add on the toolbar, and then expand an object in the Available Counters list. Select the Show Description check box, and then scroll through the list of counters for this object.

When Performance Monitor is monitoring a particular object, it can track all instances of all counters for that object. Instances are multiple occurrences of a particular counter. For example, when you track counters for the Processor object on a multiprocessor system, you have a choice of tracking all processor instances or specific processor instances. If you think a particular processor is going bad or experiencing other problems, you could monitor just that processor instance.

To select which counters you want to monitor, follow these steps:

1. Performance Monitor has several views and view types. Be sure that current activity is displayed by clicking View Current Activity on the toolbar or pressing Ctrl+T. You can switch between the view types (Line, Histogram Bar, and Report) by clicking Change Graph Type or pressing Ctrl+G.

2. To add counters, click Add on the toolbar or press Ctrl+N. This displays the Add Counters dialog box, shown in Figure 4-17.

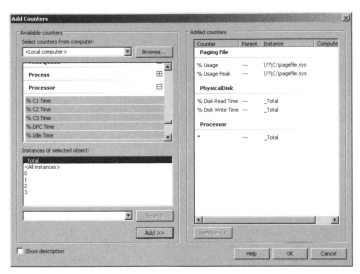

FIGURE 4-17 Select the objects and counters you want to monitor.

3. In the Select Counters From Computer list, enter the Universal Naming Convention (UNC) name of the server you want to work with, such as \\CorpServer84, or choose <Local Computer> to work with the local computer.

   NOTE You need to be at least a member of the Performance Monitor Users group in the domain or on the local computer to perform remote monitoring. When you use performance logging, you need to be at least a member of the Performance Log Users group in the domain or on the local computer to work with performance logs on remote computers.

4. In the Available Counters panel, performance objects are listed alphabetically. If you select an object entry by clicking it, all related counters are selected. If you expand an object entry, you can see all the related counters and can then select individual counters by clicking them. For example, you could expand the entry for the Active Server Pages object and then select the Requests Failed Total, Requests Not Found, Requests Queued, and Requests Total counters.

5. When you select an object or any of its counters, you see the related instances. Choose All Instances to select all counter instances for monitoring, or select one or more counter instances to monitor. For example, you could select instances of Anonymous Users/Sec for individual Web sites or for all Web sites.

6. When you've selected an object or a group of counters for an object as well as the object instances, click Add to add the counters to the graph.

7. Repeat steps 4–6 to add other performance parameters.

8. Click OK when you have finished.

TIP Don't try to chart too many counters or counter instances at once. You'll make the display too difficult to read, and you'll use system resources—namely, CPU time and memory—that might affect server responsiveness.

Performance Logging

Windows Server 2008 R2 introduces data collector sets and reports. Data collector sets allow you to specify sets of performance objects and counters that you want to track. Once you've created a data collector set, you can easily start or stop monitoring the performance objects and counters included in the set. In a way, this makes data collector sets similar to the performance logs used in earlier releases of Windows. However, data collector sets are much more sophisticated. You can use a single data set to generate multiple performance counter and trace logs. You can also do the following:

- Assign access controls to manage who can access collected data
- Create multiple run schedules and stop conditions for monitoring
- Use data managers to control the size of collected data and reporting
- Generate reports based on collected data

In the Performance tool, you can review currently configured data collector sets and reports under the Data Collector Sets and Reports nodes, respectively. As shown in Figure 4-18, you'll find data sets and reports that are user-defined and system-defined. User-defined data sets are created by users for general monitoring and performance tuning. System-defined data sets are created by the operating system to aid in automated diagnostics.

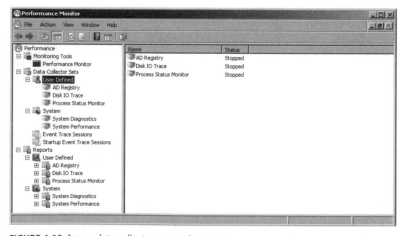

FIGURE 4-18 Access data collector sets and reports.

Creating and Managing Data Collector Sets

To view the currently configured data collector sets, select the Performance Monitor option in the Administrative Tools program group, and then expand the Data Collector Sets node. You can work with data collectors in a variety of ways.

- You can view currently defined user or system data collector sets by selecting either User Defined or System as appropriate. When you select a data collector set in the left pane, you'll see the related data collectors in the main pane listed by name and type. The Trace type is for data collectors that record performance data whenever related events occur. The Performance Counter type is for data collectors that record data on selected counters when a predetermined interval has elapsed. The Configuration type is for data collectors that record changes to particular registry paths.

- You can view running event traces by selecting Event Trace Sessions. You can then stop a data collector that is running a trace by right-clicking it and selecting Stop.

- You can view the enabled or disabled status of event traces configured to run automatically when you start the computer by selecting Startup Event Trace Sessions. You can start a trace by right-clicking a startup data collector and selecting Start As Event Trace Session. You can delete a startup data collector by right-clicking it and then clicking Delete.

- You can save a data collector as a template that can be used as the basis of other data collectors by right-clicking the data collector and selecting Save Template. In the Save As dialog box, select a directory, type a name for the template, and then click Save. The data collector template is saved as an XML file that can be copied to other systems.

- You can delete a user-defined data collector by right-clicking it and selecting Delete. If a data collector is running, you need to stop collecting data first and then delete the collector. Deleting a collector deletes the related reports as well.

Collecting Performance Counter Data

Data collectors can be used to record performance data on the selected counters at a specific sampling interval. For example, you could sample performance data for the CPU every 15 minutes.

To collect performance counter data, follow these steps:

1. In Performance Monitor, under the Data Collector Sets node, right-click the User-Defined node in the left pane, point to New, and then choose Data Collector Set.

2. In the Create New Data Collector Set Wizard, type a name for the data collector, such as **System Performance Monitor** or **Processor Status Monitor**. Note that if you type an invalid name, such as one with a nonalphanumeric character, you won't be able to continue.

3. Select the Create Manually option, and then click Next.

4. On the What Type Of Data Do You Want To Include page, the Create Data Logs option is selected by default. Select the Performance Counter check box, and then click Next.

5. On the Which Performance Counters Would You Like To Log page, click Add. This displays the Add Counters dialog box, which you can use as previously discussed to select the performance counters to track. When you have finished selecting counters, click OK.

6. On the Which Performance Counters Would You Like To Log page, enter a sampling interval and select a time unit in seconds, minutes, hours, days, or weeks. The sampling interval specifies when new data is collected. For example, if you sample every 15 minutes, the data log is updated every 15 minutes. Click Next when you are ready to continue.

7. On the Where Would You Like The Data To Be Saved page, type the root path to use for logging collected data. Alternatively, click Browse, and then use the Browse For Folder dialog box to select the logging directory. Click Next when you are ready to continue.

   BEST PRACTICES The default location for logging is %SystemDrive%\Perf-Logs\Admin. Log files can grow in size very quickly. If you plan to log data for an extended period, be sure to place the log file on a drive with lots of free space. Remember, the more frequently you update the log file, the greater the drive space and CPU resource usage on the system.

8. On the Create Data Collector Set page, the Run As box lists <Default> to indicate that the log will run under the privileges and permissions of the default system account. To run the log with the privileges and permissions of another user, click Change. Type the user name and password for the account, and then click OK. User names can be entered in domain\user-name format, such as cpandl\williams for the Williams account in the Cpandl domain.

9. Select the Open Properties For This Data Collector Set option, and then click Finish. This saves the data collector set, closes the wizard, and then opens the related Properties dialog box.

10. By default, logging is configured to start manually. To configure a logging schedule, click the Schedule tab, and then click Add. You can now set the Active Range, Start Time, and run days for data collection.

11. By default, logging stops only if you set an expiration date as part of the logging schedule. Using the options on the Stop Condition tab, you can configure the log file to stop automatically after a specified period of time, such as seven days, or when the log file is full (if you've set a maximum size limit).

12. Click OK when you've finished setting the logging schedule and stop conditions. You can manage the data collector as explained previously.

NOTE You can configure Windows to run a scheduled task when data collection stops. You configure tasks to run on the Tasks tab in the Properties dialog box.

Collecting Performance Trace Data

You can use data collectors to record performance trace data whenever events related to their source providers occur. A source provider is an application or operating system service that has traceable events.

To collect performance trace data, follow these steps:

1. In Performance Monitor, under the Data Collector Sets node, right-click the User-Defined node in the left pane, point to New, and then choose Data Collector Set.

2. In the Create New Data Collector Set Wizard, type a name for the data collector, such as **Logon Trace** or **Disk IO Trace**. Note that if you type an invalid name, such as one with a nonalphanumeric character, you won't be able to continue.

3. Select the Create Manually option, and then click Next.

4. On the What Type Of Data Do You Want To Include page, the Create Data Logs option is selected by default. Select the Event Trace Data check box, and then click Next.

5. On the Which Event Trace Providers Would You Like To Enable page, click Add. Select an event trace provider to track, and then click OK. By selecting individual properties in the Properties list and clicking Edit, you can track particular property values rather than all values for the provider. Repeat this process to select other event trace providers to track. Click Next when you are ready to continue.

6. Complete steps 7–12 from the procedure in the previous section, "Collecting Performance Counter Data."

Collecting Configuration Data

You can use data collectors to record changes in registry configuration. To collect configuration data, follow these steps:

1. In Performance Monitor, under the Data Collector Sets node, right-click the User-Defined node in the left pane, point to New, and then choose Data Collector Set.

2. In the Create New Data Collector Set Wizard, type a name for the data collector, such as **AD Registry** or **Registry Adapter Info**.

3. Select the Create Manually option, and then click Next.

4. On the What Type Of Data Do You Want To Include page, the Create Data Logs option is selected by default. Select the System Configuration Information check box, and then click Next.

5. On the Which Registry Keys Would You Like To Record page, click Add. Type the registry path to track. Repeat this process to add other registry paths to track. Click Next when you are ready to continue.

6. Complete steps 7–12 from the procedure in the section "Collecting Performance Counter Data."

Viewing Data Collector Reports

When you troubleshoot problems, you'll often want to log performance data over an extended period of time and then review the data to analyze the results. For each data collector that has been or is currently active, you'll find related data collector reports. As with data collector sets themselves, data collector reports are organized into two general categories: user-defined and system.

You can view data collector reports in Performance Monitor. Expand the Reports node, and then expand the individual report node for the data collector you want to analyze. Under the data collector's report node, you'll find individual reports for each logging session. A logging session begins when logging starts and ends when logging is stopped.

The most recent log is the one with the highest log number. If a data collector is actively logging, you won't be able to view the most recent log. You can stop collecting data by right-clicking a data collector set and selecting Stop. Collected data is shown by default in a graph view from the start of data collection to the end of data collection, as shown in Figure 4-19.

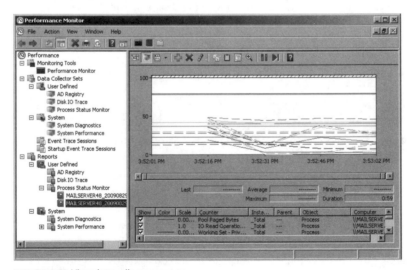

FIGURE 4-19 View data collector reports.

You can modify the report details using the following techniques:

1. In the monitor pane, press Ctrl+Q or click the Properties button on the toolbar. This displays the Performance Monitor Properties dialog box.

2. Click the Source tab.

3. Specify data sources to analyze. Under Data Source, click Log Files and then click Add to open the Select Log File dialog box. You can now select additional log files to analyze.

4. Specify the time window that you want to analyze. Click Time Range, and then drag the Total Range bar to specify the appropriate starting and ending times. Drag the left edge to the right to move up the start time. Drag the right edge to the left to make the end time later.

5. Click the Data tab. You can now select counters to view. Select a counter, and then click Remove to remove it from the graph view. Click Add to display the Add Counter dialog box, which you can use to select the counters that you want to analyze.

   NOTE Only counters that you selected for logging are available. If you don't see a counter that you want to work with, you need to modify the data collector properties, restart the logging process, and then check the logs at a later date.

6. Click OK. In the monitor pane, click the Change Graph Type button to select the type of graph.

Configuring Performance Counter Alerts

You can configure alerts to notify you when certain events occur or when certain performance thresholds are reached. You can send these alerts as network messages and as events that are logged in the application event log. You can also configure alerts to start applications and performance logs.

To configure an alert, follow these steps:

1. In Performance Monitor, under the Data Collector Sets node, right-click the User-Defined node in the left pane, point to New, and then choose Data Collector Set.

2. In the Create New Data Collector Set Wizard, type a name for the data collector, such as **Processor Alert** or **Disk IO Alert**.

3. Select the Create Manually option, and then click Next.

4. On the What Type Of Data Do You Want To Include page, select the Performance Counter Alert option, and then click Next.

5. On the Which Performance Counters Would You Like To Monitor page, click Add to display the Add Counters dialog box. This dialog box is identical to the Add Counters dialog box discussed previously. Use the dialog box to add counters that trigger the alert. Click OK when you have finished.

6. In the Performance Counters panel, select the first counter, and then use the Alert When Value Is text box to set the occasion when an alert for this counter is triggered. Alerts can be triggered when the counter is above or below a specific value. Select Above or Below, and then set the trigger value. The unit of measurement is whatever makes sense for the currently selected counter or counters. For example, to generate an alert if processor time is over 95 percent, select Over, and then type **95**. Repeat this process to configure other counters you've selected.

7. Complete steps 8–12 from the procedure in the section "Collecting Performance Counter Data."

Tuning System Performance

Now that you know how to monitor your system, let's look at how you can tune the operating system and hardware performance. I'll examine the following areas:

- Memory usage and caching
- Processor utilization
- Disk I/O
- Network bandwidth and connectivity

Monitoring and Tuning Memory Usage

Memory is often the source of performance problems, and you should always rule out memory problems before examining other areas of the system. Systems use both physical and virtual memory. To rule out memory problems with a system, you should configure application performance, memory usage, and data throughput settings and then monitor the server's memory usage to check for problems.

Application performance and memory usage settings determine how system resources are allocated. In most cases, you want to give the operating system and background applications the lion's share of resources. This is especially true for Active Directory, file, print, and network and communications servers. On the other hand, for application, database, and streaming media servers, you should give the programs a server is running the most resources, as discussed in "Setting Application Performance" in Chapter 3.

Using the monitoring techniques discussed previously in this chapter, you can determine how the system is using memory and check for problems. Table 4-1 provides an overview of counters that you'll want to track to uncover memory, caching, and virtual memory (paging) bottlenecks. The table is organized by issue category.

TABLE 4-1 Uncovering Memory-Related Bottlenecks

ISSUE	COUNTERS TO TRACK	DETAILS
Physical and virtual memory usage	Memory\ Available Kbytes Memory\Committed Bytes	Memory\Available Kbytes is the amount of physical memory available to processes running on the server. Memory\Committed Bytes is the amount of committed virtual memory. If the server has very little available memory, you might need to add memory to the system. In general, you want the available memory to be no less than 5 percent of the total physical memory on the server. If the server has a high ratio of committed bytes to total physical memory on the system, you might need to add memory as well. In general, you want the committed bytes value to be no more than 75 percent of the total physical memory.
Memory page faults	Memory\Page Faults/sec Memory\Pages Input/sec Memory\Page Reads/sec	A page fault occurs when a process requests a page in memory and the system can't find it at the requested location. If the requested page is elsewhere in memory, the fault is called a *soft page fault*. If the requested page must be retrieved from disk, the fault is called a *hard page fault*. Most processors can handle large numbers of soft faults. Hard faults, however, can cause significant delays. Page Faults/sec is the overall rate at which the processor handles all types of page faults. Pages Input/sec is the total number of pages read from disk to resolve hard page faults. Page Reads/sec is the total disk reads needed to resolve hard page faults. Pages Input/sec will be greater than or equal to Page Reads/sec and can give you a good idea of your hard page fault rate. A high number of hard page faults could indicate that you need to increase the amount of memory or reduce the cache size on the server.

ISSUE	COUNTERS TO TRACK	DETAILS
Memory paging	Memory\Pool Paged Bytes Memory\Pool Nonpaged Bytes	These counters track the number of bytes in the paged and nonpaged pool. The paged pool is an area of system memory for objects that can be written to disk when they aren't used. The nonpaged pool is an area of system memory for objects that can't be written to disk. If the size of the paged pool is large relative to the total amount of physical memory on the system, you might need to add memory to the system. If the size of the nonpaged pool is large relative to the total amount of virtual memory allocated to the server, you might want to increase the virtual memory size.

Monitoring and Tuning Processor Usage

The CPU does the actual processing of information on your server. As you examine a server's performance, you should focus on the CPU after you have eliminated memory bottlenecks. If the server's processors are the performance bottleneck, adding memory, drives, or network connections won't overcome the problem. Instead, you might need to upgrade the processors to faster clock speeds or add processors to increase the server's upper capacity. You could also move processor-intensive applications, such as SQL Server, to another server.

Before you make a decision to upgrade CPUs or add CPUs, you should rule out problems with memory and caching. If signs still point to a processor problem, you should monitor the performance counters listed in Table 4-2. Be sure to monitor these counters for each CPU installed on the server.

TABLE 4-2 Uncovering Processor-Related Bottlenecks

ISSUE	COUNTERS TO TRACK	DETAILS
Thread queuing	System\Processor Queue Length	This counter displays the number of threads waiting to be executed. These threads are queued in an area shared by all processors on the system. If this counter has a sustained value of more than 10 threads per processor, you need to upgrade or add processors.

ISSUE	COUNTERS TO TRACK	DETAILS
CPU usage	Processor\ % Processor Time	This counter displays the percentage of time the selected CPU is executing a nonidle thread. You should track this counter separately for all processor instances on the server. If the % Processor Time values are high while the network interface and disk I/O throughput rates are relatively low, you need to upgrade or add processors.

Monitoring and Tuning Disk I/O

With today's high-speed disks, the disk throughput rate is rarely the cause of a bottleneck. That said, accessing memory is much faster than accessing disks. So, if the server has to do a lot of disk reads and writes, a server's overall performance can be degraded. To reduce the amount of disk I/O, you want the server to manage memory very efficiently and page to disk only when necessary. You monitor and tune memory usage as discussed in "Monitoring and Tuning Memory Usage."

In addition to memory tuning, you can monitor some counters to gauge disk I/O activity. Specifically, you should monitor the counters listed in Table 4-3.

TABLE 4-3 Uncovering Drive-Related Bottlenecks

ISSUE	COUNTERS TO TRACK	DETAILS
Overall drive performance	PhysicalDisk\% Disk Time in conjunction with Processor\% Processor Time and Network Interface Connection\Bytes Total/sec	If the % Disk Time value is high and the processor and network connection values aren't high, the system's hard disk drives might be creating a bottleneck. Be sure to monitor % Disk Time for all hard disk drives on the server.
Disk I/O	PhysicalDisk\Disk Writes/sec, PhysicalDisk\Disk Reads/sec PhysicalDisk\Avg. DiskWrite Queue Length PhysicalDisk\Avg. DiskRead Queue Length PhysicalDisk\ CurrentDisk Queue Length	The number of writes and reads per second tell you how much disk I/O activity there is. The write and read queue lengths tell you how many write or read requests are waiting to be processed. In general, you want very few waiting requests. Keep in mind that the request delays are proportional to the length of the queues minus the number of drives in a redundant array of independent disks (RAID) set.

Monitoring and Tuning Network Bandwidth and Connectivity

No other factor matters more to the way a user perceives your server's performance than the network that connects your server to the user's computer. The delay, or latency, between when a request is made and the time it's received can make all the difference. With a high degree of latency, it doesn't matter if you have the fastest server on the planet: the user experiences a delay and perceives that your servers are slow.

Generally speaking, the latency that the user experiences is beyond your control. It's a function of the type of connection the user has and the route the request takes to your server. The total capacity of your server to handle requests and the amount of bandwidth available to your servers are factors under your control, however. Network bandwidth availability is a function of your organization's network infrastructure. Network capacity is a function of the network cards and interfaces configured on the servers.

The capacity of your network card can be a limiting factor in some instances. Most servers use 100/1000 network cards, which can be configured in many ways. Someone might have configured a card for 100 Mbps, or the card might be configured for half duplex instead of full duplex. If you suspect a capacity problem with a network card, you should always check the configuration.

To determine the throughput and current activity on a server's network cards, you can check the following counters:

- Network\Bytes Received/sec
- Network\Bytes Sent/sec
- Network\Bytes Total/sec
- Network Current Bandwidth

If the total bytes per second value is more than 50 percent of the total capacity under average load conditions, your server might have problems under peak load conditions. You might want to ensure that operations that take a lot of network bandwidth, such as network backups, are performed on a separate interface card. Keep in mind that you should compare these values in conjunction with PhysicalDisk\% Disk Time and Processor\% Processor Time. If the disk time and processor time values are low but the network values are very high, you might have a capacity problem. Solve the problem by optimizing the network card settings or by adding a network card. Remember, planning is everything—it isn't always as simple as inserting a card and plugging it into the network.

CHAPTER 5

Automating Administrative Tasks, Policies, and Procedures

Performing routine tasks day after day, running around policing systems, and walking users through the basics aren't efficient uses of your time. You'd be much more effective if you could automate these chores and focus on issues that are more important. Support services are all about increasing productivity and allowing you to focus less on mundane matters and more on what's important.

Windows Server 2008 Release 2 (R2) includes many roles, role services, and features that help you support server installations. You can easily install and use some of these components. If you need an administrative tool to manage a role or feature on a remote computer, you can select the tool to install as part of the Remote Server Administration Tools feature. If a server has a wireless adapter, you can install the Wireless LAN Service feature to enable wireless connections. Beyond these and other basic support components, you can use many other support features, including:

- **Automatic Updates** Ensures that the operating system is up to date and has the most recent security updates. If you update a server by using Microsoft Update instead of the standard Windows Updates, you can get updates for additional products. By default, Automatic Updates is installed but not enabled on servers running Windows Server 2008 R2. You can configure Automatic Updates by using the Windows Update utility in Control Panel. Click Start, All Programs, and then click Windows Update to start this utility. To learn how to configure Automatic Updates through Group Policy, see "Configuring Automatic Updates" later in this chapter.

- **BitLocker Drive Encryption** Provides an extra layer of security for a server's hard disks. This protects the disks from attackers who have physical access to the server. BitLocker encryption can be used on servers with or without a Trusted Platform Module (TPM). When you add this feature to a server using the Add Features Wizard, you can manage it using the BitLocker Drive Encryption utility in Control Panel. Click Start, click Control Panel, System And Security, and then click BitLocker Drive Encryption. Windows Server 2008 R2 (like Windows 7) includes BitLockerToGo, which allows you to encrypt USB flash drives. To use BitLockerToGo, you must install the BitLocker feature.

- **Remote Assistance** Provides an assistance feature that allows an administrator to send a remote assistance invitation to a more senior administrator. The senior administrator can then accept the invitation to view the user's desktop and temporarily take control of the computer to resolve a problem. When you add this feature to a server using the Add Features Wizard, you can manage it by using options on the Remote tab of the System Properties dialog box. In Control Panel, System And Security, click System, and then click Remote Settings under Tasks to view the related options.

- **Remote Desktop** Provides a remote connectivity feature that allows you to connect to and manage a server from another computer. By default, Remote Desktop is installed but not enabled on servers running Windows Server 2008 R2. You can manage the Remote Desktop configuration with the options on the Remote tab of the System Properties dialog box. In Control Panel, click System, and then click Remote Settings to view the related options. You can establish remote connections using the Remote Desktop Connection utility. Click Start, click All Programs, click Accessories, and then click Remote Desktop Connection.

- **Task Scheduler** Allows you to schedule execution of one-time and recurring tasks, such as tasks for performing routine maintenance. Like Windows 7, Windows Server 2008 R2 makes extensive use of the scheduled task facilities. You can view and work with scheduled tasks in Server Manager. Expand the Configuration, Task Scheduler, and Task Scheduler Library nodes to view configured scheduled tasks.

- **Windows Defender** Helps protect a server from spyware and other potentially unwanted software. You can run Windows Defender manually or configure it to run automatically according to a schedule. By default, Windows Defender is not enabled on server installations. When Windows Defender is installed as part of the Desktop Experience feature, you can start it from the All Programs menu.

- **Desktop Experience**   Installs Windows 7 desktop functionality on the server. You can use this feature when you use Windows Server 2008 R2 as your desktop operating system. When you add this feature using the Add Features Wizard, the server's desktop functionality is enhanced, and the following programs are installed as well: Windows Media Player, Desktop Themes, Video for Windows (AVI support), Windows SideShow, Windows Defender, Disk Cleanup, Sync Center, Sound Recorder, Character Map, and Snipping Tool.

- **Windows Firewall**   Helps protect a computer from attack by unauthorized users. Windows Server 2008 R2 includes a basic firewall called Windows Firewall and an advanced firewall called Windows Firewall With Advanced Security. By default, the firewalls are not enabled on server installations. To access the basic firewall, click Windows Firewall in Control Panel. To access the advanced firewall, select Windows Firewall With Advanced Security on the Administrative Tools menu.

- **Windows Time**   Synchronizes the system time with world time to ensure that the system time is accurate. You can configure computers to synchronize with a specific time server. The way Windows Time works depends on whether a computer is a member of a domain or a workgroup. In a domain, domain controllers are used for time synchronization, and you can manage this feature through Group Policy. In a workgroup, Internet time servers are used for time synchronization, and you can manage this feature through the Date And Time utility.

You can configure and manage these support components in the same way on Windows 7 and Windows Server 2008 R2. You'll find extensive coverage of these support components in *Windows 7 Administrator's Pocket Consultant* (Microsoft Press, 2009).

Many other components provide support services. However, you need these additional support services only in specific scenarios. You can use Windows System Resource Manager (WSRM) to manage server processor and memory usage when you want to help ensure the availability of a busy server. You can use Remote Desktop Services when you want to allow users to run applications on a remote server. You can use Windows Deployment Services when you want to enable automated deployment of Windows-based operating systems. The one always-on support service that you must master to succeed with Windows Server 2008 R2 is Group Policy.

NOTE   Group Policy settings for Windows Server 2008 R2 have changed considerably from previous versions of Windows Server. Under the Computer Configuration and User Configuration nodes, you'll find two new nodes: Policies and Preferences. Settings for general policies are listed under the Policies node. Settings for general preferences are listed under the Preferences node. When I reference settings under the Policies node, I'll use a shortcut such as User Configuration\Administrative Templates\Windows Components rather than User Configuration\Policies\Administrative Templates: Policy Definitions\Windows Components. This shortcut tells you that the policy setting being discussed is under User Configuration rather than Computer Configuration and can be found under Administrative Templates\Windows Components.

Understanding Group Policies

Group policies simplify administration by giving administrators centralized control over privileges, permissions, and capabilities of both users and computers. Through group policies, you can do the following:

- Control access to Windows components, system resources, network resources, Control Panel utilities, the desktop, and the Start menu. See "Using Administrative Templates to Set Policies" later in this chapter for more details.

- Create centrally managed directories for special folders, such as a user's Documents folder. See "Centrally Managing Special Folders" later in the chapter for more details.

- Define user and computer scripts to run at specified times. This is covered in "User and Computer Script Management" later in the chapter.

- Configure policies for account lockout and passwords, auditing, user rights assignment, and security. These topics are covered in Chapter 9, "Understanding User and Group Accounts," and Chapter 10, "Creating User and Group Accounts."

The sections that follow explain how you can work with and apply group policies.

Group Policy Essentials

You can think of a policy as a set of rules that helps you manage users and computers. You can apply group policies to multiple domains, to individual domains, to subgroups within a domain, or to individual systems. Policies that apply to individual systems are referred to as *local group policies* and are stored on the local system only. Other group policies are linked as objects in the Active Directory data store.

To understand group policies, you need to know a bit about the structure of Active Directory. In Active Directory, sites represent the physical structure of your network. A site is a group of TCP/IP subnets, with each subnet representing a physical network segment. A domain is a logical grouping of objects for centralized management, and subgroups within a domain are called *organizational units* (OUs). Your network might have sites called NewYorkMain, CaliforniaMain, and WashingtonMain. Within the WashingtonMain site you could have domains called Seattle-East, SeattleWest, SeattleNorth, and SeattleSouth. Within the SeattleEast domain you could have organizational units called Information Services (IS), Engineering, and Sales.

Group policies apply only to systems running Windows 2000 and later versions of Windows. Group Policy settings are stored in a Group Policy object (GPO). You can think of a GPO as a container for the policies you apply and their settings. You can apply multiple GPOs to a single site, domain, or organizational unit. Because Group Policy is described using objects, many object-oriented concepts apply. If you know a bit about object-oriented programming, you might expect the concepts of parent-child relationships and inheritance to apply to GPOs—and you'd be right.

A *container* is a top-level object that contains other objects. Through inheritance, a policy applied to a parent container is inherited by a child container. Essentially, this means that a policy setting applied to a parent object is passed down to a child object. For example, if you apply a policy setting in a domain, the setting is inherited by organizational units within the domain. In this case, the GPO for the domain is the parent object, and the GPOs for the organizational units are the child objects.

The order of inheritance is site, domain, organizational unit. This means that the Group Policy settings for a site are passed down to the domains within that site, and the settings for a domain are passed down to the organizational units within that domain.

As you might expect, you can override inheritance. To do this, you specifically assign a policy setting for a child container that is different from the policy setting for the parent. As long as overriding the policy is allowed (that is, overriding isn't blocked), the child container's policy setting will be applied appropriately. To learn more about overriding and blocking GPOs, see "Blocking, Overriding, and Disabling Policies" later in this chapter.

In What Order Are Multiple Policies Applied?

When multiple policies are in place, policies are applied in the following order:

1. Local group policies
2. Site group policies
3. Domain group policies
4. Organizational unit group policies
5. Child organizational unit group policies

If policy settings conflict, the policy settings applied later have precedence and overwrite previously set policy settings. For example, organizational unit policies have precedence over domain group policies. As you might expect, there are exceptions to the precedence rule. These exceptions are discussed in "Blocking, Overriding, and Disabling Policies" later in this chapter.

When Are Group Policies Applied?

As you'll discover when you start working with group policies, policy settings are divided into two broad categories:

- Those that apply to computers
- Those that apply to users

Computer policies are normally applied during system startup, and user policies are normally applied during logon. The exact sequence of events is often important in troubleshooting system behavior. The events that take place during startup and logon are as follows:

1. The network starts, and then Windows Server 2008 R2 applies computer policies. By default, computer policies are applied one at a time in the previously specified order. No user interface is displayed while computer policies are being processed.

2. Windows Server 2008 R2 runs startup scripts. By default, startup scripts are executed one at a time, with each completing or timing out before the next one starts. Script execution isn't displayed to the user unless specified.

3. A user presses Ctrl+Alt+Del to log on. After the user is validated, Windows Server 2008 R2 loads the user profile.

4. Windows Server 2008 R2 applies user policies. By default, user policies are applied one at a time in the previously specified order. The user interface is displayed while user policies are being processed.

5. Windows Server 2008 R2 runs logon scripts. Logon scripts for Group Policy are executed simultaneously by default. Script execution isn't displayed to the user unless specified. Scripts in the Netlogon share run last in a normal command shell window.

6. Windows Server 2008 R2 displays the start shell interface configured in Group Policy.

7. By default, Group Policy is refreshed when a user logs off or a computer is restarted and automatically within a 90 to 120 minute period. You can change this behavior by setting a Group Policy refresh interval, as discussed in "Refreshing Group Policy" later in this chapter. To do this, open a command prompt and type **gpupdate**.

REAL WORLD Some user settings, such as Folder Redirection, can't be updated when a user is logged on. The user must log off and then log back on for these settings to be applied. You can type **gpupdate /logoff** at a command prompt to log off the user automatically after the refresh. Similarly, some computer settings can be updated only at startup. The computer must be restarted for these settings to be applied. You can enter **gpupdate /boot** at a command prompt to restart the computer after the refresh.

Group Policy Requirements and Version Compatibility

Group policies were introduced with Windows 2000 and apply only to systems running workstation and server versions of Windows 2000 and later. As you might expect, each new version of the Windows operating system has brought with it changes to Group Policy. Sometimes these changes have made older policies obsolete on newer versions of Windows. In this case, the policy works only on specific versions of Windows, such as only on Windows XP Professional and Windows Server 2003.

Generally speaking, most policies are forward compatible. This means that in most cases, policies introduced in Windows Server 2003 can be used on Windows Vista, Windows 7, Windows Server 2008, and Windows Server 2008 R2. It also means that policies for Windows Server 2008 or later versions usually aren't applicable to earlier releases of Windows. If a policy isn't applicable to a particular version of the Windows operating system, you can't enforce the policy on computers running those versions of Windows.

How will you know if a policy is supported on a particular version of Windows? Easy. The Properties dialog box for each policy setting has a Supported On field on the Settings tab. This text-only field lists the policy's compatibility with various versions of Windows. If you select a policy with the Extended display in any of the Group Policy editors, you'll also see a Requirements entry that lists compatibility.

You can also install new policies when you add a service pack, install Windows applications, or add Windows components. This means that you'll see a wide range of compatibility entries.

Navigating Group Policy Changes

In an effort to streamline management of Group Policy, Microsoft removed management features from Active Directory–related tools and moved to a primary console called the Group Policy Management Console (GPMC) starting with Windows Vista and Windows Server 2008. The GPMC is a feature that you can add to any installation of Windows Server 2008 or Windows Server 2008 R2 by using the Add Features Wizard. The GPMC is available on Windows Vista and Windows 7 when you install the Remote Server Administration Tools (RSAT). Once you add the GPMC to a computer, it is available on the Administrative Tools menu.

When you want to edit a GPO in the GPMC, the GPMC opens the Group Policy Management Editor, which you use to manage the policy settings. If Microsoft had stopped with these two tools, we'd have a wonderful and easy-to-use policy management environment. Unfortunately, several other, nearly identical editors also exist, including:

- **Group Policy Starter GPO Editor** An editor that you can use to create and manage starter policy objects. As the name implies, starter GPOs are meant to provide a starting point for policy objects that you'll use throughout your organization. When you create a policy object, you can specify a starter GPO as the source or basis of the object.

- **Local Group Policy Object Editor** An editor that you can use to create and manage policy objects for the local computer. As the name implies, local GPOs are meant to provide policy settings for a specific computer as opposed to settings for a site, domain, or organizational unit.

If you've worked with earlier versions of Windows, you might also be familiar with the Group Policy Object Editor (GPOE). With Windows Server 2003 and earlier versions of Windows, the GPOE is the primary editing tool for policy objects. The Group Policy Object Editor, Group Policy Management Editor, Group Policy Starter GPO Editor, and Local Group Policy Object Editor are essentially identical except for the set of policy objects you have access to. For this reason, and because you use these tools to manage individual policy objects in the same way, I won't differentiate between them unless necessary. As a matter of preference, I refer to these tools collectively as policy editors. Sometimes, I might use the acronym GPOE to refer to policy editors in general because it is more easily distinguished from the management console, the GPMC.

You can manage Windows Vista and later policy settings only from computers running Windows Vista or later. The reason for this is that Windows Vista and later releases have new versions of the GPOE and the GPMC, and these versions have been updated to work with the new XML-based administrative templates format called ADMX.

NOTE You cannot use older versions of the policy editors with ADMX. You can edit GPOs using ADMX files only on a computer running Windows Vista or later.

Microsoft had many reasons for going to a new format. The key reasons were to allow greater flexibility and extensibility. Because ADMX files are created using XML, the files are strictly structured and can be more easily and rapidly parsed during initialization. This can help to improve performance when the operating system processes Group Policy during the startup, logon, logoff, and shutdown phases, as well as during policy refreshes. Further, the strict structure of ADMX files makes it possible for Microsoft to continue in its internationalization efforts.

ADMX files are divided into language-neutral files ending with the .admx file extension and language-specific files ending with the .adml extension. The language-neutral files ensure that a GPO has identical core policies. The language-specific files allow policies to be viewed and edited in multiple languages. Because the language-neutral files store a policy's core settings, policies can be edited in any language for which a computer is configured, thus allowing one user to view and edit policies in English and another to view and edit policies in Spanish, for example. The mechanism that determines the language used is the language pack installed on the computer.

Language-neutral ADMX files are installed on computers running Windows Vista or later in the %SystemRoot%\PolicyDefinitions folder. Language-specific ADMX files are installed on computers running Windows 7 and Windows Server 2008 R2 in the %SystemRoot%\PolicyDefinitions*LanguageCulture* folder. Each subfolder is named using the corresponding International Organization for Standardization (ISO) language/culture name, such as EN-US for U.S. English.

When you start a policy editor, it automatically reads ADMX files from the policy definitions folders. Because of this, you can copy ADMX files that you want to use to an appropriate policy definitions folder to make them available when you are editing GPOs. If the policy editor is running when you copy the file or files, you must restart the policy editor to force it to read the file or files.

In domains, ADMX files can be stored in a central store—the domainwide directory created in the SYSVOL directory (%SystemRoot%\Sysvol\Domain\Policies). When you use a central store, administrative templates are no longer stored with each GPO. Instead, only the current state of the setting is stored in the GPO, and the ADMX files are stored centrally. This reduces the amount of storage space used as the number of GPOs increases and also reduces the amount of data being replicated throughout the enterprise. As long as you edit GPOs using Windows Vista or later, new GPOs will not contain ADM or ADMX files inside the GPO. For more information, see Chapter 2, "Deploying Group Policy" in *Group Policy Administrator's Pocket Consultant* (Microsoft Press, 2009).

When running in Windows Server 2008 or higher domain functional level, servers running Windows Server 2008 or later implement a new replication mechanism for Group Policy called Distributed File System (DFS) Replication Service. With DFS replication, only the changes in GPOs are replicated, thereby eliminating the need to replicate an entire GPO after a change.

Unlike Windows XP and Windows Server 2003, Windows Vista and later releases use the Group Policy client service to isolate Group Policy notification and processing from the Windows logon process. Separating Group Policy from the Windows logon process reduces the resources used for background processing of policy while increasing overall performance and allowing delivery and application of new Group Policy files as part of the update process without requiring a restart.

Computers running Windows Vista or later don't use the trace logging functionality in Userenv.dll and instead write Group Policy event messages to the System log. Further, the Group Policy operational log replaces previous Userenv logging. When you are troubleshooting Group Policy issues, you use the detailed event messages in the operational log rather than the Userenv log. In Event Viewer, you can access the operational log under Applications And Services Logs\Microsoft\Windows\ GroupPolicy.

Computers running Windows Vista or later use Network Location Awareness instead of ICMP protocol (ping). With Network Location Awareness, a computer is aware of the type of network it is connected to and can be responsive to changes in the system status or network configuration. By using Network Location Awareness, the Group Policy client can determine the computer state, the network state, and the available network bandwidth for slow-link detection.

Managing Local Group Policies

Computers running Windows Vista or later allow the use of multiple local Group Policy objects on a single computer (as long as the computer is not a domain controller). Previously, computers had only one local GPO. Windows allows you to assign a different local GPO to each local user or general user type. This allows the application of policy to be more flexible and supports a wider array of implementation scenarios.

Local Group Policy Objects

When computers are being used in a stand-alone configuration rather than a domain configuration, you might find that multiple local GPOs are useful because you no longer have to explicitly disable or remove settings that interfere with your ability to manage a computer before performing administrator tasks. Instead, you can implement one local GPO for administrators and another local GPO for nonadministrators. In a domain configuration, however, you might not want to use multiple local GPOs. In domains, most computers and users already have multiple GPOs applied to them—adding multiple local GPOs to this already varied mix can make managing Group Policy confusing.

Computers running Windows Vista or later have three layers of local Group Policy objects:

- **Local Group Policy**   Local Group Policy is the only local Group Policy object that allows both computer configuration and user configuration settings to be applied to all users of the computer.

- **Administrators and Non-Administrators local Group Policy**   Administrators and Non-Administrators local Group Policy contains only user configuration settings. This policy is applied based on whether the user account being used is a member of the local Administrators group

- **User-specific local Group Policy**   User-specific local Group Policy contains only user configuration settings. This policy is applied to individual users and groups.

These layers of local Group Policy objects are processed in the following order: Local Group Policy, Administrators and Non-Administrators local Group Policy, user-specific local Group Policy.

Because the available user configuration settings are the same for all local GPOs, a setting in one GPO might conflict with a setting in another GPO. Windows resolves conflicts in settings by overwriting any previous setting with the last read and most-current setting. The final setting is the one that Windows uses. When Windows resolves conflicts, only the enabled or disabled state of settings matter. A setting set as Not Configured has no effect on the state of the setting from a previous policy application. To simplify domain administration, you can disable processing of local Group Policy objects on computers running Windows Vista or later releases by enabling the Turn Off Local Group Policy Objects Processing policy setting in a domain GPO. In Group Policy, this setting is located under Computer Configuration\ Administrative Templates\System\Group Policy.

Accessing the Top-Level Local Policy Settings

With the exception of domain controllers, all computers running Windows 2000 and later releases of Windows have an editable local Group Policy object. The quickest way to access the local GPO on a computer is to type the following command at a command prompt:

```
gpedit.msc /gpcomputer: "%ComputerName%"
```

This command starts the GPOE in a Microsoft Management Console (MMC) with its target set to the local computer. Here, *%ComputerName%* is an environment variable that sets the name of the local computer; it must be enclosed in double quotation marks as shown. To access the top-level local GPO on a remote computer, type the following command at a command prompt:

```
gpedit.msc /gpcomputer: "RemoteComputer"
```

where *RemoteComputer* is the host name or fully qualified domain name (FQDN) of the remote computer. Again, the double quotation marks are required, as shown in the following example:

```
gpedit.msc /gpcomputer: "corpsvr82"
```

You can also manage the top-level local GPO on a computer by following these steps:

1. Click Start, type **mmc** into the Search box, and then press Enter.

2. In the Microsoft Management Console, click File, and then click Add/Remove Snap-In.

3. In the Add Or Remove Snap-Ins dialog box, click Group Policy Object Editor, and then click Add.

4. In the Select Group Policy Object dialog box, click Finish because the local computer is the default object. Click OK.

As shown in Figure 5-1, you can now manage local policy settings using the options provided.

TIP   You can use the same MMC snap-in to manage more than one local Group Policy object. In the Add Or Remove Snap-Ins dialog box, you simply add one instance of the Local Group Policy Object Editor for each object you want to work with.

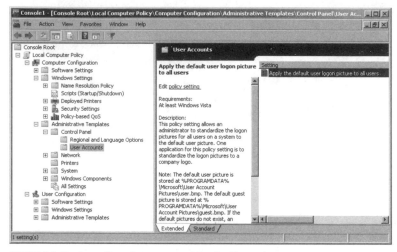

FIGURE 5-1 Use the policy editor to manage local policy settings.

Local Group Policy Object Settings

Local group policies are stored in the %SystemRoot%\System32\GroupPolicy folder on each Windows Server 2008 R2 computer. In this folder you'll find the following subfolders:

- **Machine** Stores computer scripts in the Script folder and registry-based policy information for HKEY_LOCAL_MACHINE (HKLM) in the Registry.pol file.

- **User** Stores user scripts in the Script folder and registry-based policy information for HKEY_CURRENT_USER (HKCU) in the Registry.pol file.

CAUTION You shouldn't edit these folders and files directly. Instead, you should use the appropriate features of one of the Group Policy management tools. By default, these files and folders are hidden. If you want to view hidden files and folders in Windows Explorer, choose Folder Options from the Tools menu, click the View tab, select Show Hidden Files And Folders, clear Hide Protected Operating System Files (Recommended), click Yes in the warning dialog box, and then click OK.

Accessing Administrator, Non-Administrator, and User-Specific Local Group Policy

By default, the only local policy object that exists on a computer is the Local Group Policy object. You can create and manage other local objects as necessary. You can create or access the Administrator local Group Policy object, the Non-Administrator local Group Policy object, or a user-specific local Group Policy object by following these steps:

1. Click Start, type **mmc** into the Search box, and then press Enter. In the Microsoft Management Console, click File, and then click Add/Remove Snap-In.

2. In the Add Or Remove Snap-Ins dialog box, click Group Policy Object Editor, and then click Add.

3. In the Select Group Policy Object dialog box, click Browse. In the Browse For A Group Policy Object dialog box, click the Users tab.

4. On the Users tab, the entries in the Group Policy Object Exists column specify whether a particular local policy object has been created. Do one of the following:

   - Select Administrators to create or access the Administrator local Group Policy object.

   - Select Non-Administrators to create or access the Non-Administrator local Group Policy object.

   - Select the local user whose user-specific local Group Policy object you want to create or access.

5. Click OK. If the selected object doesn't exist, it will be created. Otherwise, the existing object opens for review and editing.

Policy settings for administrators, nonadministrators, and users are stored in the %SystemRoot%\System32\GroupPolicyUsers folder on each Windows Server 2008 R2 computer. Because these local GPOs apply only to user configuration settings, user-specific policy settings under %SystemRoot%\System32\GroupPolicyUsers have only a User subfolder, and this subfolder stores user scripts in the Script folder and registry-based policy information for HKEY_CURRENT_USER in the Registry.pol file.

Managing Site, Domain, and Organizational Unit Policies

When you deploy Active Directory Domain Services (AD DS), you can use Active Directory–based Group Policy. Each site, domain, and organizational unit can have one or more group policies. Group policies listed higher in the Group Policy list have higher precedence than policies listed lower in the list. This ensures that policies are applied appropriately throughout the related sites, domains, and organizational units.

Understanding Domain and Default Policies

When you work with Active Directory–based Group Policy, you'll find that each domain in your organization has two default GPOs:

- **Default Domain Controllers Policy GPO**   A default GPO created for and linked to the Domain Controllers organizational unit. This GPO is applicable to all domain controllers in a domain (as long as they aren't moved from this organizational unit). Use it to manage security settings for domain controllers in a domain.

- **Default Domain Policy GPO**   A default GPO created for and linked to the domain itself within Active Directory. Use this GPO to establish baselines for a wide variety of policy settings that apply to all users and computers in a domain.

Typically, the Default Domain Policy GPO is the highest-precedence GPO linked to the domain level, and the Default Domain Controllers Policy GPO is the highest-precedence GPO linked to the Domain Controllers container. You can link additional GPOs to the domain level and to the Domain Controllers container. When you do this, the settings in the highest-precedence GPO override settings in lower-precedence GPOs. These GPOs aren't meant for general management of Group Policy.

The Default Domain Policy GPO is used only to manage the default Account Policies settings and, in particular, three specific areas of Account Policies: password policy, account lockout policy, and Kerberos policy. Several security options are managed through this GPO as well. These include Accounts: Rename Administrator Account, Accounts: Administrator Account Status, Accounts: Guest Account Status, Accounts: Rename Guest Account, Network Security: Force Logoff When Logon Hours Expire, Network Security: Do Not Store LAN Manager Hash Value On Next Password Change, and Network Access: Allow Anonymous SID/Name Translation. One way to override these settings is to create a GPO with the overriding settings and link it with a higher precedence to the domain container.

The Default Domain Controllers Policy GPO includes specific User Rights Assignment and Security Options settings that limit the ways domain controllers can be used. One way to override these settings is to create a GPO with the overriding settings and link it with a higher precedence to the Domain Controllers container.

To manage other areas of policy, you should create a GPO and link it to the domain or to an appropriate organizational unit within the domain.

Site, domain, and organizational unit group policies are stored in the %SystemRoot%\Sysvol\Domain\Policies folder on domain controllers. In this folder you'll find one subfolder for each policy you've defined on the domain controller. The policy folder name is the policy's globally unique identifier (GUID). You can find the policy's

GUID on the policy's Properties page on the General tab in the Summary frame. Within these individual policy folders, you'll find the following subfolders:

- **Machine** Stores computer scripts in the Script folder and registry-based policy information for HKEY_LOCAL_MACHINE (HKLM) in the Registry.pol file.

- **User** Stores user scripts in the Script folder and registry-based policy information for HKEY_CURRENT_USER (HKCU) in the Registry.pol file.

CAUTION Do not edit these folders and files directly. Instead, use the appropriate features of one of the Group Policy management tools.

Using the Group Policy Management Console

You can run the GPMC from the Administrative Tools menu. Click Start, All Programs, Administrative Tools, and then click Group Policy Management. As shown in Figure 5-2, the console root node is labeled Group Policy Management and below this node is the Forest node. The Forest node represents the forest to which you are currently connected and is named after the forest root domain for that forest. If you have appropriate credentials, you can add connections to other forests. To do this, right-click the Group Policy Management node, and then click Add Forest. In the Add Forest dialog box, type the name of the forest root domain in the Domain text box, and then click OK.

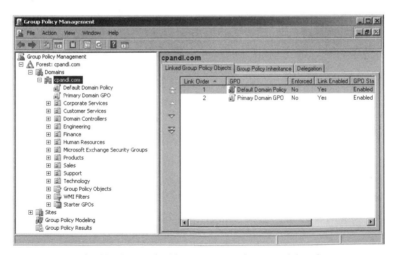

FIGURE 5-2 Use the GPMC to work with GPOs in sites, forests, and domains.

When you expand the Forest node, you see the following nodes:

- **Domains** Provides access to the policy settings for domains in the related forest. You are connected to your logon domain by default. If you have appropriate credentials, you can add connections to other domains in the related forest. To do this, right-click the Domains node, and then click Show

Domains. In the Show Domains dialog box, select the check boxes for the domains you want to add, and then click OK.

- **Sites** Provides access to the policy settings for sites in the related forest. Sites are hidden by default. If you have appropriate credentials, you can add connections for sites. To do this, right-click the Sites node, and then click Show Sites. In the Show Sites dialog box, select the check boxes for the sites you want to add, and then click OK.

- **Group Policy Modeling** Provides access to the Group Policy Modeling Wizard, which helps you plan policy deployment and simulate settings for testing purposes. Any saved policy models are also available.

- **Group Policy Results** Provides access to the Group Policy Results Wizard. For each domain you are connected to, all related GPOs and OUs are available to work with in one location.

GPOs listed under the domain, site, and OU containers in the GPMC are GPO links and not the GPOs themselves. You can access the actual GPOs through the Group Policy Objects container of the selected domain. Note that the icons for GPO links have small arrows at the bottom left, similar to shortcut icons, while GPOs themselves do not.

When you start the GPMC, the console connects to Active Directory running on the domain controller that is acting as the PDC emulator for your logon domain and obtains a list of all GPOs and OUs in that domain. It does this by using LDAP to access the directory store and the Server Message Block (SMB) protocol to access the SYSVOL directory. If the PDC emulator isn't available for some reason, such as when the server is offline, the GPMC displays a prompt so that you can choose to work with policy settings on the domain controller you are currently connected to or on any available domain controller. To change the domain controller you are connected to, right-click the domain node for which you want to set the domain controller focus, and then click Change Domain Controller. In the Change Controller dialog box, the domain controller you are currently connected to is listed under Current Domain Controller. Using the Change To options, specify the domain controller to use, and then click OK.

Getting to Know the Policy Editor

With the GPMC, you can edit a GPO by right-clicking it and then selecting Edit on the shortcut menu. As Figure 5-3 shows, the policy editor has two main nodes:

- **Computer Configuration** Allows you to set policies that should be applied to computers, regardless of who logs on.

- **User Configuration** Allows you to set policies that should be applied to users, regardless of which computer they log on to.

The exact configuration of Computer Configuration and User Configuration depends on the add-ons installed and which type of policy you're creating. Still, you'll usually find that both Computer Configuration and User Configuration have subnodes for the following:

- **Software Settings** Sets policies for software settings and software instal- lation. When you install software, subnodes might be added to Software Settings.

- **Windows Settings** Sets policies for folder redirection, scripts, and security.

- **Administrative Templates** Sets policies for the operating system, Windows components, and programs. Administrative templates are config- ured through template files. You can add or remove template files whenever you need to.

NOTE A complete discussion of all the available options is beyond the scope of this book. The sections that follow focus on using folder redirection and administrative templates. Scripts are discussed in "User and Computer Script Management" later in this chapter. Security is covered in chapters later in this book.

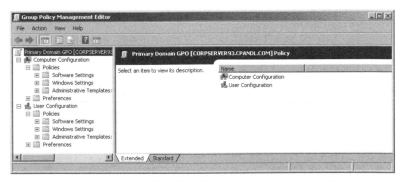

FIGURE 5-3 The configuration of the policy editor depends on the type of policy you're creating and the add-ons installed.

Using Administrative Templates to Set Policies

Administrative templates provide easy access to registry-based policy settings that you might want to configure. A default set of administrative templates is configured for users and computers in the policy editor. You can add or remove administrative templates as well. Any changes you make to policies available through adminis- trative templates are saved in the registry. Computer configurations are saved in HKEY_LOCAL_MACHINE, and user configurations are saved in HKEY_CURRENT_USER.

You can view the currently configured templates in the Administrative Templates node of the policy editor. This node contains policies that you can configure for local systems, organizational units, domains, and sites. Different sets of templates are found under Computer Configuration and User Configuration. You can add tem- plates containing new policies in the policy editor when you install new Windows components.

You can use administrative templates to manage the following:

- **Control Panel**   Determine the available options and configuration of Control Panel and Control Panel utilities.

- **Desktop**   Configure the Windows desktop and the available options from the desktop.

- **Network**   Configure networking and network client options for offline files, DNS clients, and network connections.

- **Printers**   Configure printer settings, browsing, spooling, and directory options.

- **Shared folders**   Allow publishing of shared folders and Distributed File System (DFS) roots.

- **Start menu and taskbar**   Control the available options and configuration of the Start menu and the taskbar.

- **System**   Configure system settings for disk quotas, user profiles, user logon, system restore, error reporting, and so on.

- **Windows components**   Determine the available options and configuration of various Windows components, including Event Viewer, Internet Explorer, Task Scheduler, Windows Installer, and Windows Updates.

The best way to get to know which administrative template policies are available is to browse the Administrative Templates nodes. As you browse the templates, you'll find that policies are in one of three states:

- **Not Configured**   The policy isn't used and no settings for it are saved in the registry.

- **Enabled**   The policy is actively being enforced and its settings are saved in the registry.

- **Disabled**   The policy is turned off and isn't enforced unless overridden. This setting is saved in the registry.

You can enable, disable, and configure policies by following these steps:

1. In the policy editor, open the Administrative Templates folder in the Computer Configuration or User Configuration node, whichever is appropriate for the type of policy you want to set.

2. In the left pane, select the subfolder containing the policies you want to work with. The related policies are then displayed in the right pane.

3. Double-click a policy to display its related Properties dialog box.

   You can read a description of the policy in the Help pane. The description is available only if one is defined in the related template file.

4. To set the policy's state, select the following options:

   - **Not Configured**   The policy isn't configured.
   - **Enabled**   The policy is enabled.
   - **Disabled**   The policy is disabled.

5. If you enable the policy, set any additional parameters, and then click OK.

NOTE Normally, computer policies have precedence in Windows Server 2008 R2. If there's a conflict between a computer policy setting and a user policy setting, the computer policy is enforced.

Creating and Linking GPOs

When you work with a policy object, creating an object and linking an object to a specific container within Active Directory are two different actions. You can create a GPO without linking it to any domain, site, or OU. Then, as appropriate, you can link the GPO to a specific domain, site, or OU. You can also create a GPO and link it automatically to a domain, site, or OU. The technique that you choose primarily depends on your personal preference and how you plan to work with the GPO. Keep in mind that when you create and link a GPO to a site, domain, or OU, the GPO is applied to the user and computer objects in that site, domain, or OU according to the Active Directory options governing inheritance, the precedence order of GPOs, and other settings.

You can create and then link a GPO to a site, domain, or OU by following these steps:

1. In the GPMC, expand the entry for the forest you want to work with, and then expand the related Domains node by double-clicking each node in turn.

2. Right-click Group Policy Objects, and then click New. In the New GPO dialog box, type a descriptive name for the GPO, such as **Secure Workstation GPO**. If you want to use a starter GPO as the source for the initial settings, select the starter GPO to use in the Source Starter GPO list. When you click OK, the new GPO is added to the Group Policy Objects container.

3. Right-click the new GPO, and then click Edit. In the policy editor, configure the necessary policy settings, and then close the policy editor.

4. In the GPMC, select the site, domain, or OU. Expand the Sites node you want to work with. In the right pane, the Linked Group Policy Objects tab shows the GPOs that are currently linked to the selected container (if any).

5. Right-click the site, domain, or OU to which you want to link the GPO, and then click Link An Existing GPO. In the Select GPO dialog box, select the GPO you want to link with, and then click OK. When Group Policy is refreshed for computers and users in the applicable site, domain, or OU, the policy settings in the GPO are applied.

You can create and link a GPO as a single operation by following these steps:

1. In the GPMC, right-click the site, domain, or OU for which you want to create and link the GPO, and then click Create A GPO In This Domain, And Link It Here.

2. In the New GPO dialog box, type a descriptive name for the GPO, such as **Secure Workstation GPO**. If you want to use a starter GPO as the source for the initial settings, select the starter GPO to use in the Source Starter GPO list. When you click OK, the new GPO is added to the Group Policy Objects container and linked to the previously selected site, domain, or OU.

3. Right-click the new GPO, and then click Edit. In the policy editor, configure the necessary policy settings, and then close the policy editor. When Group Policy is refreshed for computers and users in the applicable site, domain, or OU, the policy settings in the GPO are applied.

Creating and Using Starter GPOs

When you create a GPO in the GPMC, you can base the GPO on a starter GPO. The settings for the starter GPO are then imported into the new GPO, which allows you to use a starter GPO to define the base configuration settings for a new GPO. In a large organization, you should create different categories of starter GPOs based on the users and computers they will be used with or on the required security configuration.

You can create a starter GPO by following these steps:

1. In the GPMC, expand the entry for the forest you want to work with, and then double-click the related Domains node to expand it.

2. Right-click Starter GPOs, and then click New. In the New Starter GPO dialog box, type a descriptive name for the GPO, such as **General Management User GPO**. You can also enter comments describing the GPO's purpose. Click OK.

3. Right-click the new GPO, and then click Edit. In the policy editor, configure the necessary policy settings, and then close the policy editor.

Delegating Privileges for Group Policy Management

In Active Directory, all administrators have some level of privileges for performing Group Policy management tasks. Through delegation, other individuals can be granted permissions to perform any or all of the following tasks:

- Create GPOs and manage the GPOs they create
- View settings, modify settings, delete a GPO, and modify security
- Manage links to existing GPOs or generate Resultant Set of Policy (RSoP)

In Active Directory, administrators can create GPOs, and anyone who has created a GPO has the right to manage that GPO. In the GPMC, you can determine who can create GPOs in a domain by selecting the Group Policy Objects node for that domain and then clicking the Delegation tab. On the Delegation tab, you'll see a list of groups and users that can create GPOs in the domain. To grant GPO creation permission to a user or group, click Add. In the Select User, Computer, Or Group dialog box, select the user or group, and then click OK.

In the GPMC, you have several ways to determine who has access permissions for Group Policy management. For domain, site, and OU permissions, select the domain, site, or OU you want to work with, and then click the Delegation tab in the right pane, as shown in Figure 5-4. In the Permission list, select the permission you want to check. The options are as follows:

- **Link GPOs**   Lists users and groups that can create and manage links to GPOs in the selected site, domain, or OU.

- **Perform Group Policy Modeling Analyses**   Lists users and groups that can determine RSoP for the purposes of planning.

- **Read Group Policy Results Data**   Lists users and groups that can determine RSoP that is currently being applied, for the purposes of verification or logging.

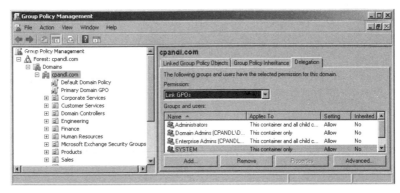

FIGURE 5-4   Review permissions for Group Policy management.

To grant domain, site, or OU permissions, complete the following steps:

1. In the GPMC, select the domain, site, or OU you want to work with, and then click the Delegation tab in the right pane.

2. In the Permission list, select the permission you want to grant. The options are Link GPOs, Perform Group Policy Modeling Analyses, and Read Group Policy Results Data.

3. Click Add. In the Select User, Computer, Or Group dialog box, select the user or group, and then click OK.

4. In the Add Group Or User dialog box, specify how the permission should be applied. To apply the permission to the current container and all child containers, select This Container And All Child Containers. To apply the permission only to the current container, select This Container Only. Click OK.

For individual GPO permissions, select the GPO you want to work with in the GPMC, and then click the Delegation tab in the right pane. You then see one or more of the following permissions for individual users and groups:

- **Read**   Indicates that the user or group can view the GPO and its settings.

- **Edit Settings**   Indicates that the user or group can view the GPO and change its settings. The user or group cannot delete the GPO or modify security.

- **Edit Settings, Delete, Modify Security**   Indicates that the user or group can view the GPO and change its settings. The user or group can also delete the GPO and modify security.

To grant permissions for working with the GPO, complete the following steps:

1. In the GPMC, select the domain, site, or OU you want to work with, and then click the Delegation tab in the right pane. Click Add.

2. To grant GPO creation permission to a user or group, click Add. In the Select User, Computer, Or Group dialog box, select the user or group, and then click OK.

3. In the Add Group Or User dialog box, select the permission level, and then click OK.

Blocking, Overriding, and Disabling Policies

Inheritance ensures that every computer and user object in a domain, site, or OU is affected by Group Policy. Most policies have three configuration options: Not Configured, Enabled, or Disabled. Not Configured is the default state for most policy settings. If a policy is enabled, the policy is enforced and is applied directly or through inheritance to all users and computers that are subject to the policy. If a policy is disabled, the policy is not enforced or applied.

You can change the way inheritance works in four key ways:

- Change link order and precedence
- Override inheritance (as long as there is no enforcement)
- Block inheritance (to prevent inheritance completely)
- Enforce inheritance (to supersede and prevent overriding or blocking)

For Group Policy, the order of inheritance goes from the site level to the domain level and then to each nested OU level. Keep the following in mind:

- When multiple policy objects are linked to a particular level, the link order determines the order in which policy settings are applied. Linked policy objects are always applied in link-ranking order. Lower-ranking policy objects are processed first, and then higher-ranking policy objects are processed. The policy object processed last has priority, so any policy settings config-ured in this policy object are final and override those of other policy objects (unless you use inheritance blocking or enforcing).

- When multiple policy objects can be inherited from a higher level, the precedence order shows exactly how policy objects are being processed. As with link order, lower-ranking policy objects are processed before higher-ranking policy objects. The policy object processed last has precedence, so any policy settings configured in this policy object are final and override those of other policy objects (unless you use inheritance blocking or enforcing).

When multiple policy objects are linked at a specific level, you can change the link order (and thus the precedence order) of policy objects by following these steps:

1. In the GPMC, select the container for the site, domain, or OU with which you want to work.

2. In the right pane, the Linked Group Policy Objects tab (shown in Figure 5-5) should be selected by default. Click the policy object you want to work with.

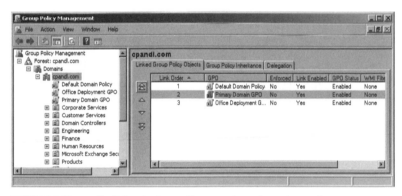

FIGURE 5-5 Change the link order to modify processing order and precedence.

3. Click the Move Link Up or Move Link Down buttons as appropriate to change the link order of the selected policy object.

4. When you are done changing the link order, confirm that policy objects are being processed in the expected order by checking the precedence order on the Group Policy Inheritance tab.

Overriding inheritance is a basic technique for changing the way inheritance works. When a policy is enabled in a higher-level policy object, you can override inheritance by disabling the policy in a lower-level policy object. When a policy is disabled in a higher-level policy object, you can override inheritance by enabling the policy in a lower-level policy object. As long as a policy is not blocked or enforced, this technique achieves the effects you want.

Sometimes you will want to block inheritance so that no policy settings from higher-level containers are applied to users and computers in a particular container. When inheritance is blocked, only configured policy settings from policy objects linked at that level are applied, and settings from all high-level containers are blocked (as long as there is no policy enforcement).

Domain administrators can use inheritance blocking to block inherited policy settings from the site level. OU administrators can use inheritance blocking to block inherited policy settings from both the domain and the site level. By using blocking to ensure the autonomy of a domain or OU, you can ensure that domain or OU administrators have full control over the policies that apply to users and computers under their administration.

Using the GPMC, you can block inheritance by right-clicking the domain or OU that should not inherit settings from higher-level containers and selecting Block Inheritance. If Block Inheritance is already selected, selecting it again removes the setting. When you block inheritance in the GPMC, a blue circle with an exclamation point is added to the container's node in the console tree. This notification icon provides a quick way to tell whether any domain or OU has the Block Inheritance setting enabled.

To prevent administrators who have authority over a container from overriding or blocking inherited Group Policy settings, you can enforce inheritance. When inheritance is enforced, all configured policy settings from higher-level policy objects are inherited and applied regardless of the policy settings configured in lower-level policy objects. Thus, enforcement of inheritance is used to supersede overriding and blocking of policy settings.

Forest administrators can use inheritance enforcement to ensure that configured policy settings from the site level are applied and to prevent overriding or blocking of policy settings by domain and OU administrators. Domain administrators can use inheritance enforcement to ensure that configured policy settings from the domain level are applied and to prevent overriding or blocking of policy settings by OU administrators.

Using the GPMC, you can enforce policy inheritance by expanding the top-level container from which to begin enforcement, right-clicking the link to the GPO, and then clicking Enforced. For example, if you want to ensure that a domain-level GPO is inherited by all OUs in the domain, expand the domain container, right-click the domain-level GPO, and then click Enforced. If Enforced is already selected, selecting it again removes the enforcement. In the GPMC, you can easily determine which policies are inherited and which policies are enforced. Simply select a policy object anywhere in the GPMC, and then view the related Scope tab in the right pane. If the policy is enforced, the Enforced column under Links will display Yes, as shown in Figure 5-6.

After you select a policy object, you can right-click a location entry on the Scope tab to display a shortcut menu that allows you to manage linking and policy enforcement. Enable or disable links by selecting or clearing the Link Enabled option. Enable or disable enforcement by selecting or clearing the Enforced option.

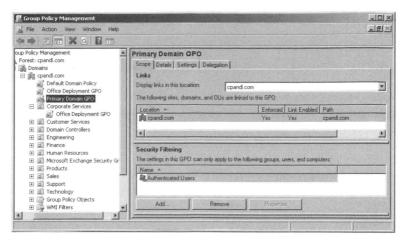

FIGURE 5-6 Enforce policy inheritance to ensure that settings are applied.

Maintaining and Troubleshooting Group Policy

Group Policy is a broad area of administration that requires careful management. Like any area of administration, Group Policy must also be carefully maintained to ensure proper operation, and you must diagnose and resolve any problems that occur. To troubleshoot Group Policy, you need a strong understanding of how policy is refreshed and processed. You also need a strong understanding of general maintenance and troubleshooting tasks.

Refreshing Group Policy

When you make changes to a policy, those changes are immediate. However, they aren't propagated automatically. Client computers request policies at the following times:

- When the computer starts
- When a user logs on
- When an application or user requests a refresh
- When a refresh interval is set for Group Policy and the interval has elapsed

Computer configuration settings are applied during startup of the operating system. User configuration settings are applied when a user logs on to a computer. Normally, if there is a conflict between computer and user settings, computer settings have priority and take precedence.

Once policy settings are applied, the settings are refreshed automatically to ensure that they are current. The default refresh interval for domain controllers is 5 minutes. For all other computers, the default refresh interval is 90 minutes, with up to a 30-minute variation to avoid overloading the domain controller with numerous concurrent client requests. This means that an effective refresh window for non-domain-controller computers is 90 to 120 minutes.

During a Group Policy refresh, the client computer contacts an available domain controller in its local site. If one or more of the policy objects defined in the domain have changed, the domain controller provides a list of the policy objects that apply to the computer and to the user who is currently logged on, as appropriate. The domain controller does this regardless of whether the version numbers on all the listed policy objects have changed. By default, the computer processes the policy objects only if the version number of at least one of the policy objects has changed. If any one of the related policies has changed, all the policies have to be processed again because of inheritance and the interdependencies between policies.

Security settings are a notable exception to the processing rule. By default, these settings are refreshed every 16 hours (960 minutes) regardless of whether policy objects contain changes. A random offset of up to 30 minutes is added to reduce impact on domain controllers and the network during updates (making the effective refresh window 960 to 990 minutes). Also, if the client computer detects that it is connecting over a slow network connection, it informs the domain controller, and only the security settings and administrative templates are transferred over the network. This means that by default, only the security settings and administrative templates are applied when a computer is connected over a slow link. You can configure the way slow-link detection works in Group Policy.

You must carefully balance update frequency with the actual rate of policy change. If policy is changed infrequently, you might want to increase the refresh window to reduce resource usage. For example, you might want to use a refresh interval of 20 minutes on domain controllers and 180 minutes on other computers.

Configuring the Refresh Interval

You can change the Group Policy refresh interval on a per–policy object basis. To set the refresh interval for domain controllers, follow these steps:

1. In the GPMC, right-click the Group Policy object you want to modify, and then click Edit. This GPO should be linked to a container that contains domain controller computer objects.

2. In the Computer Configuration\Administrative Templates\System\Group Policy folder, double-click the Group Policy Refresh Interval For Domain Controllers policy. This displays a properties dialog box for the policy, shown in Figure 5-7.

3. Define the policy by selecting Enabled. Set the base refresh interval in the first Minutes box. You usually want this value to be between 5 and 59 minutes.

4. In the other Minutes box, set the minimum or maximum time variation for the refresh interval. The variation effectively creates a refresh window with the goal of avoiding overload resulting from numerous clients simultaneously requesting a Group Policy refresh. Click OK.

NOTE A faster refresh rate increases the likelihood that a computer has the most current policy configuration. A slower refresh rate reduces the frequency of policy refreshes, which can reduce overhead with regard to resource usage but also increase the likelihood that a computer won't have the most current policy configuration.

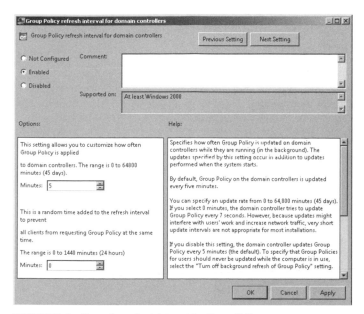

FIGURE 5-7 Configure the refresh interval for Group Policy.

To set the refresh interval for member servers and workstations, follow these steps:

1. In the GPMC, right-click the Group Policy object you want to modify, and then click Edit. This GPO should be linked to a container that contains computer objects.

2. In the Computer Configuration\Administrative Templates\System\Group Policy folder, double-click the Group Policy Refresh Interval For Computers policy. This displays a dialog box similar to the one in Figure 5-7.

3. Define the policy by selecting Enabled. In the first Minutes box, set the base refresh interval. You usually want this value to be between 60 and 240 minutes.

4. In the other Minutes box, set the minimum or maximum time variation for the refresh interval. The variation effectively creates a refresh window with the goal of avoiding overload resulting from numerous clients simultaneously requesting a Group Policy refresh. Click OK.

REAL WORLD You want to be sure that updates don't occur too frequently yet are timely enough to meet expectations or requirements. The more often a policy is refreshed, the more traffic is generated over the network. In a large installation, you typically want to set a refresh rate that is longer than the default to reduce network traffic, particularly if the policy affects hundreds of users or computers. In any installation where users complain about their computers periodically being sluggish, you might want to increase the policy refresh interval as well. Consider that a once-a-day or once-a-week update might be all that it takes to keep policies current enough to meet your organization's needs.

As an administrator, you might often need or want to refresh Group Policy manually. For example, you might not want to wait for Group Policy to be refreshed at the automatic interval, or you might be trying to resolve a problem with refreshes and want to force a Group Policy refresh. You can refresh Group Policy manually by using the Gpupdate command-line utility.

You can initiate a refresh in several ways. Typing **gpupdate** at a command prompt refreshes settings in both Computer Configuration and User Configuration on the local computer. Only policy settings that have changed are processed and applied when you run Gpupdate. You can change this behavior using the /Force parameter to force a refresh of all policy settings.

You can refresh user and computer configuration settings separately. To refresh only computer configuration settings, type **gpupdate /target:computer** at the command prompt. To refresh only user configuration settings, type **gpupdate /target:user** at the command prompt.

You can also use Gpupdate to log off a user or restart a computer after Group Policy is refreshed. This is useful because some group policies are applied only when a user logs on or when a computer starts. To log off a user after a refresh, add the /Logoff parameter. To restart a computer after a refresh, add the /Boot parameter.

Modeling Group Policy for Planning Purposes

Modeling Group Policy for planning is useful when you want to test various implementation and configuration scenarios. For example, you might want to model the effect of loopback processing or slow-link detection. You can also model the effect of moving users or computers to another container in Active Directory or the effect of changing security group membership for users and computers.

All domain and enterprise administrators have permission to model Group Policy for planning, as do those who have been delegated the Perform Group Policy Modeling Analyses permission. To model Group Policy and test various implementation and update scenarios, follow these steps:

1. In the GPMC, right-click the Group Policy Modeling node, select Group Policy Modeling Wizard, and then click Next.

2. On the Domain Controller Selection page, select the domain you want to model in the Show Domain Controllers In This Domain list. By default,

you will simulate policy on any available domain controller in the selected domain. If you want to use a specific domain controller, select This Domain Controller, and then click the domain controller to use. Click Next.

3. On the User And Computer Selection page, shown in Figure 5-8, you have the option of simulating policy based on containers or individual accounts. Use one of the following techniques to choose accounts, and then click Next:

   ■ Use containers to simulate changes for entire organizational units or other containers. Under User Information, select Container, and then click Browse to display the Choose User Container dialog box. Use the dialog box to choose any of the available user containers in the selected domain. Under Computer Information, select Container, click Browse to display the Choose Computer Container dialog box, and then choose any of the available computer containers in the selected domain.

   ■ Select specific accounts to simulate changes for a specific user and computer. Under User Information, select User, click Browse to display the Select User dialog box, and then specify a user account. Under Computer Information, select Computer, click Browse to display the Select Computer dialog box, and then specify a computer account.

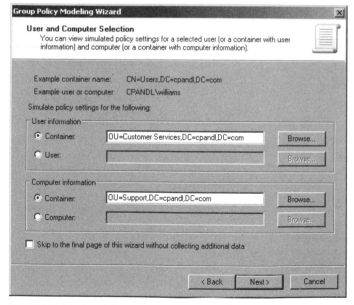

FIGURE 5-8 Select containers or accounts to use in the simulation.

4. On the Advanced Simulation Options page, select any advanced options for Slow Network Connections, Loopback Processing, and Site as necessary, and then click Next.

5. On the User Security Groups page, you can simulate changes to the applicable user or users security group membership. Any changes you make to group membership affect the previously selected user or user container. For example, if you want to see what happens if a user in the designated user container is a member of the CorpManagers group, add this group to the Security Groups list. Click Next.

6. On the Computer Security Groups page, you can simulate changes to the applicable security group membership for a computer or computers. Any changes you make to group membership affect the previously selected computer or computer container. For example, if you want to see what happens if a computer in the designated computer container is a member of the RemoteComputers group, add this group to the Security Groups list. Click Next.

7. You can link WMI filters to Group Policy objects. By default, the selected users and computers are assumed to meet all the WMI filter requirements, which is want you want in most cases for planning purposes. Click Next twice to accept the default options.

8. Review the selections you've made, and then click Next. After the wizard gathers policy information, click Finish. When the wizard finishes generating the report, the report is selected in the left pane, and the results are displayed in the right pane. (See Figure 5-9.)

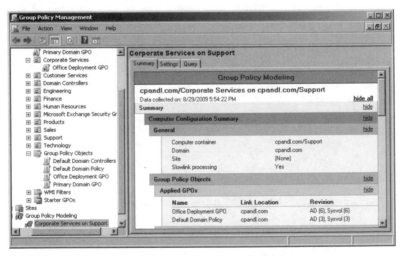

FIGURE 5-9 Review the report to determine the effects of modeling.

9. You can determine the settings that would be applied by browsing the report. Computer policy information is listed under Computer Configuration Summary. User policy information is listed under User Configuration Summary.

Copying, Pasting, and Importing Policy Objects

The GPMC features built-in copy, paste, and import operations. Using the copy and paste features is fairly straightforward. The Copy and Paste options are available when you right-click a GPO in the GPMC. You can copy a policy object and all its settings in one domain and then navigate to the domain into which you want to paste the copy of the policy object. The source and target domains can be any domains that you can connect to in the GPMC and for which you have permission to manage related policy objects. In the source domain, you need Read permission to create a copy of a policy object. In the target domain, you need Write permission to write (paste) the copied policy object. Administrators have this privilege, as do those who have been delegated permission to create policy objects.

Copying policy objects between domains works well when you have connectivity between domains and the appropriate permissions. If you are an administrator at a remote office or have been delegated permissions, however, you might not have access to the source domain to create a copy of a policy object. In this case, another administrator can make a backup copy of a policy object for you and then send you the related data. When you receive the related data, you can import the backup copy of the policy object into your domain to create a policy object with the same settings.

Anyone with the Edit Settings Group Policy management privilege can perform an import operation. The import operation overwrites all the settings of the policy object you select. To import a backup copy of a policy object into a domain, follow these steps:

1. In the GPMC, right-click Group Policy Objects, and then select New. In the New GPO dialog box, type a descriptive name for the new GPO, and then click OK.

2. The new GPO is now listed in the Group Policy Objects container. Right-click the new policy object, and then click Import Settings. This starts the Import Settings Wizard.

3. Click Next twice to bypass the Backup GPO page. You don't need to create a backup of the GPO at this time because it's new.

4. On the Backup Location page, click Browse. In the Browse For Folder dialog box, select the folder containing the backup copy of the policy object you want to import, and then click OK. Click Next to continue.

5. If multiple backups are stored in the designated backup folder, you'll see a list of them on the Source GPO page. Click the one you want to use, and then click Next.

6. The Import Settings Wizard scans the policy object for references to security principals and UNC paths that might need to be migrated. If any are found, you are given the opportunity to create migration tables or use existing migration tables.

7. Continue through the wizard by clicking Next, and then click Finish to begin the import process. When importing is complete, click OK.

Backing Up and Restoring Policy Objects

As part of your periodic administration tasks, you should back up GPOs to protect them. You can use the GPMC to back up individual policy objects in a domain or all policy objects in a domain by following these steps:

1. In the GPMC, expand and then select the Group Policy Objects node. If you want to back up all policy objects in the domain, right-click the Group Policy Objects node, and then click Back Up All. If you want to back up a specific policy object in the domain, right-click the policy object and select Back Up.

2. In the Back Up Group Policy Object dialog box, click Browse. In the Browse For Folder dialog box, set the location where the GPO backup should be stored.

3. In the Description field, type a description of the contents of the backup. Click Back Up to start the backup process.

4. The Backup dialog box shows the progress and status of the backup. Click OK when the backup is complete. If a backup fails, check the permissions on the policy and the folder to which you are writing the backup. You need Read permission on a policy and Write permission on the backup folder to create a backup. By default, members of the Domain Admins and Enterprise Admins groups should have these permissions.

Using the GPMC, you can restore a policy object to the state it was in when it was backed up. The GPMC tracks the backup of each policy object separately, even if you back up all policy objects at once. Because version information is also tracked according to the backup time stamp and description, you can restore the last version of each policy object or a particular version of any policy object.

You can restore a policy object by following these steps:

1. In the GPMC, right-click the Group Policy Objects node, and then click Manage Backups. This displays the Manage Backups dialog box.

2. In the Backup Location field, click Browse. In the Browse For Folder dialog box, find the backup folder, and then click OK.

3. All policy object backups in the designated folder are listed under Backup Policy Objects. To show only the latest version of the policy objects according to the time stamp, select Show Only The Latest Version Of Each GPO.

4. Select the GPO you want to restore. If you want to confirm its settings, click View Settings, and then use Internet Explorer to verify that the settings are as expected. When you are ready to continue, click Restore. Confirm that you want to restore the selected policy object by clicking OK.

5. The Restore dialog box shows the progress and status of the restore operation. If a restore operation fails, check the permissions on the policy object

and the folder from which you are reading the backup. To restore a GPO, you need Edit Settings, Delete, and Modify Security permissions on the policy object and Read permission on the folder containing the backup. By default, members of the Domain Admins and Enterprise Admins groups should have these permissions.

Determining Current Group Policy Settings and Refresh Status

You can use Group Policy modeling for logging Resultant Set of Policy (RSoP). When you use Group Policy modeling in this way, you can review all the policy objects that apply to a computer and the last time the applicable policy objects were processed (refreshed). All domain and enterprise administrators have permission to model Group Policy for logging, as do those who have been delegated the permission Read Group Policy Results Data. In the GPMC, you can model Group Policy for the purpose of logging RSoP by right-clicking the Group Policy Results node and selecting Group Policy Results Wizard. When the Group Policy Results Wizard starts, follow the prompts.

Disabling an Unused Part of Group Policy

Another way to disable a policy is to disable an unused part of the GPO. When you do this, you block computer configuration or user configuration settings, or both, and don't allow them to be applied. When you disable part of a policy that isn't used, the application of GPOs will be faster.

You can enable and disable policies partially or entirely by following these steps:

1. In the GPMC, select the container for the site, domain, or OU with which you want to work.

2. Select the policy object you want to work with, and then click the Details tab in the right pane.

3. Choose one of the following status settings from the GPO Status list, and then click OK when prompted to confirm that you want to change the status of this GPO:

    - **All Settings Disabled**   Disallows processing of the policy object and all its settings.

    - **Computer Configuration Settings Disabled**   Disables processing of computer configuration settings. This means that only user configuration settings are processed.

    - **Enabled**   Allows processing of the policy object and all its settings.

    - **User Configuration Settings Disabled**   Disables processing of user configuration settings. This means that only computer configuration settings are processed.

Changing Policy Processing Preferences

In Group Policy, computer configuration settings are processed when a computer starts and accesses the network. User configuration settings are processed when a user logs on to the network. In the event of a conflict between settings in Computer Configuration and User Configuration, the computer configuration settings win. It is also important to remember that computer settings are applied from the computer's GPOs and user settings are applied from the user's GPOs.

In some special situations you might not want this behavior. On a shared computer you might want the user settings to be applied from the computer's GPOs, but you might also want to allow user settings from the user's GPOs to be applied. In a secure lab or kiosk environment you might want the user settings to be applied from the computer's GPOs to ensure compliance with strict security rules or guidelines for the lab. By using loopback processing, you can allow for these types of exceptions and obtain user settings from a computer's GPOs.

To change the way loopback processing works, follow these steps:

1. In the GPMC, right-click the Group Policy object you want to modify, and then click Edit.

2. In the Computer Configuration\Administrative Templates\System\Group Policy folder, double-click the User Group Policy Loopback Processing Mode policy. This displays a Properties dialog box for the policy.

3. Define the policy by selecting Enabled, select one of the following processing modes from the Mode list, and then click OK:

   - **Replace** Select the Replace option to ensure that user settings from the computer's GPOs are processed and that user settings in the user's GPOs are not processed. This means that the user settings from the computer's GPOs replace the user settings normally applied to the user.

   - **Merge** Select the Merge option to ensure that the user settings in the computer's GPOs are processed first, then user settings in the user's GPOs, and then user settings in the computer's GPOs again. This processing technique serves to combine the user settings in both the computer's and the user's GPOs. In the event of a conflict, the user settings in the computer's GPOs take precedence and overwrite the user settings in the user's GPOs.

Configuring Slow-Link Detection

Slow-link detection is used by Group Policy clients to detect increased latency and reduced responsiveness on the network and to take corrective action to reduce the likelihood that processing of Group Policy will further saturate the network. Once a slow link is detected, Group Policy clients reduce their network communications and requests, thereby reducing the overall network traffic load by limiting the amount of policy processing they do.

By default, if the connection speed is determined to be less than 500 kilobits per second (which could also be interpreted as high latency/reduced responsiveness on a fast network), the client computer interprets this as a slow network connection and notifies the domain controller. As a result, only security settings and administrative templates in the applicable policy objects are sent by the domain controller during a policy refresh.

You can configure slow-link detection by using the Group Policy Slow Link Detection policy, which is stored in the Computer Configuration\Administrative Templates\System\Group Policy folder. If you disable this policy or do not configure it, clients use the default value of 500 kilobits per second to determine whether they are on a slow link. If you enable this policy, you can set a specific slow-link value, such as 384 kilobits per second. On the other hand, if you want to disable slow-link detection completely, set the Connection Speed option to 0. This setting effectively tells clients not to detect slow links and to consider all links to be fast.

You can optimize slow-link detection for various areas of Group Policy processing as necessary. By default, policy areas that are not processed when a slow link is detected include:

- Disk Quota Policy Processing
- EFS Recovery Policy Processing
- Folder Redirection Policy Processing
- Scripts Policy Processing
- Software Installation Policy Processing

Security Policy Processing is always enabled automatically for slow links. By default, security policy is refreshed every 16 hours even if security policy has not changed. The only way to stop the forced refresh is to configure security policy processing so that it is not applied during periodic background refreshes. To do this, select the policy setting Do Not Apply During Periodic Background Processing. However, because security policy is so important, the Do Not Apply setting means only that security policy processing is stopped when a user is logged on and using the computer. One of the only reasons you'll want to stop security policy refreshes is if applications are failing during refresh operations.

You can configure slow-link detection and related policy processing by following these steps:

1. In the GPMC, right-click the policy object you want to modify, and then click Edit.

2. In the Computer Configuration\Administrative Templates\System\Group Policy folder, double-click the Group Policy Slow Link Detection policy.

3. Select Enabled to define the policy, as shown in Figure 5-10. In the Connection Speed box, specify the speed that should be used to determine whether a computer is on a slow link. Click OK.

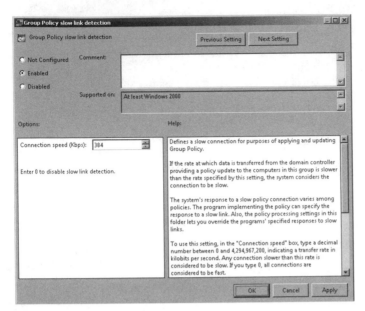

FIGURE 5-10 Configure slow-link detection.

To configure slow-link and background policy processing of key areas of Group Policy, follow these steps:

1. In the GPMC, right-click the policy object you want to modify, and then click Edit.

2. Expand Computer Configuration\Administrative Templates\System\Group Policy.

3. Double-click the processing policy you want to configure. Select Enabled to define the policy, as shown in Figure 5-11, and then make your configuration selections. The options differ slightly depending on the policy selected and might include the following:

    - **Allow Processing Across A Slow Network Connection**   Ensures that the related policy settings are processed even on a slow network.

    - **Do Not Apply During Periodic Background Processing**   Overrides refresh settings when related policies change after startup or logon.

    - **Process Even If The Group Policy Objects Have Not Changed**   Forces the client computer to process the related policy settings during a refresh even if the settings haven't changed.

4. Click OK to save your settings.

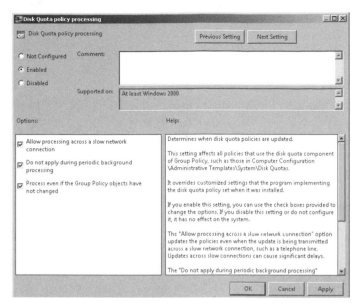

FIGURE 5-11 Configure policy processing for slow links.

Removing Links and Deleting GPOs

In the GPMC, you can stop using a linked GPO in two ways:

- Remove a link to a GPO but not the GPO itself.
- Permanently delete the GPO and all links to it.

Removing a link to a GPO stops a site, domain, or OU from using the related policy settings but does not delete the GPO. Because of this, the GPO remains linked to other sites, domains, or OUs as appropriate. In the GPMC, you can remove a link to a GPO by right-clicking the GPO link in the container that it is linked to and then selecting Delete. When prompted to confirm that you want to remove the link, click OK. If you remove all links to the GPO from sites, domains, and OUs, the GPO continues to exist in the Group Policy Objects container but its policy settings have no effect in your organization.

Permanently deleting a GPO removes the GPO and all links to it. The GPO will not exist in the Group Policy Objects container and will not be linked to any sites, domains, or OUs. The only way to recover a deleted GPO is to restore it from a backup (if one is available). In the GPMC, you can remove a GPO and all links to the object from the Group Policy Objects node. Right-click the GPO, and then select Delete. When prompted to confirm that you want to remove the GPO and all links to it, click Yes.

Troubleshooting Group Policy

When you are trying to determine why policy is not being applied as expected, one of first things you should do is examine the Resultant Set of Policy for the user and computer experiencing problems with policy settings. You can determine the GPO that a setting is applied from by following these steps:

1. In the GPMC, right-click the Group Policy Results node, and then click Group Policy Results Wizard. When the wizard starts, click Next.

2. On the Computer Selection page, select This Computer to view information for the local computer. To view information for a remote computer, select Another Computer, and then click Browse. In the Select Computer dialog box, type the name of the computer, and then click Check Names. After you select the correct computer account, click OK, and then click Next.

3. On the User Selection page, select the user whose policy information you want to view. You can view policy information for any user who has logged on to the previously selected computer. Click Next.

4. Review the selections you've made, and then click Next. After the wizard gathers policy information, click Finish. When the wizard finishes generating the report, the report is selected in the left pane and the results are displayed in the right pane.

5. To determine the settings that are being applied, browse the report. Computer and user policy information is listed separately. Computer policy information is listed under Computer Configuration Summary. User policy information is listed under User Configuration Summary.

Using the Gpresult command-line utility, you can view RsOP as well. Gpresult provides details on the following:

- Special settings applied for folder redirection, software installation, disk quota, IPSec, and scripts
- The last time Group Policy was applied
- The domain controller from which policy was applied and the security group memberships for the computer and user
- The complete list of GPOs that were applied as well as the complete list of GPOs that were not applied because of filters

Gpresult has the following basic syntax:

```
gpresult /s ComputerName /user Domain\UserName
```

where *ComputerName* is the name of the computer that you want to log policy results for and *Domain\UserName* indicates the user that you want to log policy results for. For example, to view the RSoP for CorpPC85 and the user Tedg in the Cpandl domain, you would type the following command:

```
gpresult /s corppc85 /user cpandl\tedg
```

You can view more detailed output by using one of the two verbose options. The /v parameter turns on verbose output, and results are displayed only for policy settings in effect. The /z parameter turns on verbose output with settings for policy settings in effect and all other GPOs that have the policy set. Because Gpresult output can be fairly long, you should create an HTML report using the /h parameter or an XML report using the /x parameter. The following examples use these parameters:

```
gpresult /s corppc85 /user cpand1\tedg /h gpreport.html
gpresult /s corppc85 /user cpand1\tedg /x gpreport.xml
```

Fixing Default Group Policy Objects

The Default Domain Policy and Default Domain Controller Policy GPOs are vital to the health of Active Directory Domain Services. If for some reason these policies become corrupted, Group Policy will not function properly. To resolve this, you must use the GPMC to restore a backup of these GPOs. If you are in a disaster recovery scenario and you do not have any backups of the Default Domain Policy or the Default Domain Controller Policy, you can use Dcgpofix to restore the security settings in these policies. The state that Dcgpofix restores these objects to depends on how you modified security and on the security state of the domain controller before you ran Dcgpofix. You must be a member of Domain Admins or Enterprise Admins to run Dcgpofix.

When you run Dcgpofix, both the Default Domain Policy and Default Domain Controller Policy GPOs are restored by default and you lose any base changes made to these GPOs. Some policy settings are maintained separately and are not lost, including Windows Deployment Services (WDS), Security Settings, and Encrypting File System (EFS). Nondefault Security Settings are not maintained, however, which means that other policy changes could be lost as well. All other policy settings are restored to their previous values, and any changes you've made are lost.

To run Dcgpofix, log on to a domain controller in the domain in which you want to fix default Group Policy, and then type **dcgpofix** at an elevated command prompt. Dcgpofix checks the Active Directory schema version number to ensure compatibility between the version of Dcgpofix you are using and the Active Directory schema configuration. If the versions are not compatible, Dcgpofix exits without fixing the default Group Policy objects. By specifying the /Ignoreschema parameter, you can enable Dcgpofix to work with different versions of Active Directory. However, default policy objects might not be restored to their original state. Because of this, you should always be sure to use the version of Dcgpofix that is installed with the current operating system.

You also have the option of fixing only the Default Domain Policy or only the Default Domain Controller Policy GPO. If you want to fix only the Default Domain Policy, type **dcgpofix/target: domain**. If you want to fix only the Default Domain Controller Policy, type **dcgpofix/target: dc**.

Managing Users and Computers with Group Policy

You can use Group Policy to manage users and computers in many different ways. In the sections that follow, I'll describe some specific management areas, including the following:

- Folder redirection
- Computer and user scripts
- Software deployment
- Computer and user certificate enrollment
- Automatic update settings

Centrally Managing Special Folders

You can centrally manage special folders used by Windows Server 2008 R2 through folder redirection. You do this by redirecting special folders to a central network location instead of using multiple default locations on each computer. For Windows XP Professional and earlier releases of Windows, the special folders you can centrally manage are Application Data, Start Menu, Desktop, My Documents, and My Pictures. For Windows Vista and later releases of Windows, the special folders you can manage are AppData(Roaming), Desktop, Start Menu, Documents, Pictures, Music, Videos, Favorites, Contacts, Downloads, Links, Searches, and Saved Games.

It is important to note that even though Windows Vista and Windows 7 store personal folders in slightly different ways, you manage the folders in the same way within Group Policy.

You have two general options for redirection. You can redirect a special folder to the same network location for all users, or you can designate locations based on user membership in security groups. In either case you should make sure that the network location you plan to use is available as a network share. See Chapter 15, "Data Sharing, Security, and Auditing," for details on sharing data on a network.

Redirecting a Special Folder to a Single Location

You can redirect a special folder to a single location by following these steps:

1. In the GPMC, right-click the GPO for the site, domain, or organizational unit you want to work with, and then click Edit. This opens the policy editor for the GPO.

2. In the policy editor, expand the following nodes: User Configuration, Windows Settings, and Folder Redirection.

3. Under Folder Redirection, right-click the special folder you want to work with, such as AppData(Roaming), and then click Properties. This opens a Properties dialog box similar to the one shown in Figure 5-12.

4. In the Setting list on the Target tab, choose Basic—Redirect Everyone's Folder To The Same Location.

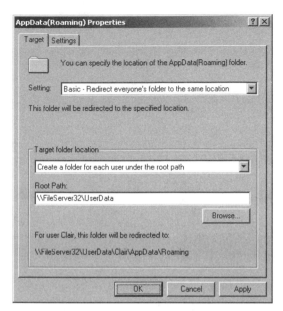

FIGURE 5-12 Set options for redirection using a special folder's Properties dialog box.

5. Under Target Folder Location, you have several options. The options available depend on the folder you're working with and include the following:

- **Redirect To The User's Home Directory** If you select this option, the folder is redirected to a subdirectory within the user's home directory. You set the location of the user's home directory with the %HomeDrive% and %HomePath% environment variables.

- **Create A Folder For Each User Under The Root Path** If you select this option, a folder is created for each user at the location you enter in the Root Path field. The folder name is the user account name as specified by %UserName%. Thus, if you enter the root path value \\Zeta\UserDocuments, the folder for Williams will be located at \\Zeta\ UserDocuments\Williams.

- **Redirect To The Following Location** If you select this option, the folder is redirected to the location you enter in the Root Path field. Here, you typically want to use an environment variable to customize the folder location for each user. For example, you could use the root path value \\Zeta\UserData\%UserName%\docs.

- **Redirect To The Local Userprofile Location** If you select this option, the folder is redirected to a subdirectory within the user profile directory. You set the location of the user profile with the %UserProfile% variable.

6. Click the Settings tab, configure additional options using the following fields, and then click OK to complete the process.

- **Grant The User Exclusive Rights To** Gives users full rights to access their data in the special folder.

- **Move The Contents Of *FolderName* To The New Location** Moves the data in the special folders from the individual systems on the network to the central folder or folders.

- **Also Apply Redirection Policy To** Applies the redirection policy to previous releases of Windows as well.

Redirecting a Special Folder Based on Group Membership

You can redirect a special folder based on group membership by following these steps:

1. In the GPMC, right-click the GPO for the site, domain, or organizational unit you want to work with, and then click Edit. This opens the policy editor for the GPO.

2. In the policy editor, expand the following nodes: User Configuration, Windows Settings, and Folder Redirection.

3. Under Folder Redirection, right-click the special folder you want to work with, such as AppData(Roaming), and then click Properties.

4. On the Target tab, choose Advanced—Specify Locations For Various User Groups in the Setting list. As shown in Figure 5-13, a Security Group Membership panel is added to the Properties dialog box.

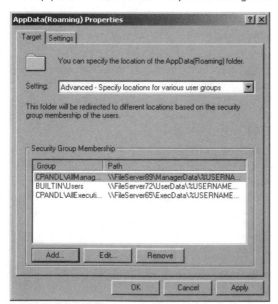

FIGURE 5-13 Configure advanced redirection using the Security Group Membership panel.

5. Click Add to open the Specify Group And Location dialog box. Or select a group entry, and then click Edit to modify its settings.

6. In the Security Group Membership field, type the name of the security group for which you want to configure redirection, or click Browse to find a security group to add.

7. As with basic redirection, the options available depend on the folder you're working with and include the following:

   - **Redirect To The User's Home Directory**   If you select this option, the folder is redirected to a subdirectory within the user's home directory. You set the location of the user's home directory with the %HomeDrive% and %HomePath% environment variables.

   - **Create A Folder For Each User Under The Root Path**   If you select this option, a folder is created for each user at the location you enter in the Root Path field. The folder name is the user account name as specified by %UserName%. Thus, if you enter the root path value \\Zeta\UserDocuments, the folder for Williams will be located at \\Zeta\ UserDocuments\Williams.

   - **Redirect To The Following Location**   If you select this option, the folder is redirected to the location you enter in the Root Path field. Here, you typically want to use an environment variable to customize the folder location for each user. For example, you could use the root path value \\Zeta\UserData\%UserName%\docs.

   - **Redirect To The Local Userprofile Location**   If you select this option, the folder is redirected to a subdirectory within the user profile directory. You set the location of the user profile with the %UserProfile% variable.

8. Click OK. Repeat steps 5–7 for other groups that you want to configure.

9. When you're done creating group entries, click the Settings tab, configure additional options using the following fields, and then click OK to complete the process.

   - **Grant The User Exclusive Rights To**   Gives users full rights to access their data in the special folder.

   - **Move The Contents Of *FolderName* To The New Location**   Moves the data in the special folders from the individual systems on the network to the central folder or folders.

   - **Also Apply Redirection Policy To**   Applies the redirection policy to early releases of Windows as well.

Removing Redirection

Sometimes you might want to remove redirection from a particular special folder. You remove redirection by following these steps:

1. In the GPMC, right-click the GPO for the site, domain, or organizational unit you want to work with. Then click Edit to open the policy editor for the GPO.

2. In the policy editor, expand the following nodes: User Configuration, Windows Settings, and Folder Redirection.

3. Under Folder Redirection, right-click the special folder you want to work with, and then click Properties.

4. Click the Settings tab, and then make sure that an appropriate Policy Removal option is selected. Two options are available:

   - **Leave The Folder In The New Location When Policy Is Removed**   When you select this option, the folder and its contents remain at the redirected location and current users are still permitted to access the folder and its contents at this location.

   - **Redirect The Folder Back To The Local Userprofile Location When Policy Is Removed**   When you select this option, the folder and its contents are copied back to the original location. The contents aren't deleted from the previous location, however.

5. If you changed the Policy Removal option, click Apply, and then click the Target tab. Otherwise, just click the Target tab.

6. To remove all redirection definitions for the special folder, choose Not Configured in the Setting list.

7. To remove redirection for a particular security group, select the security group in the Security Group Membership panel, and then click Remove. Click OK.

User and Computer Script Management

With Windows Server 2008 R2 you can configure four types of scripts:

- **Computer Startup**   Executed during startup
- **Computer Shutdown**   Executed prior to shutdown
- **User Logon**   Executed when a user logs on
- **User Logoff**   Executed when a user logs off

Windows 2000 and later releases support scripts written as command-shell batch scripts ending with the .bat or .cmd extension or scripts that use the Windows Script Host (WSH). WSH is a feature of Windows Server 2008 R2 that lets you use scripts written in a scripting language, such as VBScript, without needing to insert the script into a Web page. To provide a multipurpose scripting environment, WSH relies on scripting engines. A scripting engine is the component that defines the core syntax and structure of a particular scripting language. Windows Server ships with scripting engines for VBScript and JScript. Other scripting engines are also available.

Windows 7 and Windows Server 2008 R2 also support Windows PowerShell scripts. If you've installed Windows PowerShell on computers that process a particular GPO, you can use Windows PowerShell scripts in much the same way as you use other scripts. You have the option of running Windows PowerShell scripts before or after other types of scripts.

Assigning Computer Startup and Shutdown Scripts

Computer startup and shutdown scripts are assigned as part of a GPO. In this way, all computers that are members of the site, domain, or organizational unit—or all three—execute scripts automatically when they're booted or shut down.

To assign a computer startup or shutdown script, follow these steps:

1. Open the folder containing the script or scripts you want to use in Windows Explorer.

2. In the GPMC, right-click the GPO for the site, domain, or organizational unit you want to work with, and then click Edit. This opens the policy editor for the GPO.

3. In the Computer Configuration node, double-click the Windows Settings folder, and then click Scripts.

4. To work with startup scripts, right-click Startup, and then click Properties. To work with shutdown scripts, right-click Shutdown and select Properties. This opens a dialog box similar to the one shown in Figure 5-14.

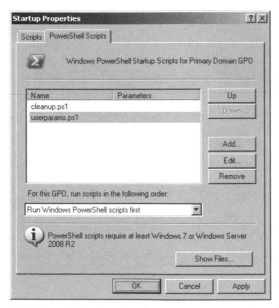

FIGURE 5-14 Add, edit, and remove computer startup scripts using the Startup Properties dialog box.

5. On the Scripts tab, you can manage command-shell batch scripts ending with the .bat or .cmd extension and scripts that use the Windows Script Host. On the PowerShell Scripts tab, you can manage Windows PowerShell scripts. When working with either tab, click Show Files.

6. Copy the files in the open Windows Explorer window, and then paste them into the window that opened when you clicked Show Files.

7. Click Add to assign a script. This opens the Add A Script dialog box. In the Script Name field, type the name of the script you copied to the Machine\Scripts\Startup or the Machine\Scripts\Shutdown folder for the related policy. In the Script Parameters field, enter any parameters to pass to the script. Repeat this step to add other scripts.

8. During startup or shutdown, scripts are executed in the order in which they're listed in the Properties dialog box. On the Scripts tab, use the Up and Down buttons to reorder scripts as necessary. Do the same on the PowerShell Scripts tab. On the PowerShell Scripts tab, you can also use the selection list to specify whether Windows PowerShell scripts should run before or after other types of scripts.

9. If you want to edit the script name or parameters later, select the script in the Script For list, and then click Edit. To delete a script, select the script in the Script For list and click Remove.

10. To save your changes, click OK.

Assigning User Logon and Logoff Scripts

You can assign user scripts in one of three ways:

- You can assign logon and logoff scripts as part of a GPO. In this way, all users who are members of the site, domain, or organizational unit—or all three—execute scripts automatically when they log on or log off.

- You can also assign logon scripts individually through the Active Directory Users And Computers console. In this way, you can assign each user or group a separate logon script. For details, see "Configuring the User's Environment Settings" in Chapter 11.

- You can also assign individual logon scripts as scheduled tasks. You schedule tasks using the Scheduled Task Wizard.

To assign a logon or logoff script in a GPO, follow these steps:

1. Open the folder containing the script or scripts you want to use in Windows Explorer.

2. In the GPMC, right-click the GPO for the site, domain, or organizational unit you want to work with, and then click Edit. This opens the policy editor for the GPO.

3. Double-click the Windows Settings folder in the User Configuration node, and then click Scripts.

4. To work with logon scripts, right-click Logon, and then click Properties. To work with logoff scripts, right-click Logoff, and then click Properties. This opens a dialog box similar to the one shown in Figure 5-15.

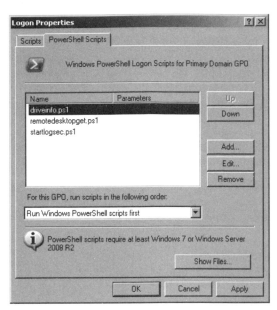

FIGURE 5-15 Add, edit, and remove user logon scripts using the Logon Properties dialog box.

5. On the Scripts tab, you can manage command-shell batch scripts ending with the .bat or .cmd extension and scripts that use the Windows Script Host. On the PowerShell Scripts tab, you can manage Windows PowerShell scripts. When working with either tab, click Show Files.

6. Copy the files in the open Windows Explorer window, and then paste them into the window that opened when you clicked Show Files.

7. Click Add to assign a script. This opens the Add A Script dialog box. In the Script Name field, type the name of the script you copied to the User\Scripts\ Logon or the User\Scripts\Logoff folder for the related policy. In the Script Parameter field, enter any parameters to pass to the script. Repeat this step to add other scripts.

8. During logon or logoff, scripts are executed in the order in which they're listed in the Properties dialog box. On the Scripts tab, use the Up and Down buttons to reorder scripts as necessary. Do the same on the PowerShell Scripts tab. On the PowerShell Scripts tab, you can also use the selection list to specify whether Windows PowerShell scripts should run before or after other types of scripts.

9. If you want to edit the script name or parameters later, select the script in the Script For list, and then click Edit. To delete a script, select the script in the Script For list, and then click Remove.

10. To save your changes, click OK.

Deploying Software Through Group Policy

Group Policy includes basic functionality, called Software Installation policy, for deploying software. Although Software Installation policy is not designed to replace enterprise solutions such as Systems Management Server (SMS), you can use it to automate the deployment and maintenance of software in just about any size organization, provided that your computers are running business editions of Windows 2000 or later.

Getting to Know Software Installation Policy

In Group Policy, you can deploy software on a per-computer or per-user basis. Per-computer applications are available to all users of a computer and configured under Computer Configuration\Software Settings\Software Installation. Per-user applications are available to individual users and configured under User Configuration\Software Settings\Software Installation.

You deploy software in three key ways:

- **Computer assignment**   Assigns the software to client computers so that it is installed when the computer starts. This technique requires no user intervention, but it does require a restart to install the software. Installed software is then available to all users on the computer.

- **User assignment**   Assigns the software to users so that it is installed when a user logs on. This technique requires no user intervention, but it does require the user to log on to install or advertise the software. The software is associated with the user only and not the computer.

- **User publishing**   Publishes the software so that users can install it manually through Programs And Features. This technique requires the user to explicitly install software or activate installation. The software is associated with the user only.

When you use user assignment or user publishing, you can advertise the software so that a computer can install the software when it is first used. With advertisements, the software can be installed automatically in the following situations:

- When a user accesses a document that requires the software
- When a user opens a shortcut to the application
- When another application requires a component of the software

When you configure Software Installation policy, you should generally not use existing GPOs. Instead, you should create GPOs that configure software installation and then link those GPOs to the appropriate containers in Group Policy. When you use this approach, it is much easier to redeploy software and apply updates.

After you create a GPO for your software deployment, you should set up a distribution point. A distribution point is a shared folder that is available to the computers and users to which you are deploying software. With basic applications, you prepare the distribution point by copying the installer package file and all required application files to the share and configuring permissions so that these files can be accessed. With other applications, such as Microsoft Office, you prepare the distribution point by performing an administrative installation to the share. With Microsoft Office, you can do this by running the application's Setup program with the /a parameter and designating the share as the install location. The advantage of an administrative installation is that the software can be updated and redeployed through Software Installation policy.

You can update applications deployed through Software Installation policy by using an update or service pack or by deploying a new version of the application. Each task is performed in a slightly different way.

Deploying Software Throughout Your Organization

Software Installation policy uses either Windows Installer Packages (.msi) or ZAW Down-Level Application Packages (.zap) files. When you use computer assignment, user assignment, or user publishing, you can deploy software using Windows Installer Packages. When you use user publishing, you can deploy software using either Windows Installer Packages or ZAW Down-Level Application Packages. With either technique, you must set file permissions on the installer package so that the appropriate computer and user accounts have read access.

Because Software Installation policy is applied only during foreground processing of policy settings, per-computer application deployments are processed at startup and per-user application deployments are processed at logon. You can customize installation using transform (.mst) files. Transform files modify the installation process according to the settings you've defined for specific computers and users.

You can deploy software by following these steps:

1. In the GPMC, right-click the GPO you want to use for the deployment, and then click Edit.

2. In the policy editor, open Computer Configuration\Software Settings\Software Installation or User Configuration\Software Settings\Software Installation as appropriate for the type of software deployment.

3. Right-click Software Installation. On the shortcut menu, click New, and then click Package.

4. In the Open dialog box, navigate to the network share where your package is located, click the package to select it, and then click Open.

    NOTE Windows Installer Packages (.msi) is selected by default in the Files Of Type list. If you are performing a user publishing deployment, you can also choose ZAW Down-Level Application Packages (.zap) as the file type.

5. In the Deploy Software dialog box, shown in Figure 5-16, select one of the following deployment methods, and then click OK:

    ▪ **Published** To publish the application without modifications

- **Assigned**   To assign the application without modifications
- **Advanced**   To deploy the application using advanced configuration options

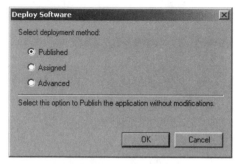

FIGURE 5-16 Select the deployment method.

Configuring Software Deployment Options

You can view and set general options for a software package by following these steps:

1. In the GPMC, right-click the GPO you want to use for the deployment, and then click Edit.

2. In the policy editor, access Computer Configuration\Software Settings\Software Installation or User Configuration\Software Settings\Software Installation as appropriate for the type of software deployment.

3. Double-click the Software Installation package. In the Properties dialog box, review or modify software deployment options.

4. On the Deployment tab, shown in Figure 5-17, you can change the deployment type and configure the following deployment and installation options:

   - **Auto-Install This Application By File Extension Activation**   Advertises any file extensions associated with this package for install-on-first-use deployment. This option is selected by default.

   - **Uninstall This Application When It Falls Out Of The Scope Of Management**   Removes the application if it no longer applies to the user.

   - **Do Not Display This Package In The Add/Remove Programs Control Panel**   Prevents the application from appearing in Add/Remove Programs, which prevents a user from uninstalling an application.

   - **Install This Application At Logon**   Configures full installation—rather than advertisement—of an application when the user logs on. This option cannot be set when you publish a package for users.

- **Installation User Interface Options** Controls how the installation is performed. With the default setting, Maximum, the user sees all setup screens and messages during installation. With the Basic option, the user sees only error and completion messages during installation.

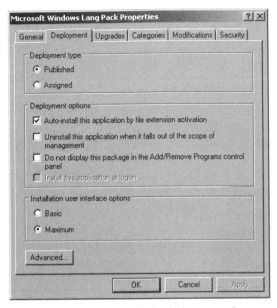

FIGURE 5-17 Review and modify the deployment options as necessary.

5. Click OK.

Updating Deployed Software

When an application uses a Windows Installer package, you can apply an update or service pack to a deployed application by following these steps:

1. After you obtain an .msi file or .msp (patch) file containing the update or service pack to be applied, copy the .msi or .msp file and any new installation files to the folder containing the original .msi file. Overwrite any duplicate files as necessary.

2. In the GPMC, right-click the GPO you want to use for the deployment, and then click Edit.

3. In the policy editor, access Computer Configuration\Software Settings\Software Installation or User Configuration\Software Settings\Software Installation as appropriate for the type of software deployment.

4. Right-click the package you want to work with. On the shortcut menu, click All Tasks, and then click Redeploy Application.

5. When prompted to confirm the action, click Yes. The application is then redeployed to all users and computers as appropriate for the GPO you are working with.

When an application uses a non-Windows Installer package, you can update a deployed application or apply a service pack by following these steps:

1. In the GPMC, right-click the GPO you want to use for the deployment, and then click Edit.

2. In the policy editor, access Computer Configuration\Software Settings\Software Installation or User Configuration\Software Settings\Software Installation as appropriate for the type of software deployment.

3. Right-click the package. On the shortcut menu, click All Tasks, and then click Remove. Click OK to accept the default option of immediate removal.

4. Copy the new .zap file and all related files to a network share and redeploy the application.

Upgrading Deployed Software

You can upgrade a previously deployed application to a new version by following these steps:

1. Obtain a Windows Installer file for the new software version and copy it along with all required files to a network share. Alternatively, you can perform an administrative installation to the network share.

2. In the GPMC, right-click the GPO you want to use for the deployment, and then click Edit.

3. In the policy editor, access Computer Configuration\Software Settings\Software Installation or User Configuration\Software Settings\Software Installation as appropriate for the type of software deployment.

4. Right-click Software Installation. On the shortcut menu, click New, and then click Package. Create an assigned or published application by using the Windows Installer file for the new software version.

5. Right-click the upgrade package, and then click Properties. On the Upgrades tab, click Add. In the Add Upgrade Package dialog box, do one of the following:

   - If the original application and the upgrade are in the current GPO, select Current Group Policy Object, and then select the previously deployed application in the Package To Upgrade list.

   - If the original application and the upgrade are in different GPOs, select A Specific GPO, click Browse, and then select the GPO from the Browse For A Group Policy Object dialog box. Select the previously deployed application in the Package To Upgrade list.

6. Choose an upgrade option. If you want to replace the application with the new version, select Uninstall The Existing Package, Then Install The Upgrade

Package. If you want to perform an in-place upgrade over the existing installation, select Package Can Upgrade Over The Existing Package.

7. Click OK to close the Add Upgrade Package dialog box. If you want to make this a required upgrade, select the Required Upgrade For Existing Packages check box, and then click OK to close the upgrade package's Properties dialog box.

Automatically Enrolling Computer and User Certificates

A server designated as a certificate authority (CA) is responsible for issuing digital certificates and managing certificate revocation lists (CRLs). Servers running Windows Server 2008 R2 can be configured as certificate authorities by installing Active Directory Certificate Services. Computers and users can use certificates for authentication and encryption.

In an enterprise configuration, enterprise CAs are used for autoenrollment. This means authorized users and computers can request a certificate, and the certificate authority can automatically process the certificate request so that the users and computers can immediately install the certificate.

Group Policy controls the way autoenrollment works. When you install enterprise CAs, autoenrollment policies for users and computers are enabled automatically. The policy for computer certificate enrollment is Certificate Services Client–Auto-Enrollment Settings under Computer Configuration\Windows Settings\Security Settings\Public Key Policies. The policy for user certificate enrollment is Certificate Services Client–AutoEnrollment under User Configuration\Windows Settings\Security Settings\Public Key Policies.

You can configure autoenrollment by following these steps:

1. In the GPMC, right-click the GPO you want to work with, and then click Edit.

2. In the policy editor, access User Configuration\Windows Settings\Security Settings\Public Key Policies or Computer Configuration\Windows Settings\Security Settings\Public Key Policies as appropriate for the type of policy you want to review.

3. Double-click Certificate Services Client–Auto-Enrollment. To disable automatic enrollment, select Disabled from the Configuration Model list, click OK, and then skip the remaining steps in this procedure. To enable automatic enrollment, select Enabled from the Configuration Model list.

4. To automatically renew expired certificates, update pending certificates, and remove revoked certificates, select the related check box.

5. To ensure that the latest version of certificate templates are requested and used, select the Update Certificates That Use Certificate Templates check box.

6. To notify users when a certificate is about to expire, select the Expiration Notification check box, and then specify when notifications are sent using

the box provided. By default, if notification is enabled, notifications are sent when 10 percent of the certificate lifetime remains.

7. Click OK to save your settings.

Managing Automatic Updates in Group Policy

Automatic Updates help you keep the operating system up to date. Although you can configure Automatic Updates on a per-computer basis, you'll typically want to configure this feature for all users and computers that process a GPO—this is a much more efficient management technique.

Configuring Automatic Updates

When you manage Automatic Updates through Group Policy, you can set the update configuration to any of the following options:

- **Auto Download And Schedule The Install** Updates are automatically downloaded and installed according to a schedule that you specify. When updates have been downloaded, the operating system notifies the user so that he or she can review the updates that are scheduled to be installed. The user can install the updates then or wait for the scheduled installation time.

- **Auto Download And Notify For Install** The operating system retrieves all updates as they become available and then prompts the user when they're ready to be installed. The user can then accept or reject the updates. Accepted updates are installed. Rejected updates aren't installed but remain on the system, where they can be installed later.

- **Notify For Download And Notify For Install** The operating system notifies the user before retrieving any updates. If a user elects to download the updates, the user still has the opportunity to accept or reject them. Accepted updates are installed. Rejected updates aren't installed but remain on the system, where they can be installed later.

- **Allow Local Admin To Choose Setting** Allows the local administrator to configure Automatic Updates on a per-computer basis. Note that if you use any other setting, local users and administrators are unable to change settings for Automatic Updates.

You can configure Automatic Updates in Group Policy by following these steps:

1. In the GPMC, right-click the GPO you want to work with, and then click Edit.

2. In the policy editor, access Computer Configuration\Administrative Templates\Windows Components\Windows Update.

3. Double-click Configure Automatic Updates. In the Properties dialog box, you can now enable or disable Group Policy management of Automatic Updates. To enable management of Automatic Updates, select Enabled. To disable management of Automatic Updates, select Disabled, click OK, and then skip the remaining steps.

4. Choose an update configuration from the options in the Configure Automatic Updating list.

5. If you select Auto Download And Schedule The Install, you can schedule the installation day and time by using the lists provided. Click OK to save your settings.

Optimizing Automatic Updates

Generally, most automatic updates are installed only when a computer is shut down and restarted. Some automatic updates can be installed immediately without interrupting system services or requiring system restart. To ensure that some updates can be installed immediately, follow these steps:

1. In the GPMC, right-click the GPO you want to work with, and then click Edit.

2. In the policy editor, access Computer Configuration\Administrative Templates\Windows Components\Windows Update.

3. Double-click Allow Automatic Updates Immediate Installation. In the Properties dialog box, select Enabled, and then click OK.

By default, only users with local administrator privileges receive notifications about updates. You can allow any user logged on to a computer to receive update notifications by following these steps:

1. In the GPMC, right-click the GPO you want to work with, and then click Edit.

2. In the policy editor, access Computer Configuration\Administrative Templates\Windows Components\Windows Update.

3. Double-click Allow Non-Administrators To Receive Update Notifications. In the Properties dialog box, select Enabled, and then click OK.

Another useful policy is Remove Access To Use All Windows Update Features. This policy prohibits access to all Windows Update features. If enabled, all Automatic Updates features are removed and can't be configured. This includes the Automatic Updates tab in the System utility, the Windows Update link on the Start menu and on the Tools menu in Internet Explorer, and driver updates from the Windows Update Web site in Device Manager. This policy is located in User Configuration\Administrative Templates\Windows Components\Windows Update.

Using Intranet Update Service Locations

On networks with hundreds or thousands of computers, the Automatic Updates process can use a considerable amount of network bandwidth, and having all the computers check for updates and install them over the Internet doesn't make sense. Instead, consider using the Specify Intranet Microsoft Update Service Location policy, which tells individual computers to check a designated internal server for updates.

The designated update server must run Windows Server Update Services (WSUS), be configured as a Web server running Microsoft Internet Information Services (IIS), and be able to handle the additional workload, which might be considerable on a large network during peak usage times. Additionally, the update server must have access to the external network on port 80. The use of a firewall or proxy server on this port shouldn't present any problems.

The update process also tracks configuration information and statistics for each computer. This information is necessary for the update process to work properly and can be stored on a separate statistics server (an internal server running IIS) or on the update server itself.

To specify an internal update server, follow these steps:

1. After you install and configure an update server, open the GPO you want to work with for editing. In the policy editor, access Computer Configuration\ Administrative Templates\Windows Components\Windows Update.

2. Double-click Specify Intranet Microsoft Update Service Location. In the Properties dialog box, select Enabled.

3. In the Set The Intranet Update Service For Detecting Updates text box, type the URL of the update server. In most cases, this is http://*servername*, such as http://CorpUpdateServer01.

4. Type the URL of the statistics server in the Set The Intranet Statistics Server text box. This doesn't have to be a separate server; you can specify the update server in this text box.

    NOTE If you want a single server to handle both updates and statistics, enter the same URL in both fields. Otherwise, if you want a different server for updates and statistics, enter the URL for each server in the appropriate field.

5. Click OK. After the applicable Group Policy object is refreshed, systems running appropriate versions of Windows will look to the update server for updates. You'll want to monitor the update and statistics servers closely for several days or weeks to ensure that everything is working properly. Directories and files will be created on the update and statistics servers.

Enhancing Computer Security

Sound security practices and settings are essential to successful system adminis-tration. Two key ways to configure security settings are to use security tem-plates and security policies. Both of these features manage system settings that you would typically manage through Group Policy otherwise.

Using Security Templates

Security templates provide a centralized way to manage security-related settings for workstations and servers. You use security templates to apply customized sets of Group Policy definitions to specific computers.

These policy definitions generally affect the following policies:

- **Account policies**   Control security for passwords, account lockout, and Kerberos security.

- **Local policies**   Control security for auditing, user rights assignment, and other security options.

- **Event log policies**   Control security for event logging.

- **Restricted groups policies**   Control security for local group membership administration.

- **System services policies**   Control security and startup mode for local services.

- **File system policies**   Control security for file and folder paths in the local file system.

- **Registry policies**   Control the permissions on security-related registry keys.

NOTE Security templates are available in all Windows Server 2008 R2 installations and can be imported into any Group Policy object. Security templates apply only to the Computer Configuration area of Group Policy. They do not apply to the User Configuration area. In Group Policy, you'll find applicable settings under Computer Configuration\Windows Settings\Security Settings. Some security settings are not included, such as those that apply to wireless networks, public keys, software restrictions, and IP security.

Working with security templates is a multipart process that involves the following steps:

1. Use the Security Templates snap-in to select a template and review its settings.

2. Use the Security Templates snap-in to make necessary changes to the template settings.

3. Use the Security Configuration And Analysis snap-in to analyze the differences between the template you are working with and the current computer security settings.

4. Revise the template as necessary after you review the differences between the template settings and the current computer settings.

5. Use the Security Configuration And Analysis snap-in to apply the template and overwrite existing security settings.

When you first start working with security templates, you should determine whether you can use an existing template as a starting point. Other administrators might have created templates, or your organization might have baseline templates that should be used. You can also use the blank template stored in the %System-Root%\Security\Templates\Policies directory as your starting point. If you do, you should create a copy of the blank template and then work with the copy, as shown in Figure 6-1.

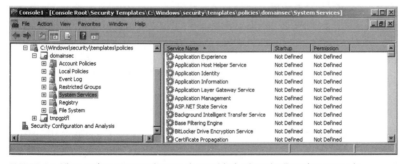

FIGURE 6-1 View and create security templates with the Security Templates snap-in.

TIP If you select a template that you want to use as a starting point, you should go through each setting that the template applies and evaluate how the setting affects your environment. If a setting doesn't make sense, you should modify it appropriately or delete it.

You don't use the Security Templates snap-in to apply templates. You use the Security Configuration And Analysis snap-in to apply templates. You can also use the Security Configuration And Analysis snap-in to compare the settings in a template to the current settings on a computer. The results of the analysis highlight areas where the current settings don't match those in the template. This is useful to determine whether security settings have changed over time.

Using the Security Templates and Security Configuration And Analysis Snap-Ins

You can open the security snap-ins by following these steps:

1. Click Start, type **mmc** into the Search box, and then press Enter.

2. In the Microsoft Management Console, click File, and then click Add/Remove Snap-In.

3. In the Add Or Remove Snap-Ins dialog box, click Security Templates, and then click Add.

4. Click Security Configuration And Analysis, and then click Add. Click OK.

By default, the Security Templates snap-in looks for security templates in the %SystemDrive%\Users\%UserName%\Documents\Security\Templates folder. You can add other search paths for templates by following these steps:

1. In the Security Templates snap-in, choose New Template Search Path from the Action menu.

2. In the Browse For Folder dialog box, select the template location to add, such as %SystemRoot%\Security\Templates\Policies. Click OK.

    Now that you've located the template search path you want to work with, you can select a template and expand the related notes to review its settings.

You can create a template by following these steps:

1. In the Security Templates snap-in, right-click the search path where the template should be created, and then click New Template.

2. Type a name and description for the template in the text boxes provided.

3. Click OK to create the template. The template will have no settings configured, so you need to modify the settings carefully before the template is ready for use.

Reviewing and Changing Template Settings

The sections that follow discuss how to work with template settings. As you'll learn, you manage each type of template setting in a slightly different way.

Changing Settings for Account, Local, and Event Log Policies

Account policy settings control security for passwords, account lockout, and Kerberos security. Local policy settings control security for auditing, user rights assignment, and other security options. Event log policy settings control security for event logging. For detailed information on account policy and local policy settings, see Chapter 10, "Creating User and Group Accounts." For detailed information on configuring event logging, see Chapter 4, "Monitoring Processes, Services, and Events."

With account, local, and event log policies, you can change template settings by following these steps:

1. In the Security Templates snap-in, expand the Account Policies or Local Policies node as necessary, and then select a related subnode, such as Password Policy or Account Lockout Policy.

2. In the right pane, policy settings are listed alphabetically. The value in the Computer Setting column shows the current settings. If the template changes the setting so that it is no longer defined, the value is listed as Not Defined.

3. Double-click a setting to display its Properties dialog box, shown in Figure 6-2. To determine the purpose of the setting, click the Explain tab. To define and apply the policy setting, select the Define This Policy Setting In The Template check box. To clear this policy and not apply it, clear this check box.

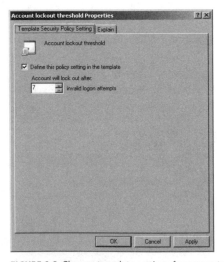

FIGURE 6-2 Change template settings for account and local policies.

4. If you enable the policy setting, specify how the policy setting is to be used by configuring any additional options.

5. Click OK to save your changes. You might see the Suggested Value Changes dialog box, shown in Figure 6-3. This dialog box informs you of other values that are changed to suggested values based on your setting change. For example, when you change the Account Lockout Threshold setting, Windows might also change the Account Lockout Duration and Reset Account Lockout Counter After settings, as shown in the figure.

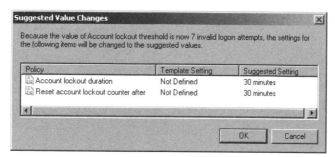

FIGURE 6-3 Review the suggested value changes.

Configuring Restricted Groups

Restricted groups policy settings control the list of members of groups as well as the groups to which the configured group belongs. You can restrict a group by following these steps:

1. In the Security Templates snap-in, select the Restricted Groups node. In the right pane, any currently restricted groups are listed by name. Members of the group are listed as well, and so are groups of which the restricted group is a member.

2. You can add a restricted group by right-clicking the Restricted Groups node in the left pane and then clicking Add Group. In the Add Group dialog box, click Browse.

3. In the Select Groups dialog box, type the name of a group you want to restrict, and then click Check Names. If multiple matches are found, select the account you want to use, and then click OK. If no matches are found, update the name you entered and try searching again. Repeat this step as necessary, and then click OK.

4. In the Properties dialog box, you can use the Add Members option to add members to the group. Click Add Members, and then specify the members of the group. If the group should not have any members, remove all members by clicking Remove. Any members who are not specified in the policy

setting for the restricted group are removed when the security template is applied.

5. In the Properties dialog box, click Add Groups to specify the groups to which this group belongs. If you specify membership in groups, the groups to which this group belongs are listed exactly as you've applied them (provided that the groups are valid in the applicable workgroup or domain). If you do not specify membership in groups, the groups to which this group belongs are not modified when the template is applied.

6. Click OK to save your settings.

You can remove a restriction on a group by following these steps:

1. In the Security Templates snap-in, select the Restricted Groups node. In the right pane, any currently restricted groups are listed by name. Members of the group are listed along with the groups of which the restricted group is a member.

2. Right-click the group that should not be restricted, and then click Delete. When prompted to confirm the action, click Yes.

Enabling, Disabling, and Configuring System Services

Policy settings for system services control the general security and startup mode for local services. You can enable, disable, and configure system services by following these steps:

1. In the Security Templates snap-in, select the System Services node. In the right pane, all currently installed services on the computer you are working with are listed by name, startup setting, and permission configuration. Keep the following in mind when working with system services:

   - If the template does not change the startup configuration of the service, the value for the Startup column is listed as Not Defined. Otherwise, the startup configuration is listed as one of the following values: Automatic, Manual, or Disabled.

   - If the template does not change the security configuration of the service, the value for the Permission column is listed as Not Defined. Otherwise, the security configuration is listed as Configured.

2. Double-click the entry for a system service to display its Properties dialog box, shown in Figure 6-4. To define and apply the policy setting, select the Define This Policy Setting In The Template check box. To clear this policy and not apply it, clear this check box.

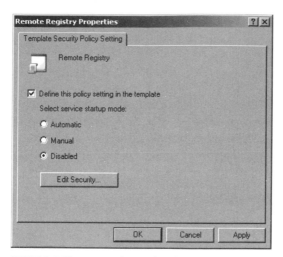

FIGURE 6-4 Change template settings for system services.

3. If you enable the policy setting, specify the service startup mode by selecting Automatic, Manual, or Disabled. Keep the following in mind:

   - Automatic ensures that the service starts automatically when the operating system starts. Choose this setting for essential services that you know are secure and that you want to be sure are run if they are installed on the computer that the template is being applied to.

   - Manual prevents the service from starting automatically and allows the service only to be started manually, either by a user, application, or other service. Choose this setting when you want to restrict unnecessary or unused services or when you want to restrict services that you know are not entirely secure.

   - Disabled prevents the service from starting automatically or manually. Choose this setting only with unnecessary or unused services that you want to prevent from running.

4. If you know the security configuration that the service should use, click Edit Security, and then set the service permissions in the Security For dialog box. You can set permissions to allow specific users and groups to start, stop, and pause the service on the computer.

5. Click OK.

Configuring Security Settings for Registry and File System Paths

Policy settings for the file system control security for file and folder paths in the local file system. Policy settings for the registry control the values of security-related registry keys. You can view or change security settings for currently defined registry and file system paths by following these steps:

1. In the Security Templates snap-in, select the Registry node or the File System node, depending on which type of file path you want work with. In the right pane, all currently secured paths are listed.

2. Double-click a registry or file path to view its current settings, as shown in Figure 6-5.

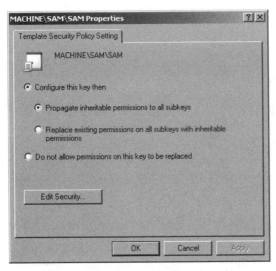

FIGURE 6-5 Change template settings for paths and keys.

3. To ensure that permissions on the path or key are not replaced, select Do Not Allow Permissions On This Key To Be Replaced, and then click OK. Skip the remaining steps in this procedure.

4. To configure the path or key and replace permissions, select Configure This Key Then, and then choose one of the following options:

   - **Propagate Inheritable Permissions To All Subkeys**   Choose this option to apply all inheritable permissions to this registry or file path and to all registry and file paths below this path. Existing permissions are replaced only if they conflict with a security permission set for this path.

   - **Replace Existing Permissions On All Subkeys With Inheritable Permissions**   Choose this option to replace all existing permissions on this registry or file path and on all registry and file paths below this path.

Any existing permissions are removed, and only the current permissions remain.

5. Click Edit Security. In the Security For dialog box, configure security permissions for users and groups. You have the same options for permissions, auditing, and ownership as you do for files and folders used with NTFS. See Chapter 15, "Data Sharing, Security, and Auditing," for details on permissions, auditing, and ownership.

6. Click OK twice to save the settings.

You can define security settings for registry paths by following these steps:

1. In the Security Templates snap-in, select and then right-click the Registry node, and then click Add Key. This displays the Select Registry Key dialog box, shown in Figure 6-6.

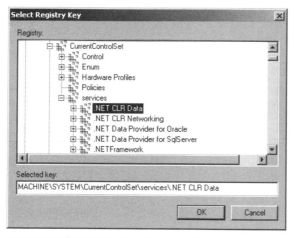

FIGURE 6-6 Select the registry path or value to secure.

2. In the Select Registry Key dialog box, select the registry path or value you want to work with, and then click OK. Entries under CLASSES_ROOT are for HKEY_CLASSES_ROOT. Entries under MACHINE are for HKEY_LOCAL_MACHINE. Entries under USERS are for HKEY_USERS.

3. In the Database Security For dialog box, configure security permissions for users and groups. You have the same options for permissions, auditing, and ownership as you do for files and folders used with NTFS. See Chapter 15 for details on permissions, auditing, and ownership.

4. Click OK. The Add Object dialog box is displayed. To ensure that permissions on the path or key are not replaced, select Do Not Allow Permissions On This Key To Be Replaced, and then click OK. Skip the remaining steps in this procedure.

5. To configure the path or key and replace permissions, select Configure This Key Then, and then do one of the following:

   - Choose Propagate Inheritable Permissions To All to apply all inheritable permissions to this registry path and all registry paths below this path. Existing permissions are replaced only if they conflict with a security permission set for this path.

   - Choose Replace Existing Permissions On All . . . With Inheritable Permissions to replace all existing permissions on this registry path and on all registry paths below this path. Any existing permissions are removed, and only the current permissions remain.

6. Click OK.

You can define security settings for file paths by following these steps:

1. In the Security Templates snap-in, select and then right-click the File System node, and then click Add File. This displays the Add A File Or Folder dialog box, shown in Figure 6-7.

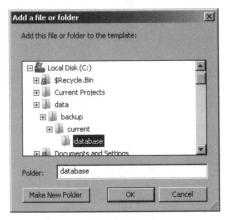

FIGURE 6-7 Select the file or folder path to secure.

2. In the Add A File Or Folder dialog box, select the file or folder path or value you want to work with, and then click OK.

3. In the Database Security For dialog box, configure security permissions for users and groups. You have the same options for permissions, auditing, and ownership as you do for files and folders used with NTFS. See Chapter 15 for details on permissions, auditing, and ownership.

4. Click OK. The Add Object dialog box is displayed. To ensure that permissions on the path are not replaced, select Do Not Allow Permissions On This File Or Folder To Be Replaced, and then click OK. Skip the remaining steps in this procedure.

5. To configure the path and replace permissions, select Configure This Path Then, and then do one of the following:

- Choose Propagate Inheritable Permissions To All to apply all inheritable permissions to this file path and all file paths below this path. Existing permissions are replaced only if they conflict with a security permission set for this path.

- Choose Replace Existing Permissions On All . . .With Inheritable Permissions to replace all existing permissions on this file path and on all file paths below this path. Any existing permissions are removed, and only the current permissions remain.

6. Click OK.

Analyzing, Reviewing, and Applying Security Templates

As stated previously, you use the Security Configuration And Analysis snap-in to apply templates and to compare the settings in a template to the current settings on a computer. Applying a template ensures that a computer conforms to a specific security configuration. Comparing settings can help you identify any discrepancies between what is implemented currently and what is defined in a security template. This can also be useful to determine whether security settings have changed over time.

REAL WORLD The key drawback to using the Security Configuration And Analysis snap-in is that you cannot configure multiple computers at once. You can configure security only on the computer on which you are running the snap-in. If you want to use this tool to deploy security configurations, you must log on to and run the tool on each computer. Although this technique works for stand-alone computers, it is not the optimal approach in a domain. In a domain setting, you'll want to import the security template settings into a Group Policy object (GPO) and then deploy the security configuration to multiple computers. For more information, see "Deploying Security Templates to Multiple Computers" later in this chapter.

The Security Configuration And Analysis snap-in uses a working database to store template security settings and then applies the settings from this database. For analysis and comparisons, the template settings are listed as the effective database settings, and the current computer settings are listed as the effective computer settings.

After you create a template or determine that you want to use an existing template, you can configure and analyze the template by following these steps:

1. Open the Security Configuration And Analysis snap-in.

2. Right-click the Security Configuration And Analysis node, and then click Open Database. This displays the Open Database dialog box.

3. By default, the Open Database dialog box's search path is set to %System-Drive%\Users\%UserName%\Documents\Security*Database*. As necessary,

select options in the Open Database dialog box to navigate to a new save location. In the File Name field, type a descriptive name for the database, such as **Current Config Comparison**, and then click Open. The security database is created in the Security Database Files format with the .sdb file extension.

4. The Import Template dialog box is displayed with the default search path set to %SystemDrive%\Users\%UserName%\Documents\Security\Templates. As necessary, select options in the Import Template dialog box to navigate to a new template location. Select the security template that you want to use, and then click Open. Security template files end with the .inf file extension.

5. Right-click the Security Configuration And Analysis node, and then click Analyze Computer Now. When prompted to set the error log path, type a new path or click OK to use the default path.

6. Wait for the snap-in to complete the analysis of the template. If an error occurs during the analysis, you can view the error log by right-clicking the Security Configuration And Analysis node and choosing View Log File.

When you are working with the Security Configuration And Analysis snap-in, you can review the differences between the template settings and the current computer settings. As Figure 6-8 shows, the template settings stored in the analysis database are listed in the Database Setting column, and the current computer settings are listed in the Computer Setting column. If a setting has not been analyzed, it is listed as Not Defined.

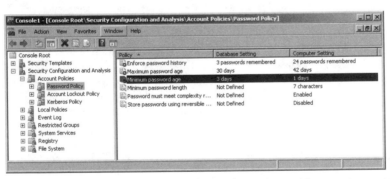

FIGURE 6-8 Review the differences between the template settings and the current computer settings.

You can make changes to a setting stored in the database by following these steps:

1. In the Security Configuration And Analysis snap-in, double-click the setting you want to work with.

2. In the Properties dialog box, shown in Figure 6-9, note the current computer setting listed in the Computer Setting text box. If information about the purpose of the setting is available, you can view this by clicking the Explain tab.

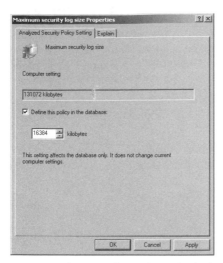

FIGURE 6-9 Change a policy setting in the database before applying the template.

3. To define and apply the policy setting, select the Define This Policy Setting In The Database check box. To clear this policy and not apply it, clear this check box.

4. If you enable the policy setting, specify how the policy setting is to be used by configuring any additional options.

5. Repeat this process as necessary. To save your database changes to the template, right-click the Security Configuration And Analysis node, and then click Save.

Before applying a template, you might want to create a rollback template. A rollback template is a reverse template that allows you to remove most settings applied with a template. The only settings that cannot be removed are those for access control lists on file system and registry paths.

You can create a rollback template by using the Secedit command-line utility. Type the following:

```
secedit /generaterollback /cfg TemplateName /rbk RollBackName /log LogName
```

where *TemplateName* is the name of the security template for which you are creating a rollback template, *RollBackName* sets the name of a security template in which the reverse settings should be stored, and *LogName* sets the name of an optional log file to use.

In the following example, you create a rollback template for the "dc security" template:

```
secedit /generaterollback /cfg "dc security.inf"
/rbk dc-orig.inf /log rollback.log
```

When you're ready to apply the template, right-click the Security Configuration And Analysis node, and then click Configure Computer Now. When prompted to set the error log path, click OK because the default path should be sufficient. To view the configuration error log, right-click the Security Configuration And Analysis node, and then click View Log File. Note any problems and take action as necessary.

If you created a rollback template prior to applying a security template, you can restore the computer's security settings to their previous state. To apply a rollback template, follow these steps:

1. In the Security Configuration And Analysis snap-in, right-click the Security Configuration And Analysis node, and then click Import Template.

2. In the Import Template dialog box, select the rollback template.

3. Select the Clear This Database Before Importing check box, and then click Open.

4. Right-click the Security Configuration And Analysis node, and then click Configure Computer Now. Click OK.

The only settings that cannot be restored are for access control lists on file system and registry paths. Once the permissions on file system and registry paths have been applied, you cannot reverse the process automatically and must instead manually reverse the changes one at a time.

Deploying Security Templates to Multiple Computers

Rather than applying security templates to one computer at a time, you can deploy your security configurations to multiple computers through Group Policy. To do this, you need to import the security template into a GPO processed by the computers that the template settings should apply to. Then, when policy is refreshed, all computers within the scope of the GPO receive the security configuration.

Security templates apply only to the Computer Configuration portion of Group Policy. Before you deploy security configurations in this way, you should take a close look at the domain and organizational unit (OU) structure of your organization and make changes as necessary to ensure that the security configuration is applied only to relevant types of computers. Essentially, this means that you need to create OUs for the different types of computers in your organization and then move the computer accounts for these computers into the appropriate OUs. Afterward, you need to create and link a GPO for each of the computer OUs. For example, you could create the following computer OUs:

- **Domain Controllers** An OU for your organization's domain controllers. This OU is created automatically in a domain.

- **High Security Member Servers** An OU for servers that require higher than normal security configurations.

- **Member Servers** An OU for servers that require standard server security configurations.

- **High Security User Workstations** An OU for workstations that require higher than normal security configurations.

- **User Workstations** An OU for workstations that require standard workstation security configurations.

- **Remote Access Computers** An OU for computers that remotely access the organization's network.

- **Restricted Computers** An OU for computers that require restrictive security configurations, such as computers that are used in labs or kiosks.

REAL WORLD You need to be extra careful when you deploy security templates through GPOs. If you haven't done this before, practice in a test environment first, and be sure to also practice recovering computers to their original security settings. If you create a GPO and link the GPO to the appropriate level in the Active Directory structure, you can recover the computers to their original state by removing the link to the GPO. This is why it is extremely important to create and link a new GPO rather than use an existing GPO.

To deploy a security template to a computer GPO, follow these steps:

1. After you configure a security template and have tested it to ensure that it is appropriate, open the GPO you previously created and linked to the appropriate level of your Active Directory structure. In the policy editor, open Computer Configuration\Windows Settings\Security Settings.

2. Right-click Security Settings, and then click Import Policy.

3. In the Import Policy From dialog box, select the security template to import, and then click Open. Security templates end with the .inf file extension.

4. Check the configuration state of the security settings to verify that the settings were imported as expected, and then close the policy editor. Repeat this process for each security template and computer GPO you've configured. In the default configuration of Group Policy, it will take 90 to 120 minutes for the settings to be pushed out to computers in the organization.

Using the Security Configuration Wizard

The Security Configuration Wizard can help you create and apply a comprehensive security policy. A security policy is an XML file that you can use to configure services, network security, registry values, and audit policies. Because security policies are role-based and feature-based, you generally need to create a separate policy for each of your standard server configurations. For example, if your organization uses domain controllers, file servers, and print servers, you might want to create a separate policy for each of these server types. If your organization has mail servers, database servers, and combined file/print servers as well as domain controllers, you should create separate policies tailored to these server types.

You can use the Security Configuration Wizard to do the following:

- Create a security policy.
- Edit a security policy.
- Apply a security policy.
- Roll back the last-applied security policy.

Security policies can incorporate one or more security templates. Much like you can with security templates, you can apply a security policy to the currently logged-on computer using the Security Configuration Wizard. Through Group Policy, you can apply a security policy to multiple computers as well.

Creating Security Policies

The Security Configuration Wizard allows you to configure policy only for roles and features that are installed on a computer when you run the wizard. The precise step-by-step process for creating security policies depends on the server roles and features available on the currently logged-on computer. That said, the general configuration sections presented in the wizard are the same regardless of the computer configuration.

The Security Configuration Wizard has the following configuration sections:

- **Role-Based Service Configuration** Configures the startup mode of system services based on a server's installed roles, installed features, installed options, and required services.

- **Network Security** Configures inbound and outbound security rules for Windows Firewall With Advanced Security based on installed roles and installed options.

- **Registry Settings** Configures protocols used to communicate with other computers based on installed roles and installed options.

- **Audit Policy** Configures auditing on the selected server based on your preferences.

- **Save Security Policy** Allows you to save and view the security policy. You can also include one or more security templates.

With this in mind, you can create a security policy by following these steps:

1. Start the Security Configuration Wizard by clicking Start, Administrative Tools, Security Configuration Wizard. On the Welcome page of the wizard, click Next.

2. On the Configuration Action page, review the actions you can perform. (See Figure 6-10.) Create A New Security Policy is selected by default. Click Next.

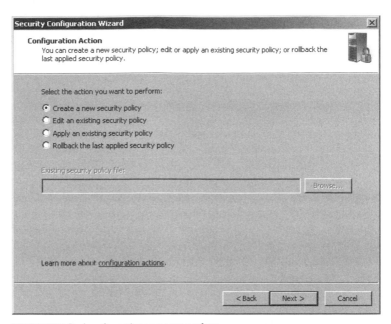

3. On the Select Server page, select the server you want to use as a baseline for this security policy. The baseline server is the server on which the roles, features, and options you want to work with are installed. The currently logged-on computer is selected by default. To choose a different computer, click Browse. In the Select Computer dialog box, type the name of the computer, and then click Check Names. Select the computer account you want to use, and then click OK.

4. When you click Next, the wizard collects the security configuration and stores it in a security configuration database. On the Processing Security Configuration Database page, click View Configuration Database to view the settings in the database. After you review the settings in the SCW Viewer, return to the wizard and click Next to continue.

5. Each configuration section has an introductory page. The first introductory page is the one for Role-Based Service Configuration. Click Next.

6. The Select Server Roles page, shown in Figure 6-11, lists the installed server roles. Select each role that should be enabled. Clear each role that should be disabled. Selecting a role enables services, inbound ports, and settings required for that role. Clearing a role disables services, inbound ports, and settings required for that role, provided that they aren't required by an enabled role. Click Next.

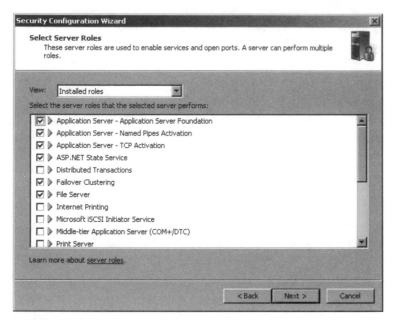

FIGURE 6-11 Select server roles to enable.

7. On the Select Client Features page, you'll see the installed client features used to enable services. Select each feature that should be enabled. Clear each feature that should be disabled. Selecting a feature enables services required for that feature. Clearing a feature disables services required for that feature, provided that they aren't required by an enabled feature. Click Next.

8. On the Select Administration And Other Options page, you'll see the installed options used to enable services and open ports. Select each option that should be enabled. Clear each option that should be disabled. Selecting an option enables services required for that option. Clearing an option disables services required for that option, provided that they aren't required by an enabled option. Click Next.

9. On the Select Additional Services page, you'll see a list of additional services found on the selected server while processing the security configuration database. Select each service that should be enabled. Clear each service that should be disabled. Selecting a service enables services required for that service. Clearing a service disables services required for that service, provided that they aren't required by an enabled service. Click Next.

10. On the Handling Unspecified Services page, indicate how unspecified services should be handled. Unspecified services are services that are not installed on the selected server and are not listed in the security configuration database. By default, the startup mode of unspecified services is not

changed. To disable unspecified services instead, select Disable The Service. Click Next.

11. On the Confirm Service Changes page, review the services that will be changed on the selected server if the security policy is applied. Note the current startup mode and the startup mode that will be applied by the policy. Click Next.

12. On the introductory page for Network Security, click Next. On the Network Security Rules page, you'll see a list of firewall rules needed for the roles, features, and options you previously selected. You can add, edit, or remove inbound and outbound rules using the options provided. Click Next when you are ready to continue.

13. On the introductory page for Registry Settings, click Next. On the Require SMB Security Signatures page, review the SMB security signature options. By default, minimum operating system requirements and digital signing are used, and you won't want to change these settings. Click Next.

14. On the Require LDAP Signing page, you can set minimum operating system requirements for all directory enabled computers that access Active Directory.

15. On the Outbound Authentication Methods page, choose the methods that the selected server uses to authenticate with remote computers. Your choices set the outbound LAN Manager authentication level that will be used. If the computer communicates only with domain computers, select Domain Accounts but do not select the other options. This will ensure that the computer uses the highest level of outbound LAN Manager authentication. If the computer communicates with both domain and workgroup computers, select Domain Accounts and Local Accounts On The Remote Computers. In most cases, you won't want to select the file-sharing option because this will result in a substantially lowered authentication level. Click Next.

16. On the Outbound Authentication Using Domain Accounts page, choose the types of computers from which the selected server will accept connections. Your choices set the inbound LAN Manager authentication level that will be used. If the computer communicates only with Windows XP Professional or later computers, clear both options. This ensures that the computer uses the highest level of inbound LAN Manager authentication. If the computer communicates with older PCs, accept the default selections. Click Next.

17. On the Registry Settings Summary page, review the values that will be changed on the selected server if the security policy is applied. Note the current value and the value that will be applied by the policy. Click Next.

18. On the introductory page for Audit Policy, click Next. On the System Audit Policy page, configure the level of auditing you want. To disable auditing, select Do Not Audit. To enable auditing for successful events, select Audit

Successful Activities. To enable auditing for all events, select Audit Successful And Unsuccessful Activities. Click Next.

19. On the Audit Policy Summary page, review the settings that will be changed on the selected server if the security policy is applied. Note the current setting and the setting that will be applied by the policy. Click Next.

20. On the introductory page for Save Security Policy, click Next. On the Security Policy File Name page, you can configure options for saving the security policy and adding one or more security templates to the policy. To view the security policy in the SCW Viewer, click View Security Policy. When you have finished viewing the policy, return to the wizard.

21. To add security templates to the policy, click Include Security Templates. In the Include Security Templates dialog box, click Add. In the Open dialog box, select a security template to include in the security policy. If you add more than one security template, you can prioritize them in case any security configuration conflicts occur between them. Settings from templates higher in the list have priority. Select a template, and then click the Up and Down buttons to prioritize the templates. Click OK.

22. By default, the security policy is saved in the %SystemRoot%\Security\ Msscw\Policies folder. Click Browse. In the Save As dialog box, select a different save location for the policy if necessary. After you type a name for the security policy, click Save. The default or selected folder path and file name are then listed in the Security Policy File Name text box.

23. Click Next. On the Apply Security Policy page, you can choose to apply the policy now or later. Click Next, and then click Finish.

Editing Security Policies

You can use the Security Configuration Wizard to edit a security policy by following these steps:

1. Start the Security Configuration Wizard by clicking Start, Administrative Tools, and then Security Configuration Wizard. When the wizard starts, click Next.

2. On the Configuration Action page, select Edit An Existing Security Policy, and then click Browse. In the Open dialog box, select the security policy you want to work with, and then click Open. Security policies end with the .xml extension. Click Next.

3. Follow steps 3-23 of the procedure in the section "Creating Security Policies" to edit the configuration of the security policy.

Applying Security Policies

You can use the Security Configuration Wizard to apply a security policy by following these steps:

1. Start the Security Configuration Wizard by clicking Start, Administrative Tools, and then Security Configuration Wizard. When the wizard starts, click Next.

2. On the Configuration Action page, select Apply An Existing Security Policy, and then click Browse. In the Open dialog box, select the security policy you want to work with, and then click Open. Security policies end with the .xml extension. Click Next.

3. On the Select Server page, select the server that you want to apply the security policy to. The currently logged-on computer is selected by default. To choose a different computer, click Browse. In the Select Computer dialog box, type the name of the computer, and then click Check Names. Select the computer account you want to use, and then click OK.

4. Click Next. On the Apply Security Policy page, click View Security Policy to view the security policy in the SCW Viewer. When you have finished viewing the policy, return to the wizard.

5. Click Next to apply the policy to the selected server. When the wizard finishes applying the policy, click Next, and then click Finish.

Rolling Back the Last-Applied Security Policy

You can use the Security Configuration Wizard to roll back the last security policy you applied by following these steps:

1. Start the Security Configuration Wizard by clicking Start, Administrative Tools, and then Security Configuration Wizard. When the wizard starts, click Next.

2. On the Configuration Action page, select Rollback The Last Applied Security Policy, and then click Next.

3. On the Select Server page, select the server on which you want to roll back the last security policy you applied. The currently logged-on computer is selected by default. To choose a different computer, click Browse. In the Select Computer dialog box, type the name of the computer, and then click Check Names. Select the computer account you want to use, and then click OK.

4. Click Next. On the Rollback Security Configuration page, click View Rollback File to view the details of the last-applied security policy in the SCW Viewer. When you have finished viewing the policy, return to the wizard.

5. Click Next to roll back the policy to the selected server. When the wizard finishes the rollback process, click Next, and then click Finish.

Deploying a Security Policy to Multiple Computers

In an organization with many computers, you probably won't want to apply a security policy to each computer separately. As discussed in "Deploying Security Templates to Multiple Computers" earlier in this chapter, you might want to apply a security policy through Group Policy, and you might want to create computer OUs for this purpose.

Once you've created the necessary OUs, you can use the Scwcmd utility's transform command to create a GPO that includes the settings in the security policy (and any security templates attached to the policy). You then deploy the settings to computers by linking the new GPO to the appropriate OU or OUs.

Use the following syntax to transform a security policy:

```
scwcmd transform /p:FullFilePathToSecurityPolicy /g:GPOName
```

where *FullFilePathToSecurityPolicy* is the full file path to the security policy's .xml file, and *GPOName* is the display name for the new GPO. Consider the following example:

```
scwcmd transform /p:"c:\users\wrs\documents\fspolicy.xml"
/g: "FileServer GPO"
```

When you create the GPO, you can link the GPO by following these steps:

1. In the Group Policy Management Console (GPMC), select the OU you want to work with. In the right pane, the Linked Group Policy Objects tab shows the GPOs that are currently linked to the selected OU (if any).

2. Right-click the OU to which you want to link the previously created GPO, and then select Link An Existing GPO. In the Select GPO dialog box, select the GPO you want to link to, and then click OK.

   When Group Policy is refreshed for computers in the applicable OU, the policy settings in the GPO are applied.

Because you created a new GPO and linked the GPO to the appropriate level in the Active Directory structure, you can restore the computers to their original state by removing the link to the GPO. To remove a link to a GPO, follow these steps:

1. In the GPMC, select and then expand the OU you want to work with. In the right pane, the Linked Group Policy Objects tab shows the GPOs that are currently linked to the selected OU.

2. Right-click the GPO. On the shortcut menu, the Link Enabled option should have a check mark to show it is enabled. Clear this option to remove the link.

CHAPTER 7

Using Active Directory

Active Directory Domain Services (AD DS) is an extensible and scalable directory service that you can use to efficiently manage network resources. As an administrator, you need to be deeply familiar with how Active Directory technology works, and that's exactly what this chapter is about. If you haven't worked with Active Directory technology before, you'll notice immediately that the technology is fairly advanced and has many features. To help manage this complex technology, I'll start with an overview of Active Directory and then explore its components.

Introducing Active Directory

Since Windows 2000, Active Directory has been the heart of Windows-based domains. Just about every administrative task you perform affects Active Directory in some way. Active Directory technology is based on standard Internet protocols and is designed to help you clearly define your network's structure.

Active Directory and DNS

Active Directory uses Domain Name System (DNS). DNS is a standard Internet service that organizes groups of computers into domains. DNS domains are organized into a hierarchical structure. The DNS domain hierarchy is defined on an Internet-wide basis, and the different levels within the hierarchy identify computers, organizational domains, and top-level domains. DNS is also used to map host names, such as zeta.microsoft.com, to numeric TCP/IP addresses, such as 192.168.19.2. Through DNS, an Active Directory domain hierarchy can also be defined on an Internet-wide basis, or the domain hierarchy can be separate from the Internet and private.

When you refer to computer resources in a DNS domain, you use a fully qualified domain name (FQDN), such as zeta.microsoft.com. Here, *zeta* represents the name of an individual computer, *microsoft* represents the organizational domain, and *com* is the top-level domain. Top-level domains (TLDs) are at the base of the DNS hierarchy. TLDs are organized geographically by using two-letter country codes, such as *CA* for Canada; by organization type, such as *com* for commercial organizations; and by function, such as *mil* for U.S. military installations.

Normal domains, such as microsoft.com, are also referred to as *parent domains* because they're the parents of an organizational structure. You can divide parent domains into subdomains, which you can then use for different offices, divisions, or geographic locations. For example, the FQDN for a computer at Microsoft's Seattle office could be designated as jacob.seattle.microsoft.com. Here, *jacob* is the computer name, *seattle* is the subdomain, and *microsoft.com* is the parent domain. Another term for a subdomain is a *child domain*.

DNS is an integral part of Active Directory technology—so much so that you must configure DNS on the network before you can install Active Directory. Working with DNS is covered in Chapter 20, "Optimizing DNS."

With Windows Server 2008 R2, you install Active Directory in a two-part process. First you use the Add Roles Wizard to add the Active Directory Domain Services role to the server. Then you run the Active Directory Installation Wizard (click Start, type **dcpromo** in the Search field, and then press Enter). If DNS isn't already installed, you are prompted to install it. If no domain exists, the wizard helps you create a domain and configure Active Directory in the new domain. The wizard can also help you add child domains to existing domain structures. To verify that a domain controller is installed correctly, you can:

- Check the Directory Service event log for errors.
- Ensure that the SYSVOL folder is accessible to clients.
- Verify that name resolution is working through DNS.
- Verify the replication of changes to Active Directory.

NOTE In the rest of this chapter, I'll use the terms *directory* and *domains* to refer to Active Directory and Active Directory domains, respectively, except when I need to distinguish Active Directory structures from DNS or other types of directories.

Read-Only Domain Controller Deployment

As discussed in Chapter 1, "Windows Server 2008 R2 Administration Overview," domain controllers running Windows Server 2008 R2 can be configured as read-only domain controllers (RODCs). When you install the DNS Server service on an

RODC, the RODC can act as a read-only DNS (RODNS) server. In this configuration, the following conditions are true:

- The RODC replicates the application directory partitions that DNS uses, including the ForestDNSZones and DomainDNSZones partitions. Clients can query an RODNS server for name resolution. However, the RODNS server does not support client updates directly because the RODNS server does not register resource records for any Active Directory–integrated zone that it hosts.

- When a client attempts to update its DNS records, the server returns a referral. The client can then attempt to update against the DNS server that is provided in the referral. Through replication in the background, the RODNS server then attempts to retrieve the updated record from the DNS server that made the update. This replication request is only for the changed DNS record. The entire list of data changed in the zone or domain is not replicated during this special request.

The first Windows Server 2008 R2 domain controller installed in a forest or domain cannot be an RODC. However, you can configure subsequent domain controllers as read-only. For planning purposes, keep the following in mind:

- Prior to adding AD DS to a server that is running Windows Server 2008 R2 in a Windows Server 2003 or Windows 2000 Server forest, you must update the schema on the schema operations master in the forest by running adprep /forestprep.

- Prior to adding AD DS to a server that is running Windows Server 2008 R2 in a Windows Server 2003 or Windows 2000 Server domain, you must update the infrastructure master in the domain by running adprep /domainprep /gpprep.

- Prior to installing AD DS to create your first RODC in a forest, you must prepare the forest by running adprep /rodcprep.

New Active Directory Features

Active Directory Domain Service in Windows Server 2008 R2 has many new features that give administrators additional options for implementing and managing Active Directory. When you are using Windows Server 2008 R2 and have deployed the operating system on all domain controllers throughout the domains in your Active Directory forest, your domains can operate at the Windows Server 2008 R2 domain functional level, and the forest can operate at the Windows Server 2008 R2 forest functional level. These operating levels allow you to take advantage of Active Directory enhancements that improve manageability, performance, and supportability, including the following:

- **Active Directory Recycle Bin** Allows administrators to undo the accidental deletion of Active Directory objects in much the same way as they can recover deleted files from the Windows Recycle Bin. For more information, see "Using the Active Directory Recycle Bin" later in this chapter.

- **Managed service accounts** Introduces a special type of domain user account for managed services that reduces service outages and other issues by having Windows manage the account password and related Service Principal Names (SPNs) automatically. For more information, see "Implementing Managed Accounts" in Chapter 10.

- **Managed virtual accounts** Introduces a special type of local computer account for managed services that provides the ability to access the network with a computer identity in a domain environment. For more information, see "Using Virtual Accounts" in Chapter 10.

REAL WORLD Technically, you can use managed service accounts and managed virtual accounts in a mixed-mode domain environment. However, you must update the Active Directory schema for Windows Server 2008 R2 and you have to manually manage SPNs for managed service accounts.

- **Authentication Mechanism Assurance** Improves the authentication process by allowing administrators to control resource access based on whether a user logs on using a certificate-based logon method. Thus, an administrator can specify that a user has one set of access permissions when logged on using a smart card and a different set of access permissions when not logged on using a smart card.

Other improvements don't require that you raise domain or forest functional levels, but they do require that you use Windows Server 2008 R2. These include:

- **Offline domain join** Allows administrators to preprovision computer accounts in the domain to prepare operating systems for deployment. This allows computers to join a domain without having to contact a domain controller.

- **Active Directory module for Windows PowerShell** Provides cmdlets for managing Active Directory when you are working with Windows PowerShell. A related option is on the Administrative Tools menu.

- **Active Directory Administrative Center** Provides a task-orientated interface for managing Active Directory. A related option is on the Administrative Tools menu.

- **Active Directory Web Services** Introduces a Web service interface for Active Directory domains.

These features are discussed in more detail in Chapter 8, "Core Active Directory Administration." Also keep in mind that you must prepare Active Directory schema for the Active Directory Recycle Bin. The preparation procedures are the same as those discussed for RODCs in the previous section.

Working with Domain Structures

Active Directory provides both logical and physical structures for network components. Logical structures help you organize directory objects and manage network accounts and shared resources. Logical structures include the following:

- **Organizational units**   A subgroup of domains that often mirrors the organization's business or functional structure.
- **Domains**   A group of computers that share a common directory database.
- **Domain trees**   One or more domains that share a contiguous namespace.
- **Domain forests**   One or more domain trees that share common directory information.

Physical structures serve to facilitate network communication and to set physical boundaries around network resources. Physical structures that help you map the physical network structure include the following:

- **Subnets**   A network group with a specific IP address range and network mask.
- **Sites**   One or more subnets. Sites are used to configure directory access and replication.

Understanding Domains

An Active Directory domain is simply a group of computers that share a common directory database. Active Directory domain names must be unique. For example, you can't have two microsoft.com domains, but you can have a parent domain microsoft.com, with the child domains seattle.microsoft.com and ny.microsoft.com. If the domain is part of a private network, the name assigned to a new domain must not conflict with any existing domain name on the private network. If the domain is part of the Internet, the name assigned to a new domain must not conflict with any existing domain name throughout the Internet. To ensure uniqueness on the Internet, you must register the parent domain name before using it. You can register a domain through any designated registrar. You can find a current list of designated registrars at InterNIC (*www.internic.net*).

Each domain has its own security policies and trust relationships with other domains. Domains can also span more than one physical location, which means that a domain can consist of multiple sites and those sites can have multiple subnets, as shown in Figure 7-1. Within a domain's directory database, you'll find objects defining accounts for users, groups, and computers as well as shared resources such as printers and folders.

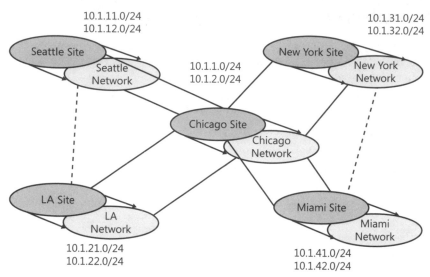

FIGURE 7-1 This network diagram depicts a wide area network (WAN) with multiple sites and subnets.

NOTE User and group accounts are discussed in Chapter 9, "Understanding User and Group Accounts." Computer accounts and the various types of computers used in Windows Server 2008 R2 domains are discussed in "Working with Active Directory Domains" later in this chapter.

Domain functions are limited and controlled by the domain functional level. Several domain functional levels are available, including the following:

- **Windows Server 2003** Supports domain controllers running Windows Server 2003, Windows Server 2008, and Windows Server 2008 R2.

- **Windows Server 2008** Supports domain controllers running Windows Server 2008 and Windows Server 2008 R2.

- **Windows Server 2008 R2** Supports domain controllers running Windows Server 2008 R2.

For further discussion of domain functional levels, see "Working with Domain Functional Levels" later in this chapter.

Understanding Domain Forests and Domain Trees

Each Active Directory domain has a DNS domain name, such as microsoft.com. One or more domains sharing the same directory data are referred to as a *forest*. The domain names within this forest can be discontiguous or contiguous in the DNS naming hierarchy.

When domains have a contiguous naming structure, they're said to be in the same *domain tree*. Figure 7-2 shows an example of a domain tree. In this example, the root domain msnbc.com has two child domains—seattle.msnbc.com and ny.msnbc.com. These domains in turn have subdomains. All the domains are part of the same tree because they have the same root domain.

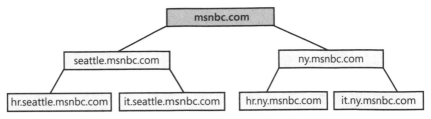

FIGURE 7-2 Domains in the same tree share a contiguous naming structure.

If the domains in a forest have discontiguous DNS names, they form separate domain trees within the forest. As shown in Figure 7-3, a domain forest can have one or more domain trees. In this example, the msnbc.com and microsoft.com domains form the roots of separate domain trees in the same forest.

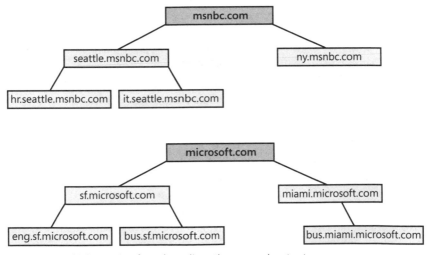

FIGURE 7-3 Multiple trees in a forest have discontiguous naming structures.

You can access domain structures by using Active Directory Domains And Trusts, shown in Figure 7-4. Active Directory Domains And Trusts is a snap-in for the Microsoft Management Console (MMC). You can also start it from the Administrative Tools menu. You'll find separate entries for each root domain. In Figure 7-4, the active domain is cpandl.com.

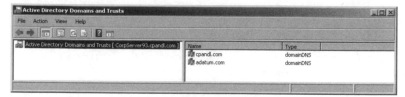

FIGURE 7-4 Use Active Directory Domains And Trusts to work with domains, domain trees, and domain forests.

Forest functions are limited and controlled by the forest functional level. Several forest functional levels are available, including:

- **Windows Server 2003** Supports domain controllers running Windows Server 2003, Windows Server 2008, and Windows Server 2008 R2.

- **Windows Server 2008** Supports domain controllers running Windows Server 2008 and Windows Server 2008 R2.

- **Windows Server 2008 R2** Supports domain controllers running Windows Server 2008 and Windows Server 2008 R2.

When all domains within a forest are operating in Windows Server 2003 forest functional level, you'll see improvements over earlier implementations in global catalog replication and replication efficiency. Because link values are replicated, you might see improved intersite replication as well. You can deactivate schema class objects and attributes; use dynamic auxiliary classes; rename domains; and create one-way, two-way, and transitive forest trusts.

The Windows Server 2008 forest functional level offers incremental improve-ments over the Windows Server 2003 forest functional level in Active Directory per-formance and features. When all domains within a forest are operating in this mode, you'll see improvements in both intersite and intrasite replication throughout the organization. Domain controllers can use Distributed File System (DFS) replication rather than File Replication Service (FRS) replication as well. In addition, Windows Server 2008 security principals are not created until the primary domain controller (PDC) emulator operations master in the forest root domain is running Windows Server 2008.

The Windows Server 2008 R2 forest functional level has several new features. These features include the Active Directory Recycle Bin, managed service accounts, and Authentication Mechanism Assurance.

Understanding Organizational Units

Organizational units (OUs) are subgroups within domains that often mirror an organization's functional or business structure. You can also think of OUs as logi-cal containers into which you place accounts, shared resources, and other OUs. For example, you could create OUs named HumanResources, IT, Engineering, and

Marketing for the microsoft.com domain. You could later expand this scheme to include child units. Child OUs for Marketing could include OnlineSales, Channel-Sales, and PrintSales.

Objects placed in an OU can only come from the parent domain. For example, OUs associated with seattle.microsoft.com can contain objects for this domain only. You can't add objects from ny.microsoft.com to these containers, but you could create separate OUs to mirror the business structure of seattle.microsoft.com.

OUs are helpful in organizing objects to reflect a business or functional structure. Still, this isn't the only reason to use OUs. Other reasons include:

- OUs allow you to assign group policies to a small set of resources in a domain without applying the policies to the entire domain. This helps you set and manage group policies at the appropriate level in the enterprise.

- OUs create smaller, more manageable views of directory objects in a domain. This helps you manage resources more efficiently.

- OUs allow you to delegate authority and to easily control administrative access to domain resources. This helps you control the scope of administrator privileges in the domain. You could grant user A administrative authority for one OU and not for others. Meanwhile, you could grant user B administrative authority for all OUs in the domain.

OUs are represented as folders in Active Directory Users And Computers, as shown in Figure 7-5. This utility is a snap-in for the MMC, and you can also start it from the Administrative Tools menu.

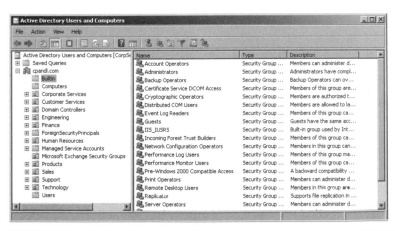

FIGURE 7-5 Use Active Directory Users And Computers to manage users, groups, computers, and organizational units.

Understanding Sites and Subnets

A site is a group of computers in one or more IP subnets. You use sites to map your network's physical structure. Site mappings are independent of logical domain structures, so there's no necessary relationship between a network's physical structure and its logical domain structure. With Active Directory, you can create multiple sites within a single domain or create a single site that serves multiple domains. The IP address ranges used by a site and the domain namespace also have no connection.

You can think of a subnet as a group of network addresses. Unlike sites, which can have multiple IP address ranges, subnets have a specific IP address range and network mask. Subnet names are shown in the form *network/bits-masked*, such as 192.168.19.0/24. Here, the network address 192.168.19.9 and network mask 255.255.255.0 are combined to create the subnet name 192.168.19.0/24.

NOTE Don't worry, you don't need to know how to create a subnet name. In most cases you enter the network address and the network mask, and then Windows Server 2008 R2 generates the subnet name for you.

Computers are assigned to sites based on their location in a subnet or a set of subnets. If computers in subnets can communicate efficiently with one another over the network, they're said to be *well connected*. Ideally, sites consist of subnets and computers that are all well connected. If the subnets and computers aren't well connected, you might need to set up multiple sites. Being well connected gives sites several advantages:

- When clients log on to a domain, the authentication process first searches for domain controllers that are in the same site as the client. This means that local domain controllers are used first, if possible, which localizes network traffic and can speed up the authentication process.

- Directory information is replicated more frequently within sites than between sites. This reduces the network traffic load caused by replication while ensuring that local domain controllers get up-to-date information quickly. You can also use site links to customize how directory information is replicated between sites. A domain controller designated to perform intersite replication is called a *bridgehead server*. By designating a bridgehead server to handle replication between sites, you place the bulk of the intersite replication burden on a specific server rather than on any available server in a site.

You access sites and subnets through Active Directory Sites And Services, shown in Figure 7-6. Because this is a snap-in for the MMC, you can add it to any updateable console. You can also open Active Directory Sites And Services from the Administrative Tools menu.

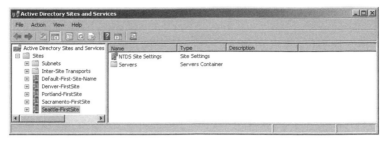

FIGURE 7-6 Use Active Directory Sites And Services to manage sites and subnets.

Working with Active Directory Domains

Although you must configure both Active Directory and DNS on a Windows Server 2008 R2 network, Active Directory domains and DNS domains have different purposes. Active Directory domains help you manage accounts, resources, and security. DNS domains establish a domain hierarchy that is primarily used for name resolution. Windows Server 2008 R2 uses DNS to map host names, such as zeta.microsoft.com, to numeric TCP/IP addresses, such as 172.16.18.8. To learn more about DNS and DNS domains, see Chapter 20.

Using Windows 2000 and Later Computers with Active Directory

User computers running professional or business editions of Windows 2000, Windows XP, Windows Vista, or Windows 7 can make full use of Active Directory. These computers access the network as Active Directory clients and have full use of Active Directory features. As clients, these systems can use transitive trust relationships that exist within the domain tree or forest. A transitive trust is one that isn't established explicitly. Rather, the trust is established automatically based on the forest structure and permissions set in the forest. These relationships allow authorized users to access resources in any domain in the forest.

Server computers running Windows 2000 Server, Windows Server 2003, and Windows Server 2008 or later provide services to other systems and can act as domain controllers or member servers. A domain controller is distinguished from a member server because it runs Active Directory Domain Services. You promote member servers to domain controllers by installing Active Directory Domain Services. You demote domain controllers to member servers by uninstalling Active Directory Domain Services. You use the Add Role and Remove Role wizards to add or remove Active Directory Domain Services. You promote or demote a server through the Active Directory Installation Wizard (Dcpromo.exe).

Domains can have one or more domain controllers. When a domain has multiple domain controllers, the controllers automatically replicate directory data with one another using a multimaster replication model. This model allows any domain controller to process directory changes and then replicate those changes to other domain controllers.

Because of the multimaster domain structure, all domain controllers have equal responsibility by default. You can, however, give some domain controllers precedence over others for certain tasks, such as specifying a bridgehead server that has priority in replicating directory information to other sites. In addition, some tasks are best performed by a single server. A server that handles this type of task is called an *operations master*. There are five flexible single master operations (FSMO) roles, and you can assign each to a different domain controller. For more information, see "Understanding Operations Master Roles" later in this chapter.

Every Windows 2000 or later computer that joins a domain has a computer account. Like other resources, computer accounts are stored in Active Directory as objects. You use computer accounts to control access to the network and its resources. A computer accesses a domain by using its account, which is authenticated before the computer can access the network.

REAL WORLD   Domain controllers use Active Directory's global catalog to authenticate both computer and user logons. If the global catalog is unavailable, only members of the Domain Admins group can log on to the domain because the universal group membership information is stored in the global catalog, and this information is required for authentication. In Windows Server 2003 and later servers, you have the option of caching universal group membership locally, which solves this problem. For more information, see "Understanding the Directory Structure" later in this chapter.

Working with Domain Functional Levels

To support domain structures, Active Directory includes support for several domain functional levels, including:

- **Windows Server 2003 mode**   When the domain is operating in Windows Server 2003 mode, the directory supports domain controllers running Windows Server 2008 R2, Windows Server 2008, and Windows Server 2003. Windows NT and Windows 2000 domain controllers are no longer supported. A domain operating in Windows Server 2003 mode can use universal groups, group nesting, group type conversion, easy domain controller renaming, update logon time stamps, and Kerberos KDC key version numbers.

- **Windows Server 2008 mode**   When the domain is operating in Windows Server 2008 mode, the directory supports Windows Server 2008 and Windows Server 2008 R2 domain controllers. Windows NT, Windows 2000, and Windows Server 2003 domain controllers are no longer supported. The good news is that a domain operating in Windows Server 2008 mode can use additional Active Directory features, including the DFS replication service for enhanced intersite and intrasite replication.

- **Windows Server 2008 R2 mode**   When the domain is operating in Windows Server 2008 R2 mode, the directory supports only Windows Server 2008 R2 domain controllers. Windows NT, Windows 2000, Windows Server 2003, and Windows Server 2008 domain controllers are no longer supported. The good news is that a domain operating in Windows Server 2008 R2 mode can use all the latest Active Directory features, including the Active Directory Recycle Bin.

Using Windows Server 2003 Functional Level

After you upgrade the Windows NT structures in your organization, you can begin upgrading to Windows Server 2003 domain structures by upgrading Windows 2000 domain controllers to Windows Server 2003 or Windows Server 2008 domain controllers. Then, if you want to, you can change the functional level to Windows Server 2003 mode operations. Note that since Windows Server 2008 R2 runs only on 64-bit hardware, you'll likely need to install Windows Server 2008 R2 on new hardware rather than hardware designed for Windows NT, Windows 2000, or Windows Server 2003.

Before updating Windows 2000 domain controllers, you should prepare the domain for upgrade. To do this, you need to update the forest and the domain schema so that they are compatible with Windows Server 2003 domains. A tool called Adprep.exe is provided to automatically perform the update for you. All you need to do is run the tool on the schema operations master in the forest and then on the infrastructure operations master for each domain in the forest. As always, you should test any procedure in a lab before performing it in a production environment. On Windows Server 2003 installation media, you'll find Adprep in the i386 subfolder.

NOTE   To determine which server is the current schema operations master for the domain, open a command prompt and type **dsquery server –hasfsmo schema**. A directory service path string is returned containing the name of the server, such as "CN=CORPSERVER01,CN=Servers,CN=Default-First-Site-Name,CN=Sites, CN=Configuration,DC=microsoft,DC=com." This string tells you that the schema operations master is CORPSERVER01 in the microsoft.com domain.

NOTE   To determine which server is the current infrastructure operations master for the domain, start a command prompt and type **dsquery server –hasfsmo infr**.

After upgrading your servers, you can raise the domain and forest level functionality to take advantage of the latest Active Directory features. If you do this, you can use only Windows Server 2003, Windows Server 2008, and Windows Server 2008 R2 resources in the domain and you can't go back to any other mode. You should use Windows Server 2003 mode only when you're certain that you don't need old Windows NT domain structures, Windows NT backup domain controllers (BDCs), or Windows 2000 domain structures.

Using Windows Server 2008 Functional Level

After you upgrade the Windows NT and Windows 2000 structures in your organization, you can begin upgrading to Windows Server 2008 domain structures by upgrading Windows Server 2003 domain controllers to Windows Server 2008 or Windows Server 2008 R2 domain controllers. Then, if you want to, you can change the functional level to Windows Server 2008 mode operations.

Before updating Windows Server 2003 domain controllers, you should prepare the domain for Windows Server 2008. To do this, you need to use Adprep.exe to update the forest and the domain schema so that they are compatible with Windows Server 2008 domains. Follow these steps:

1. On the schema operations master in the forest, copy the contents of the Sources\Adprep folder from the Windows Server 20008 installation media to a local folder, and then run **adprep /forestprep**. If you plan to install any read-only domain controllers, you should also run **adprep /rodcprep**. You need to use an administrator account that is a member of Enterprise Admins, Schema Admins, or Domain Admins in the forest root domain.

2. On the infrastructure operations master for each domain in the forest, copy the contents of the Sources\Adprep folder from the Windows Server 2008 installation media to a local folder, and then run **adprep /domainprep /gpprep**. You need to use an account that is a member of the Domain Admins group in an applicable domain.

As always, you should test any procedure in a lab before performing it in a production environment.

> **NOTE** To determine which server is the current schema operations master for the domain, start a command prompt and type **dsquery server –hasfsmo schema**. To determine which server is the current infrastructure operations master for the domain, start a command prompt and type **dsquery server –hasfsmo infr**.

After upgrading all domain controllers to Windows Server 2008, you can raise the domain and forest level functionality to take advantage of additional Active Directory features. If you do this, you can use only Windows Server 2008 or later resources in the domain and you can't go back to any other mode. You should use Windows Server 2008 mode only when you're certain that you don't need old Windows NT domain structures, Windows NT BDCs, or Windows 2000 or Windows Server 2003 domain structures.

Using Windows Server 2008 R2 Functional Level

Windows Server 2008 R2 runs only on 64-bit hardware. You'll likely need to install Windows Server 2008 R2 on new hardware rather than on hardware designed for Windows NT, Windows 2000, or Windows Server 2003.

Before updating Windows Server 2008 domain controllers, you should prepare the domain for Windows Server 2008 R2. To do this, you need to use Adprep.exe to update the forest and the domain schema so that they are compatible with Windows Server 2008 R2 domains. Follow these steps:

1. On the schema operations master in the forest, copy the contents of the Support\Adprep folder from the Windows Server 2008 R2 installation media to a local folder, and then run **adprep /forestprep**. If you plan to install any read-only domain controllers, you should also run **adprep /rodcprep**. You need to use an administrator account that is a member of Enterprise Admins, Schema Admins, or Domain Admins in the forest root domain.

2. On the infrastructure operations master for each domain in the forest, copy the contents of the Support\Adprep folder from the Windows Server 2008 R2 installation media to a local folder, and then run **adprep /domainprep /gpprep**. You need to use an account that is a member of the Domain Admins group in an applicable domain.

As always, you should test any procedure in a lab before performing it in a production environment.

NOTE To determine which server is the current schema operations master for the domain, start a command prompt and type **dsquery server –hasfsmo schema**. To determine which server is the current infrastructure operations master for the domain, start a command prompt and type **dsquery server –hasfsmo infr**.

After upgrading all domain controllers to Windows Server 2008 R2, you can raise the domain and forest level functionality to take advantage of the latest Active Directory features. If you do this, you can use only Windows Server 2008 R2 resources in the domain and you can't go back to any other mode. You should use Windows Server 2008 R2 mode only when you're certain that you don't need old Windows NT domain structures; Windows NT BDCs; or Windows 2000, Windows Server 2003, or Windows Server 2008 domain structures.

Raising Domain and Forest Functionality

Domains operating in Windows Server 2003 or higher functional level can use universal groups, group nesting, group type conversion, update logon time stamps, and Kerberos KDC key version numbers. In this mode or higher, administrators can do the following:

- Rename domain controllers without having to demote them first
- Rename domains running on Windows Server 2003 or higher domain controllers

- Create extended two-way trusts between two forests
- Restructure domains in the domain hierarchy by renaming them and putting them at different levels
- Take advantage of replication enhancements for individual group members and global catalogs

As compared to earlier implementations, forests operating in Windows Server 2003 or higher functional level have better global catalog replication and intrasite and intersite replication efficiency, as well as the ability to establish one-way, two-way, and transitive forest trusts.

REAL WORLD The domain and forest upgrade process can generate a lot of network traffic as information is being replicated around the network. Sometimes the entire upgrade process can take 15 minutes or longer. During this time you might experience delayed responsiveness when communicating with servers and higher latency on the network, so you might want to schedule the upgrade outside normal business hours. It's also a good idea to thoroughly test compatibility with existing applications (especially legacy applications) before performing this operation.

You can raise the domain level functionality by following these steps:

1. Click Start, point to Administrative Tools, and then click Active Directory Domains And Trusts.

2. In the console tree, right-click the domain you want to work with, and then click Raise Domain Functional Level.

   The current domain name and functional level are displayed in the Raise Domain Functional Level dialog box.

3. To change the domain functionality, select the new domain functional level from the list provided, and then click Raise. You can't reverse this action. Consider the implications carefully before you do this.

4. Click OK. The new domain functional level is replicated to each domain controller in the domain. This operation can take some time in a large organization.

You can raise the forest level functionality by following these steps:

1. Click Start, point to Administrative Tools, and then click Active Directory Domains And Trusts.

2. In the console tree, right-click the Active Directory Domains And Trusts node, and then click Raise Forest Functional Level.

   The current forest name and functional level are displayed in the Raise Forest Functional Level dialog box.

3. To change the forest functionality, select the new forest functional level by using the list provided, and then click Raise. You can't reverse this action. Consider the implications carefully before you do this.

4. Click OK. The new forest functional level is replicated to each domain controller in each domain in the forest. This operation can take some time in a large organization.

Understanding the Directory Structure

Active Directory has many components and is built on many technologies. Directory data is made available to users and computers through data stores and global catalogs. Although most Active Directory tasks affect the data store, global catalogs are equally important because they're used during logon and for information searches. In fact, if the global catalog is unavailable, standard users can't log on to the domain. The only way to change this behavior is to cache universal group membership locally. As you might expect, caching universal group membership has advantages and disadvantages, which I'll discuss in a moment.

You access and distribute Active Directory data by using directory access protocols and replication. Directory access protocols allow clients to communicate with computers running Active Directory. Replication is necessary to ensure that updates to data are distributed to domain controllers. Although multimaster replication is the primary technique that you use to distribute updates, some changes to data can be handled only by individual domain controllers called *operations masters*. A feature of Windows Server 2008 called *application directory partitions* also changes the way multimaster replication works.

With application directory partitions, enterprise administrators (those belonging to the Enterprise Admins group) can create replication partitions in the domain forest. These partitions are logical structures used to control replication of data within a domain forest. For example, you could create a partition to strictly control the replication of DNS information within a domain, thereby preventing other systems in the domain from replicating DNS information.

An application directory partition can appear as a child of a domain, a child of another application partition, or a new tree in the domain forest. Replicas of the application directory partition can be made available on any Active Directory domain controller running Windows Server 2008 or Windows Server 2008 R2, including global catalog servers. Although application directory partitions are useful in large domains and forests, they add overhead in terms of planning, administration, and maintenance.

Exploring the Data Store

The data store contains information about objects such as accounts, shared resources, OUs, and group policies. Another name for the data store is the *directory*, which refers to Active Directory itself.

Domain controllers store the directory in a file called Ntds.dit. This file's location is set when Active Directory is installed, and it should be on an NTFS file system drive formatted for use with Windows Server 2008 or later. You can also save directory data separately from the main data store. This is true for group policies, scripts, and other types of public information stored on the shared system volume (SYSVOL).

Sharing directory information is called *publishing*. For example, you publish information about a printer by sharing the printer over the network. Similarly, you publish information about a folder by sharing the folder over the network.

Domain controllers replicate most changes to the data store in multimaster fashion. Administrators for small or medium-size organizations rarely need to manage replication of the data store. Replication is handled automatically, but you can customize it to meet the needs of large organizations or organizations with special requirements.

Not all directory data is replicated. Instead, only public information that falls into one of the following three categories is replicated:

- **Domain data**   Contains information about objects within a domain. This includes objects for accounts, shared resources, organizational units, and group policies.
- **Configuration data**   Describes the directory's topology. This includes a list of all domains, domain trees, and forests, as well as the locations of the domain controllers and global catalog servers.
- **Schema data**   Describes all objects and data types that can be stored in the directory. The default schema provided with Windows Server 2008 R2 describes account objects, shared resource objects, and more. You can extend the default schema by defining new objects and attributes or by adding attributes to existing objects.

Exploring Global Catalogs

When universal group membership isn't cached locally, global catalogs enable network logon by providing universal group membership information when a logon process is initiated. Global catalogs also enable directory searches throughout the domains in a forest. A domain controller designated as a global catalog stores a full replica of all objects in the directory for its host domain and a partial replica for all other domains in the domain forest.

NOTE   Partial replicas are used because only certain object properties are needed for logon and search operations. Partial replication also means that less information needs to be circulated on the network, reducing the amount of network traffic.

By default, the first domain controller installed on a domain is designated as the global catalog. If only one domain controller is in the domain, the domain controller and the global catalog are the same server. Otherwise, the global catalog is on the domain controller that you've configured as such. You can also add global catalogs to a domain to help improve response time for logon and search requests. The recommended technique is to have one global catalog per site within a domain.

Domain controllers hosting the global catalog should be well connected to domain controllers acting as infrastructure masters. The role of infrastructure master is one of the five operations master roles that you can assign to a domain controller. In a domain, the infrastructure master is responsible for updating object references. The infrastructure master does this by comparing its data with that of a global catalog. If the infrastructure master finds outdated data, it requests updated data from a global catalog. The infrastructure master then replicates the changes to the other domain controllers in the domain. For more information on operations master roles, see "Understanding Operations Master Roles" later in this chapter.

When only one domain controller is in a domain, you can assign the infrastructure master role and the global catalog to the same domain controller. When two or more domain controllers are in the domain, however, the global catalog and the infrastructure master must be on separate domain controllers. If they aren't, the infrastructure master won't find out-of-date data and will never replicate changes. The only exception is when all domain controllers in the domain host the global catalog. In this case, it doesn't matter which domain controller serves as the infrastructure master.

One of the key reasons to configure additional global catalogs in a domain is to ensure that a catalog is available to service logon and directory search requests. Again, if the domain has only one global catalog and the catalog isn't available, and there's no local caching of universal group membership, standard users can't log on and those who are logged on can't search the directory. In this scenario, the only users who can log on to the domain when the global catalog is unavailable are members of the Domain Admins group.

Searches in the global catalog are very efficient. The catalog contains information about objects in all domains in the forest. This allows directory search requests to be resolved in a local domain rather than in a domain in another part of the network. Resolving queries locally reduces the network load and allows for quicker responses in most cases.

> **TIP** If you notice slow logon or query response times, you might want to configure additional global catalogs. But more global catalogs usually means more replication data being transferred over the network.

Universal Group Membership Caching

In a large organization, having global catalogs at every office location might not be practical. Not having global catalogs at every office location presents a problem, however, if a remote office loses connectivity with the main office or a designated branch office where global catalog servers reside. If this occurs, standard users won't be able to log on; only members of Domain Admins will be able to log on.

This happens because logon requests must be routed over the network to a global catalog server at a different office, and this isn't possible with no connectivity.

As you might expect, you can resolve this problem in many ways. You can make one of the domain controllers at the remote office a global catalog server by following the procedure discussed in "Configuring Global Catalogs" in Chapter 8. The disadvantage of this approach is that the designated server or servers will have an additional burden placed on them and might require additional resources. You also have to manage more carefully the up time of the global catalog server.

Another way to resolve this problem is to cache universal group membership locally. Here, any domain controller can resolve logon requests locally without having to go through a global catalog server. This allows for faster logons and makes managing server outages much easier because your domain isn't relying on a single server or a group of servers for logons. This solution also reduces replication traffic. Instead of replicating the entire global catalog periodically over the network, only the universal group membership information in the cache is refreshed. By default, a refresh occurs every eight hours on each domain controller that's caching membership locally.

Universal group membership caching is site-specific. Remember, a site is a physical directory structure consisting of one or more subnets with a specific IP address range and network mask. The domain controllers running Windows Server and the global catalog they're contacting must be in the same site. If you have multiple sites, you need to configure local caching in each site. Additionally, users in the site must be part of a Windows domain running in Windows Server 2003 or higher functional mode. To learn how to configure caching, see "Configuring Universal Group Membership Caching" in Chapter 8.

Replication and Active Directory

Regardless of whether you use FRS or DFS replication, the three types of information stored in the directory are domain data, schema data, and configuration data.

Domain data is replicated to all domain controllers within a particular domain. Schema and configuration data are replicated to all domains in the domain tree or forest. In addition, all objects in an individual domain and a subset of object properties in the domain forest are replicated to global catalogs.

This means that domain controllers store and replicate the following:

- Schema information for the domain tree or forest
- Configuration information for all domains in the domain tree or forest
- All directory objects and properties for their respective domains

However, domain controllers hosting a global catalog store and replicate schema information for the forest, configuration information for all domains in the forest, a subset of the properties for all directory objects in the forest that's replicated only between servers hosting global catalogs, and all directory objects and properties for their respective domain.

To get a better understanding of replication, consider the following scenario, in which you're installing a new network:

1. Start by installing the first domain controller in domain A. The server is the only domain controller and also hosts the global catalog. No replication occurs because no other domain controllers are on the network.

2. Install a second domain controller in domain A. Because there are now two domain controllers, replication begins. To make sure that data is replicated properly, assign one domain controller as the infrastructure master and the other as the global catalog. The infrastructure master watches for updates to the global catalog and requests updates to changed objects. The two domain controllers also replicate schema and configuration data.

3. Install a third domain controller in domain A. This server isn't a global catalog. The infrastructure master watches for updates to the global catalog, requests updates to changed objects, and then replicates those changes to the third domain controller. The three domain controllers also replicate schema and configuration data.

4. Install a new domain, domain B, and add domain controllers to it. The global catalog hosts in domain A and domain B begin replicating all schema and configuration data as well as a subset of the domain data in each domain. Replication within domain A continues as previously described. Replication within domain B begins.

Active Directory and LDAP

The Lightweight Directory Access Protocol (LDAP) is a standard Internet communications protocol for TCP/IP networks. LDAP is designed specifically for accessing directory services with the least amount of overhead. LDAP also defines operations that can be used to query and modify directory information.

Active Directory clients use LDAP to communicate with computers running Active Directory whenever they log on to the network or search for shared resources. You can also use LDAP to manage Active Directory.

LDAP is an open standard that many other directory services use. This makes interdirectory communications easier and provides a clearer migration path from other directory services to Active Directory. You can also use Active Directory Service Interface (ADSI) to enhance interoperability. ADSI supports the standard application programming interfaces (APIs) for LDAP that are specified in Internet standard Request for Comments (RFC) 1823. You can use ADSI with Windows Script Host to create and manage objects in Active Directory.

Understanding Operations Master Roles

Operations master roles accomplish tasks that are impractical to perform in multi-master fashion. Five operations master roles are defined, and you can assign these roles to one or more domain controllers. Although certain roles can be assigned only once in a domain forest, other roles must be defined once in each domain.

Every Active Directory forest must have the following roles:

- **Schema master** Controls updates and modifications to directory schema. To update directory schema, you must have access to the schema master. To determine which server is the current schema master for the domain, start a command prompt and type **dsquery server –hasfsmo schema**.

- **Domain naming master** Controls the addition or removal of domains in the forest. To add or remove domains, you must have access to the domain naming master. To determine which server is the current domain naming master for the domain, start a command prompt and type **dsquery server –hasfsmo name**.

These forestwide roles must be unique in the forest. This means that you can assign only one schema master and one domain naming master in a forest.

Every Active Directory domain must have the following roles:

- **Relative ID master** Allocates relative IDs to domain controllers. Whenever you create a user, group, or computer object, domain controllers assign a unique security ID to the related object. The security ID consists of the domain's security ID prefix and a unique relative ID allocated by the relative ID master. To determine which server is the current relative ID master for the domain, start a command prompt and type **dsquery server –hasfsmo rid**.

- **PDC emulator** When you use mixed-mode or interim-mode operations, the PDC emulator acts as a Windows NT PDC. Its job is to authenticate Windows NT logons, process password changes, and replicate updates to BDCs. The PDC emulator is the default time server, and as such also performs time synchronization in a domain. To determine which server is the current PDC emulator master for the domain, start a command prompt and type **dsquery server –hasfsmo pdc**.

- **Infrastructure master** Updates object references by comparing its directory data with that of a global catalog. If the data is outdated, the infrastructure master requests updated data from a global catalog and then replicates the changes to the other domain controllers in the domain. To determine which server is the current infrastructure operations master for the domain, start a command prompt and type **dsquery server –hasfsmo infr**.

These domainwide roles must be unique in each domain. This means that you can assign only one relative ID master, one PDC emulator, and one infrastructure master in each domain.

Operations master roles are usually assigned automatically, but you can reassign them. When you install a new network, the first domain controller in the first domain is assigned all the operations master roles. If you later create a child domain or a root domain in a new tree, the first domain controller in the new domain is automatically assigned operations master roles as well. In a new domain forest, the domain controller is assigned all operations master roles. If the new domain is in the same forest, the assigned roles are relative ID master, PDC emulator, and infrastructure master. The schema master and domain naming master roles remain in the first domain in the forest.

When a domain has only one domain controller, that computer handles all the operations master roles. If you're working with a single site, the default operations master locations should be sufficient. As you add domain controllers and domains, however, you'll probably want to move the operations master roles to other domain controllers.

When a domain has two or more domain controllers, you should configure two domain controllers to handle operations master roles. Here, you would make one domain controller the operations master, and you would designate the second as your standby operations master. The standby operations master could then be used if the primary one fails. Be sure that the domain controllers are direct replication partners and are well connected.

As the domain structure grows, you might want to split up the operations master roles and place them on separate domain controllers. This can improve the responsiveness of the operations masters. Pay particular attention to the current responsibilities of the domain controller you plan to use.

BEST PRACTICES Two roles that you should not separate are schema master and domain naming master. Always assign these roles to the same server. For the most efficient operations, you usually want the relative ID master and PDC emulator to be on the same server as well. But you can separate these roles if necessary. For example, on a large network where peak loads are causing performance problems, you would probably want to place the relative ID master and PDC emulator on separate domain controllers. Additionally, you usually shouldn't place the infrastructure master on a domain controller hosting a global catalog. See "Exploring Global Catalogs" earlier in this chapter for details.

Using the Active Directory Recycle Bin

When your Active Directory forest is operating in the Windows Server 2008 R2 mode, you can use the Active Directory Recycle Bin. The Active Directory Recycle Bin adds an easy-to-use recovery feature for Active Directory objects. When you enable this feature, all link-valued and non-link-valued attributes of a deleted object are preserved, allowing you to restore the object to the same state it was in before it was deleted. You can also recover objects from the recycle bin without having to initiate an authoritative restore. This differs substantially from the previously available technique, which used an authoritative restore to recover deleted objects from the Deleted Objects container. Previously, when you deleted an object, most of its non-link-valued attributes were cleared and all of its link-valued attributes were removed, which meant that although you could recover a deleted object, it was not restored to its previous state.

Preparing Schema for the Recycle Bin

Before you can make the recycle bin available, you must update Active Directory schema with the required recycle bin attributes, as discussed earlier in "Using Windows Server 2008 R2 Functional Level." When you do this, the schema is updated, and then every object in the forest is updated with the recycle bin attributes as well. This process is irreversible once it is started.

After you prepare Active Directory, you need to upgrade all domain controllers in your Active Directory forest to Windows Server 2008 R2 and then raise the domain and forest functional levels to the Windows Server 2008 R2 level.

After these operations, you can access the recycle bin. From now on, when an Active Directory object is deleted, the object is put in a state referred to as *logically deleted*, moved to the Deleted Objects container, and its distinguished name is altered. A deleted object remains in the Deleted Objects container for the period of time set in the delete object lifetime value, which is 180 days by default.

REAL WORLD The msDS-deletedObjectLifetime attribute replaces the tombstone-Lifetime attribute. However, when msDS-deletedObjectLifetime is set to $null, the lifetime value comes from the tombstoneLifetime. If the tombstoneLifetime is also set to $null, the default value is 180 days.

Recovering Deleted Objects

You can recover deleted objects from the Deleted Objects container by using an authoritative restore. The procedure has not changed from previous releases of Windows Server. What has changed, however, is the fact that the objects are restored to their previous state with all link-valued and non-link-valued attributes preserved. To perform an authoritative restore, the domain controller must be in Directory Services Restore Mode.

Rather than using an authoritative restore and taking a domain controller offline, you can recover deleted objects by using the Ldp.exe administration tool or the Active Directory cmdlets for Windows PowerShell. Keep in mind that Active Directory blocks access to an object for a short while after it is deleted. During this time, Active Directory processes the object's link-value table to maintain referential integrity on the linked attribute's values. Active Directory then permits access to the deleted object.

Using Ldp.exe for Basic Recovery

You can use Ldp.exe to display the Deleted Objects container and recover a deleted object by following these steps:

1. Click Start, type **Ldp.exe** in the Search box, and then press Enter.

2. On the Options menu, click Controls. In the Controls dialog box, select Return Deleted Objects in the Load Predefined list, and then click OK.

3. Bind to the server that hosts the forest root domain by choosing Bind from the Connection menu. Select the Bind type, and then click OK.

4. On the View menu, click Tree. In the Tree View dialog box, use the BaseDN list to select the appropriate forest root domain name, such as DC=Cpandl,DC=Com, and then click OK.

5. In the console tree, double-click the root distinguished name and locate the CN=Deleted Objects container.

6. Locate and right-click the Active Directory object that you want to restore, and then click Modify. This displays the Modify dialog box.

7. In the Edit Entry Attribute text box, type **isDeleted**. Do not enter anything in the Values text box.

8. Under Operation, click Delete, and then click Enter.

9. In the Edit Entry Attribute text box, type **distinguishedName**. In Values, type the original distinguished name of this Active Directory object.

10. Under Operation, click Replace. Select the Extended check box, click Enter, and then click Run.

Using Windows PowerShell for Basic and Advanced Recovery

You can also use the Active Directory cmdlets for Windows PowerShell to recover deleted objects. You use Get-ADObject to retrieve the object or objects you want to restore, pass that object or objects to Restore-ADObject, and then Restore-ADObject restores the object or objects to the directory database.

NOTE The Active Directory module is not imported into Windows PowerShell by default. You need to import the module before you can use the cmdlets it provides. For more information, see "Active Directory Administrative Center and Windows PowerShell" in Chapter 8.

To use the Active Directory cmdlets for recovery, you need to open an elevated, administrator PowerShell prompt by right-clicking the Windows PowerShell entry on the menu and clicking Run As Administrator. The basic syntax for recovering an object is as follows:

```
Get-ADObject -Filter {ObjectId} -IncludeDeletedObjects | Restore-ADObject
```

ObjectId is a filter value that identifies the object you want to restore. For example, you could restore a deleted user account by display name or SAM account name as shown in these examples:

```
Get-ADObject -Filter {DisplayName -eq "Rich Haddock"}
-IncludeDeletedObjects | Restore-ADObject

Get-ADObject -Filter {SamAccountName -eq "richh"} -IncludeDeletedObjects
| Restore-ADObject
```

It's important to note that nested objects must be recovered from the highest-level of the deleted hierarchy to a live parent container. For example, if you accidentally deleted an OU and all its related accounts, you need to restore the OU before you can restore the related accounts.

The basic syntax for restoring container objects such as an OU is as follows:

```
Get-ADObject -ldapFilter:"(msDS-LastKnownRDN=ContainerID)"
-IncludeDeletedObjects | Restore-ADObject
```

ContainerID is a filter value that identifies the container object you want to restore. For example, you could restore the Corporate Services OU as shown in this example:

```
Get-ADObject -ldapFilter:"(msDS-LastKnownRDN=Corporate_Services)"
-IncludeDeletedObjects | Restore-ADObject
```

If the OU contains accounts you also want to restore, you can now restore the accounts by using the technique discussed previously, or you can restore all accounts at the same time. The basic syntax requires that you establish a search base and associate the accounts with their last known parent, as shown here:

```
Get-ADObject -SearchBase "CN=Deleted Objects,ForestRootDN" -Filter
{lastKnownParent -eq "ContainerCN,ForestRootDN"} -IncludeDeletedObjects |
Restore-ADObject
```

ForestRootDN is the distinguished name of the forest root domain, such as DC=Cpandl,DC=Com, and *ContainerCN* is the common name of the container, such as OU=Corporate_Services or CN=Users. The following example restores all the accounts that were in the Corporate Services OU when it was deleted:

```
Get-ADObject -SearchBase "CN=Deleted Objects,DC=Cpandl,DC=com" -Filter
{lastKnownParent -eq "OU=Corporate_Services,DC=Cpandl,DC=com"}
-IncludeDeletedObjects | Restore-ADObject
```

Core Active Directory Administration

C ore Active Directory administration focuses on key tasks that you perform routinely with Active Directory Domain Services (AD DS), such as creating computer accounts or joining computers to a domain. In this chapter, you'll learn about the tools you can use to manage Active Directory as well as about specific techniques for managing computers, domain controllers, and organizational units.

Tools for Managing Active Directory

Several sets of tools are available for managing Active Directory, including graphical administration tools, command-line tools, support tools, and Windows Power-Shell cmdlets.

Active Directory Administration Tools

Active Directory administration tools are provided as snap-ins for the Microsoft Management Console (MMC). You use the following key tools to manage Active Directory:

- **Active Directory Administrative Center** For performing task-orientated management tasks.

- **Active Directory Domains And Trusts** For working with domains, domain trees, and domain forests.

- **Active Directory Module For Windows PowerShell** For managing Active Directory when you are working with Windows PowerShell.

- **Active Directory Sites And Services** For managing sites and subnets.

- **Active Directory Users And Computers** For managing users, groups, computers, and organizational units.

- **Group Policy Management** For managing the way Group Policy is used in the organization. Provides access to Resultant Set of Policy (RSoP) for modeling and logging.

SECURITY ALERT Windows Firewall can affect remote administration with some MMC snap-ins. If Windows Firewall is enabled on a remote computer and you receive an error message stating that you don't have appropriate rights, the network path isn't found, or access is denied, you might need to configure an exception on the remote computer for incoming TCP port 445. To resolve this problem, you can enable the Windows Firewall: Allow Remote Administration Exception policy setting within Computer Configuration\Administrative Templates\Network\Network Connections\Windows Firewall\Domain Profile. Alternatively, type the following at a command prompt on the remote computer: **netsh firewall set portopening tcp 445 smb enable**. See Microsoft Knowledge Base Article 840634 for more details (*support.microsoft.com/default.aspx?scid=kb;en-us;840634*).

You can access the Active Directory administration tools through the Administrative Tools menu or add them to any updateable MMC. If you're using another computer with access to a Windows Server 2008 R2 domain, the tools won't be available until you install them. One technique for installing these tools is to use the Add Features Wizard.

Active Directory Command-Line Tools

Several tools are provided to let you manage Active Directory from the command line:

- **Adprep** Prepares a Windows forest or domain for installation of Windows domain controllers (DCs). To prepare a forest or a domain, use **adprep /forestprep** and **adprep /domainprep**, respectively.

SECURITY ALERT   For Windows Server 2003 SP1 or later, a domain's Group Policy isn't automatically updated. To prepare Group Policy for the domain, you must use the command **adprep /domainprep /gpprep**. This modifies the access control entries (ACEs) for all Group Policy object (GPO) folders in the SYSVOL directory to grant read access to all enterprise domain controllers. This level of access is required to support RSoP for site-based policy. Because this security change causes the NT File Replication Service (NTFRS) to resend all GPOs to all domain controllers, you should use adprep /domainprep /gpprep only after careful planning.

- **Dsadd**   Adds computers, contacts, groups, organizational units, and users to Active Directory. Type **dsadd *objectname* /?** at a command prompt to display help information about using the command, such as **dsadd computer /?**.

- **Dsget**   Displays properties of computers, contacts, groups, organizational units, users, sites, subnets, and servers registered in Active Directory. Type **dsget *objectname* /?** at a command prompt to display help information about using the command, such as **dsget subnet /?**.

- **Dsmod**   Modifies properties of computers, contacts, groups, organizational units, users, and servers that exist in Active Directory. Type **dsmod *objectname* /?** at a command prompt to display help information about using the command, such as **dsmod server /?**.

- **Dsmove**   Moves a single object to a new location within a single domain or renames the object without moving it. Type **dsmove /?** at a command prompt to display help information about using the command.

- **Dsquery**   Uses search criteria to find computers, contacts, groups, organizational units, users, sites, subnets, and servers in Active Directory. Type **dsquery /?** at a command prompt to display help information about using the command.

- **Dsrm**   Removes objects from Active Directory. Type **dsrm /?** at a command prompt to display help information about using the command.

- **Ntdsutil**   Allows the user to view site, domain, and server information; manage operations masters; and perform database maintenance of Active Directory. Type **ntdsutil /?** at a command prompt to display help information about using the command.

Active Directory Support Tools

Many Active Directory tools are included with Windows Server 2008 R2. Table 8-1 lists some of the most useful support tools for configuring, managing, and troubleshooting Active Directory.

TABLE 8-1 Quick Reference for Active Directory Support Tools

SUPPORT TOOL	EXECUTABLE NAME	DESCRIPTION
ADSI Edit	Adsiedit.msc	Opens and edits the Active Directory Services Interface for domain, schema, and configuration containers
Active Directory Administration Tool	Ldp.exe	Performs Lightweight Directory Access Protocol (LDAP) operations on Active Directory
Directory Services Access Control Lists Utility	Dsacls.exe	Manages access control lists (ACLs) for objects in Active Directory
Distributed File System Utility	Dfsutil.exe	Manages the Distributed File System (DFS) and displays DFS information
DNS Server Troubleshooting Tool	Dnscmd.exe	Manages properties of Domain Name System (DNS) servers, zones, and resource records
Replication Diagnostics Tool	Repadmin.exe	Manages and monitors replication using the command line
Windows Domain Manager	Netdom.exe	Allows domain and trust relationships management from the command line

Active Directory Administrative Center and Windows PowerShell

Active Directory Administrative Center, shown in Figure 8-1, provides a task-orientated interface for managing Active Directory. To start this tool, click Start, Administrative Tools, Active Directory Administrative Center. You can use this tool to do the following:

- Connect to one or more domains
- Create and manage user accounts
- Create and manage groups
- Create and manage organizational units
- Perform global searches of Active Directory

Active Directory Administrative Center is installed by default on Windows Server 2008 R2 and is available on Windows 7 when you install the Remote Server Administration Tools (RSAT). This tool uses Windows PowerShell to perform administration tasks and relies on the .NET Framework 3.5.1. Both of these features must be installed and properly configured for you to use Active Directory Administrative Center.

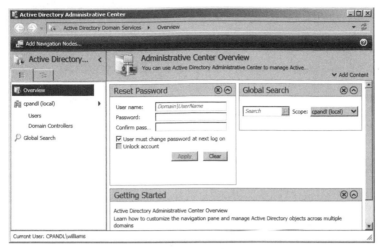

FIGURE 8-1 Perform task-oriented management of Active Directory.

Additionally, Active Directory Administrative Center makes use of the Web services provided by Active Directory Web Services (ADWS). At least one domain controller in each Active Directory domain you want to manage must have ADWS installed and have the related services running. Connections are made over TCP port 9389 by default, and firewall policies must enable an exception on this port for ADWS.

You can also work with Active Directory by using the Active Directory module for Windows PowerShell. The module is automatically imported when you select the related option on the Administrative Tools menu. Otherwise, this module is not imported into Windows PowerShell by default, and you need to import it before you can work with any Active Directory cmdlets.

At the Windows PowerShell prompt, you can import the Active Directory module by entering **Import-Module ActiveDirectory**. Once the module is imported, you can use it with the currently running instance of Windows PowerShell. The next time you start Windows PowerShell, you need to import the module again if you want to use its features. Alternatively, you can select the Active Directory Module For Windows PowerShell option on the Administrative Tools menu to import the module when Windows PowerShell starts.

At the Windows PowerShell prompt, you can list all available cmdlets by typing **get-command**. Use Get-Help to get more information about how cmdlets are used. If you enter **get-help *-***, you get a list of all cmdlets that includes a synopsis of the purpose of each cmdlet. To get help documentation on a specific cmdlet, type **get-help** followed by the cmdlet name. Several dozen Active Directory cmdlets are available, and you can get a list of the ones you'll use the most by entering **get-help** ***-ad*** at the Windows PowerShell prompt.

NOTE The Active Directory module for Windows PowerShell is installed by default on Windows Server 2008 R2 and is available on Windows 7 when you install the Remote Server Administration Tools and select the related options. Windows PowerShell relies on the .NET Framework 3.5.1 and Windows Remote Management (WinRM) to perform administrative tasks.

Using Active Directory Users And Computers

Active Directory Users And Computers is the primary administration tool you use to manage Active Directory. With this utility, you can handle all user, group, and computer-related tasks and manage organizational units.

You can start Active Directory Users And Computers by selecting its related option on the Administrative Tools menu. You can also add Active Directory Users And Computers as a snap-in to any console that can be updated.

Getting Started with Active Directory Users And Computers

By default, Active Directory Users And Computers works with the domain to which your computer is currently connected. You can access computer and user objects in this domain through the console tree, as shown in Figure 8-2. If you can't find a domain controller or if the domain you want to work with isn't shown, you might need to connect to a domain controller in the current domain or a domain controller in a different domain. Other high-level tasks you might want to perform with Active Directory Users And Computers are viewing advanced options or searching for objects.

When you access a domain in Active Directory Users And Computers, you'll see the following standard set of folders:

- **Builtin** The list of built-in user accounts and groups.
- **Computers** The default container for computer accounts.
- **Domain Controllers** The default container for domain controllers.
- **ForeignSecurityPrincipals** Contains information on objects from a trusted external domain. Normally, these objects are created when an object from an external domain is added to a group in the current domain.
- **Managed Service Accounts** The default container for managed service accounts.
- **Microsoft Exchange Security Groups** The default container for groups used by Microsoft Exchange Server. This folder is listed only if Exchange Server is running in the environment.

- **Saved Queries** Contains saved search criteria so that you can quickly perform previously run Active Directory searches.
- **Users** The default container for users.

Active Directory Users And Computers has advanced options that aren't displayed by default. To access these options, click View and then select Advanced Features. You now see the following additional folders:

- **LostAndFound** Contains objects that have been orphaned. You can delete or recover them.
- **NTDS Quotas** Contains directory service quota data.
- **Program Data** Contains stored Active Directory data for Microsoft applications.
- **System** Contains built-in system settings.

You can also add folders for organizational units. In Figure 8-2, there are multiple administrator-created organizational units are in the cpandl.com domain. These include Corporate Services, Customer Services, Engineering, Human Resources, Products, Sales, Support, and Technology.

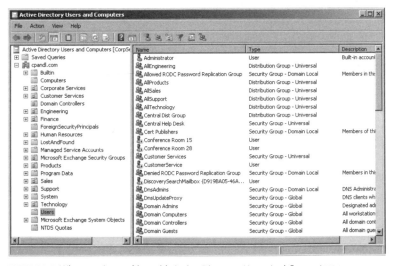

FIGURE 8-2 When you're working with Active Directory Users And Computers, you can access computer and user objects through the console tree.

Connecting to a Domain Controller

Connecting to a domain controller serves several purposes. If you start Active Directory Users And Computers and no objects are available, you can connect to a domain controller to access user, group, and computer objects in the current domain. You might also want to connect to a domain controller when you suspect that replication isn't working properly and want to inspect the objects on a specific controller. After you're connected, you can look for discrepancies in recently updated objects.

To connect to a domain controller, follow these steps:

1. In the console tree, right-click Active Directory Users And Computers, and then click Change Domain Controller.

    You'll see the current domain and domain controller you're working with in the Change Directory Server dialog box.

2. The Change To list displays the available controllers in the domain. The default selection is Any Writable Domain Controller. If you select this option, you'll be connected to the domain controller that responds to your request first. Otherwise, choose a specific domain controller to which you want to connect.

3. If you always want to use this domain controller when working with Active Directory Users And Computers, select the Save This Setting For The Current Console check box, and then click OK. Otherwise, just click OK.

NOTE The Change Directory Server dialog box now shows you the site associated with domain controllers as well as the domain controller type, version, and status. If the domain controller type is listed as GC, the domain controller is also hosting a global catalog.

Connecting to a Domain

In Active Directory Users And Computers, you can work with any domain in the forest provided that you have the proper access permissions. You connect to a domain by following these steps:

1. In the console tree, right-click Active Directory Users And Computers, and then click Change Domain.

2. The Change Domain dialog box displays the current (or default) domain. Type a new domain name, or click Browse, select a domain in the Browse For Domain dialog box, and then click OK.

3. If you always want to use this domain when working with Active Directory Users And Computers, select the Save This Domain Setting For The Current Console check box, and then click OK. Otherwise, just click OK.

Searching for Accounts and Shared Resources

Active Directory Users And Computers has a built-in search feature that you can use to find accounts, shared resources, and other directory objects. You can easily search the current domain, a specific domain, or the entire directory.

You search for directory objects by following these steps:

1. In the console tree, right-click the current domain or a specific container that you want to search, and then click Find. This opens a Find dialog box similar to the one shown in Figure 8-3.

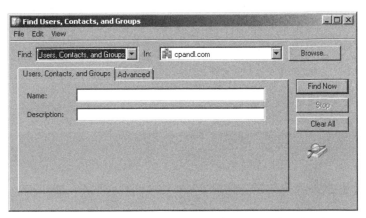

FIGURE 8-3 In the Find dialog box, you can search for resources in Active Directory.

2. In the Find list, choose the type of search you want. The options include the following:

   - **Users, Contacts, And Groups**   Search for user and group accounts, as well as contacts listed in the directory service.

   - **Computers**   Search for computer accounts by type, name, and owner.

   - **Printers**   Search for printers by name, model, and features.

   - **Shared Folders**   Search for shared folders by name or keyword.

   - **Organizational Units**   Search for organizational units by name.

   - **Custom Search**   Perform an advanced search or LDAP query.

   - **Common Queries**   Allows you to search quickly for account names, account descriptions, disabled accounts, nonexpiring passwords, and days since the last logon.

3. Using the In list, select the location that you want to search. If you chose a container to search in step 2, such as Computers, this container is selected by default. To search all objects in the directory, click Entire Directory.

4. Enter your search parameters, and then click Find Now. As shown in Figure 8-4, any matching entries are displayed in the search results. Double-click an object to view or modify its property settings. Right-click the object to display a shortcut menu of options for managing the object.

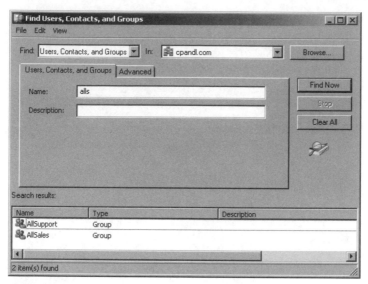

FIGURE 8-4 Objects that match search criteria are displayed in the search results; you can manage them by right-clicking their entries.

NOTE The search type determines which fields and tabs are available in the Find dialog box. In most cases you'll simply want to type the name of the object you're looking for in the Name field, but other search options are available. For example, with printers, you can search for a color printer, a printer that can print on both sides of the paper, a printer that can staple, and more.

Managing Computer Accounts

Computer accounts are stored in Active Directory as objects. You use them to control access to the network and its resources. You can add computer accounts to any container displayed in Active Directory Users And Computers. The best folders to use are Computers, Domain Controllers, and any organizational units that you've created.

Creating Computer Accounts on a Workstation or Server

The easiest way to create a computer account is to log on to the computer you want to configure and then join a domain, as described in "Joining a Computer to a Domain or Workgroup" later in this chapter. When you do this, the necessary computer account is created automatically and placed in the Computers folder or the Domain Controllers folder, as appropriate. You can also create a computer account in Active Directory Users And Computers before you try to install the computer.

Creating Computer Accounts in Active Directory Users And Computers

You can create two types of computer accounts: standard computer accounts and managed computer accounts. Using Active Directory Users And Computers, you can create a standard computer account by following these steps:

1. In the Active Directory Users And Computers console tree, right-click the container in which you want to place the computer account, click New, and then click Computer. This starts the New Object—Computer Wizard shown in Figure 8-5.

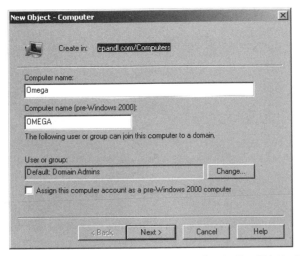

FIGURE 8-5 Create new computer accounts using the New Object—Computer Wizard.

2. Type the computer name.

3. By default, only members of Domain Admins can join this computer to the domain. To allow a different user or group to join the computer to the domain, click Change, and then select a user or group account in the Select User Or Group dialog box.

   NOTE You can select any existing user or group account. This allows you to delegate the authority to join this computer account to the domain.

4. If Windows NT systems can use this account, select Assign This Computer Account As A Pre–Windows 2000 Computer.

5. If Windows Deployment Services are not installed, click OK to create the computer account. Otherwise, click Next twice, and then click Finish.

When you are working with remote installation servers and Windows Deployment Services, managed computer accounts are used to prestage computer accounts so that a computer can be automatically installed. Using Active Directory

Users And Computers, you can create a managed computer account by following these steps:

1. Complete steps 1 to 4 in the previous procedure. Click Next to display the Managed page.

2. Select the This Is A Managed Computer check box, and then type the computer's globally unique identifier/universally unique identifier (GUID/UUID). You'll find the GUID/UUID in the system BIOS or displayed on the computer case. Click Next.

3. On the Host Server page, you have the option to specify which host server to use or to allow any available host server to be used for remote installation. To select a host server, select The Following Remote Installation Server. In the Find dialog box, click Find Now to display a list of all remote installation servers in the organization. Click the host server you want to use, and then click OK to close the Find dialog box.

4. Click Next, and then click Finish.

Viewing and Editing Computer Account Properties

You can view and edit computer account properties by following these steps:

1. Open Active Directory Users And Computers. In the console tree, expand the domain node.

2. Select the container or organizational unit in which the computer account is located.

3. Right-click the account you want to work with, and then click Properties. This displays a Properties dialog box that allows you to view and edit settings.

Deleting, Disabling, and Enabling Computer Accounts

If you no longer need a computer account, you can delete it permanently from Active Directory. You can also temporarily disable the account and later enable it to be used again.

To delete, disable, or enable computer accounts, follow these steps:

1. Open Active Directory Users And Computers. In the console tree, select the container in which the computer account is located.

2. Right-click the computer account, and then do one of the following:

   - Click Delete to delete the account permanently. Click Yes to confirm the deletion.

   - Click Disable Account to temporarily disable the account, Click Yes to confirm the action. A red circle with an X indicates that the account is disabled.

   - Click Enable Account to enable the account so that it can be used again.

TIP If an account is currently in use, you might not be able to disable it. Try shutting down the computer or disconnecting the computer session in the Sessions folder of Computer Management.

Resetting Locked Computer Accounts

Computer accounts have passwords, just like user accounts. Unlike user accounts, however, computer account passwords are managed and maintained automatically. To perform this automated management, computers in the domain store a computer account password, which is changed every 30 days by default, and a secure channel password for establishing secure communications with domain controllers. The secure channel password is also updated by default every 30 days, and both passwords must be synchronized. If the secure channel password and the computer account password get out of sync, the computer won't be allowed to log on to the domain, and a domain authentication error message will be logged for the Netlogon service with an event ID of 3210 or 5722.

If this happens, you need to reset the computer account password. One way to do this is to right-click the computer account in Active Directory Users And Computers and select Reset Account. You then need to remove the computer from the domain (by making the computer a member of a workgroup or another domain) and then rejoin the computer to the domain. You can use the Netdom command-line utility to reset a computer's password. See Microsoft Knowledge Base Article 325850 for more details (*support.microsoft.com/default.aspx?scid=kb;en-us;325850*).

For a member server, you can reset the computer account password by following these steps:

1. Log on locally to the computer. At a command prompt, type **netdom resetpwd /s:*ServerName* /ud:*domain\UserName* /pd:***, where *ServerName* is the name of the domain controller to use to set the password, *domain\UserName* specifies an administrator account with the authority to change the password, and * indicates that Netdom should prompt you for the account password before continuing.

2. Type your password when prompted. Netdom changes the computer account password locally and on the domain controller. The domain controller distributes the password change to other domain controllers in the domain.

3. Restart the computer.

For domain controllers, you must perform additional steps. After you log on locally, you must stop the Kerberos Key Distribution Center service and set its startup type to Manual. After you restart the computer and verify that the password has been successfully reset, you can restart the Kerberos Key Distribution Center service and set its startup type back to Automatic.

Moving Computer Accounts

Computer accounts are normally placed in the Computers or Domain Controllers containers or in customized organizational unit containers. You can move an account to a different container by selecting the computer account in Active Directory Users And Computers and then dragging the account to the new location.

You can also use the following technique to move computer accounts:

1. Open Active Directory Users And Computers.

2. In the console tree, select the container in which the computer account is located.

3. Right-click the computer account you want to move, and then click Move. This displays the Move dialog box, shown in Figure 8-6.

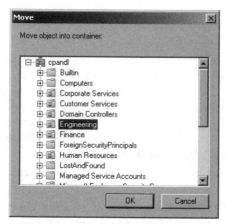

FIGURE 8-6 In the Move dialog box, you can move computer accounts to different containers.

4. In the Move dialog box, expand the domain node, and then select the container to which you want to move the computer. Click OK.

Managing Computers

As its name indicates, you use Computer Management to manage computers. When you're working with Active Directory Users And Computers, you can open Computer Management and connect to a specific computer by right-clicking the computer entry and selecting Manage from the shortcut menu. This launches Computer Management and automatically connects to the selected computer.

Joining a Computer to a Domain or Workgroup

Joining a computer to a domain or workgroup allows a Windows NT, Windows 2000, Windows XP, Windows Server 2003, Windows Vista, Windows 7, Windows Server 2008, or Windows Server 2008 R2 computer to log on and access the network.

Windows 95 and Windows 98 computers don't need computer accounts and don't join the network with this technique. For Windows 95 and Windows 98 computers, you must configure the computer as an Active Directory client.

Before you get started, make sure that networking components are properly installed on the computer. These should have been installed during the setup of the operating system. You might also want to refer to Chapter 17, "Managing TCP/IP Networking," for details on configuring TCP/IP connections. TCP/IP settings must be correct and permit communications between the computer you're configuring and a controller in the domain. If Dynamic Host Configuration Protocol (DHCP), Windows Internet Name Service (WINS), and DNS are properly installed on the network, workstations don't need to be assigned a static IP address or have a special configuration. The only requirements are a computer name and a domain name, which you can specify when joining the computer to the domain.

REAL WORLD Windows Server 2008 R2 automatically grants the Add Workstations To The Domain user right to the implicit group Authenticated Users. This means that any user who logs on to the domain as a User and is authenticated can add workstations to the domain without needing administration privileges. However, as a security precaution, the number of workstations any such user can add to the domain is limited to 10. If an authenticated user exceeds this limit, an error message is displayed. For Windows NT workstations this message states "The machine account for this computer either does not exist or is unavailable." For Windows 2000 and Windows XP workstations, this message states "Your computer could not be joined to the domain; you have exceeded the maximum number of computer accounts you are allowed to create in this domain." Although you can use the Ldp.exe tool from the Windows Server 2008 R2 Support Tools to override the default limit on the number of computers an authenticated user can join to a domain (as set by the *ms-DS-MachineAccountQuota* attribute), this isn't a good security practice. A better technique, and a more appropriate technique where security is a concern, is to create the necessary computer account in a specific OU beforehand or to grant the user the advanced security privilege Create Computer Objects in a specific OU.

During installation of the operating system, a network connection was probably configured for the computer, or you might have previously joined the computer to a domain or a workgroup. If so, you can join the computer to a new domain or workgroup. For joining a Windows Vista, Windows 7, or Windows Server 2008 or later computer to a domain, see "The Computer Name Tab" in Chapter 3. The process is nearly identical for configuring Windows 2000 Professional, Windows 2000 Server, Windows XP Professional, and Windows Server 2003 computers as well. A key difference is that clicking System And Security, System in Control Panel opens the System Properties dialog box directly.

If the name change is unsuccessful, you'll see a message informing you that the change was unsuccessful or a message telling you that the account credentials already exist. This problem can occur when you're changing the name of a computer that's already connected to a domain and when the computer has active sessions in that domain. Close applications that might be connected to the domain, such as Windows Explorer accessing a shared folder over the network. Then repeat the process for changing the computer's name.

If you have other problems joining a domain, be sure that the computer you're configuring has the proper networking configuration. The computer must have Networking Services installed, and TCP/IP properties must have the correct DNS server settings, as discussed in Chapter 17.

Using Offline Domain Join

Computers running Windows 7 Professional, Enterprise, or Ultimate edition or any edition of Windows Server 2008 R2 support offline domain join. The related utility, Djoin.exe, is included with these editions of Windows. Any member of Domain Admins can perform offline domain joins (as can anyone who is granted the appropriate user rights).

The basic steps for performing an offline domain join operation follow:

1. Create the computer account in Active Directory, and then force replication of the shared secrets of the computer that is to join the domain.

2. Write the relevant state information that the computer needs to join the domain to a text file, and then make the state information available to the computer.

3. When the computer starts, Windows reads the provisioning data, and the computer is joined to the domain.

You run Djoin.exe at an elevated, administrator command prompt to provision the computer account metadata. The computer account metadata is written to a .txt file. After provisioning the computer, you can run Djoin.exe again to request the computer account metadata and insert it into the Windows directory of the destination computer. Alternatively, you can save the computer account metadata in an Unattend.xml file and then specify the Unattend.xml file during an unattended operating system installation.

You can use a .txt file for provisioning by following these steps:

1. Using an account that is allowed to join computers to the domain, log on to a computer that is a member of the domain.

2. Use Djoin.exe to create a text file that contains the computer account metadata. To do this, at an elevated, administrator command prompt, enter **djoin /provision /domain** *DomainName* **/machine** *MachineName* **/savefile** *FileName*, where *DomainName* is the name of the domain to join, *MachineName* is the computer name, and *FileName* is name of the .txt file where the metadata should be saved, such as:

```
djoin /provision /domain cpandl /machine HrComputer15 /savefile
Hrcomputer15.txt
```

TIP By default, computer accounts are created in the Computers container. If you want to use a different container, you can add the /Machineou parameter and then specify the container to use. If the computer account object is already created, you can still generate the required metadata by adding the /reuse parameter. If your domain controller is not yet running Windows Server 2008 R2, add the /downlevel command.

3. On the new computer, use Djoin.exe to import the .txt file. At an elevated, administrator command prompt, enter **djoin /requestODJ /loadfile *FileName* /windowspath %SystemRoot% /localosCaution**, where *File-Name* is the name of the metadata file, such as:

```
djoin /requestODJ /loadfile HrComputer15.txt /windowspath
%SystemRoot% /localos
```

4. Ensure that the new computer is connected to the network, and then reboot it. During startup, the computer will be joined to the domain.

You can use an Unattend.xml file for provisioning by creating a section in the Unattend.xml file and then adding the contents of the metadata .txt file to the AccountData element, as shown in this example:

```
<Component>
<Component name=Microsoft-Windows-UnattendedJoin>
    <Identification>
        <Provisioning>
            <AccountData> Insert metadata here! </AccountData>
        </Provisioning>
    </Identification>
</Component>
```

After you create the Unattend.xml file, start the new computer in Safe Mode or start the computer in the Windows Preinstallation Environment (Windows PE), and then run the Setup command with an answer file, as shown in the following example:

```
setup /unattend: FullPathToAnswerFile
```

where *FullPathToAnswerFile* is the full file path to the Unattend.xml file.

Managing Domain Controllers, Roles, and Catalogs

Domain controllers perform many important tasks in Active Directory domains. Many of these tasks are discussed in Chapter 7, "Using Active Directory."

Installing and Demoting Domain Controllers

You install a domain controller by configuring Active Directory Domain Services on a server. Later, if you don't want the server to handle controller tasks, you can demote the server. It will then act as a member server again. You follow a similar procedure to install or demote servers, but before you do, you should consider the impact on the network and read "Understanding the Directory Structure" in Chapter 7.

As that section explains, when you install a domain controller, you might need to transfer operations master roles and reconfigure the global catalog structure. Also, before you can install Active Directory Domain Services, DNS must be working on the network. Similarly, before you demote a domain controller, you should shift any key responsibilities to other domain controllers. This means moving the global catalog off the server and transferring any operations master roles, if necessary. You must also remove any application directory partitions that are on the server.

REAL WORLD It's important to note that in Windows Server 2003, Windows Server 2008, and Windows Server 2008 R2, you no longer have to demote a domain controller to rename it. You can rename a domain controller at any time. The only problem is that the server is unavailable to users during the renaming process and you might need to force a directory refresh to reestablish proper communications with the server. You can't, however, move a domain controller to a different domain. You must demote the domain controller, update the domain settings for the server and its computer account, and then promote the server to be a domain controller once more.

To install a domain controller, follow these steps:

1. Log on to the server you want to reconfigure. In Server Manager, select the Roles node in the left pane, and then click Add Roles. This starts the Add Roles Wizard. If the wizard displays the Before You Begin page, read the Welcome message, and then click Next.

2. On the Select Server Roles page, select Active Directory Domain Services, and then click Next twice. Click Install.

3. Click Start, type **dcpromo** in the Search box, and then press Enter. This starts the Active Directory Domain Services Installation Wizard.

4. If the computer is currently a member server, the wizard takes you through the steps needed to install Active Directory. You need to specify whether this is a domain controller for a new domain or an additional domain controller for an existing domain. To verify that a domain controller is installed correctly, you should do the following: check the Directory Service event log for errors, ensure that the SYSVOL folder is accessible to clients, verify that name resolution is working through DNS, and verify replication of changes to Active Directory.

To demote a domain controller, follow these steps:

1. Log on to the server you want to reconfigure. Click Start, type **dcpromo** in the Search box, and then press Enter. This starts the Active Directory Domain Services Installation Wizard.

2. If the computer is currently a domain controller, the Active Directory Installation Wizard takes you through the process of demoting the domain controller. After the computer is demoted, it acts as a member server.

3. In Server Manager, select the Roles node in the left pane, and then click Remove Roles. This starts the Remove Roles Wizard. If the wizard displays the Before You Begin page, read the Welcome message, and then click Next.

4. On the Remove Server Roles page, clear the Active Directory Domain Services check box, and then click Next twice. Click Finish.

CAUTION Demoting a server using Dcpromo gracefully transfers any roles held by the server. Microsoft Knowledge Base article 332199 *(support.microsoft.com/ kb/332199)* describes how to force demotion using **dcpromo /forceremoval**. However, if you use **dcpromo /forceremoval**, the FSMO roles of the demoted server are left in an invalid state until they are reassigned by an administrator. If you forcefully demote a domain controller and the demotion fails, or you are unable to demote a server, the domain data may be in an inconsistent state. See Microsoft Knowledge Base article 216498 for details on how to resolve this issue *(support.microsoft.com/ kb/216498/en-us)*.

REAL WORLD An alternative technique for installing domain controllers is to use backup media. This option was introduced in Windows Server 2003. To install a domain controller from backup media, create a backup of the system state data of a domain controller and restore it on a different server running Windows Server 2003, Windows Server 2008, or Windows Server 2008 R2. When you create a domain controller from backup media, you eliminate the need to replicate the entire directory database over the network to the new domain controller. This can really save the day when you have bandwidth limitations or the directory database has thousands of entries.

Viewing and Transferring Domainwide Roles

You can use Active Directory Users And Computers to view or change the location of domainwide operations master roles. At the domain level, you can work with roles for relative ID (RID) masters, primary domain controller (PDC) emulator masters, and infrastructure masters.

NOTE Operations master roles are discussed in "Understanding Operations Master Roles" in Chapter 7. You use Active Directory Domains And Trusts to set the domain naming master role and Active Directory Schema to change the schema master role. The fastest way to determine the current FSMO for all roles is to type **netdom query fsmo** at a command prompt.

You can view the current operations master roles by following these steps:

1. In Active Directory Users And Computers, right-click Active Directory Users And Computers in the console tree. On the shortcut menu, point to All Tasks, and then click Operations Masters. This opens the Operations Masters dialog box, shown in Figure 8-7.

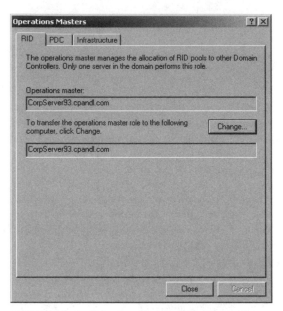

FIGURE 8-7 In the Operations Masters dialog box, transfer operations masters to new locations or simply view their current locations.

2. The Operations Masters dialog box has three tabs. The RID tab shows the location of the current RID master. The PDC tab shows the location of the current PDC emulator master. The Infrastructure tab shows the location of the current infrastructure master.

You can transfer the current operations master roles by following these steps:

1. Start Active Directory Users And Computers. In the console tree, right-click Active Directory Users And Computers, and then click Change Domain Controller.

2. In the Change Directory Server dialog box, click This Domain Controller, select the domain controller to which you want to transfer an operations master role, and then click OK.

3. In the console tree, right-click Active Directory Users And Computers. On the shortcut menu, point to All Tasks, and then click Operations Masters.

4. In the Operations Masters dialog box, click the RID, PDC, or Infrastructure tab as appropriate for the type of role you want to transfer.

5. Click Change to transfer the role to the previously selected domain controller. Click OK.

Viewing and Transferring the Domain Naming Master Role

You can use Active Directory Domains And Trusts to view or change the location of the domain naming master in the domain forest. In Active Directory Domains And Trusts, the root level of the control tree shows the currently selected domain.

TIP If you need to connect to a different domain, connect to a domain controller following steps similar to those described in "Connecting to a Domain Controller" earlier in this chapter. The only difference is that you right-click Active Directory Domains And Trusts in the console tree.

To transfer the domain naming master role, follow these steps:

1. Start Active Directory Domains And Trusts. In the console tree, right-click Active Directory Domains And Trusts, and then click Change Active Directory Domain Controller.

2. In the Change Directory Server dialog box, select the This Domain Controller Or AD LDS Instance option, and then select the domain controller to which you want to transfer the domain naming master role. Click OK.

3. In the console tree, right-click Active Directory Domains And Trusts, and then click Operations Master. This opens the Operations Master dialog box.

4. The Domain Naming Operations Master field displays the current domain naming master. Click Change to transfer this role to the previously selected domain controller.

5. Click Close.

Viewing and Transferring Schema Master Roles

You use Active Directory Schema to view or change the schema master's location. Type **regsvr32 schmmgmt.dll** at a command prompt to register Active Directory Schema. You can then transfer the schema master role by following these steps:

1. Add the Active Directory Schema snap-in to an MMC.

2. In the console tree, right-click Active Directory Schema, and then click Change Active Directory Domain Controller.

3. Select Any Writable Domain Controller to let Active Directory select the new schema master, or select This Domain Controller Or AD LDS Instance and then select the new schema master, such as **zeta.seattle.cpandl.com**.

4. Click OK. In the console tree, right-click Active Directory Schema, and then click Operations Master.

5. Click Change in the Change Schema Master dialog box. Click OK, and then click Close.

Transferring Roles Using the Command Line

Another way to transfer roles is to use Netdom to list current FSMO role holders and then Ntdsutil.exe to transfer roles. Ntdsutil is a command-line tool for managing Active Directory. Follow these steps to transfer roles at the command line:

1. Get a list of the current FSMO role holders by typing **netdom query fsmo** at a command prompt.

2. It is recommended (but not required) that you log on to the console of the server you want to assign as the new operations master. You can log on to the console locally or use Remote Desktop Connection.

3. Click Start, type **cmd** in the Search box, and then click OK.

4. At the command prompt, type **ntdsutil**. This starts the Directory Services Management Tool.

5. At the ntdsutil prompt, type **roles**. This puts the utility in Operations Master Maintenance mode.

6. At the fsmo maintenance prompt, type **connections**. At the server connections prompt, type **connect to server** followed by the fully qualified domain name of the domain controller to which you want to assign the FSMO role, such as:

   ```
   connect to server engdc01.technology.adatum.com
   ```

7. After you've established a successful connection, type **quit** to exit the server connections prompt. At the fsmo maintenance prompt, type **transfer**, and then type the identifier for the role to transfer. The identifiers are as follows:

   - **pdc**   For the PDC emulator role
   - **rid master**   For the RID master role
   - **infrastructure master**   For the infrastructure master role
   - **schema master**   For the schema master role
   - **domain naming master**   For the domain naming master role

8. Type **quit** at the fsmo maintenance prompt, and then type **quit** at the ntdsutil prompt.

Seizing Roles Using the Command Line

Occasionally, you might find yourself in a situation where you can't gracefully transfer server roles. For example, a domain controller acting as the RID master might have a drive failure that takes down the entire server. If you're unable to get the server back online, you might need to seize the RID master role and assign this role to another domain controller.

> **NOTE**   Seize a server role only if the domain controller managing the current role is out of service. When the original server comes back online, it will recognize the change and accept it.

Don't seize a role without first determining how up to date the domain controller that will take over the role is with respect to the previous role owner. Active Directory tracks replication changes using update sequence numbers (USNs). Because replication takes time, not all domain controllers will necessarily be up to date. If you compare a domain controller's USN to that of other servers in the domain, you can determine whether the domain controller is the most up to date with respect to changes from the previous role owner. If the domain controller is up to date, you can transfer the role safely. If the domain controller isn't up to date, you can wait for replication to occur and then transfer the role to the domain controller.

Windows Server 2008 R2 includes Repadmin for working with Active Directory replication. To display the highest sequence number for a specified naming context on each replication partner of a designated domain controller, type the following at a command prompt:

```
repadmin /showutdvec DomainControllerName NamingContext
```

where *DomainControllerName* is the fully qualified domain name of the domain controller, and *NamingContext* is the distinguished name of the domain in which the server is located, such as:

```
repadmin /showutdvec server252.cpandl.com dc=cpandl,dc=com
```

The output shows the highest USN on replication partners for the domain partition:

```
Default-First-Site-Name\SERVER252 @ USN    45164 @ Time 2008-03-30 14:25:36

Default-First-Site-Name\SERVER147 @ USN    45414 @ Time 2008-03-30 14:25:36
```

If Server252 was the previous role owner and the domain controller you are examining has an equal or larger USN for Server252, the domain controller is up to date. However, if Server252 was the previous role owner and the domain controller you are examining has a lower USN for Server252, the domain controller is not up to date, and you should wait for replication to occur before seizing the role. You can also use Repadmin /Syncall to force the domain controller that is the most up to date with respect to the previous role owner to replicate with all of its replication partners.

Follow these steps to seize a server role:

1. Type **netdom query fsmo** at a command prompt to get a list of the current FSMO role holders.

2. Ensure that the current domain controller with the role you want to seize is permanently offline. If the server can be brought back online, don't perform this procedure unless you intend to completely reinstall this server.

3. It is recommended that you log on to the console of the server you want to assign as the new operations master. You can log on to the console locally or use Remote Desktop Connection.

4. Open a Command Prompt window.

5. At the command prompt, type **ntdsutil**. This starts the Directory Services Management Tool.

6. At the ntdsutil prompt, type **roles**. This puts the utility in Operations Master Maintenance mode.

7. At the fsmo maintenance prompt, type **connections**. At the server connections prompt, type **connect to server** followed by the fully qualified domain name of the domain controller to which you want to assign the FSMO role, such as:

```
connect to server engdc01.technology.adatum.com
```

8. After you've established a successful connection, type **quit** to exit the server connections prompt. At the fsmo maintenance prompt, type **seize**, and then type the identifier for the role to seize. The identifiers are as follows:

   - **pdc**   For the PDC emulator role
   - **rid master**   For the RID master role
   - **infrastructure master**   For the infrastructure master role
   - **schema master**   For the schema master role
   - **domain naming master**   For the domain naming master role

9. Type **quit** at the fsmo maintenance prompt, and then type **quit** at the ntdsutil prompt.

Configuring Global Catalogs

Global catalogs have an important role on the network. This role is discussed in "Understanding the Directory Structure" in Chapter 7. You configure additional global catalogs by enabling domain controllers to host the global catalog. In addition, if you have two or more global catalogs within a site, you might want a domain controller to stop hosting the global catalog. You do this by disabling the global catalog on the domain controller.

You enable or disable a global catalog by following these steps:

1. In Active Directory Sites And Services, expand the site you want to work with in the console tree.

2. Expand the Servers folder for the site, and then select the server you want to configure to host the global catalog.

3. In the details pane, right-click NTDS Settings, and then click Properties.

4. To enable the server to host the global catalog, select the Global Catalog check box on the General tab.

5. To disable the global catalog, clear the Global Catalog check box on the General tab.

CAUTION Don't enable or disable global catalogs without proper planning and analysis of the impact on the network. In a large enterprise environment, designating a domain controller as a global catalog can cause data related to thousands of Active Directory objects to be replicated across the network.

Configuring Universal Group Membership Caching

Universal membership caching eliminates the dependency on the availability of a global catalog server during logons. When you enable this feature on a domain operating in Windows Server 2003 or higher functional level, any domain controller can resolve logon requests locally without having to go through the global catalog server. As discussed in "Universal Group Membership Caching" in Chapter 7, this has advantages and disadvantages.

You can enable or disable universal group membership caching by following these steps:

1. In Active Directory Sites And Services, expand and then select the site you want to work with.

2. In the details pane, right-click NTDS Site Settings, and then click Properties.

3. To enable universal group membership caching, select the Enable Universal Group Membership Caching check box on the Site Settings tab. Then, in the Refresh Cache From list, choose a site from which to cache universal group memberships. The selected site must have a working global catalog server.

4. To disable universal group membership caching, clear the Enable Universal Group Membership Caching check box on the Site Settings tab.

5. Click OK.

Managing Organizational Units

As discussed in Chapter 7, organizational units help you organize objects, set Group Policy with a limited scope, and more. In this section you'll learn how to create and manage organizational units.

Creating Organizational Units

You usually create organizational units to mirror your organization's business or functional structure. You may also want to create units for administrative reasons, such as if you want to delegate rights to users or administrators. You can create organizational units as subgroups of a domain or as child units within an existing organizational unit.

To create an organizational unit, follow these steps:

1. In Active Directory Users And Computers, right-click the domain node or existing organizational unit folder in which you want to add an organizational unit. Click New on the shortcut menu, and then click Organizational Unit.

2. Type the name of the organizational unit, and then click OK.

3. You can now move accounts and shared resources to the organizational unit. See "Moving Computer Accounts" earlier in this chapter for an example.

Viewing and Editing Organizational Unit Properties

You can view and edit organizational unit properties by following these steps:

1. Open Active Directory Users And Computers.

2. Right-click the organizational unit you want to work with, and then click Properties. This displays a Properties dialog box that lets you view and edit settings.

Renaming and Deleting Organizational Units

You can rename or delete an organizational unit by following these steps:

1. In Active Directory Users And Computers, right-click the organizational unit folder you want to work with.

2. To delete the organizational unit, click Delete. Then confirm the action by clicking Yes.

3. To rename the organizational unit, click Rename. Type a new name for the organizational unit, and then press Enter.

Moving Organizational Units

You can move organizational units to different locations within a domain by selecting the organizational unit in Active Directory Users And Computers and then dragging the account to the new location.

You can also follow these steps to move organizational units:

1. In Active Directory Users And Computers, right-click the organizational unit folder you want to move, and then click Move.

2. In the Move dialog box, expand the domain, and then select the container to which you want to move the organizational unit. Click OK.

Managing Sites

The Active Directory Installation Wizard creates a default site and a default site link when you install Active Directory Domain Services on the first domain controller in a site. The default site is named Default-First-Site-Name, and the default site link is called DEFAULTIPSITELINK. You can rename the default site and site link as necessary. You must create subsequent sites and site links manually.

Configuring a site is a multipart process that includes the following steps:

1. Creating the site.

2. Creating one or more subnets and associating them with the site.

3. Associating a domain controller with the site.

4. Linking the site to other sites using site links and, if necessary, creating site link bridges.

I discuss these tasks in the sections that follow.

Creating Sites

Any administrator who is a member of Domain Admins or Enterprise Admins can create sites. You can create a site by following these steps:

1. In Active Directory Sites And Services, right-click the Sites container in the console root, and then click New Site.

2. In the New Object—Site dialog box, shown in Figure 8-8, type a name for the site, such as **ChicagoSite**. Site names cannot contain spaces or any special characters other than a dash.

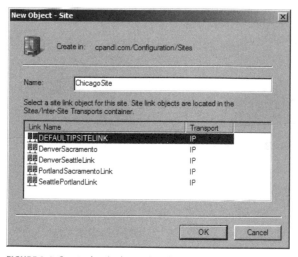

FIGURE 8-8 Create the site by setting the site name and a related site link.

3. Click the site link that you will use to connect this site to other sites. If the site link you want to use doesn't exist, select the default site link and change the site link settings later.

4. Click OK. A prompt is displayed detailing the steps you must complete to finish site configuration. Click OK again.

5. To complete site configuration, you must complete the remaining configuration tasks.

TIP You can rename a site at any time. In Active Directory Sites And Services, right-click the site and then select Rename. Type the new name for the site, and then press Enter.

Creating Subnets

Each site you define must have associated subnets that detail the network segments that belong to the site. Any computer with an IP address on a network segment associated with a site is considered to be located in the site. Although a single site can have multiple subnets associated with it, a subnet can be associated with only one site.

To create a subnet and associate it with a site, follow these steps:

1. In Active Directory Sites And Services, right-click the Subnets container in the console tree, and then click New Subnet. This displays the New Object—Subnet dialog box, shown in Figure 8-9.

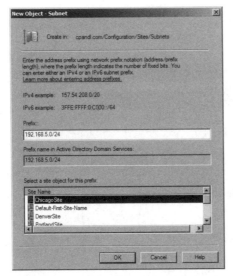

FIGURE 8-9 Create the subnet by entering the network prefix and selecting an associated site.

2. In the Prefix field, type the IPv4 or IPv6 network address prefix using the network prefix notation. In network prefix notation, you type the network ID and then a forward slash, and then you specify which bits are used for the network ID. For example, if the network ID is 192.168.5.0 and the first 24 bits identify the network ID, you would enter **192.168.5.0/24** as the network prefix notation.

3. Select the site with which the subnet should be associated, and then click OK.

TIP You can change the site association for a subnet at any time. In Active Directory Sites And Services, double-click the subnet in the Subnets folder, and then, on the General tab, change the site association in the Site list.

Associating Domain Controllers with Sites

Every site should have at least one domain controller associated with it. By adding a second domain controller to a site, you provide fault tolerance and redundancy. If at least one domain controller in the site is also a global catalog server, you can ensure that directory searches and authentication traffic are isolated to the site.

You can add domain controllers to sites automatically or manually. When you associate subnets with a site, any new domain controllers you install are placed in the site automatically if the domain controller's IP address is within the valid range of IP addresses for the subnet. Existing domain controllers are not automatically associated with sites, however. You must manually associate any existing domain controllers with a new site by moving the domain controller object into the site.

Before you can move a domain controller from one site to another, you must determine in which site the domain controller is currently located. A quick way to do that is to type the following command at a command prompt:

```
dsquery server -s DomainControllerName | dsget server -site
```

where *DomainControllerName* is the fully qualified domain name of the domain controller, such as:

```
dsquery server -s server241.cpandl.com | dsget server -site
```

The output of this command is the name of the site in which the designated domain controller is located.

To move a domain controller from one site to another site, follow these steps:

1. In Active Directory Sites And Services, any domain controllers associated with a site are listed in the site's Servers node. Select the site that the domain controller is currently associated with.

2. Right-click the domain controller, and then click Move. In the Move Server dialog box, click the site that should contain the server, and then click OK.

NOTE Don't move a domain controller to a site if it is not on a subnet associated with the site. If you change subnet and site associations, you need to move domain controllers in the affected subnets to the appropriate site containers.

Configuring Site Links

Sites are groups of IP subnets that are connected by reliable, high-speed links. Most of the time, all subnets on the same local network are part of the same site. Networks with multiple sites are connected via site links. Site links are logical, transitive connections between two or more sites. Each site link has a replication schedule, a replication interval, a link cost, and a replication transport.

Because site links are used over wide area network links, bandwidth availability and usage are important considerations when configuring site links. By default, site links are scheduled to replicate data 24 hours a day, 7 days a week at an interval of at least 180 minutes. If you know a link has bandwidth limitations, you may need to alter the schedule to allow user traffic to have priority during peak usage times.

When you have multiple links between sites, you need to consider the relative priority of each link. You assign priority based on availability and reliability of the connection. The default link cost is set to 100. If there are multiple possible routes to a site, the route with the lowest site link cost is used first. Therefore, the most reliable paths with the most bandwidth between sites should be configured in most cases to have the lowest site link cost.

You can configure site links to use either RPC over IP or Simple Mail Transfer Protocol (SMTP) as the transport protocol. With IP as the transport, domain controllers establish an RPC over IP connection with a single replication partner at a time and replicate Active Directory changes synchronously. Because RPC over IP is synchronous, both replication partners must be available at the time the connection is established. You should use RPC over IP when there are reliable, dedicated connections between sites.

With SMTP as the transport, domain controllers convert all replication traffic to e-mail messages that are sent between the sites asynchronously. Because SMTP replication is asynchronous, both replication partners do not have to be available at the time the connection is established, and replication transactions can be stored until a destination server is available. You should use SMTP when links are unreliable or not always available.

NOTE If you plan to use SMTP, you must set up a certificate authority (CA). Certificates from the CA are used to digitally sign and encrypt the SMTP messages sent between the sites. With IP, CAs are not required by default.

You can create a site link between two or more sites by following these steps:

1. In Active Directory Sites And Services, expand the Sites container, and then expand the Inter-Site Transports container.

2. Right-click the container for the transport protocol you want to use (either IP or SMTP), and then click New Site Link.

3. In the New Object—Site Link dialog box, shown in Figure 8-10, type a name for the site link, such as **ChicagotoSeattleLink**. Site link names cannot contain spaces or special characters other than a dash.

4. In the Sites Not In This Site Link list, click the first site that should be included in the link, and then click Add to add the site to the Sites In This Site Link list. Repeat this process for each site you want to add to the link. You must include at least two sites. Click OK.

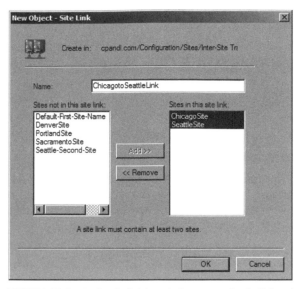

FIGURE 8-10 Create the site link by entering a name for the link and selecting the associated sites.

When you finish creating the site link, you should configure the link's properties. This allows you to specify the link cost, replication schedule, and replication interval. To configure site link properties, follow these steps:

1. In Active Directory Sites And Services, right-click the site link in the details pane, and then click Properties.

2. In the Properties dialog box, the General tab is selected by default. In the Cost box, set the relative cost of the link. The default cost is 100.

3. In the Replicate Every box, set the replication interval. The default interval is 180 minutes.

4. The default replication schedule is 24 hours a day, 7 days a week. To set a different schedule, click Change Schedule, and then set the replication schedule in the Schedule For dialog box. Click OK.

You can change the sites associated with a site link at any time by following these steps:

1. In Active Directory Sites And Services, right-click the site link in the details pane, and then click Properties.

2. In the Properties dialog box, the General tab is selected by default. In the Sites Not In This Site Link list, click the first site that should be included in the link, and then click Add to add the site to the Sites In This Site Link list. Repeat this process for each site you want to add to the link.

3. In the Sites In This Site Link list, click the first site that should not be included in the link, and then click Remove to add the site to the Sites Not In This Site

Link list. Repeat this process for each site you want to remove from the link. Click OK.

Configuring Site Link Bridges

All site links are transitive by default. This means that when more than two sites are linked for replication and use the same transport, site links are bridged automatically, allowing links to be transitive between sites. Because of transitivity, any two domain controllers can make a connection across any consecutive series of links. For example, a domain controller in site A could connect to a domain controller in site C through site B.

The link path domain controllers choose for connections across sites is largely determined by the site link bridge cost. The site link bridge cost is the sum of all the links included in the bridge; generally, the path with the lowest total site link bridge cost is used.

Knowing the costs of links and link bridges, you can calculate the effects of a network link failure and determine the paths that will be used when a connection is down. For example, a domain controller in site A would normally connect to a domain controller in site C through site B. However, if the connection to site B is down, the two domain controllers would choose an alternate path automatically if one is available, such as going through site D and site E to establish a connection.

Intersite replication topology is optimized for a maximum of three hops by default. In large-site configurations, this can have unintended consequences, such as the same replication traffic going over the same link several times. In this case, you should disable automatic site link bridging and manually configure site link bridges. Otherwise you typically do not want to disable automatic site link bridging.

Within an Active Directory forest, you can enable or disable site link transitivity on a per-transport protocol basis. This means all site links that use a particular transport use site link transitivity or they don't. You can configure transitivity for a transport protocol by following these steps:

1. In Active Directory Sites And Services, expand the Sites container, and then expand the Inter-Site Transports container.

2. Right-click the container for the transport protocol you want to work with (either IP or SMTP), and then click Properties.

3. To enable site link transitivity, select Bridge All Site Links, and then click OK. When site link transitivity is enabled, any site link bridges you've created for a particular transport protocol are ignored.

4. To disable site link transitivity, clear the Bridge All Site Links check box, and then click OK. When site link transitivity is disabled, you must configure site link bridges for the affected protocol.

Once you've disabled transitive links, you can manually create a site link bridge between two or more sites by following these steps:

1. In Active Directory Sites And Services, expand the Sites container, and then expand the Inter-Site Transports container.

2. Right-click the container for the transport protocol you want to work with (either IP or SMTP), and then click New Site Link Bridge.

3. In the New Object—Site Link Bridge dialog box, type a name for the site link bridge. Bridge names cannot contain spaces or special characters other than a dash.

4. In the Site Links Not In This Site Link Bridge list, select a site link that should be included in the bridge, and then click Add to add the site link to the Site Links In This Site Link Bridge list. Repeat this process for each site link you want to add to the bridge. A bridge must include at least two site links. Click OK.

You can change the site links associated with a site link bridge at any time by following these steps:

1. In Active Directory Sites And Services, right-click the container for the transport protocol you want to work with, and then click Properties.

2. In the Properties dialog box, the General tab is selected by default. In the Site Links Not In This Site Link Bridge list, click the first site link that should be included in the bridge, and then click Add to add the site link to the Site Links In This Site Link Bridge list. Repeat this process for each site link you want to add to the bridge.

3. In the Site Links In This Site Link Bridge list, click the first site link that should not be included in the bridge, and then click Remove to add the site link to the Site Links Not In This Site Link Bridge list. Repeat this process for each site link you want to remove from the bridge. Click OK.

Maintaining Active Directory

To ensure proper operations of Active Directory, you need to perform periodic monitoring and maintenance. In your monitoring and maintenance efforts, you'll find that some tools are instrumental to your success. In this section, I'll introduce these tools as well as some general maintenance tasks.

Using ADSI Edit

When you are diagnosing problems and troubleshooting, the Active Directory administration tool you should use is ADSI Edit. You can use ADSI Edit to manage the definitions of object classes and their attributes in schema and to work with other naming contexts, including the default naming context, the Configuration naming context, and the RootDSE naming context. If you want to create custom attributes for users or groups, use ADSI Edit, which you can start using the related option on the Administrative Tools menu.

You can use the ADSI Edit snap-in to connect to a naming context by following these steps:

1. Right-click the ADSI Edit node in the console tree, and then click Connect To. This displays the Connection Settings dialog box, shown in Figure 8-11.

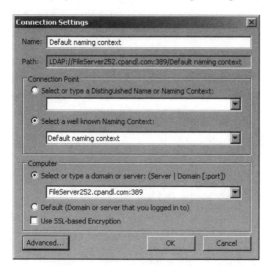

FIGURE 8-11 Connect to a naming context in ADSI Edit.

2. In the Connection Settings dialog box, the Select A Well Known Naming Context list is enabled by default. Choose the naming context you want to work with.

3. When you click OK, you are connected to any available domain controller in your logon domain. To connect to a different domain or server, select Select Or Type A Domain Or Server, and then choose the server or domain you want to work with along with an optional port number for the connection, such as FileServer252.cpandl.com:389. Port 389 is the default port for LDAP.

After you select a naming context, domain, and server, you are connected to and can work with the naming context. As Figure 8-12 shows, when you connect to multiple naming contexts, you have separate nodes for managing each context. For troubleshooting, you can connect to the same naming context on different servers in the same domain as well. By comparing the values associated with properties on one server with those on another, you can identify a replication problem.

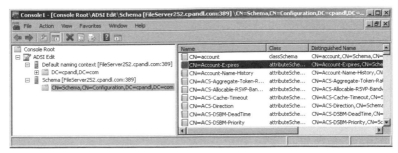

FIGURE 8-12 Navigate the naming contexts to examine related containers and properties.

Examining Intersite Topology

The Inter-Site Topology Generator (ISTG) in a site is responsible for generating the intersite replication topology. When calculating the replication topology, the ISTG can use considerable processing power, especially as the size of the network grows. Because of this, you should closely monitor the ISTGs in each site to ensure that they are not overloaded.

You can determine which domain controller is the ISTG by following these steps:

1. In Active Directory Sites And Services, expand the Sites container, and then expand the site for the ISTG you want to locate in the console tree.

2. In the details pane, double-click NTDS Site Settings. In the NTDS Site Settings dialog box, the current ISTG is listed in the Inter-Site Topology Generator panel.

Replication between sites is performed by bridgehead servers. A bridgehead server is a domain controller designated by the ISTG to perform intersite replication. When two sites are connected by a site link, the ISTG selects one bridgehead server in each site and creates inbound-only connection objects between the servers for intersite replication.

The ISTG configures a bridgehead server for each Active Directory partition that needs to be replicated and maintains a separate replication topology for each type of partition. Although a single bridgehead server can be responsible for replicating multiple directory partitions, the replication topology for each partition is maintained separately.

Domain controllers that operate as bridgehead servers have an additional workload that increases with the number and frequency of replication changes. As you should do with the ISTG, you should closely monitor designated bridgehead servers to ensure that they do not become overloaded. You can list the bridgehead servers in a site by entering the following command at a command prompt:

```
repadmin /bridgeheads site:SiteName
```

where *SiteName* is the name of the site, such as:

```
repadmin /bridgeheads site:SacramentoSite
```

If current bridgehead servers become overloaded, or if you have domain control-lers that you would prefer to be bridgehead servers, you can designate preferred bridgehead servers to use. Once you designate a preferred bridgehead server for a site, the ISTG will use only the preferred bridgehead server for intersite replication. If the preferred bridgehead server goes offline or is unable to replicate for any reason, intersite replication will stop until the server is again available or you change the preferred bridgehead server configuration.

When you designate preferred bridgeheads, you should always configure multiple preferred bridgehead servers in each site. The ISTG will then choose one of the serv-ers you've designated as the preferred bridgehead server. If this server fails, the ISTG would then choose another server from the list of preferred bridgehead servers.

You must configure a bridgehead server for each partition that needs to be rep-licated. This means you must configure at least one domain controller with a replica of each directory partition as a bridgehead server. If you don't do this, replication of the partition will fail and the ISTG will log an event in the Directory Services event log detailing the failure.

You can configure a domain controller as a preferred bridgehead server by fol-lowing these steps:

1. In Active Directory Sites And Services, domain controllers associated with a site are listed in the site's Servers node. Right-click the server you want to designate as a preferred bridgehead, and then click Properties.

2. In the Properties dialog box, select the intersite transport protocol for which the server should be a preferred bridgehead in the Transports Available For Inter-Site Data Transfer list, and then click Add. Repeat as necessary to specify both IP and SMTP. Click OK.

When you've designated preferred bridgehead servers, you can recover from replication failure in several different ways. You can remove the failed servers as preferred bridgehead servers and then specify different preferred bridgehead serv-ers, or you can remove all servers as preferred bridgehead servers and then allow the ISTG to select the bridgehead servers that should be used. To stop a server from being a preferred bridgehead for a particular transport protocol, follow these steps:

1. In Active Directory Sites And Services, domain controllers associated with a site are listed in the site's Servers node. Right-click the server you want to stop using as a preferred bridgehead, and then click Properties.

2. Select the transport protocol in the This Server Is A Preferred Bridgehead Server For The Following Transports list, and then click Remove. Click OK.

Troubleshooting Active Directory

As part of routine maintenance, you need to monitor domain controllers, global cat-alog servers, bridgehead servers, and site links. If you suspect problems with Active Directory, you should look at replication in most cases as the starting point for your diagnostics and troubleshooting. By configuring monitoring of Active Directory intrasite and intersite replication, you can diagnose and resolve most replication problems. Keep in mind, though, that Active Directory replication has several service dependencies, including LDAP, Domain Name System (DNS), Kerberos version 5 authentication, and Remote Procedure Call (RPC).

These important services must be functioning properly to allow directory updates to be replicated. During replication, Active Directory relies on various TCP and UDP ports being open between domain controllers. By default, the ports used are as follows:

- LDAP uses TCP and UDP on port 389 for standard traffic and TCP on port 686 for secure traffic.

- Global catalogs use TCP on port 3268. Kerberos version 5 uses TCP and UDP on port 88.

- DNS uses TCP and UDP on port 53.

- SMB over IP uses TCP and UDP on port 445.

Additionally, for replication of files in the System Volume (SYSVOL) shared folders on domain controllers, Active Directory uses either the File Replication Service (FRS) or the DFS Replication Service. The appropriate replication service must be running and properly configured to replicate the SYSVOL.

Active Directory tracks changes using update sequence numbers (USNs). Any time a change is made to the directory, the domain controller processing the change assigns the change a USN. Each domain controller maintains its own local USNs and increments the value each time a change occurs. The domain controller also assigns the local USN to the object attribute that changed. Each object has a related attribute called *uSNChanged,* which is stored with the object and identifies the highest USN that has been assigned to any of the object's attributes.

Each domain controller tracks its local USN and also the local USNs of other domain controllers. During replication, domain controllers compare the USN values received to what is stored. If the current USN value for a particular domain controller is higher than the stored value, changes associated with that domain controller need to be replicated. If the current value for a particular domain controller is the same as the stored value, changes for that domain controller do not need to be replicated.

You can monitor replication from the command line using Repadmin. With Repadmin, most command-line parameters accept a list of the domain controllers you want to work with, called DCList. You can specify the values for DCList as follows:

- * A wildcard that includes all domain controllers in the organization.

- ***PartialName*** A partial server name followed by the * wildcard character to match the remainder of the server name.

- **Site:*SiteName*** The name of the site for which you want to include domain controllers.
- **Gc:** Includes all global catalog servers in the organization.

Although Repadmin has many parameters and you can use it in many ways, you'll perform certain tasks more than others. Table 8-2 shows some of these tasks.

TABLE 8-2 Common Replication Tasks and Commands

TASK	COMMAND
Forcing the Knowledge Consistency Checker (KCC) to recalculate the intrasite replication topology for a specified domain controller.	repadmin /kcc DCList [/async]
Listing bridgehead servers that match the DCList.	repadmin /bridgeheads [DCList] [/verbose]
Listing calls made but not yet answered by the specified server to other servers.	repadmin /showoutcalls [DCList]
Listing domains trusted by a specified domain.	repadmin /showtrust [DCList]
Listing failed replication events that were detected by the KCC.	repadmin /failcache [DCList]
Listing connection objects for the specified domain controllers. Defaults to the local site.	repadmin /showconn [DCList]
Listing computers that have opened sessions with a specified domain controller.	repadmin /showctx [DCList]
Listing the name of the ISTG for a specified site.	repadmin istg [DCList] [/verbose]
Listing replication partners for each directory partition on the specified domain controller.	repadmin /showrepl [DCList]
Listing a summary of the replication state.	repadmin /replsummary [DCList]
Listing server certificates loaded on the specified domain controllers.	repadmin /showcert [DCList]
Listing tasks waiting in the replication queue.	repadmin /queue [DCList]
Listing the time between intersite replications using the ISTG Keep Alive time stamp.	repadmin /latency [DCList] [/verbose]

CHAPTER 9

Understanding User and Group Accounts

M anaging accounts is one of your primary tasks as a Windows administrator. Chapter 8, "Core Active Directory Administration," discusses computer accounts. This chapter examines user and group accounts. With user accounts, you can enable individual users to log on to the network and access network resources. With group accounts, you manage resources for multiple users. The permissions and privileges you assign to user and group accounts determine which actions users can perform as well as which computer systems and resources they can access.

Although you might be tempted to give users wide access, you need to balance a user's need for job-related resources with your need to protect sensitive resources or privileged information. For example, you don't want everyone in the company to have access to payroll data. Consequently, you should be sure that only those who need that information have access to it.

The Windows Server Security Model

You control access to network resources with the components of the Windows Server security model. The key components you need to know about are those used for authentication and access controls.

Authentication Protocols

Windows Server authentication is implemented as a two-part process consisting of an interactive logon and network authentication. When a user logs on to a computer using a domain account, the interactive logon process authenticates the user's logon credentials, which confirms the user's identity to the local computer and grants access to Active Directory Domain Services. Afterward, whenever the user attempts to access network resources, network authentication is used to determine whether the user has permission to do so.

Windows Server 2008 Release 2 supports many network authentication protocols. Active Directory uses Kerberos version 5 as the default authentication protocol. NTLM authentication is maintained only for backward compatibility. In Group Policy, you can control how NTLM is used with the security option Network Security: LAN Manager Authentication Level. The default authentication level in most cases is Send NTLMv2 Response Only. With this authentication level, clients use NTLM version 2 for authentication and session security if the server supports it. Active Directory can also use client certificates for authentication.

A key feature of the Windows Server authentication model is that it supports single sign-on, which works as follows:

1. A user logs on to the domain by using a logon name and password or by inserting a smart card into a card reader.

2. The interactive logon process authenticates the user's access. With a local account, the credentials are authenticated locally, and the user is granted access to the local computer. With a domain account, the credentials are authenticated in Active Directory, and the user has access to local and network resources.

3. Now the user can authenticate to any computer in the domain through the network authentication process.

With domain accounts, the network authentication process typically is automatic (through single sign-on). With local accounts, on the other hand, users must provide a user name and password every time they access a network resource.

Windows Server includes Active Directory Federation Services (AD FS), which extends single sign-on to trusted resources on the Internet. Using AD FS, organizations can extend their existing Active Directory infrastructure to provide access to trusted Internet resources, which can include third parties as well as geographically separated units of the same organization. After you configure federated servers, users at the organization can sign on once to the organization's network and are then automatically logged on to trusted Web applications hosted by partners on the Internet. Federated Web Single Sign-On uses federated authorization for seamless access. In addition to user identity and account information, security tokens used in federated authorization include authorization claims that detail user authorization and specific application entitlement.

Access Controls

Active Directory is object-based. Users, computers, groups, shared resources, and many other entities are all defined as objects. Access controls are applied to these objects with security descriptors. Security descriptors do the following:

- List the users and groups that are granted access to objects
- Specify permissions the users and groups have been assigned
- Track events that should be audited for objects
- Define ownership of objects

Individual entries in the security descriptor are referred to as *access control entries* (ACEs). Active Directory objects can inherit ACEs from their parent objects. This means that permissions for a parent object can be applied to a child object. For example, all members of the Domain Admins group inherit permissions granted to this group.

When working with ACEs, keep the following points in mind:

- ACEs are created with inheritance enabled by default.
- Inheritance takes place immediately after the ACE is created and saved.
- All ACEs contain information specifying whether the permission is inherited or explicitly assigned to the related object.

Differences Between User and Group Accounts

Windows Server 2008 R2 provides user accounts and group accounts (of which users can be a member). User accounts are designed for individuals. Group accounts are designed to make the administration of multiple users easier. Although you can log on with user accounts, you can't log on with a group account. Group accounts are usually referred to simply as *groups*.

> **REAL WORLD** Windows Server supports the InetOrgPerson object. Essentially, this object is the same as a user object, and you can use it as such. However, the real purpose for the InetOrgPerson object is to allow for compatibility and transition from third-party X.500 and Lightweight Directory Access Protocol (LDAP) directory services that use this object to represent users. If you are migrating from a third-party directory service and end up with many InetOrgPerson objects, don't worry. You can use these objects as security principals just like user accounts. The InetOrg-Person object is fully enabled only when working in Windows Server 2003 or higher domain operations mode. In this mode, you can set passwords for InetOrgPerson objects and you can change the object class if you want to. When you change the object class, the InetOrgPerson object is converted to a user object, and from then on it is listed as the User type in Active Directory Users And Computers.

User Accounts

Two types of user accounts are defined in Windows Server:

- User accounts defined in Active Directory are called *domain user accounts*. Through single sign-on, domain user accounts can access resources throughout the domain. You create domain user accounts in Active Directory Users And Computers.

- User accounts defined on a local computer are called *local user accounts*. Local user accounts have access to the local computer only, and they must authenticate themselves before they can access network resources. You create local user accounts with the Local Users And Groups utility.

NOTE In a domain, only member servers and workstations have local user and group accounts. On the initial domain controller for a domain, these accounts are moved from the local Security Account Manager (SAM) database to Active Directory and then become domain accounts.

Logon Names, Passwords, and Public Certificates

All user accounts are identified with a logon name. In Windows Server, this logon name has two parts:

- **User name**   The text label for the account
- **User domain or workgroup**   The workgroup or domain where the user account exists

For the user wrstanek, whose account is created in the cpandl.com domain, the full logon name is wrstanek@cpandl.com. The pre–Windows 2000 logon name is CPANDL\wrstanek.

When working with Active Directory, you might also need to specify the *fully qualified domain name* (FQDN) for a user. The FQDN for a user is the combination of the Domain Name System (DNS) domain name, the container or organizational unit that contains the user, and the user name. For the user cpandl.com\users\wrstanek, *cpandl.com* is the DNS domain name, *users* is the container or organizational unit location, and *wrstanek* is the user name.

User accounts can also have passwords and public certificates associated with them. Passwords are authentication strings for an account. Public certificates combine a public and private key to identify a user. You log on with a password interactively. You log on with a public certificate using a smart card and a smart card reader.

Security Identifiers and User Accounts

Although Windows Server displays user names to describe privileges and permissions, the key identifiers for accounts are *security identifiers* (SIDs). SIDs are unique identifiers that are generated when you create accounts. Each account's SID consists of the domain's security ID prefix and a unique relative ID (RID), which is allocated by the relative ID master.

Windows Server uses these identifiers to track accounts independently from user names. SIDs serve many purposes. The two most important purposes are to allow you to change user names easily and to allow you to delete accounts without worrying that someone might gain access to resources simply by re-creating an account with the same name.

When you change a user name, you tell Windows Server to map a particular SID to a new name. When you delete an account, you tell Windows Server that a particular SID is no longer valid. Afterward, even if you create an account with the same user name, the new account won't have the same privileges and permissions as the previous one. That's because the new account will have a new SID.

Group Accounts

In addition to user accounts, Windows Server provides groups. Generally speaking, you use groups to grant permissions to similar types of users and to simplify account administration. If a user is a member of a group that can access a resource, that particular user can access the same resource. Thus, you can give a user access to various work-related resources just by making the user a member of the correct group. Note that although you can log on to a computer with a user account, you can't log on to a computer with a group account.

Because different Active Directory domains might have groups with the same name, groups are often referred to by *domain\groupname*, such as cpandl\ gmarketing for the Gmarketing group in the cpandl domain. When you work with Active Directory, you might also need to specify the FQDN for a group. The FQDN for a group is the concatenation of the DNS domain name, the container or organizational unit location, and the group name. For the group cpandl.com\users\ gmarketing, *cpandl.com* is the DNS domain name, *users* is the container or organizational unit location, and *gmarketing* is the group name.

> **REAL WORLD** Employees in a marketing department probably need access to all marketing-related resources. Instead of granting access to these resources to each individual employee, you could make the users members of a marketing group. That way they automatically obtain the group's privileges. Later, if a user moves to a different department, you simply remove the user from the group, thus revoking all access permissions. Compared to having to revoke access for each individual resource, this technique is pretty easy, so you'll want to use groups whenever possible.

Group Types

Windows Server supports three types of groups:

- **Local groups** Groups that are defined on a local computer. Local groups are used on the local computer only. You create local groups with the Local Users And Groups utility.

- **Security groups** Groups that can have security descriptors associated with them. You define security groups in domains by using Active Directory Users And Computers.

- **Distribution groups** Groups that are used as e-mail distribution lists. They can't have security descriptors associated with them. You define distribution groups in domains by using Active Directory Users And Computers.

NOTE Most general discussions about groups focus on local groups and security groups rather than distribution groups. Distribution groups are only for e-mail distribution and are not for assigning or managing access.

Group Scope

In Active Directory, groups can have different scopes—domain local, built-in local, global, and universal. That is, the groups are valid in different areas.

- **Domain local groups** Groups primarily used to assign access permissions to resources within a single domain. Domain local groups can include members from any domain in the forest and from trusted domains in other forests. Typically, global and universal groups are members of domain local groups.

- **Built-in local groups** Groups with a special group scope that have domain local permissions and, for simplicity, are often included in the term *domain local groups*. The difference between built-in local groups and other groups is that you can't create or delete built-in local groups. You can only modify built-in local groups. References to domain local groups apply to built-in local groups unless otherwise noted.

- **Global groups** Groups that are used primarily to define sets of users or computers in the same domain that share a similar role, function, or job. Members of global groups can include only accounts and groups from the domain in which they're defined.

- **Universal groups** Groups that are used primarily to define sets of users or computers that should have wide permissions throughout a domain or forest. Members of universal groups include accounts, global groups, and other universal groups from any domain in the domain tree or forest.

BEST PRACTICES Universal groups are very useful in large enterprises where you have multiple domains. If you plan properly, you can use universal groups to simplify system administration. You shouldn't change the members of universal groups frequently. Each time you change the members of a universal group, you need to replicate those changes to all the global catalogs in the domain tree or forest. To reduce changes, assign other groups rather than user accounts to the universal group. For more information, see "When to Use Domain Local, Global, and Universal Groups" later in this chapter.

When you work with groups, the group's scope restricts what you can and cannot do. Table 9-1 offers a quick summary of these items. For complete details on creating groups, see Chapter 10, "Creating User and Group Accounts."

TABLE 9-1 How Group Scope Affects Group Capabilities

GROUP CAPABILITY	DOMAIN LOCAL SCOPE	GLOBAL SCOPE	UNIVERSAL SCOPE
Members	Accounts, global groups, and universal groups from any domain; domain local groups from the same domain only.	Accounts and global groups from the same domain only.	Accounts from any domain, as well as global and universal groups from any domain.
Member of	Can be put into other domain local groups and assigned permissions only in the same domain.	Can be put into other groups and assigned permissions in any domain.	Can be put into other groups and assigned permissions in any domain.
Scope conversion	Can be converted to universal scope provided that it doesn't have as its member another group having domain local scope.	Can be converted to universal scope provided that it's not a member of any other group having global scope.	Can't be converted to any other group scope.

Security Identifiers and Group Accounts

As with user accounts, Windows Server tracks group accounts with unique SIDs. This means that you can't delete a group account, re-create it, and then expect all the permissions and privileges to remain the same. The new group will have a new SID, and all the permissions and privileges of the old group are lost.

Windows Server creates a security token for each user logon. The security token specifies the user account ID and the SIDs of all the security groups to which the user belongs. The token's size grows as the user is added to additional security groups, which has the following consequences:

- The security token must be passed to the user logon process before logon can be completed. As the number of security group memberships grows, the logon process takes longer.

- To determine access permissions, the security token is sent to every computer that the user accesses. Therefore, the size of the security token has a direct impact on the network traffic load.

When to Use Domain Local, Global, and Universal Groups

Domain local, global, and universal groups provide many options for configuring groups in the enterprise. Although these group scopes are designed to simplify administration, poor planning can make them your worst administration nightmare. Ideally, you'll use group scopes to help you create group hierarchies that are similar to your organization's structure and the responsibilities of particular groups of users. The best uses for domain local, global, and universal groups are as follows:

- **Domain local groups** Groups with domain local scope have the smallest extent. Use groups with domain local scope to help you manage access to resources such as printers and shared folders.

- **Global groups** Use groups with global scope to help you manage user and computer accounts in a particular domain. Then you can grant access permissions to a resource by making the group with global scope a member of the group with domain local scope.

- **Universal groups** Groups with universal scope have the largest extent. Use groups with universal scope to consolidate groups that span domains. Normally, you do this by adding global groups as members. Now, when you change membership of the global groups, the changes aren't replicated to all global catalogs because the membership of the universal group didn't change.

TIP If your organization doesn't have two or more domains, you don't really need to use universal groups. Instead, build your group structure with domain local and global groups. Then, if you ever bring another domain into your domain tree or forest, you can easily extend the group hierarchy to accommodate the integration.

To put this in perspective, consider the following scenario. Say that you have branch offices in Seattle, Chicago, and New York. Each office has its own domain, which is part of the same domain tree or forest. These domains are called Seattle, Chicago, and NY. You want to make it easy for any administrator (from any office) to manage network resources, so you create a group structure that is very similar at each location. Although the company has marketing, IT, and engineering departments, let's focus on the structure of the marketing department. At each office, members of the marketing department need access to a shared printer called MarketingPrinter and a shared data folder called MarketingData. You also want users to be able to share and print documents. For example, Bob in Seattle should be able to print documents so that Ralph in New York can pick them up on his local printer, and Bob should also be able to access the quarterly report in the shared folder at the New York office.

To configure the groups for the marketing departments at the three offices, you'd follow these steps:

1. Start by creating global groups for each marketing group. In the Seattle domain, create a group called GMarketing and add the members of the Seattle marketing department to it. In the Chicago domain, create a group called GMarketing and add the members of the Chicago marketing department to it. In the NY domain, create a group called GMarketing and add the members of the New York marketing department to it.

2. In each location, create domain local groups that grant access to the shared printers and shared folders. Call the printer group LocalMarketingPrinter. Call the shared folder group LocalMarketingData. The Seattle, Chicago, and NY domains should each have their own local groups.

3. Create a group with universal scope in the domain at any branch office. Call the group UMarketing. Add Seattle\GMarketing, Chicago\GMarketing, and NY\GMarketing to this group.

4. Add UMarketing to the LocalMarketingPrinter and LocalMarketingData groups at each office. Marketing users should now be able to share data and printers.

Default User Accounts and Groups

When you install Windows Server, the operating system installs default users and groups. These accounts are designed to provide the basic setup necessary to grow your network. Three types of default accounts are provided:

- **Built-in**   User and group accounts installed with the operating system, applications, and services

- **Predefined**   User and group accounts installed with the operating system

- **Implicit**   Special groups, also known as *special identities*, created implicitly when accessing network resources

NOTE Although you can modify default users and groups, you can't delete default users and groups created by the operating system because you wouldn't be able to re-create them. The SIDs of the old and new accounts wouldn't match, and the permissions and privileges of these accounts would be lost.

Built-in User Accounts

Built-in user accounts have special purposes in Windows Server. All Windows Server systems have three built-in user accounts:

- **LocalSystem**   LocalSystem is a pseudoaccount for running system processes and handling system-level tasks. This account is part of the Administrators group on the server and has all user rights on the server. If you configure applications or services to use this account, the related processes have full access to the server system. Many services run under the LocalSystem account. In some cases, these services have the privilege to interact with the desktop as well. Services that need alternative privileges or logon rights run under the LocalService or NetworkService account.

- **LocalService** LocalService is a pseudoaccount with limited privileges. This account grants access to the local system only. The account is part of the Users group on the server and has the same rights as the NetworkService account, except that it is limited to the local computer. Configure applications or services to use this account when related processes don't need to access other servers.

- **NetworkService** NetworkService is a pseudoaccount for running services that need additional privileges and logon rights on a local system and the network. This account is part of the Users group on the server and provides fewer permissions and privileges than the LocalSystem account (but more than the LocalService account). Specifically, processes running under this account can interact throughout a network using the credentials of the computer account.

When you install add-ons or other applications on a server, other default accounts might be installed.

Predefined User Accounts

Several predefined user accounts are installed with Windows Server, including Administrator and Guest. With member servers, predefined accounts are local to the individual system they're installed on.

Predefined accounts have counterparts in Active Directory. These accounts have domainwide access and are completely separate from the local accounts on individual systems.

The Administrator Account

Administrator is a predefined account that provides complete access to files, directories, services, and other facilities. In Active Directory, the Administrator account has domainwide access and privileges. Otherwise, the Administrator account generally has access only to the local system. Although files and directories can be protected from the Administrator account temporarily, the Administrator account can take control of these resources at any time by changing the access permissions. By default, the Administrator account is enabled for use, but you can disable or rename it to enhance security.

> **SECURITY ALERT** To prevent unauthorized access to the system or domain, be sure to give the Administrator account an especially secure password. Also, because this is a known Windows account, you might want to rename the account as an extra security precaution. If you rename the original Administrator account, you might also want to create a dummy Administrator account. This dummy account should have no permissions, rights, or privileges, and you should disable it.

You usually won't need to change the basic settings for the Administrator account. However, you might need to change its advanced settings, such as membership in particular groups. By default, the Administrator account for a domain is a member of these groups: Administrators, Domain Admins, Domain Users, Enterprise Admins, Group Policy Creator Owners, and Schema Admins. You'll find more information about these groups in the next section.

REAL WORLD In a domain environment, you use the local Administrator account primarily to manage the system when you first install it. This allows you to set up the system without getting locked out. You probably won't use the account once the system has been installed. Instead, you should make your administrators members of the Administrators group. This ensures that you can revoke administrator privileges without having to change the passwords for all the Administrator accounts.

For a system that's part of a workgroup where each individual computer is managed separately, you typically rely on this account any time you need to perform your system administration duties. Here, you probably don't want to set up individual accounts for each person who has administrative access to a system. Instead, use a separate administrator account on each computer.

The Guest Account

The Guest account is designed for users who need one-time or occasional access. Although guests have limited system privileges, you should be very careful about using this account. Whenever you use this account, you open the system to potential security problems. The risk is so great that the account is initially disabled when you install Windows Server.

The Guest account is a member of the Domain Guests and Guests groups by default. It is important to note that the Guest account—like all other named accounts—is also a member of the implicit group Everyone. The Everyone group typically has access to files and folders by default. The Everyone group also has a default set of user rights.

SECURITY ALERT If you decide to enable the Guest account, be sure to restrict its use and to change the password regularly. As with the Administrator account, you might want to rename the account as an added security precaution.

Built-in and Predefined Groups

Built-in groups are installed with all Windows Server systems. Use built-in and predefined groups to grant a user the group's privileges and permissions. You do this by making the user a member of the group. For example, you give a user administrative access to the system by making a user a member of the local Administrators group. You give a user administrative access to the domain by making a user a member of the Domain Admins group in Active Directory.

Implicit Groups and Special Identities

In Windows NT, implicit groups were assigned implicitly during logon and were based on how a user accessed a network resource. For example, if a user accessed a resource through an interactive logon, the user was automatically a member of the implicit group called Interactive. In Windows 2000 and later releases, the object-based approach to the directory structure has changed the original rules for implicit groups. Although you still can't view the membership of special identities, you can grant membership in implicit groups to users, groups, and computers.

To reflect the modified role, implicit groups are also referred to as *special identities*. A special identity is a group whose membership can be set implicitly, such as during logon, or explicitly through security access permissions. As with other default groups, the availability of a specific implicit group depends on the current configuration. Implicit groups are discussed later in this chapter.

Account Capabilities

When you set up a user account, you can grant the user specific capabilities. You generally assign these capabilities by making the user a member of one or more groups, thus giving the user the capabilities of these groups. You withdraw capabilities by removing group membership.

In Windows Server, you can assign the following types of capabilities to an account:

- **Privileges**   A type of user right that grants permissions to perform specific administrative tasks. You can assign privileges to both user and group accounts. An example of a privilege is the ability to shut down the system.

- **Logon rights**   A type of user right that grants logon permissions. You can assign logon rights to both user and group accounts. An example of a logon right is the ability to log on locally.

- **Built-in capabilities**   A type of user right that is assigned to groups and includes the group's automatic capabilities. Built-in capabilities are predefined and unchangeable, but they can be delegated to users with permission to manage objects, organizational units, or other containers. An example of a built-in capability is the ability to create, delete, and manage user accounts. This capability is assigned to administrators and account operators. Thus, if a user is a member of the Administrators group, the user can create, delete, and manage user accounts.

- **Access permissions**   A type of user right that defines the operations that can be performed on network resources. You can assign access permissions to users, computers, and groups. An example of an access permission is the ability to create a file in a directory. Access permissions are discussed in Chapter 15 "Data Sharing, Security, and Auditing."

As an administrator, you deal with account capabilities every day. To help track built-in capabilities, refer to the following sections. Keep in mind that although you can't change a group's built-in capabilities, you can change a group's default rights. For example, an administrator could revoke network access to a computer by removing a group's right to access the computer from the network.

Privileges

A privilege is a user right assignment that grants permissions to perform a specific administrative task. You assign privileges through group policies, which can be applied to individual computers, organizational units, and domains. Although you can assign privileges to both users and groups, you'll usually want to assign privileges to groups. In this way, users are automatically assigned the appropriate privileges when they become members of a group. Assigning privileges to groups also makes it easier to manage user accounts.

Table 9-2 provides a brief summary of each privilege that you can assign to users and groups. To learn how to assign privileges, see Chapter 10.

TABLE 9-2 Windows Server 2008 R2 Privileges for Users and Groups

PRIVILEGE	DESCRIPTION
Act As Part Of The Operating System	Allows a process to authenticate as any user and gain access to resources as any user. Processes that require this privilege should use the LocalSystem account, which already has this privilege.
Add Workstations To Domain	Allows users to add computers to the domain.
Adjust Memory Quotas For A Process	Allows users to adjust process-based memory usage quotas.
Back Up Files And Directories	Allows users to back up the system regardless of the permissions set on files and directories.
Bypass Traverse Checking	Allows users to pass through directories while navigating an object path regardless of permissions set on the directories. The privilege doesn't allow the user to list directory contents.
Change The System Time	Allows users to set the time for the system clock.
Change The Time Zone	Allows users to set the time zone for the system clock. All users have this privilege by default.
Create A Pagefile	Allows users to create and change paging file size for virtual memory.

PRIVILEGE	DESCRIPTION
Create A Token Object	Allows processes to create token objects that can be used to gain access to local resources. Processes that require this privilege should use the LocalSystem account, which already has this privilege.
Create Global Objects	Allows processes to create global objects. LocalService and NetworkService have the privilege by default.
Create Permanent Shared Objects	Allows processes to create directory objects in the object manager. Most components already have this privilege; it's not necessary to specifically assign it.
Create Symbolic Links	Allows an application that a user is running to create symbolic links. Symbolic links make it appear as though a document or folder is in a specific location when it actually resides in another location. Use of symbolic links is restricted by default to enhance security.
Debug Programs	Allows users to perform debugging.
Enable User And Computer Accounts To Be Trusted For Delegation	Allows users and computers to change or apply the trusted-for-delegation setting, provided they have write access to the object.
Force Shutdown Of A Remote System	Allows users to shut down a computer from a remote location on the network.
Generate Security Audits	Allows processes to make security log entries for auditing object access.
Impersonate A Client After Authentication	Allows Web applications to act as clients during processing of requests. Services and users can also act as clients.
Increase A Process Working Set	Allows an application that a user is running to increase the memory that the related process working set uses. A process working set is the set of memory pages currently visible to a process in physical memory. Allowing for increases in memory pages reduces page faults and enhances performance.
Increase Scheduling Priority	Allows processes to increase the scheduling priority assigned to another process, provided that they have write access to the process.

PRIVILEGE	DESCRIPTION
Load And Unload Device Drivers	Allows users to install and uninstall Plug and Play device drivers. This doesn't affect device drivers that aren't Plug and Play, which can be installed only by administrators.
Lock Pages In Memory	Allows processes to keep data in physical memory, preventing the system from paging data to virtual memory on disk.
Manage Auditing And Security Log	Allows users to specify auditing options and access the security log. You must turn on auditing in the group policy first.
Modify An Object Label	Allows a user process to modify the integrity label of objects, such as files, registry keys, or processes owned by other users. This privilege can be used to lower the priority of other processes. Processes running under a user account can modify the label of any object the user owns without requiring this privilege.
Modify Firmware Environment Values	Allows users and processes to modify system environment variables.
Perform Volume Maintenance Tasks	Allows administration of removable storage, disk defragmenter, and disk management.
Profile A Single Process	Allows users to monitor the performance of nonsystem processes.
Profile System Performance	Allows users to monitor the performance of system processes.
Remove Computer From Docking Station	Allows a laptop to be undocked and removed from the network.
Replace A Process Level Token	Allows processes to replace the default token for subprocesses.
Restore Files And Directories	Allows users to restore backed-up files and directories, regardless of the permissions set on files and directories.
Shut Down The System	Allows users to shut down the local computer.
Synchronize Directory Service Data	Allows users to synchronize directory service data on domain controllers.
Take Ownership Of Files Or Other Objects	Allows users to take ownership of files and any other Active Directory objects.

Logon Rights

A *logon right* is a user right assignment that grants logon permissions. You can assign logon rights to both user and group accounts. As with privileges, you assign logon rights through group policies, and you'll usually want to assign logon rights to groups rather than to individual users.

Table 9-3 provides a brief summary of each logon right that you can assign to users and groups. To learn how to assign logon rights, see Chapter 10.

TABLE 9-3 Windows Server 2008 R2 Logon Rights for Users and Groups

LOGON RIGHT	DESCRIPTION
Access Credential Manager As A Trusted Caller	Grants permission to establish a trusted connection to Credential Manager. Credentials, such as a user name and password or smart card, provide identification and proof of identification.
Access This Computer From The Network	Grants remote access to the computer.
Allow Log On Locally	Grants permission to log on at the computer's keyboard. On domain controllers, this right is restricted by default and only members of the following groups can log on locally: Administrators, Account Operators, Backup Operators, Print Operators, and Server Operators.
Allow Log On Through Remote Desktop Services	Grants access through Remote Desktop Services; necessary for remote assistance and remote desktop.
Deny Access To This Computer From The Network	Denies remote access to the computer through network services.
Deny Logon As Batch Job	Denies the right to log on through a batch job or script.
Deny Logon As Service	Denies the right to log on as a service.
Deny Logon Locally	Denies the right to log on by using the computer's keyboard.
Deny Logon Through Remote Desktop Services	Denies the right to log on through Remote Desktop Services.
Log On As A Batch Job	Grants permission to log on as a batch job or script.
Log On As A Service	Grants permission to log on as a service. The LocalSystem account has this right. A service that runs under a separate account should be assigned this right.

Built-in Capabilities for Groups in Active Directory

The built-in capabilities that are assigned to groups in Active Directory depend on a computer's configuration. Using the Local Group Policy Editor, shown in Figure 9-1, you can view the capabilities that have been assigned to each group by expanding Computer Configuration\Windows Settings\Security Settings\Local Policies and then selecting the User Rights Assignment node.

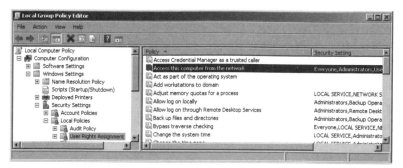

FIGURE 9-1 View the built-in capabilities that are used with groups.

Note that any action that's available to the Everyone group is available to all groups, including the Guests group. This means that although the Guests group doesn't have explicit permission to access the computer from the network, a member of the Guests group can still access the system because the Everyone group has this right.

Table 9-4 summarizes capabilities that you can delegate to other users and groups. As you study the table, note that restricted accounts include the Administrator user account, the user accounts of administrators, and the group accounts for Administrators, Server Operators, Account Operators, Backup Operators, and Print Operators. Because these accounts are restricted, Account Operators can't create or modify them.

TABLE 9-4 Other Capabilities for Built-in and Local Groups

TASK	DESCRIPTION	GROUP NORMALLY ASSIGNED
Assign User Rights	Allows users to assign user rights to other users	Administrators
Create And Delete Groups	Allows users to create new groups and delete existing groups	Administrators, Account Operators
Create And Delete Printers	Allows users to create and delete printers	Administrators, Server Operators, Printer Operators

TASK	DESCRIPTION	GROUP NORMALLY ASSIGNED
Create, Delete, And Manage User Accounts	Allows users to administer domain user accounts	Administrators, Account Operators
Manage Group Policy Links	Allows users to apply existing group policies to sites, domains, and organizational units for which they have write access to the related objects	Administrators
Manage Network Configuration	Allows users to configure networking	Administrators, Network Configuration Operators
Manage Performance Logs	Allows users to configure performance logging	Administrators, Performance Log Users
Manage Printers	Allows users to modify printer settings and manage print queues	Administrators, Server Operators, Printer Operators
Modify The Membership Of A Group	Allows users to add and remove users from domain groups	Administrators, Account Operators
Monitor Performance Logs	Allows users to monitor performance logging	Administrators, Performance Monitor Users
Perform Cryptographic Operations	Allows users to manage cryptographic options	Administrators, Cryptographic Operators
Read All User Information	Allows users to view user account information	Administrators, Server Operators, Account Operators
Read Event Logs	Allows users to read event logs	Administrators, Event Log Readers
Reset Passwords On User Accounts	Allows users to reset passwords on user accounts	Administrators, Account Operators

Using Default Group Accounts

The default group accounts are designed to be versatile. By assigning users to the correct groups, you can make managing your Windows Server 2008 R2 workgroup or domain a lot easier. Unfortunately, with so many groups, understanding the purpose of each isn't easy. To help, let's take a closer look at groups used by administrators and groups that are implicitly created.

Groups Used by Administrators

An administrator is someone who has wide access to network resources. Administrators can create accounts, modify user rights, install printers, manage shared resources, and more. The main administrator groups are Administrators, Domain Admins, and Enterprise Admins. Table 9-5 compares the administrator groups.

TABLE 9-5 Administrator Groups Overview

ADMINISTRATOR GROUP TYPE	NETWORK ENVIRONMENT	GROUP SCOPE	MEMBERSHIP	ACCOUNT ADMINISTRATION
Administrators	Active Directory domains	Domain local	Administrator, Domain Admins, Enterprise Admins	Administrators
Administrators	Workgroups, computers not part of a domain	Local	Administrator	Administrators
Domain Admins	Active Directory domains	Global	Administrator	Administrators
Enterprise Admins	Active Directory domains	Global or universal	Administrator	Administrators

TIP The Administrator account and the global groups Domain Admins and Enterprise Admins are members of the Administrators group. The Administrator account is used to access the local computer. Domain Admins membership allows other administrators to access the system from elsewhere in the domain. Enterprise Admins membership allows other administrators to access the system from other domains in the current domain tree or forest. To prevent enterprise-wide access to a domain, you can remove Enterprise Admins from this group.

Administrators is a local group that provides full administrative access to an individual computer or a single domain, depending on its location. Because this account has complete access, you should be very careful about adding users to this group.

To make someone an administrator for a local computer or domain, all you need to do is make that person a member of this group. Only members of the Administrators group can modify this account.

Domain Admins is a global group designed to help you manage resources in a domain. Members of this group have full control of a domain. This group has administrative control over all computers in a domain because it's a member of the Administrators group by default on all domain controllers, all domain workstations, and all domain member servers at the time they join the domain. To make someone an administrator for a domain, make that person a member of this group.

> **TIP** The Administrator account is a member of Domain Admins by default. This means that if a user logs on to a computer as the administrator and the computer is a member of the domain, the user will have complete access to all resources in the domain.

Enterprise Admins is a global group designed to help you manage resources in a forest. Members of this group have full control of all domains in a forest. This group has administrative control over all domain controllers in the enterprise because the group is a member of the Administrators group by default on all domain controllers in a forest. To make someone an administrator for the enterprise, make that person a member of this group.

> **TIP** The Administrator account is a member of Enterprise Admins by default. This means that if someone logs on to a computer as the administrator and the computer is a member of the domain, the user will have complete access to the domain tree or forest.

Implicit Groups and Identities

Windows Server defines a set of special identities that you can use to assign permissions in certain situations. You usually assign permissions implicitly to special identities. However, you can assign permissions to special identities directly when you modify Active Directory objects. The special identities include the following:

- **The Anonymous Logon identity** Any user accessing the system through anonymous logon has the Anonymous Logon identity. This identity allows anonymous access to resources, such as a Web page published on the corporate presence servers.

- **The Authenticated Users identity** Any user accessing the system through a logon process has the Authenticated Users identity. This identity allows access to shared resources within the domain, such as files in a shared folder that should be accessible to all the workers in the organization.

- **The Batch identity** Any user or process accessing the system as a batch job (or through the batch queue) has the Batch identity. This identity allows batch jobs to run scheduled tasks, such as a nightly cleanup job that deletes temporary files.

- **The Creator Group identity** Windows Server uses this special identity group to automatically grant access permissions to users who are members of the same group or groups as the creator of a file or a directory.

- **The Creator Owner identity** The person who created the file or the directory is a member of this special identity group. Windows Server uses this identity to automatically grant access permissions to the creator of a file or directory.

- **The Dial-Up identity** Any user accessing the system through a dial-up connection has the Dial-Up identity. This identity distinguishes dial-up users from other types of authenticated users.

- **The Enterprise Domain Controllers identity** Domain controllers with enterprise-wide roles and responsibilities have the Enterprise Domain Controllers identity. This identity allows them to perform certain tasks in the enterprise using transitive trusts.

- **The Everyone identity** All interactive, network, dial-up, and authenticated users are members of the Everyone group. This special identity group gives wide access to a system resource.

- **The Interactive identity** Any user logged on to the local system has the Interactive identity. This identity allows only local users to access a resource.

- **The Network identity** Any user accessing the system through a network has the Network identity. This identity allows only remote users to access a resource.

- **The Proxy identity** Users and computers accessing resources through a proxy have the Proxy identity. This identity is used when proxies are implemented on the network.

- **The Remote Desktop Services User identity** Any user accessing the system through Remote Desktop Services has the Remote Desktop Services User identity. This identity allows Remote Desktop Services users to access Remote Desktop Services applications and to perform other necessary tasks with Remote Desktop Services.

- **The Restricted identity** Users and computers with restricted capabilities have the Restricted identity.

- **The Self identity** The Self identity refers to the object itself and allows the object to modify itself.

- **The Service identity** Any service accessing the system has the Service identity. This identity grants access to processes being run by Windows Server services.

- **The System identity** The Windows Server operating system itself has the System identity. This identity is used when the operating system needs to perform a system-level function.

Creating User and Group Accounts

A key part of your job as an administrator is to create accounts, and this chapter shows you how. User and group accounts allow Windows Server 2008 R2 to track and manage information about users, including permissions and privileges. To create user accounts, you primarily use the following two account administration tools:

- Active Directory Users And Computers, which is designed to administer accounts throughout an Active Directory Domain Services domain
- Local Users And Groups, which is designed to administer accounts on a local computer

This chapter covers creating domain accounts as well as local users and groups.

User Account Setup and Organization

The most important aspects of account creation are account setup and account organization. Without the appropriate guidelines and policies, you might quickly find that you need to rework all your user accounts. Before you create accounts, determine the policies you'll use for setup and organization.

Account Naming Policies

A key policy you need to set is the naming scheme for accounts. User accounts have display names and logon names. The *display name* (or full name) is the name displayed to users and the name referenced in user sessions. The *logon name* is the name used to log on to the domain. Logon names are discussed briefly in "Logon Names, Passwords, and Public Certificates" in Chapter 9.

Rules for Display Names

For domain accounts, the display name is normally the concatenation of the user's first name, middle initial, and last name, but you can set it to any string value. The display names must follow these rules:

- Local display names must be unique on an individual computer.
- Display names must be unique throughout a domain.
- Display names must be no more than 64 characters.
- Display names can contain alphanumeric characters and special characters.

Rules for Logon Names

Logon names must follow these rules:

- Local logon names must be unique on an individual computer, and global logon names must be unique throughout a domain.
- Logon names can contain as many as 256 characters. However, it isn't practical to use logon names that have more than 64 characters.
- A pre–Windows 2000 logon name is given to all accounts. By default, this logon name is set to the first 20 characters of the Windows logon name. The pre–Windows 2000 logon name must be unique throughout a domain.
- Users logging on to the domain using a computer that runs Windows 2000 or a later release can use their standard logon names or their pre–Windows 2000 logon names, regardless of the domain operations mode.
- Logon names can't contain certain characters. The following characters are invalid:

  " / \ [ ] ; | = , + * ? < >

- Logon names can contain all other special characters, including spaces, periods, dashes, and underscores. Generally, however, it is not a good idea to use spaces in account names.

NOTE Although Windows Server 2008 R2 stores user names in the case that you enter, user names aren't case sensitive. For example, you can access the Administrator account with the user name Administrator, administrator, or ADMINISTRATOR. Thus, user names are case aware but not case sensitive.

Naming Schemes

Most small organizations tend to assign logon names that use the user's first or last name. But you can have more than one person with the same name in an organization of any size. Rather than having to rework your logon naming scheme when you run into problems, select a good naming scheme now and make sure that other administrators use it. You should use a consistent procedure for naming accounts—one that allows your user base to grow, limits the possibility of name conflicts, and ensures that your accounts have secure names that aren't easily exploited. If you follow these guidelines, the types of naming schemes you might want to use include the following:

- User's first name and last initial
- User's first initial and last name
- User's first initial, middle initial, and last name
- User's first initial, middle initial, and first five characters of the last name
- User's first name and last name

SECURITY ALERT In environments with strict security, you can assign a numeric code for the logon name. This numeric code should be at least 20 characters. Combine this strict naming method with smart cards and smart card readers to allow users to quickly log on to the domain without having to type in all those characters. Don't worry, users can still have a display name that humans can read.

Password and Account Policies

Domain accounts use passwords or private keys from certificates to authenticate access to network resources. This section focuses on passwords.

Using Secure Passwords

A password is a case-sensitive string that can contain more than 127 characters with Active Directory and up to 14 characters with Windows NT Security Manager. Valid characters for passwords are letters, numbers, and symbols. When you set a password for an account, Windows Server 2008 R2 stores the password in an encrypted format in the account database.

But simply having a password isn't enough. The key to preventing unauthorized access to network resources is to use secure passwords. The difference between an average password and a secure password is that secure passwords are difficult to guess and crack. You make passwords difficult to guess and crack by using combinations of all the available character types—including lowercase letters, uppercase letters, numbers, and symbols. For example, instead of using happydays for a password, you would use haPPy2Days&, Ha**y!day5, or even h*99Y%d*ys.

You might also want to use password phrases. With a password phrase, the password contains multiple words and punctuation, like a sentence. For example, you might use the password phrase *This problem is 99 times ten!* A password phrase that includes punctuation and numbers meets all complexity requirements and is incredibly difficult to crack.

Unfortunately, no matter how secure you make a user's password initially, the user will eventually choose his or her own password. Therefore, you should set account policies that define a secure password for your systems. Account policies are a subset of the policies configurable in Group Policy.

Setting Account Policies

As I've mentioned in earlier chapters, you can apply group policies at various levels within the network structure. You manage local group policies in the manner discussed in "Managing Local Group Policies" in Chapter 5. You manage global group policies as explained in "Managing Site, Domain, and Organizational Unit Policies," also in Chapter 5.

Account policies should be configured in the highest precedence GPO linked to a domain. By default, the highest precedence GPO linked to a domain is the Default Domain Policy GPO. Once you access the Default Domain Policy GPO or other appropriate GPO, you can set account policies by following these steps:

1. In the Group Policy Management Editor, shown in Figure 10-1, open the Account Policies node by expanding Computer Configuration, Windows Settings, and Security Settings. The console tree shows the name of the computer or domain you are configuring. Be sure that this is the appropriate network resource to configure.

    NOTE Domain policies have precedence over local policies. The GPO with a link order of 1 in the domain always has the highest precedence.

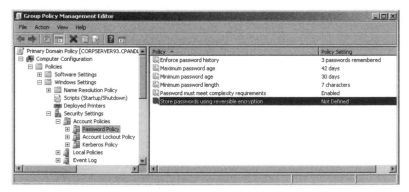

FIGURE 10-1 Use the Account Policies node to set policies for passwords and general account use.

2. You can now manage account policies through the Password Policy, Account Lockout Policy, and Kerberos Policy nodes. To configure a policy, double-click

its entry, or right-click it and then click Properties. This opens a Properties dialog box for the policy, shown in Figure 10-2.

All policies are either defined or not defined. That is, they are either configured for use or not configured for use. A policy that isn't defined in the current container could be inherited from another container.

NOTE Kerberos policies aren't used with local computers. Kerberos policies are available only with group policies that affect domains. For stand-alone servers, you can change the local policy settings. However, you cannot change the local policy settings for domain controllers or member servers.

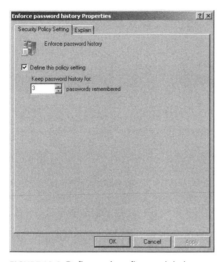

FIGURE 10-2 Define and configure global group policies in the Properties dialog box.

3. Select or clear the Define This Policy Setting check box to specify whether a policy is defined.

TIP Policies can have additional fields for configuration. Often these fields are buttons labeled Enabled and Disabled. Clicking Enabled turns on the policy restriction. Clicking Disabled turns off the policy restriction. Some policies are negations, which means that by enabling them you are actually negating the item. For example, Disable Log On As A Service is the negation of the item Log On As A Service.

Specific procedures for working with account policies are discussed in the following sections, "Configuring Password Policies," "Configuring Account Lockout Policies," and "Configuring Kerberos Policies."

Configuring Account Policies

As you learned in the previous section, there are three types of account policies: password policies, account lockout policies, and Kerberos policies. The sections that follow show you how to configure each of these policies.

Configuring Password Policies

Password policies, listed here, control security for passwords:

- Enforce Password History
- Maximum Password Age
- Minimum Password Age
- Minimum Password Length
- Passwords Must Meet Complexity Requirements
- Store Password Using Reversible Encryption For All Users In The Domain

The uses of these policies are discussed in the following sections.

Enforce Password History

Enforce Password History sets how frequently old passwords can be reused. With this policy, you can discourage users from alternating between several common passwords. Windows Server 2008 R2 can store up to 24 passwords for each user in the password history.

To disable this feature, set the value of the password history to 0. To enable this feature, set the value of the password history using the Passwords Remembered field. Windows Server 2008 R2 then tracks old passwords using a password history that's unique for each user, and users aren't allowed to reuse any of the stored passwords.

> **NOTE** To prevent users from bypassing settings for Enforce Password History, don't allow them to change passwords immediately. This stops users from changing their passwords several times to get back to an old password. You can set the time required to keep a password with the Minimum Password Age policy as discussed later in the chapter.

Maximum Password Age

Maximum Password Age determines how long users can keep a password before they have to change it. The aim is to force users to change their passwords periodically. When you use this feature, set a value that makes sense for your network. Generally, you use a shorter period when security is very important and a longer period when security is less important.

You can set the maximum password age to any value from 0 to 999. A value of 0 specifies that passwords don't expire. Although you might be tempted to set no expiration date, users should change passwords regularly to ensure the network's security. Where security is a concern, good values are 30, 60, or 90 days. Where security is less important, good values are 120, 150, or 180 days.

NOTE Windows Server 2008 R2 notifies users when the password expiration date is approaching. Any time the expiration date is less than 30 days away, users see a warning when they log on that they have to change their password within a specific number of days.

Minimum Password Age

Minimum Password Age determines how long users must keep a password before they can change it. You can use this field to prevent users from bypassing the password system by entering a new password and then changing it right back to the old one.

If the minimum password age is set to 0, users can change their passwords immediately. To prevent this, set a specific minimum age. Reasonable settings are from three to seven days. In this way you make sure that users are less inclined to switch back to an old password but are able to change their passwords in a reasonable amount of time if they want to. Keep in mind that a minimum password age could prevent a user from changing a compromised password. If a user can't change the password, an administrator has to make the change.

Minimum Password Length

Minimum Password Length sets the minimum number of characters for a password. If you haven't changed the default setting, you should do so immediately. The default in some cases is to allow empty passwords (passwords with zero characters), which is definitely not a good idea.

For security reasons you'll generally want passwords of at least eight characters because long passwords are usually harder to crack than short ones. If you want greater security, set the minimum password length to 14 characters.

Passwords Must Meet Complexity Requirements

Beyond the basic password and account policies, Windows Server 2008 R2 includes facilities for creating additional password controls. These facilities enforce the use of secure passwords that follow these guidelines:

- Passwords must have at least six characters.

- Passwords can't contain the user name, such as *stevew*, or parts of the user's full name, such as *steve*.

- Passwords must use at least three of the four available character types: lowercase letters, uppercase letters, numbers, and symbols.

To enforce these rules, enable Passwords Must Meet Complexity Requirements.

Store Password Using Reversible Encryption For All Users

Passwords in the password database are encrypted. This encryption can't normally be reversed. The only time you would want to change this setting is when your organization uses applications that need to read the password. If this is the case, enable Store Password Using Reversible Encryption For All Users.

With this policy enabled, passwords might as well be stored as plain text—it presents the same security risks. With this in mind, a much better technique is to enable the option on a per-user basis and then only as required to meet the user's actual needs.

Configuring Account Lockout Policies

Account lockout policies, listed here, control how and when accounts are locked out of the domain or the local system:

- Account Lockout Threshold
- Account Lockout Duration
- Reset Account Lockout Counter After

These policies are discussed in the sections that follow.

Account Lockout Threshold

Account Lockout Threshold sets the number of logon attempts that are allowed before an account is locked out. If you decide to use lockout controls, you should set this field to a value that balances the need to prevent account cracking with the needs of users who are having difficulty accessing their accounts.

The main reason users might not be able to access their accounts properly the first time is that they forgot their passwords. If this is the case, they might need several attempts to log on properly. Workgroup users could also have problems accessing a remote system if their current passwords don't match the passwords that the remote system expects. For example, the remote system might record several bad logon attempts before a user receives a prompt to enter the correct password because Windows Server 2008 R2 has attempted to automatically log on to the remote system. In a domain environment this normally doesn't happen because of the single sign-on feature.

You can set the lockout threshold to any value from 0 to 999. The lockout threshold is set to 0 by default, which means that accounts won't be locked out because of invalid logon attempts. Any other value sets a specific lockout threshold. Keep in mind that the higher the lockout value, the higher the risk that a hacker might be able to break into your system. A reasonable range of values for this threshold is from 7 to 15. This is high enough to rule out user error and low enough to deter hackers.

Account Lockout Duration

If someone violates the lockout controls, Account Lockout Duration sets the length of time that the account is locked. You can set the lockout duration to a specific length of time using a value between 1 and 99,999 minutes or to an indefinite length of time by setting the lockout duration to 0.

The best security policy is to lock the account indefinitely. When you do, only an administrator can unlock the account. This prevents hackers from trying to access the system again and forces users who are locked out to seek help from an administrator, which is usually a good idea. By talking to the user, you can determine what the user is doing wrong and help the user avoid further problems.

TIP When an account is locked out, open the Properties dialog box for the account in Active Directory Users And Computers. Click the Account tab, and then select the Unlock Account check box.

Reset Account Lockout Counter After

Every time a logon attempt fails, Windows Server 2008 R2 raises the value of a threshold that tracks the number of bad logon attempts. To maintain a balance between potential lockouts from valid security concerns and lockouts that could occur from simple human error, another policy determines how long to maintain information regarding bad logon attempts. This policy is called Reset Account Lockout Counter After, and you use it to reset the bad logon attempts counter to 0 after a certain waiting period. The way the policy works is simple: If the waiting period for Reset Account Lockout Counter After has elapsed since the last bad logon attempt, the bad logon attempts counter is reset to 0. The bad logon attempts counter is also reset when a user logs on successfully.

If the Reset Account Lockout Counter After policy is enabled, you can set it to any value from 1 to 99,999 minutes. As with Account Lockout Threshold, you need to select a value that balances security needs against user access needs. A good value is from one to two hours. This waiting period should be long enough to force hackers to wait longer than they want to before trying to access the account again.

If the Reset Account Lockout Counter After policy isn't set or is disabled, the bad logon attempts counter is reset only when a user successfully logs on.

NOTE Bad logon attempts against a password-protected screen saver at a workstation don't increase the lockout threshold. Similarly, if you press Ctrl+Alt+Delete to lock a server or workstation, bad logon attempts against the Unlock dialog box don't count.

Configuring Kerberos Policies

Kerberos v5 is the primary authentication mechanism used in an Active Directory domain. The Kerberos protocol uses tickets to verify the identification of users and network services. Tickets contain encrypted data that confirms identity for the purposes of authentication and authorization.

You can control ticket duration, renewal, and enforcement with the following policies:

- Enforce User Logon Restrictions
- Maximum Lifetime For Service Ticket
- Maximum Lifetime For User Ticket
- Maximum Lifetime For User Ticket Renewal
- Maximum Tolerance For Computer Clock Synchronization

These policies are discussed in the sections that follow.

SECURITY ALERT Only administrators with an intimate understanding of Kerberos security should change these policies. If you change these policies to inefficient settings, you might cause serious problems on the network. The default Kerberos policy settings usually work just fine.

Enforce User Logon Restrictions

Enforce User Logon Restrictions ensures that any restrictions placed on a user account are enforced. For example, if the user's logon hours are restricted, this policy enforces the restriction. By default, the policy is enabled and you should disable it only in rare circumstances.

Maximum Lifetime

Maximum Lifetime For Service Ticket and Maximum Lifetime For User Ticket set the maximum duration for which a service or user ticket is valid. By default, service tickets have a maximum duration of 600 minutes, and user tickets have a maximum duration of 10 hours.

You can change the duration of tickets. For service tickets, the valid range is from 0 to 99,999 minutes. For user tickets, the valid range is from 0 to 99,999 hours. A value of 0 effectively turns off expiration. Any other value sets a specific ticket lifetime.

A user ticket that expires can be renewed, provided that the renewal takes place within the time set for Maximum Lifetime For User Ticket Renewal. By default, the maximum renewal period is seven days. You can change the renewal period to any value from 0 to 99,999 days. A value of 0 effectively turns off the maximum renewal period, and any other value sets a specific renewal period.

Maximum Tolerance

Maximum Tolerance For Computer Clock Synchronization is one of the few Kerberos policies that you might need to change. By default, computers in the domain must be synchronized within five minutes of one another. If they aren't, authentication fails.

If you have remote users who log on to the domain without synchronizing their clocks to the network time server, you might need to adjust this value. You can set any value from 0 to 99,999. A value of 0 indicates that there's no tolerance for a time difference, which means the remote user's system must be precisely time-synchronized or authentication will fail.

Configuring User Rights Policies

Chapter 9, "Understanding User and Group Accounts," covers built-in capabilities and user rights. Although you can't change built-in capabilities for accounts, you can administer user rights for accounts. Normally, you apply user rights to users by making them members of the appropriate group or groups. You can also apply rights directly, and you do this by managing the user rights for the user's account.

SECURITY ALERT Any user who's a member of a group that's assigned a certain right also has that right. For example, if the Backup Operators group has the right and jsmith is a member of this group, jsmith has this right as well. Keep in mind that changes that you make to user rights can have a far-reaching effect. Because of this, only experienced administrators should make changes to the user rights policy.

You assign user rights through the Local Policies node of Group Policy. As the name implies, local policies pertain to a local computer. However, you can configure local policies and then import them into Active Directory. You can also configure these local policies as part of an existing Group Policy object (GPO) for a site, a domain, or an organizational unit. When you do this, the local policies apply to computer accounts in the site, domain, or organizational unit.

To administer user rights policies, follow these steps:

1. Open the GPO you want to work with, and then open the Local Policies node by working your way down the console tree. To do so, expand Computer Configuration, Windows Settings, Security Settings, and Local Policies.

2. Select User Rights Assignment to manage user rights. To configure a user rights assignment, double-click a user right, or right-click it and then click Properties. This opens a Properties dialog box.

3. You can now configure the user rights. To configure local user rights, follow steps 1–4 in "Configuring Local User Rights." To configure global user rights, follow steps 1–6 in the following section.

Configuring Global User Rights

For a site, a domain, or an organizational unit, you configure individual user rights by following these steps:

1. Open the Properties dialog box for the user right, which is similar to the one shown in Figure 10-3. If the policy isn't defined, select Define These Policy Settings.

FIGURE 10-3 In the Properties dialog box, define the user right, and then apply the right to users and groups.

2. To apply the right to a user or group, click Add User Or Group. Then, in the Add User Or Group dialog box, click Browse. This opens the Select Users, Computers, Service Accounts, Or Groups dialog box, shown in Figure 10-4.

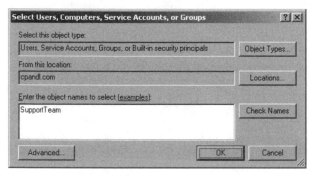

FIGURE 10-4 In the Select Users, Computers, Service Accounts, Or Groups dialog box, apply the user right to users and groups.

SECURITY ALERT Windows Firewall running on a domain controller might prevent you from using the Select Users, Computers, Service Accounts, Or Groups dialog box. This can occur when you aren't logged on locally to the domain controller and are working remotely. You might need to configure an exception on the domain controller for incoming TCP port 445. You can do this by expanding Computer Configuration\Administrative Templates\Network\Network Connections\ Windows Firewall\Domain Profile. In the details pane, double-click the Windows Firewall: Allow Remote Administration Exception policy, and then select Enabled.

Alternatively, you can configure an exception by typing the following at a command prompt on the remote computer: **netsh firewall set portopening tcp 445 smb enable**. See Microsoft Knowledge Base Article 840634 (*support.microsoft.com/ default.aspx?scid=kb;en-us;840634*) for more details.

3. Type the name of the user or group you want to use in the field provided, and then click Check Names. By default, the search is configured to find built-in security principals and user accounts. To add groups to the search, click Object Types, select Groups in the list box, and then click OK.

4. After you select the account names or groups to add, click OK. The Add User Or Group dialog box should now show the selected accounts. Click OK again.

5. The Properties dialog box is updated to reflect your selections. If you made a mistake, select a name and remove it by clicking Remove.

6. When you have finished granting the right to users and groups, click OK.

Configuring Local User Rights

For local computers, apply user rights by following these steps:

1. Open the Properties dialog box for the user right, which is similar to the one shown in Figure 10-5. Remember that site, domain, and organizational unit policies have precedence over local policies.

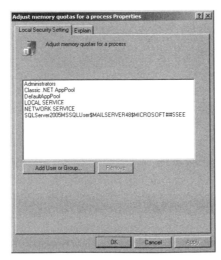

FIGURE 10-5 In the Properties dialog box, define the user right and then apply the right to users and groups.

2. The Properties dialog box shows current users and groups that have been given a user right. To remove the user right, select a user or group, and then click Remove.

3. You can apply the user right to additional users and groups by clicking Add User Or Group. This opens the Select Users, Computers, Services Accounts, Or Groups dialog box shown previously in Figure 10-4. You can now add users and groups.

Adding a User Account

You need to create a user account for each user who wants to use your network resources. You create domain user accounts with Active Directory Users And Computers. You create local user accounts with Local Users And Groups.

Creating Domain User Accounts

Generally, you can create new domain accounts in two ways:

- **Create a completely new user account**   Right-click the container in which you want to place the user account, click New, and then click User. This opens the New Object—User Wizard, shown in Figure 10-6. When you create a new account, the default system settings are used.

- **Base the new account on an existing account**   Right-click the user account you want to copy in Active Directory Users And Computers, and then click Copy. This starts the Copy Object—User Wizard, which is essentially the same as the New Object—User Wizard. However, when you create a copy of an account, the new account gets most of its environment settings from the existing account. For more information on copying accounts, see "Copying Domain User Accounts" in Chapter 11.

With either the New Object—User Wizard or the Copy Object—User Wizard, you can create an account by following these steps:

1. As shown in Figure 10-6, the first wizard page lets you configure the user display name and logon name.

2. Type the user's first name, middle initial, and last name in the fields provided. These fields are used to create the full name, which is the user's display name.

3. Make changes to the Full Name field as necessary. For example, you might want to type the name in LastName FirstName MiddleInitial format or in FirstName MiddleInitial LastName format. The full name must be unique in the domain and must have 64 or fewer characters.

4. In the User Logon Name field, type the user's logon name. Use the drop-down list to select the domain to associate the account with. This sets the fully qualified logon name.

5. The first 20 characters of the logon name are used to set the pre–Windows 2000 logon name. This logon name must be unique in the domain. If necessary, change the pre–Windows 2000 logon name.

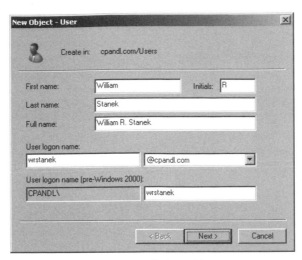

FIGURE 10-6 Configure the user display and logon names.

6. Click Next, and then configure the user's password on the page shown in Figure 10-7.

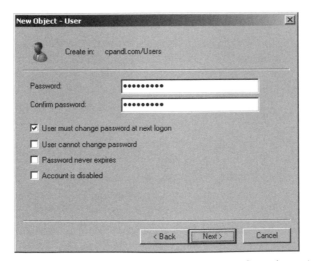

FIGURE 10-7 Use the New Object—User Wizard to configure the user's password.

The options for this page are as follows:

- **Password** The password for the account. This password should follow the conventions of your password policy.

- **Confirm Password** A field to ensure that you assign the account password correctly. Simply reenter the password to confirm it.

- **User Must Change Password At Next Logon**   If selected, the user must change the password upon logon.

- **User Cannot Change Password**   If selected, the user can't change the password.

- **Password Never Expires**   If selected, the password for this account never expires. This setting overrides the domain account policy. Generally, it's not a good idea to set a password so that it doesn't expire—this defeats the purpose of having passwords in the first place.

- **Account Is Disabled**   If selected, the account is disabled and can't be used. Use this field to temporarily prevent anyone from using an account.

7. Click Next, and then click Finish to create the account. If you have problems creating the account, you'll see a warning, and you need to use the Back button to retype information in the user name and password pages as necessary.

After you create the account, you can set advanced properties for the account as discussed later in this chapter.

Creating Local User Accounts

You create local user accounts with Local Users And Groups. You can open this utility and create an account by following these steps:

1. Click Start, All Programs, Administrative Tools, and then Computer Management. Or select Computer Management in the Administrative Tools folder.

2. Right-click the Computer Management entry in the console tree, and then click Connect To Another Computer. You can now choose the system whose local accounts you want to manage. Domain controllers don't have local users and groups.

3. Expand the System Tools node by clicking the plus sign (+) next to it, and then choose Local Users And Groups.

4. Right-click Users, and then click New User. This opens the New User dialog box, shown in Figure 10-8. You use each of the fields in the dialog box as follows:

   - **User Name**   The logon name for the user account. This name should follow the conventions for the local user name policy.

   - **Full Name**   The full name of the user, such as William R. Stanek.

   - **Description**   A description of the user. Normally you'd type the user's job title, such as Webmaster. You could also type the user's job title and department.

   - **Password**   The password for the account. This password should follow the conventions of your password policy.

- **Confirm Password**   A field to ensure that you assign the account password correctly. Simply reenter the password to confirm it.

- **User Must Change Password At Next Logon**   If selected, the user must change the password upon logon.

- **User Cannot Change Password**   If selected, the user can't change the password.

- **Password Never Expires**   If selected, the password for this account never expires. This setting overrides the local account policy.

- **Account Is Disabled**   If selected, the account is disabled and can't be used. Use this field to temporarily prevent anyone from using an account.

FIGURE 10-8 Configuring a local user account is different from configuring a domain user account.

5. Click Create when you have finished configuring the new account.

Adding a Group Account

You use group accounts to manage privileges for multiple users. You create global group accounts in Active Directory Users And Computers. You create local group accounts in Local Users And Groups.

As you set out to create group accounts, remember that you create group accounts for similar types of users. The types of groups you might want to create include the following:

- **Groups for departments within the organization**   Generally, users who work in the same department need access to similar resources. You'll often create groups that are organized by department, such as Business Development, Sales, Marketing, and Engineering.

- **Groups for users of specific applications** Users often need access to an application and resources related to the application. If you create application-specific groups, you can be sure that users have proper access to the necessary resources and application files.

- **Groups for roles within the organization** You can also organize groups by user roles within the organization. For example, executives probably need access to different resources than supervisors and general users. By creating groups based on roles within the organization, you can ensure that proper access is given to the users who need it.

Creating a Global Group

To create a global group, follow these steps:

1. Start Active Directory Users And Computers. Right-click the container in which you want to place the user account, click New, and then click Group. This opens the New Object—Group dialog box, shown in Figure 10-9.

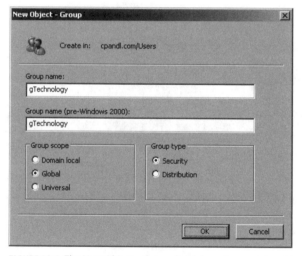

FIGURE 10-9 The New Object—Group dialog box allows you to add a new global group to the domain.

2. Type a name for the group. Global group account names follow the same naming rules as display names for user accounts. They aren't case sensitive and can be up to 64 characters.

3. The first 20 characters of the group name are used to set the pre–Windows 2000 group name. This group name must be unique in the domain. If necessary, change the pre–Windows 2000 group name.

4. Select a group scope (Domain Local, Global, or Universal).

5. Select a group type (either Security or Distribution).

6. Click OK to create the group. After you create the account, you can add members and set additional properties, as discussed later in this chapter.

Creating a Local Group and Assigning Members

You create local groups with Local Users And Groups. You can access this utility and create a group by following these steps:

1. Click Start, All Programs, Administrative Tools, and then Computer Management. Or select Computer Management in the Administrative Tools folder.

2. Right-click the Computer Management entry in the console tree, and then click Connect To Another Computer. You can now choose the system whose local accounts you want to manage. Domain controllers don't have local users and groups.

3. Expand the System Tools node by clicking the plus sign (+) next to it, and then choose Local Users And Groups.

4. Right-click Groups, and then click New Group. This opens the New Group dialog box, shown in Figure 10-10.

FIGURE 10-10 In the New Group dialog box, you can add a new local group to a computer.

5. After you type a name and description of the group, click the Add button to add names to the group. This opens the Select Users dialog box.

6. In the Select Users dialog box, type the name of a user you want to use in the Name field, and then click Check Names. If matches are found, select the account you want to use, and then click OK. If no matches are found, update

the name you entered and try searching again. Repeat this step as necessary, and then click OK.

7. The New Group dialog box is updated to reflect your selections. If you made a mistake, select a name and click Remove.

8. Click Create when you've finished adding or removing group members.

Handling Global Group Membership

To configure group membership, you use Active Directory Users And Computers. When working with groups, keep the following points in mind:

- All new domain users are members of the group Domain Users, and their primary group is specified as Domain Users.

- All new domain workstations and member servers are members of Domain Computers, and their primary group is Domain Computers.

- All new domain controllers are members of Domain Controllers, and their primary group is Domain Controllers.

With Active Directory Users And Computers, you can manage group membership several ways:

- Manage individual membership
- Manage multiple memberships
- Set primary group membership for individual users and computers

Managing Individual Membership

You can quickly add a user or a group to one or more groups by right-clicking the account and selecting Add To A Group. This opens the Select Groups dialog box. You can now choose groups that the currently selected account should be a member of.

You can manage group membership for any type of account by following these steps:

1. Double-click the user, computer, or group entry in Active Directory Users And Computers. This opens the account's Properties dialog box.

2. Click the Member Of tab.

3. To make the account a member of a group, click Add. This opens the Select Groups dialog box. You can now choose groups that the currently selected account should be a member of.

4. To remove the account from a group, select a group, and then click Remove.

5. Click OK.

If you're working exclusively with user accounts, you can add users to groups by following these steps:

1. Select the user accounts that you want to work with in Active Directory Users And Computers.

   TIP To select multiple users individually, hold down the Ctrl key and then click the left mouse button on each user account that you want to select. To select a sequence of accounts, hold down the Shift key, select the first user account, and then click the last user account.

2. Right-click one of the selections, and then click Add To A Group. This opens the Select Groups dialog box. You can now choose groups that the currently selected accounts should be members of.

3. Click OK.

Managing Multiple Memberships in a Group

Another way to manage group membership is to use a group's Properties dialog box to add or remove multiple accounts. To do this, follow these steps:

1. Double-click the group entry in Active Directory Users And Computers. This opens the group's Properties dialog box.

2. Click the Members tab.

3. To add accounts to the group, click Add. This opens the Select Users, Computers, Service Accounts, Or Groups dialog box. You can now choose users, computers, service accounts, and groups that should be members of the currently selected group.

4. To remove members from a group, select an account, and then click Remove.

5. Click OK.

Setting the Primary Group for Users and Computers

Users who access Windows Server through Services for Macintosh use primary groups. When a Macintosh user creates files or directories on a system running Windows Server, the primary group is assigned to these files or directories.

NOTE Windows Server 2008 and Windows Server 2008 R2 do not include Services for Macintosh. Services for Macintosh is only included with earlier releases of Windows Server. All user and computer accounts must have a primary group whether or not the accounts access Windows Server systems through Macintosh. This group must be a group with global or universal scope, such as the global group Domain Users or the global group Domain Computers.

To set the primary group, follow these steps:

1. Double-click the user or computer entry in Active Directory Users And Computers. This opens the account's Properties dialog box.

2. Click the Member Of tab.

3. Select a group with global or universal scope in the Member Of list.

4. Click Set Primary Group.

All users must be a member of at least one primary group. You can't revoke membership in a primary group without first assigning the user to another primary group. To do this, follow these steps:

1. Select a different group with global or universal scope in the Member Of list, and then click Set Primary Group.

2. In the Member Of list, click the former primary group, and then click Remove. The group membership is now revoked.

Implementing Managed Accounts

Microsoft Exchange Server, Internet Information Services, SQL Server, and other types of applications often use service accounts. On a local computer, you can configure the application to run as a built-in user account, such as Local Service, Network Service, or Local System. Although these service accounts are easy to configure and use, they usually are shared among multiple applications and services and cannot be managed on a domain level. If you configure the application to use a domain account, you can isolate the privileges for the application, but then you must manually manage the account password and any service principal names (SPNs) required for Kerberos authentication.

Windows 7 and Windows Server 2008 R2 support two new types of accounts:

- Managed service accounts
- Managed virtual accounts

Managed service accounts are a special type of domain user account for managed services. These accounts reduce service outages and other issues by having Windows manage the account password and related SPNs automatically.

Managed virtual accounts are a special type of local computer account for managed services. These accounts provide the ability to access the network with a computer identity in a domain environment. Because the computer identity is used, no password management is required.

Windows 7 and Windows Server 2008 R2 do not have a user interface for creating and managing these accounts. Future service packs or releases may provide a user interface, but until this happens you need to use Windows PowerShell to manage these accounts. You manage these accounts using the Active Directory module for Windows PowerShell.

NOTE The Active Directory module is not imported into Windows PowerShell by default. You need to import the module before you can use the cmdlets it provides. For more information, see "Active Directory Administrative Center and Windows PowerShell" in Chapter 8.

Creating and Using Managed Service Accounts

With managed service accounts, you create an actual account, which is stored by default in the Managed Service Accounts organizational unit in Active Directory. Next, you install the managed service account on a local server to add it to the account as a local user. Finally, you configure the local service to use the account.

You use Windows PowerShell cmdlets to install, uninstall, and reset passwords for managed service accounts. After a managed service account has been installed, you can configure a service or application to use the account and no longer have to specify or change passwords because the account password is maintained by the computer. You can also configure the SPN on the service account without requiring domain administrator privileges.

You create a managed service account using New-ADServiceAccount. The basic syntax is as follows:

```
New-ADServiceAccount –DisplayName DisplayName -SamAccountName SAMName
-Name Name
```

DisplayName is the display name for the account, *SAMName* is the pre–Windows 2000 name of the account, and *Name* is the pre–Windows 2000 name of the account, such as:

```
New-ADServiceAccount –DisplayName "SQL Agent Account"
-SamAccountName sqlagent –Name "SQL Agent"
```

The account will have a randomly generated 240-character password and be created in the Managed Service Accounts organizational unit. By default, the account is enabled, but you can create the account in a disabled state by adding –Enabled $false. If you need to pass in credentials to create the account, use the –Credential parameter as shown in this example:

```
$cred = Get-Credential
New-ADServiceAccount –DisplayName "IIS App Pool 1"
-SamAccountName pool1 –Name "IIS Pool 1" –Credential $cred
```

Although the account is listed in Active Directory Users And Computers, you shouldn't use this management tool to work with the account. Instead, you should use the following Windows PowerShell cmdlets:

- Get-ADServiceAccount to get information about one or more managed service accounts.

- Set-ADServiceAccount to set properties on an existing managed service account.

- Remove-ADServiceAccount to remove a managed service account from Active Directory.

After you create a managed service account in Active Director, you can install the account on a local computer by using Install-ADServiceAccount. The basic syntax is:

```
Install-ADServiceAccount -Identity ServiceAccountId
```

ServiceAccountId is the display name or SAM account name of the service account, such as:

```
Install-ADServiceAccount -Identity sqlagent
```

If you need to pass in credentials to create the account, use the –Credential parameter.

Configuring Services to Use Managed Service Accounts

You can configure a service to run with the managed service account by following these steps:

1. Click Start, Administrative Tools, and then Server Manager. Or click Server Manager on the Quick Launch toolbar.

2. As necessary, connect to the computer you want to manage. In the left pane, right-click the Server Manager node, and then click Connect To Another Computer. Enter the host name, fully qualified domain name, or IP address of the remote server, and then click OK.

3. In the left pane, click the plus sign (+) next to the Configuration node, and then select the Services node.

4. Right-click the name of the service that you want to work with, and then click Properties.

5. On the Log On tab, select This Account, and then type the name of the managed service account in the format DomainName\AccountName, or click Browse to search for the account.

6. Confirm that the password field is blank, and then click OK.

7. Select the name of the service, and then click Start to start the service, or click Restart to restart the service as appropriate. Confirm that the newly configured account name appears in the Log On As column for the service.

NOTE A dollar sign ($) appears at the end of the account name in the Services snap-in console. When you use the Services snap-in console to configure the logon as an account, the Service Logon Right logon right is automatically assigned to the account. If you use a different tool, the account has to be explicitly granted this right.

Removing Managed Service Accounts

If a managed service account is no longer being used on a computer, you might want to uninstall the account. Before you do this, however, you should check the Services snap-in to ensure that the account isn't being used. To uninstall a managed service account from a local computer, use Uninstall-ADServiceAccount. The basic syntax is:

```
Uninstall-ADServiceAccount -Identity ServiceAccountId
```

where *ServiceAccountId* is the display name or SAM account name of the service account, such as:

```
Uninstall-ADServiceAccount -Identity sqlagent
```

If you need to pass in credentials to create the account, use the –Credential parameter.

Managed service account passwords are reset on a regular basis based on the password reset requirements of the domain, but you can reset the password manually if needed. To reset the password for a managed service account, use Reset-ADServiceAccountPassword. The basic syntax is:

```
Reset-ADServiceAccountPassword -Identity ServiceAccountId
```

where *ServiceAccountId* is the display name or SAM account name of the service account, such as:

```
Reset-ADServiceAccountPassword -Identity sqlagent
```

If you need to pass in credentials to create the account, use the –Credential parameter. You can modify the default password change interval for managed service accounts by using the domain policy Domain Member: Maximum Machine Account Password Age under Local Policy\Security Options. Group Policy settings under Account Policies\Password Policy are not used to modify managed service account password reset intervals nor can the NLTEST /SC_CHANGE_PWD command be used to reset managed service account passwords.

Moving Managed Service Accounts

To move a managed service account from a source computer to a new destination computer, you need to do the following:

1. On the source computer, configure any services that are using the managed account to use a different account, and then run Uninstall-ADServiceAccount.

2. On the new destination computer, run Install-ADServiceAccount, and then use the Services snap-in console to configure the service to run with the managed service account.

To migrate a service from a user account to a managed service account, you need to do the following:

1. Create a new managed service account in Active Directory by using New-ADServiceAccount.

2. Install the managed service account on the appropriate computer by using Install-ADServiceAccount, and then use the Services snap-in console to configure the service to run with the managed service account.

3. You also may need to configure the access control lists on the service resources for the service management account.

Using Virtual Accounts

Virtual accounts require very little management. They cannot be created or deleted, and they do not require any password management. Instead, they exist automatically and are represented by the machine identity of the local computer.

With virtual accounts, you configure a local service to access the network with a computer identity in a domain environment. Because the computer identity is used, no account needs to be created and no password management is required.

You can configure a service to run with a virtual account by following these steps:

1. Click Start, Administrative Tools, and then Server Manager, or click Server Manager on the Quick Launch toolbar.

2. As necessary, connect to the computer you want to manage. In the left pane, right-click the Server Manager node, and then click Connect To Another Computer. Enter the host name, fully qualified domain name, or IP address of the remote server, and then click OK.

3. In the left pane, click the plus sign (+) next to the Configuration node, and then select the Services node.

4. Right-click the name of the service that you want to work with, and then click Properties.

5. On the Log On tab, select This Account, and then type the name of the service account in the format SERVICE\ComputerName.

6. Confirm that the password field is blank, and then click OK.

7. Select the name of the service, and then click Start to start the service, or click Restart to restart the service. Confirm that the newly configured account name appears in the Log On As column for the service.

NOTE A dollar sign ($) appears at the end of the account name in the Services snap-in console. When you use the Services snap-in console to configure the logon as an account, the Service Logon Right logon right is automatically assigned to the account. If you use a different tool, the account has to be explicitly granted this right.

CHAPTER 11

Managing User and Group Accounts

In a perfect world, you could create user and group accounts and never have to touch them again. Unfortunately, we live in the real world. After you create accounts, you'll spend a lot of time managing them. This chapter provides guidelines and tips to make that task easier.

Managing User Contact Information

Active Directory is a directory service. When you create user accounts, those accounts can have detailed contact information associated with them. The contact information is then available for anyone in the domain tree or forest to use as criteria to search for users and to create address book entries.

Setting Contact Information

You can set contact information for a user account by following these steps:

1. Double-click the user name in Active Directory Users And Computers. This opens the account's Properties dialog box.

2. Click the General tab, shown in Figure 11-1. Set general contact information in the following fields:

- **First Name, Initials, Last Name**   Sets the user's full name.

- **Display Name**   Sets the user's display name as seen in logon sessions and in Active Directory Domain Services.

- **Description**   Sets a description of the user.

- **Office**   Sets the user's office location.

- **Telephone Number**   Sets the user's primary business telephone number. If the user has other business telephone numbers that you want to track, click Other, and then enter additional phone numbers in the Phone Number (Others) dialog box.

- **E-Mail**   Sets the user's business e-mail address.

- **Web Page**   Sets the URL of the user's home page, which can be on the Internet or on the company intranet. If the user has other Web pages that you want to track, click Other, and then enter additional Web page addresses in the Web Page Address (Others) dialog box.

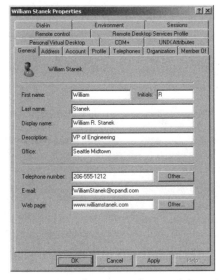

FIGURE 11-1 Configure general contact information for the user on the General tab.

TIP You must fill in the E-Mail and Web Page fields if you want to use the Send Mail and Open Home Page features of Active Directory Users And Computers. For more information, see "Updating User and Group Accounts" later in this chapter.

3. Click the Address tab. Set the user's business or home address in the fields provided. You'll usually want to enter the user's business address. You can then track the business locations and mailing addresses of users at various offices.

NOTE You need to consider privacy issues before you enter users' home addresses. Discuss the matter with your human resources and legal departments. You might also want to get user consent before releasing home addresses.

4. Click the Telephones tab. Enter the primary telephone numbers that should be used to contact the user, such as home, pager, mobile, fax, and IP phone.

5. You can configure other numbers for each type of telephone number. Click the associated Other buttons, and then enter additional phone numbers in the dialog box provided.

6. Click the Organization tab. As appropriate, enter the user's title, department, and company.

7. To specify the user's manager, click Change, and then select the user's manager in the Select User Or Contact dialog box. When you specify a manager, the user shows up as a direct report in the manager's account.

8. Click Apply or OK to apply the changes.

Searching for Users and Groups in Active Directory

Active Directory makes it easy for you to find users and groups in the directory, which you can do by following these steps:

1. In Active Directory Users And Computers, right-click the domain or container, and then click Find.

2. In the Find Users, Contacts, And Groups dialog box, the In list shows the previously selected domain or container. If you want to search the entire directory instead, select Entire Directory, or click Browse to select a domain or container to search.

3. On the Users, Contacts, And Groups tab, type the name of the user, contact, or group you want to search for.

4. Click Find Now to begin the search. If matches are found, the search results are displayed, as shown in Figure 11-2. Otherwise, type new search parameters and search again.

5. To manage an account, right-click its entry. If you right-click an account entry and then select Properties, you can open the account's Properties dialog box.

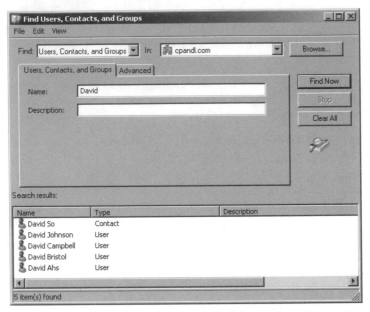

FIGURE 11-2 Search for users in Active Directory, and then use the results to create address book entries.

Configuring the User's Environment Settings

User accounts can also have profiles, logon scripts, and home directories associated with them. To configure these optional settings, double-click a display name in Active Directory Users And Computers, and then click the Profile tab, shown in Figure 11-3. On the Profile tab, you can set the following fields:

- **Profile Path** The path to the user's profile. Profiles provide the environment settings for users. Each time a user logs on to a computer, that user's profile is used to determine desktop and Control Panel settings, the availability of menu options and applications, and more. Setting the profile path is covered later in the chapter in "Managing User Profiles."

- **Logon Script** The path to the user's logon script. Logon scripts are batch files that run whenever a user logs on. You use logon scripts to set commands that should be executed each time a user logs on. Chapter 5, "Automating Administrative Tasks, Policies, and Procedures," discusses logon scripts in detail.

- **Home Folder** The directory the user should use for storing files. Here, you assign a specific directory for the user's files as a local path on the user's system or on a connected network drive. If the directory is available to the network, the user can access the directory from any computer on the network, which is a definite advantage.

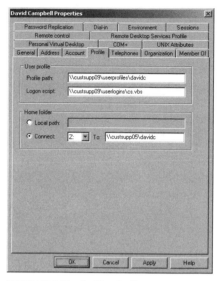

FIGURE 11-3 The Profile tab allows you to create a user profile and thereby configure the network environment for a user.

System Environment Variables

System environment variables often come in handy when you're setting up the user's environment, especially when you work with logon scripts. You use environment variables to specify path information that can be dynamically assigned. You use the following environment variables the most:

- **%SystemRoot%** The base directory for the operating system, such as C:\Windows. Use it with the Profile tab of the user's Properties dialog box and logon scripts.

- **%UserName%** The user account name, such as wrstanek. Use it with the Profile tab of the user's Properties dialog box and logon scripts.

- **%HomeDrive%** The drive letter of the user's home directory followed by a colon character, such as C:. Use it with logon scripts.

- **%HomePath%** The full path to the user's home directory on the respective home drive, such as \Users\Mkg\Georgej. Use it with logon scripts.

- **%Processor_Architecture%** The processor architecture of the user's computer, such as x86. Use it with logon scripts.

Figure 11-4 shows how you might use environment variables when creating user accounts. Note that by using the %UserName% variable, you allow the system to determine the full path information on a user-by-user basis. If you use this technique, you can use the same path information for multiple users, and all the users will have unique settings.

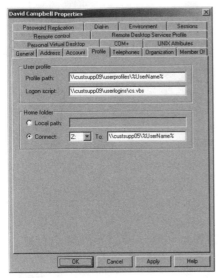

FIGURE 11-4 When you use the Profile tab, environment variables can lessen the information you need to type, especially when you create an account based on another account.

Logon Scripts

Logon scripts set commands that should be executed each time a user logs on. You can use logon scripts to set the system time, network drive paths, network printers, and more. Although you can use logon scripts to execute one-time commands, you shouldn't use them to set environment variables. Any environment settings used by scripts aren't maintained for subsequent user processes. Also, you shouldn't use logon scripts to specify applications that should run at startup. You should set startup applications by placing the appropriate shortcuts in the user's Startup folder.

Normally, logon scripts contain Windows commands. However, logon scripts can be any of the following:

- PowerShell scripts with a .ps1 or other valid extension
- Windows Script Host files with the .vbs, .js, or another valid script extension
- Batch files with the .bat extension
- Command files with the .cmd extension
- Executable programs with the .exe extension

One user or many users can use a single logon script. As the administrator, you control which users use which scripts. As the name implies, logon scripts are accessed when users log on to their accounts. You can specify a logon script by following these steps:

1. Open the user's Properties dialog box in Active Directory Users And Computers, and then click the Profile tab.

2. Type the path to the logon script in the Logon Script field. Be sure to set the full path to the logon script, such as **\\Zeta\User_Logon\Eng.vbs**.

NOTE You can use other techniques to specify logon and logoff scripts. For complete details, see "User and Computer Script Management" in Chapter 5.

Creating logon scripts is easier than you might think, especially when you use the Windows command language. Just about any command that you can type into a command prompt can be set to run in a logon script. The most common tasks you'll want logon scripts to handle are to set the default printers and network paths for users. You can set this information with the NET USE command. The following NET USE commands define a network printer and a network drive:

```
net use lpt1: \\zeta\techmain
net use G: \\gamma\corp\files
```

If these commands were in the user's logon script, the user would have a network printer on LPT1 and a network drive on G. You can create similar connections in a script. With VBScript, you need to initialize the variables and objects you plan to use and then call the appropriate methods of the Network object to add the connections. Consider the following example:

```
Option Explicit
Dim wNetwork, printerPath
Set wNetwork = WScript.CreateObject("WScript.Network")

printerPath = "\\zeta\techmain"
wNetwork.AddWindowsPrinterConnection printerPath
wNetwork.SetDefaultPrinter printerPath

wNetwork.MapNetworkDrive "G:", "\\gamma\corpfiles"

Set wNetwork = vbEmpty
Set printerPath = vbEmpty
```

Here, you use the AddWindowsPrinterConnection method to add a connection to the TechMain printer on Zeta, and the SetDefaultPrinter method to set the printer as the default for the user. You then use the MapNetworkDrive method to define a network drive on G.

Assigning Home Directories

Windows Server 2008 R2 lets you assign a home directory for each user account. Users can store and retrieve their personal files in this directory. Many applications use the home directory as the default for File Open and File Save As operations, which helps users find their resources easily. The command prompt also uses the home directory as the initial current directory.

Home directories can be located on a user's local hard disk drive or on a shared network drive. On a local drive the directory is accessible only from a single workstation. On the other hand, shared network drives can be accessed from any computer on the network, which makes for a more versatile user environment.

TIP Although users can share home directories, it's not a good idea. You'll usually want to provide each user with a unique home directory.

You don't need to create the user's home directory ahead of time. Active Directory Users And Computers automatically creates the directory for you. If there's a problem creating the directory, Active Directory Users And Computers will instruct you to create it manually.

To specify a local home directory, follow these steps:

1. Open the user's Properties dialog box in Active Directory Users And Computers, and then click the Profile tab.

2. Select Local Path in the Home Folder section, and then type the path to the home directory in the associated text box, such as **C:\Home\%UserName%**.

To specify a network home directory, follow these steps:

1. Open the user's Properties dialog box in Active Directory Users And Computers, and then click the Profile tab.

2. In the Home Folder section, select the Connect option, and then select a drive letter for the home directory. For consistency, you should use the same drive letter for all users. Also, be sure to select a drive letter that won't conflict with any currently configured physical or mapped drives. To avoid problems, you might want to use Z as the drive letter.

3. Type the complete path to the home directory using Universal Naming Convention (UNC) notation, such as **\\Gamma\User_Dirs\%UserName%**. You include the server name in the drive path to ensure that the user can access the directory from any computer on the network.

NOTE If you don't assign a home directory, Windows Server 2008 R2 uses the default local home directory.

Setting Account Options and Restrictions

Windows Server 2008 R2 gives you many ways to control user accounts and their access to the network. You can define logon hours, permitted workstations for logon, dial-in privileges, and more.

Managing Logon Hours

Windows Server 2008 R2 lets you control when users can log on to the network. You do this by setting their valid logon hours. You can use logon hour restrictions to tighten security and prevent system cracking or malicious conduct after normal business hours.

During valid logon hours, users can work as they normally do. They can log on to the network and access network resources. During restricted logon hours, users can't work. They can't log on to the network or make connections to network resources. If users are logged on when their logon time expires, what happens depends on the account policy you've set for them. Generally, one of two things happens to the user:

- **Forcibly disconnected** You can set a policy that tells Windows Server 2008 R2 to forcibly disconnect users when their logon hours expire. If this policy is set, remote users are disconnected from all network resources and logged off the system when their hours expire.

- **Not disconnected** Users aren't disconnected from the network when their logon hours expire. Instead, Windows Server 2008 R2 doesn't allow them to make any new network connections.

Configuring Logon Hours

To configure the logon hours, follow these steps:

1. Open the user's Properties dialog box in Active Directory Users And Computers, and then click the Account tab.

2. Click Logon Hours. You can now set the valid and invalid logon hours using the Logon Hours dialog box, shown in Figure 11-5. In this dialog box, each hour of the day or night is a field that you can turn on or off.

   - Hours that are allowed are filled in with a dark bar—you can think of these hours as being turned on.

   - Hours that are disallowed are blank—you can think of these hours as being turned off.

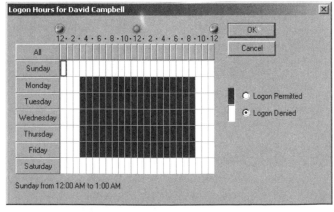

FIGURE 11-5 Configure logon hours for users.

3. To change the setting for an hour, click it, and then select either Logon Permitted or Logon Denied.

Table 11-1 lists Logon Hours dialog box options.

TABLE 11-1 Logon Hours Dialog Box Options

FEATURE	FUNCTION
All	Allows you to select all the time periods
Days of the week buttons	Allow you to select all the hours in a particular day
Hourly buttons	Allow you to select a particular hour for all the days of the week
Logon Permitted	Sets the allowed logon hours
Logon Denied	Sets the disallowed logon hours

TIP When you set logon hours, you'll save yourself a lot of work in the long run if you give users a moderately restricted time window. For example, rather than explicit 9–5 hours, you might want to allow a few hours on either side of the normal work hours. This lets early birds onto the system and allows night owls to keep working until they finish for the day.

Enforcing Logon Hours

To forcibly disconnect users when their logon hours expire, follow these steps:

1. Access the Group Policy object (GPO) you want to work with, as detailed in "Managing Site, Domain, and Organizational Unit Policies" in Chapter 5.

2. Open the Security Options node by working your way down through the console tree. Expand Computer Configuration, Windows Settings, and Security Settings. In Security Settings, expand Local Policies, and then select Security Options.

3. Double-click Network Security: Force Logoff When Logon Hours Expire. This opens a Properties dialog box for the policy.

4. Select the Define This Policy Setting check box, and then click Enabled. This turns on the policy restriction and enforces the logon hours. Click OK.

Setting Permitted Logon Workstations

Windows Server 2008 R2 has a formal policy that allows users to log on to systems locally. This policy controls whether a user can sit at the computer's keyboard and log on. By default, you can use any valid user account, including the Guest account, to log on locally to a workstation.

As you might imagine, allowing users to log on to any workstation is a security risk. Unless you restrict workstation use, anyone who obtains a user name and password can use them to log on to any workstation in the domain. By defining a permitted workstation list, you close the opening in your domain and reduce the security risk. Now, not only must hackers find a user name and password, but they must also find the permitted workstations for the account.

For domain users, you define permitted logon workstations by following these steps:

1. Open the user's Properties dialog box in Active Directory Users And Computers, and then click the Account tab.

2. Open the Logon Workstations dialog box by clicking Log On To.

3. Select The Following Computers, as shown in Figure 11-6.

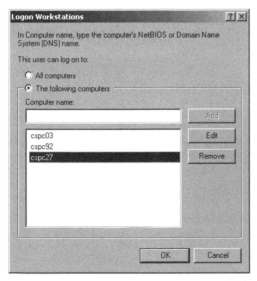

FIGURE 11-6 To restrict access to workstations, specify the permitted logon workstations.

4. Type the name of a permitted workstation, and then click Add. Repeat this procedure to specify additional workstations.

5. If you make a mistake, select the erroneous entry, and then click Edit or Remove.

Setting Dial-In and VPN Privileges

Windows Server 2008 R2 lets you set remote access privileges for accounts on the Dial-In tab of the user's Properties dialog box. These settings control access for dial-in and virtual private networks (VPNs). As shown in Figure 11-7, remote access privileges are controlled through Network Policy Server (NPS) Network Policy by default. This is the preferred method of controlling remote access. You can explicitly grant or deny dial-in privileges by selecting Allow Access or Deny Access. In any event, before users can remotely access the network, you need to follow these steps:

1. In Server Manager, add the role of Network Policy and Access Services.

2. To enable remote access connections, access the GPO for the site, domain, or organizational unit you want to work with, as specified in "Managing Site, Domain, and Organizational Unit Policies" in Chapter 5. In the policy editor, expand User Configuration, Administrative Templates, and then Network. Select Network Connections, and then configure the Network Connections policies as appropriate for the site, domain, or organizational unit.

3. Configure remote access using Routing And Remote Access. In Computer Management, expand Services And Applications, and then select Routing And Remote Access. Configure Routing And Remote Access as appropriate.

After you grant a user permission to access the network remotely, follow these steps to configure additional dial-in parameters on the Dial-In tab of the user's Properties dialog box (see Figure 11-7):

1. If the user must dial in from a specific phone number, select Verify Caller-ID, and then type the telephone number from which this user is required to log on. Your telephone system must support Caller ID for this feature to work.

2. Define callback parameters using the following options:

   - **No Callback**   Allows the user to dial in directly and remain connected. The user pays the long-distance telephone charges, if applicable.

   - **Set By Caller**   Allows the user to dial in directly, and then the server prompts the user for a callback number. Once the number is entered, the user is disconnected, and the server dials the user back at the specified number to reestablish the connection. The company pays the long-distance telephone charges, if applicable.

   - **Always Callback To**   Allows you to set a predefined callback number for security purposes. When a user dials in, the server calls back the preset number. The company pays the long-distance telephone charges, if applicable, and reduces the risk of an unauthorized person accessing the network.

   NOTE   You shouldn't assign callback numbers for users who dial in through a switchboard. The switchboard might not allow the user to properly connect to the network. You also shouldn't use preset callback numbers with multilinked lines. The multilinked lines won't function properly.

   If necessary, you can also assign static IP addresses and static routes for dial-in connections by selecting Assign Static IP Address and Apply Static Routes, respectively.

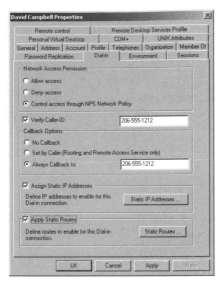

FIGURE 11-7 Dial-in privileges control remote access to the network.

Setting Account Security Options

The Account tab of the user's Properties dialog box has the following options, which are designed to help you maintain a secure network environment and control how user accounts are used:

- **User Must Change Password At Next Logon**   Forces the user to change his or her password when the user logs on next.

- **User Cannot Change Password**   Doesn't allow the user to change the account password.

- **Password Never Expires**   Ensures that the account password never expires, which overrides the normal password expiration period.

   CAUTION   Selecting this option creates a security risk on the network. Although you might want to use Password Never Expires with administrator accounts, you usually shouldn't use this option with normal user accounts.

- **Store Password Using Reversible Encryption**   Saves the password as encrypted clear text.

- **Account Is Disabled**   Disables the account, which prevents the user from accessing the network and logging on.

- **Smart Card Is Required For Interactive Logon**   Requires the user to log on to a workstation using a smart card. The user can't log on to the workstation by typing a logon name and password at the keyboard.

- **Account Is Sensitive And Cannot Be Delegated** Specifies that the user's account credentials cannot be delegated using Kerberos. Use this for sensitive accounts that should be carefully controlled.

- **Use Kerberos DES Encryption Types For This Account** Specifies that the user account will use Data Encryption Standard (DES) encryption.

- **This Account Supports Kerberos AES 128 Bit Encryption** Specifies that the account supports Advanced Encryption Standard (AES) 128-bit encryption.

- **This Account Supports Kerberos AES 256 Bit Encryption** Specifies that the account supports AES 256-bit encryption.

- **Do Not Require Kerberos Preauthentication** Specifies that the user account doesn't need Kerberos preauthentication to access network resources. Preauthentication is part of the Kerberos version 5 security procedure. The option to log on without it allows authentication from clients using a previous, or nonstandard, implementation of Kerberos.

REAL WORLD AES is one of several encryption standards. Another encryption standard is Data Encryption Standard (DES). Most computers running older versions of Windows support DES.

Computers running Windows Vista, Windows 7, or Windows Server 2008 or later releases support AES, which provides more secure encryption than DES. While U.S. versions support both 128-bit and 256-bit AES, versions exported for use outside the United States typically support only 128-bit encryption.

Managing User Profiles

User profiles contain settings for the network environment, such as desktop configuration and menu options. Problems with a profile can sometimes prevent a user from logging on. For example, if the display size in the profile isn't available on the system being used, the user might not be able to log on properly. In fact, the user might get nothing but a blank screen. You could reboot the computer, go into Video Graphics Adapter (VGA) mode, and then reset the display manually, but solutions for profile problems aren't always this easy, and you might need to update the profile itself.

Windows Server 2008 R2 provides several ways to manage user profiles:

- You can assign profile paths in Active Directory Users And Computers.

- You can copy, delete, and change the type of an existing local profile with the System utility in Control Panel.

- You can set system policies that prevent users from manipulating certain aspects of their environment.

Local, Roaming, and Mandatory Profiles

In Windows Server 2008 R2, every user has a profile. Profiles control startup features for the user's session, the types of programs and applications that are available, the desktop settings, and a lot more. Each computer that a user logs on to has a copy of the user's profile. Because this profile is stored on the computer's hard disk, users who access several computers have a profile on each computer. Another computer on the network can't access a locally stored profile—called a *local profile*—and, as you might expect, this has some drawbacks. For example, if a user logs on to three different workstations, the user could have three very different profiles—one on each system. As a result, the user might get confused about what network resources are available on a given system.

To reduce the confusion caused by multiple profiles, you can create a profile that other computers can access. This type of profile is called a *roaming profile*. With a roaming profile, users can access the same profile no matter which computer they're using within the domain. Roaming profiles are server-based and can be stored only on a server running Windows 2000, Windows Server 2003, Windows Server 2008, or Windows Server 2008 R2. When a user with a roaming profile logs on, the profile is downloaded, which creates a local copy on the user's computer. When the user logs off, changes to the profile are updated both on the local copy and on the server.

> **REAL WORLD** When your organization uses the Encrypting File System (EFS) to make file access more secure, the use of roaming profiles becomes extremely important for users who log on to multiple computers. This is because encryption certificates are stored in user profiles, and the encryption certificate is needed to access and work with the user's encrypted files. If a user has encrypted files and doesn't have a roaming profile, that user won't be able to work with these encrypted files on another computer (unless he or she uses credential roaming with Digital ID Management Service (DIMS)).

As an administrator, you can control user profiles or let users control their own profiles. One reason to control profiles yourself is to make sure that all users have a common network configuration, which can reduce the number of environment-related problems.

Profiles controlled by administrators are called *mandatory profiles*. Users who have a mandatory profile can make only transitory changes to their environment. Any changes that users make to the local environment aren't saved, and the next time they log on, they're back to the original profile. The idea is that if users can't permanently modify the network environment, they can't make changes that cause problems. A key drawback to mandatory profiles is that the user can log on only if the profile is accessible. If, for some reason, the server that stores the profile is inaccessible and a cached profile isn't accessible, the user normally won't be able to log on. If the server is inaccessible, but a cached profile is accessible, the user receives a warning message and is logged on to the local system using the system's cached profile.

NOTE Mandatory profiles are deleted when you restart a computer running Windows XP. Users may receive an unrestricted temporary profile when they log on to a computer running Windows XP. This can occur if no network connection to the domain or a domain controller is available and if a cached profile isn't available. See Microsoft Knowledge Base article 893243 for more details at *support.microsoft.com/ default.aspx?scid=kb;en-us;893243.*

Creating Local Profiles

In Windows 2000 or later, user profiles are maintained either in a default directory or in the location set by the Profile Path field in the user's Properties dialog box. For Windows 7 and Windows Server 2008 R2, the default location for profiles is %SystemDrive%\Users\%UserName%\. A key part of the profile is the Ntuser.dat file in this location, such as C:\Users\wrstanek\Ntuser.dat. If you don't change the default location, the user will have a local profile.

Creating Roaming Profiles

Roaming profiles are stored on servers running Windows 2000, Windows Server 2003, Windows Server 2008, or Windows Server 2008 R2. When users log on to multiple computers and use EFS, they need a roaming profile to ensure that the certificates necessary to read and work with encrypted files are available on computers other than their primary work computers.

If you want a user to have a roaming profile, you must set a server-based location for the profile directory by following these steps:

1. Create a shared directory on a server running Windows Server 2008 R2, and make sure that the group Everyone has at least Change and Read access.

2. Open the user's Properties dialog box in Active Directory Users And Computers, and then click the Profile tab. Type the path to the shared directory in the Profile Path field. The path should have the form *server name\profile folder name\user name*. An example is \\Zeta\User_Profiles\Georgej, where *Zeta* is the server name, *User_Profiles* is the shared directory, and *Georgej* is the user name.

The roaming profile is then stored in the Ntuser.dat file in the designated directory, such as \\Zeta\User_Profiles\Georgej\Ntuser.dat.

NOTE You don't usually need to create the profile directory. The directory is created automatically when the user logs on, and NTFS permissions are set so that only the user has access. You can select multiple user accounts for simultaneous editing by holding down the Shift key or the Ctrl key when clicking the user names. When you right-click one of the selected users and then click Properties, you can edit properties for all the selected users. Be sure to use %UserName% in the profile path, such as \\Zeta\User_Profiles\%UserName%.

3. As an optional step, you can create a profile for the user or copy an existing profile to the user's profile folder. If you don't create an actual profile for the user, the next time the user logs on, the user will use the default local profile. Any changes the user makes to this profile are saved when the user logs off. The next time the user logs on, the user has a personal profile.

Creating Mandatory Profiles

Mandatory profiles are stored on servers running Windows Server 2008 R2. If you want a user to have a mandatory profile, you define the profile as follows:

1. Follow steps 1 and 2 in the previous section, "Creating Roaming Profiles."

2. Create a mandatory profile by renaming the Ntuser.dat file as %UserName%\ Ntuser.man. The next time the user logs on, he or she will have a mandatory profile.

NOTE Ntuser.dat contains the registry settings for the user. When you change the extension for the file to Ntuser.man, you tell Windows Server 2008 R2 to create a mandatory profile.

Using the System Utility to Manage Local Profiles

To manage local profiles, you need to log on to the user's computer. Then you can use the System utility in Control Panel to manage local profiles. To view current profile information, click Start, click Control Panel, click System And Security, and then click System. On the System page in Control Panel, click Advanced System Settings. In the System Properties dialog box, under User Profiles, click Settings.

As shown in Figure 11-8, the User Profiles dialog box displays information about the profiles stored on the local system. You can use this information to help you manage profiles. The fields have the following meanings:

- **Name** The local profile's name, which generally includes the name of the originating domain or computer and the user account name. For example, the name ADATUM\Wrstanek tells you that the original profile is from the domain adatum and the user account is wrstanek.

   NOTE If you delete an account but don't delete the associated profile, you might also see an entry that says Account Deleted or Account Unknown. Don't worry, the profile is still available for copying if you need it, or you can delete the profile here.

- **Size** The profile's size. Generally, the larger the profile, the more the user has customized the environment.
- **Type** The profile type, which is either local or roaming.
- **Status** The profile's current status, such as whether it's from a local cache.
- **Modified** The date that the profile was last modified.

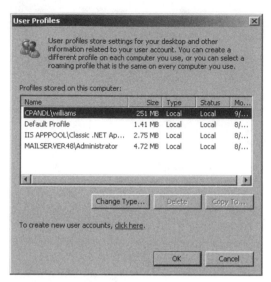

FIGURE 11-8 The User Profiles dialog box lets you manage existing local profiles.

Creating a Profile by Hand

Sometimes you might want to create the profile manually. You do this by logging on to the user account, setting up the environment, and then logging off. As you might guess, creating accounts in this manner is time-consuming. A better way to handle account creation is to create a base user account, set up the account environment, and then use this account as the basis of other accounts.

Copying an Existing Profile to a New User Account

If you have a base user account or a user account that you want to use in a similar manner, you can copy an existing profile to the new user account. To do this, follow these steps to use the System Control Panel utility:

1. Start the System Control Panel utility. On the System page in Control Panel, click Advanced System Settings. In the System Properties dialog box, under User Profiles, click Settings.

2. Select the profile you want to copy from the Profiles Stored On This Computer list. (See Figure 11-8.)

3. Copy the profile to the new user's account by clicking Copy To. In the Copy Profile To field, shown in Figure 11-9, type the path to the new user's profile directory. For example, if you were creating the profile for georgej, you'd type **\\Zeta\User_Profiles\Georgej**.

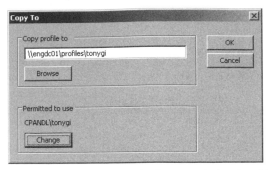

FIGURE 11-9 In the Copy To dialog box, enter the location of the profile directory and assign access permissions to the user.

4. Now you need to give the user permission to access the profile. In the Permitted To Use area, click Change, and then use the Select User Or Group dialog box to grant access to the new user account.

5. Click OK to close the Copy To dialog box. Windows then copies the profile to the new location.

TIP If you know the name of the user or group you want to use, you can save time by typing it directly into the Name field.

Copying or Restoring a Profile

When you work with workgroups where each computer is managed separately, you often have to copy a user's local profile from one computer to another. Copying a profile allows users to maintain environment settings when they use different computers. Of course, in a Windows Server 2008 R2 domain, you can use a roaming profile to create a single profile that can be accessed from anywhere within the domain. The problem is that sometimes you might need to copy an existing local profile to replace a user's roaming profile (when the roaming profile becomes corrupt), or you might need to copy an existing local profile to create a roaming profile in another domain.

You can copy a profile to a new location by following these steps:

1. Log on to the user's computer and start the System Control Panel utility. On the System page in Control Panel, click Advanced System Settings. In the System Properties dialog box, under User Profiles, click Settings.

2. In the Profiles Stored On This Computer list, select the profile you want to copy.

3. Copy the profile to the new location by clicking Copy To, and then type the path to the new profile directory in the Copy Profile To field. For example, if you're creating the profile for janew, you could type **\\Gamma\ User_Profiles\Janew**.

4. To give the user permission to access the profile, click the Change button in the Permitted To Use area, and then grant access to the appropriate user account in the Select User Or Group dialog box.

5. When you have finished, click OK to close the Copy To dialog box. Windows then copies the profile to the new location.

Deleting a Local Profile and Assigning a New One

Profiles are accessed when a user logs on to a computer. Windows Server 2008 R2 uses local profiles for all users who don't have roaming profiles. Generally, local profiles are also used if the local profile has a more recent modification date than the user's roaming profile. Therefore, sometimes you might need to delete a user's local profile. For example, if a user's local profile becomes corrupt, you can delete the profile and assign a new one. Keep in mind that when you delete a local profile that isn't stored anywhere else on the domain, you can't recover the user's original environment settings.

To delete a user's local profile, follow these steps:

1. Log on to the user's computer using an account with administrator privileges, and then start the System utility.

2. Click Advanced System Settings. In the System Properties dialog box, under User Profiles, click Settings.

3. Select the profile you want to delete, and then click Delete. When asked to confirm that you want to delete the profile, click Yes.

NOTE You can't delete a profile that's in use. If the user is logged on to the local system (the computer you're deleting the profile from), the user needs to log off before you can delete the profile. In some instances, Windows Server 2008 R2 marks profiles as in use when they aren't. This typically results from an environment change for the user that wasn't properly applied. To correct this, you might need to reboot the computer.

The next time the user logs on, Windows Server 2008 R2 does one of two things. Either the operating system gives the user the default local profile for that system, or it retrieves the user's roaming profile stored on another computer. To prevent the use of either of these profiles, you need to assign the user a new profile. To do this, you can do one of the following:

- Copy an existing profile to the user's profile directory. Copying profiles is covered in "Copying or Restoring a Profile."

- Update the profile settings for the user in Active Directory Users And Computers. Setting the profile path is covered in "Creating Roaming Profiles."

Changing the Profile Type

With roaming profiles, the System utility lets you change the profile type on the user's computer. To do this, select the profile, and then click Change Type. The options in this dialog box allow you to do the following:

- **Change a roaming profile to a local profile** If you want the user to always work with the local profile on this computer, specify that the profile is for local use. All changes to the profile are then made locally, and the original roaming profile is left untouched.

- **Change a local profile (that was defined originally as a roaming profile) to a roaming profile** The user will use the original roaming profile for the next logon. Windows Server 2008 R2 then treats the profile like any other roaming profile, which means that any changes to the local profile are copied to the roaming profile.

NOTE If these options aren't available, the user's original profile is defined locally.

Updating User and Group Accounts

Active Directory Users And Computers is the tool to use when you want to update a domain user or group account. If you want to update a local user or group account, use Local Users And Groups.

When you work with Active Directory, you'll often want to get a list of accounts and then do something with those accounts. For example, you might want to list all the user accounts in the organization and then disable the accounts of users who have left the company. One way to perform this task is to follow these steps:

1. In Active Directory Users And Computers, right-click the domain name, and then click Find.

2. In the Find list, select Custom Search. This updates the Find dialog box to display a Custom Search tab.

3. In the In list, select the area you want to search. To search the enterprise, select Entire Directory.

4. On the Custom Search tab, click Field to display a menu. Select User, and then select Logon Name (Pre–Windows 2000).

   TIP Be sure to select Logon Name (Pre–Windows 2000). Don't use Logon Name. User accounts aren't required to have a Windows Server 2008 R2 logon name, but they are required to have a pre–Windows 2000 logon name.

5. In the Condition list, select Present, and then click Add. If prompted to confirm, click Yes.

6. Click Find Now. Active Directory Users And Computers gathers a list of all users in the designated area.

7. You can now work with the accounts one by one or several at a time. To select multiple resources not in sequence, hold down the Ctrl key and then click each object you want to select. To select a series of resources at once, hold down the Shift key, click the first object, and then click the last object.

8. Right-click a user account, and then select an action on the shortcut menu that's displayed, such as Disable Account.

TIP The actions you can perform on multiple accounts include Add To Group (used to add the selected accounts to a designated group), Enable Account, Disable Account, Delete, Move, and Send Mail. By choosing Properties, you can edit the properties of multiple accounts.

Use this same procedure to get a list of computers, groups, or other Active Directory resources. With computers, do a custom search, click Field, choose Computer, and then select Computer Name (Pre–Windows 2000). With groups, do a custom search, click Field, choose Group, and then select Group Name (Pre–Windows 2000).

The sections that follow examine other techniques that you can use to update (rename, copy, delete, and enable) accounts as well as to change and reset passwords. You'll also learn how to troubleshoot account logon problems.

Renaming User and Group Accounts

When you rename a user account, you give the account a new label. As discussed in Chapter 10, "Creating User and Group Accounts," user names are meant to make managing and using accounts easier. Behind the scenes, Windows Server 2008 R2 uses security identifiers (SIDs) to identify, track, and handle accounts independently from user names. SIDs are unique identifiers that are generated when accounts are created.

Because SIDs are mapped to account names internally, you don't need to change the privileges or permissions on renamed accounts. Windows Server 2008 R2 simply maps the SIDs to the new account names as necessary.

One common reason for changing the name of a user account is that the user gets married and decides to change her last name. For example, if Kim Akers (kima) gets married, she might want her user name to be changed to Kim Ralls (kimr). When you change the user name from kima to kimr, all associated privileges and permissions will reflect the name change. If you view the permissions on a file that kima had access to, kimr now has access (and kima is no longer listed).

To simplify the process of renaming user accounts, Active Directory Users And Computers provides a Rename User dialog box that you can use to rename a user's account and all the related name components. To rename an account, follow these steps:

1. Find the user account that you want to rename in Active Directory Users And Computers.

2. Right-click the user account, and then click Rename. Active Directory Users And Computers highlights the account name for editing. Press Backspace or Delete to erase the existing name, and then press Enter to open the Rename User dialog box.

3. Make the necessary changes to the user's name information, and then click OK. If the user is logged on, you'll see a warning prompt telling you that the user should log off and then log back on using the new account logon name.

4. The account is renamed, and the SID for access permissions remains the same. You might still need to modify other data for the user in the account Properties dialog box, including:

   - **User Profile Path** Change the Profile Path in Active Directory Users And Computers, and then rename the corresponding directory on disk.

   - **Logon Script Name** If you use individual logon scripts for each user, change the Logon Script Name in Active Directory Users And Computers, and then rename the logon script on disk.

   - **Home Directory** Change the home directory path in Active Directory Users And Computers, and then rename the corresponding directory on disk.

NOTE Changing directory and file information for an account when a user is logged on might cause problems. You might want to update this information after hours or ask the user to log off for a few minutes and then log back on. You can usually write a simple Windows script that can perform the tasks for you automatically.

Copying Domain User Accounts

Creating domain user accounts from scratch can be tedious. Instead of starting anew each time, you might want to use an existing account as a starting point. To do this, follow these steps:

1. In Active Directory Users And Computers, right-click the account you want to copy, and then click Copy. This opens the Copy Object—User dialog box.

2. Create the account as you would any other domain user account, and then update the properties of the account as appropriate.

As you might expect, when you create a copy of an account, Active Directory Users And Computers doesn't retain all the information from the existing account. Instead, Active Directory Users And Computers tries to copy only the information you need and to discard the information that you need to update. The following properties are retained:

- City, state, ZIP code, and country values set on the Address tab
- Department and company set on the Organization tab
- Account options set using the Account Options fields on the Account tab
- Logon hours and permitted logon workstations

- Account expiration date
- Group account memberships
- Profile settings
- Dial-in privileges

NOTE If you used environment variables to specify the profile settings in the original account, the environment variables are used for the copy of the account as well. For example, if the original account used the %UserName% variable, the copy of the account will also use this variable.

Importing and Exporting Accounts

Windows Server 2008 R2 includes the Comma-Separated Value Directory Exchange (CSVDE) command-line utility for importing and exporting Active Directory objects. For import operations, CSVDE uses a comma-delimited text file as the import source. You can run CSVDE using these general parameters:

- **–i** Turns on import mode (rather than export, which is the default mode).
- **–f** *filename* Sets the source for an import or the output file for an export.
- **–s** *servername* Sets the server to use for the import or export (rather than the default domain controller for the domain).
- **–v** Turns on verbose mode.

For import operations, the source file's first row defines the list of LDAP attributes for each object defined. Each successive line of data provides the details for a specific object to import and must contain exactly the attributes listed. Here is an example:

```
DN,objectClass,sAMAccoutName,sn,givenName,userPrincipalName
"CN=William Stanek,OU=Eng,DC=cpandl,DC=com",user,williams,William,Stanek,
williams@cpandl.com
```

Given this listing, if the import source file is named newusers.csv, you could import the file into Active Directory by entering the following command at an elevated command prompt:

```
csvde -i -f newusers.csv
```

For export operations, CSVDE writes the exported objects to a comma-delimited text file. You can run CSVDE using the general parameters listed previously as well as export-specific parameters, which include the following:

- **–d** *RootDN* Sets the starting point for the export, such as –d "OU=Sales,DC=domain,DC=local". The default is the current naming context.
- **–l** *list* Provides a comma-separated list of attributes to output.
- **–r** *Filter* Sets the LDAP search filter, such as –r "(objectClass=user)".
- **–m** Configures output for the Security Accounts Manager (SAM) rather than Active Directory.

To create an export file for the current naming context (the default domain), you could enter the following at an elevated command prompt:

```
csvde -f newusers.csv
```

However, this could result in a very large export dump. Thus, in most cases you should specify at a minimum the RootDN and an object filter, such as:

```
csvde -f newusers.csv -d "OU=Service,DC=cpand1,DC=com" -r
"(objectClass=user)" Deleting User and Group Accounts
```

Deleting an account permanently removes the account. Once you delete an account, you can't create an account with the same name to get the same permissions. That's because the SID for the new account won't match the SID for the old account.

Because deleting built-in accounts can have far-reaching effects on the domain, Windows Server 2008 R2 doesn't let you delete built-in user accounts or group accounts. You can remove other types of accounts by selecting them and pressing the Delete key or by right-clicking and selecting Delete. When prompted, click Yes.

With Active Directory Users And Computers, you can work with multiple accounts by doing one of the following:

- Select multiple user names for editing by holding down the Ctrl key and clicking each account you want to select.
- Select a range of user names by holding down the Shift key, selecting the first account name, and then clicking the last account in the range.

NOTE When you delete a user account, Windows Server 2008 R2 doesn't delete the user's profile, personal files, or home directory. If you want to delete these files and directories, you have to do it manually. If this is a task you perform routinely, you might want to create a script that performs the necessary procedures for you. However, don't forget to back up files or data that might be needed before you do this.

Changing and Resetting Passwords

As an administrator, you often have to change or reset user passwords. This usually happens when users forget their passwords or when their passwords expire.

To change or reset a password, follow these steps:

1. Open Active Directory Users And Computers or Local Users And Groups (whichever is appropriate for the type of account you're renaming).

2. Right-click the account name, and then click Reset Password or Set Password.

3. Type a new password for the user and confirm it. The password should conform to the password complexity policy set for the computer or domain.

4. Double-click the account name, and then select the Unlock Account check box. In Active Directory Users And Computers, this check box is on the Account tab.

Enabling User Accounts

User accounts can become disabled for several reasons. If a user forgets his password and tries to guess it, the user might exceed the account policy for bad logon attempts. Another administrator could have disabled the account while the user was on vacation, or the account could have expired. The following sections describe what to do when an account is disabled, locked out, or expired.

Account Disabled

Active Directory Users And Computers depicts disabled accounts with a down arrow next to the user icon in the main view. When an account is disabled, follow these steps to enable it:

1. Open Active Directory Users And Computers or Local Users And Groups (whichever is appropriate for the type of account you're restoring).

2. Right-click the user's account name, and then click Enable Account.

TIP To quickly search the current domain for disabled accounts, type **dsquery user –disabled** at a command prompt.

Account Locked Out

When an account is locked out, follow these steps to unlock it:

1. Open Active Directory Users And Computers or Local Users And Groups (whichever is appropriate for the type of account you're restoring).

2. Double-click the user's account name, and then select the Unlock Account check box. In Active Directory Users And Computers, this check box is on the Account tab.

NOTE If users frequently get locked out of their accounts, consider adjusting the account policy for the domain. You might want to increase the value for acceptable bad logon attempts and reduce the duration for the associated counter. For more information on setting account policy, see "Configuring Account Policies" in Chapter 10.

Account Expired

Only domain accounts have an expiration date. (Local user accounts don't have an expiration date.) When a domain account expires, follow these steps to change the expiration date:

1. Open Active Directory Users And Computers.

2. Double-click the user's account name, and then click the Account tab.

3. In the Account Expires panel, select End Of, and then click the down arrow on the related field. This displays a calendar that you can use to set a new expiration date.

Managing Multiple User Accounts

You can use Active Directory Users And Computers to modify the properties of multiple accounts simultaneously. Any changes you make to the property settings are applied to all the selected accounts. When you right-click the selected accounts, the following options are available:

- **Add To A Group** Displays the Select Group dialog box, which you can use to designate the groups the selected users should be members of.
- **Disable Account** Disables all the selected accounts.
- **Enable Account** Enables all the selected accounts.
- **Move** Moves the selected accounts to a new container or organizational unit.
- **Properties** Allows you to configure a limited set of properties for multiple accounts.

The Properties option is the one we'll look at in the sections that follow. As shown in Figure 11-10, the Properties For Multiple Items dialog box has a different interface than the Properties dialog box for standard users.

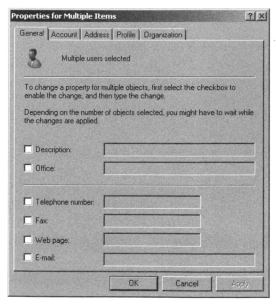

FIGURE 11-10 The Properties dialog box has a different interface when you work with multiple accounts.

You should note the following differences:

- Account name and password fields are no longer available. You can, however, set the Domain Name System (DNS) domain name (user principal name

[UPN] suffix), logon hours, computer restrictions, account options, account expiration, and profiles.

■ You must specifically select fields that you want to work with by selecting the fields' check boxes. After you do this, the value you enter in the field is applied to all the selected accounts.

Setting Profiles for Multiple Accounts

You set the profile information for multiple accounts with the options on the Profile tab. One of the best reasons to work with multiple accounts in Active Directory Users And Computers is that you can set all their environment profiles using a single interface. To do this, you usually rely on the %UserName% environment variable, which lets you assign paths and file names that are based on individual user names. For example, if you assign the logon script name as %UserName%.cmd, Windows replaces this value with the user name, and it does so for each user you're managing. Thus, the users bobs, janew, and ericl would all be assigned the following unique logon scripts: Bobs.cmd, Janew.cmd, and Ericl.cmd.

Figure 11-11 shows an example of setting environment profile information for multiple accounts. Note that the %UserName% variable is used to assign the user profile path, the user logon script name, and the home folder.

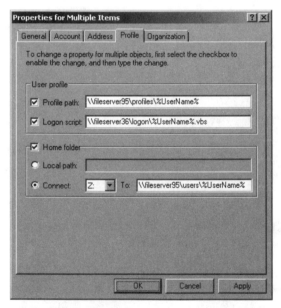

FIGURE 11-11 Use the %UserName% environment variable to assign paths and file names based on individual user names.

Although you might want all users to have unique file names and paths, sometimes you want users to share this information. For example, if you're using mandatory profiles for users, you might want to assign a specific user profile path rather than one that's dynamically created.

Setting Logon Hours for Multiple Accounts

When you select multiple user accounts in Active Directory Users And Computers, you can manage their logon hours collectively. To do this, follow these steps:

1. Select the accounts you want to work with in Active Directory Users And Computers.

2. Right-click the highlighted accounts, and then click Properties. In the Properties dialog box, click the Account tab.

3. Select the Logon Hours check box, and then click Logon Hours. You can then set the logon hours as discussed in "Configuring Logon Hours" earlier in the chapter.

NOTE Active Directory Users And Computers doesn't tell you the previous logon hour designations for the selected accounts, and it doesn't warn you if the logon hours for the accounts are different.

Setting Permitted Logon Workstations for Multiple Accounts

You set the permitted logon workstations for multiple accounts with the Logon Workstations dialog box. To open this dialog box, follow these steps:

1. Select the accounts you want to work with in Active Directory Users And Computers.

2. Right-click the highlighted accounts, and then click Properties. In the Properties dialog box, click the Account tab.

3. Select the Computer Restrictions check box, and then click Log On To.

4. If you want to allow the users to log on to any workstation, select All Computers. If you want to specify which workstations users are permitted to use, click The Following Computers button, and then enter the names of up to eight workstations. When you click OK, these settings are applied to all the selected user accounts.

Setting Logon, Password, and Expiration Properties for Multiple Accounts

User accounts have many options that control logon, passwords, and account expiration. You set these values on the Account tab of the Properties dialog box. When you work with multiple accounts, you must enable the option you want to work with by selecting the corresponding check box in the leftmost column. You now have two choices:

- Enable the option by selecting its check box. For example, if you are working with the Password Never Expires option, a flag is set so that the password for the selected users won't expire when you click OK.

- Don't set the option, which effectively clears the option. For example, if you are working with the Account Is Disabled option, the accounts for the selected users are reenabled when you click OK.

If you want to set the expiration date of the selected accounts, start by selecting Account Expires, and then select the appropriate expiration value. The Never option removes any current account expiration values. Select the End Of option to set a specific expiration date.

Troubleshooting Logon Problems

The previous section listed ways in which accounts can become disabled. Active Directory Users And Computers shows disabled accounts with a red warning icon next to the account name. To enable a disabled account, right-click the account in Active Directory Users And Computers, and then click Enable Account.

You can also search the entire domain for users with disabled accounts by typing **dsquery user –disabled** at a command prompt. To enable a disabled account from the command line, type **dsmod user UserDN –disabled no**.

When a user account has been locked out by the Account Lockout policy, the account cannot be used for logging until the lockout duration has elapsed or an administrator resets the account. If the account lockout duration is indefinite, the only way to unlock the account is to have an administrator reset it as discussed previously.

Windows Server 2008 R2 can record logon success and failure through auditing. When you enable account logon failure auditing, logon failure is recorded in the security log on the login domain controller. Auditing policies for a site, domain, or organizational unit GPO are found under Computer Configuration\Windows Settings\Security Settings\Local Policies\Audit Policy.

When a user logs on to the network by using his or her domain user account, the account credentials are validated by a domain controller. By default, users can log on using their domain user accounts even if the network connection is down or no domain controller is available to authenticate the user's logon.

The user must have previously logged on to the computer and have valid, cached credentials. If the user has no cached credentials on the computer and the network connection is down or no domain controller is available, the user will not be able to log on. Each member computer in a domain can cache up to 10 credentials by default.

When a domain is operating in Windows 2000 native or Windows Server 2003 mode, authentication can also fail if the system time on the member computer deviates from the logon domain controller's system time by more than is allowed in the Kerberos Policy: Maximum Tolerance For Computer Clock Synchronization. The default tolerance is 5 minutes for member computers.

Beyond these typical reasons for an account being disabled, some system settings can also cause access problems. Specifically, you should look for the following:

- **A user gets a message that says that the user can't log on interactively**   The user right to log on locally isn't set for this user, and the user isn't a member of a group that has this right.

  The user might be trying to log on to a server or domain controller. If so, keep in mind that the right to log on locally applies to all domain controllers in the domain. Otherwise, this right applies only to the single workstation.

  If the user is supposed to have access to the local system, configure the Logon Locally user right as described in "Configuring User Rights Policies" in Chapter 10.

- **A user gets a message that the system could not log on the user**   If you've already checked the password and account name, you might want to check the account type. The user might be trying to access the domain with a local account. If this isn't the problem, the global catalog server might be unavailable, which means that only users with administrator privileges can log on to the domain.

- **A user has a mandatory profile and the computer storing the profile is unavailable**   When a user has a mandatory profile, the computer storing the profile must be accessible during the logon process. If the computer is shutdown or otherwise unavailable, users with mandatory profiles may not be able to log on. See "Local, Roaming, and Mandatory Profiles" earlier in the chapter.

- **A user gets a message saying the account has been configured to prevent the user from logging on to the workstation**   The user is trying to access a workstation that isn't defined as a permitted logon workstation. If the user is supposed to have access to this workstation, change the logon workstation information as described in "Setting Permitted Logon Workstations for Multiple Accounts" earlier in the chapter.

Viewing and Setting Active Directory Permissions

As you know from previous discussions, user, group, and computer accounts are represented in Active Directory as objects. Active Directory objects have standard and advanced security permissions. These permissions grant or deny access to the objects.

Permissions for Active Directory objects aren't as straightforward as other permissions. Different types of objects can have sets of permissions that are specific to the type of object. They can also have general permissions that are specific to the container they're defined in.

You can view and set standard security permissions for objects by following these steps:

1. Start Active Directory Users And Computers, and then display advanced options by choosing Advanced Features from the View menu. Next, right-click the user, group, or computer account you want to work with, and then click Properties.

2. In the Properties dialog box, click the Security tab. As shown in Figure 11-12, you should now see a list of groups and users that have been assigned permissions on the object you previously selected. If the permissions are dimmed, it means the permissions are inherited from a parent object.

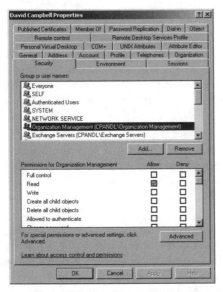

FIGURE 11-12 View and configure object permissions on the Security tab.

3. Users or groups with access permissions are listed in the Group Or User Names list box. You can change permissions for these users and groups by doing the following:

   - Select the user or group you want to change.

   - Grant or deny access permissions in the Permissions list.

   - When inherited permissions are not available, override inherited permissions by selecting the opposite permissions.

4. To set access permissions for additional users, computers, or groups, click Add. In the Select Users, Computers, Service Accounts, Or Groups dialog box, add users, computers, or groups.

5. In the Group Or User Names list, select the user, computer, or group you want to configure. Click Check Names, and then click OK. In the fields in the Permissions area, allow or deny permissions. Repeat this step for other users, computers, or groups.

6. Click OK when you have finished.

CAUTION Only administrators who have a solid understanding of Active Directory and Active Directory permissions should manipulate object permissions. Setting object permissions incorrectly can cause problems that are very difficult to track down.

You can view and set advanced security permissions for objects by following these steps:

1. Start Active Directory Users And Computers, and then display advanced options by choosing Advanced Features from the View menu. Next, right-click the user, group, or computer account you want to work with, and then click Properties.

2. In the Properties dialog box, click the Security tab, and then click Advanced. You should now see a list of individual permission entries for the previously selected object. Permission entries that are inherited are listed as being inherited from a specific parent object.

3. To view and set the individual permissions associated with a permission entry, select the entry, and then click Edit. You can change advanced permissions for the selected user or group by granting or denying access permissions in the Permissions list. When inherited permissions are not available, override inherited permissions by selecting the opposite permissions.

4. Click OK twice when you have finished.

Managing File Systems and Drives

A hard disk drive is the most common storage device used on network workstations and servers. Users depend on hard disk drives to store their word-processing documents, spreadsheets, and other types of data. Drives are organized into file systems that users can access either locally or remotely.

Local file systems are installed on a user's computer and can be accessed without remote network connections. The C drive available on most workstations and servers is an example of a local file system. You access the C drive using the file path C:\.

On the other hand, you access remote file systems through a network connection to a remote resource. You can connect to a remote file system using the Map Network Drive feature of Windows Explorer.

Wherever disk resources are located, your job as a system administrator is to manage them. The tools and techniques you use to manage file systems and drives are discussed in this chapter. Chapter 13, "Administering Volume Sets and RAID Arrays," looks at volume sets and fault tolerance.

Managing the File Services Role

A file server provides a central location for storing and sharing files across the network. When many users require access to the same files and application data, you should configure file servers in the domain. In earlier releases of the Windows

Server operating system, all servers were installed with basic file services. With Windows Server 2008 R2, you must specifically configure a server to be a file server by adding the File Services role and configuring this role to use the appropriate role services.

Table 12-1 provides an overview of the role services associated with the File Services role. When you install the File Services role, you might also want to install the following optional features, available through the Add Features Wizard:

- **Windows Server Backup** The backup utility included with Windows Server 2008 R2.

- **Storage Manager for SANs** Allows you to provision storage for storage area networks (SANs).

- **Multipath I/O** Provides support for using multiple data paths between a file server and a storage device. Servers use multiple I/O paths for redundancy in case of the failure of a path and to improve transfer performance.

TABLE 12-1 Role Services for File Servers

ROLE SERVICE	DESCRIPTION
BranchCache For Network Files	Enables computers in a branch office to cache commonly used files from shared folders.
Distributed File System (DFS)	Provides tools and services for DFS Namespaces and DFS Replication. DFS Replication is a newer and preferred replication technology. When a domain is running in Windows 2008 domain functional level, domain controllers use DFS Replication to provide more robust and granular replication of the SYSVOL directory.
DFS Namespaces	Allows you to group shared folders located on different servers into one or more logically structured namespaces. Each namespace appears as a single shared folder with a series of subfolders. However, the underlying structure of a namespace can come from shared folders on multiple servers in different sites.
DFS Replication	Allows you to synchronize folders on multiple servers across local or wide area network connections using a multimaster replication engine. The replication engine uses the Remote Differential Compression (RDC) protocol to synchronize only the portions of files that have changed since the last replication. You can use DFS Replication with DFS Namespaces or by itself.

ROLE SERVICE	DESCRIPTION
File Server Resource Manager (FSRM)	Installs a suite of tools that administrators can use to better manage data stored on servers. Using FSRM, administrators can generate storage reports, configure quotas, and define file-screening policies.
Indexing Service	Allows indexing of files and folders for faster searching. Using the related query language, users can find files quickly. You cannot install Indexing Service and Windows Search Service on the same computer.
Services for Network File System	Provides a file sharing solution for enterprises with a mixed Windows and UNIX environment. When you install Services for Network File System (NFS), users can transfer files between Windows Server 2008 R2 and UNIX operating systems by using the NFS protocol.
Windows Search Service	Enables fast file searches of resources on the server from clients that are compatible with Windows Search Service. This feature is designed primarily for desktop and small office implementations.
Windows Server 2003 File Services	Provides file services that are compatible with Windows Server 2003. This allows you to use a server running Windows Server 2008 R2 with servers running Windows Server 2003.

You can add the File Services role to a server by following these steps:

1. In Server Manager, select the Roles node in the left pane, and then click Add Roles. This starts the Add Roles Wizard. If the wizard displays the Before You Begin page, read the Welcome text, and then click Next.

   NOTE During the setup process, shared files are created on the server. If you encounter a problem that causes the setup process to fail, you need to resume the setup process using the Add Role Services Wizard. After you restart Server Manager, select the File Services node under Roles. In the main pane, scroll down and then click Add Role Services. You can continue with the installation starting with step 3. If you were in the process of configuring domain-based DFS, you need to provide administrator credentials.

2. On the Select Server Roles page, select File Services, and then click Next twice.

3. On the Select Role Services page, select one or more role services to install. A summary of each role service is provided in Table 12-1. To allow for interoperability with UNIX, be sure to add Services for Network File System. Click Next.

4. A DFS namespace is a virtual view of shared folders located on different servers. To install DFS Namespaces, you work with several additional configuration pages:

- On the Create A DFS Namespace page, set the root name for the first namespace or elect to create a namespace later, as shown in the following screen. The namespace root name should be something that is easy for users to remember, such as CorpData. In a large enterprise, you may need to create separate namespaces for each major division.

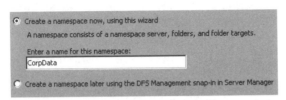

- On the Select Namespace Type page, specify whether you want to create a domain-based namespace or a stand-alone namespace, as shown in the following screen. Domain-based namespaces can be replicated with multiple namespace servers to provide high availability, but they can have only up to 5,000 DFS folders. Stand-alone namespaces can have up to 50,000 DFS folders, but they are replicated only when you use failover server clusters and configure replication.

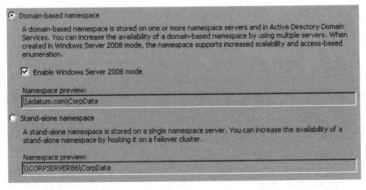

- If you are creating a domain-based namespace, on the Provide Credentials To Create A Namespace page, click Select, and then specify the user name and password for an account that is a member of the Domain Admins groups. This account is used to create the namespace.

- On the Configure Namespace page, you can add shared folders to the namespace as well as namespaces that are associated with a DFS folder, as shown in the following screen. Click Add. In the Add Folder To Namespace dialog box, click Browse. In the Browse For Shared Folders dialog box, select the shared folder to add, and then click OK. Type a name for the folder to add, and then click OK. Next, type a name for the folder in the namespace. This name can be the same as the original folder name or a new name that will be associated with the original folder in the namespace. After you type a name, click OK to add the folder and complete the process.

NOTE You do not have to configure DFS Namespaces at this time. Once you install DFS Namespaces, DFS Replication, or both, you can use the DFS Management console to manage the related features. This console is installed and available on the Administrative Tools menu. See Chapter 15, "Data Sharing, Security, and Auditing," for more information.

5. With File Server Resource Manager, you can monitor the amount of space used on disk volumes and create storage reports. To install File Server Resource Manager, you work with two additional configuration pages:

- On the Configure Storage Usage Monitoring page, select disk volumes for monitoring as shown in the following screen. When you select a volume and then click Options, you can set the volume usage threshold and choose the reports to generate when the volume reaches the threshold value. By default, the usage threshold is 85 percent.

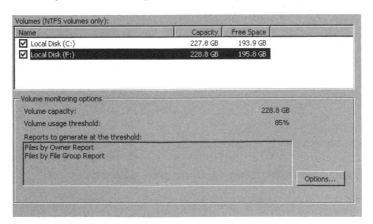

- On the Set Report Options page, you can select a save location for usage reports, as shown in the following screen. One usage report of each type you select is generated each time a volume reaches its threshold. Old reports are not automatically deleted. The default save location is %SystemDrive%\StorageReports. To change the default location, click Browse, and then select the new save location in the Browse For Folder dialog box. You can also elect to receive reports by e-mail. To do this, you must specify the recipient e-mail addresses and the SMTP server to use.

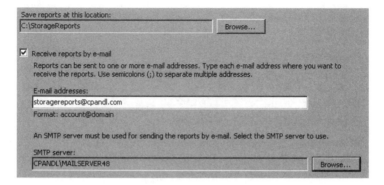

NOTE You do not have to configure monitoring and reporting at this time. After you install FSRM, you can use the File Server Resource Manager console to manage the related features. This console is installed and available on the Administrative Tools menu.

6. To install Windows Search Service, you work with an additional configuration page that allows you to select the volumes to index. Indexing a volume makes it possible for users to search a volume quickly. However, indexing entire volumes can affect service performance, especially if you index the system volume. Therefore, you may want to index only specific shared folders on volumes, which you can do later on a per-folder basis.

NOTE You do not have to configure indexing at this time. After you install Windows Search Service, you can use the Indexing Options utility in Control Panel to manage the related features.

7. After you complete the optional pages, click Next. You'll see the Confirm Installation Options page. Click Install to begin the installation process. When Setup finishes installing the server with the features you selected, you'll see the Installation Results page. Review the installation details to ensure that all phases of the installation were completed successfully.

If the File Services role is installed already on a server and you want to install additional services for a file server, you can add role services to the server by using a similar process. In Server Manager, expand the Roles node, and then select the File

Services node. In the main pane, the window is divided into several panels. Scroll down until you see the Role Services panel, and then click Add Role Services. You can then follow the previous procedure starting with step 3 to add role services.

Adding Hard Disk Drives

Before you make a hard disk drive available to users, you need to configure it and consider how it will be used. With Windows Server 2008 R2, you can configure hard disk drives in a variety of ways. The technique you choose depends primarily on the type of data you're working with and the needs of your network environment. For general user data stored on workstations, you might want to configure individual drives as stand-alone storage devices. In that case, user data is stored on a workstation's hard disk drive, where it can be accessed and stored locally.

Although storing data on a single drive is convenient, it isn't the most reliable way to store data. To improve reliability and performance, you might want a set of drives to work together. Windows Server 2008 R2 supports drive sets and arrays using redundant array of independent disks (RAID) technology, which is built into the operating system.

Physical Drives

Whether you use individual drives or drive sets, you need physical drives. Physical drives are the actual hardware devices that are used to store data. The amount of data a drive can store depends on its size and whether it uses compression. Typical drives have capacities of 500 gigabytes (GB) to 2 terabytes (TB). Many drive types are available for use with Windows Server 2008 R2, including Small Computer System Interface (SCSI), Parallel ATA (PATA), and Serial ATA (SATA).

The terms SCSI, PATA, and SATA designate the interface type used by the hard disk drives. This interface is used to communicate with a drive controller. SCSI drives use SCSI controllers, PATA drives use PATA controllers, and so on. When setting up a new server, you should give considerable thought to the drive configuration. Start by choosing drives or storage systems that provide the appropriate level of performance. There really is a substantial difference in speed and performance among various drive specifications.

You should consider not only the capacity of the drive but also the following:

- **Rotational speed** A measurement of how fast the disk spins

- **Average seek time** A measurement of how long it takes to seek between disk tracks during sequential input/output (I/O) operations

Generally speaking, when comparing drives that conform to the same specification, such as Ultra320 SCSI or SATA II, the higher the rotational speed (measured in thousands of rotations per minute) and the lower the average seek time (measured in milliseconds, or msecs), the better. As an example, a drive with a rotational speed of 15,000 RPM gives you 45–50 percent more I/O per second than the average 10,000 RPM drive, all other things being equal. A drive with a seek time of 3.5 msec gives you a 25–30 percent response time improvement over a drive with a seek time of 4.7 msec.

Other factors to consider include the following:

- **Maximum sustained data transfer rate**   A measurement of how much data the drive can continuously transfer

- **Mean time to failure (MTTF)**   A measurement of how many hours of operation you can expect to get from the drive before it fails

- **Nonoperational temperatures**   Measurements of the temperatures at which the drive fails

Most drives of comparable quality have similar transfer rates and MTTF. For example, if you compare Ultra320 SCSI drives with 15,000 RPM rotational speed from different vendors, you will probably find similar transfer rates and MTTF. For example, the Maxtor Atlas 15K II has a maximum sustained data transfer rate of up to 98 megabytes per second (MBps). The Seagate Cheetah 15K.4 has a maximum sustained data transfer rate of up to 96 MBps. Both have an MTTF of 1.4 million hours. Transfer rates can also be expressed in gigabits per second (Gbps). A rate of 1.5 Gbps is equivalent to a data rate of 187.5 MBps, and 3.0 Gbps is equivalent to 375 MBps. Sometimes you'll see a maximum external transfer rate (per the specification to which the drive complies) and an average sustained transfer rate. The average sustained transfer rate is the most important factor. The Seagate Barracuda 7200 SATA II drive has a rotational speed of 7,200 RPM and an average sustained transfer rate of 58 MBps. With an average seek time of 8.5 msec and an MTTF of 1 million hours, the drive performs comparably to other 7,200 RPM SATA II drives. However, most Ultra320 SCSI drives perform better and are better at multiuser read/ write operations, too.

> **NOTE**   Don't confuse MBps and Mbps. MBps is megabytes per second. Mbps is megabits per second. Because there are 8 bits in a byte, a 100 MBps transfer rate is equivalent to an 800 Mbps transfer rate. With SATA, the maximum data transfer rate is usually around 150 MBps or 300 MBps. With PATA, the maximum data transfer rate is usually around 100 MBps.

Temperature is another important factor to consider when you're selecting a drive, but it's a factor few administrators take into account. Typically, the faster a drive rotates, the hotter it runs. This is not always the case, but it is certainly something you should consider when making your choice. For example, 15K drives tend to run hot, and you must be sure to carefully regulate temperature. Both the Maxtor Atlas 15K II and the Seagate Cheetah 15K.4 can become nonoperational at temperatures of 70 degrees Centigrade or higher (as would most other drives).

Preparing a Physical Drive for Use

After you install a drive, you need to configure it for use. You configure the drive by partitioning it and creating file systems in the partitions as needed. A partition is a section of a physical drive that functions as if it were a separate unit. After you create a partition, you can create a file system in the partition.

Two partition styles are used for disks: master boot record (MBR) and GUID partition table (GPT). The MBR contains a partition table that describes where the partitions are located on the disk. With this partition style, the first sector on a hard disk contains the master boot record and a binary code file called the *master boot code* that's used to boot the system. This sector is unpartitioned and hidden from view to protect the system.

With the MBR partitioning style, disks support volumes of up to 4 terabytes (TB) and use one of two types of partitions—primary or extended. Each MBR drive can have up to four primary partitions or three primary partitions and one extended partition. Primary partitions are drive sections that you can access directly for file storage. You make a primary partition accessible to users by creating a file system on it. Although you can access primary partitions directly, you can't access extended partitions directly. Instead, you can configure extended partitions with one or more logical drives that are used to store files. Being able to divide extended partitions into logical drives allows you to divide a physical drive into more than four sections.

GPT was originally developed for high-performance Itanium-based computers. GPT is recommended for disks larger than 2 TB on x86 and x64 systems or any disks used on Itanium-based computers. The key difference between the GPT partition style and the MBR partition style has to do with how partition data is stored. With GPT, critical partition data is stored in the individual partitions, and redundant primary and backup partition tables are used for improved structural integrity. Additionally, GPT disks support volumes of up to 18 exabytes and as many as 128 partitions. Although the GPT and MBR partitioning styles have underlying differences, most disk-related tasks are performed in the same way.

Using Disk Management

You use the Disk Management snap-in for the Microsoft Management Console (MMC) to configure drives. Disk Management makes it easy to work with the internal and external drives on a local or remote system. Disk Management is included as part of the Computer Management console and the Server Manager console. You can also add it to custom MMCs. In Computer Management and in Server Manager, you can access Disk Management by expanding the Storage node and then selecting Disk Management.

Regardless of whether you are using Computer Management or Server Manager, Disk Management has three views: Disk List, Graphical View, and Volume List. With remote systems you're limited in the tasks you can perform with Disk Management. Remote management tasks you can perform include viewing drive details, changing drive letters and paths, and converting disk types. With removable media drives, you can also eject media remotely. To perform more advanced manipulation of remote drives, you can use the DiskPart command-line utility.

NOTE Before you work with Disk Management, you should know several things. If you create a partition but don't format it, the partition is labeled as Free Space. If you haven't assigned a portion of the disk to a partition, this section of the disk is labeled Unallocated.

In Figure 12-1, the Volume List view is in the upper-right corner and Graphical View is used in the lower-right corner. This is the default configuration. You can change the view for the top or bottom pane as follows:

- To change the top view, select View, choose Top, and then select the view you want to use.

- To change the bottom view, select View, choose Bottom, and then select the view you want to use.

- To hide the bottom view, select View, choose Bottom, and then select Hidden.

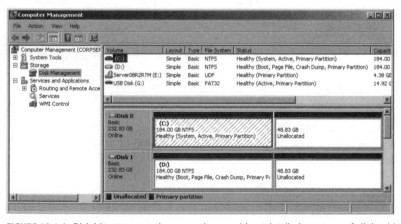

FIGURE 12-1 In Disk Management, the upper view provides a detailed summary of all the drives on the computer and the lower view provides an overview of the same drives by default.

Windows Server 2008 R2 supports four types of disk configurations:

- **Basic** The standard fixed disk type used in previous versions of Windows. Basic disks are divided into partitions and can be used with previous versions of Windows.

- **Dynamic** An enhanced fixed disk type for Windows Server 2008 R2 that you can update without having to restart the system (in most cases). Dynamic disks are divided into volumes and can be used only with Windows 2000 and later releases of Windows.

- **Removable**   The standard disk type associated with removable storage devices. Removable storage devices can be formatted with exFAT, FAT, FAT32, or NTFS.

- **Virtual**   The virtual hard disk (VHD) disk type associated with virtualization can be used when a computer is running Windows 7, Windows Server 2008 R2, or later releases. Computers can use VHDs just like they use regular fixed disks and can even be configured to boot from a VHD.

REAL WORLD   Windows Vista with SP1 or later, Windows 7, and Windows Server 2008 or later all support exFAT with removable storage devices. The exFAT file system is the next generation file system in the FAT (FAT12/16, FAT32) family. While retaining the ease-of-use advantages of FAT32, exFAT overcomes the 4-GB file size limit on FAT32 and its 32-GB partition size limit on Windows systems. The exFAT file system also supports allocation unit sizes of up to 32,768 KB.

The exFAT file system is designed so that it can be used with any compliant operating system or device. This means you can remove an exFAT storage device from a compliant camera and insert it into a compliant phone or vice versa without having to do any reformatting. It also means that you can remove an exFAT storage device from a computer running Mac OS or Linux and insert it into a computer running Windows.

From the Disk Management window, you can get more detailed information on a drive section by right-clicking it and then selecting Properties. When you do this, you see a dialog box. With fixed disks, the dialog box is much like the one shown on the left in Figure 12-2. With removable disks, the dialog box is much like the one shown on the right in Figure 12-2. This is the same dialog box that you can open from Windows Explorer (by selecting the top-level folder for the drive and then choosing Properties from the File menu).

FIGURE 12-2 The General tab of the Properties dialog box provides detailed information about a drive.

If you've configured remote management through Server Manager and MMCs, as discussed in Chapter 3, "Managing Servers Running Windows Server 2008 R2," you can use Disk Management to configure and work with disks on remote computers. Keep in mind, however, that your options are slightly different from when you are working with the disks on a local computer. Tasks you can perform include:

- Viewing limited disk properties but not volume properties. When you are viewing disk properties, you'll see only the General and Volumes tabs. You won't be able to see volume properties.

- Changing drive letters and mount paths.

- Formatting, shrinking, and extending volumes. With mirrored, spanned, and striped volumes, you are able to add and configure related options.

- Deleting volumes (except for system and boot volumes)

- Creating, attaching, and detaching VHDs. When you create and attach VHDs, you need to enter the full file path and won't be able to browse for the .vhd file.

Some tasks you perform with disks and volumes depend on the Plug and Play and Remote Registry services.

Removable Storage Devices

Removable storage devices can be formatted with NTFS, FAT, FAT32, or exFAT. You connect external storage devices to a computer rather than installing them inside the computer. This makes external storage devices easier and faster to install than most fixed disk drives. Most external storage devices have either a universal serial bus (USB) or a FireWire interface. When working with USB and FireWire, the transfer speed and overall performance of the device from a user's perspective depends primarily on the version supported. Currently, several versions of USB and FireWire are used, including USB 1.0, USB 1.1, USB 2.0, FireWire 400, and FireWire 800.

USB 2.0 is the industry standard, and it supports data transfers at a maximum rate of 480 Mbps, with sustained data transfer rates usually from 10–30 Mbps. The actual sustainable transfer rate depends on many factors, including the type of device, the data you are transferring, and the speed of a computer. Each USB controller on a computer has a fixed amount of bandwidth, which all devices attached to the controller must share. The data transfer rates are significantly slower if a computer's USB port is an earlier version than the device you are using. For example, if you connect a USB 2.0 device to a USB 1.0 port or vice versa, the device operates at the significantly reduced USB 1.0 transfer speed.

USB 1.0, 1.1, and 2.0 ports all look alike. The best way to determine which type of USB ports a computer has is to refer to the documentation that comes with the computer. Newer LCD monitors have USB 2.0 ports to which you can connect devices as well. When you have USB devices connected to a monitor, the monitor acts like a USB hub device. As with any USB hub device, all devices attached to the hub share the same bandwidth, and the total available bandwidth is determined by the speed of the USB input to which the hub is connected on a computer.

FireWire (IEEE 1394) is a high-performance connection standard that uses a peer-to-peer architecture in which peripherals negotiate bus conflicts to determine which device can best control a data transfer. Like USB, several versions of FireWire currently are used, including FireWire 400 and FireWire 800. FireWire 400 (IEEE 1394a) has maximum sustained transfer rates of up to 400 Mbps. FireWire 800 (IEEE 1394b) has maximum sustained transfer rates of up to 800 Mbps. As with USB, if you connect a FireWire 800 device to a FireWire 400 port or vice versa, the device operates at the significantly reduced FireWire 400 transfer speed.

FireWire 400 and FireWire 800 ports and cables have different shapes, making it easier to tell the difference between them—if you know what you're looking for. FireWire 400 cables without bus power have four pins and four connectors. FireWire 400 cables with bus power have six pins and six connectors. FireWire 800 cables always have bus power and have nine pins and nine connectors.

Another option is External Serial ATA (eSATA), which is available on newer computers and is an ultra-high-performance connection for data transfer to and from external mass storage devices. eSATA operates at speeds up to 3 Gbps. You can add support for eSATA devices by installing an eSATA controller card.

When you are purchasing an external device for a computer, you'll also want to consider what interfaces it supports. In some cases, you may be able to get a device with a dual interface that supports USB 2.0 and FireWire 400, or a triple interface that supports USB 2.0, FireWire 400, and FireWire 800. A device with dual or triple interfaces gives you more options. There also are devices with quadruple interfaces.

Working with removable disks is similar to working with fixed disks. You can do the following:

- Right-click a removable disk and select Open or Explore to examine the disk's contents in Windows Explorer.

- Right-click a removable disk and select Format to format a removable disk as discussed in "Formatting Partitions" later in this chapter. Removable disks generally are formatted with a single partition.

- Right-click a removable disk and select Properties to view or set properties. On the General tab of the Properties dialog box, you can set the volume label as discussed in "Changing or Deleting the Volume Label" later in this chapter.

When you work with removable disks, you can customize disk and folder views. To do this, right-click the disk or folder, select Properties, and then click the Customize tab. You can then specify the default folder type to control the default details displayed. For example, you can set the default folder type as Documents or Pictures And Videos. You can also set folder pictures and folder icons.

Removable disks support network file and folder sharing. You configure sharing on removable disks in the same way that you configure standard file sharing. You can assign share permissions, configure caching options for offline file use, and limit the number of simultaneous users. You can share an entire removable disk as well as individual folders stored on the removable disk. You can also create multiple share instances.

Removable disks differ from standard NTFS sharing in that they don't necessarily have an underlying security architecture. With exFAT, FAT, or FAT32, folders and files stored on a removable disk do not have any security permissions or features other than the basic read-only or hidden attribute flags that you can set.

Installing and Checking for a New Drive

Hot swapping is a feature that allows you to remove devices without shutting off the computer. Typically, hot-swappable drives are installed and removed from the front of the computer. If your computer supports hot swapping of drives, you can install drives without having to shut down. After you do this, open Disk Management, and then choose Rescan Disks from the Action menu. New disks that are found are added with the appropriate disk type. If a disk that you've added isn't found, reboot.

If the computer doesn't support hot swapping of drives, you must turn the computer off and then install the new drives. Then you can scan for new disks as described previously. If you are working with new disks that have not been initialized—meaning they don't have disk signatures—Disk Management will start the Initialize Disk dialog box as soon it starts up and detects the new disks.

You can initialize the disks by following these steps:

1. Each disk you install needs to be initialized. Select the disk or disks that you installed.

2. Disks can use either the MBR or GPT partition style. Select the partition style you want to use for the disk or disks you are initializing.

3. Click OK. If you elected to initialize disks, Windows writes a disk signature to the disks and initializes the disks with the basic disk type.

If you don't want to use the Initialize Disk dialog box, you can close it and use Disk Management instead to view and work with the disk. In the Disk List view, the disk is marked with a red downward pointing arrow icon, the disk's type is listed as Unknown, and the disk's status is listed as Not Initialized. You can then right-click the disk's icon and select Online. Right-click the disk's icon again, and select Initialize Disk. You can then initialize the disk as discussed previously.

Understanding Drive Status

Knowing the status of a drive is useful when you install new drives or troubleshoot drive problems. Disk Management shows the drive status in Graphical View and Volume List view. Table 12-2 summarizes the most common status values.

TABLE 12-2 Common Drive Status Values

STATUS	DESCRIPTION	RESOLUTION
Online	The normal disk status. It means the disk is accessible and doesn't have problems. Both dynamic disks and basic disks display this status.	The drive doesn't have any known problems. You don't need to take any corrective action.
Online (Errors)	I/O errors have been detected on a dynamic disk.	You can try to correct temporary errors by right-clicking the disk and selecting Reactivate Disk. If this doesn't work, the disk might have physical damage or you might need to run a thorough check of the disk.
Offline	The disk isn't accessible and might be corrupted or temporarily unavailable. If the disk name changes to Missing, the disk can no longer be located or identified on the system.	Check for problems with the drive, its controller, and cables. Make sure that the drive has power and is connected properly. Use the Reactivate Disk command to bring the disk back online (if possible).
Foreign	The disk has been moved to your computer but hasn't been imported for use. A failed drive brought back online might sometimes be listed as Foreign.	Right-click the disk, and then click Import Foreign Disks to add the disk to the system.
Unreadable	The disk isn't accessible currently, which can occur when disks are being rescanned. Both dynamic and basic disks display this status.	With FireWire and USB card readers, you might see this status if the card is unformatted or improperly formatted. You might also see this status after the card is removed from the reader. Otherwise, if the drives aren't being scanned, the drive might be corrupted or have I/O errors. Right-click the disk, and then click Rescan Disk (on the Action menu) to try to correct the problem. You might also want to reboot the system.

STATUS	DESCRIPTION	RESOLUTION
Unrecognized	The disk is of an unknown type and can't be used on the system. A drive from a non-Windows system might display this status.	If the disk is from another operating system, don't do anything. You can't use the drive on the computer, so try a different drive.
Not Initialized	The disk doesn't have a valid signature. A drive from a non-Windows system might display this status.	If the disk is from another operating system, don't do anything. You can't use the drive on the computer, so try a different drive. To prepare the disk for use on Windows Server 2008 R2, right-click the disk, and then click Initialize Disk.
No Media	No media has been inserted into the CD-ROM or removable drive, or the media has been removed. Only CD-ROM and removable disk types display this status.	Insert a CD-ROM, a floppy disk, or a removable disk to bring the disk online. With FireWire and USB card readers, this status is usually (but not always) displayed when the card is removed.

Working with Basic, Dynamic, and Virtual Disks

Windows Server 2008 R2 supports basic, dynamic, and virtual disk configurations. This section discusses techniques for working with each disk configuration type.

NOTE You can't use dynamic disks on portable computers or with removable media.

Using Basic and Dynamic Disks

Normally, Windows Server 2008 R2 disk partitions are initialized as basic disks. You can't create new fault-tolerant drive sets using the basic disk type. You need to convert to dynamic disks and then create volumes that use striping, mirroring, or striping with parity (referred to as RAID 0, 1, and 5 respectively). The fault-tolerant features and the ability to modify disks without having to restart the computer are the key capabilities that distinguish dynamic disks from basic disks. Other features available on a disk depend on the disk formatting.

You can use both basic and dynamic disks on the same computer. However, volume sets must use the same disk type and partitioning style. For example, if you want to mirror drives C and D, both drives must have the dynamic disk type and use the same partitioning style, which can be either MBR or GPT. Note that Disk Management allows you to start many disk configuration tasks regardless of whether the disks you are working with use the dynamic disk type. The catch is that during the configuration process Disk Management will convert the disks to the dynamic disk type. To learn how to convert a disk from basic to dynamic, see "Changing Drive Types" on the next page.

You can perform different disk configuration tasks with basic and dynamic disks. With basic disks, you can do the following:

- Format partitions and mark them as active
- Create and delete primary and extended partitions
- Create and delete logical drives within extended partitions
- Convert from a basic disk to a dynamic disk

With dynamic disks, you can do the following:

- Create and delete simple, striped, spanned, mirrored, and RAID-5 volumes
- Remove a mirror from a mirrored volume
- Extend simple or spanned volumes
- Split a volume into two volumes
- Repair mirrored or RAID-5 volumes
- Reactivate a missing or offline disk
- Revert to a basic disk from a dynamic disk (requires deleting volumes and restoring from backup)

With either disk type, you can do the following:

- View properties of disks, partitions, and volumes
- Make drive letter assignments
- Configure security and drive sharing

Special Considerations for Basic and Dynamic Disks

Whether you're working with basic or dynamic disks, you need to keep in mind five special types of drive sections:

- **Active**   The active partition or volume is the drive section for system caching and startup. Some devices with removable storage may be listed as having an active partition.
- **Boot**   The boot partition or volume contains the operating system and its support files. The system and boot partition or volume can be the same.
- **Crash dump**   The partition to which the computer attempts to write dump files in the event of a system crash. By default, dump files are written to the %SystemRoot% folder, but they can be located on any partition or volume.

- **Page file** A partition containing a paging file used by the operating system. Because a computer can page memory to multiple disks, according to the way virtual memory is configured, a computer can have multiple page file partitions or volumes.

- **System** The system partition or volume contains the hardware-specific files needed to load the operating system. The system partition or volume can't be part of a striped or spanned volume.

NOTE You can mark a partition as active using Disk Management. In Disk Management, right-click the primary partition you want to mark as active, and then click Mark Partition As Active. You can't mark dynamic disk volumes as active. When you convert a basic disk containing the active partition to a dynamic disk, this partition becomes a simple volume that's active automatically.

Changing Drive Types

Basic disks are designed to be used with previous versions of Windows. Dynamic disks are designed to let you take advantage of the latest Windows features. Only computers running Windows 2000 or later releases of Windows can use dynamic disks. However, you can use dynamic disks with other operating systems, such as UNIX. To do this, you need to create a separate volume for the non-Windows operating system. You can't use dynamic disks on portable computers.

Windows Server 2008 R2 provides the tools you need to convert a basic disk to a dynamic disk and to change a dynamic disk back to a basic disk. When you convert to a dynamic disk, partitions are changed to volumes of the appropriate type automatically. You can't change these volumes back to partitions. Instead, you must delete the volumes on the dynamic disk and then change the disk back to a basic disk. Deleting the volumes destroys all the information on the disk.

Converting a Basic Disk to a Dynamic Disk

Before you convert a basic disk to a dynamic disk, you should make sure that you don't need to boot the computer to other versions of Windows. Only computers running Windows 2000 and later releases of Windows can use dynamic disks.

With MBR disks, you should also make sure that the disk has 1 MB of free space at the end of the disk. Although Disk Management reserves this free space when creating partitions and volumes, disk management tools on other operating systems might not. Without the free space at the end of the disk, the conversion will fail.

With GPT disks, you must have contiguous, recognized data partitions. If the GPT disk contains partitions that Windows doesn't recognize, such as those created by another operating system, you can't convert to a dynamic disk.

With either type of disk, the following holds true:

- There must be at least 1 MB of free space at the end of the disk. Disk Management reserves this free space automatically, but other disk management tools might not.

- You can't use dynamic disks on portable computers or with removable media. You can configure these drives only as basic drives with primary partitions.

- You shouldn't convert a disk if it contains multiple installations of the Windows operating system. If you do, you might be able to start the computer only using Windows Server 2008 R2.

To convert a basic disk to a dynamic disk, follow these steps:

1. In Disk Management, right-click a basic disk that you want to convert, either in the Disk List view or in the left pane of the Graphical View. Then click Convert To Dynamic Disk.

2. In the Convert To Dynamic Disk dialog box, select the check boxes for the disks you want to convert. If you're converting a spanned, striped, mirrored, or RAID-5 volume, be sure to select all the basic disks in this set. You must convert the set together. Click OK to continue.

    The Disks To Convert dialog box shows the disks you're converting. The buttons and columns in this dialog box contain the following information:

    - **Name**   Shows the disk number.

    - **Disk Contents**   Shows the type and status of partitions, such as boot, active, or in use.

    - **Will Convert**   Specifies whether the drive will be converted. If the drive doesn't meet the criteria, it won't be converted, and you might need to take corrective action, as described previously.

    - **Details**   Shows the volumes on the selected drive.

    - **Convert**   Starts the conversion.

3. To begin the conversion, click Convert. Disk Management warns you that after the conversion is complete, you won't be able to boot previous versions of Windows from volumes on the selected disks. Click Yes to continue.

4. Disk Management restarts the computer if a selected drive contains the boot partition, system partition, or a partition in use.

Changing a Dynamic Disk Back to a Basic Disk

Before you can change a dynamic disk back to a basic disk, you must delete all dynamic volumes on the disk. After you do this, right-click the disk and select Convert To Basic Disk. This changes the dynamic disk to a basic disk. You can then create new partitions and logical drives on the disk.

Reactivating Dynamic Disks

If the status of a dynamic disk is Online (Errors) or Offline, you can often reactivate the disk to correct the problem. You reactivate a disk by following these steps:

1. In Disk Management, right-click the dynamic disk you want to reactivate, and then click Reactivate Disk. Confirm the action when prompted.

2. If the drive status doesn't change, you might need to reboot the computer. If this still doesn't resolve the problem, check for problems with the drive, its controller, and the cables. Also make sure that the drive has power and is connected properly.

Rescanning Disks

Rescanning all drives on a system updates the drive configuration information on the computer. Rescanning can sometimes resolve a problem with drives that show a status of Unreadable. You rescan disks on a computer by choosing Rescan Disks from the Action menu in Disk Management.

Moving a Dynamic Disk to a New System

An important advantage of dynamic disks over basic disks is that you can easily move them from one computer to another. For example, if after setting up a computer you decide that you don't really need an additional hard disk, you can move it to another computer where it can be better used.

Windows Server 2008 R2 greatly simplifies the task of moving drives to a new system. Before moving disks, you should follow these steps:

1. Open Disk Management on the system where the dynamic drives are currently installed. Check the status of the drives and ensure that they're marked as Healthy. If the status isn't Healthy, you should repair partitions and volumes before you move the disk drives.

   NOTE Drives with BitLocker Drive Encryption cannot be moved using this technique. BitLocker Driver Encryption wraps drives in a protected seal so that any offline tampering is detected and results in the disk being unavailable until an administrator unlocks it.

2. Check the hard disk subsystems on the original computer and the computer to which you want to transfer the disk. Both computers should have identical hard disk subsystems. If they don't, the Plug and Play ID on the system disk from the original computer won't match what the destination computer is expecting. As a result, the destination computer won't be able to load the right drivers, and boot might fail.

3. Check whether any dynamic disks that you want to move are part of a spanned, extended, or striped set. If they are, you should make a note of which disks are part of which set and plan on moving all disks in a set

together. If you are moving only part of a disk set, you should be aware of the consequences. For spanned, extended, or striped volumes, moving only part of the set will make the related volumes unusable on the current computer and on the computer to which you are planning to move the disks.

When you are ready to move the disks, follow these steps:

1. On the original computer, start Computer Management. Then, in the left pane, select Device Manager. In the Device list, expand Disk Drives. This shows a list of the physical disk drives on the computer. Right-click each disk that you want to move, and then click Uninstall. If you are unsure which disks to uninstall, right-click each disk and click Properties. In the Properties dialog box, click the Volumes tab, and then select Populate. This shows you the volumes on the selected disk.

2. Next, on the original computer, select the Disk Management node in Computer Management. If the disk or disks that you want to move are still listed, right-click each disk, and then click Remove Disk.

3. After you perform these procedures, you can move the dynamic disks. If the disks are hot-swappable disks and this feature is supported on both computers, remove the disks from the original computer and then install them on the destination computer. Otherwise, turn off both computers, remove the drives from the original computer, and then install them on the destination computer. When you have finished, restart the computers.

4. On the destination computer, access Disk Management, and then choose Rescan Disks from the Action menu. When Disk Management finishes scanning the disks, right-click any disk marked Foreign, and then click Import. You should now be able to access the disks and their volumes on the destination computer.

NOTE In most cases, the volumes on the dynamic disks should retain the drive letters that they had on the original computer. However, if a drive letter is already used on the destination computer, a volume receives the next available drive letter. If a dynamic volume previously did not have a drive letter, it does not receive a drive letter when moved to the destination computer. Additionally, if automounting is disabled, the volumes aren't automatically mounted, and you must manually mount volumes and assign drive letters.

Managing Virtual Hard Disks

Using Disk Management, you can create, attach, and detach virtual hard disks. You can create a virtual hard disk by choosing Create VHD from the Action menu. In the Create And Attach Virtual Hard Disk dialog box, click Browse. Use the Browse Virtual Disk Files dialog box to select the location where you want to create the .vhd file for the virtual hard disk, and then click Save.

In the Virtual Hard Disk Size list, enter the size of the disk in MB, GB, or TB. Specify whether the size of the VHD dynamically expands to its fixed maximum size as data is saved to it or uses a fixed amount of space regardless of the amount of data stored on it. When you click OK, Disk Management creates the virtual hard disk.

The VHD is attached automatically and added as a new disk. To initialize the disk for use, right-click the disk entry in Graphical View, and then click Initialize Disk. In the Initialize Disk dialog box, the disk is selected for initialization. Specify the disk type as MBR or GPT, and then click OK.

After initializing the disk, right-click the unpartitioned space on the disk and create a volume of the appropriate type. After you create the volume, the VHD is available for use.

Once you've created, attached, initialized, and formatted a VHD, you can work with a virtual disk in much the same way as you work with other disks. You can write data to and read data from a VHD. You can boot the computer from a VHD. You are able to take a VHD offline or put a VHD online by right-clicking the disk entry in Graphical View and selecting Offline or Online, respectively. If you no longer want to use a VHD, you can detach it by right-clicking the disk entry in Graphical View, selecting Detach VHD, and then clicking OK in the Detach Virtual Hard Disk dialog box.

You can use VHDs created with other programs as well. If you created a VHD using another program or have a detached VHD that you want to attach, you can work with the VHD by completing the following steps:

1. In Disk Management, click the Attach VHD option on the Action menu.

2. In the Attach Virtual Hard Disk dialog box, click Browse. Use the Browse Virtual Disk Files dialog box to select the .vhd file for the virtual hard disk, and then click Open.

3. If you want to attach the VHD in read-only mode, select Read-Only. Click OK to attach the VHD.

Using Basic Disks and Partitions

When you install a new computer or update an existing computer, you often need to partition the drives on the computer. You partition drives using Disk Management.

Partitioning Basics

In Windows Server 2008 R2, a physical drive using the MBR partition style can have up to four primary partitions and one extended partition. This allows you to configure MBR drives in one of two ways: by using one to four primary partitions, or by using one to three primary partitions and one extended partition. A primary partition can fill an entire disk, or you can size it as appropriate for the workstation or server you're configuring. Within an extended partition, you can create one or more logical drives. A logical drive is simply a section of a partition with its own file system. Generally, you use logical drives to divide a large drive into manageable sections. With this in mind, you might want to divide a 600-GB extended partition into three logical drives of 200 GB each. Physical disks with the GPT partition style can have up to 128 partitions.

After you partition a drive, you format the partitions to assign drive letters. This is a high-level formatting that creates the file system structure rather than a low-level formatting that sets up the drive for initial use. You're probably very familiar with the C drive used by Windows Server 2008 R2. Well, the C drive is simply the designator for a disk partition. If you partition a disk into multiple sections, each section can have its own drive letter. You use the drive letters to access file systems in various partitions on a physical drive. Unlike MS-DOS, which assigns drive letters automatically starting with the letter C, Windows Server 2008 R2 lets you specify drive letters. Generally, the drive letters C through Z are available for your use.

NOTE The drive letter A is usually assigned to a system's floppy disk drive. If the system has a second floppy disk drive, the letter B is assigned to it, so you can use only the letters C through Z. Don't forget that CD-ROMs, Zip drives, and other types of media drives need drive letters as well. The total number of drive letters you can use at one time is 24. If you need additional volumes, you can create them by using drive paths.

Using drive letters, you can have only 24 active volumes. To get around this limitation, you can mount disks to drive paths. A drive path is set as a folder location on another drive. For example, you might mount additional drives as E:\Data1, E:\Data2, and E:\Data3. You can use drive paths with basic and dynamic disks. The only restriction for drive paths is that you mount them on empty folders that are on NTFS drives.

To help you differentiate between primary partitions and extended partitions with logical drives, Disk Management color codes the partitions. For example, primary partitions might be color coded with a dark-blue band and logical drives in extended partitions might be color coded with a light-blue band. The key for the color scheme is shown at the bottom of the Disk Management window. You can change the colors in the Settings dialog box by choosing Settings from the View menu.

Creating Partitions and Simple Volumes

Windows Server 2008 R2 simplifies the Disk Management user interface by using one set of dialog boxes and wizards for both partitions and volumes. The first three volumes on a basic drive are created automatically as primary partitions. If you try to create a fourth volume on a basic drive, the remaining free space on the drive is converted automatically to an extended partition with a logical drive of the size you designate by using the new volume feature in the extended partition. Any subsequent volumes are created in the extended partitions as logical drives automatically.

In Disk Management, you create partitions, logical drives, and simple volumes by following these steps:

1. In Disk Management's Graphical View, right-click an unallocated or free area, and then click New Simple Volume. This starts the New Simple Volume Wizard. Read the Welcome page, and then click Next.

2. The Specify Volume Size page, shown in Figure 12-3, specifies the minimum and maximum size for the volume in megabytes and lets you size the volume within these limits. Size the partition in megabytes in the Simple Volume Size In MB field, and then click Next.

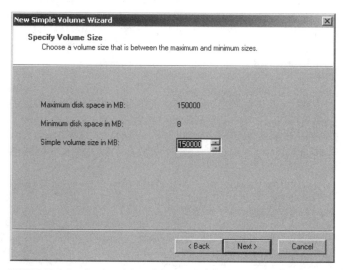

FIGURE 12-3 Set the size of the volume on the Specify Volume Size page.

3. On the Assign Drive Letter Or Path page, shown in Figure 12-4, specify whether you want to assign a drive letter or path, and then click Next. The following options are available:

   - **Assign The Following Drive Letter** Choose this option to assign a drive letter. Then select an available drive letter in the list provided. By default, Windows Server 2008 R2 selects the lowest available drive letter and excludes reserved drive letters as well as those assigned to local disks or network drives.

   - **Mount In The Following Empty NTFS Folder** Choose this option to mount the partition in an empty NTFS folder. You must then type the path to an existing folder or click Browse to search for or create a folder to use.

   - **Do Not Assign A Drive Letter Or Drive Path** Choose this option if you want to create the partition without assigning a drive letter or path. If you later want the partition to be available for storage, you can assign a drive letter or path at that time.

NOTE You don't have to assign volumes a drive letter or a path. A volume with no designators is considered to be unmounted and is for the most part unusable. An unmounted volume can be mounted by assigning a drive letter or a path at a later date. See "Assigning Drive Letters and Paths" later in this chapter.

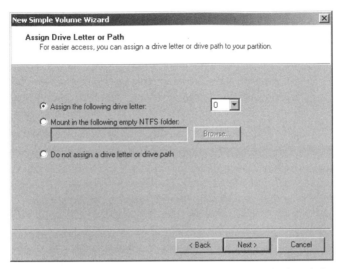

FIGURE 12-4 On the Assign Drive Letter Or Path page, assign the drive designator or choose to wait until later.

4. On the Format Partition page, shown in Figure 12-5, determine whether and how the volume should be formatted. If you want to format the volume, select Format This Volume With The Following Settings, and then configure the following options:

- **File System** Sets the file system type as FAT32 or NTFS. NTFS is selected by default in most cases. If you use FAT32, you can later convert to NTFS with the Convert utility. You can't, however, convert NTFS partitions to FAT32.

- **Allocation Unit Size** Sets the cluster size for the file system. This is the basic unit in which disk space is allocated. The default allocation unit size is based on the size of the volume and is set dynamically prior to formatting by default. To override this feature, you can set the allocation unit size to a specific value. If you use many small files, you might want to use a smaller cluster size, such as 512 or 1,024 bytes. With these settings, small files use less disk space.

- **Volume Label** Sets a text label for the partition. This label is the partition's volume name and is set to New Volume by default. You can change the volume label at any time by right-clicking the volume in Windows Explorer, clicking Properties, and typing a new value in the Label field provided on the General tab.

- **Perform A Quick Format** Tells Windows Server 2008 R2 to format without checking the partition for errors. With large partitions, this option can save you a few minutes. However, it's usually better to check for errors, which enables Disk Management to mark bad sectors on the disk and lock them out.

- **Enable File And Folder Compression** Turns on compression for the disk. Built-in compression is available only for NTFS. Under NTFS, compression is transparent to users and compressed files can be accessed just like regular files. If you select this option, files and directories on this drive are compressed automatically. For more information on compressing drives, files, and directories, see "Compressing Drives and Data" later in this chapter.

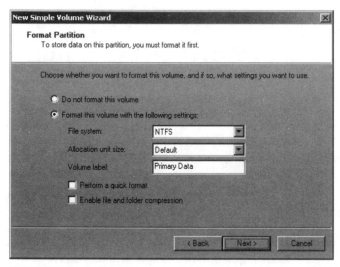

FIGURE 12-5 Set the formatting options for the partition on the Format Partition page.

5. Click Next, confirm your options, and then click Finish.

Formatting Partitions

Formatting creates a file system on a partition and permanently deletes any existing data. This is a high-level formatting that creates the file system structure rather than a low-level formatting that initializes a drive for use. To format a partition, right-click the partition and then click Format. This opens the Format dialog box, shown in Figure 12-6.

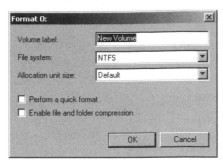

FIGURE 12-6 Format a partition in the Format dialog box by specifying its file system type and volume label.

You use the formatting fields as follows:

- **Volume Label**   Specifies a text label for the partition. This label is the partition's volume name.

- **File System**   Specifies the file system type as FAT32 or NTFS. NTFS is the native file system type for Windows NT and later releases of Windows.

- **Allocation Unit Size**   Specifies the cluster size for the file system. This is the basic unit in which disk space is allocated. The default allocation unit size is based on the size of the volume and is set dynamically prior to formatting. To override this feature, you can set the allocation unit size to a specific value. If you use lots of small files, you might want to use a smaller cluster size, such as 512 or 1,024 bytes. With these settings, small files use less disk space.

- **Perform A Quick Format**   Tells Windows Server 2008 R2 to format without checking the partition for errors. With large partitions, this option can save you a few minutes. However, it's more prudent to check for errors, which allows Disk Management to mark bad sectors on the disk and lock them out.

- **Enable File And Folder Compression**   Turns on compression for the disk. Built-in compression is available only for NTFS. Under NTFS, compression is transparent to users, and compressed files can be accessed just like regular files. If you select this option, files and directories on this drive are compressed automatically. For more information on compressing drives, files, and directories, see "Compressing Drives and Data" later in this chapter.

When you're ready to proceed, click OK. Because formatting a partition destroys any existing data, Disk Management gives you one last chance to cancel the procedure. Click OK to start formatting the partition. Disk Management changes the drive's status to reflect the formatting and the percentage of completion. When formatting is complete, the drive status changes to reflect this.

Managing Existing Partitions and Drives

Disk Management provides many ways to manage existing partitions and drives. Use these features to assign drive letters, delete partitions, set the active partition, and more. In addition, Windows Server 2008 R2 provides other utilities to carry out common tasks such as converting a volume to NTFS, checking a drive for errors, and cleaning up unused disk space.

NOTE Windows Vista, Windows 7, Windows Server 2008, and later releases of Windows support hot-pluggable media that use NTFS volumes. This new feature allows you to format USB flash devices and other similar media with NTFS. There are also enhancements to prevent data loss when ejecting NTFS-formatted removable media.

Assigning Drive Letters and Paths

You can assign drives one drive letter and one or more drive paths, provided that the drive paths are mounted on NTFS drives. Drives don't have to be assigned a drive letter or path. A drive with no designators is considered to be unmounted, and you can mount it by assigning a drive letter or path at a later date. You need to unmount a drive before moving it to another computer.

Windows cannot modify the drive letter of system, boot, or page file volumes. To change the drive letter of a system or boot volume, you need to edit the registry as described in Microsoft Knowledge Base article 223188 (*support.microsoft.com/ kb/223188/en-us*). Before you can change the drive letter of a page file volume, you might need to move the page file to a different volume.

To manage drive letters and paths, right-click the drive you want to configure in Disk Management, and then click Change Drive Letter And Paths. This opens the dialog box shown in Figure 12-7. You can now do the following:

- **Add a drive path**   Click Add, select Mount In The Following Empty NTFS Folder, and then type the path to an existing folder, or click Browse to search for or create a folder.

- **Remove a drive path**   Select the drive path to remove, click Remove, and then click Yes.

- **Assign a drive letter**   Click Add, select Assign The Following Drive Letter, and then choose an available letter to assign to the drive.

- **Change the drive letter**   Select the current drive letter, and then click Change. Select Assign The Following Drive Letter, and then choose a different letter to assign to the drive.

- **Remove a drive letter**   Select the current drive letter, click Remove, and then click Yes.

NOTE If you try to change the letter of a drive that's in use, Windows Server 2008 R2 displays a warning. You need to exit programs that are using the drive and try again or allow Disk Management to force the change by clicking Yes when prompted.

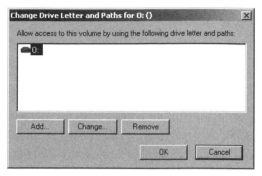

FIGURE 12-7 You can change the drive letter and path assignment in the Change Drive Letter And Paths dialog box.

Changing or Deleting the Volume Label

The volume label is a text descriptor for a drive. With FAT32, the volume label can be up to 11 characters and can include spaces. With NTFS, the volume label can be up to 32 characters. Additionally, although FAT32 doesn't allow you to use some special characters, including * / \ [ ] : ; | = , . + " ? < >, NTFS does allow you to use these special characters.

Because the volume label is displayed when the drive is accessed in various Windows Server 2008 R2 utilities, including Windows Explorer, it can provide information about a drive's contents. You can change or delete a volume label using Disk Management or Windows Explorer.

Using Disk Management, you can change or delete a label by following these steps:

1. Right-click the partition, and then click Properties.

2. On the General tab of the Properties dialog box, type a new label for the volume in the Label text box or delete the existing label. Click OK.

Using Windows Explorer, you can change or delete a label by following these steps:

1. Right-click the drive icon, and then click Properties.

2. On the General tab of the Properties dialog box, type a new label for the volume in the Label text box or delete the existing label. Click OK.

Deleting Partitions and Drives

To change the configuration of a drive that's fully allocated, you might need to delete existing partitions and logical drives. Deleting a partition or a drive removes the associated file system, and all data in the file system is lost. Before you delete a partition or a drive, you should back up any files and directories that the partition or drive contains.

> **NOTE** To protect the integrity of the system, you can't delete the system or boot partition. However, Windows Server 2008 R2 does let you delete the active partition or volume if it is not designated as boot or system. Always check to be sure that the partition or volume you are deleting doesn't contain important data or files.

You can delete a primary partition, a volume, or a logical drive by following these steps:

1. In Disk Management, right-click the partition, volume, or drive you want to delete, and then click Explore. Using Windows Explorer, move all the data to another volume or verify an existing backup to ensure that the data was properly saved.

2. In Disk Management, right-click the partition, volume, or drive again, and then click Delete Partition, Delete Volume, or Delete Logical Drive as appropriate.

3. Confirm that you want to delete the selected item by clicking Yes.

The steps for deleting an extended partition differ slightly from those for deleting a primary partition or a logical drive. To delete an extended partition, follow these steps:

1. Delete all the logical drives on the partition following the steps listed in the previous procedure.

2 Select the extended partition area itself and delete it.

Converting a Volume to NTFS

Windows Server 2008 R2 provides a utility for converting FAT volumes to NTFS. This utility, Convert (Convert.exe), is located in the %SystemRoot% folder. When you convert a volume using this tool, the file and directory structure is preserved and no data is lost. Keep in mind, however, that Windows Server 2008 R2 doesn't provide a utility for converting NTFS to FAT. The only way to go from NTFS to FAT is to delete the partition by following the steps listed in the previous section and then to re-create the partition as a FAT volume.

The Convert Utility Syntax

Convert is run at the command prompt. If you want to convert a drive, use the following syntax:

```
convert volume /FS:NTFS
```

where *volume* is the drive letter followed by a colon, drive path, or volume name. For example, if you want to convert the D drive to NTFS, use the following command:

```
convert D: /FS:NTFS
```

If the volume has a label, you are prompted to enter the volume label for the drive. You are not prompted for a volume label if the disk doesn't have a label.

The complete syntax for Convert is shown here:

```
convert volume /FS:NTFS [/V] [/X] [/CvtArea:filename] [/NoSecurity]
```

The options and switches for Convert are used as follows:

volume	Sets the volume to work with
/FS:NTFS	Converts to NTFS
/V	Sets verbose mode
/X	Forces the volume to dismount before the conversion (if necessary)
/CvtArea: *filename*	Sets the name of a contiguous file in the root directory to be a placeholder for NTFS system files
/NoSecurity	Removes all security attributes and makes all files and directories accessible to the group Everyone

The following sample statement uses Convert:

```
convert C: /FS:NTFS /V
```

Using the Convert Utility

Before you use the Convert utility, determine whether the partition is being used as the active boot partition or a system partition containing the operating system. You can convert the active boot partition to NTFS. Doing so requires that the system gain exclusive access to this partition, which can be obtained only during startup. Thus, if you try to convert the active boot partition to NTFS, Windows Server 2008 R2 displays a prompt asking if you want to schedule the drive to be converted the next time the system starts. If you click Yes, you can restart the system to begin the conversion process.

> **TIP** Often, you will need to restart a system several times to completely convert the active boot partition. Don't panic. Let the system proceed with the conversion.

Before the Convert utility actually converts a drive to NTFS, the utility checks whether the drive has enough free space to perform the conversion. Generally, Convert needs a block of free space that's roughly equal to 25 percent of the total space used on the drive. For example, if the drive stores 200 GB of data, Convert needs about 50 GB of free space. If the drive doesn't have enough free space, Convert aborts and tells you that you need to free up some space. On the other hand, if the drive has enough free space, Convert initiates the conversion. Be patient. The conversion process takes several minutes (longer for large drives). Don't access files or applications on the drive while the conversion is in progress.

You can use the /CvtArea option to improve performance on the volume so that space for the master file table (MFT) is reserved. This option helps to prevent fragmentation of the MFT. How? Over time, the MFT might grow larger than the space allocated to it. The operating system must then expand the MFT into other areas of the disk. Although the Disk Defragmenter utility can defragment the MFT, it cannot move the first section of the MFT, and it is very unlikely that there will be space after the MFT because this will be filled by file data.

To help prevent fragmentation in some cases, you might want to reserve more space than the default (12.5 percent of the partition or volume size). For example, you might want to increase the MFT size if the volume will have many small or average-size files rather than a few large files. To specify the amount of space to reserve, you can use FSUtil to create a placeholder file equal in size to that of the MFT you want to create. You can then convert the volume to NTFS and specify the name of the placeholder file to use with the /CvtArea option.

In the following example, you use FSUtil to create a 1.5-GB (1,500,000,000 bytes) placeholder file named Temp.txt:

```
fsutil file createnew c:\temp.txt 1500000000
```

To use this placeholder file for the MFT when converting drive C to NTFS, you would then type the following command:

```
convert c: /fs:ntfs /cvtarea:temp.txt
```

Notice that the placeholder file is created on the partition or volume that is being converted. During the conversion process, the file is overwritten with NTFS metadata and any unused space in the file is reserved for future use by the MFT.

Resizing Partitions and Volumes

Windows Server 2008 R2 doesn't user Ntldr and Boot.ini to load the operating system. Instead, Windows Server 2008 R2 has a preboot environment in which Windows Boot Manager is used to control startup and load the boot application you've selected. Windows Boot Manager also finally frees the Windows operating system from its reliance on MS-DOS so that you can use drives in new ways. With Windows Server 2008 R2, you can extend and shrink both basic and dynamic disks. You can use either Disk Management or DiskPart to extend and shrink volumes. You cannot shrink or extend striped, mirrored, or striped-with-parity volumes.

In extending a volume, you convert areas of unallocated space and add them to the existing volume. For spanned volumes on dynamic disks, the space can come from any available dynamic disk, not only from those on which the volume was originally created. Thus, you can combine areas of free space on multiple dynamic disks and use those areas to increase the size of an existing volume.

CAUTION Before you try to extend a volume, be aware of several limitations. First, you can extend simple and spanned volumes only if they are formatted and the file system is NTFS. You can't extend striped volumes. You can't extend volumes that aren't formatted or that are formatted with FAT32. Additionally, you can't extend a system or boot volume, regardless of its configuration.

You can shrink a simple volume or a spanned volume by following these steps:

1. In Disk Management, right-click the volume that you want to shrink, and then click Shrink Volume. This option is available only if the volume meets the previously discussed criteria.

2. In the field provided in the Shrink dialog box, shown in Figure 12-8, enter the amount of space to shrink.

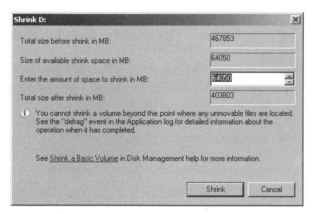

FIGURE 12-8 Specify the amount of space to shrink from the volume.

The Shrink dialog box provides the following information:

- **Total Size Before Shrink In MB**   Lists the total capacity of the volume in megabytes. This is the formatted size of the volume.

- **Size Of Available Shrink Space In MB**   Lists the maximum amount by which the volume can be shrunk. This doesn't represent the total amount of free space on the volume; rather, it represents the amount of space that can be removed, not including any data reserved for the master file table, volume snapshots, page files, and temporary files.

- **Enter The Amount Of Space To Shrink In MB**   Lists the total amount of space that will be removed from the volume. The initial value defaults to the maximum amount of space that can be removed from the volume. For optimal drive performance, you'll want to ensure that the drive has at least 10 percent of free space after the shrink operation.

- **Total Size After Shrink In MB**   Lists what the total capacity of the volume will be (in megabytes) after the shrink. This is the new formatted size of the volume.

3. Click Shrink to shrink the volume.

You can extend a simple volume or a spanned volume by following these steps:

1. In Disk Management, right-click the volume that you want to extend, and then click Extend Volume. This option is available only if the volume meets the previously discussed criteria and free space is available on one or more of the system's dynamic disks.

2. In the Extend Volume Wizard, read the introductory message, and then click Next.

3. On the Select Disks page, select the disk or disks from which you want to allocate free space. Any disks currently being used by the volume are automatically selected. By default, all remaining free space on those disks is selected for use.

4. With dynamic disks, you can specify the additional space that you want to use on other disks by performing the following tasks:

   - Click the disk, and then click Add to add the disk to the Selected list.
   - Select each disk in the Selected list, and then, in the Select The Amount Of Space In MB list, specify the amount of unallocated space to use on the selected disk.

5. Click Next, confirm your options, and then click Finish.

Repairing Disk Errors and Inconsistencies

Windows Server 2008 R2 includes feature enhancements that reduce the amount of manual maintenance you must perform on disk drives. The following enhancements have the most impact on the way you work with disks:

- Transactional NTFS
- Self-healing NTFS

Transactional NTFS allows file operations on an NTFS volume to be performed transactionally. This means programs can use a transaction to group sets of file and registry operations so that all of them succeed or none of them succeed. While a transaction is active, changes are not visible outside the transaction. Changes are committed and written fully to disk only when a transaction is completed successfully. If a transaction fails or is incomplete, the program rolls back the transactional work to restore the file system to the state it was in prior to the transaction.

Transactions that span multiple volumes are coordinated by the Kernel Transaction Manager (KTM). The KTM supports independent recovery of volumes if a transaction fails. The local resource manager for a volume maintains a separate transaction log and is responsible for maintaining threads for transactions separate from threads that perform the file work.

Traditionally, you have had to use the Check Disk tool to fix errors and inconsistencies in NTFS volumes on a disk. Because this process can disrupt the availability of Windows systems, Windows Server 2008 R2 uses self-healing NTFS to protect file systems without requiring you to use separate maintenance tools to fix problems. Because much of the self-healing process is enabled and performed automatically, you might need to perform volume maintenance manually only when you are notified by the operating system that a problem cannot be corrected automatically. If such an error occurs, Windows Server 2008 R2 notifies you about the problem and provides possible solutions.

Self-healing NTFS has many advantages over Check Disk, including the following:

- Check Disk must have exclusive access to volumes, which means system and boot volumes can be checked only when the operating system starts up. On the other hand, with self-healing NTFS, the file system is always available and does not need to be corrected offline (in most cases).

- Self-healing NTFS attempts to preserve as much data as possible if corruption occurs and reduces failed file system mounting that previously could occur if a volume was known to have errors or inconsistencies. During restart, self-healing NTFS repairs the volume immediately so that it can be mounted.

- Self-healing NTFS reports changes made to the volume during repair through existing Chkdsk.exe mechanisms, directory notifications, and update sequence number (USN) journal entries. This feature also allows authorized users and administrators to monitor repair operations through Verification, Waiting For Repair Completion, and Progress Status messages.

- Self-healing NTFS can recover a volume if the boot sector is readable but does not identify an NTFS volume. In this case, you must run an offline tool that repairs the boot sector and then allow self-healing NTFS to initiate recovery.

Although self-healing NTFS is a terrific enhancement, at times you may want to (or may have to) manually check the integrity of a disk. In these cases, you can use Check Disk (Chkdsk.exe) to check for and (optionally) repair problems found on FAT, FAT32, and NTFS volumes. Although Check Disk can check for and correct many types of errors, the utility primarily looks for inconsistencies in the file system and its related metadata. One of the ways Check Disk locates errors is by comparing the volume bitmap to the disk sectors assigned to files in the file system. Beyond this, the usefulness of Check Disk is rather limited. For example, Check Disk can't repair corrupted data within files that appear to be structurally intact.

Running Check Disk from the Command Line

You can run Check Disk from the command prompt or within other utilities. At a command prompt, you can test the integrity of the E drive by typing the following command:

```
chkdsk E:
```

To find and repair errors that are on the E drive, use the following command:

```
chkdsk /f E:
```

> **NOTE** Check Disk can't repair volumes that are in use. If a volume is in use, Check Disk displays a prompt that asks if you want to schedule the volume to be checked the next time you start the system. Click Yes to schedule this.

The complete syntax for Check Disk is shown here:

```
chkdsk [volume[[path]filename]]] [/F] [/V] [/R] [/X] [/I] [/C] [/L[:size]]
```

The options and switches for Check Disk are used as follows:

volume	Sets the volume to work with.
[path]filename	FAT/FAT32 only: Specifies files to check for fragmentation.
/F	Fixes errors on the disk.
/V	On FAT/FAT32: Displays the full path and name of every file on the disk. On NTFS: Displays cleanup messages, if any.
/R	Locates bad sectors and recovers readable information (implies /F).
/X	Forces the volume to dismount first if necessary (implies /F).
/I	NTFS only: Performs a minimum check of index entries.
/C	NTFS only: Skips checking of cycles within the folder structure.
/L:*size*	NTFS only: Changes the log file size.

Running Check Disk Interactively

You can run Check Disk interactively by using Windows Explorer or Disk Management. Follow these steps:

1. Right-click the drive, and then click Properties.
2. On the Tools tab of the Properties dialog box, click Check Now.
3. As shown in Figure 12-9, you can now do the following:
   - Check for errors without repairing them. Click Start without selecting either of the check boxes.
   - Check for errors and fix them. Make the appropriate selections in the check boxes to fix file system errors, recover bad sectors, or both, and then click Start.

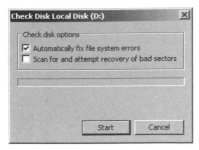

FIGURE 12-9 Use Check Disk to check a disk for errors and repair them.

Defragmenting Disks

Any time you add files to or remove files from a drive, the data on the drive can become fragmented. When a drive is fragmented, large files can't be written to a single continuous area on the disk. As a result, the operating system must write the file to several smaller areas on the disk, which means more time is spent reading the file from the disk. To reduce fragmentation, Windows Server 2008 R2 can manually or automatically defragment disks using Disk Defragmenter. The more frequently data is updated on drives, the more often you should run this tool.

You can manually defragment a disk by following these steps:

1. In Server Manager, select the Storage node and then the Disk Management node. Right-click a drive, and then click Properties.

2. On the Tools tab, click Defragment Now. In the Disk Defragmenter dialog box, select a disk, and then click Analyze Disk. Disk Defragmenter then analyzes the disk to determine whether it needs to be defragmented. If so, it recommends that you defragment now.

3. In the Disk Defragmenter dialog box, select a disk, and then click Defragment Disk.

NOTE Depending on the size of the disk, defragmentation can take several hours. You can click Stop Operation at any time to stop defragmentation.

When you enable automatic defragmentation, Windows Server 2008 R2 runs Disk Defragmenter automatically on a specific schedule, such as at 1:00 A.M. every Wednesday. As long as the computer is powered on at the scheduled run time, automatic defragmentation occurs. You can configure and manage automated defragmentation by following these steps:

1. In Server Manager, select the Storage node and then the Disk Management node. Right-click a drive, and then click Properties.

2. On the Tools tab, click Defragment Now. This displays the Disk Defragmenter dialog box, shown in Figure 12-10.

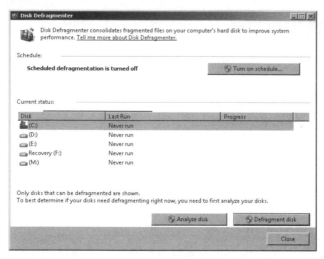

FIGURE 12-10 Disk Defragmenter analyzes and defragments disks efficiently.

3. To cancel automated defragmentation, click Configure Schedule, clear Run On A Schedule, and then click OK. Click Close, and skip the remaining steps.

4. To enable automated defragmentation, click Turn On Schedule. In the Modify Schedule dialog box, shown in Figure 12-11, select Run On A Schedule, and then set the run schedule. In the Frequency list, you can choose Daily, Weekly, or Monthly. If you choose a weekly or monthly run schedule, you need to select the run day of the week or month from the Day list. Finally, the Time list lets you set the time of the day that automated defragmentation should occur.

5. If you want to modify the run schedule, click Configure Schedule. In the Modify Schedule dialog box, shown in Figure 12-11, set the run schedule as discussed in the previous step.

6. If you want to manage which disks are defragmented, click Select Disks. In the Select Disks For Schedule dialog box, select which disks should be defragmented. By default, all disks installed within or connected to the computer are defragmented, and any new disks are defragmented automatically as well. In the Disks To Include In Schedule list, select the check boxes for disks that should be defragmented automatically and clear the check boxes for disks that should not be defragmented automatically. Click OK.

7. Click OK, and then click Close to save your settings.

NOTE Windows Vista with SP1 or later, Windows 7, and Windows Server 2008 or later releases of Windows automatically perform cyclic pickup defragmentation. With this feature, when a scheduled defragmentation pass is stopped and rerun, the computer automatically picks up the next unfinished volume in line to be defragmented.

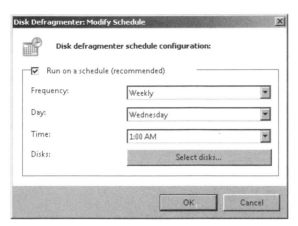

FIGURE 12-11 Set the run schedule for automated defragmentation.

Compressing Drives and Data

When you format a drive for NTFS, Windows Server 2008 R2 allows you to turn on the built-in compression feature. With compression, all files and directories stored on a drive are automatically compressed when they're created. Because this compression is transparent to users, compressed data can be accessed just like regular data. The difference is that you can store more information on a compressed drive than you can on an uncompressed drive.

> **REAL WORLD** Although compression is certainly a useful feature when you want to save disk space, you can't encrypt compressed data. Compression and encryption are mutually exclusive alternatives for NTFS volumes, which means you have the choice of using compression or using encryption. You can't use both techniques. For more information on encryption, see "Encrypting Drives and Data" later in this chapter. If you try to compress encrypted data, Windows Server 2008 R2 automatically decrypts the data and then compresses it. Likewise, if you try to encrypt compressed data, Windows Server 2008 R2 uncompresses the data and then encrypts it.

Compressing Drives

To compress a drive and all its contents, follow these steps:

1. In Windows Explorer or Disk Management, right-click the drive that you want to compress, and then click Properties.

2. On the General tab, select Compress Drive To Save Disk Space, and then click OK.

3. In the Confirm Attribute Changes dialog box, select whether to apply the changes to subfolders and files, and then click OK.

Compressing Directories and Files

If you decide not to compress a drive, Windows Server 2008 R2 lets you selectively compress directories and files. To compress a file or directory, follow these steps:

1. In Windows Explorer, right-click the file or directory that you want to compress, and then click Properties.

2. On the General tab of the Properties dialog box, click Advanced. In the Advanced Attributes dialog box, select the Compress Contents To Save Disk Space check box, as shown in Figure 12-12. Click OK twice.

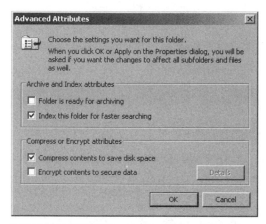

FIGURE 12-12 With NTFS, you can compress a file or directory by selecting the Compress Contents To Save Disk Space check box in the Advanced Attributes dialog box.

For an individual file, Windows Server 2008 R2 marks the file as compressed and then compresses it. For a directory, Windows Server 2008 R2 marks the directory as compressed and then compresses all the files in it. If the directory contains subfolders, Windows Server 2008 R2 displays a dialog box that allows you to compress all the subfolders associated with the directory. Simply select Apply Changes To This Folder, Subfolders, And Files, and then click OK. Once you compress a directory, any new files added or copied to the directory are compressed automatically.

NOTE If you move an uncompressed file from a different drive, the file is compressed. However, if you move an uncompressed file to a compressed folder on the same NTFS drive, the file isn't compressed. Note also that you can't encrypt compressed files.

Expanding Compressed Drives

You can remove compression from a drive by following these steps:

1. In Windows Explorer or Disk Management, right-click the drive that contains the data you want to expand, and then click Properties.

2. Clear the Compress Drive To Save Disk Space check box, and then click OK.

3. In the Confirm Attribute Changes dialog box, select whether to apply the change to subfolders and files, and then click OK.

TIP Windows always checks the available disk space before expanding compressed data. You should too. If less free space is available than used space, you might not be able to complete the expansion. For example, if a compressed drive uses 150 GB of space and has 70 GB of free space available, you won't have enough free space to expand the data.

Expanding Compressed Directories and Files

If you decide that you want to expand a compressed file or directory, follow these steps:

1. Right-click the file or directory in Windows Explorer, and then click Properties.

2. On the General tab of the Properties dialog box, click Advanced. Clear the Compress Contents To Save Disk Space check box. Click OK twice.

With files, Windows Server 2008 R2 removes compression and expands the file. With directories, Windows Server 2008 R2 expands all the files within the directory. If the directory contains subfolders, you also have the opportunity to remove compression from the subfolders. To do this, select Apply Changes To This Folder, Subfolders, And Files when prompted, and then click OK.

TIP Windows Server 2008 R2 also provides command-line utilities for compressing and uncompressing data. The compression utility is called Compact (Compact.exe). The uncompression utility is called Expand (Expand.exe).

Encrypting Drives and Data

NTFS has many advantages over other file systems that you can use with Windows Server 2008 R2. One of the major advantages is the capability to automatically encrypt and decrypt data using the Encrypting File System (EFS). When you encrypt data, you add an extra layer of protection to sensitive data, and this extra layer acts as a security blanket blocking all other users from reading the contents of the encrypted files. Indeed, one of the great benefits of encryption is that only the designated user can access the data. This benefit is also a disadvantage in that the user must remove encryption before authorized users can access the data.

NOTE As discussed previously, you can't compress encrypted files. The encryption and compression features of NTFS are mutually exclusive. You can use one feature or the other but not both.

Understanding Encryption and the Encrypting File System

File encryption is supported on a per-folder or per-file basis. Any file placed in a folder marked for encryption is automatically encrypted. Files in encrypted format can be read only by the person who encrypted the file. Before other users can read an encrypted file, the user must decrypt the file or grant special access to the file by adding a user's encryption key to the file.

Every encrypted file has the unique encryption key of the user who created the file or currently has ownership of the file. An encrypted file can be copied, moved, or renamed just like any other file, and in most cases these actions don't affect the encryption of the data. (For details, see "Working with Encrypted Files and Folders" later in this chapter.) The user who encrypts a file always has access to the file, provided that the user's public-key certificate is available on the computer that he or she is using. For this user, the encryption and decryption process is handled automatically and is transparent.

EFS is the process that handles encryption and decryption. The default setup for EFS allows users to encrypt files without needing special permission. Files are encrypted using a public/private key that EFS automatically generates on a per-user basis.

Encryption certificates are stored as part of the data in user profiles. If a user works with multiple computers and wants to use encryption, an administrator needs to configure a roaming profile for that user. A roaming profile ensures that the user's profile data and public-key certificates are accessible from other computers. Without this, users won't be able to access their encrypted files on another computer.

SECURITY ALERT An alternative to a roaming profile is to copy the user's encryption certificate to the computers that the user uses. You can do this by using the certificate backup and restore process discussed in "Backing Up and Restoring the System State" in Chapter 16. Simply back up the certificate on the user's original computer and then restore the certificate on each of the other computers the user logs on to.

EFS has a built-in data recovery system to guard against data loss. This recovery system ensures that encrypted data can be recovered in the event that a user's public-key certificate is lost or deleted. The most common scenario for this is when a user leaves the company and the associated user account is deleted. A manager might have been able to log on to the user's account, check files, and save important files to other folders, but if the user account has been deleted, encrypted files will be accessible only if the encryption is removed or if the files are moved to a FAT or FAT32 volume (where encryption isn't supported).

To access encrypted files after the user account has been deleted, you need to use a recovery agent. Recovery agents have access to the file encryption key necessary to unlock data in encrypted files. To protect sensitive data, however, recovery agents don't have access to a user's private key or any private key information.

Windows Server 2008 R2 won't encrypt files without designated EFS recovery agents. Therefore, recovery agents are designated automatically, and the necessary recovery certificates are generated automatically as well. This ensures that encrypted files can always be recovered.

EFS recovery agents are configured at two levels:

- **Domain** The recovery agent for a domain is configured automatically when the first Windows Server 2008 R2 domain controller is installed. By default, the recovery agent is the domain administrator. Through Group Policy, domain administrators can designate additional recovery agents. Domain administrators can also delegate recovery agent privileges to designated security administrators.

- **Local computer** When a computer is part of a workgroup or in a stand-alone configuration, the recovery agent is the administrator of the local computer by default. Additional recovery agents can be designated. Further, if you want local recovery agents in a domain environment rather than domain-level recovery agents, you must delete the recovery policy from Group Policy for the domain.

You can delete recovery agents if you don't want them to be used. However, if you delete all recovery agents, EFS will no longer encrypt files. One or more recovery agents must be configured for EFS to function.

Encrypting Directories and Files

With NTFS volumes, Windows Server 2008 R2 lets you select files and folders for encryption. When a file is encrypted, the file data is converted to an encrypted format that can be read only by the person who encrypted the file. Users can encrypt files only if they have the proper access permissions. When you encrypt folders, the folder is marked as encrypted, but only the files within it are actually encrypted. All files that are created in or added to a folder marked as encrypted are encrypted automatically.

To encrypt a file or directory, follow these steps:

1. Right-click the file or directory that you want to encrypt, and then click Properties.

2. On the General tab of the Properties dialog box, click Advanced, and then select the Encrypt Contents To Secure Data check box. Click OK twice.

NOTE You can't encrypt compressed files, system files, or read-only files. If you try to encrypt compressed files, the files are automatically uncompressed and then encrypted. If you try to encrypt system files, you get an error.

For an individual file, Windows Server 2008 R2 marks the file as encrypted and then encrypts it. For a directory, Windows Server 2008 R2 marks the directory as encrypted and then encrypts all the files in it. If the directory contains subfolders, Windows Server 2008 R2 displays a dialog box that allows you to encrypt all the subfolders associated with the directory. Simply select Apply Changes To This Folder, Subfolders, And Files, and then click OK.

NOTE On NTFS volumes, files remain encrypted even when they're moved, copied, or renamed. If you copy or move an encrypted file to a FAT or FAT32 drive, the file is automatically decrypted before being copied or moved. Thus, you must have proper permissions to copy or move the file.

You can grant special access to an encrypted file or folder by right-clicking the file or folder in Windows Explorer and then selecting Properties. On the General tab of the Properties dialog box, click Advanced. In the Advanced Attributes dialog box, click Details. In the Encryption Details For dialog box, users who have access to the encrypted file are listed by name. To allow another user access to the file, click Add. If a user certificate is available for the user, select the user's name in the list provided, and then click OK. Otherwise, click Find User to locate the certificate for the user.

Working with Encrypted Files and Folders

Previously, I said that you can copy, move, and rename encrypted files and folders just like any other files. This is true, but I qualified this by saying "in most cases." When you work with encrypted files, you'll have few problems as long as you work with NTFS volumes on the same computer. When you work with other file systems or other computers, you might run into problems. Two of the most common scenarios are the following:

- **Copying between volumes on the same computer** When you copy or move an encrypted file or folder from one NTFS volume to another NTFS volume on the same computer, the files remain encrypted. However, if you copy or move encrypted files to a FAT or FAT32 volume, the files are decrypted before transfer and then transferred as standard files. FAT and FAT32 don't support encryption.

- **Copying between volumes on a different computer** When you copy or move an encrypted file or folder from one NTFS volume to another NTFS volume on a different computer, the files remain encrypted as long as the destination computer allows you to encrypt files and the remote computer is trusted for delegation. Otherwise, the files are decrypted and then transferred as standard files. The same is true when you copy or move encrypted files to a FAT or FAT32 volume on another computer. FAT and FAT32 don't support encryption.

After you transfer a sensitive file that has been encrypted, you might want to confirm that the encryption is still applied. Right-click the file and then select Properties. On the General tab of the Properties dialog box, click Advanced. The Encrypt Contents To Secure Data option should be selected.

Configuring Recovery Policy

Recovery policies are configured automatically for domain controllers and workstations. By default, domain administrators are the designated recovery agents for domains, and the local administrator is the designated recovery agent for a standalone workstation.

Through the Group Policy console, you can view, assign, and delete recovery agents. To do that, follow these steps:

1. Open the Group Policy console for the local computer, site, domain, or organizational unit you want to work with. For details on working with Group Policy, see "Understanding Group Policies" in Chapter 5.

2. Open the Encrypted Data Recovery Agents node in Group Policy. To do this, expand Computer Configuration, Windows Settings, Security Settings, and Public Key Policies, and then select Encrypting File System.

3. The pane at the right lists the recovery certificates currently assigned. Recovery certificates are listed according to who issued them, who they are issued to, expiration data, purpose, and more.

4. To designate an additional recovery agent, right-click Encrypting File System, and then click Add Data Recovery Agent. This starts the Add Recovery Agent Wizard, which you can use to select a previously generated certificate that has been assigned to a user and mark it as a designated recovery certificate. Click Next.

5. On the Select Recovery Agents page, you can select certificates published in Active Directory or use certificate files. If you want to use a published certificate, click Browse Directory, and then, in the Find Users, Contacts, And Groups dialog box, select the user you want to work with. You'll then be able to use the published certificate of that user. If you want to use a certificate file, click Browse Folders. In the Open dialog box, use the options provided to select and open the certificate file you want to use.

   SECURITY ALERT Before you designate additional recovery agents, you should consider setting up a root certificate authority (CA) in the domain. Then you can use the Certificates snap-in to generate a personal certificate that uses the EFS Recovery Agent template. The root CA must then approve the certificate request so that the certificate can be used.

6. To delete a recovery agent, select the recovery agent's certificate in the right pane, and then press Delete. When prompted to confirm the action, click Yes to permanently and irrevocably delete the certificate. If the recovery policy is empty (meaning that it has no other designated recovery agents), EFS will be turned off so that files can no longer be encrypted.

Decrypting Files and Directories

If you want to decrypt a file or directory, follow these steps:

1. In Windows Explorer, right-click the file or directory, and then click Properties.

2. On the General tab of the Properties dialog box, click Advanced. Clear the Encrypt Contents To Secure Data check box. Click OK twice.

With files, Windows Server 2008 R2 decrypts the file and restores it to its original format. With directories, Windows Server 2008 R2 decrypts all the files within the directory. If the directory contains subfolders, you also have the option to remove encryption from the subfolders. To do this, select Apply Changes To This Folder, Subfolders, And Files when prompted, and then click OK.

TIP Windows Server 2008 R2 also provides a command-line utility called Cipher (Cipher.exe) for encrypting and decrypting your data. Typing **cipher** at a command prompt without additional parameters shows you the encryption status of all folders in the current directory.

Administering Volume Sets and RAID Arrays

When you work with fixed disk drives on Windows Server 2008 R2, you often need to perform advanced disk setup procedures, such as creating a volume set or setting up a redundant array of independent disks (RAID) array.

With a volume set, you can create a single volume that spans multiple drives. Users can access this volume as if it were a single drive, regardless of how many drives the volume is spread over. A volume that's on a single drive is referred to as a *simple volume*. A volume that spans multiple drives is referred to as a *spanned volume*.

With RAID arrays, you can protect important business data and sometimes improve the performance of drives. RAID can be implemented using the built-in feature of the operating system (a software approach) or by using hardware. Windows Server 2008 R2 supports three levels of software RAID: 0, 1, and 5. RAID arrays are implemented as mirrored, striped, and striped with parity volumes.

You create volume sets and RAID arrays on dynamic drives, which are accessible only by Windows 2000 and later releases. If you dual boot a computer to an earlier version of Windows, the dynamic drives are unavailable. However, computers running earlier versions of Windows can access the drives over the network, just as they can any other network drive.

Using Volumes and Volume Sets

You create and manage volumes in much the same way that you create and manage partitions. A volume is a drive section that you can use to store data directly.

NOTE With spanned and striped volumes on basic disks, you can delete a volume but you can't create or extend volumes. With mirrored volumes on basic disks, you can delete, repair, and resync the mirror. You can also break the mirror. For striped with parity volumes (RAID 5) on basic disks, you can delete or repair the volume, but you can't create new volumes.

Understanding Volume Basics

Disk Management color codes volumes by type, much like it does partitions. As Figure 13-1 shows, volumes also have the following properties:

- **Layout** Volume layouts include simple, spanned, mirrored, striped, and striped with parity.
- **Type** Volumes always have the type dynamic.
- **File System** Like partitions, each volume can have a different file system type, such as FAT, FAT32, or NTFS file system. Note that FAT is only available when the partition or volume is 2 GB or less in size.
- **Status** The state of the drive. In Graphical View, the state is shown as Healthy, Failed Redundancy, and so on. The next section, "Understanding Volume Sets," discusses volume sets and the various states you might see.
- **Capacity** Total storage size of the drive.

An important advantage of dynamic volumes over basic volumes is that they let you make changes to volumes and drives without having to restart the system (in most cases). Volumes also let you take advantage of the fault tolerance enhancements of Windows Server 2008 R2. You can install other operating systems and dual boot a Windows Server 2008 R2 system. To do this, you should create a separate volume for the other operating system. For example, you could install Windows Server 2008 R2 on volume C and Windows 7 on volume D.

With volumes, you can do the following:

- Assign drive letters and drive paths as discussed in "Assigning Drive Letters and Paths" in Chapter 12
- Create any number of volumes on a disk as long as you have free space
- Create volumes that span two or more disks and, if necessary, configure fault tolerance
- Extend volumes to increase the volume's capacity
- Designate active, system, and boot volumes as described in "Special Considerations for Basic and Dynamic Disks" in Chapter 12

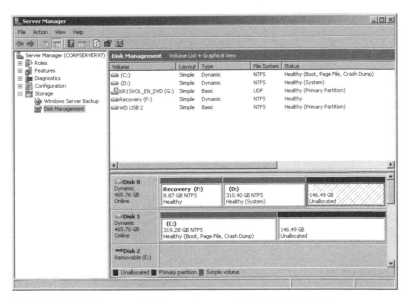

FIGURE 13-1 Disk Management displays volumes much like it does partitions.

Understanding Volume Sets

With volume sets, you can create volumes that span several drives. To do this, you use free space on different drives to create what users see as a single volume. Files are stored on the volume set segment by segment, with the first segment of free space being used to store files before other segments. When the first segment fills up, the second segment is used, and so on.

You can create a volume set using free space on up to 32 hard disk drives. The key advantage to volume sets is that they let you tap into unused free space and create a usable file system. The key disadvantage is that if any hard disk drive in the volume set fails, the volume set can no longer be used, which means that essentially all the data on the volume set is lost.

Understanding the volume status is useful when you install new volumes or are trying to troubleshoot problems. Disk Management shows the drive status in Graphical View and Volume List view. Table 13-1 summarizes status values for dynamic volumes.

TABLE 13-1 Understanding and Resolving Volume Status Issues

STATUS	DESCRIPTION	RESOLUTION
Data Incomplete	Spanned volumes on a foreign disk are incomplete. You must have forgotten to add the other disks from the spanned volume set.	Add the disks that contain the rest of the spanned volume, and then import all the disks at one time.
Data Not Redundant	Fault-tolerant volumes on a foreign disk are incomplete. You must have forgotten to add the other disks from a mirror or RAID-5 set.	Add the remaining disks, and then import all the disks at one time.
Failed	An error disk status. The disk is inaccessible or damaged.	Ensure that the related dynamic disk is online. As necessary, right-click the volume and then click Reactivate Volume. For a basic disk, you might need to check the disk for a faulty connection.
Failed Redundancy	An error disk status. One of the disks in a mirror or RAID-5 set is offline.	Ensure that the related dynamic disk is online. If necessary, reactivate the volume. Next, you might need to replace a failed mirror or repair a failed RAID-5 volume.
Formatting	A temporary status that indicates the volume is being formatted.	The progress of the formatting is indicated as the percent complete unless you choose the Perform A Quick Format option.
Healthy	The normal volume status.	The volume doesn't have any known problems. You don't need to take any corrective action.
Healthy (At Risk)	Windows had problems reading from or writing to the physical disk on which the dynamic volume is located. This status appears when Windows encounters errors.	Right-click the volume, and then click Reactivate Volume. If the disk continues to have this status or has this status periodically, the disk might be failing, and you should back up all data on the disk.

STATUS	DESCRIPTION	RESOLUTION
Healthy (Unknown Partition)	Windows does not recognize the partition. This can occur because the partition is from a different operating system or is a manufacturer-created partition used to store system files.	No corrective action is necessary.
Initializing	A temporary status that indicates the disk is being initialized.	The drive status should change after a few seconds.
Regenerating	A temporary status that indicates that data and parity for a RAID-5 volume are being regenerated.	Progress is indicated as the percent complete. The volume should return to Healthy status.
Resynching	A temporary status that indicates that a mirror set is being resynchronized.	Progress is indicated as the percent complete. The volume should return to Healthy status.
Stale Data	Data on foreign disks that are fault tolerant are out of sync.	Rescan the disks or restart the computer, and then check the status. A new status should be displayed, such as Failed Redundancy.
Unknown	The volume cannot be accessed. It might have a corrupted boot sector.	The volume might have a boot sector virus. Check it with an up-to-date antivirus program. Rescan the disks or restart the computer, and then check the status.

Creating Volumes and Volume Sets

You can format simple volumes as FAT32 or NTFS. To make management easier, you should format volumes that span multiple disks as NTFS. NTFS formatting allows you to expand the volume set if necessary. If you find that you need more space on a volume, you can extend simple and spanned volumes. You do this by selecting an area of free space and adding it to the volume. You can extend a simple volume within the same disk. You can also extend a simple volume onto other disks. When you do this, you create a spanned volume, which you must format as NTFS.

You create volumes and volume sets by following these steps:

1. In Disk Management's Graphical View, right-click an unallocated area, and then click New Spanned Volume or New Striped Volume as appropriate. Read the Welcome page, and then click Next.

2. You should see the Select Disks page, shown in Figure 13-2. Select disks that you want to be part of the volume and size the volume segments on those disks.

3. Available disks are shown in the Available list. If necessary, select a disk in this list, and then click Add to add the disk to the Selected list. If you make a mistake, you can remove disks from the Selected list by selecting the disk and then clicking Remove.

CAUTION Unlike in earlier versions of Windows, the disk wizards in Windows Server 2008 R2 show both basic and dynamic disks with available disk space. If you add space from a basic disk, the wizard converts the disk to a dynamic disk before creating the volume set. Before clicking Yes to continue, be sure you really want to do this because it can affect how the disk is used by the operating system.

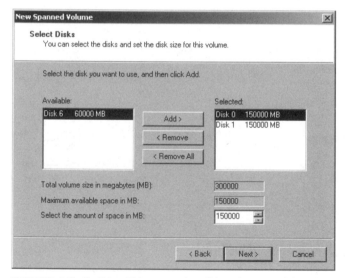

FIGURE 13-2 On the Select Disks page, select disks to be a part of the volume, and then size the volume on each disk.

4. Select a disk in the Selected list, and then specify the size of the volume on the disk in the Select The Amount Of Space In MB box. The Maximum Available Space In MB field shows you the largest area of free space available on the disk. The Total Volume Size field shows you the total disk space selected for use with the volume. Click Next.

TIP Although you can size a volume set any way you want, consider how you'll use volume sets on the system. Simple and spanned volumes aren't fault tolerant, and rather than creating one monstrous volume with all the available free space, you might want to create several smaller volumes to help ensure that losing one volume doesn't mean losing all your data.

5. Specify whether you want to assign a drive letter or path to the volume, and then click Next. You use these options as follows:

   - **Assign The Following Drive Letter** To assign a drive letter, choose this option, and then select an available drive letter in the list provided.

   - **Mount In The Following Empty NTFS Folder** To assign a drive path, choose this option and then type the path to an existing folder on an NTFS drive, or click Browse to search for or create a folder.

   - **Don't Assign A Drive Letter Or Drive Path** To create the volume without assigning a drive letter or path, choose this option. You can assign a drive letter or path later if necessary.

6. As shown in Figure 13-3, determine whether the volume should be formatted. If you elect to format the volume, set the formatting options in the following fields:

   - **File System** Specifies the file system type. The NTFS file system is the only option within Disk Management.

   - **Allocation Unit Size** Specifies the cluster size for the file system. This is the basic unit in which disk space is allocated. The default allocation unit size is based on the volume's size and is set dynamically prior to formatting. To override this feature, you can set the allocation unit size to a specific value. If you use lots of small files, you might want to use a smaller cluster size, such as 512 or 1,024 bytes. With these settings, small files use less disk space.

   - **Volume Label** Specifies a text label for the partition. This label is the partition's volume name.

   - **Perform A Quick Format** Tells Windows to format without checking the partition for errors. With large partitions, this option can save you a few minutes. However, it's more prudent to check for errors, which allows Disk Management to mark bad sectors on the disk and lock them out.

   - **Enable File And Folder Compression** Turns on compression for the disk. Compression is transparent to users, and compressed files can be accessed just like regular files. If you select this option, files and directories on this drive are compressed automatically. For more information on compressing drives, files, and directories, see "Compressing Drives and Data" in Chapter 12.

7. Click Next, and then click Finish.

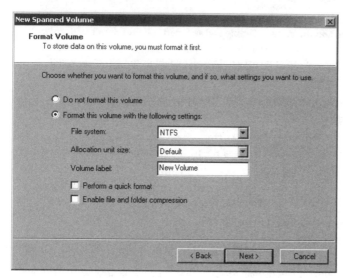

FIGURE 13-3 Format a volume by specifying its file system type and volume label.

Deleting Volumes and Volume Sets

You use the same technique to delete all volumes, whether they're simple, spanned, mirrored, striped, or RAID 5 (striped with parity). Deleting a volume set removes the associated file system, and all associated data is lost. Before you delete a volume set, you should back up any files and directories that the volume set contains.

You can't delete a volume that contains the system, boot, or active paging files for Windows Server 2008 R2.

To delete volumes, follow these steps:

1. In Disk Management, right-click any volume in the set, and then click Delete Volume. You can't delete a portion of a spanned volume without deleting the entire volume.

2. Click Yes to confirm that you want to delete the volume.

Managing Volumes

You manage volumes much like you manage partitions. Follow the techniques outlined in "Managing Existing Partitions and Drives" in Chapter 12.

Improving Performance and Fault Tolerance with RAID

You'll often want to give important data increased protection from drive failures. To do this, you can use RAID technology to add fault tolerance to your file systems. With RAID, you increase data integrity and availability by creating redundant copies of the data. You can also use RAID to improve your disks' performance.

Different implementations of RAID technology are available. These implementations are described in terms of levels. Currently, RAID levels 0 to 5 are defined. Each RAID level offers different features. Windows Server 2008 R2 supports RAID levels 0, 1, and 5. You can use RAID 0 to improve the performance of your drives. You use RAID 1 and 5 to provide fault tolerance for data.

Table 13-2 provides a brief overview of the supported RAID levels. This support is completely software-based.

TABLE 13-2 Windows Server 2008 R2 Support for RAID

RAID LEVEL	RAID TYPE	DESCRIPTION	MAJOR ADVANTAGES
0	Disk striping	Two or more volumes, each on a separate drive, are configured as a striped set. Data is broken into blocks, called *stripes*, and then written sequentially to all drives in the striped set.	Speed and performance.
1	Disk mirroring	Two volumes on two drives are configured identically. Data is written to both drives. If one drive fails, no data loss occurs because the other drive contains the data. (Doesn't include disk striping.)	Redundancy. Better write performance than disk striping with parity.
5	Disk striping with parity	Uses three or more volumes, each on a separate drive, to create a striped set with parity error checking. In the case of failure, data can be recovered.	Fault tolerance with less overhead than mirroring. Better read performance than disk mirroring.

The most common RAID levels in use on servers running Windows Server 2008 R2 are level 1, disk mirroring, and level 5, disk striping with parity. With respect to upfront costs, disk mirroring is the least expensive way to increase data protection with redundancy. Here, you use two identically sized volumes on two different drives to create a redundant data set. If one of the drives fails, you can still obtain the data from the other drive.

On the other hand, disk striping with parity requires more disks—a minimum of three—but offers fault tolerance with less overhead than disk mirroring. If any of the drives fail, you can recover the data by combining blocks of data on the remaining disks with a parity record. Parity is a method of error checking that uses an exclusive OR operation to create a checksum for each block of data written to the disk. This checksum is used to recover data in case of failure.

REAL WORLD Although it's true that the upfront costs for mirroring should be less than the upfront costs for disk striping with parity, the actual cost per megabyte might be higher with disk mirroring. With disk mirroring you have an overhead of 50 percent. For example, if you mirror two 300-gigabyte (GB) drives (a total storage space of 600 GB), the usable space is only 300 GB. With disk striping with parity, on the other hand, you have an overhead of around 33 percent. For example, if you create a RAID-5 set using three 300-GB drives (a total storage space of 900 GB), the usable space (with one-third lost for overhead) is 600 GB.

Implementing RAID on Windows Server 2008 R2

Windows Server 2008 R2 supports disk mirroring, disk striping, and disk striping with parity. Implementing these RAID techniques is discussed in the sections that follow.

CAUTION Some operating systems, such as MS-DOS, don't support RAID. If you dual boot your system to one of these noncompliant operating systems, your RAID-configured drives will be unavailable.

Implementing RAID 0: Disk Striping

RAID level 0 is disk striping. With disk striping, two or more volumes—each on a separate drive—are configured as a striped set. Data written to the striped set is broken into blocks called *stripes*. These stripes are written sequentially to all drives in the striped set. You can place volumes for a striped set on up to 32 drives, but in most circumstances sets with 2 to 5 volumes offer the best performance improvements. Beyond this, the performance improvement decreases significantly.

The major advantage of disk striping is speed. Data can be accessed on multiple disks using multiple drive heads, which improves performance considerably. However, this performance boost comes with a price tag. As with volume sets, if any hard disk drive in the striped set fails, the striped set can no longer be used, which essentially means that all data in the striped set is lost. You need to re-create the striped set and restore the data from backups. Data backup and recovery is discussed in Chapter 16, "Data Backup and Recovery."

CAUTION The boot and system volumes shouldn't be part of a striped set. Don't use disk striping with these volumes.

When you create striped sets, you should use volumes that are approximately the same size. Disk Management bases the overall size of the striped set on the smallest volume size. Specifically, the maximum size of the striped set is a multiple of the smallest volume size. For example, if the smallest volume is 50 MB and you want to create a three-volume striped set, the maximum size for the striped set is 150 MB.

You can maximize performance of the striped set in a couple of ways:

- Use disks that are on separate disk controllers. This allows the system to simultaneously access the drives.

- Don't use the disks containing the striped set for other purposes. This allows the disk to dedicate its time to the striped set.

You can create a striped set by following these steps:

1. In Disk Management's Graphical View, right-click an area marked Unallocated on a dynamic disk, and then click New Striped Volume. This starts the New Striped Volume Wizard. Read the Welcome page, and then click Next.

2. Create the volume as described in "Creating Volumes and Volume Sets" earlier in this chapter. The key difference is that you need at least two dynamic disks to create a striped volume.

3. After you create a striped volume, you can use the volume as you would any other volume. You can't extend a striped set once it's created. Therefore, you should carefully consider the setup before you implement it.

Implementing RAID 1: Disk Mirroring

RAID level 1 is disk mirroring. With disk mirroring, you use identically sized volumes on two different drives to create a redundant data set. The drives are written with identical sets of information, and if one of the drives fails, you can still obtain the data from the other drive.

Disk mirroring offers about the same fault tolerance as disk striping with parity. Because mirrored disks don't need to write parity information, they can offer better write performance in most circumstances. However, disk striping with parity usually offers better read performance because read operations are spread over multiple drives.

The major drawback to disk mirroring is that it effectively cuts the amount of storage space in half. For example, to mirror a 500-GB drive, you need another 500-GB drive. That means you use 1000 GB of space to store 500 GB of information.

> **TIP** If possible, it's a good idea to mirror boot and system volumes. Mirroring these volumes ensures that you are able to boot the server in case of a single drive failure.

As with disk striping, you'll often want the mirrored disks to be on separate disk controllers. This provides increased protection against failure of the disk controller. If one of the disk controllers fails, the disk on other controller is still available.

Technically, when you use two separate disk controllers to duplicate data, you're using a technique known as *disk duplexing*. Figure 13-4 shows the difference between the two techniques. Where disk mirroring typically uses a single drive controller, disk duplexing uses two drive controllers. Otherwise, the two techniques are essentially the same.

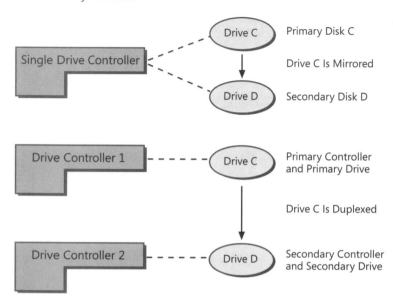

FIGURE 13-4 Although disk mirroring typically uses a single drive controller to create a redundant data set, disk duplexing uses two drive controllers.

If one of the mirrored drives in a set fails, disk operations can continue. Here, when users read and write data, the data is written to the remaining disk. You need to break the mirror before you can fix it. To learn how, see "Managing RAID and Recovering from Failures" later in this chapter.

Creating a Mirror Set in Disk Management

You create a mirror set by following these steps:

1. In Disk Management's Graphical View, right-click an area marked Unallocated on a dynamic disk, and then click New Mirrored Volume. This starts the New Mirrored Volume Wizard. Read the Welcome page, and then click Next.

2. Create the volume as described in "Creating Volumes and Volume Sets" earlier in this chapter. The key difference is that you must create two identically sized volumes, and these volumes must be on separate dynamic drives. You won't be able to continue past the Select Disks window until you select the two disks that you want to work with.

3. Like other RAID techniques, mirroring is transparent to users. Users see the mirrored set as a single drive that they can access and use like any other drive.

NOTE The status of a normal mirror is Healthy. During the creation of a mirror, you'll see a status of Resynching, which tells you that Disk Management is creating the mirror.

Mirroring an Existing Volume

Rather than create a new mirrored volume, you can use an existing volume to create a mirrored set. To do this, the volume you want to mirror must be a simple volume and you must have an area of unallocated space on a second dynamic drive of equal or larger size than the existing volume.

In Disk Management you mirror an existing volume by following these steps:

1. Right-click the simple volume you want to mirror, and then click Add Mirror. This displays the Add Mirror dialog box.

2. In the Disks list, shown in Figure 13-5, select a location for the mirror, and then click Add Mirror. Windows Server 2008 R2 begins the mirror creation process. In Disk Management you'll see a status of Resynching on both volumes. The disk on which the mirrored volume is being created has a warning icon.

FIGURE 13-5 Select the location for the mirror.

Implementing RAID 5: Disk Striping with Parity

RAID level 5 is disk striping with parity. With this technique you need a minimum of three hard disk drives to set up fault tolerance. Disk Management sizes the volumes on these drives identically.

RAID 5 is essentially an enhanced version of RAID 1, with the key addition of fault tolerance. Fault tolerance ensures that the failure of a single drive won't bring down the entire drive set. Instead, the set continues to function with disk operations directed at the remaining volumes in the set.

To allow for fault tolerance, RAID 5 writes parity checksums with the blocks of data. If any of the drives in the striped set fails, you can use the parity information to recover the data. (This process, called *regenerating the striped set,* is covered in "Managing RAID and Recovering from Failures.") If two disks fail, however, the parity information isn't sufficient to recover the data, and you'll need to rebuild the striped set from backup.

Creating a Striped Set with Parity in Disk Management

In Disk Management you can create a striped set with parity by following these steps:

1. In Disk Management's Graphical View, right-click an area marked Unallocated on a dynamic disk, and then click New RAID-5 Volume. This starts the New RAID-5 Volume Wizard. Read the Welcome page, and then click Next.

2. Create the volume as described previously in "Creating Volumes and Volume Sets." The key difference is that you must select free space on three separate dynamic drives.

After you create a striped set with parity (RAID 5), users can use the set just like they would a normal drive. Keep in mind that you can't extend a striped set with parity after you create it. Therefore, you should carefully consider the setup before you implement it.

Managing RAID and Recovering from Failures

Managing mirrored drives and striped sets is somewhat different from managing other drive volumes, especially when it comes to recovering from failure. The techniques you use to manage RAID arrays and to recover from failure are covered in this section.

Breaking a Mirrored Set

You might want to break a mirror for two reasons:

- If one of the mirrored drives in a set fails, disk operations can continue. When users read and write data, these operations use the remaining disk. At some point, however, you need to fix the mirror, and to do this you must first break the mirror, replace the failed drive, and then reestablish the mirror.

- If you no longer want to mirror your drives, you might also want to break a mirror. This allows you to use the disk space for other purposes.

BEST PRACTICES Although breaking a mirror doesn't delete the data in the set, you should always back up the data before you perform this procedure. This ensures that if you have problems, you can recover your data.

In Disk Management you can break a mirrored set by following these steps:

1. Right-click one of the volumes in the mirrored set, and then click Break Mirrored Volume.

2. Confirm that you want to break the mirror by clicking Yes. If the volume is in use, you'll see another warning dialog box. Confirm that it's okay to continue by clicking Yes.

   Windows Server 2008 R2 breaks the mirror, creating two independent volumes.

Resynchronizing and Repairing a Mirrored Set

Windows Server 2008 R2 automatically synchronizes mirrored volumes on dynamic drives. However, data on mirrored drives can become out of sync. For example, if one of the drives goes offline, data is written only to the drive that's online.

You can resynchronize and repair mirrored sets, but you must rebuild the set using disks with the same partition style—either master boot record (MBR) or GUID partition table (GPT). You need to get both drives in the mirrored set online. The mirrored set's status should read Failed Redundancy. The corrective action you take depends on the failed volume's status:

- If the status is Missing or Offline, be sure that the drive has power and is connected properly. Then start Disk Management, right-click the failed volume, and click Reactivate Volume. The drive status should change to Regenerating and then to Healthy. If the volume doesn't return to the Healthy status, right-click the volume, and then click Resynchronize Mirror.

- If the status is Online (Errors), right-click the failed volume, and then click Reactivate Volume. The drive status should change to Regenerating and then to Healthy. If the volume doesn't return to the Healthy status, right-click the volume, and then click Resynchronize Mirror.

- If one of the drives shows a status of Unreadable, you might need to rescan the drives on the system by choosing Rescan Disks from Disk Management's Action menu. If the drive status doesn't change, you might need to reboot the computer.

- If one of the drives still won't come back online, right-click the failed volume, and then click Remove Mirror. Next, right-click the remaining volume in the original mirror, and then click Add Mirror. You now need to mirror the volume on an unallocated area of free space. If you don't have free space, you need to create space by deleting other volumes or replacing the failed drive.

Repairing a Mirrored System Volume to Enable Boot

The failure of a mirrored drive might prevent your system from booting. Typically, this happens when you're mirroring the system or boot volume, or both, and the primary mirror drive has failed. In previous versions of the Windows operating system, you often had to go through several procedures to get the system back up and running. With Windows Server 2008 R2, the failure of a primary mirror is usually much easier to resolve.

When you mirror a system volume, the operating system should add an entry to the system's boot manager that allows you to boot to the secondary mirror. Resolving a primary mirror failure is much easier with this entry in the boot manager file than without it because all you need to do is select the entry to boot to the secondary mirror. If you mirror the boot volume and a secondary mirror entry is not created for you, you can modify the boot entries in the boot manager to create one by using the BCD Editor (Bcdedit.exe).

If a system fails to boot to the primary system volume, restart the system and select the Windows Server 2008 R2—Secondary Plex option for the operating system you want to start. The system should start up normally. After you successfully boot the system to the secondary drive, you can schedule the maintenance necessary to rebuild the mirror. You need to follow these steps:

1. Shut down the system and replace the failed volume or add a hard disk drive. Then restart the system.

2. Break the mirror set, and then re-create the mirror on the drive you replaced, which is usually drive 0. Right-click the remaining volume that was part of the original mirror, and then click Add Mirror. Next, follow the technique in "Mirroring an Existing Volume."

3. If you want the primary mirror to be on the drive you added or replaced, use Disk Management to break the mirror again. Be sure that the primary drive in the original mirror set has the drive letter that was previously assigned to the complete mirror. If it doesn't, assign the appropriate drive letter.

4. Right-click the original system volume, and then click Add Mirror. Now re-create the mirror.

5. Check the boot entries in the boot manager and use the BCD Editor to ensure that the original system volume is used during startup.

Removing a Mirrored Set

Using Disk Management, you can remove one of the volumes from a mirrored set. When you do this, all data on the removed mirror is deleted, and the space it used is marked as Unallocated.

To remove a mirror, follow these steps:

1. In Disk Management, right-click one of the volumes in the mirrored set, and then click Remove Mirror. This displays the Remove Mirror dialog box.

2. In the Remove Mirror dialog box, select the disk from which to remove the mirror.

3. Confirm the action when prompted. All data on the removed mirror is deleted.

Repairing a Striped Set Without Parity

A striped set without parity doesn't have fault tolerance. If a drive that's part of a striped set fails, the entire striped set is unusable. Before you try to restore the striped set, you should repair or replace the failed drive. Then you need to re-create the striped set and recover the data contained on the striped set from backup.

Regenerating a Striped Set with Parity

With RAID 5 you can recover the striped set with parity if a single drive fails. You'll know that a striped set with parity drive has failed because the set's status changes to Failed Redundancy and the individual volume's status changes to Missing, Offline, or Online (Errors).

You can repair RAID-5 disks, but you must rebuild the set using disks with the same partition style—either MBR or GPT. You need to get all drives in the RAID-5 set online. The set's status should read Failed Redundancy. The corrective action you take depends on the failed volume's status.

- If the status is Missing or Offline, make sure that the drive has power and is connected properly. Then start Disk Management, right-click the failed volume, and select Reactivate Volume. The drive's status should change to Regenerating and then to Healthy. If the drive's status doesn't return to Healthy, right-click the volume and select Regenerate Parity.

- If the status is Online (Errors), right-click the failed volume and select Reactivate Volume. The drive's status should change to Regenerating and then to Healthy. If the drive's status doesn't return to Healthy, right-click the volume and select Regenerate Parity.

- If one of the drives shows as Unreadable, you might need to rescan the drives on the system by choosing Rescan Disks from Disk Management's Action menu. If the drive status doesn't change, you might need to reboot the computer.

- If one of the drives still won't come back online, you need to repair the failed region of the RAID-5 set. Right-click the failed volume, and then select Remove Volume. You now need to select an unallocated space on a separate dynamic disk for the RAID-5 set. This space must be at least as large as the region to repair, and it can't be on a drive that the RAID-5 set is already using. If you don't have enough space, the Repair Volume command is unavailable, and you need to free space by deleting other volumes or by replacing the failed drive.

BEST PRACTICES If possible, you should back up the data before you perform this procedure. This ensures that if you have problems, you can recover your data.

Managing LUNs on SANs

With storage area networks (SANs), a logical unit number (LUN) is a logical reference to a portion of the storage subsystem. A LUN is fairly analogous to a volume in that you can use it to represent all or part of a disk as well as all or part of an array of disks. As with volumes, you can assign access and control privileges on a per-LUN basis.

Like volumes, LUNs come in several varieties:

- **Simple** A simple LUN uses only one physical drive or one portion of a physical drive.

- **Spanned** A spanned LUN is a simple LUN that spans multiple physical drives.

- **Striped** A striped LUN writes data across multiple physical drives. Striped LUNs don't offer fault tolerance and can't be extended or mirrored. If one of the disks containing a striped LUN fails, the entire LUN fails.

- **Mirrored** A mirrored LUN is a fault-tolerant LUN that provides data redundancy by creating identical copies of the LUN on two physical drives. If one of the physical disks fails, the data on the failed disk becomes unavailable, but the LUN continues to be available using the unaffected disk.

- **Striped with parity** A striped LUN with parity is a fault-tolerant LUN with data and parity spread intermittently across three or more physical disks. If a portion of a physical disk fails, you can re-create the data that was on the failed portion from the remaining data and parity information.

With Windows Server 2008 R2, you can use the Storage Manager For SANs console, shown in Figure 13-6, to manage Fibre Channel and iSCSI SANs that support the Virtual Disk Service (VDS) and have a configured VDS hardware provider. Before you can use this console, you must use the Add Features Wizard to add the Storage Manager For SANs feature to the server. After you add this feature, you can open Storage Manager For SANs as a separate console by selecting the related option on the Administrative Tools menu or by expanding the Storage node in Server Manager and then clicking the Storage Manager For SANs node. You may need to close and then reopen Server Manager for the node to appear.

For Windows Server 2008 R2, you have additional options for working with the iSCSI Initiator, including:

- Quick Connect, which allows one-click connections to basic storage devices.
- Support for up to 32 paths at boot time
- Support for header and data digest offloading

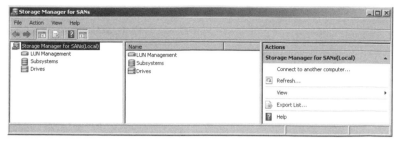

FIGURE 13-6 Use Storage Manager For SANs to manage Fibre Channel and iSCSI SANs.

The iSCSI control panel is included in Server Core installations of Windows Server 2008 R2. Using the control panel, you can more easily configure iSCSI connections.

Multipath I/O (MPIO) is a related feature that makes it possible to use multiple data paths to a storage device. Before a server can access LUNs with Fibre Channel or iSCSI, you must install MPIO by using the Add Features Wizard.

Windows Server 2008 R2 includes improved MPIO health reporting and now also provides configuration reporting. These changes make it easier to get path data. You can also configure load-balance policies using the MPClaim command-line utility.

Configuring Fibre Channel SAN Connections

With Fibre Channel SANs, the server attached to the SAN accesses the LUN directly through one or more Fibre Channel host bus adapter (HBA) ports. Therefore, you only need to identify the server that will access the LUN and then select which HBA ports on that server will be used for LUN traffic. When you identify a server, Storage Manager For SANs attempts to automatically detect available Fibre Channel HBA ports on that server. You can also add ports manually using the World Wide Name (WWN) of the port.

To add and configure a server with Fibre Channel connections, follow these steps:

1. In Storage Manager For SANs, select LUN Management. In the Actions pane or on the Action menu, click Manage Server Connections.

2. In the Manage Server Connections dialog box, click Add.

3. In the Add Server dialog box, type the name or IP address of the server that you want to add. You can also browse for the server.

4. Optionally, type a description for the server.

5. Click OK. The server should now be listed under Manage Server Connections. All ports that were automatically discovered are listed on the Fibre Channel Ports tab.

To add a Fibre Channel port manually, follow these steps:

1. In Storage Manager For SANs, select LUN Management. In the Actions pane or on the Action menu, click Manage Server Connections.

2. In the server list, select a server you previously configured. On the Fibre Channel Ports tab, click Add, and then enter the WWN of the new port.

3. Optionally, type a description for the new port.

4. Click OK.

To enable Fibre Channel ports for LUN access, follow these steps:

1. In Storage Manager For SANs, select LUN Management. In the Actions pane or on the Action menu, click Manage Server Connections.

2. In the server list, select a server you previously configured. On the Fibre Channel Ports tab, select the ports to enable.

3. Click OK.

NOTE Before selecting multiple initiators, you must ensure that multipath input/output (I/O) is configured for the server. If multipath I/O is not configured, data corruption might occur.

Configuring iSCSI SAN Connections

With iSCSI, LUNs created on an iSCSI disk storage subsystem aren't directly assigned to a server. Instead, they're assigned to logical entities called *targets*. You use targets to manage the connections between an iSCSI device and the servers that need to access it. A target identifies the IP address portals that can be used to connect to the iSCSI device and any applicable security settings that the iSCSI device requires to authenticate the servers requesting resource access.

Generally, you create and manage targets manually. However, some iSCSI SANs support only a simple target configuration in which the necessary targets are created automatically when you create a LUN. With simple target configurations, you only need to identify the server or servers that need to access a particular LUN.

A server attached to an iSCSI SAN accesses a LUN through an iSCSI initiator. After you identify the server that will access a LUN, Storage Manager For SANs attempts to automatically detect the iSCSI initiator that should be used for communications and lists all available adapters for a particular initiator. You can then specify which adapter to use for the LUN.

To add and configure a server with iSCSI connections, follow these steps:

1. In Storage Manager For SANs, select LUN Management. In the Actions pane or on the Action menu, click Manage Server Connections.

2. In the Manage Server Connections dialog box, click Add.

3. In the Add Server dialog box, type the name or IP address of the server that you want to add. You can also browse for the server.

4. Optionally, type a description for the server.

5. Click OK. The server should now be listed under Manage Server Connections. All initiators that were automatically discovered are listed on the iSCSI Initiator Adapters tab.

To enable iSCSI initiator adapters for LUN access, follow these steps:

1. In Storage Manager For SANs, select LUN Management. In the Actions pane or on the Action menu, click Manage Server Connections.

2. In the server list, select a server you previously configured. On the Initiator Adapters tab, select the initiator adapters to enable.

   NOTE Before selecting multiple initiators, you must ensure that multipath I/O is configured for the server. If multipath I/O is not configured, data corruption might occur.

3. Click OK.

Adding and Removing Targets

When working with iSCSI, you can perform a variety of tasks using Manage iSCSI Targets. In Storage Manager For SANs, select LUN Management. In the Actions pane or on the Action menu, click Manage iSCSI Targets. After you select a subsystem to manage, you can do the following:

- Click Add to create an iSCSI target. In the Add Target dialog box, type a descriptive name for the target, select IP address portals to enable for the target, and then click OK.

- Select an existing target, and then click Remove to remove the iSCSI target. In the Remove Target dialog box, confirm that you want to delete the target by selecting the check box provided and then clicking OK.

Creating, Extending, Assigning, and Deleting LUNs

After you've configured the required SAN connections, you can perform a variety of tasks using Manage Server Connections. In Storage Manager For SANs, select LUN Management. In the Actions pane or on the Action menu, click Manage Server Connections. You can then do the following:

- Click Create LUN, and then select the subsystem on which to create the LUN. Specify the LUN type, size, and name. As necessary, you can assign the LUN to a target, assign the LUN to a server or cluster, and specify the formatting for the LUN volume. To complete the process, click Create LUN.

- Click Action, and then click Extend LUN to display the Extend LUN dialog box. In the dialog box, type a new size for the LUN.

- Click Action, click Assign LUN, and then select the server, target, or cluster to which you want to assign the LUN. To complete the process, click Assign LUN.

- Click Action, and then click Delete LUN to display the Delete LUN dialog box. Confirm that you want to delete the LUN by selecting the check box provided, and then click OK.

Defining a Server Cluster in Storage Manager For SANs

A group of clustered servers can access LUNs as well. You create server clusters by defining them in Storage Manager For SANs and by enabling clustering services on each individual server in the cluster. Each server should be a member of only one cluster, and clustering services should be active on all cluster nodes. After you create server clusters, you can assign LUNs to the cluster the same way that you assign LUNs to individual servers.

To define a server cluster in Storage Manager For SANs, follow these steps:

1. In Storage Manager For SANs, select LUN Management. In the Actions pane or on the Action menu, click Manage Server Connections.

2. In the Manage Server Connections dialog box, click Manage Clusters.

3. In the Manage Clusters dialog box, click Add.

4. In the Add New Cluster dialog box, type a name for the cluster or type a general description that will help you identify the cluster.

5. In the server list, select the servers that you want to include in the new cluster.

6. Click OK to create the new cluster, and then click OK again.

7. Configure cluster connections as appropriate for Fibre Channel ports or iSCSI initiator adapters by following the procedures discussed previously.

The new cluster is listed under Manage Server Connections. You can now assign LUNs to the cluster as discussed previously in this chapter.

CHAPTER 14

Managing File Screening and Storage Reporting

W indows Server 2008 R2 provides a robust environment for working with files and folders. For maximum control and flexibility, you'll usually format volumes with the NTFS file system. NTFS gives you many advanced options, including the option to configure file screening and storage reporting. File screening and storage reporting are available when you add the File Server Resource Manager role service to a server as part of the File Services role.

Understanding File Screening and Storage Reporting

When you work with Windows Server 2008 R2, file screening is another tool you can use in your effort to keep networks safe from malicious programs and to block unauthorized types of content. You can use file screening in conjunction with quotas and storage reports as discussed in Chapter 15, "Data Sharing, Security, and Auditing." Using file screening, you can monitor and block the use of certain types of files. You can configure file screening in one of two modes:

- **Active screening**   Does not allow users to save unauthorized files.

- **Passive screening**   Allows users to save unauthorized files but monitors or warns about using the files (or both).

You actively or passively screen files by defining a file screen. All file screens have a *file screen path*, which is a folder that defines the base file path to which the screen is applied. Screening applies to the designated folder and all subfolders of the designated folder. The particulars of how screening works and what is screened are derived from a source template that defines the file screen's properties.

Windows Server 2008 R2 includes the file screen templates listed in Table 14-1. Using the File Server Resource Manager, you can easily define additional templates to use when you define file screens, or you can set single-user custom file screen properties when defining the file screen.

TABLE 14-1 File Screen Templates

FILE SCREEN TEMPLATE NAME	SCREENING TYPE	FILE GROUP ACTION
Block Audio And Video Files	Active	Block: Audio and Video Files
Block E-Mail Files	Active	Block: E-Mail Files
Block Executable Files	Active	Block: Executable Files
Block Image Files	Active	Block: Image Files
Monitor Executable And System Files	Passive	Warn: Executable Files, System Files

File screen templates or custom properties define the following:

- Screening type, active or passive
- File groups to which screening is applied
- Notifications using e-mail, an event log, a command, a report, or any combination of these

Table 14-2 lists the standard file groups for screening. Each file group has a predefined set of files to which it applies. You can modify the included file types and create additional file groups by using File Server Resource Manager.

TABLE 14-2 File Screen Groups and the File Types to Which They Apply

FILE GROUP	APPLIES TO
Audio and video files	.aac, .aif, .aifft, .asf, .asx, .au, .avi, .flac, .m3u, .mid, .midi, .mov, .mp1, .mp2, .mp3, .mp4, .mpa, .mpe, .mpeg, .mpeg2, .mpeg3, .mpg, .ogg, .qt, .qtw, .ram, .rm, .rmi, .rmvb, .snd, .swf, .vob, .wav, .wax, .wma, .wmv, .wvx
Backup files	.bak, .bck, .bkf, .old
Compressed files	.ace, .arc, .arj, .bhx, .bz2, .cab, .gz, .gzip, .hpk, .hqx, .jar, .lha, .lzh, .lzx, .pak, .pit, .rar, .sea, .sit, .sqz, .tgz, .uu, .uue, .z, .zip, .zoo
E-mail files	.eml, .idx, .mbox, .mbx, .msg, .ost, .otf, .pab, .pst
Executable files	.bat, .cmd, .com, .cpl, .exe, .inf, .js, .jse, .msh, .msi, .msp, .ocx, .pif, .pl, .scr, .vb, .vbs, .wsf, .wsh

FILE GROUP	APPLIES TO
Image files	.bmp, .dib, .eps, .gif, .img, .jfif, .jpe, .jpeg, .jpg, .pcx, .png, .ps, .psd, .raw, .rif, .spiff, .tif, .tiff
Office files	.accdb, .accde, .accdr, .accdt, .adn, .adp, .doc, .docm, .docx, .dot, .dotm, .dotx, .grv, .gsa, .gta, .mad, .maf, .mda, .mdb, .mde, .mdf, .mdm, .mdt, .mdw, .mdz, .mpd, .mpp, .mpt, .obt, .odb, .one, .onepkg, .pot, .potm, .potx, .ppa, .ppam, .pps, .ppsm, .ppsx, .ppt, .pptn, .pptx, .pwz, .rqy, .rtf, .rwz, .sldm, .sldx, .slk, .thmx, .vdx, .vsd, .vsl, .vss, .vst, .vsu, .vsw, .vsx, .vtx, .wbk, .wri, .xla, .xlam, .xlb, .xlc, .xld, .xlk, .xll, .xlm, .xls, .xlsb, .xlsm, .xlsx, .xlt, .xltm, .xltx, .xlv, .xlw, .xsf, .xsn
System files	.acm, .dll, .ocx, .sys, .vxd
Temporary files	.temp, .tmp, ~*
Text files	.asc, .text, .txt
Web page files	.asp, .aspx, .cgi, .css, .dhtml, .hta, .htm, .html, .mht, .php, .php3, .shtml, .url

You can configure exception paths as well to designate specifically allowed locations for saving blocked file types. You can use this feature to allow specific users to save blocked file types to designated locations or to allow all users to save blocked file types to designated locations. As an example, you might want to deter illegal downloading of music and movies within the organization by preventing users from saving audio and video files. However, if your organization has an audio/video department that needs to be able to save audio and video files, you can configure an exception to allow files to be saved on a folder accessible only to members of this department.

You can generate storage reports as part of quota and file screening management. Table 14-3 provides a summary of the standard storage reports and their purposes. Using one of the standard storage reports, you can generate three general types of storage reports:

- **Incident reports** Generated automatically when a user tries to save an unauthorized file or when a user exceeds a quota

- **Scheduled reports** Generated periodically based on a scheduled report task

- **On-demand reports** Generated manually upon request

TABLE 14-3 Standard Storage Reports

REPORT NAME	DESCRIPTION
Duplicate Files	Lists files that appear to be duplicates based on the file size and last modification time. Helps reclaim wasted space resulting from duplication.
File Screening Audit	Lists file screening audit events on the server for a specified period. Helps identify users and applications that violate screening policies. You can set report parameters to filter events based on the minimum days since the screening event occurred and the user.
Files By File Group	Lists files by file group. Helps identify usage patterns and types of files that are using large amounts of disk space. You can set report parameters to include or exclude specific file groups.
Files By Owner	Lists files by users who own them. Helps identify users who use large amounts of disk space. You can set report parameters to include or exclude specific users as well as specific files by name pattern.
Files By Property	Lists files by a particular classification property. Helps identify users who use large amounts of disk space. You can set report parameters to include or exclude specific users as well as specific files by name pattern.
Large Files	Lists files that are of a specified size or larger. Helps identify file classification usage patterns. You can set report parameters to generate a report about a specified classification property. You can include and exclude files only by name pattern.
Least Recently Accessed Files	Lists files that haven't been accessed recently. Helps identify files that you might be able to delete or archive. You can set report parameters to define what constitutes a least recently used file. By default, any file that hasn't been accessed in the last 90 days is considered to be a least recently used file. You can also include or exclude specific files by name pattern.
Most Recently Accessed Files	Lists files that have been accessed recently. Helps identify frequently used files. You can set report parameters to define what constitutes a most recently used file. By default, any file that has been accessed within the last seven days is considered to be a most recently used file. You can also include or exclude specific files by name pattern.
Quota Usage	Lists the quotas that exceed a minimum quota usage value. Helps identify file usage according to quotas. You can set report parameters to define the quotas that should be included according to the percentage of the quota limit used.

You manage file screening and storage reporting using the File Server Resource Manager console. This console is installed and available on the Administrative Tools menu when you add the File Server Resource Manager role service to the server as part of the File Services role. When you select the File Server Resource Manager node in the console, you'll see five additional nodes (see Figure 14-1):

- **Quota Management**   Used to manage the quota features of Windows Server 2008 R2 and discussed in Chapter 15

- **File Screening Management**   Used to manage the file screening features of Windows Server 2008 R2 and discussed in this chapter

- **Storage Reports Management**   Used to manage the storage reporting features of Windows Server 2008 R2 and discussed in this chapter

- **Classification Management**   Used to manage the file classification features of Windows Server 2008 R2

- **File Management Tasks**   Used to find subsets of files and then manage the files in some way

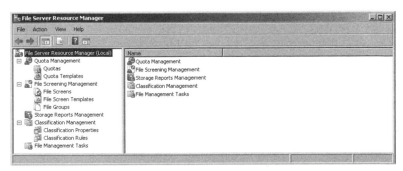

FIGURE 14-1 Use File Server Resource Manager to manage quotas, file screening, and storage reports.

Managing File Screening and Storage Reporting

File screening and storage reporting management can be divided into the following key areas:

- **Global options**   Control global settings for file server resources, including e-mail notification, storage report default parameters, report locations, and file screen auditing

- **File groups**   Control the types of files to which screens are applied

- **File screen templates**   Control screening properties (screening type: active or passive, file groups to which screening is applied; notifications: e-mail, event log, or both)

- **File screens**   Control file paths that are screened

- **File screen exceptions**   Control file paths that are screening exceptions
- **Report generation**   Controls whether and how storage reports are generated

The following sections discuss each of these management areas.

Managing Global File Resource Settings

You use global file resource options to configure e-mail notification, storage report default parameters, report locations, and file screen auditing. You should configure these global settings prior to configuring quotas, file screens, and storage reporting.

Configuring E-Mail Notifications

Notifications and storage reports are e-mailed through a Simple Mail Transfer Protocol (SMTP) server. For this process to work, you must designate which organizational SMTP server to use, default administrative recipients, and the From address to be used in mailing notifications and reports. To configure these settings, follow these steps:

1. Open File Server Resource Manager. On the Action menu or in the Actions pane, click Configure Options. This displays the File Server Resource Manager Options dialog box with the Email Notifications tab selected by default, as shown in Figure 14-2.

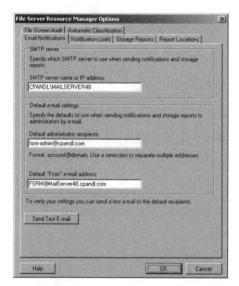

FIGURE 14-2 Set e-mail notification and other global file resource settings on the Email Notifications tab.

2. In the SMTP Server Name Or IP Address text box, type the host name of the organization's mail server in Domain\ServerName format, such as **CPANDL\ MailServer48**, or type the IP address of this server, such as **192.168.10.52**.

3. In the Default Administrator Recipients field, type the e-mail address of the default administrator for notification, such as **filescreens@cpandl.com**. Typically, you'll want this to be a separate mailbox that is monitored by an administrator or a distribution group that goes to the specific administrators responsible for file server resource management. You can also enter multiple e-mail addresses. Be sure to separate each e-mail address with a semicolon.

4. In the Default "From" E-Mail Address field, type the e-mail address you want the server to use in the From field of notification messages. Remember, users as well as administrators may receive notifications.

5. To test the settings, click Send Test E-Mail. The test e-mail message should be delivered to the default administrator recipients almost immediately. If it isn't, check to be sure that the e-mail addresses used are valid and that the From e-mail address is acceptable to the SMTP server as a valid sender.

6. Click OK.

Configuring Notification Limits

When a quota is exceeded or an unauthorized file is detected, File Server Resource Manager sends a notification to administrators by performing one or more of the following actions:

- Sending an e-mail message to the user who attempted to save an unauthorized file, a designated list of administrators, or both

- Recording a warning message in the event logs

- Executing a command that performs administrative tasks under the LocalService, NetworkService, or LocalSystem account

- Generating one or more notification reports and optionally sending those reports to an authorized list of recipients

To reduce the number of notifications, you can set notification limits that specify a period of time that must elapse before a subsequent notification of the same type is raised for the same issue. The default notification limit for e-mail notification, event log notification, command notification, and report notification is 60 minutes.

You can configure notification limits by following these steps:

1. Open File Server Resource Manager. On the Action menu or in the Actions pane, click Configure Options.

2. In the File Server Resource Manager Options dialog box, click the Notification Limits tab.

3. You can now configure limits for the following types of notifications:
   - **Email Notification**   Sets the interval between e-mail notifications
   - **Event Log Notification**   Sets the interval between event log notifications
   - **Command Notification**   Sets the interval between command notifications
   - **Report Notification**   Sets the interval between report notifications
4. Click OK to save your settings.

Reviewing Reports and Configuring Storage Report Parameters

Each storage report has a default configuration that you can review and modify using File Server Resource Manager Options. Default parameter changes apply to all future incident reports and any existing report tasks that use the default configuration. You're able to override the default settings as necessary if you subsequently schedule a report task or generate a report on demand.

You can access the standard storage reports and change their default parameters by following these steps:

1. Open File Server Resource Manager. On the Action menu or in the Actions pane, click Configure Options.
2. In the File Server Resource Manager Options dialog box, click the Storage Reports tab.
3. To review a report's current settings, select the report name in the Reports list, and then click Review Reports.
4. To modify a report's default parameters, select the report name in the Reports list, and then click Edit Parameters. You can then modify the report parameters as necessary.
5. When you finish, click Close or OK as appropriate.

Configuring Report Locations

By default, incident, scheduled, and on-demand reports are stored on the server on which notification is triggered in separate subfolders under %SystemDrive%\StorageReports. You can review or modify this configuration by following these steps:

1. Open File Server Resource Manager. On the Action menu or in the Actions pane, click Configure Options.
2. In the File Server Resource Manager Options dialog box, click the Report Locations tab.

3. The report folders currently in use are listed under Report Locations. To specify a different local folder for a particular report type, type a new folder path, or click Browse to search for the folder path you want to use.

4. Click OK.

NOTE You can use only local paths for report storage. Nonlocal folder paths are considered invalid.

Configuring File Screen Auditing

By running a File Screen Auditing Report, you can record file screening activity in an auditing database for later review. This auditing data is tracked on a per-server basis, so the server on which the activity occurs is the one where the activity is audited. To enable or disable file screen auditing, follow these steps:

1. Open File Server Resource Manager. On the Action menu or in the Actions pane, click Configure Options.

2. In the File Server Resource Manager Options dialog box, click the File Screen Audit tab.

3. To enable auditing, select the Record File Screening Activity In Auditing Database check box.

4. To disable auditing, clear the Record File Screening Activity In Auditing Database check box.

5. Click OK to save your settings.

Managing the File Groups to Which Screens Are Applied

You use file groups to designate sets of similar file types to which screening can be applied. In File Server Resource Manager you can view the currently defined screening file groups by expanding the File Server Resource Manager and File Screening Management nodes and then selecting File Groups. Table 14-2, shown previously, lists the default file groups and the included file types.

You can modify existing file groups by following these steps:

1. Open File Server Resource Manager. Expand the File Server Resource Manager and File Screening Management nodes, and then select File Groups.

2. Currently defined file groups are listed along with included and excluded files.

3. To modify file group properties, double-click the file group name. This displays a Properties dialog box similar to the one shown in Figure 14-3.

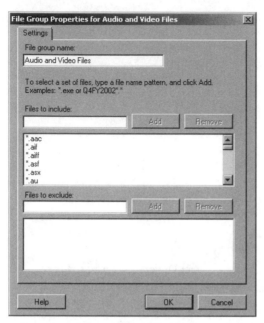

FIGURE 14-3 Include and exclude file types by modifying file group properties.

4. In the Files To Include text box, type the file extension of an additional file type to screen, such as **.pdf**, or the file name pattern, such as **Archive*.***. Click Add. Repeat this step to specify other file types to screen.

5. In the Files To Exclude text box, type the file extension of a file type to exclude from screening, such as **.doc**, or the file name pattern, such as **Report*.***. Click Add. Repeat this step to specify other file types to exclude from screening.

6. Click OK to save the changes.

You can specify additional file groups to screen by following these steps:

1. Open File Server Resource Manager. Expand the File Server Resource Manager and File Screening Management nodes and then select File Groups.

2. On the Action menu or in the Actions pane, click Create File Group. This displays the Create File Group Properties dialog box.

3. In the File Group Name text box, type the name of the file group you're creating.

4. In the Files To Include field, type the file extension to screen, such as **.pdf**, or the file name pattern, such as **Archive*.***. Click Add. Repeat this step to specify other file types to screen.

5. In the Files To Exclude text box, type the file extension to exclude from screening, such as **.doc**, or the file name pattern, such as **Report*.***. Click Add. Repeat this step to specify other file types to exclude from screening.

6. Click OK to create the file group.

Managing File Screen Templates

You use file screen templates to define screening properties, including the screening type, the file groups to which a screen is applied, and notification. In File Server Resource Manager, you can view the currently defined file screen templates by expanding the File Server Resource Manager and File Screening Management nodes and then selecting File Screen Templates. Table 14-1, shown previously, provides a summary of the default file screen templates.

You can modify existing file screen templates by following these steps:

1. Open File Server Resource Manager. Expand the File Server Resource Manager and File Screening Management nodes, and then select File Screen Templates.

2. Currently defined file screen templates are listed by name, screening type, and file groups affected.

3. To modify file screen template properties, double-click the file screen template name. This displays a Properties dialog box (shown in Figure 14-4).

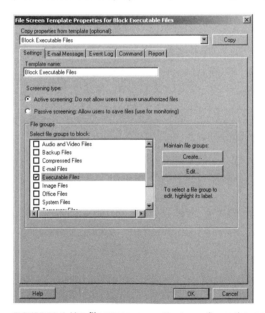

FIGURE 14-4 Use file screen properties to configure the screening type, the file groups to which a screen is applied, and notification.

4. On the Settings tab, you can set the template name, screen type, and file groups affected using the controls provided.

5. On the E-Mail Message tab, you can configure the following notifications:

   - To notify an administrator when the file screen is triggered, select the Send E-Mail To The Following Administrators check box, and then type the e-mail address or addresses to use. Be sure to separate multiple e-mail addresses with a semicolon. Use the value [Admin Email] to specify the default administrator as configured previously under the global options.

   - To notify users, select the Send E-Mail To The User Who Attempted To Save An Unauthorized File check box. In the Subject and Message Body text boxes, specify the contents of the user notification message. Table 14-4 lists available variables and their meanings.

6. On the Event Log tab, you can configure event logging. Select Send Warning To Event Log to enable logging, and then specify the text of the log entry in the Log Entry field. Table 14-4 lists available variables and their meanings.

7. On the Report tab, select the Generate Reports check box to enable incident reporting, and then select the check boxes for the types of reports you want to generate. Incident reports are stored under %SystemDrive%\StorageRe-ports\Incident by default and can also be sent to designated administrators as well as to the user who attempted to save an unauthorized file. Use the value [Admin Email] to specify the default administrator as configured previously under the global options.

8. Click OK when you have finished modifying the template.

You can create a new file screen template by following these steps:

1. Open File Server Resource Manager. Expand the File Server Resource Manager and File Screening Management nodes, and then select File Screen Templates.

2. On the Action menu or in the Actions pane, click Create File Screen Template. This displays the Create File Screen Template dialog box.

3. Follow steps 4–8 of the previous procedure.

TABLE 14-4 File Screen Variables

VARIABLE NAME	DESCRIPTION
[Admin Email]	Inserts the e-mail addresses of the administrators defined under the global options
[File Screen Path]	Inserts the local file path where the user attempted to save the file, such as C:\Data
[File Screen Remote Path]	Inserts the remote file path where the user attempted to save the file, such as \\server\share
[File Screen System Path]	Inserts the canonical file path where the user attempted to save the file, such as \\?\VolumeGUID
[Server Domain]	Inserts the domain of the server on which the notification occurred
[Server]	Inserts the server on which the notification occurred
[Source File Owner]	Inserts the user name of the owner of the unauthorized file
[Source File Owner Email]	Inserts the e-mail address of the owner of the unauthorized file
[Source File Path]	Inserts the source path of the unauthorized file
[Source Io Owner Email]	Inserts the e-mail address of the user who caused notification
[Source Io Owner]	Inserts the name of the user who caused notification
[Source Process Id]	Inserts the process ID (PID) of the process that caused notification
[Source Process Image]	Inserts the executable for the process that caused notification
[Violated File Group]	Inserts the name of the file group in which the file type is defined as unauthorized

Creating File Screens

You use file screens to designate file paths that are screened. In File Server Resource Manager, you can view current file screens by expanding the File Server Resource Manager and File Screening Management nodes and then selecting File Screens. Before you define file screens, you should specify screening file groups and file screen templates that you will use, as discussed in "Managing the File Groups to Which Screens Are Applied" and "Managing File Screen Templates."

After you've defined the necessary file groups and file screen templates, you can create a file screen by following these steps:

1. Open File Server Resource Manager. Expand the File Server Resource Manager and File Screening Management nodes, and then select File Screens.

2. Click Create File Screen on the Action menu or in the Actions pane.

3. In the Create File Screen dialog box, set the local computer path to screen by clicking Browse. In the Browse For Folder dialog box, select the path to screen, such as C:\Data.

4. In the Derive Properties selection list, choose the file screen template that defines the screening properties you want to use.

5. Click Create.

Defining File Screening Exceptions

You use exception paths to specifically designate folder locations where it's permitted to save blocked file types. Based on the NTFS permissions on the excepted file path, you can use this feature to allow specific users to save blocked file types to designated locations or to allow all users to save blocked file types to designated locations.

You can create a file screen exception by following these steps:

1. Open File Server Resource Manager. Expand the File Server Resource Manager and File Screening Management nodes, and then select File Screens.

2. Click Create File Screen Exception on the Action menu or in the Actions pane.

3. In the Create File Screen Exception dialog box, set the local path to exclude from screening by clicking Browse. Then, in the Browse For Folder dialog box, select the path to exclude from screening, such as C:\Data\Images.

4. Select the file groups to exclude from screening on the designated path.

5. Click OK.

Scheduling and Generating Storage Reports

Incident reports are generated automatically when triggered, as defined in the Reports tab properties of a file screen template. (For details, see "Understanding File Screening and Storage Reporting.") Scheduled and on-demand reports are configured separately. In File Server Resource Manager, you can view currently scheduled reports by expanding the File Server Resource Manager node and then selecting Storage Reports Management.

You can schedule reports on a per-volume or per-folder basis by following these steps:

1. Open File Server Resource Manager. Expand the File Server Resource Manager node and then select Storage Reports Management.

2. On the Action menu or in the Actions pane, click Schedule A New Report Task. This displays the Storage Reports Task Properties dialog box, shown in Figure 14-5.

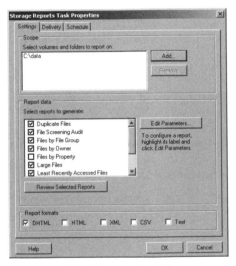

FIGURE 14-5 Schedule reports for delivery on a per-volume or per-folder basis.

3. On the Settings tab, under Scope, click Add. In the Browse For Folder dialog box, select the volume or folder on which you want to generate scheduled storage reports. Repeat to add other volumes or folders.

   NOTE On clustered file servers, you can report only on volumes that belong to the same cluster resource group.

4. Under Report Data, select the types of reports to generate.

5. Under Report Formats, select the format for the report, such as Dynamic HTML (DHTML).

6. By default, Windows Server 2008 R2 stores scheduled storage reports as they're generated in the %SystemDrive%\StorageReports\Scheduled folder. If you'd also like to deliver reports by e-mail to administrators, click the Delivery tab, and then select the Send Reports To The Following Administrators check box. Enter the e-mail address or addresses to which reports should be delivered, being sure to separate each e-mail address with a semicolon.

7. On the Schedule tab, click Create Schedule. In the Schedule dialog box, click New, and then define the run schedule for reporting.

8. Click OK twice to schedule the report task.

You can generate an on-demand report by following these steps:

1. Open File Server Resource Manager. Expand the File Server Resource Manager node, and then select Storage Reports Management.

2. On the Action menu or in the Actions pane, click Generate Reports Now. This displays the Storage Reports Task Properties dialog box.

3. On the Settings tab, under Scope, click Add. In the Browse For Folder dialog box, select the volume or folder on which you want to generate the on-demand storage reports. Repeat to add other volumes or folders.

4. Under Report Data, select the types of reports to generate.

5. Under Report Formats, select the format for the report, such as DHTML.

6. Windows Server 2008 R2 stores on-demand storage reports in the %SystemDrive%\StorageReports\Interactive folder. If you'd also like to deliver reports by e-mail to administrators, click the Delivery tab, and then select the Send Reports To The Following Administrators check box. Enter the e-mail address or addresses to which reports should be delivered, being sure to separate each email address with a semicolon.

7. Click OK. When prompted, specify whether to wait for the reports to be generated and then display them or to generate the reports in the background for later access. Click OK.

Data Sharing, Security, and Auditing

W indows Server 2008 Release 2 (R2) supports two file-sharing models: *standard file sharing* and *public folder sharing*. Standard file sharing allows remote users to access network resources such as files, folders, and drives. When you share a folder or a drive, you make all its files and subfolders available to a specified set of users. Because you don't need to move files from their current location, standard file sharing is also referred to as *in-place file sharing*.

You can enable standard file sharing on removable disks formatted with exFAT, FAT, or FAT32 and on any type of disk formatted with NTFS. One set of permissions apply to removable disks formatted with exFAT, FAT, or FAT32. These permissions are called *share permissions*. Two sets of permissions apply to disks formatted with NTFS: *NTFS permissions* (also referred to as *access permissions*) and share permissions. Having two sets of permissions allows you to determine precisely who has access to shared files and the level of access assigned. With either NTFS permissions or share permissions, you do not need to move the files you are sharing.

With public folder sharing, you share files simply by copying or moving files to the computer's Public folder. Public files are available to anyone who logs on to a computer locally regardless of whether he or she has a standard user account or an administrator user account on the computer. You can also grant network access to the Public folder. If you do this, however, there are no access restrictions. The Public folder and its contents are open to everyone who can access the computer over the local network.

Using and Enabling File Sharing

The sharing settings on a computer determine the way files can be shared. The two file-sharing models that Windows Server 2008 R2 supports have the following differences:

- **Standard (in-place) file sharing** Allows remote users to access files, folders, and drives over the network. When you share a folder or a drive, you make all its files and subfolders available to a specified set of users. Share permissions and access permissions together enable you to control who has access to shared files and the level of access assigned. You do not need to move the files you are sharing.

- **Public folder sharing** Allows local users and (optionally) remote users to access any files placed in the computer's %SystemDrive%\Users\Public folder. Access permissions on the Public folder determine which users and groups have access to publicly shared files as well as the level of access those users and groups have. When you copy or move files to the Public folder, access permissions are changed to match those of the Public folder. Some additional permissions are added as well. When a computer is part of a workgroup, you can add password protection to the Public folder. Separate password protection isn't needed in a domain. In a domain, only domain users can access Public folder data.

With standard file sharing, local users don't have automatic access to any data stored on a computer. You control local access to files and folders by using the security settings on the local disk. With public folder sharing, on the other hand, files copied or moved to the Public folder are available to anyone who logs on locally. You can grant network access to the Public folder as well. Doing so, however, makes the Public folder and its contents open to everyone who can access the computer over the network.

Public folder sharing is designed to allow users to share files and folders from a single location. With public folder sharing, you copy or move files that you want to share to a computer's %SystemDrive%\Users\Public folder. You can access public folders in Windows Explorer by clicking Start and then clicking Computer. In

Windows Explorer, double-click the system drive and then access the Users\Public folder.

The Public folder has several subfolders that you can use to help organize public files, including:

- **Public Desktop**   Used for shared desktop items. Any files and program shortcuts placed in the Public Desktop folder appear on the desktop of all users who log on to the computer (and to all network users if network access has been granted to the Public folder).

- **Public Documents, Public Music, Public Pictures, Public Videos**   Used for shared document and media files. All files placed in one of these sub-folders are available to all users who log on to the computer (and to all network users if network access has been granted to the Public folder).

- **Public Downloads**   Used for shared downloads. Any downloads placed in the Public Downloads subfolder are available to all users who log on to the computer (and to all network users if network access has been granted to the Public folder).

By default, anyone with a user account and password on a computer can access that computer's Public folder. When you copy or move files to the Public folder, access permissions are changed to match that of the Public folder, and some additional permissions are added as well.

You can change the default Public folder sharing configuration in two key ways:

- Allow users logged on to the computer to view and manage public files but restrict network users from accessing public files. When you configure this option, the implicit groups Interactive, Batch, and Service are granted special permissions on public files and public folders.

- Allow users with network access to view and manage public files. This allows network users to open, change, create, and delete public files. When you configure this option, the implicit group Everyone is granted Full Control permission to public files and public folders.

Windows Server 2008 R2 can use either or both sharing models at any time. However, standard file sharing offers more security and better protection than public folder sharing, and increasing security is essential to protecting your organization's data. With standard file sharing, share permissions are used only when a user attempts to access a file or folder from a different computer on the network. Access permissions are always used, whether the user is logged on to the console or is using a remote system to access a file or folder over the network. When data is accessed remotely, first the share permissions are applied and then the access permissions are applied.

You can configure the basic file-sharing settings for a server by using Advanced Sharing Settings in Network And Sharing Center. Separate options are provided for network discovery, file and printer sharing, and public folder sharing, as shown in Figure 15-1.

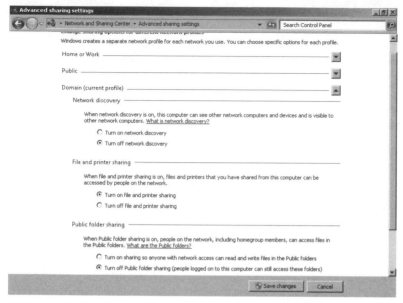

FIGURE 15-1 Network And Sharing Center shows the current sharing configuration.

You can manage a computer's sharing configuration by following these steps:

1. Open Network And Sharing Center by clicking Start and then clicking Network. On the toolbar in the Network console, click Network And Sharing Center.

2. In Network And Sharing Center, click Change Advanced Sharing Settings in the left pane. Select the network profile for the network on which you want to enable file and printer sharing. Typically, this will be the Domain profile.

3. Standard file and printer sharing controls network access to shared resources. To configure standard file sharing, do one of the following:

   - Select Turn On File And Printer Sharing to enable file sharing.
   - Select Turn Off File And Printer Sharing to disable file sharing.

4. Public folder sharing controls access to a computer's Public folder. To configure public folder sharing, expand the Public Folder Sharing panel by clicking the related expand button. Choose one of the following options:

   - **Turn On Sharing So Anyone With Network Access Can Read And Write Files In The Public Folders**   Enables public folder sharing by granting access to the Public folder and all public data to anyone who can access the computer over the network. Windows Firewall settings might prevent external access.

- **Turn Off Public Folder Sharing** Disables public folder sharing, preventing local network access to the Public folder. Anyone who logs on locally to your computer can still access the Public folder and its files.

5. Click Save Changes.

Configuring Standard File Sharing

You use shares to control access for remote users. Permissions on shared folders have no effect on users who log on locally to a server or to a workstation that has shared folders.

Viewing Existing Shares

You can use both Computer Management and Share And Storage Management to work with shares. You can also view current shares on a computer by typing **net share** at a command prompt.

In Computer Management, you can view the shared folders on a local or remote computer by following these steps:

1. You're connected to the local computer by default. If you want to connect to a remote computer, right-click the Computer Management node, and then click Connect To Another Computer. Choose Another Computer, type the name or IP address of the computer you want to connect to, and then click OK.

2. In the console tree, expand System Tools, expand Shared Folders, and then select Shares. The current shares on the system are displayed, as shown in Figure 15-2.

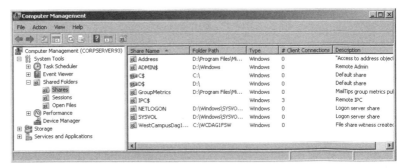

FIGURE 15-2 Available shares are listed in the Shared Folders node.

3. The columns for the Shares node provide the following information:

- **Share Name** Name of the shared folder
- **Folder Path** Complete path to the folder on the local system

- **Type** What kind of computers can use the share, such as Macintosh or Windows

- **# Client Connections** Number of clients currently accessing the share

- **Description** Description of the share

NOTE An entry of Windows in the Type column means that all clients can use the share, including those running Windows or Macintosh operating systems. An entry of Macintosh in the Type column means that only Macintosh clients can use the share.

In Share And Storage Management, you can view the shared folders on a local or remote computer by following these steps:

1. You're connected to the local computer by default. To connect to a remote computer, right-click the Share And Storage Management node, and then click Connect To Another Computer. Choose Another Computer, type the name or IP address of the computer you want to connect to, and then click OK.

2. When you click the Shares tab in the main pane, the current shares on the system are displayed, as shown in Figure 15-3.

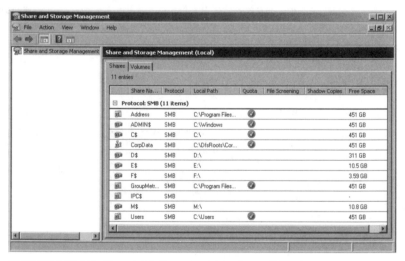

FIGURE 15-3 Click the Shares tab in the main pane to view available shares.

3. The columns on the Shares tab provide the following information:

- **Share Name** Name of the shared folder.

- **Protocol** Name of the protocol used for sharing the folder, such as Server Message Block (SMB) or Network File System (NFS).

- **Local Path** Complete path to the folder on the local system.

- **Quota** Summary status of Resource Manager quotas that are being applied to the shared folder.

- **File Screening** Summary status of file screens that are being applied to the shared folder.

- **Shadow Copies** Summary status of shadow copies that are being applied to the shared folder.

- **Free Space** The amount of unused (available) space on the related disk, except when quotas are applied. When quotas are applied, the field lists the available space according to the space limit you've defined.

REAL WORLD Network File System (NFS) is the file sharing protocol used by UNIX systems. As discussed in "Configuring NFS Sharing" later in this chapter, you can enable support for NFS by installing the Services for Network File System (NFS) role service as part of the file server configuration. Server Message Block (SMB) is the file sharing protocol used by Windows operating systems. Windows Vista, Windows 7, Windows Server 2008, and later releases support SMB version 2, which enhances the performance of the original SMB protocol. Support for the SMB Helper Class is part of the Network Diagnostics Framework (NDF). This helper class provides diagnostic information that users will find useful when they are having problems connecting to file shares. Specifically, this helper class can help diagnose failures when a user is trying to access a server that does not exist, when a user is trying to access a nonexisting share on an existing server, and when a user misspells a share name and there is a similarly named share available.

Creating Shared Folders

Windows Server 2008 R2 provides several ways to share folders. You can share local folders using Windows Explorer, and you can share local and remote folders using Computer Management or Share And Storage Management.

When you create a share with Computer Management, you can configure its share permissions and offline settings. When you create a share with Share And Storage Management, you provision all aspects of sharing, including NTFS permissions, share protocols, user limits, offline settings, and share permissions. You can also configure Resource Manager quotas, file screens, NFS permissions, and DFS Namespace publishing.

To share folders on a server running Windows Server 2008 R2, you must be a member of the Administrators or the Server Operators group. In Computer Management you share a folder by following these steps:

1. If necessary, connect to a remote computer. In the console tree, expand System Tools, expand Shared Folders, and then select Shares. The current shares on the system are displayed.

2. Right-click Shares, and then click New Share. This starts the Create A Shared Folder Wizard. Click Next.

3. In the Folder Path text box, type the local file path to the folder you want to share. The file path must be exact, such as **C:\Data\CorpDocuments**. If you don't know the full path, click Browse, use the Browse For Folder dialog box to find the folder you want to share, and then click OK. Click Next.

TIP If the file path doesn't exist, the wizard can create it for you. Click Yes when prompted to create the necessary folders.

4. In the Share Name text box, type a name for the share, as shown in Figure 15-4. This is the name of the folder to which users will connect. Share names must be unique for each system.

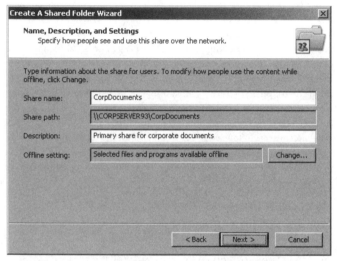

FIGURE 15-4 Use the Create A Shared Folder Wizard to configure the essential share properties, including name, description, and offline resource usage.

TIP If you want to hide a share from users (which means that they won't be able to see the shared resource when they try to browse to it in Windows Explorer or at the command line), type a dollar sign ($) as the last character of the shared resource name. For example, you could create a share called PrivEngData$, which would be hidden from Windows Explorer, Net View, and other similar utilities. Users can still connect to the share and access its data if they've been granted access permission and they know the share's name. Note that the $ must be typed as part of the share name when mapping to the shared resource.

5. If you want to, type a description of the share in the Description text box. When you view shares on a particular computer, the description is displayed in Computer Management.

6. By default, the share is configured so that only files and programs that users specify are available for offline use. If you want to prohibit the offline use of files or programs in the share or specify that all files and programs in the share are available for offline use, click Change, and then select the appropriate options in the Offline Settings dialog box.

7. Click Next, and then set basic permissions for the share. You'll find helpful pointers in "Managing Share Permissions" on the next page. As shown in Figure 15-5, the available options are as follows:

- **All Users Have Read-Only Access**   Gives users access to view files and read data. They can't create, modify, or delete files and folders.

- **Administrators Have Full Access; Other Users Have Read-Only Access**   Gives administrators complete control over the share. Full access allows administrators to create, modify, and delete files and folders. On an NTFS volume or partition, it also gives administrators the right to change permissions and to take ownership of files and folders. Other users can only view files and read data. They can't create, modify, or delete files and folders.

- **Administrators Have Full Access; Other Users Have No Access**   Gives administrators complete control over the share but prevents other users from accessing the share.

- **Customize Permissions**   Allows you to configure access for specific users and groups, which is usually the best technique to use. Setting share permissions is discussed fully in "Managing Share Permissions."

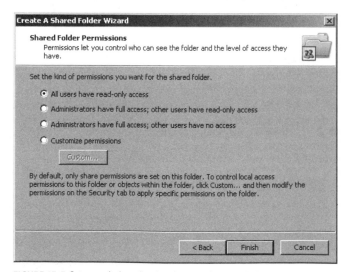

FIGURE 15-5 Set permissions for the share on the Permissions page.

8. When you click Finish, the wizard displays a status report, which should state "Sharing Was Successful." Click Finish.

NOTE If you view the shared folder in Windows Explorer, you'll see that the folder icon now depicts a padlock to indicate a share. Through Computer Management, you can also view shared resources. To learn how, see "Viewing Existing Shares" earlier in this chapter.

TIP If you're creating a share for general use and general access, you should publish the shared resource in Active Directory. Publishing the resource in Active Directory makes finding the share easier for users. To publish a share in Active Directory, right-click the share in Computer Management, and then click Properties. On the Publish tab, select the Publish This Share In Active Directory check box, add an optional description and owner information, and then click OK.

Creating Additional Shares on an Existing Share

Individual folders can have multiple shares. Each share can have a different name and a different set of access permissions. To create additional shares on an existing share, simply follow the steps for creating a share outlined in the previous section with these changes:

- In step 4, when you name the share, make sure that you use a different name.
- In step 5, when you add a description for the share, use a description that explains what the share is used for and how it's different from the other shares for the same folder.

Managing Share Permissions

Share permissions set the maximum allowable actions available within a shared folder. By default, when you create a share, everyone with access to the network has Read access to the share's contents. This is an important security change—in previous editions of Windows Server, the default permission was Full Control.

With NTFS volumes, you can use file and folder permissions and ownership, as well as share permissions, to further constrain actions within the share. With FAT volumes, share permissions only control access.

The Different Share Permissions

From the most restrictive to the least restrictive, the share permissions available are:

- **No Access**   No permissions are granted for the share.
- **Read**   With this permission, users can do the following:
  - View file and subfolder names
  - Access the subfolders in the share
  - Read file data and attributes
  - Run program files
- **Change**   Users have Read permission and the ability to do the following:
  - Create files and subfolders
  - Modify files
  - Change attributes on files and subfolders
  - Delete files and subfolders
- **Full Control**   Users have Read and Change permissions, as well as the following additional capabilities on NTFS volumes:
  - Change file and folder permissions
  - Take ownership of files and folders

You can assign share permissions to users and groups. You can even assign permissions to implicit groups. For details on implicit groups, see "Implicit Groups and Special Identities" in Chapter 9.

Viewing Share Permissions

To view share permissions, follow these steps:

1. In Computer Management, connect to the computer on which the share is created.
2. In the console tree, expand System Tools, expand Shared Folders, and then select Shares.
3. Right-click the share you want to view, and then click Properties.
4. In the Properties dialog box, click the Share Permissions tab, shown in Figure 15-6. You can now view the users and groups that have access to the share and the type of access they have.

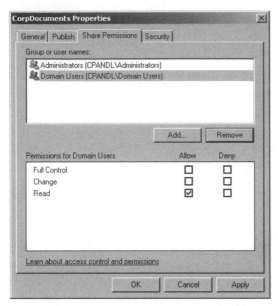

FIGURE 15-6 The Share Permissions tab shows which users and groups have access to the share and what type of access they have.

Configuring Share Permissions

In Computer Management, you can add user, computer, and group permissions to shares by following these steps:

1. Right-click the share you want to manage, and then click Properties.

2. In the Properties dialog box, click the Share Permissions tab.

3. Click Add. This opens the Select Users, Computers, Service Accounts, Or Groups dialog box, shown in Figure 15-7.

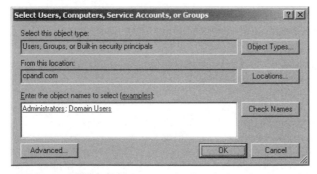

FIGURE 15-7 Add users and groups to the share in the Select Users, Computers, Service Accounts, Or Groups dialog box.

4. Type the name of a user, computer, or group in the current domain, and then click Check Names.

- If a single match is found, the dialog box is automatically updated and the entry is underlined.

- If no matches are found, you've either entered an incorrect name part or you're working with an incorrect location. Modify the name and try again, or click Locations to select a new location.

- If multiple matches are found, select the name or names you want to use, and then click OK. To assign permissions to other users, computers, or groups, type a semicolon (;), and then repeat this step.

NOTE The Locations button allows you to access account names in other domains. Click Locations to see a list of the current domain, trusted domains, and other resources that you can access. Because of the transitive trusts in Windows Server 2008 R2, you can usually access all the domains in the domain tree or forest.

5. Click OK. The users and groups are added to the Group Or User Names list for the share.

6. Configure access permissions for each user, computer, and group by selecting an account name and then allowing or denying access permissions. Keep in mind that you're setting the maximum allowable permissions for a particular account.

7. Click OK. To assign additional security permissions for NTFS, see "File and Folder Permissions" later in this chapter.

Modifying Existing Share Permissions

You can change the share permissions you assign to users, computers, and groups in the Properties dialog box. In Computer Management, follow these steps:

1. Right-click the share you want to manage, and then click Properties.

2. In the Properties dialog box, click the Share Permissions tab.

3. In the Group Or User Names list, select the user, computer, or group you want to modify.

4. Use the check boxes in the Permissions area to allow or deny permissions.

5. Repeat steps 3 and 4 for other users, computers, or groups, and then click OK.

Removing Share Permissions for Users and Groups

You also remove share permissions assigned to users, computers, and groups with the Properties dialog box. In Computer Management, follow these steps:

1. Right-click the share you want to manage, and then click Properties.

2. In the Properties dialog box, click the Share Permissions tab.

3. In the Group Or User Names list, select the user, computer, or group you want to remove, and then click Remove.

4. Repeat step 3 for other users or groups, and then click OK.

Managing Existing Shares

As an administrator, you often have to manage shared folders. This section covers the common administrative tasks of managing shares.

Understanding Special Shares

When you install Windows Server 2008 R2, the operating system creates special shares automatically. These shares are known as *administrative shares* and *hidden shares*. These shares are designed to help make system administration easier. You can't set access permissions on automatically created special shares; Windows Server 2008 R2 assigns access permissions. (You can create your own hidden shares by adding the $ symbol as the last character of the share name.)

You can delete special shares temporarily if you're certain the shares aren't needed. However, the shares are re-created automatically the next time the operating system starts. To permanently disable the administrative shares, change the following registry values to 0 (zero):

- HKEY_LOCAL_MACHINE\SYSTEM\CurrentControlSet\Services\lanmanserver\ parameters\AutoShareServer

- HKEY_LOCAL_MACHINE\SYSTEM\CurrentControlSet\Services\lanmanserver\ parameters\AutoShareWks

Which special shares are available depends on your system configuration. Table 15-1 lists special shares you might see and how they're used.

TABLE 15-1 Special Shares Used by Windows Server 2008 R2

SHARE NAME	DESCRIPTION	USAGE
ADMIN$	A share used during remote administration of a system. Provides access to the operating system %SystemRoot%.	On workstations and servers, administrators and backup operators can access these shares. On domain controllers, server operators also have access.
FAX$	Supports network faxes.	Used by fax clients when sending faxes.
IPC$	Supports named pipes during remote interprocess communications (IPC) access.	Used by programs when performing remote administration and when viewing shared resources.
NETLOGON	Supports the Net Logon service.	Used by the Net Logon service when processing domain logon requests. Everyone has Read access.
PRINT$	Supports shared printer resources by providing access to printer drivers.	Used by shared printers. Everyone has Read access. Administrators, server operators, and printer operators have Full Control.
PUBLIC	Supports public folder sharing.	Used to store public data.
SYSVOL	Supports Active Directory.	Used to store data and objects for Active Directory.
Driveletter$	A share that allows administrators to connect to a drive's root folder. These shares are shown as C$, D$, E$, and so on.	On workstations and servers, administrators and backup operators can access these shares. On domain controllers, server operators also have access.

Connecting to Special Shares

Special shares end with the $ symbol. Although these shares aren't displayed in Windows Explorer, administrators and certain operators can connect to them. To connect to a special share, follow these steps:

1. Click Start, and then click Computer. In the Computer console, click Map Network Drive on the toolbar. This opens the page shown in Figure 15-8.

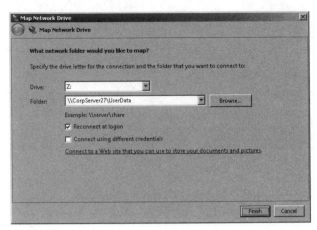

FIGURE 15-8 Connect to special shares by mapping them with the Map Network Drive page.

2. In the Drive list, select a free drive letter. This drive letter is used to access the special share.

3. In the Folder text box, type the Universal Naming Convention (UNC) path to the share. For example, to access the C$ share on a server called Twiddle, you would use the path \\TWIDDLE\C$.

4. The Reconnect At Logon check box is selected automatically to ensure the network drive is connected each time you log on. If you need to access the share only during the current logon session, clear this check box.

5. If you need to connect to the share using different user credentials, select the Connect Using Different Credentials check box.

6. Click Finish. If you are connecting using different credentials, enter the user name and password when prompted, and then click OK.

After you connect to a special share, you can access it as you would any other drive. Because special shares are protected, you don't have to worry about ordinary users accessing these shares. The first time you connect to the share, you might be prompted for a user name and password. If you are, provide that information.

Viewing User and Computer Sessions

You can use Computer Management to track all connections to shared resources on a Windows Server 2008 R2 system. Whenever a user or computer connects to a shared resource, Windows Server 2008 R2 lists a connection in the Sessions node.

To view connections to shared resources, type **net session** at a command prompt or follow these steps:

1. In Computer Management, connect to the computer on which you created the shared resource.

2. In the console tree, expand System Tools, expand Shared Folders, and then select Sessions. You can now view connections to shares for users and computers.

The columns for the Sessions node provide the following important information about user and computer connections:

- **User** The names of users or computers connected to shared resources. Computer names are shown with a $ suffix to differentiate them from users.
- **Computer** The name of the computer being used.
- **Type** The type of network connection being used.
- **# Open Files** The number of files the user is actively working with. For more detailed information, access the Open Files node.
- **Connected Time** The time that has elapsed since the connection was established.
- **Idle Time** The time that has elapsed since the connection was last used.
- **Guest** Whether the user is logged on as a guest.

Managing Sessions and Shares

Managing sessions and shares is a common administrative task. Before you shut down a server or an application running on a server, you might want to disconnect users from shared resources. You might also need to disconnect users when you plan to change access permissions or delete a share entirely. Another reason to disconnect users is to break locks on files. You disconnect users from shared resources by ending the related user sessions.

ENDING INDIVIDUAL SESSIONS

To disconnect individual users from shared resources, type **net session \\computername /delete** at a command prompt or follow these steps:

1. In Computer Management, connect to the computer on which you created the share.
2. In the console tree, expand System Tools, expand Shared Folders, and then select Sessions.
3. Right-click the user sessions you want to end, and then click Close Session.
4. Click Yes to confirm the action.

ENDING ALL SESSIONS

To disconnect all users from shared resources, follow these steps:

1. In Computer Management, connect to the computer on which you created the share.
2. In the console tree, expand System Tools, expand Shared Folders, and then right-click Sessions.

3. Click Disconnect All Sessions, and then click Yes to confirm the action.

NOTE Keep in mind that you're disconnecting users from shared resources and not from the domain. You can only use logon hours and Group Policy to force users to log off once they've logged on to the domain. Thus, disconnecting users doesn't log them off the network. It simply disconnects them from the shared resource.

Managing Open Resources

Any time users connect to shares, the individual file and object resources they are working with are displayed in the Open Files node. The Open Files node might show the files the user has open but isn't currently editing.

You can access the Open Files node by following these steps:

1. In Computer Management, connect to the computer on which you created the share.

2. In the console tree, expand System Tools, expand Shared Folders, and then select Open Files. This displays the Open Files node, which provides the following information about resource usage:

- **Open File**   The file or folder path to the open file on the local system. The path might also be a named pipe, such as \PIPE\spools, which is used for printer spooling.

- **Accessed By**   The name of the user accessing the file.

- **Type**   The type of network connection being used.

- **# Locks**   The number of locks on the resource.

- **Open Mode**   The access mode used when the resource was opened, such as read, write, or write+read.

CLOSING AN OPEN FILE

To close an open file on a computer's shares, follow these steps:

1. In Computer Management, connect to the computer you want to work with.

2. In the console tree, expand System Tools, expand Shared Folders, and then select Open Files.

3. Right-click the open file you want to close, and then click Close Open File.

4. Click Yes to confirm the action.

CLOSING ALL OPEN FILES

To close all open files on a computer's shares, follow these steps:

1. In Computer Management, connect to the computer on which the share is created.

2. In the console tree, expand System Tools, expand Shared Folders, and then right-click Open Files.

3. Click Disconnect All Open Files, and then click Yes to confirm the action.

Stopping File and Folder Sharing

To stop sharing a folder, follow these steps:

1. In Computer Management, connect to the computer on which you created the share, and then access the Shares node.

2. Right-click the share you want to remove, click Stop Sharing, and then click Yes to confirm the action.

CAUTION You should never delete a folder containing shares without first stopping the shares. If you fail to stop the shares, Windows Server 2008 R2 attempts to reestablish the shares the next time the computer is started, and the resulting error is logged in the system event log.

Configuring NFS Sharing

As discussed in Chapter 12, "Managing File Systems and Drives," you can install Services for Network File System as a role service on a file server. Services for Network File System provides a file-sharing solution for enterprises with mixed Windows and UNIX environments, allowing users to transfer files between Windows Server 2008 R2 and UNIX operating systems using the Network File System (NFS) protocol.

You can configure NFS sharing for local folders on NTFS volumes using Windows Explorer. You can also configure NFS sharing of local and remote folders on NTFS volumes by using Share And Storage Management. In Windows Explorer, follow these steps to enable and configure NFS sharing:

1. Right-click the share you want to manage, and then click Properties. This displays a Properties dialog box for the share.

2. On the NFS Sharing tab, click Manage NFS Sharing.

3. In the NFS Advanced Sharing dialog box, select the Share This Folder check box, as shown in Figure 15-9.

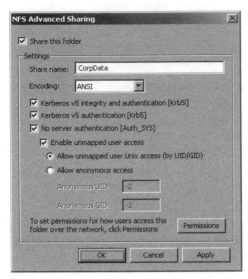

FIGURE 15-9 You can use NFS sharing to share resources between Windows and UNIX computers.

4. In the Share Name text box, type a name for the share. This is the name of the folder to which UNIX users will connect. NFS share names must be unique for each system and can be the same as those used for standard file sharing.

5. ANSI is the default encoding for text associated with directory listings and file names. If your UNIX computers use a different default encoding, you can choose that encoding in the Encoding list.

6. By default, the share is configured to allow Kerberos integrity and authentication mechanisms as well as standard Kerberos authentication. Clear the check boxes for the authentication mechanisms you don't want to use.

7. By default, the share is configured so that no server authentication is required. If you want to require server authentication, clear the No Server Authentication check box.

8. By default, unmapped user access is allowed and enabled from UNIX computers. If you want to allow anonymous access to the NFS share, select the Allow Anonymous Access option, and then enter the anonymous user UID and anonymous group GID.

9. By default, all UNIX computers have read-only access to the NFS share. If you want to modify the default permissions, click Permissions, set the permissions you want to use in the NFS Share Permissions dialog box, and then click OK. You can configure no access, read-only access, or read-write access by client computer name and client computer groups.

10. Click OK twice to close the open dialog boxes and save your settings.

In Windows Explorer, you can disable sharing by following these steps:

1. Right-click the share you want to manage, and then click Properties. This displays a Properties dialog box for the share.

2. On the NFS Sharing tab, click Manage NFS Sharing.

3. In the NFS Advanced Sharing dialog box, clear the Share This Folder check box, and then click OK twice.

With Share And Storage Management, you can configure NFS permissions as part of the initial share configuration when you are provisioning a share. You can:

- Modify NFS permissions by right-clicking the NFS share entry on the Shares tab and selecting Properties. In the Properties dialog box, click NFS Permissions on the Permissions tab to manage NFS permissions.

- Modify NFS authentication by right-clicking the NFS share entry on the Shares tab and selecting Properties. In the Properties dialog box, use the options on the NFS Authentication tab to manage NFS authentication.

- Stop sharing the folder via NFS by right-clicking the NFS share entry on the Shares tab and selecting Stop Sharing. When prompted to confirm the action, click Yes.

Using Shadow Copies

Any time your organization uses shared folders, you should consider creating shadow copies of these shared folders as well. Shadow copies are point-in-time backups of data files that users can access directly in shared folders. These point-in-time backups can save you and the other administrators in your organization a lot of work, especially if you routinely have to retrieve lost, overwritten, or corrupted data files from backups. The normal procedure for retrieving shadow copies is to use the Previous Versions or Shadow Copy client. Windows Server 2008 R2 includes a feature enhancement that allows you to revert an entire (nonsystem) volume to a previous shadow copy state.

Understanding Shadow Copies

You can create shadow copies only on NTFS volumes. You use the Shadow Copy feature to create automatic backups of the files in shared folders on a per-volume basis. For example, on a file server that has three NTFS volumes, each containing shared folders, you need to configure this feature for each volume separately.

If you enable this feature in its default configuration, shadow copies are created twice each weekday (Monday–Friday) at 7:00 A.M. and 12:00 P.M. You need at least 100 MB of free space to create the first shadow copy on a volume. The total disk space used beyond this depends on the amount of data in the volume's shared folders. You can restrict the total amount of disk space used by Shadow Copy by setting the allowable maximum size of the point-in-time backups.

You configure and view current Shadow Copy settings on the Shadow Copies tab of the disk's Properties dialog box. In Windows Explorer or Computer Management, right-click the icon for the disk you want to work with, click Properties, and then click the Shadow Copies tab. The Select A Volume panel shows the following:

- **Volume**   Volume label of NTFS volumes on the selected disk drive
- **Next Run Time**   The status of Shadow Copy as Disabled or the next time a shadow copy of the volume will be created
- **Shares**   Number of shared folders on the volume
- **Used**   Amount of disk space used by Shadow Copy

Individual shadow copies of the currently selected volume are listed in the Shadow Copies Of Selected Volume panel by date and time.

Creating Shadow Copies

To create a shadow copy on an NTFS volume with shared folders, follow these steps:

1. Start Computer Management. If necessary, connect to a remote computer.
2. In the console tree, expand Storage, and then select Disk Management. The volumes configured on the selected computer are displayed in the details pane.
3. Right-click Disk Management, point to All Tasks, and then click Configure Shadow Copies.
4. On the Shadow Copies tab, select the volume you want to work with in the Select A Volume list.
5. Click Settings to configure the maximum size of all shadow copies for this volume and to change the default schedule. Click OK twice.
6. After you configure the volume for shadow copying, click Enable if necessary. When prompted to confirm this action, click Yes. This creates the first shadow copy and sets the schedule for later shadow copies.

NOTE   If you create a run schedule when configuring the shadow copy settings, shadow copying is enabled automatically for the volume when you click OK to close the Settings dialog box.

Restoring a Shadow Copy

Users working on client computers access shadow copies of individual shared folders by using the Previous Versions or Shadow Copy client. The best way to access shadow copies on a client computer is to follow these steps:

1. In Windows Explorer, right-click the share for which you want to access previous file versions, click Properties, and then click the Previous Versions tab.

2. On the Previous Versions tab, select the folder version that you want to work with. Each folder has a date and time stamp. Click the button corresponding to the action you want to perform:

   ▪ Click Open to open the shadow copy in Windows Explorer.

   ▪ Click Copy to display the Copy Items dialog box, which lets you copy the snapshot image of the folder to the location you specify.

   ▪ Click Restore to roll back the shared folder to its state at the time of the snapshot image you selected.

Reverting an Entire Volume to a Previous Shadow Copy

Windows Server 2008 R2 features a shadow copy enhancement that allows you to revert an entire volume to the state it was in when a particular shadow copy was created. Because volumes containing operating system files can't be reverted, the volume you want to revert must not be a system volume.

To revert an entire volume to a previous state, follow these steps:

1. Start Computer Management. If necessary, connect to a remote computer.

2. In the console tree, expand Storage. Right-click Disk Management, point to All Tasks, and then click Configure Shadow Copies.

3. On the Shadow Copies tab, select the volume you want to work with in the Select A Volume list.

4. Individual shadow copies of the currently selected volume are listed by date and time in the Shadow Copies Of Selected Volume panel. Select the shadow copy with the date and time stamp to which you want to revert, and then click Revert.

5. To confirm this action, select the Check Here If You Want To Revert This Volume check box, and then click Revert Now. Click OK to close the Shadow Copies dialog box.

Deleting Shadow Copies

Each point-in-time backup is maintained separately. You can delete individual shadow copies of a volume as necessary. This recovers the disk space used by the shadow copies.

To delete a shadow copy, follow these steps:

1. Start Computer Management. If necessary, connect to a remote computer.

2. In the console tree, expand Storage. Right-click Disk Management, point to All Tasks, and then click Configure Shadow Copies.

3. On the Shadow Copies tab, select the volume you want to work with in the Select A Volume list.

4. Individual shadow copies of the currently selected volume are listed by date and time in the Shadow Copies Of Selected Volume panel. Select the shadow

copy you want to delete, and then click Delete Now. Click Yes to confirm the action.

Disabling Shadow Copies

If you no longer want to maintain shadow copies of a volume, you can disable the Shadow Copy feature. Disabling this feature turns off the scheduling of automated point-in-time backups and removes any existing shadow copies.

To disable shadow copies of a volume, follow these steps:

1. Start Computer Management. If necessary, connect to a remote computer.

2. In the console tree, expand Storage. Right-click Disk Management, point to All Tasks, and then click Configure Shadow Copies.

3. On the Shadow Copies tab, select the volume you want to work with in the Select A Volume list, and then click Disable.

4. When prompted, confirm the action by clicking Yes. Click OK to close the Shadow Copies dialog box.

Connecting to Network Drives

Users can connect to a network drive and to shared resources available on the network. This connection is shown as a network drive that users can access like any other drive on their systems.

NOTE When users connect to network drives, they're subject not only to the permissions set for the shared resources, but also to Windows Server 2008 R2 file and folder permissions. Differences in these permission sets are usually the reason users might not be able to access a particular file or subfolder within the network drive.

Mapping a Network Drive

In Windows Server 2008 R2, you connect to a network drive by mapping to it using NET USE and the following syntax:

```
net use DeviceName \\ComputerName\ShareName
```

DeviceName specifies the drive letter or an asterisk (*) to use the next available drive letter, and *ComputerName**ShareName* is the UNC path to the share, such as:

```
net use g: \\ROMEO\DOCS
```

or

```
net use * \\ROMEO\DOCS
```

NOTE To ensure that the mapped drive is available each time the user logs on, make the mapping persistent by adding the /Persistent:Yes option.

If the client computer is running Windows Vista or Windows 7, one way to map network drives is to follow these steps:

1. While the user is logged on, open any Windows Explorer view on the user's computer.

2. From the Tools menu, choose Map Network Drive. This opens the Map Network Drive dialog box.

3. Using the Drive list, you can now create a network drive for a shared resource. Select a free drive letter to create a network drive that can be accessed in Windows Explorer.

4. In the Folder text box, type the UNC path to the share. For example, to access a share called DOCS on a server called ROMEO, you would use the path **\\ROMEO\DOCS**. If you don't know the share location, click Browse to search for available shares. After selecting the appropriate share, click OK to close the Browse For Folder dialog box.

5. If you want the network drive to be automatically connected in subsequent sessions, select the Reconnect At Logon check box. Otherwise, clear this check box to later establish a connection whenever you double-click the network drive.

6. If you need to connect to the share using different user credentials, select the Connect Using Different Credentials check box.

7. Click Finish. If you are connecting using different credentials, enter the user name and password when prompted, and then click OK.

Disconnecting a Network Drive

To disconnect a network drive, follow these steps:

1. While the user is logged on, start Windows Explorer on the user's computer.

2. From the Tools menu, choose Disconnect Network Drive. This opens the Disconnect Network Drive dialog box.

3. Select the drive you want to disconnect, and then click OK.

Object Management, Ownership, and Inheritance

Windows Server 2008 R2 takes an object-based approach to describing resources and managing permissions. Objects that describe resources are defined on NTFS volumes and in Active Directory. With NTFS volumes, you can set permissions for files and folders. With Active Directory, you can set permissions for other types of objects, such as users, computers, and groups. You can use these permissions to control access with precision.

Objects and Object Managers

Whether defined on an NTFS volume or in Active Directory, each type of object has an object manager and primary management tools. The object manager controls object settings and permissions. The primary management tools are the tools of choice for working with the object. Objects, their managers, and management tools are summarized in Table 15-2.

TABLE 15-2 Windows Server 2008 R2 Objects

OBJECT TYPE	OBJECT MANAGER	MANAGEMENT TOOL
Files and folders	NTFS	Windows Explorer
Printers	Print spooler	Printers in Control Panel
Registry keys	Windows registry	Registry Editor
Services	Service controllers	Security Configuration Tool Set
Shares	Server service	Windows Explorer, Computer Management, Share And Storage Management

Object Ownership and Transfer

It's important to understand the concept of object ownership. In Windows Server 2008 R2, the object owner isn't necessarily the object's creator. Instead, the object owner is the person who has direct control over the object. Object owners can grant access permissions and give other users permission to take ownership of the object.

As an administrator, you can take ownership of objects on the network. This ensures that authorized administrators can't be locked out of files, folders, printers, and other resources. After you take ownership of files, however, you can't return ownership to the original owner (in most cases). This prevents administrators from accessing files and then trying to hide the fact.

The way ownership is assigned initially depends on the location of the resource being created. In most cases, the Administrators group is listed as the current owner, and the object's actual creator is listed as a person who can take ownership.

Ownership can be transferred in several ways:

- If the Administrators group is initially assigned as the owner, the creator of the object can take ownership, provided that he or she does this before someone else takes ownership.

- The current owner can grant the Take Ownership permission to other users, allowing those users to take ownership of the object.

- An administrator can take ownership of an object, provided that the object is under his or her administrative control.

To take ownership of an object, follow these steps:

1. Start the management tool for the object. For example, if you want to work with files and folders, start Windows Explorer.

2. Right-click the object you want to take ownership of, and then click Properties. In the Properties dialog box, click the Security tab.

3. Display the Advanced Security Settings dialog box by clicking Advanced.

4. On the Owner tab, click Edit to display an editable version of the Owner tab, as shown in Figure 15-10.

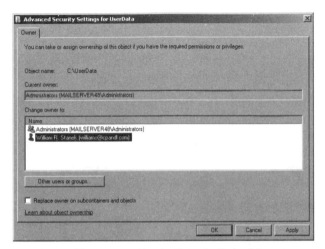

FIGURE 15-10 Change ownership of a file on the Owner tab.

5. Select the new owner in the Change Owner To list, and then click OK.

TIP If you're taking ownership of a folder, you can take ownership of all subfolders and files within the folder by selecting the Replace Owner On Subcontainers And Objects check box. This option also works with objects that contain other objects. Here, you would take ownership of all child objects.

Object Inheritance

Objects are defined using a parent-child structure. A parent object is a top-level object. A child object is an object defined below a parent object in the hierarchy. For example, the folder C:\ is the parent of the folders C:\Data and C:\Backups. Any subfolders created in C:\Data or C:\Backups are children of these folders and grandchildren of C:\.

Child objects can inherit permissions from parent objects. In fact, all Windows Server 2008 R2 objects are created with inheritance enabled by default. This means that child objects automatically inherit the permissions of the parent. Because of this, the parent object permissions control access to the child object. If you want to change permissions on a child object, you must do the following:

1. Edit the permissions of the parent object.

2. Stop inheriting permissions from the parent object, and then assign permissions to the child object.

3. Select the opposite permission to override the inherited permission. For example, if the parent allows the permission, you would deny it on the child object.

To start or stop inheriting permissions from a parent object, follow these steps:

1. Start the management tool for the object. For example, if you want to work with files and folders, start Windows Explorer.

2. Right-click the object you want to work with, and then click Properties. In the Properties dialog box, click the Security tab.

3. Click Advanced to display the Advanced Security Settings dialog box.

4. On the Permissions tab, click Change Permissions to display an editable version of the Permissions tab.

5. Select or clear the Include Inheritable Permissions From This Object's Parent check box. Click OK.

File and Folder Permissions

On NTFS volumes, you can set security permissions on files and folders. These permissions grant or deny access to the files and folders. You can view security permissions for files and folders by following these steps:

1. In Windows Explorer, right-click the file or folder you want to work with, and then click Properties. In the Properties dialog box, click the Security tab.

2. In the Group Or User Names list, select the user, computer, or group whose permissions you want to view. If the permissions are not available (dimmed), the permissions are inherited from a parent object.

Understanding File and Folder Permissions

The basic permissions you can assign to files and folders are summarized in Table 15-3. File permissions include Full Control, Modify, Read & Execute, Read, and Write. Folder permissions include Full Control, Modify, Read & Execute, List Folder Contents, Read, and Write.

TABLE 15-3 File and Folder Permissions Used by Windows Server 2008 R2

PERMISSION	MEANING FOR FOLDERS	MEANING FOR FILES
Read	Permits viewing and listing files and subfolders	Permits viewing or accessing a file's contents
Write	Permits adding files and subfolders	Permits writing to a file
Read & Execute	Permits viewing and listing files and subfolders as well as executing files; inherited by files and folders	Permits viewing and accessing a file's contents as well as executing a file
List Folder Contents	Permits viewing and listing files and subfolders as well as executing files; inherited by folders only	N/A
Modify	Permits reading and writing of files and subfolders; allows deletion of the folder	Permits reading and writing of a file; allows deletion of a file
Full Control	Permits reading, writing, changing, and deleting files and subfolders	Permits reading, writing, changing, and deleting a file

Any time you work with file and folder permissions, you should keep the following in mind:

- Read is the only permission needed to run scripts. Execute permission doesn't matter.

- Read access is required to access a shortcut and its target.

- Giving a user permission to write to a file but not to delete it doesn't prevent the user from deleting the file's contents. A user can still delete the contents.

- If a user has full control over a folder, the user can delete files in the folder regardless of the permission on the files.

The basic permissions are created by combining special permissions in logical groups. Table 15-4 shows special permissions used to create the basic permissions for files. Using advanced permission settings, you can assign these special permissions individually, if necessary. As you study the special permissions, keep the following in mind:

- By default, if no access is specifically granted or denied, the user is denied access.

- Actions that users can perform are based on the sum of all the permissions assigned to the user and to all the groups the user is a member of. For example, if the user GeorgeJ has Read access and is a member of the group Techies, which has Change access, GeorgeJ will have Change access. If Techies is a member of Administrators, which has Full Control, GeorgeJ will have complete control over the file.

TABLE 15-4 Special Permissions for Files

SPECIAL PERMISSIONS	BASIC PERMISSIONS				
	FULL CONTROL	MODIFY	READ & EXECUTE	READ	WRITE
Traverse Folder/ Execute File	Yes	Yes	Yes		
List Folder/Read Data	Yes	Yes	Yes	Yes	
Read Attributes	Yes	Yes	Yes	Yes	
Read Extended Attributes	Yes	Yes	Yes	Yes	
Create Files/Write Data	Yes	Yes			Yes
Create Folders/ Append Data	Yes	Yes			Yes
Write Attributes	Yes	Yes			Yes
Write Extended Attributes	Yes	Yes			Yes
Delete Subfolders and Files	Yes				
Delete	Yes	Yes			
Read Permissions	Yes	Yes	Yes	Yes	Yes
Change Permissions	Yes				
Take Ownership	Yes				

Table 15-5 shows special permissions used to create the basic permissions for folders. As you study the special permissions, keep the following in mind:

- When you set permissions for parent folders, you can force all files and sub-folders within the folder to inherit the permissions. You do this by selecting Replace All Child Object Permissions With Inheritable Permissions From This Object.

- When you create files in folders, these files inherit certain permission settings. These permission settings are shown as the default file permissions.

TABLE 15-5 Special Permissions for Folders

SPECIAL PERMISSIONS	BASIC PERMISSIONS					
	FULL CONTROL	MODIFY	READ & EXECUTE	LIST FOLDER CONTENTS	READ	WRITE
Traverse Folder/ Execute File	Yes	Yes	Yes	Yes		
List Folder/Read Data	Yes	Yes	Yes	Yes	Yes	
Read Attributes	Yes	Yes	Yes	Yes	Yes	
Read Extended Attributes	Yes	Yes	Yes	Yes	Yes	
Create Files/Write Data	Yes	Yes				Yes
Create Folders/ Append Data	Yes	Yes				Yes
Write Attributes	Yes	Yes				Yes
Write Extended Attributes	Yes	Yes				Yes
Delete Subfolders And Files	Yes					
Delete	Yes	Yes				
Read Permissions	Yes	Yes	Yes	Yes	Yes	Yes
Change Permissions	Yes					
Take Ownership	Yes					

Setting File and Folder Permissions

To set permissions for files and folders, follow these steps:

1. In Windows Explorer, right-click the file or folder you want to work with, and then click Properties. In the Properties dialog box, click the Security tab.

2. Click Edit to display an editable version of the Security tab, as shown in Figure 15-11.

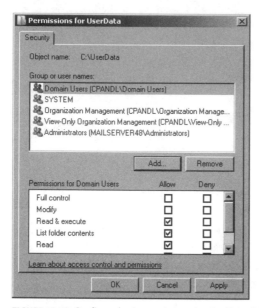

FIGURE 15-11 Configure basic permissions for the file or folder on the Security tab.

3. Users or groups that already have access to the file or folder are listed in the Group Or User Names list. You can change permissions for these users and groups by doing the following:

   a. Select the user or group you want to change.

   b. Grant or deny access permissions in the Permissions list box.

   TIP Inherited permissions are shaded. If you want to override an inherited permission, select the opposite permission.

4. To set access permissions for additional users, computers, or groups, click Add. This displays the Select Users, Computers, Service Accounts, Or Groups dialog box, shown in Figure 15-12.

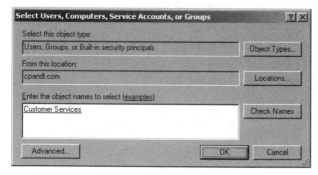

FIGURE 15-12 In the Select Users, Computers, Service Accounts, Or Groups dialog box, select accounts that should be granted or denied access.

5. Type the name of a user, computer, or group in the current domain, and then click Check Names.

- If a single match is found, the dialog box is updated and the entry is underlined.

- If no matches are found, you entered an incorrect name part or are working with an incorrect location. Modify the name and try again, or click Locations to select a new location.

- If multiple matches are found, select the name or names you want to use, and then click OK. To add more users, computers, or groups, type a semicolon (;), and then repeat this step.

NOTE The Locations button allows you to access account names in other domains. Click Locations to see a list of the current domain, trusted domains, and other resources that you can access. Because of the transitive trusts in Windows Server 2008 R2, you can usually access all the domains in the domain tree or forest.

6. In the Group Or User Names list, select the user, computer, or group you want to configure, and in the check boxes in the Permissions list, allow or deny permissions. Repeat for other users, computers, or groups.

7. Click OK.

Auditing System Resources

Auditing is the best way to track what's happening on your Windows Server 2008 R2 systems. You can use auditing to collect information related to resource usage such as file access, system logons, and system configuration changes. Any time an action occurs that you've configured for auditing, the action is written to the system's security log, where it's stored for your review. The security log is accessible from Event Viewer.

NOTE For most auditing changes, you need to be logged on using an account that's a member of the Administrators group or be granted the Manage Auditing And Security Log right in Group Policy.

Setting Auditing Policies

Auditing policies are essential to ensure the security and integrity of your systems. Just about every computer system on the network should be configured with some type of security logging. You configure auditing policies for individual computers with local Group Policy and for all computers in domains with Active Directory–based Group Policy. Through Group Policy, you can set auditing policies for an entire site, a domain, or an organizational unit. You can also set policies for an individual workstation or server.

After you access the Group Policy object (GPO) you want to work with, you can set auditing policies by following these steps:

1. In the Group Policy Management Editor, shown in Figure 15-13, access the Audit Policy node by working your way down the console tree. Expand Computer Configuration, Windows Settings, Security Settings, and Local Policies, and then select Audit Policy.

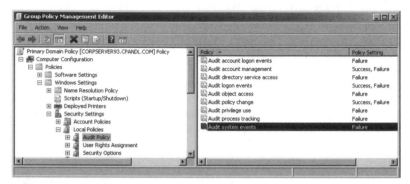

FIGURE 15-13 Set auditing policies using the Audit Policy node in Group Policy.

2. The auditing options are as follows:

- **Audit Account Logon Events**   Tracks events related to user logon and logoff.

- **Audit Account Management**   Tracks account management by means of Active Directory Users And Computers. Events are generated any time user, computer, or group accounts are created, modified, or deleted.

- **Audit Directory Service Access**   Tracks access to Active Directory. Events are generated any time users or computers access the directory.

- **Audit Logon Events**   Tracks events related to user logon, logoff, and remote connections to network systems.

- **Audit Object Access**   Tracks system resource usage for files, directories, shares, printers, and Active Directory objects.

- **Audit Policy Change**   Tracks changes to user rights, auditing, and trust relationships.

- **Audit Privilege Use**   Tracks the use of user rights and privileges, such as the right to back up files and directories.

NOTE   The Audit Privilege Use policy doesn't track system access-related events, such as the use of the right to log on interactively or the right to access the computer from the network. You track these events with logon and logoff auditing.

- **Audit Process Tracking** Tracks system processes and the resources they use.

- **Audit System Events** Tracks system startup, shutdown, and restart, as well as actions that affect system security or the security log.

3. To configure an auditing policy, double-click its entry, or right-click the entry, and then click Properties.

4. In the dialog box that is displayed, select the Define These Policy Settings check box, and then select either the Success check box, the Failure check box, or both. Success logs successful events, such as successful logon attempts. Failure logs failed events, such as failed logon attempts.

5. Click OK.

When auditing is enabled, the security event log will reflect the following:

- Event ID of 560 and 562 detailing user audits
- Event ID of 592 and 593 detailing process audits

Auditing Files and Folders

If you configure a GPO to enable the Audit Object Access option, you can set the level of auditing for individual folders and files. This allows you to control precisely how folder and file usage is tracked. Auditing of this type is available only on NTFS volumes.

You can configure file and folder auditing by following these steps:

1. In Windows Explorer, right-click the file or folder to be audited, and then click Properties.

2. Click the Security tab, and then click Advanced. This displays the Advanced Security Settings For dialog box.

3. On the Auditing tab, click Edit. You can now view and manage auditing settings by using the options shown in Figure 15-14.

4. If you want to inherit auditing settings from a parent object, ensure that the Include Inheritable Auditing Entries From This Object's Parent check box is selected.

5. If you want child objects of the current object to inherit the settings, select the Replace All Existing Inheritable Auditing Entries check box.

6. In the Auditing Entries list, select the users, groups, or computers whose actions you want to audit. To remove an account, select the account in the Auditing Entries list, and then click Remove.

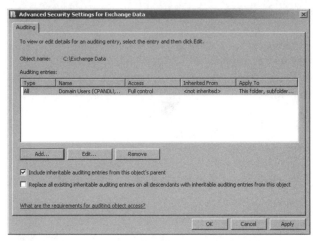

FIGURE 15-14 After you audit object access, you can set auditing policies on individual files and folders on the Auditing tab.

7. To add specific accounts, click Add. In the Select User, Computer, Service Account, Or Group dialog box, select an account name to add. When you click OK, you'll see the Auditing Entry For dialog box, shown in Figure 15-15.

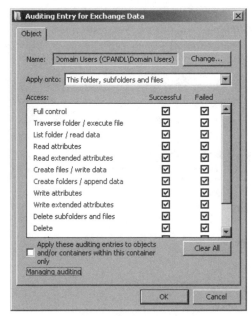

FIGURE 15-15 In the Auditing Entry For dialog box, set auditing entries for a user, computer, or group.

8. As necessary, use the Apply Onto list to specify where objects are audited.

9. Select the Successful check box, the Failed check box, or both for each of the events you want to audit. Successful logs successful events, such as successful file reads. Failed logs failed events, such as failed file deletions. The events you can audit are the same as the special permissions listed in Table 15-5, except that you can't audit the synchronizing of offline files and folders. For essential files and folders, you'll typically want to track the following:

   - Write Attributes—Successful

   - Write Extended Attributes—Successful

   - Delete Subfolders and Files—Successful

   - Delete—Successful

   - Change Permissions—Successful

10. Click OK. Repeat this process to audit other users, groups, or computers.

Auditing the Registry

If you configure a GPO to enable the Audit Object Access option, you can set the level of auditing for keys within the registry. This allows you to track when key values are set, when subkeys are created, and when keys are deleted.

You can configure registry auditing by following these steps:

1. At a command prompt, type **regedit**.

2. Browse to a key you want to audit. On the Edit menu, select Permissions.

3. In the Permissions For dialog box, click Advanced. In the Advanced Security Settings For dialog box, click the Auditing tab.

4. Click Add. In the Select User, Computer, Service Account, Or Group dialog box, type **Everyone**, click Check Names, and then click OK.

5. In the Auditing Entry For dialog box, choose the actions you want to audit. Typically, you'll want to track the following:

   - Set Value—Successful and Failed

   - Create Subkey—Successful and Failed

   - Delete—Successful and Failed

6. Click OK three times to close all open dialog boxes and apply the auditing settings.

Auditing Active Directory Objects

If you configure a GPO to enable the Audit Directory Service Access option, you can set the level of auditing for Active Directory objects. This allows you to control precisely how object usage is tracked.

To configure object auditing, follow these steps:

1. In Active Directory Users And Computers, ensure that Advanced Features is selected on the View menu, and then access the container for the object.

2. Right-click the object to be audited, and then click Properties.

3. Click the Security tab, and then click Advanced.

4. In the Advanced Settings For dialog box, click the Auditing tab. To inherit auditing settings from a parent object, make sure that the Include Inheritable Auditing Entries From This Object's Parent check box is selected.

5. In the Auditing Entries list, select the users, groups, or computers whose actions you want to audit. To remove an account, select the account in the Auditing Entries list, and then click Remove.

6. To add specific accounts, click Add, and then select an account name to add in the Select User, Computer, Service Account, Or Group dialog box. When you click OK, the Auditing Entry For dialog box is displayed.

7. In the Apply Onto list, specify where objects are audited.

8. Select the Successful check box, the Failed check box, or both for each of the events you want to audit. Successful logs successful events, such as a successful attempt to modify an object's permissions. Failed logs failed events, such as a failed attempt to modify an object's owner.

9. Click OK. Repeat this process to audit other users, groups, or computers.

Using, Configuring, and Managing NTFS Disk Quotas

Windows Server 2008 R2 supports two mutually exclusive types of disk quotas:

- **NTFS disk quotas**   NTFS disk quotas are supported on all editions of Windows Server 2008 R2 and allow you to manage disk space usage by users. You configure quotas on a per-volume basis. Although users who exceed limits see warnings, administrators are notified primarily through the event logs.

- **Resource Manager disk quotas**   Resource Manager disk quotas are supported on all editions of Windows Server 2008 R2 and allow you to manage disk space usage by folder and by volume. Users who are approaching or have exceeded a limit can be automatically notified by e-mail. The notification system also allows for notifying administrators by e-mail, triggering incident reporting, running commands, and logging related events.

The sections that follow discuss NTFS disk quotas.

NOTE Regardless of the quota system being used, you can configure quotas only for NTFS volumes. You can't create quotas for FAT or FAT32 volumes.

REAL WORLD When you apply disk quotas, you need to be particularly careful in the way you enforce quotas, especially with respect to system accounts, service accounts, or other special purpose accounts. Improper application of disk quotas to these types of accounts can cause serious problems that are difficult to diagnose and resolve. Enforcing quotas on the System, NetworkService, and LocalService accounts could prevent the computer from completing important operating system tasks. As an example, if these accounts reach their enforced quota limit, you would be unable to apply changes to Group Policy because the Group Policy client runs within a LocalSystem context by default and would not be able to write to the system disk. If the service can't write to the system disk, Group Policy changes cannot be made, and being unable to change Group Policy could have all sorts of unexpected consequences because you would be stuck with the previously configured settings. You would be unable to disable or modify the quota settings through Group Policy, for example.

In this scenario, where service contexts have reached an enforced quota limit, any other configuration settings that use these service contexts and require making changes to files on disk would likely also fail. For example, you would be unable to complete the installation or removal of roles, role services, and features. This would leave the server in a state in which Server Manager always includes a warning that you need to restart the computer to complete configuration tasks, but restarting the computer would not resolve these issues.

To address this problem, you need to edit the disk quota entries for the system disk, raise the enforced limits on the service accounts, and then restart the computer. Restarting the computer triggers the finalization tasks and allows the computer to complete any configuration tasks stuck in a pending status. Because the Group Policy client service could process changes and write them to the system disk, changes to Group Policy would then be applied as well.

Understanding NTFS Disk Quotas and How NTFS Quotas Are Used

Administrators use NTFS disk quotas to manage disk space usage for critical volumes, such as those that provide corporate data shares or user data shares. When you enable NTFS disk quotas, you can configure two values:

- **Disk quota limit** Sets the upper boundary for space usage, which you can use to prevent users from writing additional information to a volume, to log events regarding the user exceeding the limit, or both.

- **Disk quota warning** Warns users and logs warning events when users are getting close to their disk quota limit.

TIP You can set disk quotas but not enforce them, and you might be wondering why you'd do this. Sometimes you want to track disk space usage on a per-user basis and know when users have exceeded some predefined limit, but instead of denying them additional disk space, you log an event in the application log to track the overage. You can then send out warning messages or figure out other ways to reduce the space usage.

NTFS disk quotas apply only to end users. NTFS disk quotas don't apply to administrators. Administrators can't be denied disk space even if they exceed enforced disk quota limits.

In a typical environment, you would restrict disk space usage in megabytes (MB) or gigabytes (GB). For example, on a corporate data share used by multiple users in a department, you might want to limit disk space usage to 20 to 100 GB. For a user data share, you might want to set the level much lower, such as 5 to 20 GB, which would restrict the user from creating large amounts of personal data. Often you'll set the disk quota warning as a percentage of the disk quota limit. For example, you might set the warning to 90 to 95 percent of the disk quota limit.

Because NTFS disk quotas are tracked on a per-volume, per-user basis, disk space used by one user doesn't affect the disk quotas for other users. Thus, if one user exceeds his or her limit, any restrictions applied to this user don't apply to other users. For example, if a user exceeds a 1 GB disk quota limit and the volume is configured to prevent writing over the limit, the user can no longer write data to the volume. Users can, however, remove files and folders from the volume to free up disk space. They can also move files and folders to a compressed area on the volume, which might free up space, or they could elect to compress the files themselves. Moving files to a different location on the volume doesn't affect the quota restriction. The amount of file space is the same unless the user moves uncompressed files and folders to a folder with compression. In any case, the restriction on a single user doesn't affect other users' ability to write to the volume (as long as there's free space on the volume).

You can enable NTFS disk quotas on the following:

- **Local volumes** To manage disk quotas on local volumes, you work with the local disk itself. When you enable disk quotas on a local volume, the Windows system files are included in the volume usage for the user who installed those files. Sometimes this might cause the user to go over the disk quota limit. To prevent this, you might want to set a higher limit on a local workstation volume.

- **Remote volumes** To manage disk quotas on remote volumes, you must share the root directory for the volume and then set the disk quota on the volume. Remember, you set quotas on a per-volume basis, so if a remote file server has separate volumes for different types of data—that is, a corporate data volume and a user data volume—these volumes have different quotas.

Only members of the Domain Admins group or the local system Administrators group can configure disk quotas. The first step in using quotas is to enable quotas in Group Policy. You can do this at two levels:

- **Local** Through local Group Policy you can enable disk quotas for an individual computer.

- **Enterprise** Through Group Policy that applies to a site, a domain, or an organizational unit, you can enable disk quotas for groups of users and computers.

Having to keep track of disk quotas does cause some overhead on computers. This overhead is a function of the number of disk quotas being enforced, the total size of the volumes and their data, and the number of users to which the disk quotas apply.

Although on the surface disk quotas are tracked per user, behind the scenes Windows Server 2008 R2 manages disk quotas according to security identifiers (SIDs). Because SIDs track disk quotas, you can safely modify user names without affecting the disk quota configuration. Tracking by SIDs does cause some additional overhead when viewing disk quota statistics for users. That's because Windows Server 2008 R2 must correlate SIDs to user account names so that the account names can be displayed in dialog boxes. This means contacting the local user manager and the Active Directory domain controller as necessary.

After Windows Server 2008 R2 looks up names, it caches them to a local file so that they can be available immediately the next time they're needed. The query cache is infrequently updated—if you notice a discrepancy between what's displayed and what's configured, you need to refresh the information. Usually, this means choosing Refresh from the View menu or pressing F5 in the current window.

Setting NTFS Disk Quota Policies

The best way to configure NTFS disk quotas is through Group Policy. When you configure disk quotas through local policy or through unit, domain, and site policy, you define general policies that are set automatically when you enable quota management on individual volumes. Thus, rather than having to configure each volume separately, you can use the same set of rules and apply them in turn to each volume you want to manage.

Policies that control NTFS disk quotas are applied at the system level. You access these policies through Computer Configuration\Administrative Templates\System\ Disk Quotas. Table 15-6 summarizes the available policies.

TABLE 15-6 Policies for Setting NTFS Disk Quotas

POLICY NAME	DESCRIPTION
Enable Disk Quotas	Turns disk quotas on or off for all NTFS volumes of the computer and prevents users from changing the setting.
Enforce Disk Quota Limit	Specifies whether quota limits are enforced. If quotas are enforced, users will be denied disk space if they exceed the quota. This overrides settings on the Quota tab on the NTFS volume.
Default Quota Limit And Warning Level	Sets a default quota limit and warning level for all users. This setting overrides other settings and affects only new users.
Log Event When Quota Limit Exceeded	Determines whether an event is logged when users reach their limit and prevents users from changing their logging options.
Log Event When Quota Warning Level Exceeded	Determines whether an event is logged when users reach the warning level.
Apply Policy To Removable Media	Determines whether quota policies apply to NTFS volumes on removable media. If you don't enable this policy, quota limits apply only to fixed media drives.

Whenever you work with quota limits, you should use a standard set of policies on all systems. Typically, you won't want to enable all the policies. Instead, you'll selectively enable policies and then use the standard NTFS features to control quotas on various volumes. If you want to enable quota limits, follow these steps:

1. Access Group Policy for the system (for example, a file server) that you want to work with. Access the Disk Quotas node by expanding Computer Configuration, Administrative Templates, System and then selecting Disk Quotas.

2. Double-click Enable Disk Quotas. Select Enabled, and then click OK.

3. Double-click Enforce Disk Quota Limit. If you want to enforce disk quotas on all NTFS volumes residing on this computer, click Enabled. Otherwise, click Disabled, and then set specific limits on a per-volume basis. Click OK.

4. Double-click Default Quota Limit And Warning Level. In the dialog box shown in Figure 15-16 select Enabled.

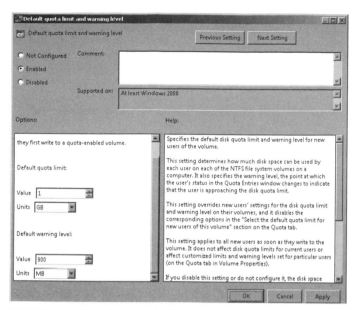

FIGURE 15-16 Enforce disk quotas in the Default Quota Limit And Warning Level dialog box.

5. Under Default Quota Limit, set a default limit that's applied to users when they first write to the quota-enabled volume. The limit doesn't apply to current users or affect current limits in place. On a corporate share, such as a share used by members of a project team, a good limit is between 500 and 1,000 MB. Of course, this depends on the size of the data files that the users routinely work with, the number of users, and the size of the disk volume. Graphic designers and data engineers might need much more disk space.

6. To set a warning limit, scroll down in the Options window. A good warning limit is about 90 percent of the default quota limit, which means that if you set the default quota limit to 1,000 MB, you'd set the warning limit to 900 MB. Click OK.

7. Double-click Log Event When Quota Limit Exceeded. Select Enabled so that limit events are recorded in the application log, and then click OK.

8. Double-click Log Event When Quota Warning Level Exceeded. Select Enabled so that warning events are recorded in the application log, and then click OK.

9. Double-click Apply Policy To Removable Media. Select Disabled so that the quota limits apply only to fixed media volumes on the computer, and then click OK.

TIP To ensure that the policies are enforced immediately, access the Computer Configuration\Administrative Templates\System\Group Policy node, and then double-click Disk Quota Policy Processing. Select Enabled, and then select the Process Even If The Group Policy Objects Have Not Changed check box. Click OK.

Enabling NTFS Disk Quotas on NTFS Volumes

You can set NTFS disk quotas on a per-volume basis. Only NTFS volumes can have disk quotas. After you've configured the appropriate group policies, you can use Computer Management to set disk quotas for local and remote volumes.

NOTE If you use the Enforce Disk Quota Limit policy setting to enforce quotas, users are denied disk space if they exceed the quota. This overrides settings on the Quota tab on the NTFS volume.

To enable NTFS disk quotas on an NTFS volume, follow these steps:

1. Start Computer Management. If necessary, connect to a remote computer.

2. In the console tree, expand Storage, and then select Disk Management. The volumes configured on the selected computer are displayed in the details pane.

3. Using Volume List view or Graphical View, right-click the volume you want to work with, and then click Properties.

4. On the Quota tab, select the Enable Quota Management check box, shown in Figure 15-17. If you've already set quota management values through Group Policy, the options are unavailable, and you can't change them. You must modify options through Group Policy instead.

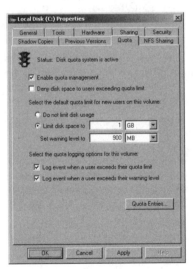

FIGURE 15-17 After you enable quota management, you can configure a quota limit and quota warning for all users.

Whenever you work with the Quota tab, pay particular attention to the Status text and the associated traffic light icon. Both change based on the state of quota management. If quotas aren't configured, the traffic light icon shows a red light and the status is inactive or not configured. If the operating system is working or updating the quotas, the traffic light icon shows a yellow light and the status shows the activity being performed. If quotas are configured, the traffic light icon shows a green light and the status text states that the quota system is active.

5. To set a default disk quota limit for all users, select Limit Disk Space To. In the text boxes provided, set a limit in kilobytes, megabytes, gigabytes, terabytes, petabytes, or exabytes. Then set the default warning limit in the Set Warning Level To text boxes. Again, you'll usually want the disk quota warning limit to be 90–95 percent of the disk quota limit.

TIP Although the default quota limit and warning apply to all users, you can configure different levels for individual users. You do this in the Quota Entries dialog box. If you create many unique quota entries and don't want to re-create them on a volume with similar characteristics and usage, you can export the quota entries and import them into a different volume.

6. To enforce the disk quota limit and prevent users from going over the limit, select the Deny Disk Space To Users Exceeding Quota Limit check box. Keep in mind that this creates an actual physical limitation for users (but not for administrators).

7. To configure logging when users exceed a warning limit or the quota limit, select the Log Event check boxes. Click OK to save your changes.

8. If the quota system isn't currently enabled, you'll see a prompt asking you to enable the quota system. Click OK to allow Windows Server 2008 R2 to rescan the volume and update disk usage statistics. Actions might be taken against users who exceed the current limit or warning levels. These actions can include preventing additional writing to the volume, notifying them the next time they access the volume, and logging applicable events to the application log.

Viewing Disk Quota Entries

Disk space usage is tracked on a per-user basis. When disk quotas are enabled, each user storing data on a volume has an entry in the disk quota file. This entry is updated periodically to show the current disk space used, the applicable quota limit, the applicable warning level, and the percentage of allowable space being used. As an administrator, you can modify disk quota entries to set different limits and warning levels for particular users. You can also create disk quota entries for users who haven't yet saved data on a volume. The key reason for creating entries is to ensure that when a user does make use of a volume, the user has an appropriate limit and warning level.

To view the current disk quota entries for a volume, follow these steps:

1. Start Computer Management. If necessary, connect to a remote computer.

2. In the console tree, expand Storage and then select Disk Management. The volumes configured on the selected computer are displayed in the details pane.

3. Using Volume List view or Graphical View, right-click the volume you want to work with, and then click Properties.

4. On the Quota tab, click Quota Entries. This displays the Quota Entries dialog box. Each quota entry is listed according to a status. The status is meant to quickly depict whether a user has gone over a limit. A status of OK means the user is working within the quota boundaries. Any other status usually means the user has reached the warning level or the quota limit.

Creating Disk Quota Entries

You can create disk quota entries for users who haven't yet saved data on a volume. This allows you to set custom limits and warning levels for a particular user. You usually use this feature when a user frequently stores more information than other users and you want to allow the user to go over the normal limit or when you want to set a specific limit for administrators. As you might recall, administrators aren't subject to disk quota limits, so if you want to enforce limits for individual administrators, you must create disk quota entries for each administrator you want to limit.

REAL WORLD You shouldn't create individual disk quota entries haphazardly. You need to track individual entries carefully. Ideally, you should keep a log that details any individual entries so that other administrators understand the policies in place and how those policies are applied. When you modify the base rules for quotas on a volume, you should reexamine individual entries to see whether they're still applicable or need to be updated as well. I've found that certain types of users are exceptions more often than not and that it's sometimes better to put different classes of users on different volumes and then apply disk quotas to each volume. In this way, each class or category of user has a quota limit that's appropriate for its members' typical usage, and you have fewer (perhaps no) exceptions. For example, you might use separate volumes for executives, managers, and standard users, or you might have separate volumes for management, graphic designers, engineers, and all other users.

To create a quota entry on a volume, follow these steps:

1. Open the Quota Entries dialog box as discussed in "Viewing Disk Quota Entries" earlier in this chapter. Current quota entries for all users are listed. To refresh the listing, press F5 or choose Refresh from the View menu.

2. If the user doesn't have an existing entry on the volume, you can create it by choosing New Quota Entry from the Quota menu. This opens the Select Users dialog box.

3. In the Select Users dialog box, type the name of a user you want to use in the Enter The Object Names To Select text box, and then click Check Names. If a match is found, select the account you want to use, and then click OK. If no matches are found, update the name you entered and try searching again. Repeat this step as necessary, and then click OK.

4. After you've selected a user, the Add New Quota Entry dialog box is displayed, as shown in Figure 15-18. You have two options. You can remove all quota restrictions for this user by selecting Do Not Limit Disk Usage, or you can set a specific limit and warning level by selecting Limit Disk Space To and then entering the appropriate values in the fields provided. Click OK.

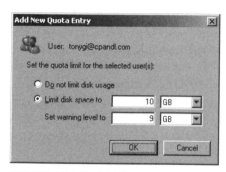

FIGURE 15-18 In the Add New Quota Entry dialog box, you can customize the user's quota limit and warning level or remove quota restrictions altogether.

Deleting Disk Quota Entries

When you've created disk quota entries on a volume and a user no longer needs to use the volume, you can delete the associated disk quota entry. When you delete a disk quota entry, all files owned by the user are collected and displayed in a dialog box so that you can permanently delete the files, take ownership of the files, or move the files to a folder on a different volume.

To delete a disk quota entry for a user and manage the user's remaining files on the volume, follow these steps:

1. Open the Quota Entries dialog box as discussed in "Viewing Disk Quota Entries" earlier in this chapter. Current quota entries for all users are listed. To refresh the listing, press F5 or choose Refresh from the View menu.

2. Select the disk quota entry that you want to delete, and then press Delete, or choose Delete Quota Entry from the Quota menu. You can select multiple entries using the Shift and Ctrl keys.

3. When prompted to confirm the action, click Yes. This displays the Disk Quota dialog box with a list of current files owned by the selected user or users.

4. In the List Files Owned By list, display files for a user whose quota entry you're deleting. You must now specify how the files for the user are to be

handled. You can handle each file separately by selecting individual files and then choosing an appropriate option. You can select multiple files by using the Shift and Ctrl keys. The following options are available:

- **Permanently Delete Files**   Select the files to delete, and then press Delete. When prompted to confirm the action, click Yes.

- **Take Ownership Of Files**   Select the files that you want to take ownership of, and then click Take Ownership Of Files.

- **Move Files To**   Select the files that you want to move, and then enter the path to a folder on a different volume in the field provided. If you don't know the path that you want to use, click Browse to display the Browse For Folder dialog box. Once you find the folder, click Move.

5. Click Close when you have finished managing the files. If you've appropriately handled all user files, the disk quota entries will be deleted.

Exporting and Importing NTFS Disk Quota Settings

Rather than re-creating custom disk quota entries on individual volumes, you can export the settings from a source volume and then import the settings onto another volume. You must format both volumes using NTFS. To export and then import disk quota entries, follow these steps:

1. Open the Quota Entries dialog box as discussed in "Viewing Disk Quota Entries" earlier in this chapter. Current quota entries for all users are listed. To refresh the listing, press F5 or choose Refresh from the View menu.

2. Select Export from the Quota menu. This displays the Export Quota Settings dialog box. Choose the save location for the file containing the quota settings, and then set a name for the file in the File Name text box. Click Save.

   NOTE   If you save the settings file to a mapped drive on the target volume, you'll have an easier time importing the settings. Quota files are usually fairly small, so you don't need to worry about disk space usage.

3. On the Quota menu, click Close to exit the Quota Entries dialog box.

4. Right-click Computer Management in the console tree, and then click Connect To Another Computer. In the Select Computer dialog box, choose the computer containing the target volume. The target volume is the one on which you want to use the exported settings.

5. As explained previously, open the Properties dialog box for the target volume. Then click Quota Entries on the Quota tab. This displays the Quota Entries dialog box for the target volume.

6. Click Import on the Quota menu. In the Import Quota Settings dialog box, select the quota settings file that you saved previously. Click Open.

7. If the volume had previous quota entries, you are given the choice to replace existing entries or keep existing entries. When prompted about a conflict, click

Yes to replace an existing entry or click No to keep the existing entry. To apply the option to replace or keep existing entries to all entries on the volume, select the Do This For All Quota Entries check box prior to clicking Yes or No.

Disabling NTFS Disk Quotas

You can disable quotas for individual users or all users on a volume. When you disable quotas for a particular user, the user is no longer subject to the quota restrictions but disk quotas are still tracked for other users. When you disable quotas on a volume, quota tracking and management are completely removed. To disable quotas for a particular user, follow the technique outlined earlier in the chapter in "Viewing Disk Quota Entries." To disable quota tracking and management on a volume, follow these steps:

1. Start Computer Management. If necessary, connect to a remote computer.

2. Open the Properties dialog box for the volume on which you want to disable NTFS quotas.

3. On the Quota tab, clear the Enable Quota Management check box. Click OK. When prompted to confirm, click OK.

Using, Configuring, and Managing Resource Manager Disk Quotas

Windows Server 2008 R2 supports an enhanced quota management system called *Resource Manager disk quotas*. Using Resource Manager disk quotas, you can manage disk space usage by folder and by volume.

TIP Because you manage Resource Manager disk quotas separately from NTFS disk quotas, you can configure a single volume to use both quota systems. However, it's recommended that you use one quota system or the other. Alternatively, if you've already configured NTFS disk quotas, you might want to continue using NTFS disk quotas on a per-volume basis and supplement this quota management with Resource Manager disk quotas for important folders.

Understanding Resource Manager Disk Quotas

When you're working with Windows Server 2008 R2, Resource Manager disk quotas are another tool you can use to manage disk usage. You can configure Resource Manager disk quotas on a per-volume basis and on a per-folder basis. You can set disk quotas with a specific hard limit—meaning a limit can't be exceeded—or a soft limit, meaning a limit can be exceeded.

Generally, you should use hard limits when you want to prevent users from exceeding a specific disk usage limitation. Use soft limits when you want to monitor usage and simply warn users who exceed or are about to exceed usage guidelines.

All quotas have a quota path, which designates the base file path on the volume or folder to which the quota is applied. The quota applies to the designated volume or folder and all subfolders of the designated volume or folder. The particulars of how quotas work and how users are limited or warned are derived from a source template that defines the quota properties.

Windows Server 2008 R2 includes the quota templates listed in Table 15-7. Using the File Server Resource Manager, you can easily define additional templates that would then be available whenever you define quotas, or you can set single-use custom quota properties when defining a quota.

TABLE 15-7 Disk Quota Templates

QUOTA TEMPLATE	LIMIT	QUOTA TYPE	DESCRIPTION
100 MB Limit	100 MB	Hard	Sends warnings to users as the limit is approached and exceeded
200 MB Limit Reports To User	200 MB	Hard	Sends storage reports to the users who exceed the threshold
200 MB Limit With 50 MB Extension	200 MB	Hard	Uses the DIRQUOTA command to grant an automatic, one-time, 50-MB extension to users who exceed the quota limit
250 MB Extended Limit	250 MB	Hard	Meant to be used by those whose limit has been extended from 200 MB to 250 MB
Monitor 200 GB Volume Usage	200 GB	Soft	Monitors volume usage and warns when the limit is approached and exceeded
Monitor 500 MB Share	500 MB	Soft	Monitors share usage and warns when the limit is approached and exceeded

Quota templates or custom properties define the following:

- **Limit**   The disk space usage limit
- **Quota type**   Hard or soft
- **Notification thresholds**   The types of notification that occur when usage reaches a specific percentage of the limit

Although each quota has a specific limit and type, you can define multiple notification thresholds as either a warning threshold or a limit threshold. Warning thresholds are considered to be any percentage of the limit that is less than 100 percent. Limit thresholds occur when the limit reached is 100 percent. For example, you could define warning thresholds that are triggered at 85 percent and 95 percent of the limit and a limit threshold that is triggered when 100 percent of the limit is reached.

Users who are approaching or have exceeded a limit can be automatically notified by e-mail. The notification system also allows for notifying administrators by e-mail, triggering incident reporting, running commands, and logging related events.

Managing Disk Quota Templates

You use disk quota templates to define quota properties, including the limit, quota type, and notification thresholds. In File Server Resource Manager, you can view the currently defined disk quota templates by expanding the Quota Management node and then selecting Quota Templates. Table 15-7, shown earlier, provides a summary of the default disk quota templates.

You can modify existing disk quota templates by following these steps:

1. In File Server Resource Manager, expand the Quota Management node, and then select Quota Templates.

   Currently defined disk quota templates are listed by name, limit, and quota type.

2. To modify disk quota template properties, double-click the disk quota template name. This displays a related Properties dialog box, as shown in Figure 15-19.

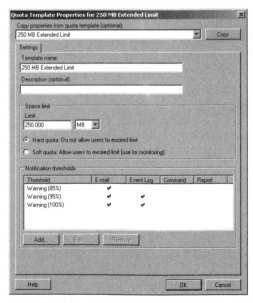

FIGURE 15-19 Use disk quota properties to configure the limit, quota type, and notification thresholds.

3. On the Settings tab, you can set the template name, limit, and quota type. Current notification thresholds are listed. To modify an existing threshold, select it, and then click Edit. To define a new threshold, click Add.

4. When you have finished modifying the quota template, click OK to save the changes.

You can create a new disk quota template by following these steps:

1. In File Server Resource Manager, expand the Quota Management node, and then select Quota Templates.

2. On the Action menu or in the Actions pane, click Create Quota Template. This displays the Create Quota Template dialog box.

3. On the Settings tab, set the template name, limit, and quota type. You should create a limit threshold first and then create additional warning thresholds as necessary. In the Limit list, type the limit value and specify whether you are setting the limit in kilobytes, megabytes, gigabytes, or terabytes.

4. Click Add to add warning thresholds. In the Add Threshold dialog box, enter a percentage value under Generate Notifications When Usage Reaches (%). Warning thresholds are considered to be any percentage of the limit that is less than 100 percent. Limit thresholds occur when the limit reached is 100 percent.

5. On the E-Mail Message tab, you can configure notification as follows:

   - To notify an administrator when the disk quota is triggered, select the Send E-Mail To The Following Administrators check box, and then type the e-mail address or addresses to use. Be sure to separate multiple e-mail addresses with a semicolon. Use the value [Admin Email] to specify the default administrator as configured previously under the global options.

   - To notify users, select the Send E-Mail To The User Who Exceeded The Threshold check box.

   - Specify the contents of the notification message in the Subject and Message Body text boxes. Table 14-4, "File Screen Variables," lists available variables and their meanings.

6. On the Event Log tab you can configure event logging. Select the Send Warning To Event Log check box to enable logging and then specify the text of the log entry in the Log Entry text box. Table 14-4 lists available variables and their meanings.

7. On the Report tab, select the Generate Reports check box to enable incident reporting, and then select the types of reports to generate. Incident reports are stored under %SystemDrive%\StorageReports\Incident by default, and they can also be sent to designated administrators. Use the value [Admin Email] to specify the default administrator as configured previously under the global options.

8. Repeat steps 5–7 to define additional notification thresholds.

9. Click OK when you have finished creating the template.

Creating Resource Manager Disk Quotas

You use disk quotas to designate file paths that have specific usage limits. In File Server Resource Manager, you can view current disk quotas by expanding the Quota Management node and then selecting Quotas. Before you define disk quotas, you should specify screening file groups and disk quota templates that you will use, as discussed in "Managing Disk Quota Templates" earlier in this chapter.

After you've defined the necessary file groups and disk quota templates, you can create a disk quota by following these steps:

1. In File Server Resource Manager, expand the Quota Management node, and then select Quotas.

2. Click Create Quota on the Action menu or in the Actions pane.

3. In the Create Quota dialog box, set the local computer path for the quota by clicking Browse and then using the Browse For Folder dialog box to select the path, such as C:\Data. Click OK.

4. In the Derive Properties From This Quota Template list, choose the disk quota template that defines the quota properties you want to use.

5. Click Create.

CHAPTER 16

Data Backup and Recovery

B ecause data is the heart of the enterprise, protecting it is crucial. And to protect your organization's data, you need to implement a data backup and recovery plan. Backing up files can protect against accidental loss of user data, database corruption, hardware failures, and even natural disasters. Your job as an administrator is to make sure that backups are performed and that backups are stored in a secure location.

Creating a Backup and Recovery Plan

Data backup is an insurance plan. Important files are accidentally deleted all the time. Mission-critical data can become corrupt. Natural disasters can leave your office in ruin. With a solid backup and recovery plan, you can recover from any of these. Without one, you're left with nothing to fall back on.

Figuring Out a Backup Plan

It takes time to create and implement a backup and recovery plan. You need to figure out what data needs to be backed up, how often the data should be backed up, and more. To help you create a plan, consider the following questions:

- **How important or sensitive is the data on your systems?** Knowing the importance of data can go a long way toward helping you determine whether you need to back it up, as well as when and how it should be backed up. For critical data, such as a database, you should have redundant backup sets that cover several backup periods. For sensitive data, you should be sure that backup data is physically secure or encrypted. For less important data, such as daily user files, you won't need such an elaborate backup plan, but you need to back up the data regularly and ensure that the data can be recovered easily.

- **What type of information does the data contain?** Data that doesn't seem important to you might be very important to someone else. The type of information the data contains can help you determine whether you need to back up the data, as well as when and how the data should be backed up.

- **How often does the data change?** The frequency of change can affect your decision on how often certain data should be backed up. For example, data that changes daily should be backed up daily.

- **Can you supplement backups with shadow copies?** *Shadow copies* are point-in-time copies of documents in shared folders. These point-in-time copies make recovering documents easy because you can quickly go back to an older version in case a document is deleted or overwritten accidentally. You should use shadow copies in addition to standard backups, not to replace backup procedures.

- **How quickly do you need to recover the data?** Recovery time is an important factor in a backup plan. For critical systems, you might need to get back online swiftly. To do this, you might need to alter your backup plan.

- **Do you have the equipment to perform backups?** You must have backup hardware to perform backups. To perform timely backups, you might need several backup devices and several sets of backup media. Backup hardware includes hard disk drives, tape drives, optical drives, and removable disk drives. In most environments, hard disk drives have become the preferred back up media.

- **Who will be responsible for the backup and recovery plan?** Ideally, someone should be a primary contact for the organization's backup and recovery plan. This person might also be responsible for performing the actual backup and recovery of data.

- **What's the best time to schedule backups?** Scheduling backups when system use is as low as possible will speed up the backup process. However, you can't always schedule backups for off-peak hours, so you need to carefully plan when key system data is backed up.

- **Do you need to store backups off-site?** Storing copies of backups off-site is essential to recovering your systems in the event of a natural disaster. In your off-site storage location, you should also include copies of the software you might need to install to reestablish operational systems.

REAL WORLD Recovery time objective (RTO) and recovery point objective (RPO) are important factors to consider. RTO represents the time to recover, which might be two hours for one server and four hours for another server. RPO represents your potential data loss, which might be one business day of data with one server or two business days with another server. A high RTO environment is an environment in which you can recover server functionality quickly after an outage. A high RPO environment is an environment in which the data recovered is as up to date as possible.

The frequency of your full server backups will vary according to the speed of your backup system and the amount of data you need to back up. The frequency at which you can create backups controls both the RPO and the RTO available to you. For example, with nightly backups, your RPO will be one business day, meaning that any server outage will likely result in the loss of an entire business day of data. Meanwhile, your RTO, indicating how long it actually takes to recover, will vary according to the amount of data you have to restore.

The Basic Types of Backup

There are many techniques for backing up files. The techniques you use depend on the type of data you're backing up, how convenient you want the recovery process to be, and more.

If you view the properties of a file or directory in Windows Explorer, you'll see an attribute called *archive*. You often use this attribute to determine whether a file or directory should be backed up. If the attribute is on, the file or directory might need to be backed up. You can perform the following basic types of backups:

- **Normal/full backups** All files that have been selected are backed up, regardless of the archive attribute's setting. When a file is backed up, the archive attribute is cleared. If the file is later modified, this attribute is set, indicating that the file needs to be backed up.

- **Copy backups** All files that have been selected are backed up, regardless of the archive attribute's setting. Unlike in a normal backup, the archive attribute on files isn't modified. This allows you to perform other types of backups on the files at a later date.

- **Differential backups** Designed to create backup copies of files that have changed since the last normal backup. The presence of the archive attribute indicates that the file has been modified, and only files with this attribute set are backed up. However, the archive attribute on files isn't modified. This allows you to perform other types of backups on the files at a later date.

- **Incremental backups** Designed to create backups of files that have changed since the most recent normal or incremental backup. The presence of the archive attribute indicates that the file has been modified, and only files with this attribute set are backed up. When a file is backed up, the archive attribute is cleared. If the file is later modified, this attribute is set, indicating that the file needs to be backed up.

- **Daily backups** Designed to back up files using the modification date on the file itself. If a file has been modified on the same day as the backup, the file will be backed up. This technique doesn't change the archive attribute of files.

As part of your backup operations, you'll probably want to perform full backups on a weekly basis and supplement this with daily, differential, or incremental backups. You might also want to create an extended backup set for monthly and quarterly backups that includes additional files that aren't being backed up regularly.

TIP You'll often find that weeks or months go by before anyone notices that a file or data source is missing. This doesn't mean the file isn't important. Although some types of data aren't used often, they're still needed. So don't forget that you might also want to create extra sets of backups for monthly or quarterly periods, or for both periods, to ensure that you can recover historical data.

Differential and Incremental Backups

The difference between differential and incremental backups is extremely important. To understand the distinction, examine Table 16-1. As you can see, with differential backups you back up all the files that have changed since the last full backup (which means that the size of the differential backup grows over time). With incremental backups, you back up only files that have changed since the most recent full or incremental backup (which means the size of the incremental backup is usually much smaller than a full backup).

TABLE 16-1 Incremental and Differential Backup Techniques

DAY OF WEEK	WEEKLY FULL BACKUP WITH DAILY DIFFERENTIAL BACKUP	WEEKLY FULL BACKUP WITH DAILY INCREMENTAL BACKUP
Sunday	A full backup is performed.	A full backup is performed.
Monday	A differential backup contains all changes since Sunday.	An incremental backup contains changes since Sunday.
Tuesday	A differential backup contains all changes since Sunday.	An incremental backup contains changes since Monday.
Wednesday	A differential backup contains all changes since Sunday.	An incremental backup contains changes since Tuesday.
Thursday	A differential backup contains all changes since Sunday.	An incremental backup contains changes since Wednesday.
Friday	A differential backup contains all changes since Sunday.	An incremental backup contains changes since Thursday.
Saturday	A differential backup contains all changes since Sunday.	An incremental backup contains changes since Friday.

After you determine what data you're going to back up and how often, you can select backup devices and media that support these choices. These are covered in the next section.

Selecting Backup Devices and Media

Many tools are available for backing up data. Some are fast and expensive. Others are slow but very reliable. The backup solution that's right for your organization depends on many factors, including the following:

- **Capacity**   The amount of data that you need to back up on a routine basis. Can the backup hardware support the required load given your time and resource constraints?

- **Reliability**   The reliability of the backup hardware and media. Can you afford to sacrifice reliability to meet budget or time needs?

- **Extensibility**   The extensibility of the backup solution. Will this solution meet your needs as the organization grows?

- **Speed**   The speed with which data can be backed up and recovered. Can you afford to sacrifice speed with server or service downtime to reduce costs?

- **Cost**   The cost of the backup solution. Does it fit your budget?

Common Backup Solutions

Capacity, reliability, extensibility, speed, and cost are the issues driving your backup plan. If you understand how these issues affect your organization, you'll be on track to select an appropriate backup solution. Some of the most commonly used backup solutions include the following:

- **Tape drives**   Tape drives are the most common backup devices. Tape drives use magnetic tape cartridges to store data. Magnetic tapes are relatively inexpensive but aren't highly reliable. Tapes can break or stretch. They can also lose information over time. The average capacity of tape cartridges ranges from 24 gigabytes (GB) to 72 GB. Compared with other backup solutions, tape drives are fairly slow. Still, the selling point is the low cost.

- **Digital audio tape (DAT) drives**   DAT drives are quickly replacing standard tape drives as the preferred backup devices. Many DAT formats are available. The most commonly used formats are Digital Linear Tape (DLT) and Super DLT (SDLT). With SDLT 320 and 600, tapes have a capacity of either 160 GB or 300 GB uncompressed (320 GB or 600 GB compressed). Large organizations might want to look at Linear Tape Open (LTO) tape technologies. LTO-3 tapes have a capacity of 400 GB uncompressed (800 GB compressed).

- **Autoloader tape systems**   Autoloader tape systems use a magazine of tapes to create extended backup volumes capable of meeting an enterprise's high-capacity needs. With an autoloader system, tapes within the magazine are automatically changed as necessary during the backup or recovery process. Most autoloader tape systems use DAT tapes formatted for DLT, SDLT, or LTO. Typical DLT drives can record up to 45 GB per hour, and you can improve that speed by purchasing a tape library system with multiple drives. In this way, you can record on multiple tapes simultaneously. In contrast, most SDLT and LTO drives record over 100 GB per hour, and by using multiple drives in a system you can record hundreds of GB per hour.

- **Disk drives**   Disk drives provide one of the fastest ways to back up and restore files. With disk drives, you can often accomplish in minutes what takes a tape drive hours. When business needs mandate a speedy recovery, nothing beats a disk drive. The drawback to disk drives is a relatively high cost compared to tape library systems.

- **Disk-based backup systems**   Disk-based backup systems provide complete backup and restore solutions using large arrays of disks to achieve high performance. High reliability can be achieved when you use redundant array of independent disks (RAID) to build in redundancy and fault tolerance. Typical disk-based backup systems use virtual library technology so that Windows sees them as autoloader tape library systems. This makes them easier to work with. A typical 20-drive system can record up to 500 GB per hour; a typical 40-drive system can record up to 2 terabytes (TB) per hour.

NOTE   Disks and disk-based backup systems can be used between the servers you are backing up and an enterprise autoloader. Servers are backed up to disk first (because this is very fast compared to tape) and later backed up to an enterprise autoloader. Having data on tapes also makes it easier to rotate backup sets to off-site storage. That said, tape backups are increasingly being replaced with disk backups. If you back up to disk arrays, you can move data off site by replicating the data to a secondary array at an alternative data center.

Before you can use a backup device, you must install it. When you install backup devices other than standard tape and DAT drives, you need to tell the operating system about the controller card and drivers that the backup device uses.

Buying and Using Backup Media

Selecting a backup device is an important step toward implementing a backup and recovery plan. But you also need to purchase the tapes, disks, or both that allow you to implement your plan. The number of tapes or disks you need depends on how much data you have to back up, how often you need to back up the data, and how long you need to keep additional data sets.

The typical way to use backup tapes is to set up a rotation schedule whereby you rotate through two or more sets of tapes. The idea is that you can increase tape longevity by reducing tape usage and at the same time reduce the number of tapes you need to ensure that you have historic data on hand when necessary.

One of the most common tape rotation schedules is the 10-tape rotation. With this rotation schedule, you use 10 tapes divided into two sets of 5 (one for each weekday). The first set of tapes is used one week and the second set of tapes is used the next week. On Fridays full backups are scheduled. On Mondays through Thursdays incremental backups are scheduled. If you add a third set of tapes, you can rotate one of the tape sets to an off-site storage location on a weekly basis.

The 10-tape rotation schedule is designed for the 9-to-5 workers of the world. If you're in a 24/7 environment, you'll definitely want extra tapes for Saturday and Sunday. In this case, use a 14-tape rotation with two sets of 7 tapes. On Sundays schedule full backups. On Mondays through Saturdays schedule incremental backups.

As disk drives have become more affordable, many organizations have been using disk backup instead of tape backup. With disks, you can use a rotation schedule similar to the one you use with tapes. You will, however, need to modify the way you rotate disks to accommodate the amount of data you are backing up. The key thing to remember is to periodically rotate disks to off-site storage.

Selecting a Backup Utility

Many backup and recovery solutions are available for use with Windows Server 2008 R2. When selecting a backup utility, you need to keep in mind the types of backups you want to perform and the types of data you are backing up. Windows Server 2008 R2 includes three installable backup and recovery features:

- **Windows Server Backup** A basic and easy to use backup and recovery utility. When this feature is installed on a server, you'll find a related option on the Administrative Tools menu. The utility is also added to Server Manager.

- **Backup Command-Line Tools** A set of backup and recovery commands accessible through the Wbadmin command-line tool. You run and use Wbadmin from an elevated, administrator command prompt. Type **wbadmin /?** for a full list of supported commands. Windows PowerShell cmdlets for managing backups are also available.

- **Repair Your Computer** You can restore a server using repair options if you cannot access recovery options provided by the server manufacturer.

Windows Server Backup is the feature you'll use the most. You can use Windows Server Backup to perform full or copy backups on both local and remote systems. You cannot use Windows Server Backup to perform differential backups. Windows Server Backup uses the Volume Shadow Copy Service (VSS) to create fast, block-level backups of the operating system, files and folders, and disk volumes. After you create the first full backup, you can configure Windows Server Backup to automatically run full or incremental backups on a recurring basis.

When you use Windows Server Backup, you need separate, dedicated media for storing archives of scheduled backups. You can back up to external and internal disks, DVDs, and shared folders. While you can recover full volumes from DVD backups, you cannot recover individual files, folders, or application data from DVD backups.

NOTE You cannot back up to tape using Windows Server Backup. If you want to back up to tape, you need a third-party backup utility.

You can use Windows Server Backup to easily recover individual folders and files. Rather than manually restoring files from multiple backups if the files are stored in incremental backups, you can recover folders and files by choosing the date on which you backed up the version of the item or items you want to restore. Windows Server Backup also works with the new Windows Recovery tools, making it easier for you to recover the operating system. You can recover to the same server or to a new server that has no operating system. Because Windows Server Backup uses VSS, you can easily back up data from compliant applications, such as Microsoft SQL Server and Windows SharePoint Services.

Windows Server Backup also includes automatic disk management. You can run backups to multiple disks in rotation simply by adding each disk as a scheduled backup location. Once you configure a disk as a scheduled backup location, Windows Server Backup automatically manages the disk storage, ensuring that you no longer need to worry about a disk running out of space. Windows Server Backup reuses the space of older backups when creating newer backups. To help ensure that you can plan for additional storage needs, Windows Server Backup displays the backups that are available and the current disk usage information.

Backing Up Your Data: The Essentials

Windows Server 2008 R2 provides Windows Server Backup for creating backups on local and remote systems. You use Windows Server Backup to archive files and folders, restore archived files and folders, create snapshots of the system state for backup and restore, and schedule automated backups.

Installing the Windows Backup and Recovery Utilities

The Windows Server backup and recovery tools are available in all editions of Windows Server 2008 R2. However, you cannot install the graphical components of these utilities on core installations of Windows Server 2008 R2. On servers running with a core installation, you need to use the command line or manage backups remotely from another computer.

You can install the Windows backup and recovery tools by following these steps:

1. In Server Manager, select the Features node in the left pane, and then click Add Features. This starts the Add Features Wizard.

2. On the Select Features page, select Windows Server Backup Features. When you select Windows Server Backup Features, the Windows Server Backup and Command-Line Tools options are selected. Click Next.

3. Click Install. When the wizard finishes installing the selected features, click Close. From now on, Windows Server Backup is available as an option on the Administrative Tools menu.

REAL WORLD When you use Windows Server Backup with Microsoft Exchange Server 2010, you can use only full (normal) backups. Using the Windows Server Backup command-line tools with Exchange Server 2010 also is not supported. For more information on backing up Exchange Server 2010, see Chapter 15, "Backing Up and Restoring Exchange Server 2010," in *Microsoft Exchange Server 2010 Administrator's Pocket Consultant* (Microsoft Press, 2009).

TIP You cannot use Windows Server Backup to recover backups created with the previous backup feature (Ntbackup.exe). At *microsoft.com/downloads*, a version of Ntbackup.exe is available for Windows Server 2008 and later releases. The downloadable version of Ntbackup.exe is only for recovering backups created with older versions of Windows; you cannot use it to create new backups in Windows Server 2008 R2.

Getting Started with Windows Server Backup

The first time you use Windows Server Backup, you'll see a warning that no backup has been configured for the computer. (See Figure 16-1.) You clear this warning by creating a backup using the Backup Once feature or by scheduling backups to run automatically using the Backup Schedule feature.

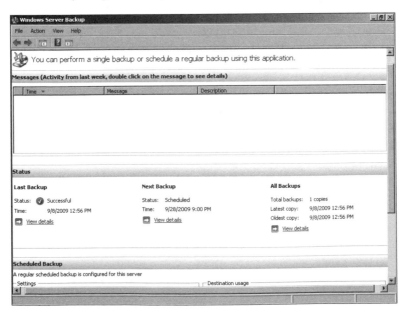

FIGURE 16-1 Windows Server Backup provides a user-friendly interface for backup and restore.

To perform backup and recovery operations, you must have certain permissions and user rights. Members of the Administrators and the Backup Operators groups have full authority to back up and restore any type of file, regardless of who owns the file and the permissions set on it. File owners and those who have been given control over files can also back up files, but only those files that they own or those for which they have Read, Read & Execute, Modify, or Full Control permissions.

NOTE Keep in mind that although local accounts can work only with local systems, domain accounts have domainwide privileges. Therefore, a member of the local Administrators group can work only with files on the local system, but a member of the Domain Admins group can work with files throughout the domain.

Windows Server Backup provides extensions for working with the following special types of data:

- **System state data** Includes essential system files needed to recover the local system. All computers have system state data, which must be backed up in addition to other files to restore a complete working system.

- **Application data** Includes application data files. You must back up application data if you want to be able to fully recover applications. Windows Server Backup creates block-level backups of application data using VSS.

Windows Server Backup allows you to perform full, copy, and incremental backups. While you can schedule a full or incremental backup to be performed one or more times each day, you cannot use this feature to create separate run schedules for performing both full and incremental backups. Further, you cannot select the day or days of the week to run backups. This occurs because each server has a single master schedule that is set to run one or more times daily. If your servers have a single master schedule, you can work around this limitation by configuring Windows Server Backup to perform daily incremental backups and then creating a scheduled task via the Task Scheduler that uses Wbadmin to create a full backup on the day of the week or month you want to use.

When you start Windows Server Backup, the utility connects to the local computer by default. This allows you to easily manage backups on the local computer. If you want to manage backups on a remote computer, you need to connect to it by following these steps:

1. Start Windows Server Backup. In the Actions pane or on the Action menu, click Connect To Another Computer. (This option is available only after an initial backup is performed.)

2. Select Another Computer, and then type the server's name or IP address. Alternatively, if network discovery is enabled, click Browse, choose the remote computer in the dialog box provided, and then click OK.

3. Click Finish to establish a connection to the remote computer.

When you use Windows Server Backup, the first backup of a server is always a full backup. This is because the full backup process clears the archive bits on files so that Windows Server Backup can track which files are updated subsequently. Whether Windows Server Backup performs full or incremental backups subsequently depends on the default performance settings that you configure. You can configure the default performance settings by following these steps:

1. Start Windows Server Backup. In the Actions pane or on the Action menu, click Configure Performance Settings. This displays the Optimize Backup Performance dialog box, shown in Figure 16-2.

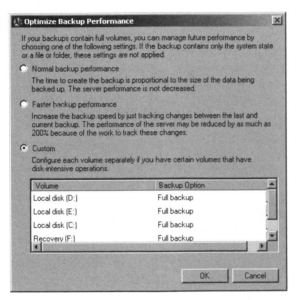

FIGURE 16-2 Configure the default backup settings.

2. Do one of the following, and then click OK:

   - Choose Normal Backup Performance to perform full backups of all attached drives.

   - Choose Faster Backup Performance to perform incremental backups of all attached drives.

   - Choose Custom. In the option lists provided, specify whether to perform full or incremental backups for individual attached drives.

3. Once you configure the default performance settings, you can start a full or copy backup by clicking Backup Once on the Action menu or in the Actions pane. You can configure a backup schedule by clicking Backup Schedule on the Action menu or in the Actions pane.

Getting Started with the Backup Command-Line Utility

Wbadmin is the command-line counterpart to Windows Server Backup. You use Wbadmin to manage all aspects of backup configuration that you would otherwise manage in Windows Server Backup. This means that you can typically use either tool to manage backup and recovery.

After you install the Backup Command-Line Tools feature as discussed earlier in the chapter, you can use Wbadmin to manage backup and recovery. Wbadmin is located in the %SystemRoot%\System32\ directory. This directory is in your command path by default, so you do not need to add it. You can run Wbadmin by following these steps:

1. Click Start, click All Programs, and then click Accessories.

2. Right-click Command Prompt, and then click Run As Administrator to start an elevated command prompt.

3. In the Command Prompt window, enter the necessary command text or run a script that invokes Wbadmin.

Wbadmin has a number of associated commands, summarized in Table 16-2.

When you are working with Wbadmin, you can get help on available commands:

- To view a list of management commands, type **wbadmin /?** at the command prompt.

- To view the syntax for a specific management command, type **wbadmin Command /?**, where *Command* is the name of the management command you want to examine, such as **wbadmin stop job /?**.

When you work with Wbadmin, you'll find that just about every command accepts parameters and specific parameter values that qualify what you want to work with. To see more clearly how this works, consider the following syntax example:

```
wbadmin get versions [-backupTarget:{VolumeName | NetworkSharePath}]
    [-machine:BackupMachineName]
```

The brackets tell you that –backupTarget and –machine are optional. Thus, you could type the following to get information on recoverable backups on the local computer:

```
wbadmin get versions
```

You could type the following to get information on recoverable backups for C:

```
wbadmin get versions -backupTarget:f:
```

Or you could type the following to get information on recoverable backups for C on Server96:

```
wbadmin get versions -backupTarget:f: -machine:server96
```

Many Wbadmin commands use the –backupTarget and –machine parameters. The backup target is the storage location you want to work with and can be expressed as a local volume name, such as F:, or as a network share path, such as \\FileServer32\backups\Server85. The –machine parameter identifies the computer you want to work with for backup or recovery operations.

TABLE 16-2 Wbadmin Management Commands

COMMAND	DESCRIPTION
DELETE SYSTEMSTATEBACKUP	Deletes the system state backup or backups from a specified location.
DISABLE BACKUP	Disables scheduled daily backups so that they no longer run.
ENABLE BACKUP	Enables or modifies a scheduled daily backup.
GET DISKS	Lists the disks that are currently online for the local computer. Disks are listed by manufacturer name, type, disk number, GUID, total space, used space, and associated volumes.
GET ITEMS	Lists items contained in a specified backup.
GET STATUS	Reports the status of the currently running backup or recovery job.
GET VERSIONS	Lists details about the available backups stored in a specific location, including the backup time and backup destination.
START BACKUP	Starts a one-time backup using the specified parameters. If no parameters are passed and scheduled backups are enabled, the backup uses the settings for scheduled backups.
START RECOVERY	Initiates a recovery of volumes, applications, or files using the specified parameters.
START SYSTEMSTATEBACKUP	Starts a system state backup using the options specified.
START SYSTEMSTATERECOVERY	Starts a system state recovery using the specified parameters.
STOP JOB	Stops the currently running backup or recovery job. Stopped jobs cannot be restarted from where they were stopped.

Working with Wbadmin Commands

You use Wbadmin commands to manage the backup configuration of your servers. These commands work with a specific set of parameters. The following sections provide an overview of the available commands with their most commonly used syntaxes.

Using General-Purpose Commands

The following general-purpose commands are provided for getting information about backups and the system you are working with:

- GET DISKS   Lists the disks that are currently online for the local computer. Disks are listed by manufacturer name, type, disk number, GUID, total space, used space, and associated volumes.

  ```
  wbadmin get disks
  ```

- GET ITEMS   Lists items contained in a specified backup.

  ```
  wbadmin get items  -version:VersionIdentifier
    [-backupTarget:{VolumeName | NetworkSharepath}]
    [-machine:BackupMachineName]
  ```

- GET STATUS   Reports the status of the currently running backup or recovery job.

  ```
  wbadmin get status
  ```

- GET VERSIONS   Lists details about the available backups stored in a specific location, including the backup time and backup destination.

  ```
  wbadmin get versions [-backupTarget:{VolumeName | NetworkSharepath}]
    [-machine:BackupMachineName]
  ```

Using Backup Management Commands

You can manage backups and their configurations using the following commands and command-line syntaxes:

- DELETE SYSTEMSTATEBACKUP   Deletes the system state backup or backups from a specified location.

  ```
  wbadmin delete systemstateBackup [-backupTarget:{VolumeName}]
    [-machine:BackupMachineName]
    [-keepVersions:NumberOfBackupsToKeep | -version:VersionIdentifier |
    -deleteOldest]
    [-quiet]
  ```

- DISABLE BACKUP   Disables scheduled daily backups so that they no longer run.

  ```
  wbadmin disable backup [-quiet]
  ```

- ENABLE BACKUP Enables or modifies a scheduled daily backup.

```
wbadmin enable backup [-addTarget:{BackupTargetDisk}]
  [-removeTarget:{BackupTargetDisk}]
  [-schedule:TimeToRunBackup]
  [-include:VolumesToInclude]
  [-allCritical]
  [-quiet]
```

- START BACKUP Starts a one-time backup using the specified parameters. If no parameters are passed and scheduled backups are enabled, the backup uses the settings for scheduled backups.

```
wbadmin start backup [-backupTarget:{TargetVolume |
TargetNetworkShare}]
  [-include:VolumesToInclude]
  [-allCritical]
  [-noVerify]
  [-user:username]
  [-password:password]
  [-inheritAcl:InheritAcl]
  [-vssFull]
  [-quiet]
```

- STOP JOB Stops the currently running backup or recovery job. Stopped jobs cannot be restarted from where they were stopped.

```
wbadmin stop job [-quiet]
```

Using Recovery Management Commands

You can recover your computers and data using the following commands and command-line syntaxes:

- START RECOVERY Initiates a recovery of volumes, applications, or files using the specified parameters.

```
wbadmin start recovery -version:VersionIdentifier
  -items:VolumesToRecover | AppsToRecover | FilesOrFoldersToRecover
  -itemType:{volume | app | file}
  [-backupTarget:{VolumeHostingBackup | NetworkShareHostingBackup}]
  [-machine:BackupMachineName]
  [-recoveryTarget:TargetVolumeForRecovery | TargetPathForRecovery]
  [-recursive]
  [-overwrite:{Overwrite | CreateCopy | skip}]
  [-notRestoreAcl]
  [-skipBadClusterCheck]
  [-noRollForward]
  [-quiet]
```

- START SYSTEMSTATEBACKUP   Starts a system state backup using the options specified.

  ```
  wbadmin start systemstateBackup -backupTarget:{VolumeName}
  [-quiet]
  ```

- START SYSTEMSTATERECOVERY   Starts a system state recovery using the specified parameters.

  ```
  wbadmin start systemstateRecovery -version:VersionIdentifier
  -showSummary
  [-backupTarget:{VolumeName | NetworkSharePath}]
  [-machine:BackupMachineName]
  [-recoveryTarget:TargetPathForRecovery]
  [-authSysvol]
  [-quiet]
  ```

Performing Server Backups

You can back up local and remote servers. If Windows Firewall is enabled and you are trying to work with a remote computer, you may need to make an exception to allow backup and recovery operations. As part of your planning for each server you plan to back up, you should consider which volumes you want to back up and whether backups will include system state recovery data, application data, or both.

Although you can manually back up to shared volumes and DVD media, you need a separate, dedicated hard disk for running scheduled backups. After you configure a disk for scheduled backups, the backup utilities automatically manage the disk usage and automatically reuse the space of older backups when creating new backups. Once you schedule backups, you need to check periodically to ensure that backups are being performed as expected and that the backup schedule meets current needs.

When you create or schedule backups, you need to specify the volumes that you want to include, and this affects the ways you can recover your servers and your data. You have the following options:

- **Full server (all volumes with application data)**   Back up all volumes with application data if you want to be able to fully recover a server, along with its system state and application data. Because you are backing up all files, the system state, and application data, you should be able to fully restore your server using only the Windows backup tools.

- **Full server (all volumes without application data)**   Back up all volumes without application data if you want to be able to restore a server and its applications separately. With this technique, you back up the server using the Windows backup tools but exclude locations where applications and application data are stored. Then you back up applications and related data using third-party tools or tools built into the applications. You can fully recover a server by using the Windows backup utilities and then use a third-party utility to restore backups of applications and application data.

- **Critical volumes/bare metal recovery**   Back up only critical volumes if you want to be able to recover only the operating system.

- **Noncritical volumes**   Back up only individual volumes if you want to be able to recover only files, applications, or data from those volumes.

As part of the backup process, you also need to specify a storage location for backups. Keep the following in mind when you choose storage locations:

- When you use an internal hard disk for storing backups, you are limited in how you can recover your system. You can recover the data from a volume, but you cannot rebuild the entire disk structure.

- When you use an external hard disk for storing backups, the disk will be dedicated for storing your backups and will not be visible in Windows Explorer. Choosing this option will format the selected disk or disks, removing any existing data.

- When you use a remote shared folder for storing backups, your backup will be overwritten each time you create a new backup. Do not choose this option if you want to store multiple backups for each server.

- When you use removable media or DVDs for storing backups, you can recover only entire volumes, not applications or individual files. The media you use must be at least 1 GB in size.

The sections that follow discuss techniques for performing backups. The procedures you use to back up servers with Windows Server Backup and Wbadmin are similar.

Configuring Scheduled Backups

With Windows Server Backup, you can schedule automated backups for a server by following these steps:

1. In Windows Server Backup, you are connected to the local server by default. As necessary, connect to the remote server with which you want to work.

2. Click Backup Schedule on the Action menu or in the Actions pane. This starts the Backup Schedule Wizard. Click Next.

3. On the Select Backup Configuration page, note the backup size listed under the Full Server option, as shown in the following screen. This is the storage space required to back up the server data, applications, and the system state. To back up all volumes on the server, select the Full Server option, and then click Next. To back up selected volumes on the server, click Custom, and then click Next.

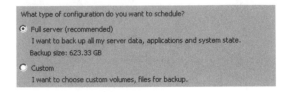

What type of configuration do you want to schedule?

○ Full server (recommended)
   I want to back up all my server data, applications and system state.
   Backup size: 623.33 GB

○ Custom
   I want to choose custom volumes, files for backup.

NOTE Volumes that contain operating system files or applications are included in the backup by default and cannot be excluded. On a server on which you installed Windows Server 2008 R2 on the D drive, this unfortunately means you must also back up the entire C drive because the C drive in this case includes the boot manager and other boot files.

4. If you select Custom, the Select Items For Backup page is displayed. Click Add Items. As shown in the following screen, select the check boxes for the volumes that you want to back up and clear the check boxes for the volumes that you want to exclude. Select the Bare Metal Recovery option if you want to be able to fully recover the operating system. Click OK, and then click Next.

   TIP After you select items, you may want to click Advanced Settings before continuing. You can then use the options on the Exclusions tab to identify locations and file types that should not be backed up. You also can then use the options on the VSS Settings tab to specify whether you want to create a full backup or a copy back up.

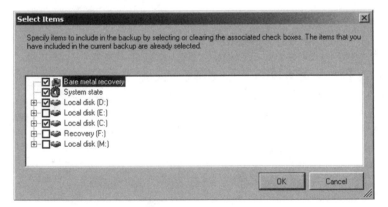

5. On the Specify Backup Time page, you can specify how often and when you want to run backups. To perform backups daily at a specific time, choose Once A Day, and then select the time to start running the daily backup. To perform backups multiple times each day, choose More Than Once A Day, as shown in the following screen. Next, click a start time under Available Time, and then click Add to move the time under Scheduled Time. Repeat for each start time that you want to add. Click Next when you are ready to continue.

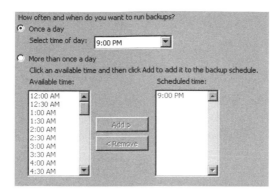

6. On the Specify Destination Type page, you have these options:

- **Backup To A Hard Disk That Is Dedicated For Backups** Allows you to specify a dedicated hard disk for backups. Although you can use multiple disks for backups, any disk that you select will be formatted and then dedicated only to backups. This option is recommended because you'll get the best performance. If you select this option, click Next, select the disk or disks to use, and then click Next again.

- **Backup To A Volume** Allows you to write backups to individual volumes on a hard disk. Because any volume you select is not dedicated to backups, it can be used for other purposes. However, the performance of any of the selected volumes is reduced while backups are being written. If you select this option, click Next, use the Add and Remove options to select the volumes to use, and then click Next again.

- **Backup To A Shared Network Folder** Allows you to specify a shared network folder for backups. With this option, you can have only one backup at a time because each new backup overwrites the previous backup. If you select this option, click Next. When prompted, click OK. Type the UNC path to the network share, such as \\FileServer25\Backups\Exchange. If you want the backup to be accessible to everyone who has access to the shared folder, select Inherit under Access Control. If you want to restrict access to the shared folder to the current user and members of the Administrators and Backup Operators groups, select Do Not Inherit under Access Control. Click Next. When prompted to provide access credentials, type the user name and password for an account authorized to access and write to the shared folder.

7. On the Confirmation page, review the details, and then click Finish. The wizard formats the disk. The formatting process may take several minutes or considerably longer depending on the size of the disk.

8. On the Summary page, click Close. Your backups are now scheduled for the selected server.

With Wbadmin, you can schedule backups using the ENABLE BACKUP command. ENABLE BACKUP accepts the following parameters:

- –addTarget Sets the storage location for backups according to the GUID of the disk you want to use. The GUID of a disk is listed as the disk identifier in the output of the Wbadmin GET DISKS command.

- –removeTarget Sets the storage location to remove from the backup schedule according to the GUID of the disk you want to use. The GUID of a disk is listed as the disk identifier in the output of the Wbadmin GET DISKS command.

- –include Sets a comma-delimited list of volume drive letters, volume mount points, and GUID volume names to back up.

- –allCritical Includes all operating system volumes in the backup automatically.

- –quiet Specifies that you want to run the command with no prompts to the user.

To see how ENABLE BACKUP is used, consider the following examples:

Schedule a backup for C and D at 9:00 P.M. daily

```
wbadmin enable backup -addTarget:{06d88776-0000-0000-0000-000000000000}
-schedule:18:00 -include:c:,d:
```

Schedule a backup for all operating system volumes at 6:00 A.M. and 9:00 P.M. daily

```
wbadmin enable backup -addTarget:{06d88776-0000-0000-0000-000000000000}
-schedule:06:00,18:00 -allCritical
```

Modifying or Stopping Scheduled Backups

Once you've configured scheduled backups on a server, you can modify or stop the scheduled backups by following these steps:

1. Start Windows Server Backup. You are connected to the local server by default. As necessary, connect to the remote server you want to work with.

2. Click Backup Schedule on the Action menu or in the Actions pane. This starts the Backup Schedule Wizard. Click Next.

3. On the Modify Scheduled Backup Settings page, click Modify Backup if you want to add or remove backup items, times, or targets, and then follow steps 3 to 10 in the section titled "Configuring Scheduled Backups" earlier in the chapter. If you want to stop the scheduled backups from running, click Stop Backup, click Next, and then click Finish. When prompted to confirm, click Yes, and then click Close.

NOTE Stopping backups releases backup disks for normal use. Backup archives are not deleted from the backup disks and remain available for use in recovery.

With Wbadmin, you can modify scheduled backups using the ENABLE BACKUP command. For targets, you must use the –addTarget and –removeTarget parameters to modify the target disks. For the run schedule and included volumes, you simply set the new values you want to use. Consider the following examples.

Adding a new target to scheduled backups

```
wbadmin enable backup -removeTarget:{06d88776-0000-0000-0000-000000000000}
```

Removing a target from scheduled backups

```
wbadmin enable backup -addTarget:{41cd2567-0000-0000-0000-000000000000}
```

Modifying the run schedule and included volumes

```
wbadmin enable backup -schedule:03:00 -include:c:,d:,e:
```

Creating and Scheduling Backups with Wbadmin

One way to create manual backups is to use the Wbadmin START BACKUP command. START BACKUP accepts the following parameters:

- –backupTarget   Sets the storage location for the backup as either a drive letter or UNC path to a shared folder on a remote server.

- –include   Sets a comma-delimited list of volume drive letters, volume mount points, and GUID volume names to back up.

- –allCritical   Includes all operating system volumes in the backup automatically.

- –inheritAcl   Specifies that you want the backup folder at the remote shared folder to inherit the security permissions of the shared folder. If you do not specify this parameter, the backup folder is accessible only to the user you specify in the –user parameter, administrators, and backup operators.

- –noVerify   Specifies that you do not want to verify backups written to removable media. If you do not specify this parameter, backups written to removable media are verified.

- –password   Sets the password to use when connecting to the remote shared folder.

- –quiet   Specifies that you want to run the command with no prompts to the user.

- –user   Sets the user name to use when connecting to the remote shared folder.

- –vssFull   Specifies that you want to perform a full backup using VSS, which ensures that all server and application data is backed up. Do not use this parameter if you are using a third-party backup utility to back up application data.

To see how START BACKUP is used, consider the following examples:

Performing a full backup of the server

`wbadmin start backup -backupTarget:f: -vssfull`

Backing up C and D to F

`wbadmin start backup -backupTarget:f: -include:c:,d:`

Backing up all critical volumes

`wbadmin start backup -backupTarget:f: -allCritical`

Backing up C and D to a remote shared folder

`wbadmin start backup -backupTarget:\\fileserver27\backups -include:c:,d: -user:williams`

If you want to create a schedule to run backups at different times on different days, you can use Task Scheduler to create the necessary tasks to run this command on the schedule you set. You can use Task Scheduler and Wbadmin to schedule tasks to run backups by following these steps:

1. Click Start, click Administrative Tools, and then click Task Scheduler. You are connected to the local computer by default. As necessary, connect to the computer that you want to access.

2. Right-click the Task Scheduler node, and then click Create Task. This opens the Create Task dialog box.

3. On the General tab, type the name of the task, and then set security options for running the task.

   - If the task should run under a user other than the current user, click Change User Or Group. In the Select User Or Group dialog box, select the user or group under which the task should run, and then provide the appropriate credentials when prompted later.

   - Set other run options as necessary. By default, tasks run only when a user is logged on. If you want to run the task regardless of whether a user is logged on, select Run Whether User Is Logged On Or Not. You can also elect to run with highest privileges and configure the task for earlier releases of Windows.

4. On the Triggers tab, click New. In the New Trigger dialog box, select On A Schedule in the Begin The Task list. Use the options provided to set the run schedule, and then click OK.

5. On the Actions tab, click New. In the New Action dialog box, select Start A Program in the Action list.

6. In the Program/Script text box, type **%windir%\System32\wbadmin.exe**.

7. In Add Arguments, type the START BACKUP command you want to use along with its parameters, such as:

```
start backup -backupTarget:f: -include:c:,d:,e:\mountpoint,
\\?\volume{be345a23-32b2-432d-43d2-7867ff3e3432}\
```

8. Click OK to close the New Action dialog box.

9. On the Conditions tab, specify any limiting conditions for starting or stopping the task.

10. On the Settings tab, choose any additional optional settings for the task.

11. Click OK to create the task.

Running Manual Backups

You can use Windows Server Backup to back up servers manually by following these steps:

1. Start Windows Server Backup. You are connected to the local server by default. As necessary, connect to the remote server with which you want to work.

2. Click Backup Once on the Action menu or in the Actions pane. This starts the Backup Once Wizard.

3. If you want to back up the server using the same options that you use for the Backup Schedule Wizard, select Scheduled Backup Options, click Next, and then click Backup to perform the backup. Skip the remaining steps.

4. If you want to back up the server using different options, select Different Options, and then click Next.

5. On the Select Backup Configuration page, note the backup size listed under the Full Server option. This is the storage space required to back up the server data, applications, and the system state. To back up all volumes on the server, select the Full Server option, and then click Next. To back up selected volumes on the server, click Custom, and then click Next.

6. If you select Custom, the Select Items For Backup page is displayed. Click Add Items. Select the check boxes for the volumes that you want to back up and clear the check boxes for the volumes that you want to exclude. Select the Bare Metal Recovery option if you want to be able to fully recover the operating system. Click OK, and then click Next.

TIP After you select items, you may want to click Advanced Settings before continuing. You can then use the options on the Exclusions tab to identify locations and file types that should not be backed up. You also can then use the options on the VSS Settings tab to specify whether you want to create a full backup or a copy backup.

7. On the Specify Destination Type page, do one of the following:

- If you want to back up to local drives, select Local Drives, and then click Next. On the Backup Destination page, select the internal or external disk or DVD drive to use as the backup target. Backups are compressed when stored on a DVD. As a result, the size of the backup on a DVD might be smaller than the volume on the server. Click Next.

- If you want to back up to a remote shared folder, select Remote Shared Folder, and then click Next. On the Specify Remote Folder page, type the UNC path to the remote folder, such as \\FileServer43\Backups. If you want the backup to be accessible to everyone who has access to the shared folder, select Inherit under Access Control. If you want to restrict access to the shared folder to the current user, administrators, and backup operators, select Do Not Inherit under Access Control. Click Next. When prompted to provide access credentials, type the user name and password for an account authorized to access and write to the shared folder.

8. Click Next, and then click Backup. The Backup Progress dialog box shows you the progress of the backup process. If you click Close, the backup will continue to run in the background.

Recovering Your Server from Hardware or Startup Failure

Like Windows 7, Windows Server 2008 R2 includes an extensive diagnostics and resolution architecture. These features can help you recover from many types of hardware, memory, and performance issues and either resolve them automatically or help users through the process of resolving them.

Windows Server 2008 R2 includes more reliable and better-performing device drivers to prevent many common causes of hangs and crashes. Improved input/output (I/O) cancellation for device drivers ensures that the operating system can recover gracefully from blocking calls and that there are fewer blocking disk I/O operations.

To reduce downtime and restarts required for application installations and updates, Windows Server 2008 R2 can use the update process to mark in-use files for update and then automatically replace the files the next time the application is started. In some cases, Windows Server 2008 R2 can save the application's data, close the application, update the in-use files, and then restart the application. To improve overall system performance and responsiveness, Windows Server 2008 R2 uses memory more efficiently, provides ordered execution for groups of threads, and provides new process scheduling mechanisms. By optimizing memory and process usage, Windows Server 2008 R2 ensures that background processes have less performance impact on system performance.

Windows Server 2008 R2 provides improved guidance on the causes of unresponsive conditions. By including additional error-reporting details in the event logs, Windows Server 2008 R2 makes it easier to identify and resolve issues. To automatically recover from service failures, Windows Server 2008 R2 uses service recovery policies more extensively than its predecessors. When recovering a failed service, Windows Server 2008 R2 automatically handles both service and nonservice dependencies. Any necessary dependent services and system components are started prior to starting the failed service.

In earlier versions of Windows, an application crash or hang is marked as not responding, and it is up to the user to exit and then restart the application. Windows Server 2008 R2 attempts to resolve the issue of unresponsive applications by using Restart Manager. Restart Manager can shut down and restart unresponsive applications automatically. Thanks to Restart Manager, you might not have to intervene to try to resolve issues with frozen applications.

Failed installation and nonresponsive conditions of applications and drivers are also tracked through Action Center, and the built-in diagnostics display a warning message. By clicking the Action Center icon in the system tray, you can view recent messages. If you click a message, Windows Server 2008 R2 opens the Message Details page in Action Center, which may provide a solution for the problem.

You also can view a list of current problems at any time by following these steps:

1. Click Start, and then click Control Panel.

2. In Control Panel, under the System And Security heading, click Review Your Computer's Status.

3. In Action Center, a list of known problems is displayed. Select the related View Message Details button to display the Message Details page. If a solution is available, click the link provided to download the solution or visit a related Web site to get more information.

While you are working with Action Center, you can have Windows Server check for solutions to problems by clicking the Check For Solutions link.

Windows Server 2008 R2 attempts to resolve issues related to running out of virtual memory by providing Resource Exhaustion Detection And Recovery. This feature monitors the systemwide virtual memory commit limit and alerts you if the computer is running low on virtual memory. To help you to correct this issue, it also identifies the processes consuming the largest amount of memory, allowing you to close any or all of these high resource-consuming applications directly from the Close Programs To Prevent Information Loss dialog box. The resource exhaustion alert is also logged in the system event log.

In early versions of Windows, corrupted system files are one of the most common causes of startup failure. Windows Server 2008 R2 includes built-in diagnostics to automatically detect corrupted system files during startup and guide you through automated or manual recovery. To resolve startup problems, Windows Server 2008 R2 uses the Startup Repair tool (StR), which is installed automatically and started when a system fails to boot. Once started, StR attempts to determine the cause of the startup failure by analyzing startup logs and error reports. Then StR attempts to fix the problem automatically. If StR is unable to resolve the problem, it restores the system to the last known working state and then provides diagnostic information and support options for further troubleshooting.

Hardware problems addressed by built-in diagnostics include error detection and disk failure detection. If a device is having problems, hardware diagnostics can detect error conditions and either repair the problem automatically or guide the user through a recovery process. With disk drives, hardware diagnostics can use fault reports provided by disk drives to detect potential failures and alert you before they happen. Hardware diagnostics can also help guide you through the backup process after alerting you that a disk might be failing.

Performance problems addressed by built-in diagnostics include slow application startup, slow boot, slow standby/resume, and slow shutdown. If a computer is experiencing degraded performance, performance diagnostics can detect the problem and provide possible solutions for resolving the problem. For advanced performance issues, you can track related performance and reliability data in the Performance Diagnostics console, which includes a performance monitor and a reliability monitor. (This is discussed in Chapter 4, "Monitoring Processes, Services, and Events.")

Memory problems addressed by built-in diagnostics include both memory leaks and failing memory. A memory leak occurs if an application or system component doesn't completely free areas of physical memory after it is done with them. If you suspect that a computer has a memory problem that is not being automatically detected, you can run Windows Memory Diagnostics manually during startup by selecting the related option. If the Windows Memory Diagnostics option is not provided during startup, you can run the program by following these steps:

1. Click Start, type **mdsched.exe** in the Search box, and then press Enter.

2. Choose whether to restart the computer now and run the tool immediately or schedule the tool to check for problems at the next restart.

3. Windows Memory Diagnostics runs automatically after the computer restarts, enabling you to choose the type of testing to perform. Three different levels of memory testing can be performed, from basic to exhaustive.

To detect system crashes possibly caused by failing memory, memory diagnostics work with the Microsoft Online Crash Analysis tool. If a computer crashes because of failing memory, and memory diagnostics detect this, you are prompted to schedule a memory test the next time the computer is restarted.

Starting a Server in Safe Mode

If a system won't boot normally, you can use safe mode to recover or troubleshoot system problems. In safe mode, Windows Server 2008 R2 loads only basic files, services, and drivers. The drivers loaded include the mouse, monitor, keyboard, mass storage, and base video. No networking services or drivers are started unless you choose the Safe Mode With Networking option. Because safe mode loads a limited set of configuration information, it can help you troubleshoot problems.

You start a system in safe mode by following these steps:

1. Start (or restart) the problem system.

2. During startup , press F8. This tells the computer to display the Advanced Boot Options menu.

3. Use the arrow keys to select the safe mode you want to use, and then press Enter. The safe mode option you use depends on the type of problem you're experiencing. The key options are as follows:

- **Safe Mode** Loads only basic files, services, and drivers during the initialization sequence. The drivers loaded include the mouse, monitor, keyboard, mass storage, and base video. No networking services or drivers are started.

- **Safe Mode With Networking** Loads basic files, services, and drivers, as well as services and drivers needed to start networking.

- **Safe Mode With Command Prompt** Loads basic files, services, and drivers, and then starts a command prompt instead of the Windows graphical interface. No networking services or drivers are started.

> **TIP** In Safe Mode With Command Prompt, you can start the Explorer shell from the command-line interface by pressing Ctrl+Shift+Esc and typing explorer.exe in the New Process window on the File menu of Task Manager.

- **Enable Boot Logging** Allows you to create a record of all startup events in a boot log.

- **Enable Low Resolution Video** Allows you to start the system in low-resolution 640 × 480 display mode, which is useful if the system display is set to a mode that can't be used with the current monitor.

- **Last Known Good Configuration** Starts the computer in safe mode using registry information that Windows saved at the last shutdown, including the HKEY_CURRENT_CONFIG (HKCC) hive. This registry hive stores information about the hardware configuration with which you previously and successfully started the computer.

- **Debugging Mode** Starts the system in debugging mode, which is useful only for troubleshooting operating system bugs.

- **Directory Services Restore Mode** Starts the system in safe mode and allows you to restore the directory service. This option is available on Windows Server 2008 R2 domain controllers.

- **Disable Automatic Restart On System Failure** Prevents Windows Server 2008 R2 from automatically restarting after an operating system crash.

- **Disable Driver Signature Enforcement** Starts the computer in safe mode without enforcing digital signature policy settings for drivers. If a driver with an invalid or missing digital signature is causing startup failure, this option resolves the problem temporarily so that you can start the computer and resolve the problem by getting a new driver or changing the driver signature enforcement settings.

4. If a problem doesn't reappear when you start in safe mode, you can eliminate the default settings and basic device drivers as possible causes. If a newly added device or updated driver is causing problems, you can use safe mode to remove the device or reverse the update.

Resuming After a Failed Start

Like Windows 7, Windows Server 2008 R2 enters Windows Error Recovery mode automatically if Windows fails to start. In this mode, you have options similar to those you have when working with the Advanced Boot Options menu. For troubleshooting, you can elect to boot the system in Safe Mode, Safe Mode With Networking, or Safe Mode With Command Prompt. You can also choose to use the last known good configuration or to start Windows normally. See "Starting a Server in Safe Mode" for more information.

TIP If you'd rather use options on the Advanced Boot Options menu, restart the server, and then press F8 before the Windows Error Recovery mode is initiated.

Backing Up and Restoring the System State

On Windows Server 2008 R2, there are approximately 50,000 system state files, which use approximately 4 GB of disk space in the default installation of an x64-based computer. The fastest and easiest way to back up and restore a server's system state is to use Wbadmin. With Wbadmin, you can use the START SYSTEMSTATEBACKUP command to create a backup of the system state for a computer and the START SYSTEMSTATERECOVERY command to restore a computer's system state.

TIP When you select a system state restore on a domain controller, you have to be in the Directory Services Restore mode. To learn how to restore Active Directory, see the next section.

To back up a server's system state, type the following at an elevated command prompt:

```
wbadmin start systemstatebackup -backupTarget:VolumeName
```

where *VolumeName* is the storage location for the backup, such as F:.

To restore a server's system state, type the following at an elevated command prompt:

```
wbadmin start systemstaterecovery -backupTarget:VolumeName
```

where *VolumeName* is the storage location that contains the backup you want to recover, such as F:. Additionally, you can do the following:

- Use the –recoveryTarget parameter to restore to an alternate location.

- Use the –machine parameter to specify the name of the computer to recover if the original backup location contains backups for multiple computers.

- Use the –authSysvol parameter to perform an authoritative restore of the SYSVOL.

You can also recover the system state by using a backup that includes the system state or by performing a recovery.

Restoring Active Directory

When restoring system state data to a domain controller, you must choose whether you want to perform an authoritative or nonauthoritative restore. The default is nonauthoritative. In this mode, Active Directory and other replicated data are restored from backup and any changes are replicated from another domain controller. Thus, you can safely restore a failed domain controller without overwriting the latest Active Directory information. On the other hand, if you're trying to restore Active Directory throughout the network using archived data, you must use authoritative restore. With authoritative restore, the restored data is restored on the current domain controller and then replicated to other domain controllers.

> **CAUTION** An authoritative restore overwrites all Active Directory data throughout the domain. Before you perform an authoritative restore, you must be certain that the archive data is the correct data to propagate throughout the domain and that the current data on other domain controllers is inaccurate, outdated, or otherwise corrupted.

To restore Active Directory on a domain controller and enable the restored data to be replicated throughout the network, follow these steps:

1. Make sure the domain controller server is shut down.

2. Restart the domain controller server. Press F8 to display the Advanced Boot Options menu.

3. Select Directory Services Restore Mode.

4. When the system starts, use the Backup utility to restore the system state data and other essential files.

5. After restoring the data but before restarting the server, use the Ntdsutil.exe tool to mark objects as authoritative. Be sure to check the Active Directory data thoroughly.

6. Restart the server. When the system finishes startup, the Active Directory data should begin to replicate throughout the domain.

Restoring the Operating System and the Full System

As discussed previously, Windows Server 2008 R2 includes startup repair features that can recover a server in case of corrupted or missing system files. The startup repair process can also recover from some types of boot failures involving the boot manager. If these processes fail and the boot manager is the reason you cannot start the server, you can use the Windows Server 2008 R2 installation disc or system recovery options to restore the boot manager and enable startup.

System recovery options are only available with full server installations and not with Server Core installations. With Server Core installations, you need to use the installation disc to initiate recovery.

System recovery options include the following tools:

- **System Image Recovery**   Allows you to recover a server's operating system or perform a full system recovery. With an operating system or full system recovery, make sure your backup data is available and that you can log on with an account that has the appropriate permissions. With a full system recovery, keep in mind that data that was not included in the original backup will be deleted when you recover the system, including any in-use volumes that were not included in the backup.

- **Windows Memory Diagnostics Tools**   Allows you to diagnose a problem with the server's physical memory. Three different levels of memory testing can be performed: basic, standard, and exhaustive.

You can also access a command prompt. This command prompt gives you access to the command-line tools available during installation as well as to these additional programs:

- **Startup Repair Wizard (X:\Sources\Recovery\StartRep.exe)**   Normally, this tool is started automatically on boot failure if Windows detects an issue with the boot sector, the boot manager, or the boot configuration data (BCD) store.

- **Startup Recovery Options (X:\Sources\Recovery\Recenv.exe)**   Allows you to start the Startup Recovery Options wizard. If you previously entered the wrong recovery settings, you can provide different options.

As an administrator, you can use these tools to recover a server. You can boot the server and initiate recovery by following these steps:

1. During startup, press F8 to access the Advanced Boot Options screen. If the computer has multiple operating systems, you'll see the Windows Boot Manager screen. Select the operating system to work with, and then press F8.

2. On the Advanced Boot Options menu, use the arrow keys to select Repair Your Computer, and then press Enter.

3. The server will load the system recovery options. In the System Recovery Options Wizard, select a language and keyboard layout, and then click Next.

4. To access recovery options, you need to log on using a local administrator account. Select the local administrator to log on as, type the password for this account, and then click OK.

5. In the System Recovery Options Wizard, note the location of the operating system, and then choose the appropriate repair option. If you want to perform a system image recovery, select the related option, and then perform steps 5 to 8 of the next procedure.

You also can recover a server's operating system or perform a full system recovery by using a Windows installation disc and a backup that you created earlier with Windows Server Backup. With an operating system recovery, you recover all critical volumes but do not recover nonsystem volumes. If you recover your full system, Windows Server Backup reformats and repartitions all disks that are attached to the server. Therefore, you should use this method only when you want to recover the server data onto separate hardware or when all other attempts to recover the server on the existing hardware have failed.

NOTE When you recover the operating system or the full system, make sure that your backup data is available and that you can log on with an account that has the appropriate permissions. With a full system recovery, keep in mind that existing data that was not included in the original backup will be deleted when you recover the system. This includes any volumes that are currently used by the server but were not included in the backup.

You can recover a server's operating system or perform a full system recovery by following these steps:

1. Insert the Windows disc into the CD or DVD drive and turn on the computer. If needed, press the required key to boot from the disc. The Install Windows Wizard should appear.

2. Specify the language settings to use, and then click Next.

3. Click Repair Your Computer. Setup searches the hard disk drives for an existing Windows installation and then displays the results in the System Recovery Options Wizard. If you are recovering the operating system onto separate hardware, the list should be empty and there should be no operating system on the computer. Click Next.

4. On the System Recovery Options page, click System Image Recovery. This starts the System Image Recovery Wizard.

5. Click Use The Latest Available System Image (Recommended), and then click Next. Or click Select A System Image, and then click Next.

6. If you select an image to restore, do one of the following on the Select The Location Of The Backup page:

   - Click the location that contains the system image that you want to use, and then click Next. On the Select The Backup To Restore page, click the system image that you want to use, and then click Next.

- To browse for a system image on the network, click Advanced, and then click Search For A System Image On The Network. When you are prompted to confirm that you want to connect to the network, click Yes. In the Network Folder text box, specify the location of the server and shared folder in which the system image is stored, such as \\FileServer22\Backups, and then click OK.

- To install a driver for a backup device that doesn't show up in the location list, click Advanced, and then click Install A Driver. Insert the installation media for the device, and then click OK. After Windows installs the device driver, the backup device should be listed in the location list.

7. On the Choose How To Restore The Backup page, do the following optional tasks, and then click Next:

   - Select the Format And Repartition Disks check box to delete existing partitions and reformat the destination disks to be the same as the backup.

   - Click the Exclude Disks button, and then select the check boxes associated with any disks that you want to exclude from being formatted and partitioned. The disk that contains the backup that you are using is automatically excluded.

   - Click Install Drivers to install device drivers for the hardware to which you are recovering.

   - Click Advanced to specify whether the computer is restarted and the disks are checked for errors immediately after the recovery operation is completed.

8. On the Confirmation page, review the details for the restoration, and then click Finish. The wizard then restores the operating system or the full server as appropriate for the options you selected.

Restoring Applications, Nonsystem Volumes, and Files and Folders

Windows Server 2008 R2 provides separate processes for system state and full server recovery and the recovery of individual volumes and files and folders. You can use the Recovery Wizard in Windows Server Backup to recover nonsystem volumes and files and folders from a backup. Before you begin, you should be sure that the computer that you are recovering files to is running Windows Server 2008 R2. If you want to recover individual files and folders, you should be sure that at least one backup exists on an internal or external disk or in a remote shared folder. You cannot recover files and folders from backups saved to DVDs or removable media.

With this in mind, you can recover nonsystem volumes, files and folders, or application data by following these steps:

1. Start Windows Server Backup. In the Actions pane or on the Action menu, click Recover. This starts the Recovery Wizard.

2. On the Getting Started page, specify whether you will recover data from the local computer or from another location, and then click Next.

3. If you are recovering data from another location, specify whether the backup that you want to restore is on a local drive or a remote shared folder, click Next, and then specify location-specific settings. When you are recovering from a local drive, on the Select Backup Location page, select the location of the backup from the drop-down list. When you are recovering from a remote shared folder, on the Specify Remote Folder page, type the path to the folder that contains the backup. In the remote folder, the backup should be stored at *BackupServer*\WindowsImageBackup*ComputerName*.

4. If you are recovering from the local computer and there are multiple backups, on the Select Backup Location page, select the location of the backup in the drop-down list.

5. On the Select Backup Date page, select the date and time of the backup you want to restore using the calendar and the time list. Backups are available for dates shown in bold. Click Next.

6. On the Select Recovery Type page, do one of the following:

   - To restore individual files and folders, click Files And Folders, and then click Next. On the Select Items To Recover page, under Available Items, click the plus sign (+) to expand the list until the folder you want is visible. Click a folder to display the contents of the folder in the adjacent pane, click each item that you want to restore, and then click Next.

   - To restore noncritical, nonoperating system volumes, click Volumes, and then click Next. On the Select Volumes page, you'll see a list of source and destination volumes. Select the check boxes associated with the source volumes that you want to recover, and then select the location to which you want to recover the volume by using the Destination Volume lists. Click Next.

   - To restore application data, click Applications, and then click Next. On the Select Application page, under Applications, click the application that you want to recover. If the backup that you are using is the most recent, you will see a check box labeled Do Not Perform A Roll-Forward Recovery Of The Application Databases. Select this check box if you want to prevent Windows Server Backup from rolling forward the application database that is currently on your server. Click Next. Because any data on the destination volume will be lost when you perform the recovery, make sure that the destination volume is empty or does not contain information that you will need later.

7. On the Specify Recovery Options page, under Recovery Destination, specify whether you want to restore data to its original location (nonsystem files only) or an alternate location. For an alternate location, type the path to the restore location or click Browse to select it. With applications, you can copy

application data to an alternate location. You cannot, however, recover applications to a different location or computer.

8. Next, choose a recovery technique to apply when files and folders already exist in the recovery location. You can create copies so that you have both versions of the file or folder, overwrite existing files with recovered files, or skip duplicate files and folders to preserve existing files.

9. On the Confirmation page, review the details, and then click Recover to restore the specified items.

Managing Encryption Recovery Policy

If you're an administrator for an organization that uses the Encrypting File System (EFS), your disaster recovery planning must include additional procedures and preparations. You need to consider how to handle issues related to personal encryption certificates, EFS recovery agents, and EFS recovery policy. These issues are discussed in the sections that follow.

Understanding Encryption Certificates and Recovery Policy

File encryption is supported on a per-folder or per-file basis. Any file placed in a folder marked for encryption is automatically encrypted. Files in encrypted format can be read only by the person who encrypted the file. Before other users can read an encrypted file, the user must decrypt the file.

Every file that's encrypted has a unique encryption key. This means that encrypted files can be copied, moved, and renamed just like any other file—and in most cases these actions don't affect the encryption of the data. The user who encrypted the file always has access to the file, provided that the user's private key is available in the user's profile on the computer or the user has credential roaming with Digital Identification Management Service (DIMS). For this user, the encryption and decryption process is handled automatically and is transparent.

EFS is the process that handles encryption and decryption. The default setup for EFS allows users to encrypt files without needing special permission. Files are encrypted using a public/private key that EFS generates automatically on a per-user basis. By default, Windows XP SP1 and later releases of Windows use the Advanced Encryption Standard (AES) algorithm for encrypting files with EFS. AES is not supported on Windows 2000 or Windows XP versions prior to SP1, and AES encrypted files viewed on these computers can appear to be corrupted when in fact they are not. Internet Information Services 7 uses an AES provider for encrypting passwords by default.

Encryption certificates are stored as part of the data in user profiles. If a user works with multiple computers and wants to use encryption, an administrator needs to configure a roaming profile for that user. A roaming profile ensures that the user's profile data and public-key certificates are accessible from other computers.

Without this, users won't be able to access their encrypted files on another computer.

> **TIP** An alternative to a roaming profile is to copy the user's encryption certificate to the computers the user uses. You can do this by using the certificate backup and restore process discussed in "Backing Up and Restoring Encrypted Data and Certificates" later in this chapter. Simply back up the certificate on the user's original computer, and then restore the certificate on each of the other computers the user logs on to.

EFS has a built-in data recovery system to guard against data loss. This recovery system ensures that encrypted data can be recovered if a user's public-key certificate is lost or deleted. The most common scenario in which this occurs is when a user leaves the company and the associated user account is deleted. Although a manager might have been able to log on to the user's account, check files, and save important files to other folders, encrypted files will be accessible afterward only if the encryption is removed by the user that encrypted them to a FAT or FAT32 volume (where encryption isn't supported).

To access encrypted files after the user account has been deleted, you need to use a recovery agent. Recovery agents have access to the file encryption key that's necessary to unlock data in encrypted files. However, to protect sensitive data, recovery agents don't have access to a user's private key or any private key information.

Recovery agents are designated automatically, and the necessary recovery certificates are generated automatically as well. This ensures that encrypted files can always be recovered.

EFS recovery agents are configured at two levels:

- **Domain** The recovery agent for a domain is configured automatically when the first Windows Server 2008 R2 domain controller is installed. By default, the recovery agent is the domain administrator. Through Group Policy, domain administrators can designate additional recovery agents. Domain administrators can also delegate recovery agent privileges to designated security administrators.

- **Local computer** When a computer is part of a workgroup or in a stand-alone configuration, the recovery agent is the administrator of the local computer by default. You can designate additional recovery agents. Further, if you want local recovery agents in a domain environment rather than domain-level recovery agents, you must delete the recovery policy from the Group Policy for the domain.

You can delete recovery policies if you don't want them to be available.

Configuring the EFS Recovery Policy

Recovery policies are configured automatically for domain controllers and workstations. By default, domain administrators are the designated recovery agents for domains, and the local administrator is the designated recovery agent for a stand-alone workstation.

Through Group Policy, you can view, assign, and delete recovery agents. Follow these steps:

1. Access the Group Policy console for the local computer, site, domain, or organizational unit you want to work with. For details on working with Group Policy, see Chapter 5, "Automating Administrative Tasks, Policies, and Procedures."

2. Expand Computer Configuration, Windows Settings, Security Settings, and Public Key Policies, and then click Encrypting File System to access the configured Recovery Agents in Group Policy.

3. The pane at the right lists the recovery certificates currently assigned. Recovery certificates are listed according to who they are issued to, who issued them, their expiration date and purpose, and more.

4. To designate an additional recovery agent, right-click Encrypting File System, and then click Add Data Recovery Agent. This starts the Add Recovery Agent Wizard, which you can use to select a previously generated certificate that has been assigned to a user and mark it as a designated recovery certificate. Click Next. On the Select Recovery Agents page, click Browse Directory, and in the Find Users, Contacts, And Groups dialog box, select the user you want to work with. Click OK, and then click Next. Click Finish to add the recovery agent.

   NOTE Before you can designate additional recovery agents, you should set up a root certificate authority (CA) in the domain. Afterward, you must use the Certificates snap-in to generate a personal certificate that uses the EFS Recovery Agent template. The root CA must then approve the certificate request so that the certificate can be used. You can also use Cipher.exe to generate the EFS recovery agent key and certificate.

5. To delete a recovery agent, select the recovery agent's certificate in the right pane, and then press Delete. When prompted to confirm the action, click Yes to permanently and irrevocably delete the certificate. If the recovery policy is empty (meaning it has no other designated recovery agents), EFS is turned off so that users can no longer encrypt files.

Backing Up and Restoring Encrypted Data and Certificates

You can back up and restore encrypted data like you can any other data. The key thing to remember is that you must use backup software that understands EFS, such as the built-in backup and restore tools. You must be careful when using this type of software, however.

The backup or restore process doesn't necessarily back up or restore the certificate needed to work with the encrypted data. The user's profile data contains that certificate. If the user's account exists and the profile still contains the necessary certificate, the user can still work with the encrypted data.

If the user's account exists and you previously backed up the user's profile and then restored the profile to recover a deleted certificate, the user can still work with the encrypted data. Otherwise, there's no way to work with the data, and you need to have a designated recovery agent access the files and then remove the encryption.

Being able to back up and restore certificates is an important part of any disaster recovery plan. The next sections examine the techniques you can use to perform these tasks.

Backing Up Encryption Certificates

You use the Certificates snap-in to back up and restore personal certificates. Personal certificates are saved with the Personal Information Exchange (.pfx) format.

To back up personal certificates, follow these steps:

1. Log on as the user to the computer where the personal certificate you want to work with is stored. Click Start, type **mmc** in the Search box, and then press Enter. This opens the Microsoft Management Console (MMC).

2. In the MMC, select File, and then select Add/Remove Snap-In. This opens the Add Or Remove Snap-Ins dialog box.

3. In the Available Snap-Ins list, select Certificates, and then click Add. Select My User Account, and then click Finish. This adds the Certificates snap-in to the Selected Snap-Ins list. The focus for the snap-in is set to the currently logged-on user account.

4. Click OK to close the Add Or Remove Snap-Ins dialog box.

5. Expand Certificates—Current User, expand Personal, and then select Certificates. Right-click the certificate you want to save, click All Tasks, and then click Export. This starts the Certificate Export Wizard. Click Next.

6. Select Yes, Export The Private Key. Click Next.

7. Click Next, accepting the default values, and then type a password for the certificate. Click Next.

8. Specify a file location for the certificate file. Be sure that this location is secure, because you don't want to compromise system security. The file is saved with the .pfx extension.

9. Click Next, and then click Finish. If the export process is successful, you'll see a message box confirming this. Click OK to close the message box.

Restoring Encryption Certificates

When you have a backup of a certificate, you can restore the certificate to any computer on the network—not just the original computer. The backup and restore process is, in fact, how you move certificates from one computer to another.

Follow these steps to restore a personal certificate:

1. Copy the Personal Information Exchange (.pfx) file onto removable media, such as a flash drive or a floppy disk, and then log on as the user to the computer where you want to use the personal certificate.

   NOTE Log on to the target computer as the user whose certificate you're restoring. If you don't do this, the user won't be able to work with his or her encrypted data.

2. Access the Certificates snap-in for My User Account as described previously.

3. Expand Certificates—Current User, and then right-click Personal. Click All Tasks, and then click Import. This starts the Certificate Import Wizard.

4. Click Next, and then insert the removable media.

5. Click Browse. In the Open dialog box, locate the personal certificate on the removable media. Be sure to select Personal Information Exchange as the file type. After you locate the file, select it, and then click Open.

6. Click Next. Type the password for the personal certificate, and then click Next again.

7. The certificate should be placed in the Personal store by default. Accept the default by clicking Next. Click Finish. If the import process is successful, you'll see a message box confirming this. Click OK.

Managing TCP/IP Networking

A s an administrator, you enable networked computers to communicate by using the basic networking protocols built into Windows Server 2008 R2. The key protocol you use is TCP/IP. TCP/IP is a suite of protocols and services used for communicating over a network and is the primary protocol used for internetwork communications. Compared to configuring other networking protocols, configuring TCP/IP communications is fairly complicated, but TCP/IP is the most versatile protocol available.

NOTE Group Policy settings can affect your ability to install and manage TCP/IP networking. The key policies you should examine are in User Configuration\ Administrative Templates\Network\Network Connections and Computer Configuration\Administrative Templates\System\Group Policy. Group Policy is discussed in Chapter 5, "Automating Administrative Tasks, Policies, and Procedures."

Navigating Networking in Windows Server 2008 R2

The networking features in Windows Server 2008 R2 are different from those in earlier releases of Windows. Windows Server 2008 R2 has an extensive set of networking tools, including:

- **Network Explorer**   Provides a central console for browsing computers and devices on the network

- **Network And Sharing Center** Provides a central console for viewing and managing a computer's networking and sharing configuration
- **Network Map** Provides a visual map of the network that depicts how computers and devices are connected
- **Network Diagnostics** Provides automated diagnostics to help diagnose and resolve networking problems

Before I describe how these networking tools are used, let's first look at the Windows Server 2008 R2 features on which these tools rely, including:

- **Network Discovery** A feature of Windows Server 2008 R2 that controls the ability to see other computers and devices
- **Network Awareness** A feature of Windows Server 2008 R2 that reports changes in network connectivity and configuration

REAL WORLD Computers running Windows Vista with SP1 or later, Windows 7, Windows Server 2008, or later releases support extensions to network awareness. These extensions allow a computer connected to one or more networks via two or more interfaces (regardless of whether they are wired or wireless) to select the route with the best performance for a particular data transfer. As part of selecting the best route, Windows chooses the best interface (either wired or wireless) for the transfer. This mechanism improves the selection of wireless over wired networks when both interfaces are present.

Network discovery settings for the computer you are working with determine the computers and devices you can browse or view in Windows Server 2008 R2 networking tools. Discovery settings work in conjunction with a computer's Windows Firewall settings to block or allow the following:

- Discovery of network computers and devices
- Discovery of your computer by others

Network discovery settings are meant to provide the appropriate level of security for each of the various categories of networks to which a computer can connect. Three categories of networks are defined:

- **Domain network** Designates a network in which computers are connected to the corporate domain they are joined to.
- **Private network** Designates a network in which computers are configured as members of a homegroup or workgroup and are not connected directly to the public Internet.
- **Public network** Designates a network in a public place, such as a coffee shop or an airport, rather than an internal network.

Because a computer saves settings separately for each category of network, different block and allow settings can be used for each network category. When you connect to a network for the first time, you see a dialog box that allows you to specify the network category as either home, work, or public. If you select home or work and the computer determines that it is connected to the corporate domain it is joined to, the network category is set as Domain Network. If you select home or work and the computer is not connected to the corporate domain, the network category is set as Private Network.

Based on the network category, Windows Server 2008 R2 automatically configures settings that turn discovery on or off. The On (Enabled) state means:

- The computer can discover other computers and devices on the network.

- Other computers on the network can discover the computer.

The Off (Disabled) state means:

- The computer cannot discover other computers and devices on the network.

- Other computers on the network cannot discover the computer.

Network Explorer, shown in Figure 17-1, displays a list of discovered computers and devices on the network. You can access Network Explorer by clicking Start and then clicking Network. The computers and devices listed in Network Explorer depend on the network discovery settings of the computer, the operating system, and whether the computer is a member of a domain. If discovery is blocked and a server running Windows Server 2008 R2 is not a member of a domain, you'll see a note about this. When you click the warning message and then select Turn On Network Discovery And File Sharing, you enable network discovery, file sharing, and printer sharing. This opens related Windows Firewall ports.

FIGURE 17-1 Use Network Explorer to browse network resources.

Network And Sharing Center, shown in Figure 17-2, provides the current network status, as well as an overview of the current network configuration. You can access Network And Sharing Center by clicking Start, clicking Network, and then clicking Network And Sharing Center on the toolbar in Network Explorer.

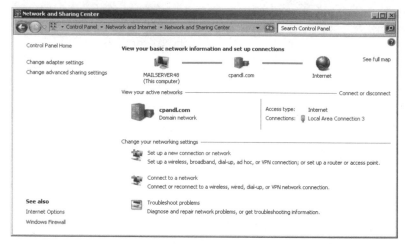

FIGURE 17-2 View and manage network settings with Network And Sharing Center.

Network And Sharing Center has two main areas:

- **Summary network map** Provides a graphical depiction of the network configuration and connections. A normal status is indicated by a line connecting the various network segments. Any problems with the network configuration or connections are depicted with warning icons. A yellow warning icon indicates a possible configuration issue. A red X indicates a lack of a connection for a particular network segment. Clicking See Full Map opens Network Map, which displays an expanded network view. Network mapping is disabled by default on domain networks and can be enabled using Group Policy.

- **Network details** Lists the current network by name and provides an overview of the network. The value below the network name shows the category of the current network as Domain Network, Private Network, or Public Network. The Access Type field specifies whether and how the computer is connected to its current network. Values for this field are No Network Access, No Internet Access, or Internet. If you click the name of a local area connection, you can display the related Local Area Connection Status dialog box.

Clicking Change Adapter Settings displays the Network Connections page, which you can use to manage network connections. Clicking Change Advanced Sharing Settings provides options for configuring the computer's sharing and discovery settings for each network profile. To manage a profile, expand the profile's view panel by clicking the Expand button (showing a down arrow), click the setting you want to work with, and then click Save Changes. To turn on or off network discovery, click Turn On Network Discovery or Turn Off Network Discovery as appropriate, and then click Save Changes.

From Network And Sharing Center, you can attempt to diagnose a warning status. To do this, click the warning icon to start Windows Network Diagnostics. Windows Network Diagnostics then attempts to identify the network problem and provide a possible solution.

NOTE In Network And Sharing Center, you can run diagnostics manually at any time by selecting Troubleshoot Problems, clicking a troubleshooter to run, and then following the prompts.

Managing Networking in Windows 7 and Windows Server 2008 R2

In Group Policy, you'll find network management policies for both wired networks (IEEE 802.3) and wireless networks (IEEE 802.11) under Computer Configuration\Windows Settings\Security Settings. Only one wired policy and one wireless policy can be created and applied at a time. This means you can establish both a wired policy and a wireless policy for computers running Windows Vista and later releases of Windows. You also can create a wireless policy for computers running Windows XP.

If you right-click the Wired Network (IEEE 802.3) node, you can create a policy for Windows Vista and later releases that specifies whether the Wire AutoConfig service is used to configure and connect these clients to 802.3 wired Ethernet networks. For Windows 7 and Windows Server 2008 R2, you have options for preventing the sharing of user credentials and for specifying whether to prohibit computers from making autoconnection attempts to the network for a specified amount of time. •

If you right-click the Wireless Network (IEEE 802.11) node, you can create separate policies for Windows XP computers and computers running later releases that enable WLAN autoconfiguration, define the specific networks that can be used, and set network permissions. For Windows 7 and Windows Server 2008 R2, you have options for preventing the sharing of user credentials, for specifying whether to prohibit computers from making autoconnection attempts to the network for a specified amount of time, and for preventing the use of hosted networks.

Windows Vista with SP1 or later and later releases of Windows support several wired and wireless enhancements. These changes allow users to change their password when connecting to a wired or wireless network (as opposed to using the Winlogon change password feature), to correct a wrong password entered during sign on, and to reset an expired password—all as part of the network logon process.

Network security enhancements include the following:

- Secure Socket Tunneling Protocol (SSTP)
- Secure Remote Access (SRA)
- CryptoAPI Version 2 (CAPI2)

- Online Certificate Status Protocol (OCSP) extensions
- Port preservation for Teredo
- Remote Desktop Protocol (RDP) file signing

SSTP allows data transmission at the data link layer over a Hypertext Transfer Protocol over Secure Sockets Layer (HTTPS) connection. SRA enables secure access to remote networks over HTTPS. Together these technologies enable users to securely access a private network using an Internet connection. SSTP and SRA represent improvements over the Point-to-Point Tunneling Protocol (PPTP) and Layer Two Tunneling Protocol/Internet Protocol Security (L2TP/IPSec) protocols because they use the standard TCP/IP ports for secure Web traffic, and this allows them to traverse most firewalls as well as Network Address Translation (NAT) and Web proxies.

SSTP uses HTTP over Secure Sockets Layer (SSL), which is also known as Transport Layer Security (TLS). HTTP over SSL (TCP port 443) is commonly used for protected communications with Web sites. Whenever users connect to a Web address that begins with *https://*, they are using HTTP over SSL. Using HTTP over SSL solves many of the virtual private network (VPN) protocol connectivity problems. Because SSTP supports both IPv4 and IPv6, users can establish secure tunnels using either IP technology. Essentially, you get VPN technology that works everywhere, which should mean far fewer support calls.

CAPI2 extends support for public key infrastructure (PKI) and X.509 certificates and implements additional functionality for certificate path validation, certificate stores, and signature verification. One of the steps during certificate path validation is revocation checking, which involves verifying the certificate status to ensure that it has not been revoked by its issuer; this is where Online Certificate Status Protocol (OCSP) comes into the picture.

OCSP is used to check the revocation status of certificates. CAPI2 also supports independent OCSP signer chains and specifying additional OCSP download locations on a per-issuer basis. Independent OCSP signer chains modify the original OCSP implementation so that it can work with OCSP responses that are signed by trusted OCSP signers that are separate from the issuer of the certificate being validated. Additional OCSP download locations make it possible to specify OCSP download locations for issuing CA certificates as URLs that are added as a property to the CA certificate.

To enhance IPv4/IPv6 coexistence, feature enhancements were implemented that allow applications to use IPv6 on an IPv4 network, such as port preservation for Teredo. Teredo is a UDP-based tunneling technology that can traverse NATs. This new feature allows Teredo communications between "port preserving" symmetric NATs and other types of NATs. A NAT is port preserving if it chooses to use the same external port number as the internal port number.

Windows Server 2008 R2 supports TCP Chimney offloading. This feature enables the networking subsystem to offload the processing of a TCP/IP connection from a server's processors to its network adapters, as long as the network adapters support

TCP/IP offload processing. Both TCP/IPv4 connections and TCP/IPv6 connections can be offloaded. By default, TCP connections are offloaded on 10 gigabits per second (Gbps) network adapters but are not offloaded on 1 Gbps network adapters. To modify the related settings, you can use Netsh.

Network Diagnostic Framework (NDF) simplifies network troubleshooting by automating many of the common troubleshooting steps and solutions. When you run Windows Network Diagnostics, each diagnostic session generates a report with diagnostics results, and you can view this information in Action Center by clicking the Troubleshooting link and then clicking View History. On the Troubleshooting History page, each diagnostic session is listed by type and date run. To get detailed information, select the session you want to review, and then click View Details.

The diagnostic information shown in Action Center comes from an Event Trace Log (ETL) file created as part of diagnostics. If you right-click a diagnostic session and then select Open File Location, you can see the files generated as part of diagnostics for the selected diagnostic session.

You can use the Netsh Trace context to perform comprehensive tracing as well as network packet capturing and filtering. You perform traces using predefined or custom scenarios and providers. Tracing scenarios are collections of providers. Providers are the actual components in the network protocol stack that you want to work with, such as TCP/IP, Windows Filtering Platform and Firewall, Wireless LAN Services, Winsock, or NDIS. Typically, you use Network Monitor (Netmon) to analyze trace data. If you collect trace data on a computer where Netmon isn't installed, you can simply copy the trace file to a computer where Netmon is installed so that you can analyze the data.

Windows Vista with SP1 or later, Windows 7, Windows Server 2008, and Windows Server 2008 R2 use the RDP 6.1 client. With this client, RDP files can be digitally signed to prevent users from opening or running potentially dangerous RDP files from unknown sources. Administrators can sign RDP files using a signing tool provided by Microsoft. Three related settings can be configured through Group Policy or through the registry. These include a comma-separated list of certificate hashes that are trusted by the administrator (known as the trusted publishers list), an option to allow users to decide to accept untrusted publishers (enabled by default), and an option to allow users to accept unsigned files (enabled by default).

Installing TCP/IP Networking

To install networking on a computer, you must install TCP/IP networking and a network adapter. Windows Server 2008 R2 uses TCP/IP as the default wide area network (WAN) protocol. Normally, you install networking during Windows Server 2008 R2 setup. You can also install TCP/IP networking through local area connection properties.

To install TCP/IP after installing Windows Server 2008 R2, log on to the computer using an account with administrator privileges and then follow these steps:

1. Click Start, and then click Network. In Network Explorer, click Network And Sharing Center on the toolbar.

2. In Network And Sharing Center, click Change Adapter Settings.

3. In Network Connections, right-click the connection you want to work with, and then click Properties. This displays the Local Area Connection Properties dialog box, shown in Figure 17-3.

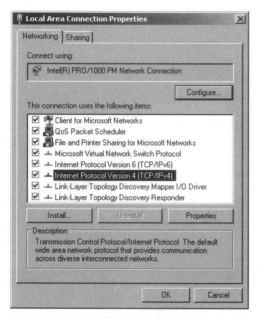

FIGURE 17-3 Install and configure TCP/IP in the Local Area Connection Properties dialog box.

4. If Internet Protocol Version 6 (TCP/IPv6), Internet Protocol Version 4 (TCP/IPv4), or both aren't shown in the list of installed components, you need to install them. Click Install. Click Protocol, and then click Add. In the Select Network Protocol dialog box, select the protocol to install, and then click OK. If you are installing both TCP/IPv6 and TCP/IPv4, repeat this procedure for each protocol.

5. In the Local Area Connection Properties dialog box, be sure that Internet Protocol Version 6 (TCP/IPv6), Internet Protocol Version 4 (TCP/IPv4), or both are selected, and then click OK.

6. As necessary, follow the instructions in the next section for configuring local area connections for the computer.

Configuring TCP/IP Networking

A local area connection is created automatically if a computer has a network adapter and is connected to a network. If a computer has multiple network adapters and is connected to a network, one local area connection is created for each adapter. If no network connection is available, you should connect the computer to the network or create a different type of connection.

Computers use IP addresses to communicate over TCP/IP. Windows Server 2008 R2 provides the following ways to configure IP addresses:

- **Manually**   IP addresses that are assigned manually are called static IP addresses. Static IP addresses are fixed and don't change unless you change them. You usually assign static IP addresses to Windows servers, and when you do this, you need to configure additional information to help the server navigate the network.

- **Dynamically**   A DHCP server (if one is installed on the network) assigns dynamic IP addresses at startup, and the addresses might change over time. Dynamic IP addressing is the default configuration.

- **Alternate addresses (IPv4 only)**   When a computer is configured to use DHCPv4 and no DHCPv4 server is available, Windows Server 2008 R2 assigns an alternate private IP address automatically. By default, the alternate IPv4 address is in the range 169.254.0.1 to 169.254.255.254 with a subnet mask of 255.255.0.0. You can also specify a user-configured alternate IPv4 address, which is particularly useful for laptop users.

Configuring Static IP Addresses

When you assign a static IP address, you need to tell the computer the IP address you want to use, the subnet mask for this IP address, and, if necessary, the default gateway to use for internetwork communications. An IP address is a numeric identifier for a computer. IP addressing schemes vary according to how your network is configured, but they're normally assigned based on a particular network segment.

IPv6 addresses and IPv4 addresses are very different. With IPv6, the first 64 bits represent the network ID and the remaining 64 bits represent the network interface. With IPv4, a variable number of the initial bits represent the network ID and the rest of the bits represent the host ID. For example, if you're working with IPv4 and a computer on the network segment 10.0.10.0 with a subnet mask of 255.255.255.0, the first three octets (8-bit groups) represent the network ID, and the address range you have available for computer hosts is 10.0.10.1 to 10.0.10.254. In this range, the address 10.0.10.255 is reserved for network broadcasts.

If you're on a private network that is indirectly connected to the Internet, you should use private IPv4 addresses. Table 17-1 summarizes private network IPv4 addresses.

TABLE 17-1 Private IPv4 Network Addressing

PRIVATE NETWORK ID	SUBNET MASK	NETWORK ADDRESS RANGE
10.0.0.0	255.0.0.0	10.0.0.0–10.255.255.255
172.16.0.0	255.240.0.0	172.16.0.0–172.31.255.255
192.168.0.0	255.255.0.0	192.168.0.0–192.168.255.255

All other IPv4 network addresses are public and must be leased or purchased. If the network is connected directly to the Internet and you've obtained a range of IPv4 addresses from your Internet service provider, you can use the IPv4 addresses you've been assigned.

Using the PING Command to Check an Address

Before you assign a static IP address, you should make sure that the address isn't already in use or reserved for use with DHCP. With the Ping command, you can check to see whether an address is in use. Open a command prompt and type **ping**, followed by the IP address you want to check.

To test the IPv4 address 10.0.10.12, you would use the following command:

`ping 10.0.10.12`

To test the IPv6 address FEC0::02BC:FF:BECB:FE4F:961D, you would use the following command:

`ping FEC0::02BC:FF:BECB:FE4F:961D`

If you receive a successful reply from the Ping test, the IP address is in use and you should try another one. If the request times out for all four Ping attempts, the IP address isn't active on the network at this time and probably isn't in use. However, a firewall could be blocking your Ping request. Your company's network administrator would also be able to confirm whether an IP address is in use.

Configuring a Static IPv4 or IPv6 Address

One local area network (LAN) connection is available for each network adapter installed. These connections are created automatically. To configure static IP addresses for a particular connection, follow these steps:

1. Click Start, and then click Network. In Network Explorer, click Network And Sharing Center on the toolbar.

2. In Network And Sharing Center, click Change Adapter Settings. In Network Connections, right-click the connection you want to work with, and then click Properties.

3. Double-click Internet Protocol Version 6 (TCP/IPv6) or Internet Protocol Version 4 (TCP/IPv4) as appropriate for the type of IP address you are
   configuring.

4. For an IPv6 address, do the following:

   ■ Click Use The Following IPv6 Address, and then type the IPv6 address in
     the IPv6 Address text box. The IPv6 address you assign to the computer
     must not be in use anywhere else on the network.

   ■ Press the Tab key. The Subnet Prefix Length field ensures that the com-
     puter communicates over the network properly. Windows Server 2008 R2
     should insert a default value for the subnet prefix into the Subnet Prefix
     Length text box. If the network doesn't use variable-length subnetting,
     the default value should suffice, but if it does use variable-length subnets,
     you'll need to change this value as appropriate for your network.

5. For an IPv4 address, do the following:

   ■ Click Use The Following IP Address, and then type the IPv4 address in the
     IP Address text box. The IPv4 address you assign to the computer must
     not be in use anywhere else on the network.

   ■ Press the Tab key. The Subnet Mask field ensures that the computer com-
     municates over the network properly. Windows Server 2008 R2 should
     insert a default value for the subnet mask into the Subnet Mask text box.
     If the network doesn't use variable-length subnetting, the default value
     should suffice, but if it does use variable-length subnets, you'll need to
     change this value as appropriate for your network.

6. If the computer needs to access other TCP/IP networks, the Internet, or other
   subnets, you must specify a default gateway. Type the IP address of the network's default router in the Default Gateway text box.

7. Domain Name System (DNS) is needed for domain name resolution. Type
   a preferred address and an alternate DNS server address in the text boxes
   provided.

8. When you have finished, click OK twice. Repeat this process for other network adapters and IP protocols you want to configure.

9. With IPv4 addressing, configure WINS as necessary.

Configuring Dynamic IP Addresses and Alternate
IP Addressing

Although most servers have static IP addresses, you can configure servers to use
dynamic addressing, alternate IP addressing, or both. You configure dynamic and
alternate addressing by following these steps:

1. Click Start, and then click Network. In Network Explorer, click Network And
   Sharing Center on the toolbar.

2. In Network And Sharing Center, click Change Adapter Settings. In Network Connections, one LAN connection is shown for each network adapter installed. These connections are created automatically. If you don't see a LAN connection for an installed adapter, check the driver for the adapter. It might be installed incorrectly. Right-click the connection you want to work with, and then click Properties.

3. Double-click Internet Protocol Version 6 (TCP/IPv6) or Internet Protocol Version 4 (TCP/IPv4) as appropriate for the type of IP address you are configuring.

4. Select Obtain An IPv6 Address Automatically or Obtain An IP Address Automatically as appropriate for the type of IP address you are configuring. You can select Obtain DNS Server Address Automatically, or you can select Use The Following DNS Server Addresses and then type a preferred and alternate DNS server address in the text boxes provided.

5. When you use dynamic IPv4 addressing, you can configure an automatic alternate address or manually configure the alternate address. To use an automatic configuration, on the Alternate Configuration tab, select Automatic Private IP Address. Click OK, click Close, and then skip the remaining step.

6. To use a manual configuration, on the Alternate Configuration tab, select User Configured, and then type the IP address you want to use in the IP Address text box. The IP address that you assign to the computer should be a private IP address, as shown earlier in Table 17-1, and it must not be in use anywhere else when the settings are applied. Complete the alternate configuration by entering a subnet mask, default gateway, DNS server, and WINS settings. When you have finished, click OK, and then click Close.

Configuring Multiple Gateways

To provide fault tolerance in case of a router outage, you can choose to configure Windows Server 2008 R2 computers so that they use multiple default gateways. When you assign multiple gateways, Windows Server 2008 R2 uses the gateway metric to determine which gateway is used and at what time. The gateway metric indicates the routing cost of using a gateway. The gateway with the lowest routing cost, or metric, is used first. If the computer can't communicate with this gateway, Windows Server 2008 R2 tries to use the gateway with the next lowest metric.

The best way to configure multiple gateways depends on the configuration of your network. If your organization's computers use DHCP, you probably want to configure the additional gateways through settings on the DHCP server. If computers use static IP addresses or you want to set gateways specifically, assign them by following these steps:

1. Click Start, and then click Network. In Network Explorer, click Network And Sharing Center on the toolbar.

2. In Network And Sharing Center, click Change Adapter Settings. In Network Connections, right-click the connection you want to work with, and then click Properties.

3. Double-click Internet Protocol Version 6 (TCP/IPv6) or Internet Protocol Version 4 (TCP/IPv4) as appropriate for the type of IP address you are configuring.

4. Click Advanced to open the Advanced TCP/IP Settings dialog box, shown in Figure 17-4.

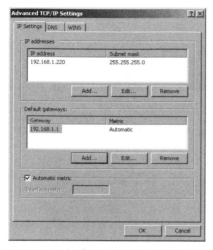

FIGURE 17-4 Configure multiple IP addresses and gateways in the Advanced TCP/IP Settings dialog box.

5. The Default Gateways panel shows the current gateways that have been manually configured (if any). You can enter additional default gateways as necessary. Click Add, and then type the gateway address in the Gateway text box.

6. By default, Windows Server 2008 R2 automatically assigns a metric to the gateway. You can also assign the metric yourself. To do this, clear the Automatic Metric check box, enter a metric in the text box provided, and then Click Add.

7. Repeat steps 5 and 6 for each gateway you want to add.

8. Click OK, and then click Close.

Configuring Networking for Hyper-V

After you install Hyper-V and create an external virtual network, your server uses a virtual network adapter to connect to the physical network. When you work with the Network Connections page, you will see the original network adapter and a new virtual network adapter. The original network adapter will have nothing bound to it except the Microsoft Virtual Network Switch Protocol, and the virtual network adapter will have all the standard protocols and services bound to it. The virtual network adapter that appears under Network Connections will have the same name as the virtual network switch with which it is associated.

> **NOTE** As part of the Hyper-V configuration, you can create an internal virtual network, which allows communications only between the server and hosted virtual machines. This configuration exposes a virtual network adapter to the parent server without the need to have a physical network adapter associated with it. Hyper-V only binds the virtual network service to a physical network adapter when an external virtual network is created.

Following this, when you install Hyper-V on a server and enable external virtual networking, you'll find that virtual network switching is being used. As shown in Figure 17-5, the server has a local area connection with the Microsoft Virtual Network Switch Protocol enabled and all other networking components not enabled and an entry for Local Area Connection—Virtual Network with all the networking components enabled except for the Microsoft Virtual Network Switch Protocol. This is the configuration you want to use to ensure proper communications for the server and any hosted virtual machines that use networking. If this configuration is changed, virtual machines won't be able to connect to the external network.

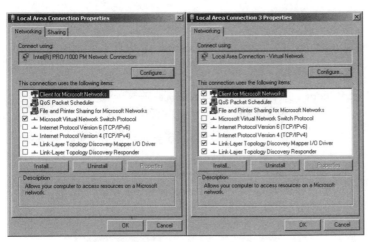

FIGURE 17-5 Use switched virtual networking to ensure communications with hosted virtual machines.

Managing Network Connections

Local area connections make it possible for computers to access resources on the network and the Internet. One local area connection is created automatically for each network adapter installed on a computer. This section examines techniques you can use to manage these connections.

Checking the Status, Speed, and Activity for Local Area Connections

To check the status of a local area connection, follow these steps:

1. Click Start, and then click Network. In Network Explorer, click Network And Sharing Center on the toolbar.

2. In Network And Sharing Center, click Change Adapter Settings. In Network Connections, right-click the connection you want to work with, and then click Status.

3. This displays the Local Area Connection Status dialog box. If the connection is disabled or the media is unplugged, you won't be able to access this dialog box. Enable the connection or connect the network cable to resolve the problem, and then try to display the Status dialog box again.

Enabling and Disabling Local Area Connections

Local area connections are created and connected automatically. If you want to disable a connection so that it cannot be used, follow these steps:

1. Click Start, and then click Network. In Network Explorer, click Network And Sharing Center on the toolbar.

2. In Network And Sharing Center, click Change Adapter Settings. In Network Connections, right-click the connection, and then click Disable to deactivate the connection and disable it.

3. If you want to enable the connection later, right-click the connection in Network Connections, and then click Enable.

If you want to disconnect from a network, follow these steps:

1. Click Start, and then click Network. In Network Explorer, click Network And Sharing Center on the toolbar.

2. In Network And Sharing Center, click Change Adapter Settings. In Network Connections, right-click the connection, and then click Disconnect. Typically, only remote access connections have a Disconnect option.

3. If you want to activate the connection later, right-click the connection in Network Connections, and then click Connect.

Renaming Local Area Connections

Windows Server 2008 R2 initially assigns default names to local area connections. In Network Connections, you can rename a connection at any time by right-clicking the connection, clicking Rename, and then typing a new name. If a computer has multiple local area connections, a descriptive name can help you and others better understand the uses of a particular connection.

CHAPTER 18

Administering Network Printers and Print Services

As an administrator, you need to take two main steps to allow users throughout a network to access print devices connected to Windows Server 2008 R2. First, you need to set up a print server, and then you need to use the print server to share print devices on the network.

This chapter covers the essentials of setting up shared printing and describes how users access it on the network. You'll also find advice on administering printers and troubleshooting printer problems, which is where we'll begin.

Managing the Print and Document Services Role

A print server provides a central location for sharing printers on a network. When many users require access to the same printers, you should configure print servers in the domain. In earlier releases of the Windows Server operating system, all servers were installed with basic print services. With Windows Server 2008 R2, you must specifically configure a server to be a print server.

Using Print Devices

Two types of print devices are used on a network:

- **Local print device** A print device that's physically attached to a user's computer and employed only by the user who's logged on to that computer.

- **Network print device** A print device that's set up for remote access over the network. This can be a print device attached directly to a print server or a print device attached directly to the network through a network interface card (NIC).

NOTE The key difference between a local printer and a network printer is that a local printer isn't shared. You can easily make a local printer a network printer. To learn how to do this, see "Starting and Stopping Printer Sharing" later in this chapter.

You install new network printers on print servers or as separate print devices attached to the network. A *print server* is a workstation or server configured to share one or more printers. These printers can be physically attached to the computer or connected to the network. The disadvantage of running a print server with a workstation operating system instead of a server operating system is the limited number of allowed connections. With Windows Server 2008 R2, you don't have to worry about operating system–enforced connection limits.

You can configure any Windows Server 2008 R2 system as a print server. The print server's primary job is to share print devices on the network and to handle print spooling. The main advantages of print servers are that printers have a centrally managed print queue and you don't have to install printer drivers on client systems.

You don't have to use a print server, however. You can connect users directly to a network-attached printer. When you do this, the network printer is handled much like a local printer attached directly to the user's computer. The key differences are that multiple users can connect to the printer and that each user has a different print queue. Each individual print queue is managed separately, which can make administration and problem resolution difficult.

Printing Essentials

An understanding of how printing works can go a long way when you're trying to troubleshoot printer problems. When you print documents, many processes, drivers, and devices work together to print the documents. If you use a printer connected to a print server, the key operations are as follows:

- **Printer driver** When you print a document in an application, your computer uses a printer driver to handle the printing process. If the print device is attached to your computer physically, the printer driver is accessed from a local disk drive. If the print device is located on a remote computer, the printer driver might be downloaded from the remote computer. The availability of printer drivers on the remote computer is configurable by operating system and chip architecture. If the computer can't obtain the latest printer driver, an administrator probably hasn't enabled the driver for the computer's operating system. For more information, see "Managing Printer Drivers" later in this chapter.

- **Local print spool and print processor**   The application you print from uses the printer driver to translate the document into a file format that the selected print device can understand. Your computer then passes the document to the local print spooler. The local spooler in turn passes the document to a print processor, which creates the raw print data necessary for printing on the print device.

- **Print router and print spooler on the print server**   The raw data is passed back to the local print spooler. If you're printing to a remote printer, the raw data is then routed to the print spooler on the print server. On Windows Server 2008 R2 systems, the printer router, Winspool.drv, handles the tasks of locating the remote printer, routing print jobs, and downloading printer drivers to the local system if necessary. If any of these tasks fails, the print router is usually the culprit. See "Solving Spooling Problems" and "Setting Printer Access Permissions" later in this chapter to learn about possible fixes for this problem. If these procedures don't work, you might want to replace or restore Winspool.drv.

  The main reason for downloading printer drivers to clients is to maintain a single location for installing driver updates. This way, instead of having to install a new driver on all the client systems, you install the driver on the print server and allow clients to download the new driver. For more information on working with printer drivers, see "Managing Printer Drivers" later in this chapter.

- **Printer (print queue)**   The document goes from the print spooler to the printer stack—which in some operating systems is called the *print queue*—for the selected print device. Once in the queue, the document is referred to as a *print job*—a task for the print spooler to handle. The length of time the document waits in the printer stack is based on its priority and position within the printer stack. For more information, see "Scheduling and Prioritizing Print Jobs" later in this chapter.

- **Print monitor**   When the document reaches the top of the printer stack, the print monitor sends the document to the print device, where it's actually printed. If the printer is configured to notify users that the document has been printed, you see a message confirming this.

  The specific print monitor used by Windows Server 2008 R2 depends on the print device configuration and type. You might also see monitors from the print device manufacturer. This dynamic-link library (DLL) is required to print to the print device. If it's corrupted or missing, you might need to reinstall it.

- **Print device** The print device is the physical device that prints documents on paper. Common print device problems and display errors include Insert Paper Into Tray *X*, Low Toner, Out Of Paper, Out Of Toner or Out Of Ink, Paper Jam, and Printer Offline.

Group Policy can affect your ability to install and manage printers. If you're having problems and believe they're related to Group Policy, you should examine the key policies in the following locations:

- Computer Configuration\Administrative Templates\Printers
- User Configuration\Administrative Templates\Control Panel\Printers
- User Configuration\Administrative Templates\Start Menu And Taskbar

Configuring Print Servers

You configure a server as a print server by adding the Print and Document Services role and configuring this role to use one or more of the following role services:

- **Print Server** Configures the server as a print server and installs the Print Management console. You can use the Print Management console to manage multiple printers and print servers, to migrate printers to and from other print servers, and to manage print jobs.

- **Line Printer Daemon (LPD) Service** Enables UNIX-based computers or other computers using the Line Printer Remote (LPR) service to print to shared printers on the server.

- **Internet Printing** Creates a Web site where authorized users can manage print jobs on the server. It also lets users who have Internet Printing Client installed to connect and print to shared printers on the server by using the Internet Printing Protocol (IPP). The default Internet address for Internet Printing is http://*ServerName*/Printers, where *ServerName* is a placeholder for the internal or external server name, such as http://PrintServer15/Printers or http://www.cpandl.com/Printers.

- **Distributed Scan Server** Establishes the server as a scan server, which is used to run scan processes. Scan processes are rules that define scan settings and control delivery of scanned documents on your network. The Scan Management snap-in is installed when you install this role service. Scan Management allows you to manage Web Services on Devices (WSD)–enabled scanners, scan servers, and scan processes.

You can add the Print and Document Services role to a server by following these steps:

1. In Server Manager, select the Roles node in the left pane, and then click Add Roles. This starts the Add Roles Wizard. If the wizard displays the Before You Begin page, read the Welcome text, and then click Next.

2. On the Select Server Roles page, select Print And Document Services, and then click Next twice.

3. On the Select Role Services page, select one or more role services to install. To allow for interoperability with UNIX, be sure to add LPD Service. Click Next.

4. When you install Internet Printing, you must also install Web Server (IIS) and some related components. You are prompted to automatically add the required role services. If you click Add Required Role Services to continue and install these role services, you're given the opportunity to add other role services for Web Server (IIS).

5. When you install Distributed Scan Server, you need to identify a service account under which the scan server runs. This service account provides the network identity for the scan server, allowing it to write files locally and communicate with network resources. The service account must have Read permission to the scan processes in Active Directory and to the scan destinations, and it should not be a user account associated with an actual user. As discussed in "Implementing Managed Accounts" in Chapter 10, you create service accounts using Windows PowerShell.

6. When you've completed all the optional pages, click Next. You see the Confirm Installation Options page. Click Install to begin the installation process. When Setup finishes installing the server with the features you selected, you see the Installation Results page. Review the installation details to ensure that all phases of the installation were completed successfully.

Enabling and Disabling File and Printer Sharing

File and printer sharing settings control access to file shares and printers that are attached to a computer. You can manage a computer's file and printer sharing configuration by following these steps:

1. Click Start, and then click Network. On the Network Explorer toolbar, click Network And Sharing Center.

2. In Network And Sharing Center, click Change Advanced Sharing Settings in the left pane. Select the network profile for the network for which file and printer sharing should be enabled. Typically, this is the Domain profile.

3. Standard file and printer sharing controls network access to shared resources. To configure standard file sharing, do one of the following:

   - Select Turn On File And Printer Sharing to enable file and printer sharing.

   - Select Turn Off File And Printer Sharing to disable file and printer sharing.

Getting Started with Print Management

Print Management should be your tool of choice for working with printers and print servers. After you install the Print and Document Services role, Print Management is available on the Administrative Tools menu as a stand-alone console. You can also add Print Management as a snap-in to any custom console you create.

Using Print Management, shown in Figure 18-1, you can install, view, and manage the printers and Windows print servers in your organization. Print Management also displays the status of printers and print servers. If a printer provides a Web-based management interface, Print Management can display additional information about the printer, including toner and paper levels.

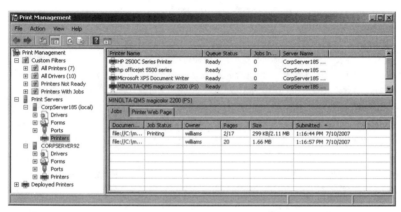

FIGURE 18-1 Use Print Management to work with print servers and printers throughout your organization.

By default, Print Management allows you to manage local print servers. You can manage and monitor other print servers in the organization by adding them to the console. However, these print servers must be running Windows 2000 or later releases. Additionally, to manage a remote print server, you must be a member of the local Administrators group on the print server or a member of the Domain Admins group in the domain of which the print server is a member.

When you select a print server's Printers node, the main pane lists the associated printer queues by printer name, queue status, number of jobs in a queue, and server name. If you right-click Printers and then click Show Extended View, you can turn on Extended view. Extended view makes it easy to track the status of both printers and print jobs by displaying information about the status of a print job, its owner, the number of pages, the size of the job, when it was submitted, its port, and its priority.

In addition, when a printer has a Web page, Extended view displays a Printer Web Page tab that lets you directly access the printer's Web page. This Web page provides details about the printer's status, its physical properties, and its configuration, and it sometimes allows remote administration.

You can add print servers to Print Management by following these steps:

1. In Print Management, right-click the Print Servers node in the left pane, and then click Add/Remove Servers.

2. In the Add/Remove Servers dialog box, shown in Figure 18-2, you'll see a list of the print servers you previously added.

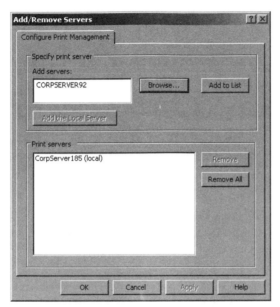

FIGURE 18-2 Add print servers to Print Management so that you can manage and monitor them.

Do one of the following, and then click Add To List:

- In the Add Servers list, type or paste the names of the print servers you want to add, using commas to separate computer names.

- Click Browse to display the Select Print Server dialog box. Click the print server you want to use, and then click Select Server.

3. Repeat the previous step as necessary, and then click OK.

You can remove print servers from Print Management by following these steps:

1. In Print Management, right-click the Print Servers node in the left pane, and then click Add/Remove Servers.

2. In the Add/Remove Servers dialog box, you'll see a list of the print servers that are being monitored. Under Print Servers, select one or more servers, and then click Remove.

Installing Printers

The following sections examine techniques you can use to install printers. Windows Server 2008 R2 allows you to install and manage printers anywhere on the network. To install or configure a new printer on Windows Server 2008 R2, you must be a member of the Administrators, Print Operators, or Server Operators group. To connect to and print documents to the printer, you must have the appropriate access permissions. See "Setting Printer Access Permissions" later in this chapter for details.

Using the Autoinstall Feature of Print Management

Print Management can automatically detect all network printers located on the same subnet as the computer on which the console is running. After detection, Print Management can automatically install the appropriate printer drivers, set up print queues, and share the printers. To automatically install network printers and configure a print server, follow these steps:

1. Start Print Management by clicking Start, pointing to Administrative Tools, and then clicking Print Management.

2. In Print Management, expand the Print Servers node by double-clicking it.

3. Right-click the entry for the local or remote server you want to work with, and then click Add Printer. This starts the Network Printer Installation Wizard.

4. On the Print Installation page, select Search The Network For Printers, and then click Next.

5. The wizard searches the local subnet for network printers. If printers are found, you'll see a list of printers by name, IP address, and status. Click a printer to install, and then click Next.

6. If there are multiple possible drivers for a detected printer, you are prompted to select the driver to use. Click Close.

Installing and Configuring Physically Attached Print Devices

Most physically attached print devices are connected to a computer directly through a universal serial bus (USB) cable or an infrared (IR) port. You can configure physically attached printers as local print devices or as network print devices. The key difference is that a local device is accessible only to users logged on to the computer and a network device is accessible to network users as a shared print device. Remember that the workstation or server you're logged on to becomes the print server for the device you're configuring. If the computer is sleeping or turned off, the printer will not be available.

You can install physically attached print devices locally by logging on to the print server you want to configure; you can install the print devices remotely through Remote Desktop. If you're configuring a local Plug and Play printer and are logged on to the print server, installing a print device is a snap. Once the printer is installed, you need to configure it for use.

You can install and configure a print device by following these steps:

1. Power on the printer, and then connect the print device to the server using the appropriate cable.

2. If Windows Server 2008 R2 automatically detects the print device, Windows begins installing the device and the necessary drivers. If the necessary drivers aren't found, you might need to insert the printer's driver disc into the CD-ROM drive.

3. If Windows Server 2008 R2 doesn't detect the print device automatically, you need to install the print device manually as described in the next set of instructions.

4. After you install the printer, you can configure the printer. In Print Management, expand the Print Servers node and the node for the server you want to work with. When you select the Printers node for the server you are configuring, you'll see a list of available printers in the main pane. Right-click the printer you want to configure, and then click Manage Sharing. This displays the printer's Properties dialog box with the Sharing tab selected, as shown in Figure 18-3.

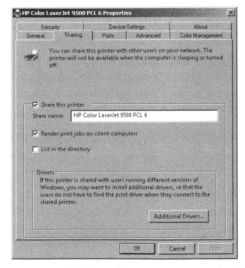

FIGURE 18-3 Configure the printer in the Properties dialog box.

5. When you select the Share This Printer check box, Windows Server 2008 R2 sets the default share name to the name of the printer. You can type a different name for the printer share in the Share Name field.

   NOTE While Windows NT–compatible share names can be only eight characters long and cannot contain spaces, share names for Windows 2000 and later releases can be up to 256 characters and can include spaces. In a large organization, you'll want the share name to be logical and helpful in locating the printer. For example, you might want to give the name Twelfth Floor NE to the printer that points to a print device in the northeast corner of the twelfth floor.

6. Listing the printer share in Active Directory allows users to search for and find the printer more easily. If you want the printer share to be listed in Active Directory, select the List In The Directory check box.

7. When you share a printer, Windows Server 2008 R2 automatically makes drivers available so that users can download them when they first connect to the printer. To make additional drivers available, click Additional Drivers. In the Additional Drivers dialog box, select operating systems that can download the printer driver. As necessary, insert the Windows Server 2008 R2 installation media, the printer driver disc, or both for the selected operating systems. The Windows Server 2008 R2 media has drivers for most Windows operating systems. Click OK twice.

Sometimes Windows won't detect your printer. In this case, follow these steps to install the print device:

1. In Print Management, expand the Print Servers node and the node for the server you want to work with.

2. Right-click the server's Printers node, and then click Add Printer. This starts the Network Printer Installation Wizard.

3. On the Printer Installation page, shown in Figure 18-4, select Add A New Printer Using An Existing Port, and then choose the appropriate LPT, COM, or USB port. You can also print to a file. If you do, Windows Server 2008 R2 prompts users for a file name each time they print. Click Next.

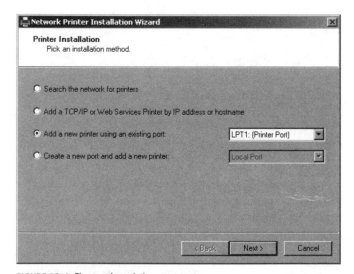

FIGURE 18-4 Choose the existing port to use.

4. On the Printer Driver page, choose one of the following options:

- If Windows detected the printer type on the selected port and a compatible driver was found automatically, a printer driver is listed that reflects the printer manufacturer and model and the Use The Printer Driver That The Wizard Selected option is selected by default. To accept this setting, simply click Next.

- If a compatible driver is not available and you want to choose an existing driver installed on the computer, select the Use An Existing Driver On The Computer option. After you choose the appropriate driver from the selection list, click Next.

- If a compatible driver is not available and you want to install a new driver, select Install A New Driver, and then click Next. As shown in Figure 18-5, you must now specify the print device manufacturer and model. This allows Windows Server 2008 R2 to assign a printer driver to the print device. After you choose a print device manufacturer, choose a printer model. For example, if you have an HP Color LaserJet 2700 Series PCL6 printer, you'd choose HP as the manufacturer and HP Color LaserJet 2700 Series PCL6 as the printer.

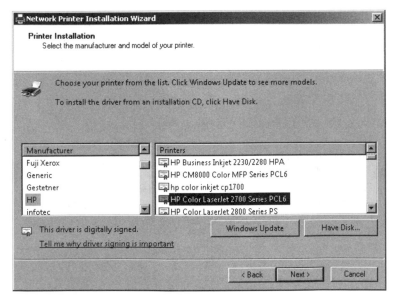

FIGURE 18-5 Select a print device manufacturer and printer model in the Network Printer Installation Wizard.

REAL WORLD If the device manufacturer and model you're using aren't displayed in the list, click Windows Update. Windows will then connect to the Windows Update Web site to update the list of printers to show additional models. This feature is part of the automatic driver provisioning feature. It can take several minutes to retrieve the updated list. You should then be able to select your printer manufacturer and model. If you can't, download the driver from the manufacturer's Web site, and then extract the driver files. Click Have Disk. In the Install From Disk dialog box, click Browse. In the Locate File dialog box, locate the .inf driver file for the device, and then click Open.

NOTE If a driver for the specific printer model you're using isn't available, you can usually select a generic driver or a driver for a similar print device. Consult the print device documentation for pointers.

5. Assign a name to the printer. This is the name you'll see in Print Management.

6. Specify whether the printer is available to remote users. To create a printer accessible to remote users, select the Share This Printer option, and then enter a name for the shared resource. In a large organization you'll want the share name to be logical and helpful in locating the printer. For example, you could give the name Twelfth Floor NE to the printer that points to the print device in the northeast corner of the twelfth floor.

7. If you like, you can enter a location description and comment. This information can help users find a printer and determine its capabilities. Click next.

8. The final page lets you review the settings. When you're ready to complete the installation, click Next.

9. After Windows installs the printer driver and configures the printer, you'll see a status page. Ensure that the driver and printer installation succeeded before continuing. If there were errors, you need to correct any problems and repeat this process. To test the printer, select Print Test Page, and then click Finish. To install another printer, select Add Another Printer, and then click Finish.

When the Network Printer Installation Wizard finishes installing the new printer, the Printers folder will have an additional icon with the name set the way you specified. You can change the printer properties and check printer status at any time. For more information, see "Configuring Printer Properties" later in this chapter.

TIP If you repeat this process, you can create additional printers for the same print device. All you need to do is change the printer name and share name. Having additional printers for a single print device allows you to set different properties to serve different needs. For example, you could have a high-priority printer for print jobs that need to be printed immediately and a low-priority printer for print jobs that aren't as urgent.

Installing Network-Attached Print Devices

A network-attached print device is attached directly to the network through a network adapter card. Network-attached printers are configured as network print devices so that they're accessible to network users as shared print devices. Remember that the server on which you configure the print device becomes the print server for the device you're configuring.

Install a network-attached print device by following these steps:

1. In Print Management, expand the Print Servers node and the node for the server you want to work with.

2. Right-click the server's Printers node, and then click Add Printer. This starts the Network Printer Installation Wizard.

3. On the Printer Installation page, select Add A TCP/IP Or Web Services Printer By IP Address Or Hostname, and then click Next.

4. On the Printer Address page, choose one of the following options in the Type Of Device list:

   - **Autodetect**   Choose this option if you are unsure of the printer device type. Windows Server 2008 R2 will try to detect the type of device automatically.

   - **TCP/IP Device**   Choose this option if you are sure the printer is a TCP/IP device.

   - **Web Services Printer**   Choose this option if you are sure the printer is an Internet print device.

5. Enter the host name or IP address for the printer, such as 192.168.1.90. With the Autodetect and TCP/IP Device options, the wizard sets the port name to the same value. You can use a different value if you want to.

   TIP   The port name doesn't matter as long as it's unique on the system. If you're configuring multiple printers on the print server, be sure to record the port-to-printer mapping.

6. Click Next, and the wizard attempts to automatically detect the print device. If the wizard is unable to detect the print device, be sure that the following are true:

   - You selected the correct type of print device.
   - The print device is turned on and connected to the network.
   - The printer is configured properly.
   - You typed the correct IP address or printer name.

7. If the device type, IP address, or printer name is incorrect, click Back, and then retype this information.

8. If the information is correct, you might need to further identify the device. In the Device Type area on the Additional Port Information Required page, click Standard, and then select the printer model or network adapter type used by the printer. Or click Custom, and then click Settings to define custom settings for the printer, such as protocol and Simple Network Management Protocol (SNMP) status.

9. On the Printer Driver page, choose one of the following options:

   - If Windows detected the printer type on the selected port and a compatible driver was found automatically, a printer driver is listed that reflects the printer manufacturer and model and the Use The Printer Driver That The Wizard Selected option is selected by default. To accept this setting, simply click Next.

   - If a compatible driver is not available and you want to choose an existing driver installed on the computer, select the Use An Existing Driver option. After you use the selection list to choose the appropriate driver, click Next.

   - If a compatible driver is not available and you want to install a new driver, select Install A New Driver, and then click Next. Specify the print device manufacturer. This allows Windows Server 2008 R2 to assign a printer driver to the print device. After you choose a print device manufacturer, choose a printer model. For example, if you have an HP LaserJet 8150 PCL printer, you'd choose HP as the manufacturer and HP LaserJet 8150 Series PCL as the printer.

   REAL WORLD If the device manufacturer and model you're using aren't displayed in the list, click Windows Update. Windows will then connect to the Windows Update Web site to update the list of printers to show additional models. This feature is part of the automatic driver provisioning feature. It can take several minutes to retrieve the updated list. You should then be able to select your printer manufacturer and model. If you can't, download the driver from the manufacturer's Web site, and then extract the driver files. Click Have Disk. In the Install From Disk dialog box, click Browse. In the Locate File dialog box, locate the .inf driver file for the device, and then click Open.

10. Assign a name to the printer. This is the name you'll see in Print Management.

11. Specify whether the printer is available to remote users. To create a printer accessible to remote users, select the Share Name option, and then enter a name for the shared resource. In a large organization, you should use a share name that is logical and helpful in locating the printer. For example, Twelfth Floor NE would be a good name for the printer that points to the print device in the northeast corner of the twelfth floor.

12. If you like, you can enter a location description and comment. This information can help users find a printer and determine its capabilities. Click Next.

13. The final page lets you review the settings. When you're ready to complete the installation, click Next.

14. After Windows installs the printer driver and configures the printer, you'll see a status page. Ensure that the driver and printer installation succeeded before continuing. If there were errors, you need to correct any problems and repeat this process. To test the printer, select Print Test Page, and then click Finish. To install another printer, select Add Another Printer, and then click Finish.

When the Network Printer Installation Wizard finishes installing the new printer, the Printers folder will have an additional icon with the name set the way you specified. You can change the printer properties and check printer status at any time. For more information, see "Configuring Printer Properties" later in this chapter.

TIP If you repeat this process, you can create additional printers for the same print device. All you need to do is change the printer name and share name. Having additional printers for a single print device allows you to set different properties to serve different needs. For example, you could have a high-priority printer for print jobs that need to be printed immediately and a low-priority printer for print jobs that aren't as urgent.

Connecting to Printers Created on the Network

After you create a network printer, remote users can connect to it and use it much as they do any other printer. You need to set up a connection on a user-by-user basis or have users do this themselves. To create a connection to the printer on a Windows Vista or Windows 7 system, follow these steps:

1. Do one of the following:

   ■ For Windows Vista, with the user logged on, click Start, click Control Panel, and then double-click Printers. In the Printers window, click Add A Printer to start the Add Printer Wizard.

   ■ For Windows 7, with the user logged on, click Start, and then click Devices And Printers. In Devices And Printers, click Add A Printer to start the Add Printer Wizard.

2. Select Add A Network, Wireless Or Bluetooth Printer. The wizard searches for available devices.

3. If the printer you want is listed in the Select A Printer list, click it, and then click Next.

4. If the printer you want is not listed in the Select A Printer list, click The Printer That I Want Isn't Listed. On the Find A Printer By Name Or TCP/IP Address page, do one of the following:

   ■ To browse the network for shared printers, choose Find A Printer In The Directory, Based On Location Or Feature, and then click Next. Click the printer to use, and then click Select.

- To specify the printer to use by its share path, choose Select A Shared Printer By Name. Type the UNC path to the shared printer, such as **\\PrintServer12\Twelfth Floor NE**, or the Web path to an Internet Printer, such as **http://PrintServer12/Printers/IPrinter52/.printer**.

- To specify a printer to use by TCP/IP address or host name, select Add A Printer Using A TCP/IP Address Or Hostname, and then click Next. Choose a device type, and then enter the host name or IP address for the printer, such as **192.168.1.90**. If you select the Autodetect or TCP/IP Device options, the wizard will set the port name to the same value. You can use a different value if you want to. Click Next.

5. On the Type A Printer Name page, the printer name is set for you. You can accept the default name or enter a new name. Click Next to install the printer, and then click Finish. The user can now print to the network printer by selecting the printer in an application. With Windows 7, the Device And Printers folder on the user's computer shows the new network printer. With Windows Vista, the Printers folder on the user's computer shows the new network printer.

To create the connection to the printer on a Windows XP system, follow these steps:

1. With the user logged on, access the Printers And Faxes folder.

2. Select or double-click Add A Printer to start the Add Printer Wizard. On the initial wizard page, select A Network Printer, and then click Next.

3. In the Specify A Printer dialog box, choose a method for finding the network printer. The following options are available:

   - **Find A Printer In The Directory** Choose this option if you want to search Active Directory for the printer. All printers configured for sharing on Windows Server 2008 R2 systems are automatically listed in Active Directory. However, you can remove printers from the directory.

   - **Type The Printer Name, Or Click Next To Browse For A Printer** Choose this option if you want to browse the network for shared printers just as you'd browse My Network Places.

   - **Connect To A Printer On The Internet Or On Your Intranet** Choose this option if you want to enter the URL of an Internet printer.

4. After you select the printer, click OK.

5. Specify whether the printer is the default used by Windows applications. Select Yes or No, and then click Next.

6. Choose Finish to complete the operation. The user can now print to the network printer by selecting the printer in an application. The Printers And Faxes folder on the user's computer shows the new network printer. You can configure local property settings by using this icon. By default, the printer name is set to *Printer* On *Computer*, such as HP DeskJet On ENGSVR01.

Deploying Printer Connections

Connecting to printers is fairly easy, but you can make the process even easier by deploying printer connections through Group Policy. You can deploy printer connections to computers or users via the Group Policy objects (GPOs) that Windows applies. Deploy the connections to groups of users when you want users to be able to access the printers from any computer they log on to. Deploy the connections to groups of computers when you want all users of the computers to access the printers. For per-computer connections, Windows adds or removes printer connections when the computer starts. For per-user connections, Windows adds or removes printer connections when the user logs on.

To deploy printer connections to computers running versions of Windows earlier than Windows Vista, you must follow these steps:

1. In the Group Policy Management Console (GPMC), right-click the GPO for the site, domain, or organizational unit you want to work with, and then click Edit. This opens the policy editor for the GPO.

2. In the Group Policy Management Editor, do one of the following:

   - To deploy the printer connections on a per-computer basis, double-click the Windows Settings folder in the Computer Configuration node, and then click Scripts.

   - To deploy the printer connections on a per-user basis, double-click the Windows Settings folder in the User Configuration node, and then click Scripts.

3. Using Windows Explorer, copy PushPrinterConnections.exe from the %SystemRoot%\System32 folder to the Computer\Scripts\Startup, User\Scripts\Logon, or User\Scripts\Logoff folder for the related policy. Policies are stored in the %SystemRoot%\Sysvol\Domain\Policies folder on domain controllers. PushPrinterConnections.exe is included with earlier versions of Windows Server and is not included with Windows Server 2008 R2.

4. In the Group Policy Management Editor, right-click Startup or Logon, and then click Properties.

5. In the Startup Properties or Logon Properties dialog box, click Show Files. If you copied the executable to the correct location in the Policies folder, you should see the executable.

6. In the Startup Properties or Logon Properties dialog box, click Add. This displays the Add A Script dialog box.

7. In the Script Name text box, type **PushPrinterConnections.exe**, and then click OK.

To deploy printer connections to computers running Windows Vista, Windows 7, Windows Server 2008, or later releases, you must follow these steps:

1. In Print Management, expand the Print Servers node and the node for the server you want to work with.

2. Select the server's Printers node. In the main pane, right-click the printer you want to deploy, and then click Deploy With Group Policy. This displays the Deploy With Group Policy dialog box, shown in Figure 18-6.

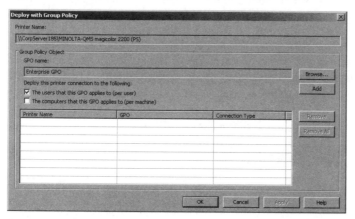

FIGURE 18-6 Select the GPO to use for deploying the printer connection.

3. Click Browse. In the Browse For Group Policy Object dialog box, select the GPO to use, and then click OK.

4. Do one or both of the following:

   - To deploy to the printer connection on a per-user basis, under Deploy This Printer Connection To The Following, select The Users That This GPO Applies To.

   - To deploy to the printer connection on a per-computer basis, under Deploy This Printer Connection To The Following, select The Computers That This GPO Applies To.

5. Click Add to create a print connection entry.

6. Repeat steps 3–5 to deploy the printer connection to other GPOs.

7. Click OK to save the changes to the GPO. In the confirmation dialog box, ensure that all operations were completed successfully. If an error occurred, click Details to see more information about the error. The most common errors involve editing permissions for the GPO you are working with. If the account you are using doesn't have appropriate permissions, you need to use an account with additional privileges. Click OK.

Configuring Point and Print Restrictions

In Group Policy, the Point And Print Restrictions setting controls several important aspects of printer security. For Windows XP Professional and later versions of Windows, the setting controls the servers to which a client computer can connect for point and print. For Windows Vista, Windows 7, and later releases, the setting controls security warnings and elevation prompts when users point and print as well as when drivers for printer connections need to be configured. Table 18-1 summarizes how this policy setting is used.

TABLE 18-1 Point and Print Restrictions

WHEN THE POLICY SETTING IS	THE POLICY WORKS AS FOLLOWS
Enabled	Windows XP and Windows Server 2003 clients can point and print only to an explicitly named list of servers in the forest. Windows Vista and later clients can point and print to any server. You can configure Windows Vista and later clients to show or hide warning and elevation prompts when users point and print and when a driver for an existing printer connection needs to be updated.
Not Configured	Windows XP and later clients can point and print to any server in the forest. Windows Vista and later clients also will not show a warning and elevation prompt when users point and print or when a driver for an existing printer connection needs to be updated.
Disabled	Windows XP and later clients can point and print to any server. Windows Vista and later clients also will not show a warning and elevation prompt when users point and print or when a driver for an existing printer connection needs to be updated.

By default, Windows Vista, Windows 7, and Windows Server 2008 allow a user who is not a member of the local Administrators group to install only trustworthy printer drivers, such as those provided by Windows or in digitally signed printer driver packages. When you enable the Point And Print Restrictions setting, you also allow users who are not members of the local Administrators group to install printer connections deployed using Group Policy that include additional or updated printer drivers that are not in the form of digitally signed printer driver packages. If you do not enable this setting, users might need to provide the credentials of a user account that belongs to the local Administrators group.

You can enable and configure the Point And Print Restrictions setting in Group Policy by following these steps:

1. In the Group Policy Management Console, right-click the GPO for the site, domain, or organizational unit you want to work with, and then click Edit. This opens the policy editor for the GPO.

2. In the Group Policy Management Editor, expand User Configuration\Administrative Templates\Control Panel, and then select the Printers node.

3. In the main pane, double-click Point And Print Restrictions.

4. In the Point And Print Restrictions dialog box, shown in Figure 18-7, select Enabled.

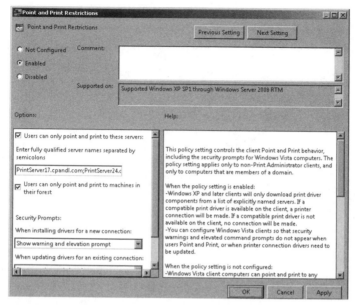

FIGURE 18-7 Configure point and print restrictions.

5. When you enable point and print restrictions, you can configure policy so that users can point and print only to a named list of servers. To enforce this restriction, select the related check box and enter a list of fully qualified server names separated by semicolons. To remove this restriction, clear the related check box.

6. When you enable point and print restrictions, you can configure policy so that users can point and print only to servers in their forest. To enforce this restriction, select the related check box. To remove this restriction, clear the related check box.

7. When you install drivers for a new connection, clients running Windows Vista or later releases can show or not show a warning or elevation prompt. Use the related selection list to choose the option you want to use.

8. When you update drivers for an existing connection, clients running Windows Vista or later releases can show or not show a warning or elevation prompt. Use the related selection list to choose the option you want to use.

9. Click OK to apply the configuration.

Moving Printers to a New Print Server

You can use the Printer Migration Wizard to move print queues, printer drivers, printer processors, and printer ports from one print server to another. This is an efficient way to consolidate multiple print servers or replace an older print server.

When you move printers, the server on which the printers are currently located is the source server, and the server to which you want to move the printers is the destination server. With this in mind, you can move printers to a new print server by following these steps:

1. In Print Management, right-click the source server, and then click Export Printers To A File. This starts the Printer Migration Wizard.

2. On the initial page, note the printer-related objects that will be exported, and then click Next.

3. On the Select The File Location page, click Browse. In the dialog box provided, select a save location for the printer migration file. After you type a name for the file, click Save.

4. Printer migration files are saved with the .printerExport extension. Click Next to save the printer settings to this file.

5. After the wizard completes the export process, click Open Event Viewer to review the events generated during the export process. If an error occurred during processing, you can use the event entries to determine what happened and possible actions to take to resolve the problem. When you have finished, exit the Event Viewer.

6. On the Exporting page, click Finish to exit the Printer Migration Wizard.

7. In Print Management, right-click the destination server, and then click Import Printers From A File. This launches the Printer Migration Wizard.

8. On the Select The File Location page, click Browse. In the dialog box provided. select the printer migration file you created in steps 3 and 4, and then click Open.

9. Click Next. Note the objects that will be imported, and then click Next. On the Select Import Options page, choose one of the following options in the Import Mode list:

   - **Keep Existing Printers** When you choose this option and existing printer queues have the same names as those you are importing, the wizard creates copies to ensure that the original printer queues and the imported printer queues are both available.

   - **Overwrite Existing Printers** When you choose this option and existing printer queues have the same names as those you are importing, the wizard overwrites the existing printer queues with the information from the printer queues you are importing.

10. On the Select Import Options page, choose one of the following options in the List In The Directory list:

- **List Printers That Were Previously Listed**   Choose this option to specify that only printers that were previously listed are listed in Active Directory.

- **List All Printers**   Choose this option to specify that all printers are listed in Active Directory.

- **Don't List Any Printers**   Choose this option to specify that no printers are listed in Active Directory.

11. Click Next to begin the import process. Once the wizard completes the import process, click Open Event Viewer to review the events generated during the import process. If an error occurred during processing, you can use the event entries to determine what happened and possible actions to take to resolve the problem. When you have finished, exit the Event Viewer.

12. On the Importing page, click Finish to exit the Printer Migration Wizard.

Monitoring Printers and Printer Queues Automatically

Printer filters display only the printers, printer queues, and printer drivers that meet specific criteria. Through automated notification, you can use printer filters to automate monitoring of printers.

In Print Management, you can view existing filters by expanding the Custom Filters node. If you expand the Custom Filters node and then select a filter, the main pane shows all printers or print drivers that match the filter criteria. Print Management includes the following default printer filters:

- **All Printers**   Lists all printers associated with print servers that have been added to the console

- **All Drivers**   Lists all printer drivers associated with print servers that have been added to the console

- **Printers Not Ready**   Lists all printers that are not in a Ready state, such as those with errors

- **Printers With Jobs**   Lists all printers associated with print servers that have active or pending print jobs

You can create a new custom filter by follow these steps:

1. In Print Management, right-click the Custom Filters node, and then click Add New Printer Filter. This starts the New Printer Filter Wizard.

2. On the Printer Filter Name And Description page, enter a filter name and description. If you'd like the number of matching items to be displayed after the filter name, select the Display The Total Number Of Printers check box. Click Next.

3. On the Define A Filter page, define the filter by specifying the field, condition, and value to match in the first row. If you want to further narrow the possible matches, define additional criteria in the second, third, and subsequent rows. Click Next when you are ready to continue.

NOTE When you use filters for monitoring and notification, you use the Queue Status field the most. This field allows you to receive a notification when a printer has a specific status. You can match the following status values: Busy, Deleting, Door Open, Error, Initializing, IO Active, Manual Feed Required, No Toner/Ink, Not Available, Offline, Out Of Memory, Out Of Paper, Output Bin Full, Page Punt, Paper Jam, Paper Problem, Paused, Printing, Processing, Ready, Toner/Ink Low, User Intervention Required, Waiting, and Warming Up.

TIP When you are matching conditions in a filter, you can match an exact condition that does exist or one that does not exist. For example, if you want to be notified only of conditions that need attention, you can look for Queue Status conditions that are not exactly the following: Deleting, Initializing, Printing, Processing, Warming Up, and Ready.

4. On the Set Notifications (Optional) page, you can specify whether to send an e-mail message, run a script, or take both actions when the specified criteria are met. Click Finish to complete the configuration.

You can modify an existing custom filter by following these steps:

1. In Print Management, expand the Custom Filters node. Select and then right-click the filter you want to work with. On the shortcut menu, click Properties.

2. In the filter's Properties dialog box, use the options provided to manage the filter settings. This dialog box has the following three tabs:

   - **General** Shows the name and description of the printer filter. Enter a new name and description as necessary.

   - **Filter Criteria** Shows the filter criteria. Enter new filter criteria as necessary.

   - **Notification** Shows the e-mail and script options. Enter new e-mail and script options as necessary.

Solving Spooling Problems

Windows Server 2008 R2 uses the Print Spooler service to control the spooling of print jobs. If this service isn't running, print jobs can't be spooled. Use the Services console to check the status of the Print Spooler. Follow these steps to check and restart the Print Spooler service:

1. On the Administrative Tools menu, click Computer Management.

2. If you want to connect to a remote computer, right-click the Computer Management entry in the console tree, and then click Connect To Another Computer. You can now choose the system whose services you want to manage.

3. Expand the Services And Applications node, and then select Services.

4. Select the Print Spooler service. The Status should be Started. If it isn't, right-click Print Spooler, and then click Start. The Startup Type should be Automatic. If it isn't, double-click Print Spooler and set Startup Type to Automatic.

TIP Spoolers can become corrupted. Symptoms of a corrupted spooler include a frozen printer or one that doesn't send jobs to the print device. Sometimes the print device might print pages of garbled data. In most of these cases, you can resolve the problem by stopping and starting the Print Spooler service. Other spooling problems might be related to permissions. See "Setting Printer Access Permissions" later in this chapter.

Configuring Printer Properties

The sections that follow explain how to set commonly used printer properties. After you install a network printer, you can set its properties by following these steps:

1. In Print Management, expand the Print Servers node and the node for the server you want to work with.

2. Select the server's Printers node. In the main pane, right-click the printer you want to work with, and then click Properties. You can now set the printer properties.

Adding Comments and Location Information

To make it easier to determine which printer to use and when, you can add comments and location information for printers. Comments provide general information about the printer, such as the type of print device and who is responsible for it. Location describes the actual site of the print device. Once set, applications can display these fields. For example, Microsoft Office Word displays this information in the Comment and Where fields when you select Print from the File menu.

You can add comments and location information to a printer by using the fields on the General tab of the printer's Properties dialog box. Type your comments in the Comment field. Type the printer location in the Location field.

Listing Printers in Active Directory

Listing printers in Active Directory makes it easier for users to locate and install printers. You can list a printer in Active Directory by doing one of the following:

- Right-click the printer's name, and then click List In Directory.
- Open the printer's Properties dialog box, and then click the Sharing tab. Select the List In Directory check box, and then click OK.

Managing Printer Drivers

In a Windows Server 2008 R2 domain you should configure and update printer drivers only on your print servers. You don't need to update printer drivers on Windows clients. Instead, you configure the network printer to provide the drivers to client systems as necessary.

Updating a Printer Driver

You can update a printer's driver by following these steps:

1. Open the printer's Properties dialog box, and then click the Advanced tab.

2. In the Driver list, you can select the driver from a list of currently installed drivers. Use the Driver list to select a new driver from a list of known drivers.

3. If the driver you need isn't listed or if you obtained a new driver, click New Driver. This starts the Add Printer Driver Wizard. Click Next.

4. If the device manufacturer and model you're using aren't displayed in the list, click Windows Update. Windows connects to the Windows Update Web site to update the list of printers to show additional models. This feature is part of the automatic driver provisioning feature. It can take several minutes to retrieve the updated list. You should then be able to select your printer manufacturer and model.

5. If the device manufacturer and model you're using still aren't displayed in the list, choose Have Disk to install the new driver from a file or disc. In the Install From Disk dialog box, type the folder path to the printer driver file or click Browse to find the printer driver file by using the Locate File dialog box. Click OK.

6. Click Next, and then click Finish.

Configuring Drivers for Network Clients

After you install a printer or change drivers, you might want to select the operating systems that should download the driver from the print server. By allowing clients to download the printer driver, you provide a single location for installing driver updates. This way, instead of having to install a new driver on all the client systems, you install the driver on the print server and allow clients to download the new driver.

You can allow clients to download the new driver by following these steps:

1. Right-click the icon of the printer you want to configure, and then click Properties.

2. Click the Sharing tab, and then click Additional Drivers.

3. In the Additional Drivers dialog box, select operating systems that can download the printer driver. As necessary, insert the Windows Server 2008 R2 installation media, printer driver discs, or both for the selected operating

systems. The Windows Server 2008 R2 installation media has drivers for most Windows operating systems.

Setting a Separator Page and Changing Print Device Mode

Separator pages have two uses on Windows Server 2008 R2 systems:

- You can use them at the beginning of a print job to make it easier for users to find a document on a busy print device.

- You can use them to change the print device mode, such as whether the print device uses PostScript or Printer Control Language (PCL).

To set a separator page for a print device, follow these steps:

1. On the Advanced tab of the printer's Properties dialog box, click Separator Page.

2. In the Separator Page dialog box, type the name of the separator file to use. Typically, you'll want to use one of these available separator pages:

   - **Pcl.sep**   Switches the print device to PCL mode and prints a separator page before each document

   - **Pscript.sep**   Sets the print device to PostScript mode but doesn't print a separator page

   - **Sysprint.sep**   Sets the print device to PostScript mode and prints a separator page before each document

   NOTE Sysprintj.sep is an alternate version of Sysprint.sep. If fonts for Japanese are available and you want to use them, you can use Sysprintj.sep.

3. To stop using the separator page, open the Separator Page dialog box and remove the file name.

NOTE When you work with a local server, click the Browse button in the Separator Page dialog box to open the %SystemRoot%\Windows\System32 folder for browsing. In this case, you can browse and select the separator page to use. On the other hand, when you work with a remote server, the Browse button is typically not available. In this case, you must type the exact file name for the separator page.

Changing the Printer Port

You can change the port used by a print device at any time by using the Properties dialog box for the printer you're configuring. Open the Properties dialog box, and then click the Ports tab. You can now add a port for printing by selecting its check box or remove a port by clearing its check box. To add a new port type, click Add Port. In the Printer Ports dialog box, select the port type, and then click New Port. Enter a valid port name, and then click OK. To remove a port permanently, select it, and then click Delete Port.

Scheduling and Prioritizing Print Jobs

You can use the Properties dialog box for the printer you're configuring to set default settings for print job priority and scheduling. Open the dialog box, and then click the Advanced tab. You can now set the default schedule and priority settings using the fields shown in Figure 18-8. Each of these fields is discussed in the sections that follow.

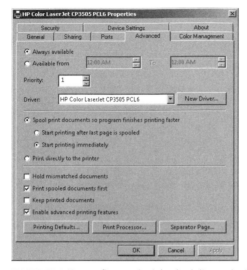

FIGURE 18-8 You configure print job scheduling and priority on the Advanced tab.

Scheduling Printer Availability

Printers are always available or available only during the hours specified. You set printer availability on the Advanced tab. Select Always Available to make the printer available at all times. Select Available From to set specific hours of operation.

Setting Printer Priority

You can set the default priority for print jobs in the Priority box on the Advanced tab. Print jobs always print in order of priority. Jobs with higher priority print before jobs with lower priority.

Configuring Print Spooling

For print devices attached to the network, you usually want the printer to spool files rather than print files directly. Print spooling makes it possible to use a printer to manage print jobs.

To enable spooling, use one of the following options:

- **Spool Print Documents So Program Finishes Printing Faster**   Select this option to spool print jobs.

- **Start Printing After Last Page Is Spooled**   Select this option if you want the entire document to be spooled before printing begins. This option ensures that the entire document makes it into the print queue before printing. If for some reason printing is canceled or not completed, the job won't be printed.

- **Start Printing Immediately**   Select this option if you want printing to begin immediately when the print device isn't already in use. This option is preferable when you want print jobs to be completed more quickly or when you want to ensure that the application returns control to users as soon as possible.

OTHER SPOOLING OPTIONS

You can disable spooling by selecting the Print Directly To The Printer option. The following additional check boxes let you configure other spooling options:

- **Hold Mismatched Documents**   If you select this option, the spooler holds print jobs that don't match the setup for the print device. Selecting this option is a good idea if you frequently have to change printer form or tray assignments.

- **Print Spooled Documents First**   If you select this option, jobs that have completed spooling will print before jobs in the process of spooling, regardless of whether the spooling jobs have higher priority.

- **Keep Printed Documents**   Normally, documents are deleted from the queue after they're printed. To keep a copy of documents in the printer, select this option. Use this option if you're printing files that can't easily be re-created. In this way, you can reprint the document without having to re-create it. For details, see "Pausing, Resuming, and Restarting Individual Document Printing" later in this chapter.

- **Enable Advanced Printing Features**   When you enable this option, you can use advanced printing options (if available), such as Page Order and Pages Per Sheet. If you note compatibility problems when using advanced options, you should disable the advanced printing features by clearing this check box.

Starting and Stopping Printer Sharing

You set printer sharing in the Properties dialog box of the printer you're configuring. Right-click the icon of the printer you want to configure, and then click Manage Sharing. This opens the printer's Properties dialog box with the Sharing tab selected.

You can use this tab to change the name of a network printer as well as to start sharing or stop sharing a printer. Printer sharing tasks that you can perform include the following:

- **Sharing a local printer (thus making it a network printer)**   To share a printer, select Share This Printer, and then specify a name for the shared resource in the Share Name field. Click OK when you have finished.

- **Changing the shared name of a printer**   To change the shared name, simply type a new name in the Share Name field, and then click OK.

- **Stopping the sharing of a printer**   To quit sharing a printer, clear the Share This Printer check box, and then click OK.

Setting Printer Access Permissions

Network printers are shared resources. As such, you can set access permissions for them. You set access permissions in the Properties dialog box of the printer you're configuring. Open the printer's Properties dialog box, and then click the Security tab. Permissions that you can grant or deny for printers are Print, Manage Documents, and Manage This Printer. Table 18-2 summarizes the capabilities of these permissions.

TABLE 18-2 Printer Permissions Used by Windows Server 2008 R2

PERMISSION	PRINT	MANAGE DOCUMENTS	MANAGE PRINTERS
Print documents	X	X	X
Pause, restart, resume, and cancel own documents	X	X	X
Connect to printers	X	X	X
Control settings for print jobs		X	X
Pause, restart, and delete print jobs		X	X
Share printers			X
Change printer properties			X
Change printer permissions			X
Delete printers			X

The default permissions are used for any new network printer you create. These settings are as follows:

- Members of the Administrators, Print Operators, and Server Operators groups have full control over printers by default. This allows you to administer a printer and its print jobs.

- The creator or owner of the document can manage his or her own document. This allows the person who printed a document to change its settings and to delete it.
- Everyone can print to the printer. This makes the printer accessible to all users on the network.

As with other permission sets, you create the basic permissions for printers by combining special permissions into logical groups. Table 18-3 shows special permissions used to create the basic permissions for printers. Using Advanced permission settings, you can assign these special permissions individually if necessary.

TABLE 18-3 Special Permissions for Printers

SPECIAL PERMISSIONS	PRINT	MANAGE DOCUMENTS	MANAGE PRINTERS
Print	X		X
Manage Documents		X	
Manage This Printer			X
Read Permissions	X	X	X
Change Permissions		X	X
Take Ownership		X	X

Auditing Print Jobs

Windows Server 2008 R2 lets you audit common printer tasks by following these steps:

1. Open the printer's Properties dialog box, and then click the Security tab. Click Advanced to open the Advanced Security Settings dialog box.

    NOTE Actions aren't audited by default. You must first enable auditing by establishing a group policy to audit the printer.

2. On the Auditing tab, add the names of users or groups you want to audit with the Add button and remove names of users or groups with the Remove button.

3. Select the events you want to audit by selecting the check boxes under the Successful and Failed headings, as appropriate.

4. Click OK.

Setting Document Defaults

Document default settings are used only when you print from non-Windows applications, such as when you print from the command prompt. You can set document defaults by following these steps:

1. Open the printer's Properties dialog box, and then click the General tab.
2. Click Preferences.
3. Use the fields on the tabs provided to configure the default settings.

Configuring Print Server Properties

Windows Server 2008 R2 allows you to control global settings for print servers by using the Print Server Properties dialog box. You can access this dialog box by doing either of the following:

- Access Devices And Printers on the print server. Under Printers And Faxes, select any available printer, and then click Print Server Properties on the toolbar.

- In Print Management, right-click the server entry for the print server you want to work with, and then click Properties. If the print server isn't listed, you can add it in the Add/Remove Servers dialog box. To open the dialog box, right-click Print Servers, and then click Add/Remove Servers.

The sections that follow examine some of the print server properties that you can configure.

Locating the Spool Folder and Enabling Printing on NTFS

The Spool folder holds a copy of all documents in the printer spool. By default, this folder is located at %SystemRoot%\System32\Spool\Printers. On the NTFS file system, all users who access the printer must have Modify permission on this directory. If they don't, they won't be able to print documents.

If you're experiencing problems, check the permission on this directory by following these steps:

1. Access the Print Server Properties dialog box.
2. Click the Advanced tab. The location of the Spool folder is shown in the Spool Folder field. Note this location.
3. Right-click the Spool folder in Windows Explorer, and then click Properties.
4. Click the Security tab. Now you can verify that the permissions are set appropriately.

Managing High-Volume Printing

Printers used in corporate environments can print hundreds or thousands of documents daily. This high volume puts a heavy burden on print servers, which can cause printing delays, document corruption, and other problems. To alleviate some of this burden, you should do the following:

- Use network-attached printers rather than printers attached through USB or IR ports. Network-attached printers use fewer system resources (namely CPU time) than other printers do.

- Dedicate the print server to handle print services only. If the print server is handling other network duties, it might not be very responsive to print requests and management. To increase responsiveness, you can move other network duties to other servers.

- Move the Spool folder to a drive dedicated to printing. By default, the Spool folder is on the same file system as the operating system. To further improve disk input/output (I/O), use a drive that has a separate controller.

Logging Printer Events

You can use the Print Server Properties dialog box to configure the logging of printer events. Open this dialog box, and then click the Advanced tab. Use the check boxes provided to determine which spooler events are logged.

Enabling Print Job Error Notification

Print servers can beep to notify users when a remote document fails to print. By default, this feature is turned off because it can be annoying. If you want to activate or remove notification, access the Advanced tab of the Print Server Properties dialog box, and then select or clear the check box labeled Beep On Errors Of Remote Documents.

Managing Print Jobs on Local and Remote Printers

You manage print jobs and printers by using the print management window. If the printer is configured on your system, you can access the print management window by using one of the following techniques:

- Access the Devices And Printers folder on the print server you want to manage. Double-click the icon of the printer you want to work with. If the printer isn't configured on your system, you can manage the printer remotely by clicking Start and then clicking Network. Double-click the icon of the print server you want to work with, and then double-click the Devices And Printers folder or the Printers folder.

- In Print Management, double-click the Print Servers node, and then double-click the entry for the print server itself. Select Printers. Right-click the printer you want to work with, and then click Open Printer Queue.

- In Print Management, right-click the Printers node, and then click Show Extended View. With the printer selected in the upper pane, the upper and lower panes in the main window provide functionality similar to that of the print management window.

Viewing Printer Queues and Print Jobs

You can now manage print jobs and printers using the print management window shown in Figure 18-9. The print management window shows information about documents in the printers. This information tells you the following:

- **Document Name**   The document file name, which can include the name of the application that printed it.

- **Status**   The status of the print job, which can include the document's status as well as the printer's status. Document status entries you'll see include Printing, Spooling, Paused, Deleting, and Restarting. Document status can be preceded by the printer status, such as Printer Off-Line.

- **Owner**   The document's owner.

- **Pages**   The number of pages in the document.

- **Size**   The document size in kilobytes or megabytes.

- **Submitted**   The time and date the print job was submitted.

- **Port**   The port used for printing, such as LPT1, COM3, File, or IP address (if applicable).

FIGURE 18-9 You manage print jobs and printers using the print management window.

Pausing the Printer and Resuming Printing

Sometimes you need to pause a printer. Using the print management window, you do this by selecting the Pause Printing option from the Printer menu. (A check mark indicates that the option is selected.) When you pause printing, the printer completes the current job and then puts all other jobs on hold.

To resume printing, select the Pause Printing option a second time. This should remove the check mark next to the option.

Emptying the Print Queue

You can use the print management window to empty the print queue and delete all its contents. To do this, choose Cancel All Documents from the Printer menu.

Pausing, Resuming, and Restarting Individual Document Printing

You set the status of individual documents using the Document menu in the print management window. To change the status of a document, right-click the document and then use one of the following options on the shortcut menu to change the status of the print job.

- **Pause**   Puts the document on hold and lets other documents print
- **Resume**   Tells the printer to resume printing the document from where it left off
- **Restart**   Tells the printer to start printing the document again from the beginning

Removing a Document and Canceling a Print Job

To remove a document from the printer or cancel a print job, select the document in the print management window. Right-click the document and select Cancel or press Delete.

> **NOTE**   When you cancel a print job that's currently printing, the print device might continue to print part or all of the document. This occurs because most print devices cache documents in an internal buffer and the print device might continue to print the contents of this cache.

Checking the Properties of Documents in the Printer

Document properties can tell you many things about documents that are in the printer, such as the page source, orientation, and size. You can check the properties of a document in the printer by doing either of the following:

- Right-click the document in the print management window, and then click Properties.
- Double-click the document name in the print management window.

Setting the Priority of Individual Documents

Scheduling priority determines when documents print. Documents with higher priority print before documents with lower priority. You can set the priority of individual documents in the printer by following these steps:

1. Right-click the document in the print management window, and then click Properties.

2. On the General tab, use the Priority slider to change the document's priority. The lowest priority is 1 and the highest is 99.

Scheduling the Printing of Individual Documents

In a busy printing environment, you might need to schedule the printing of documents in the printer. For example, you might want large print jobs of low priority to print at night. To set the printing schedule, follow these steps:

1. Right-click the document in the print management window, and then click Properties.

2. On the General tab, select the Only From option, and then specify a time interval. The time interval you set determines when the job is allowed to print. For example, you can specify that the job can print only between midnight and 5:00 A.M.

Running DHCP Clients and Servers

Y ou can use Dynamic Host Configuration Protocol (DHCP) to simplify administration of Active Directory domains, and in this chapter you'll learn how to do that. You use DHCP to dynamically assign TCP/IP configuration information to network clients. This not only saves time during system configuration, but also provides a centralized mechanism for updating the configuration. To enable DHCP on the network, you need to install and configure a DHCP server. This server is responsible for assigning the necessary network information.

Understanding DHCP

DHCP gives you centralized control over IP addressing and more. Once DHCP is installed, you rely on the DHCP server to supply the basic information necessary for TCP/IP networking, which can include the following: IP address, subnet mask, and default gateway; primary and secondary Domain Name System (DNS) servers; primary and secondary Windows Internet Name Service (WINS) servers; and the DNS domain name. With Windows Server 2008 R2, DHCP servers can assign a dynamic IP version 4 (IPv4) address, an IP version 6 (IPv6) address, or both addresses to any of the network interface cards (NICs) on a computer.

Using Dynamic IPv4 Addressing and Configuration

A computer that uses dynamic IPv4 addressing and configuration is called a *DHCPv4 client*. When you boot a DHCPv4 client, a 32-bit IPv4 address can be retrieved from a pool of IPv4 addresses defined for the network's DHCP server. The address is assigned to the client for a specified time period known as a *lease*. When the lease is approximately 50 percent expired, the client tries to renew it. If the client can't renew the lease then, it tries again before the lease expires. If this attempt fails, the client tries to contact an alternate DHCP server. IPv4 addresses that aren't renewed are returned to the address pool. If the client is able to contact the DHCP server but the current IP address can't be reassigned, the DHCP server assigns a new IPv4 address to the client.

The availability of a DHCP server doesn't affect startup or logon (in most cases). DHCPv4 clients can start and users can log on to the local computer even if a DHCP server isn't available. During startup, the DHCPv4 client looks for a DHCP server. If a DHCP server is available, the client gets its configuration information from the server. If a DHCP server isn't available and the client's previous lease is still valid, the client pings the default gateway listed in the lease. A successful ping tells the client that it's probably on the same network it was on when it was issued the lease, and the client continues to use the lease as described previously. A failed ping tells the client that it might be on a different network. In this case, the client uses IPv4 autoconfiguration. The client also uses IPv4 autoconfiguration if a DHCP server isn't available and the previous lease has expired.

IPv4 autoconfiguration works like this:

1. The client computer selects an IP address from the Microsoft-reserved class B subnet 169.254.0.0 and uses the subnet mask 255.255.0.0. Before using the IPv4 address, the client performs an Address Resolution Protocol (ARP) test to be sure that no other client is using this IPv4 address.

2. If the IPv4 address is in use, the client repeats step 1, testing up to 10 IPv4 addresses before reporting failure. When a client is disconnected from the network, the ARP test always succeeds. As a result, the client uses the first IPv4 address it selects.

3. If the IPv4 address is available, the client configures the NIC with this address. The client then attempts to contact a DHCP server, sending out a broadcast every five minutes to the network. When the client successfully contacts a server, the client obtains a lease and reconfigures the network interface.

Using Dynamic IPv6 Addressing and Configuration

On Windows Vista, Windows 7, Windows Server 2008, and later releases, both IPv4 and IPv6 are enabled by default when networking hardware is detected during installation. As discussed in Chapter 1, "Windows Server 2008 R2 Administration Overview," and Chapter 17, "Managing TCP/IP Networking," IPv4 is the primary version of IP used on most networks, and IPv6 is the next-generation version of IP.

IPv6 uses 128-bit addresses. In a standard configuration, the first 64 bits represent the network ID and the last 64 bits represent the network interface on the client computer.

You can use DHCP to configure IPv6 addressing in two key ways:

- **DHCPv6 stateful mode**   In DHCPv6 stateful mode, a client acquires its IPv6 address as well as its network configuration parameters through DHCPv6.

- **DHCPv6 stateless mode**   In DHCPv6 stateless mode, a client uses auto-configuration to acquire its IP address and acquires its network configuration parameters through DHCPv6.

A computer that uses dynamic IPv6 addressing, configuration, or both mechanisms is called a *DHCPv6 client*. As with DHCPv4, the components of the DHCPv6 infrastructure consist of DHCPv6 clients that request configuration, DHCPv6 servers that provide configuration, and DHCPv6 relay agents that convey messages between clients and servers when clients are on subnets that do not have a DHCPv6 server.

Unlike in DHCPv4, you must also configure your IPv6 routers to support DHCPv6. A DHCPv6 client performs autoconfiguration based on the following flags in the Router Advertisement message sent by a neighboring router:

- Managed Address Configuration flag, which is also known as the *M flag*. When set to 1, this flag instructs the client to use a configuration protocol to obtain stateful addresses.

- Other Stateful Configuration flag, which is also known as the *O flag*. When set to 1, this flag instructs the client to use a configuration protocol to obtain other configuration settings.

Windows Vista, Windows 7, Windows Server 2008, and later releases include a DHCPv6 client. The DHCPv6 client attempts DHCPv6-based configuration depending on the values of the M and O flags in the Router Advertisement messages it receives. If there are more than one advertising routers for a given subnet, they should be configured to advertise the same stateless address prefixes and the same values for the M and O flags. IPv6 clients running Windows XP or Windows Server 2003 do not include a DHCPv6 client and therefore ignore the values of the M and O flags in router advertisements they receive.

You can configure an IPv6 router that is running Windows Vista, Windows 7, Windows Server 2008, or a later release to set the M flag to 1 in router advertisements by typing the following command at an elevated command prompt, where *InterfaceName* is the actual name of the interface:

```
netsh interface ipv6 set interface InterfaceName managedaddress=enabled
```

Similarly, you can set the O flag to 1 in router advertisements by typing the following command at an elevated command prompt:

```
netsh interface ipv6 set interface InterfaceName otherstateful=enabled
```

If the interface name contains spaces, enclose the related value in quotation marks, as shown in the following example:

```
netsh interface ipv6 set interface "Connection 2" managedaddress=enabled
```

Keep the following in mind when you are working with the M and O flags:

- If the M and O flags are both set to 0, the network is considered not to have DHCPv6 infrastructure. Clients use router advertisements for non-link-local addresses and manual configuration to configure other settings.

- If the M and O flags are both set to 1, DHCPv6 is used for both IP addressing and other configuration settings. This combination is known as *DHCPv6 stateful mode*, in which DHCPv6 assigns stateful addresses to IPv6 clients.

- If the M flag is set to 0 and the O flag is set to 1, DHCPv6 is used only to assign other configuration settings. Neighboring routers are configured to advertise non-link-local address prefixes from which IPv6 clients derive stateless addresses. This combination is known as *DHCPv6 stateless mode*.

- If the M flag is set to 1 and the O flag is set to 0, DHCPv6 is used for IP address configuration but not for other settings. Because IPv6 clients typically need to be configured with other settings, such as the IPv6 addresses of DNS servers, this combination typically is not used.

Windows Vista, Windows 7, Windows Server 2008, and later releases obtain dynamic IPv6 addresses by using a process similar to dynamic IPv4 addresses. Typically, IPv6 autoconfiguration for DHCPv6 clients in stateful mode works like this:

1. The client computer selects a link-local unicast IPv6 address. Before using the IPv6 address, the client performs an ARP test to make sure that no other client is using this IPv6 address.

2. If the IPv6 address is in use, the client repeats step 1. Keep in mind that when a client is disconnected from the network, the ARP test always succeeds. As a result, the client uses the first IPv6 address it selects.

3. If the IPv6 address is available, the client configures the NIC with this address. The client then attempts to contact a DHCP server, sending out a broadcast every five minutes to the network. When the client successfully contacts a server, the client obtains a lease and reconfigures the network interface.

This is not how IPv6 autoconfiguration works for DHCPv6 clients in stateless mode. In stateless mode, DHCPv6 clients configure both link-local addresses and additional non-link-local addresses by exchanging Router Solicitation and Router Advertisement messages with neighboring routers.

Like DHCPv4, DHCPv6 uses User Datagram Protocol (UDP) messages. DHCPv6 clients listen for DHCP messages on UDP port 546. DHCPv6 servers and relay agents listen for DHCPv6 messages on UDP port 547. The structure for DHCPv6 messages is much simpler than for DHCPv4, which had its origins in the BOOTP protocol to support diskless workstations.

DHCPv6 messages start with a 1-byte Msg-Type field that indicates the type of DHCPv6 message. This is followed by a 3-byte Transaction-ID field determined by a client and used to group together the messages of a DHCPv6 message exchange. Following the Transaction-ID field, DHCPv6 options are used to indicate client and server identification, addresses, and other configuration settings.

Three fields are associated with each DHCPv6 option. A 2-byte Option-Code field indicates a specific option. A 2-byte Option-Len field indicates the length of the Option-Data field in bytes. The Option-Data field contains the data for the option.

Messages exchanged between relay agents and servers use a different message structure to transfer additional information. A 1-byte Hop-Count field indicates the number of relay agents that have received the message. A receiving relay agent can discard the message if the message exceeds a configured maximum hop count. A 16-byte Link-Address field contains a non-link-local address that is assigned to an interface connected to the subnet on which the client is located. Based on the Link-Address field, the server can determine the correct address scope from which to assign an address. A 16-byte Peer-Address field contains the IPv6 address of the client that originally sent the message or the previous relay agent that relayed the message. Following the Peer-Address field are DHCPv6 options. A key option is the Relay Message option. This option provides an encapsulation of the messages being exchanged between the client and the server.

IPv6 does not have broadcast addresses. The use of the limited broadcast address for some DHCPv4 messages has been replaced with the use of the All_DHCP_Relay_Agents_and_Servers address of FF02::1:2 for DHCPv6. A DHCPv6 client attempting to discover the location of the DHCPv6 server on the network sends a Solicit message from its link-local address to FF02::1:2. If there is a DHCPv6 server on the client's subnet, it receives the Solicit message and sends an appropriate reply. If the client and server are on different subnets, a DHCPv6 relay agent on the client's subnet that receives the Solicit message forwards it to a DHCPv6 server.

Checking IP Address Assignment

You can use Ipconfig to check the currently assigned IP address and other configuration information. To obtain information for all network adapters on the computer, type the command **ipconfig /all** at the command prompt. If the IP address has been assigned automatically, you'll see an entry for Autoconfiguration IP Address. In the following example, the autoconfiguration IPv4 address is 169.254.98.59:

```
Windows IP Configuration
        Host Name  . . . . . . . . . . . . . . . . :  DELTA
        Primary DNS Suffix  . . . . . . . . :  microsoft.com
        Node Type  . . . . . . . . . . . . . . . :  Hybrid
        IP Routing Enabled. . . . . . . . :  No
        WINS Proxy Enabled. . . . . . . . :  No
        DNS Suffix Search List. . . . . :  microsoft.com
```

```
Ethernet adapter Local Area Connection:
    Connection-specific DNS Suffix...:
    Description ................: Intel Pro/1000 Network Connection
    Physical Address............: 23-17-C6-F8-FD-67
    DHCP Enabled................: Yes
    Autoconfiguration Enabled...: Yes
    Autoconfiguration IP Address: 169.254.98.59
    Subnet Mask ................: 255.255.0.0
    Default Gateway ............:
    DNS Servers ................:
```

Understanding Scopes

Scopes are pools of IPv4 or IPv6 addresses that you can assign to clients through leases. DHCP also provides a way to permanently assign a lease on an address. To do this, you need to create a reservation by specifying the IPv4 address to reserve and the media access control (MAC) address of the computer that will hold the IPv4 address. The reservation thereafter ensures that the client computer with the specified MAC address always gets the designated IPv4 address. With IPv6, you can specify that a lease is temporary or nontemporary. A nontemporary lease is similar to a reservation.

You create scopes to specify IP address ranges that are available for DHCP clients. For example, you could assign the IP address range 192.168.12.2 to 192.168.12.250 to a scope called Enterprise Primary. Scopes can use public or private IPv4 addresses on the following networks:

- **Class A networks**   IP addresses from 1.0.0.0 to 126.255.255.255
- **Class B networks**   IP addresses from 128.0.0.0 to 191.255.255.255
- **Class C networks**   IP addresses from 192.0.0.0 to 223.255.255.255
- **Class D networks**   IP addresses from 224.0.0.0 to 239.255.255.255

NOTE   The IP address 127.0.0.1 is used for local loopback.

Scopes can also use link-local unicast, global unicast, and multicast IPv6 addresses. Link-local unicast addresses begin with FE80. Multicast IPv6 addresses begin with FF00. Global (site-local) unicast addresses include all other addresses except :: (unspecified) and ::1 (loopback) addresses.

A single DHCP server can manage multiple scopes. With IPv4 addresses, four types of scopes are available:

- **Normal scopes**   Used to assign IPv4 address pools for class A, B, and C networks.
- **Multicast scopes**   Used to assign IP address pools for IPv4 class D networks. Computers use multicast IP addresses as secondary IP addresses in addition to a standard IP address.

- **Superscopes**   Containers for other scopes. They are used to simplify management of multiple scopes and also support DHCP clients on a single physical network where multiple logical IP networks are used.

- **Split scopes**   Scopes split between two DHCP servers to increase fault tolerance, provide redundancy, and enable load balancing.

With IPv6, only normal scopes are available. Although you can create scopes on multiple network segments, you'll usually want these segments to be in the same network class, such as all class C IP addresses.

TIP   **Don't forget that you must configure DHCPv4 and DHCPv6 relays to relay DHCPv4 and DHCPv6 broadcast requests between network segments. You can configure relay agents with the Routing and Remote Access Service (RRAS) and the DHCP Relay Agent Service. You can also configure some routers as relay agents.**

Installing a DHCP Server

Dynamic IP addressing is available only if a DHCP server is installed on the network. Using the Add Roles Wizard, you install the DHCP server as a role service, configure its initial settings, and authorize the server in Active Directory. Only authorized DHCP servers can provide dynamic IP addresses to clients.

Installing DHCP Components

On a server running Windows Server 2008 R2, follow these steps to enable the server to function as a DHCP server:

1. DHCP servers should be assigned a static IPv4 and IPv6 address on each subnet they will service and are connected to. Be sure that the server has static IPv4 and IPv6 addresses.

2. In Server Manager, select the Roles node in the left pane, and then click Add Roles. This starts the Add Roles Wizard. If the wizard displays the Before You Begin page, read the Welcome message, and then click Next.

3. On the Select Server Roles page, select DHCP Server, and then click Next twice.

4. On the Select Network Connection Bindings page, you'll see a list of the network connections that have a static IPv4 address. As necessary, select the network connections that the server will use for servicing DHCPv4 clients, and then click Next.

5. On the Specify IPv4 DNS Server Settings page, shown in Figure 19-1, enter the default DNS settings that the server will give to DHCPv4 clients for automatic DNS configuration. In the Parent Domain text box, enter the DNS name of the parent domain, such as **cpandl.com**. In the Preferred DNS Server and Alternate DNS Server text boxes, enter the IPv4 address of the

preferred and alternate DNS servers. Click each Validate button in turn to ensure that you entered the correct DNS address. Click Next to continue.

6. On the Specify IPv4 WINS Server Settings page, use the options provided to specify whether applications on the network require WINS. If WINS is required, you need to enter the IP address of the preferred and alternate WINS servers in the Preferred WINS Server and Alternate WINS Server text boxes. Click Next to continue.

REAL WORLD With Windows Server 2008 R2, you install a WINS server by installing the WINS Server feature using the Add Features Wizard. If you don't have pre–Windows 2000 systems or applications on the network, you don't need to use WINS. Instead, you can use Link-Local Multicast Name Resolution (LLMNR) to provide peer-to-peer name resolution services for devices with IPv4 addresses, IPv6 addresses, or both. To enable LLMNR, you need to install the Peer Name Resolution Protocol feature using the Add Features Wizard.

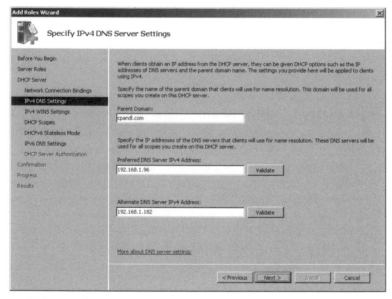

FIGURE 19-1 Configure the default DNS settings for DHCPv4 clients.

7. As discussed in Chapter 1, WINS functionality is largely being phased out. If you have applications that require WINS, you also need to ensure that you've installed and configured the WINS feature by using the Add Features Wizard.

8. On the Add Or Edit DHCP Scopes page, use the options provided to create the initial scopes for the DHCP server. If you want to create a scope for the DHCP server, click Add, and then follow the steps outlined in "Creating and Managing Scopes" later in this chapter. Otherwise, click Next and create the necessary DHCP scopes later.

9. On the Configure DHCPv6 Stateless Mode page, use the options provided to specify whether DHCPv6 stateless mode should be enabled or disabled. If you want DHCPv6 clients to obtain their IPv6 address and configuration settings from DHCPv6, disable stateless mode. Otherwise, enable stateless mode so that clients obtain configuration settings only through DHCPv6. Click Next to continue.

10. On the Specify IPv6 DNS Server Settings page, shown in Figure 19-2, enter the default DNS settings that the server will give to DHCPv6 clients for automatic DNS configuration. In the Parent Domain text box, enter the DNS name of the parent domain, such as **cpandl.com**. In the Preferred DNS Server and Alternate DNS Server text boxes, enter the IPv6 address of the preferred and alternate DNS servers. Click each Validate button in turn to ensure that you entered the right DNS address. Click Next to continue.

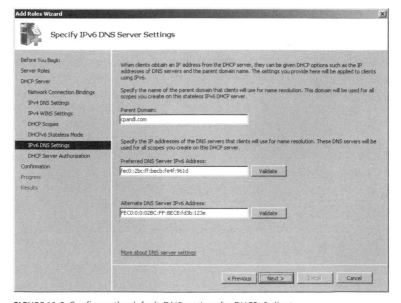

FIGURE 19-2 Configure the default DNS settings for DHCPv6 clients.

11. On the Authorize DHCP Server page, do one of the following to specify the credentials to use to authorize the DHCP server in Active Directory:

   - Your current user name is shown in the User Name text box. If you have administrator privileges in the domain that the DHCP server is a member of and you want to use your current credentials, click Next to attempt to authorize the server using these credentials.

   - If you want to use alternate credentials or if you are unable to authorize the server using your current credentials, select Use Alternate Credentials, and then click Specify. In the Windows Security dialog box, enter the user name and password for the authorized account, and then click OK. Click Next to continue.

- If you want to authorize the DHCP server later, select Skip Authorization, and then click Next. Keep in mind that only authorized DHCP servers can provide dynamic IP addresses to clients.

12. Click Install. The wizard installs DHCP and begins configuring the server. To use the server, you must authorize the server in the domain as described in "Authorizing a DHCP Server in Active Directory" later in this chapter. You must create and activate any DHCP scopes that the server will use, as discussed in "Creating and Managing Scopes." On the Installation Results page, click Close.

Starting and Using the DHCP Console

After you install a DHCP server, you use the DHCP console to configure and manage dynamic IP addressing. To start the DHCP console, click Start, point to Administrative Tools, and then click DHCP. The main window for the DHCP console is shown in Figure 19-3. As you can see, the main window is divided into two panes. The left pane lists the DHCP servers in the domain according to their fully qualified domain name (FQDN). You can expand a server listing to show subnodes for IPv4 and IPv6. If you expand the IP nodes, you'll see the scopes and options defined for the related IP version. The right pane shows the expanded view of the current selection.

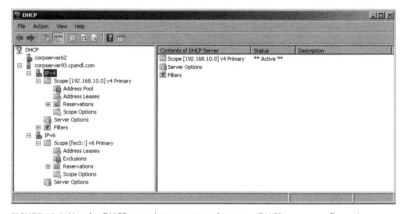

FIGURE 19-3 Use the DHCP console to create and manage DHCP server configurations.

Icons on the various nodes show the current status of the nodes. For server and IP nodes, you might see the following icons:

- A server icon with a green circle with a check mark indicates that the DHCP service is running and the server is active.

- A server icon with red circle with an X through it indicates that the console can't connect to the server. The DHCP service has been stopped or the server is inaccessible.

- A red down arrow indicates that the DHCP server hasn't been authorized.

- A blue warning icon indicates that the server's state has changed or a warning has been issued.

For scopes, you might see the following icons:

- A red down arrow indicates that the scope hasn't been activated.

- A blue warning icon indicates that the scope's state has changed or a warning has been issued.

Connecting to Remote DHCP Servers

When you start the DHCP console, you are connected directly to a local DHCP server, but you won't see entries for remote DHCP servers. You can connect to remote servers by following these steps:

1. Right-click DHCP in the console tree, and then click Add Server. This opens the dialog box shown in Figure 19-4.

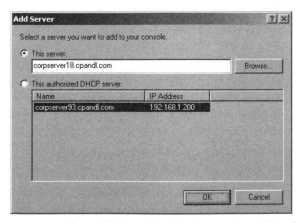

FIGURE 19-4 If your DHCP server isn't listed, you need to add it to the DHCP console by using the Add Server dialog box.

2. Select This Server, and then type the IP address or computer name of the DHCP server you want to manage.

3. Click OK. An entry for the DHCP server is added to the console tree.

TIP When you work with remote servers, you might find that you can't select certain options. A simple refresh of the server information might resolve this: right-click the server node, and then select Refresh.

Starting and Stopping a DHCP Server

You manage DHCP servers through the DHCP Server service. As with any other service, you can start, stop, pause, and resume the DHCP Server service in the Configuration\Services node of Server Manager or from the command line. You can also manage the DHCP Server service in the DHCP console. Right-click the server you want to manage in the DHCP console, point to All Tasks, and then click Start, Stop, Pause, Resume, or Restart, as appropriate.

NOTE To start and stop a DHCP server using Server Manager, expand Roles, expand DHCP Server, right-click the server, point to All Tasks, and then click Start, Stop, Pause, Resume, or Restart, as appropriate.

Authorizing a DHCP Server in Active Directory

Before you can use a DHCP server in the domain, you must authorize it in Active Directory. By authorizing the server, you specify that the server is authorized to provide dynamic IP addressing in the domain. Windows Server 2008 R2 requires authorization to prevent unauthorized DHCP servers from serving domain clients. This in turn ensures that network operations can run smoothly.

In the DHCP console, you authorize a DHCP server by right-clicking the server entry in the tree view and then selecting Authorize. To remove the authorization, right-click the server and then select Unauthorize.

NOTE To authorize a DHCP server using Server Manager, expand Roles, expand DHCP Server, right-click the server, and then select Authorize. The authorization process can take several minutes, so be patient. Press F5 to refresh the view. When the DHCP server is authorized, the scope status should change to active, and you should see a green circle with a check mark in the console tree. To remove the authorization, expand Roles, expand DHCP Server, right-click the server, and then select Unauthorize.

TIP In some scenarios, you might need to log on or remotely connect to a domain controller to authorize the DHCP server in Active Directory. After you access the domain controller, start the DHCP console and connect to the server you want to authorize. Then right-click the server and select Authorize.

Configuring DHCP Servers

When you install a new DHCP server, IP configuration options are automatically optimized for the network environment. A separate set of options are provided for IPv4 and IPv6. You don't normally need to change these settings unless you have performance problems that you need to resolve or you have options that you want to add or remove.

Binding a DHCP Server with Multiple Network Interface Cards to a Specific IP Address

A server with multiple NICs has multiple local area network connections and can provide DHCP services on any of these network connections. However, you might not want DHCP to be served over all available connections. For example, if the server has both a 100 megabits per second (Mbps) connection and a 1 gigabit per second (Gbps) connection, you might want all DHCP traffic to go over the 1 Gbps connection.

To bind DHCP to a specific network connection, follow these steps:

1. In the DHCP console, expand the node for the server you want to work with, right-click IPv4 or IPv6 as appropriate for the type of binding you want to work with, and then click Properties.

2. On the Advanced tab of the IPv4 Properties or IPv6 Properties dialog box, click Bindings.

3. The Bindings dialog box displays a list of available network connections for the DHCP server. If you want the DHCP Server service to use a connection to service clients, select the check box for the connection. If you don't want the service to use a connection, clear the related check box.

4. Click OK twice when you have finished.

Updating DHCP Statistics

The DHCP console provides statistics concerning IPv4 and IPv6 address availability and usage. By default, these statistics are updated only when you start the DHCP console or when you select the server and then click the Refresh button on the toolbar. If you monitor DHCP routinely, you might want these statistics to be updated automatically. To do that, follow these steps:

1. In the DHCP console, expand the node for the server you want to work with, right-click IPv4 or IPv6 as appropriate for the type of address you want to work with, and then click Properties.

2. On the General tab, select Automatically Update Statistics Every and enter an update interval in hours and minutes. Click OK.

DHCP Auditing and Troubleshooting

Windows Server 2008 R2 is configured to audit DHCP processes by default. Auditing tracks DHCP processes and requests in log files.

Understanding DHCP Auditing

You can use audit logs to help you troubleshoot problems with a DHCP server. Although you can enable and configure logging separately for IPv4 and IPv6, the two protocols use the same log files by default. The default location for DHCP logs is %SystemRoot%\System32\DHCP. In this directory you'll find a different log file for each day of the week. The log file for Monday is named DhcpSrvLog-Mon.log, the log file for Tuesday is named DhcpSrvLog-Tue.log, and so on.

When you start the DHCP server or a new day arrives, a header message is written to the log file. This header provides a summary of DHCP events and their meanings. Stopping and starting the DHCP Server service doesn't necessarily clear a log file. Log data is cleared only when a log hasn't been written to in the last 24 hours. You don't have to monitor space usage by the DHCP Server service. The service is configured to monitor itself and restricts disk space usage by default.

Enabling or Disabling DHCP Auditing

You can enable or disable DHCP auditing by following these steps:

1. In the DHCP console, expand the node for the server you want to work with, right-click IPv4 or IPv6 as appropriate for the type of address you want to work with, and then click Properties.

2. On the General tab, select or clear the Enable DHCP Audit Logging check box, and then click OK.

Changing the Location of DHCP Auditing Logs

By default, DHCP logs are stored in %SystemRoot%\System32\DHCP. You can change the location of DHCP logs by following these steps:

1. In the DHCP console, expand the node for the server you want to work with, right-click IPv4 or IPv6 as appropriate for the type of address you want to work with, and then click Properties.

2. Click the Advanced tab. The Audit Log File Path field shows the current folder location for log files. Enter a new folder location, or click Browse to select a new location.

3. Click OK. Windows Server 2008 R2 now needs to restart the DHCP Server service. When prompted to restart the service, click Yes. The service will be stopped and then started again.

Changing the Log Usage

DHCP Server has a self-monitoring system that checks disk space usage. By default, the maximum size of all DHCP server logs is 70 megabytes (MB), with each individual log being limited to one-seventh of this space. If the server reaches the 70 MB limit or an individual log grows beyond the allocated space, logging of DHCP activity stops until log files are cleared or space is otherwise made available. Normally, this happens at the beginning of a new day when the server clears the previous week's log file for that day.

Registry keys that control log usage and other DHCP settings are located under HKEY_LOCAL_MACHINE\SYSTEM\CurrentControlSet\Services\DHCPServer\Parameters.

The following keys control the logging:

- **DhcpLogFilesMaxSize** Sets the maximum file size for all logs. The default is 70 MB.

- **DhcpLogDiskSpaceCleanupInterval** Determines how often DHCP checks disk space usage and cleans up as necessary. The default interval is 60 minutes.

- **DhcpLogMinSpaceOnDisk** Sets the free space threshold for writing to the log. If the disk has less free space than the value specified, logging is temporarily disabled. The default value is 20 MB.

DhcpLogMinSpaceOnDisk is considered an optional key and is not created automatically. You need to create this key as necessary and set appropriate values for your network.

Integrating DHCP and DNS

DNS is used to resolve computer names in Active Directory domains and on the Internet. Thanks to the DNS dynamic update protocol, you don't need to manually register DHCP clients in DNS. The protocol allows the client or the DHCP server to register the forward lookup and reverse lookup records in DNS as necessary. When configured using the default setup for DHCP, current DHCP clients automatically update their own DNS records after receiving an IP address lease, and the DHCP server updates records for early clients after issuing a lease. You can modify this behavior globally for each DHCP server or on a per-scope basis.

Name protection is a new feature in Windows Server 2008 R2. With name protection, the DHCP server registers records on behalf of the client only if no other client with this DNS information is already registered. You can configure name protection for IPv4 and IPv6 at the network adapter level or at the scope level. Name protection settings configured at the scope level take precedence over the setting at the IPv4 or IPv6 level.

Name protection is designed to prevent name squatting. Name squatting occurs when a non-Windows-based computer registers a name in DNS that is already registered to a computer running a Windows operating system. By enabling name protection, you can prevent name squatting by non-Windows-based computers. Although name squatting generally does not present a problem when you use Active Directory to reserve a name for a single user or computer, it usually is a good idea to enable name protection on all Windows networks.

Name protection is based on the Dynamic Host Configuration Identifier (DHCID) and support for the DHCID RR (resource record) in DNS. DHCID is a resource record stored in DNS that maps names to prevent duplicate registration. DHCP uses the DHCID resource record to store an identifier for a computer along with related information for the name, such as the A and AAAA records of the computer. The DHCP server can request a DHCID record match and then refuse the registration of a computer with a different address attempting to register a name with an existing DHCID record.

You can view and change the global DNS integration settings by following these steps:

1. In the DHCP console, expand the node for the server you want to work with, right-click IPv4 or IPv6, and then click Properties.

2. Click the DNS tab. Figure 19-5 shows the default DNS integration settings for DHCP. Because these settings are configured by default, you usually don't need to modify the configuration.

3. Optionally, you can enable or disable the name protection feature. With name protection, the DHCP server registers records on behalf of the client only if no other client with this DNS information is already registered. To enable or disable name protection, click Configure. In the Name Protection dialog box, select or clear Enable Name Protection, and then click OK.

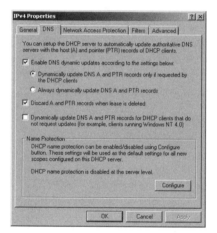 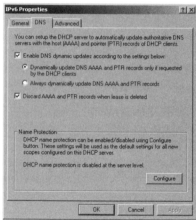

FIGURE 19-5 The DNS tab shows the default settings for DNS integration with DHCP.

You can view and change the per-scope DNS integration settings by following these steps:

1. In the DHCP console, expand the node for the server you want to work with, and then expand IPv4 or IPv6.

2. Right-click the scope you want to work with, and then click Properties.

3. Click the DNS tab. The options available are the same as those shown in Figure 19-5. Because these settings are configured by default, you usually don't need to modify the configuration.

4. Optionally, you can enable or disable the name protection feature. Click Configure. In the Name Protection dialog box, select or clear Enable Name Protection, and then click OK.

Integrating DHCP and NAP

Network Access Protection (NAP) is designed to protect the network from clients that do not have the appropriate security measures in place. The easiest way to enable NAP with DHCP is to set up the DHCP server as a Network Policy Server. To do this, you need to install the Network Policy And Access Services role, configure a compliant policy for NAP and DHCP integration on the server, and then enable NAP for DHCP. This process enables NAP for network computers that use DHCP, but it does not fully configure NAP for use.

You can create a NAP and DHCP integration policy by following these steps:

1. On the server that you want to act as the Network Policy Server, use the Add Roles Wizard to install the Network Policy And Access Services role. When you select role services, you should install the Network Policy Server role service at a minimum.

2. In the Network Policy Server Console, available from the Administrative Tools menu, select the NPS (Local) node in the console tree, and then click Configure NAP in the main pane. This starts the Configure NAP Wizard.

3. In the Network Connection Method list, choose Dynamic Host Configuration Protocol (DHCP) as the connection method that you want to deploy on your network for NAP-capable clients. As shown in Figure 19-6, the policy name is set to NAP DHCP by default. Click Next.

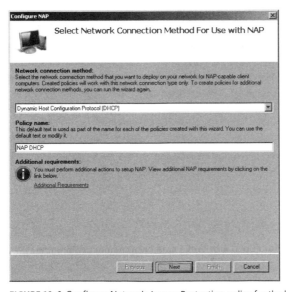

FIGURE 19-6 Configure Network Access Protection policy for the local DHCP server.

4. On the Specify NAP Enforcement Servers Running DHCP Server page, you need to identify all remote DHCP servers on your network by doing the following:

- Click Add. In the Add New RADIUS Client dialog box, type a friendly name for the remote server in the Friendly Name text box. Then type the DNS name or IP address of the remote DHCP server in the Address text box. Click Verify to ensure that the address is valid.

- In the Shared Secret panel, select Generate, and then click the Generate button to create a long shared-secret keyphrase. You need to enter this keyphrase in the NAP DHCP policy on all remote DHCP servers. Be sure to write down this keyphrase. Alternatively, copy the keyphrase to Notepad and save it in a file stored in a secure location. Click OK.

5. Click Next. On the Specify DHCP Scopes page, you can identify the DHCP scopes to which this policy should apply. If you do not specify any scopes, the policy applies to all NAP-enabled scopes on the selected DHCP servers. Click Next twice to skip the Configure Machine Groups page.

6. On the Specify A NAP Remediation Server Group And URL page, select a Remediation Server, or click New Group to define a remediation group and specify servers to handle remediation. Remediation servers store software updates for NAP clients that need them. In the text box provided, type a URL for a Web page that provides users with instructions on how to bring their computers into compliance with NAP health policy. Be sure that all DHCP clients can access this URL. Click Next to continue.

7. On the Define NAP Health Policy page, use the options provided to determine how NAP health policy works. In most cases, the default settings work fine. With the default settings, NAP-ineligible clients are denied access to the network, and NAP-capable clients are checked for compliance and automatically remediated, which allows them to get needed software updates that you've made available. Click Next, and then click Finish.

You can modify NAP settings globally for each DHCP server or on a per-scope basis. To view or change the global NAP settings, follow these steps:

1. In the DHCP console, expand the node for the server you want to work with, right-click IPv4, and then click Properties.

2. On the Network Access Protection tab, shown in Figure 19-7, click Enable On All Scopes or Disable On All Scopes to enable or disable NAP for all scopes on the server.

> **NOTE** When the local DHCP server is also a Network Policy Server, the Network Policy Server should always be reachable. If you haven't configured the server as a Network Policy Server or the DHCP server is unable to contact the designated Network Policy Server, you'll see an error stating this on the Network Access Protection tab.

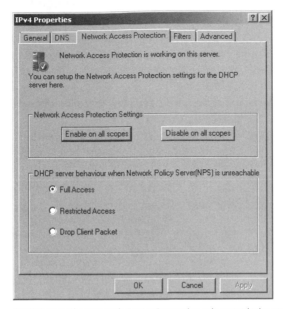

FIGURE 19-7 The Network Access Protection tab controls the protection options for DHCP.

3. Choose one of the following options to specify how the DHCP server behaves if the Network Policy Server is unreachable, and then click OK to save your settings:

- **Full Access**   Gives DHCP clients full (unrestricted) access to the network. This means clients can perform any permitted actions.

- **Restricted Access**   Gives DHCP clients restricted access to the network. This means clients can work only with the server to which they are connected.

- **Drop Client Packet**   Blocks client requests and prevents the clients from accessing the network. This means clients have no access to resources on the network.

You can view and change the NAP settings for individual scopes by following these steps:

1. In the DHCP console, expand the node for the server you want to work with, and then expand IPv4.

2. Right-click the scope you want to work with, and then click Properties.

3. On the Network Access Protection tab, click Enable For This Scope or Disable For This Scope to enable or disable NAP for this scope.

4. If you're enabling NAP and want to use a NAP profile other than the default, click Use Custom Profile on the Network Access Protection tab, and then type the name of the profile, such as **Alternate NAP DHCP**.

5. Click OK to save your settings.

Avoiding IP Address Conflicts

IPv4 address conflicts are a common cause of problems with DHCP. No two computers on the network can have the same unicast IP address. If a computer is assigned the same unicast IPv4 address as another, one or both of the computers might become disconnected from the network. To better detect and avoid potential conflicts, you can enable IPv4 address conflict detection by following these steps:

1. In the DHCP console, expand the node for the server you want to work with, right-click IPv4, and then click Properties.

2. On the Advanced tab, set Conflict Detection Attempts to a value other than 0. The value you enter determines the number of times the DHCP server checks an IP address before leasing it to a client. The DHCP server checks IP addresses by sending a ping request over the network.

REAL WORLD A unicast IPv4 address is a standard IP address for class A, B, and C networks. When a DHCP client requests a lease, a DHCP server checks its pool of available addresses and assigns the client a lease on an available IPv4 address. By default, the server checks only the list of current leases to determine whether an address is available. It doesn't actually query the network to see whether an address is in use. Unfortunately, in a busy network environment, an administrator might have assigned this IPv4 address to another computer or an offline computer might have been brought online with a lease that it believes hasn't expired, even though the DHCP server believes the lease has expired. Either way, you have an address conflict that will cause problems on the network. To reduce these types of conflicts, set the conflict detection to a value greater than 0.

Saving and Restoring the DHCP Configuration

After you configure all the necessary DHCP settings, you might want to save the DHCP configuration so that you can restore it on the DHCP server. To save the configuration, enter the following command at the command prompt:

```
netsh dump DHCP >dhcpconfig.dmp
```

In this example, *dhcpconfig.dmp* is the name of the configuration script you want to create. Once you create this script, you can restore the configuration by entering the following command at the command prompt:

```
netsh exec dhcpconfig.dmp
```

TIP You can also use this technique to set up another DHCP server with the same configuration. Simply copy the configuration script to a folder on the destination computer and then execute it.

You can save or restore the DHCP configuration by using the DHCP console as well. To save the configuration, right-click the DHCP server entry, click Backup, use the dialog box provided to select the folder for the backup, and then click OK. To restore the configuration, right-click the DHCP server entry, click Restore, use the dialog box provided to select the backup folder, and then click OK.

Managing DHCP Scopes

After you install a DHCP server, you need to configure the scopes that the DHCP server will use. Scopes are pools of IP addresses that you can lease to clients. As explained earlier in "Understanding Scopes," you can create superscopes, normal scopes, multicast scopes, and split scopes with IPv4 addresses, but you can create only normal scopes with IPv6 addresses.

Creating and Managing Superscopes

A superscope is a container for IPv4 scopes in much the same way that an organizational unit is a container for Active Directory objects. Superscopes help you manage scopes available on the network and also support DHCP clients on a single physical network where multiple logical IP networks are used. With a superscope, you can activate or deactivate multiple scopes through a single action. You can also view statistics for all scopes in the superscope rather than having to check statistics for each scope.

Creating Superscopes

After you create at least one normal or multicast IPv4 scope, you can create a superscope by following these steps:

1. In the DHCP console, expand the node for the server you want to work with, right-click IPv4, and then click New Superscope. This starts the New Superscope Wizard. Click Next.

2. Type a name for the superscope, and then click Next.

3. Select scopes to add to the superscope. Select individual scopes by clicking their entry in the Available Scopes list. Select multiple scopes by clicking entries while holding down Shift or Ctrl.

4. Click Next, and then click Finish.

Adding Scopes to a Superscope

You can add scopes to a superscope when you create it or you can do it later. To add a scope to a superscope, follow these steps:

1. Right-click the scope you want to add to a superscope, and then click Add To Superscope.

2. In the Add Scope To A Superscope dialog box, select a superscope.

3. Click OK. The scope is then added to the superscope.

Removing Scopes from a Superscope

To remove a scope from a superscope, follow these steps:

1. Right-click the scope you want to remove from a superscope, and then click Remove From Superscope.

2. Confirm the action by clicking Yes when prompted. If this is the last scope in the superscope, the superscope is deleted automatically.

Activating and Deactivating a Superscope

When you activate or deactivate a superscope, you make all the scopes within the superscope active or inactive. To activate a superscope, right-click the superscope and then select Activate. To deactivate a superscope, right-click the superscope and then select Deactivate.

Deleting a Superscope

Deleting a superscope removes the superscope container but doesn't delete the scopes it contains. If you want to delete the member scopes, you first need to delete the superscope. To delete a superscope, right-click the superscope and then select Delete. When prompted, click Yes to confirm the action.

Creating and Managing Scopes

Scopes provide a pool of IP addresses for DHCP clients. A normal scope is a scope with class A, B, or C network addresses. A multicast scope is a scope with class D network addresses. Although you create normal scopes and multicast scopes differently, you manage them in much the same way. The key differences are that multicast scopes can't use reservations and you can't set additional options for WINS, DNS, routing, and so forth.

Creating Normal Scopes for IPv4 Addresses

You can create a normal scope for IPv4 addresses by following these steps:

1. In the DHCP console, expand the node for the server you want to work with, and then select and right-click IPv4. If you want to add the new scope to a superscope automatically, select and then right-click the superscope instead.

2. On the shortcut menu, click New Scope. This starts the New Scope Wizard. Click Next.

3. Type a name and description for the scope, and then click Next.

4. The Start IP Address and End IP Address fields define the valid IP address range for the scope. On the IP Address Range page, enter a start address and an end address in these fields.

NOTE Generally, the scope doesn't include the *x.x.x.*0 and *x.x.x.*255 addresses, which are usually reserved for network addresses and broadcast messages, respectively. Accordingly, you would use a range such as 192.168.10.1 to 192.168.10.254 rather than 192.168.10.0 to 192.168.10.255.

5. When you enter an IP address range, the bit length and subnet mask are filled in for you automatically (as shown in Figure 19-8). Unless you use subnets, you should use the default values.

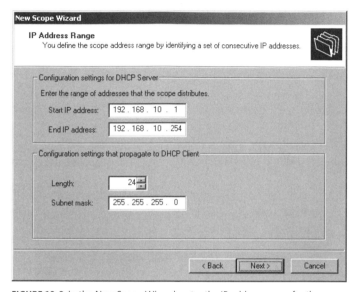

FIGURE 19-8 In the New Scope Wizard, enter the IP address range for the scope.

6. Click Next. If the IP address range you entered is on multiple networks, you're given the opportunity to create a superscope that contains separate scopes for each network. Select the Yes option button to continue, and then move on to step 8. If you make a mistake, click Back, and then modify the IP address range you entered.

7. Use the Start IP Address and End IP Address fields on the Add Exclusions And Delay page to define IP address ranges that are to be excluded from the scope. You can exclude multiple address ranges as follows:

   ▪ To define an exclusion range, type a start address and an end address in the Exclusion Range's Start IP Address and End IP Address fields, and then click Add. To exclude a single IP address, use that address as both the start IP address and the end IP address.

   ▪ To track which address ranges are excluded, use the Excluded Address Range list.

   To delete an exclusion range, select the range in the Excluded Address Range list, and then click Remove.

8. Click Next. Specify the duration of leases for the scope using the Day(s), Hour(s), and Minutes fields. The default duration is eight days. Click Next.

BEST PRACTICES Take a few minutes to plan the lease duration you want to use. A lease duration that's set too long can reduce the effectiveness of DHCP and might eventually cause you to run out of available IP addresses, especially on networks with mobile users or other types of computers that aren't fixed members of the network. A good lease duration for most networks is from one to three days.

9. You have the opportunity to set common DHCP options for DNS, WINS, gateways, and more. If you want to set these options now, select Yes, I Want To Configure These Options Now. Otherwise, select No, I Will Configure These Options Later and skip steps 10–15.

10. Click Next. The first option you can configure is the default gateway. In the IP Address field, enter the IP address of the primary default gateway, and then click Add. Repeat this process for other default gateways.

11. The first gateway listed is the one clients try to use first. If the gateway isn't available, clients try to use the next gateway, and so on. Use the Up and Down buttons to change the order of the gateways, as necessary.

12. Click Next. As shown in Figure 19-9, configure default DNS settings for DHCP clients. Enter the name of the parent domain to use for DNS resolution of computer names that aren't fully qualified.

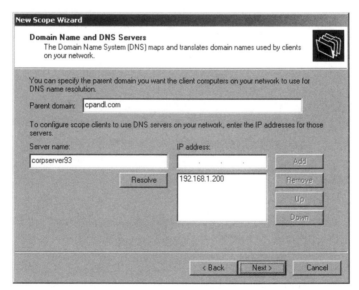

FIGURE 19-9 Use the Domain Name And DNS Servers page to configure default DNS settings for DHCP clients.

13. In the IP Address field, enter the IP address of the primary DNS server, and then click Add. Repeat this process to specify additional DNS servers. Again, the order of the entries determines which IP address is used first. Change the order as necessary by using the Up and Down buttons. Click Next.

   TIP If you know the name of a server instead of its IP address, enter the name in the Server Name field, and then click Resolve. The IP address is then entered in the IP Address field, if possible. Add the server by clicking Add.

14. Configure default WINS settings for the DHCP clients. The techniques you use are the same as those previously described. Click Next.

15. If you want to activate the scope, select Yes, I Want To Activate This Scope Now, and then click Next. Otherwise, select No, I Will Activate This Scope Later, and then click Next.

16. Click Finish to complete the process.

Creating Normal Scopes for IPv6 Addresses

You create normal scopes for IPv6 addresses by using the New Scope Wizard. When you are configuring DHCP for IPv6 addresses, you must enter the network ID and a preference value. Typically, the first 64 bits of an IPv6 address identify the network, and a 64-bit value is what the New Scope Wizard expects you to enter. The preference value sets the priority of the scope relative to other scopes. The scope with the lowest preference value will be used first. The scope with the second lowest preference will be used second, and so on.

You can create a normal scope for IPv6 addresses by following these steps:

1. In the DHCP console, expand the node for the server you want to work with.

2. Select and then right-click IPv6. On the shortcut menu, click New Scope. This starts the New Scope Wizard. Click Next.

3. Type a name and description for the scope, and then click Next.

4. On the Scope Prefix page, shown in Figure 19-10, enter the 64-bit network prefix, and then set a preference value. Click Next.

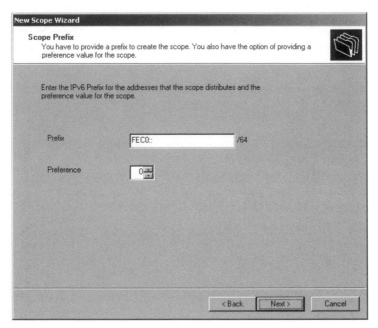

FIGURE 19-10 In the New Scope Wizard, enter the network prefix and preference value.

5. Use the Start IPv6 Address and End IPv6 Address fields on the Add Exclusions page to define IPv6 address ranges that are to be excluded from the scope. You can exclude multiple address ranges as follows:

   ■ To define an exclusion range, type a start address and an end address in the Exclusion Range's Start IPv6 Address and End IPv6 Address fields, and then click Add. To exclude a single IPv6 address, use that address as the start IPv6 address, and then click Add.

   ■ To track which address ranges are excluded, use the Excluded Address Range list.

   To delete an exclusion range, select the range in the Excluded Address Range list, and then click Remove.

6. Click Next. Dynamic IPv6 addresses can be temporary or nontemporary. A nontemporary address is similar to a reservation. On the Scope Lease page, shown in Figure 19-11, specify the duration of leases for nontemporary addresses using the Days, Hours, and Minutes fields under Preferred Life Time and Valid Life Time. The preferred lifetime is the preferred amount of time the lease should be valid. The valid lifetime is the maximum amount of time the lease is valid. Click Next.

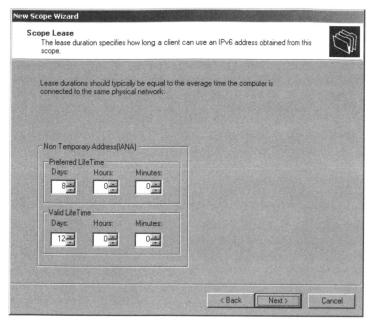

FIGURE 19-11 Specify the duration of nontemporary leases.

BEST PRACTICES Take a few minutes to plan the lease lifetime you want to use. A lease lifetime that's set too long can reduce the effectiveness of DHCP and might eventually cause you to run out of available IP addresses, especially on networks with mobile users or other types of computers that aren't fixed members of the network. A good lease duration for nontemporary leases is from 8 to 30 days.

7. If you want to activate the scope, select Yes under Activate Scope Now, and then click Finish. Otherwise, select No under Activate Scope Now, and then click Finish.

Creating Multicast Scopes

To create a multicast scope, follow these steps:

1. In the DHCP console, expand the node for the server you want to work with. Select and then right-click IPv4. If you want to add the new scope to a super-scope, select and then right-click the superscope instead.

2. On the shortcut menu, click New Multicast Scope. This starts the New Multicast Scope Wizard. Click Next.

3. Enter a name and description for the scope, and then click Next.

4. The Start IP Address and End IP Address fields define the valid IP address range for the scope. Enter a start address and an end address in these fields.

You must define multicast scopes using Class D IP addresses. This means the valid IP address range is 224.0.0.0 to 239.255.255.255.

5. Messages sent by computers using multicast IP addresses have a specific time-to-live (TTL) value. The TTL value specifies the maximum number of routers the message can go through. The default value is 32, which is sufficient on most networks. If you have a large network, you might need to increase this value to reflect the actual number of routers that might be used.

6. Click Next. If you make a mistake, click Back, and then modify the IP address range you entered.

7. Use the exclusion range fields to define IP address ranges that are to be excluded from the scope. You can exclude multiple address ranges:

   - To define an exclusion range, enter a start address and an end address in the Start IP Address and End IP Address fields, and then click Add.

   - To track which address ranges are excluded, use the Excluded Addresses list.

   To delete an exclusion range, select the range in the Excluded Addresses list, and then click Remove.

8. Click Next. Specify the duration of leases for the scope using the Day(s), Hour(s), and Minutes fields. The default duration is 30 days. Click Next.

   TIP If you haven't worked a lot with multicast, you shouldn't change the default value. Multicast leases aren't used in the same way as normal leases. Multiple computers can use a multicast IP address, and all of these computers can have a lease on the IP address. A good multicast lease duration for most networks is from 30 to 60 days.

9. If you want to activate the scope, select Yes, and then click Next. Otherwise, select No, and then click Next.

10. Click Finish to complete the process.

Setting Scope Options

Scope options allow you to precisely control a scope's functioning and to set default TCP/IP settings for clients that use the scope. For example, you can use scope options to enable clients to automatically find DNS servers on the network. You can also define settings for default gateways, WINS, and more. Scope options apply only to normal scopes, not to multicast scopes.

You can set scope options in any of the following ways:

- Globally for all scopes by setting default server options
- On a per-scope basis by setting scope options
- On a per-client basis by setting reservation options
- On a client-class basis by configuring user-specific or vendor-specific classes

IPv4 and IPv6 have different scope options. Scope options use a hierarchy to determine when certain options apply. The previous list shows the hierarchy. Basically, this means the following:

- Per-scope options override global options.
- Per-client options override per-scope and global options.
- Client-class options override all other options.

VIEWING AND ASSIGNING SERVER OPTIONS

Server options are applied to all scopes configured on a particular DHCP server. You can view and assign server options by following these steps:

1. In the DHCP console, double-click the server you want to work with, and then expand its IPv4 and IPv6 folders in the tree view.

2. To view current settings, select the Server Options node under IPv4 or IPv6, depending on the type of address you want to work with. Currently configured options are displayed in the right pane.

3. To assign new settings, right-click Server Options, and then click Configure Options. This opens the Server Options dialog box. Under Available Options, select the check box for the first option you want to configure. Then, with the option selected, enter any required information in the fields in the Data Entry panel. Repeat this step to configure other options.

4. Click OK to save your changes.

VIEWING AND ASSIGNING SCOPE OPTIONS

Scope options are specific to an individual scope and override the default server options. You can view and assign scope options by following these steps:

1. In the DHCP console, expand the entry for the scope you want to work with.

2. To view current settings, select Scope Options. Currently configured options are displayed in the right pane.

3. To assign new settings, right-click Scope Options, and then click Configure Options. This opens the Scope Options dialog box. Under Available Options, select the check box for the first option you want to configure. Then, with the

option selected, enter any required information in the fields in the Data Entry panel, as shown in Figure 19-12. Repeat this step to configure other options.

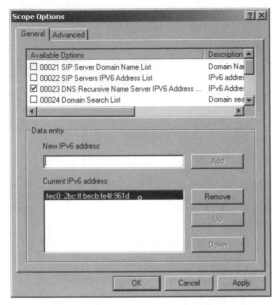

FIGURE 19-12 Select the option you want to configure in the Scope Options dialog box and then enter the required information using the fields of the Data Entry panel.

4. Click OK.

VIEWING AND ASSIGNING RESERVATION OPTIONS

You can assign reservation options to a client that has a reserved IPv4 or IPv6 address. These options are specific to an individual client and override server-specific and scope-specific options. To view and assign reservation options, follow these steps:

1. In the DHCP console, expand the entry for the scope you want to work with.

2. Double-click the Reservations folder for the scope.

3. To view current settings, click the reservation you want to examine. Currently configured options are displayed in the right pane.

4. To assign new settings, right-click the reservation, and then click Configure Options. This opens the Reservation Options dialog box. Under Available Options, select the check box for the first option you want to configure. Then, with the option selected, enter any required information in the fields in the Data Entry panel. Repeat this step to configure other options.

Modifying Scopes

You can modify an existing scope by following these steps:

1. In the DHCP console, double-click the server you want to work with, and then expand its IPv4 and IPv6 folders in the tree view. This should display the currently configured scopes for the server.

2. Right-click the scope you want to modify, and then click Properties.

3. You can now modify the scope properties. Keep the following in mind:

   - When you modify normal IPv4 scopes, you have the option of setting an unlimited lease expiration time. If you do, you create permanent leases that reduce the effectiveness of pooling IP addresses with DHCP. Permanent leases aren't released unless you physically release them or deactivate the scope. As a result, you might eventually run out of addresses, especially as your network grows. A better alternative to unlimited leases is to use address reservations, and then only for specific clients that need fixed IP addresses.

   - When you modify multicast scopes, you have the option of setting a lifetime for the scope. The scope lifetime determines the amount of time the scope is valid. By default, multicast scopes are valid as long as they're activated. To change this setting, click the Lifetime tab, select Multicast Scope Expires On, and then set an expiration date.

Activating and Deactivating Scopes

In the DHCP console, inactive scopes are displayed with an icon showing a red arrow pointing down. Active scopes display a normal folder icon.

You can activate an inactive scope by right-clicking it in the DHCP console, and then selecting Activate. You can deactivate an active scope by right-clicking it in the DHCP console, and then selecting Deactivate.

> **TIP** Deactivating turns off a scope but doesn't terminate current client leases. If you want to terminate leases, follow the instructions in "Releasing Addresses and Leases" later in this chapter.

Enabling the Bootstrap Protocol

Bootstrap Protocol (BOOTP) is a dynamic IPv4 addressing protocol that predates DHCP. Normal scopes don't support BOOTP. To enable a scope to support BOOTP, follow these steps:

1. Right-click the normal scope for IPv4 addresses that you want to modify, and then click Properties.

2. On the Advanced tab, click Both to support DHCP and BOOTP clients.

3. As necessary, set a lease duration for BOOTP clients, and then click OK.

Removing a Scope

Removing a scope permanently deletes the scope from the DHCP server. To remove a scope, follow these steps:

1. In the DHCP console, right-click the scope you want to remove, and then click Delete.

2. When prompted to confirm that you want to delete the scope, click Yes.

Configuring Multiple Scopes on a Network

You can configure multiple scopes on a single network. A single DHCP server or multiple DHCP servers can serve these scopes. However, any time you work with multiple scopes, it's extremely important that the address ranges used by different scopes not overlap. Each scope must have a unique address range. If it doesn't, the same IP address might be assigned to different DHCP clients, which can cause severe problems on the network.

To understand how you can use multiple scopes, consider the following scenario, in which each server has its respective DHCP scope IP address range on the same subnet.

Server	DHCP Scope IP Address Range
A	192.168.10.1 to 192.168.10.99
B	192.168.10.100 to 192.168.10.199
C	192.168.10.200 to 192.168.10.254

Each of these servers responds to DHCP discovery messages, and any of them can assign IP addresses to clients. If one of the servers fails, the other servers can continue to provide DHCP services to the network. To introduce fault tolerance and provide redundancy, you can use split scopes as discussed in the next section.

Creating and Managing Split Scopes

Split scopes are split between two DHCP servers to increase fault tolerance, provide redundancy over using a single DHCP server, and enable load balancing. With a split scope, you identify the two DHCP servers that split the scope. If one of the servers becomes unavailable or overloaded, the other server can take its place by continuing to lease new IP addresses and renew existing leases. A split scope can also help to balance server loads.

Creating Split Scopes

Split scopes apply only to IPv4 addresses. You cannot split a superscope or a scope that is part of a superscope. You create a split scope on the DHCP server that you want to act as the primary server by splitting an existing scope. During the split scope creation process, you need to specify the DHCP server with which you want to split the primary server's scope. This additional server acts as the secondary server for the scope. Because split scopes are a server-side enhancement, no additional configuration is required for DHCP clients.

The way scope splitting works depends on the split scope configuration settings. You can:

- **Optimize for fault tolerance**   A split scope optimized for fault tolerance has an extended time delay configured in its scope properties. The time delay on the secondary DHCP server causes the server to respond with a delay to DHCP DISCOVER requests from DHCP clients. The delay on the secondary server allows the primary DHCP server to respond to and accept the DHCPOFFER first. However, if the primary server becomes unavailable or overloaded and is unable to respond to requests, the secondary server handles requests and continues distributing addresses until the primary server is available to service clients again. Because split scopes are a server-side enhancement, no additional configuration is required for DHCP clients.

- **Optimize for load balancing**   A split scope optimized for load balancing has little or no time delay configured in its scope properties. With no time delay, both the primary and the secondary servers can respond to DHCP DISCOVER requests from DHCP clients. This allows the fastest server to respond to and accept a DHCPOFFER first. Fault tolerance continues to be a part of the scope. If one of the servers becomes unavailable or overloaded and is unable to respond to requests, the other server handles requests and continues distributing addresses until the normal process is restored.

You can create a split scope by completing the following steps:

1. In the DHCP console, connect to the primary DHCP server for the split scope. Double-click the entry for the primary server, and then expand its IPv4 folder in the tree view.

2. The scope you want to split must already be defined. Right-click the normal scope for IPv4 addresses that you want to split, point to Advanced, and then click Split-Scope. This starts the DHCP Split-Scope Configuration Wizard. Click Next.

3. On the Additional DHCP Server page, shown in Figure 19-13, note that the server on which you selected the scope to split is listed as the host DHCP server. If this is not the correct primary server for the split scope, click Cancel, and then begin this procedure again, ensuring that you select the correct primary server at the start. Otherwise, click Add Server. Use the options in the Add Server dialog box to select the secondary DHCP server for the split scope, and then click OK. Click Next.

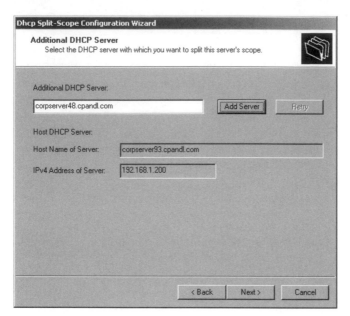

FIGURE 19-13 Identify the secondary DHCP server for the split scope.

4. On the Percentage Of Split page, shown in Figure 19-14, use the slider to specify the relative percentage for how to allocate the IP addresses to each of the servers, and then click Next. Here are configuration examples:

- An 80/20 split works best when you are configuring for fault tolerance. With an 80/20 split, the primary server is configured to handle 80 percent of the IP addresses and has exclusions set for the other 20 percent. The secondary server is configured to handle 20 percent of the IP addresses and has exclusions set for the other 80 percent.

- A 50/50 split works best when you are configuring for load balancing. With an 50/50 split, the primary server is configured to handle 50 percent of the IP addresses and has exclusions set for the other 50 percent. The secondary server is configured to handle 50 percent of the IP addresses and has exclusions set for the other 50 percent.

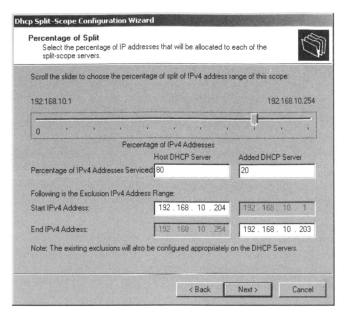

FIGURE 19-14 Specify the percentage of the split.

5. On the Delay In DHCP Offer page, specify the time delay in milliseconds for the primary DHCP server (the host server) and the secondary server (the added server). Keep the following in mind:

   - If you are optimizing for fault tolerance, you'll typically want the primary server to have no delay and the secondary server to have a short delay, such as 500 milliseconds.

   - If you are optimizing for load balancing, you'll typically want the primary server to have no delay and the secondary server to have no delay.

   - If you want to load balance but give one server a slight preference over the other, you'll want one of the servers to have a short delay, such as 100 milliseconds.

6. Click Next, and then click Finish. Review the summary of the split scope configuration. If any errors were encountered, you may need to take corrective action. Click Close.

Modifying or Removing Split Scopes

Split scopes are not identified as such in the DHCP console. You can identify a split scope by its network ID and IP address pool. Generally, you'll find a scope with the same network ID on two DHCP servers, and the scopes on those servers will have opposite inclusion and exclusion address ranges. One server will have an IP address range for distribution and a set of IP addresses excluded from distribution. On the second server, the exclusions on the first server will be allowed and inclusions on the first server will be denied. If you try to split a scope that is already split, you get an error message on the Additional DHCP Server page that states the following:

```
The scope IP address specified is already in use. Use a different DHCP
server or remove the conflicting scope.
```

You can modify the settings of a split scope:

- To modify the percentage of addresses split, you must manually make changes to the scope's included and excluded address list. For example, if you configured an 80/20 split and now want to use a 50/50 split, you need to modify the included and excluded addresses for the scope on both the primary and secondary servers.

- To change the preference for the way scope splitting works, such as to optimize for load balancing rather than fault tolerance or vice versa, you modify the subnet delay on the Advanced tab in the Scope Properties dialog box.

If you no longer want to split the scope, you can remove the scope from the primary or secondary server or both servers. Typically, when you remove the scope only from the primary or secondary server, you should remove address exclusions from the remaining scope and then include the additional addresses in the scope.

Managing the Address Pool, Leases, and Reservations

Scopes have separate folders for address pools, leases, and reservations. By accessing these folders, you can view current statistics for the related data and manage existing entries.

Viewing Scope Statistics

Scope statistics provide summary information about the address pool for the current scope or superscope. To view statistics, right-click the scope or superscope and then select Display Statistics.

The primary fields in the Scope Statistics dialog box are used as follows:

- **Total Scopes** Shows the number of scopes in a superscope.

- **Total Addresses** Shows the total number of IP addresses assigned to the scope.

- **In Use** Shows the total number (as a numerical value and as a percentage of the total available addresses) of addresses being used. If the total reaches 85 percent or more, you might want to consider assigning additional addresses or freeing up addresses for use.

- **Available** Shows the total number (as a numerical value and as a percentage of the total available addresses) of addresses available for use.

Enabling and Configuring MAC Address Filtering

MAC address filtering (aka link-layer filtering) is a feature for IPv4 addresses that allows you to include or exclude computers and devices based on their MAC address. When you configure MAC address filtering, you can specify the hardware types that are exempted from filtering. By default, all hardware types defined in RFC 1700 are exempted from filtering. To modify hardware type exemptions, follow these steps:

1. In the DHCP console, right-click the IPv4 node, and then click Properties.

2. On the Filters tab, click Advanced. In the Advanced Filter Properties dialog box, select the check box for hardware types to exempt from filtering. Clear the check box for hardware types to filter.

3. Click OK to save your changes.

Before you can configure MAC address filtering, you must do the following:

- Enable and define an explicit allow list. The DHCP server provides DHCP services only to clients whose MAC addresses are in the allow list. Any client that previously received IP addresses is denied address renewal if its MAC address isn't on the allow list.

- Enable and define an explicit deny list. The DHCP server denies DHCP services only to clients whose MAC addresses are in the deny list. Any client that previously received IP addresses is denied address renewal if its MAC address is on the deny list.

- Enable and define an allow list and a block list. The block list has precedence over the allow list. This means that the DHCP server provides DHCP services only to clients whose MAC addresses are in the allow list, provided that no corresponding matches are in the deny list. If a MAC address has been denied, the address is always blocked even if the address is on the allow list.

To enable an allow list, deny list, or both, follow these steps:

1. In the DHCP console, right-click the IPv4 node, and then click Properties.

2. On the Filters tab, you'll see the current filter configuration details. To use an allow list, select Enable Allow List. To use a deny list, select Enable Deny List.

3. Click OK to save your changes.

NOTE As an alternative, you can simply right-click the Allow or Deny node, and then select Enable to enable allow or deny lists. If you right-click the Allow or Deny node and then select Disable, you disable allow or deny lists.

Once you've enabled filtering, you define your filters using the MAC address for the client computer or device's network adapter. On a client computer, you can obtain the MAC address by typing the command **ipconfig /all** at the command prompt. The Physical Address entry shows the client's MAC address. You must type this value exactly for the address filter to work.

A MAC address is defined by eight pairings of two-digit hexadecimal numbers separated by a hyphen, such as:

FE-01-56-23-18-94-EB-F2

When you define a filter, you can specify the MAC address with or without the hyphens. This means that you could enter FE-01-56-23-18-94-EB-F2 or FE0156231894EBF2.

You also can use an asterisk (*) as a wildcard for pattern matching. To allow any value to match a specific part of the MAC address, you can insert * where the values normally would be, such as:

FE-01-56-23-18-94-*-F2

FE-*-56-23-18-94-*-*

FE-01-56-23-18-*-*-*

FE01*

To configure a MAC address filter, follow these steps:

1. In the DHCP console, double-click the IPv4 node, and then double-click the Filters node.

2. Right-click Allow or Deny as appropriate for the type of filter you are creating, and then click New Filter.

3. Enter the MAC address to filter, and then enter a comment in the Description field if you want to. Click Add. Repeat this step to add other filters.

4. Click Close when you have finished.

Setting a New Exclusion Range

You can exclude IPv4 or IPv6 addresses from a scope by defining an exclusion range. Scopes can have multiple exclusion ranges. To define an exclusion range for a scope with IPv4 addresses, follow these steps:

1. In the DHCP console, expand the scope you want to work with, and then right-click the Address Pool folder or Exclusions folder. On the shortcut menu, click New Exclusion Range.

2. Enter a start address and an end address in the Start IP Address and End IP Address fields, and then click Add. The range specified must be a subset of the range set for the current scope and must not be currently in use. Repeat this step to add other exclusion ranges.

3. Click Close when you have finished.

To define an exclusion range for a scope with IPv6 addresses, follow these steps:

1. In the DHCP console, expand the scope you want to work with, and then right-click the Exclusions folder. On the shortcut menu, click New Exclusion Range.

2. Enter a start address and an end address in the Start IPv6 Address and End IPv6 Address fields, and then click Add. The range specified must be a subset of the range set for the current scope and must not be currently in use. Repeat this step to add other exclusion ranges.

3. Click Close when you have finished.

Deleting an Exclusion Range

If you don't need an exclusion anymore, you can delete it. Select Address Pool or Exclusions as appropriate. In the main pane, right-click the exclusion, select Delete, and then click Yes in response to the confirmation message.

Reserving DHCP Addresses

DHCP provides several ways to assign permanent addresses to clients. One way is to use the Unlimited setting in the Scope dialog box to assign permanent addresses to all clients that use the scope. Another way is to reserve DHCP addresses on a per-client basis. When you reserve a DHCP address, the DHCP server always assigns the client the same IP address, and you can do so without sacrificing the centralized management features that make DHCP so attractive.

To reserve an IPv4 address for a client, follow these steps:

1. In the DHCP console, expand the scope you want to work with, and then right-click the Reservations folder. On the shortcut menu, click New Reservation.

2. In the Reservation Name field, type a short but descriptive name for the reservation. This field is used only for identification purposes.

3. In the IP Address field, enter the IPv4 address you want to reserve for the client.

   NOTE This IP address must be within the valid range of addresses for the currently selected scope.

4. The MAC Address field specifies the MAC address for the client computer's NIC. You can obtain the MAC address by typing the command **ipconfig /all** at the command prompt on the client computer. The Physical Address entry shows the client's MAC address. You must type this value exactly for the address reservation to work.

5. Enter an optional comment in the Description field.

6. By default, both DHCP and BOOTP clients are supported. This option is fine, and you need to change it only if you want to exclude a particular type of client.

7. Click Add to create the address reservation. Repeat this step to add other address reservations.

8. Click Close when you have finished.

To reserve an IPv6 address for a client, follow these steps:

1. In the DHCP console, expand the scope you want to work with, and then right-click the Reservations folder. On the shortcut menu, click New Reservation.

2. In the Reservation field, type a short but descriptive name for the reservation. This field is used only for identification purposes.

3. In the IPv6 Address field, enter the IPv6 address you want to reserve for the client.

   NOTE This IP address must be within the valid range of addresses for the currently selected scope.

4. The device unique identifier (DUID) field specifies the MAC address for the client computer's NIC. You can obtain the MAC address by typing the command **ipconfig /all** at the command prompt on the client computer. The Physical Address entry shows the client's MAC address. You must type this value exactly for the address reservation to work.

5. The identity association identifier (IAID) sets a unique identifier prefix for the client. Typically, this a nine-digit value.

6. Enter an optional comment in the Description field.

7. Click Add to create the address reservation. Repeat this step to add other address reservations.

8. Click Close when you have finished.

Releasing Addresses and Leases

When you work with reserved addresses, you should heed a couple of caveats:

- Reserved addresses aren't automatically reassigned. If the address is already in use, you need to release the address to ensure that the appropriate client can obtain it. You can force a client to release an address by terminating the client's lease or by logging on to the client and typing the command **ipconfig /release** at the command prompt.

- Clients don't automatically switch to the reserved address. If the client is using a different IP address, you need to force the client to release the current lease and request a new one. You can do this by terminating the client's lease or by logging on to the client and typing the command **ipconfig /renew** at the command prompt.

Modifying Reservation Properties

You can modify the properties of reservations by following these steps:

1. In the DHCP console, expand the scope you want to work with, and then click the Reservations folder.

2. Right-click a reservation, and then click Properties. You can now modify the reservation properties. You can't modify fields that are shaded, but you can modify other fields. These fields are the same fields described in the previous section.

Deleting Leases and Reservations

You can delete active leases and reservations by following these steps:

1. In the DHCP console, expand the scope you want to work with, and then click the Address Leases folder or Reservations folder, as appropriate.

2. Right-click the lease or reservation you want to delete, and then click Delete.

3. Confirm the deletion by clicking Yes.

4. The lease or reservation is now removed from DHCP. However, the client isn't forced to release the IP address. To force the client to release the IP address, log on to the client that holds the lease or reservation and type the command **ipconfig /release** at the command prompt.

Backing Up and Restoring the DHCP Database

DHCP servers store DHCP lease and reservation information in database files. By default, these files are stored in the %SystemRoot%\System32\DHCP directory. The key files in this directory are used as follows:

- **Dhcp.mdb**   The primary database file for the DHCP server

- **J50.log**   A transaction log file used to recover incomplete transactions in case of a server malfunction

- **J50.chk**   A checkpoint file used in truncating the transaction log for the DHCP server

- **Res1.log**   A reserved log file for the DHCP server

- **Res2.log**   A reserved log file for the DHCP server

- **Tmp.edb**   A temporary working file for the DHCP server

Backing Up the DHCP Database

The Backup directory in the %SystemRoot%\System32\DHCP folder contains backup information for the DHCP configuration and the DHCP database. By default, the DHCP database is backed up every 60 minutes automatically. To manually back up the DHCP database at any time, follow these steps:

1. In the DHCP console, right-click the server you want to back up, and then click Backup.

2. In the Browse For Folder dialog box, select the folder that will contain the backup DHCP database, and then click OK.

Registry keys that control the location and timing of DHCP backups, as well as other DHCP settings, are located under HKEY_LOCAL_MACHINE\SYSTEM\ CurrentControlSet\Services\DHCPServer\Parameters.

The following keys control the DHCP database and backup configuration:

- **BackupDatabasePath** Sets the location of the DHCP database. You should set this option through the DHCP Properties dialog box. Click the Advanced tab, and then set the Database Path field as appropriate.

- **DatabaseName** Sets the name of the primary DHCP database file. The default value is DHCP.mdb.

- **BackupInterval** Determines how often the DHCP client information database is backed up. The default is 60 minutes.

- **DatabaseCleanupInterval** Determines how often the DHCP service deletes expired records from the DHCP client information database. The default is four hours.

Restoring the DHCP Database from Backup

In the case of a server crash and recovery, you might need to restore and then reconcile the DHCP database. To force DHCP to restore the database from backup, follow these steps:

1. If necessary, restore a good copy of the %SystemRoot%\System32\DHCP\ Backup directory from the archive. Afterward, start the DHCP console, right-click the server you want to restore, and then click Restore.

2. In the Browse For Folder dialog box, select the folder that contains the backup you want to restore, and then click OK.

3. During restoration of the database, the DHCP Server service is stopped. As a result, DHCP clients are temporarily unable to contact the DHCP server to obtain IP addresses.

Using Backup and Restore to Move the DHCP Database to a New Server

If you need to rebuild a server providing DHCP services, you might want to move the DHCP services to another server prior to rebuilding the server. To do this, you need to perform several tasks on the source and destination servers. On the destination server, do the following:

1. Install the DHCP Server service on the destination server, and then restart the server.

2. Stop the DHCP Server service in the Services console.

3. Delete the contents of the %SystemRoot%\System32\DHCP folder.

On the source server, do the following:

1. Stop the DHCP Server service in the Services console.

2. After the DHCP Server service is stopped, disable the service so that it can no longer be started.

3. Copy the entire contents of the %SystemRoot%\System32\DHCP folder to the %SystemRoot%\System32\DHCP folder on the destination server.

Now all the necessary files are on the destination server. Start the DHCP Server service on the destination server to complete the migration.

Forcing the DHCP Server Service to Regenerate the DHCP Database

If the DHCP database becomes corrupt and Windows is unable to repair the database when you stop and restart the DHCP Server service, you can attempt to restore the database as described in "Restoring the DHCP Database from Backup" earlier in this chapter. If this fails or you prefer to start with a fresh copy of the DHCP database, follow these steps:

1. Stop the DHCP Server service in the Services console.

2. Delete the contents of the %SystemRoot%\System32\DHCP folder. If you want to force a complete regeneration of the database and not allow the server to restore from a previous backup, you should also delete the contents of the Backup folder.

> **CAUTION** Don't delete DHCP files if the DHCPServer registry keys aren't intact. These keys must be available to restore the DHCP database.

3. Restart the DHCP Server service.

4. No active leases or other information for scopes are displayed in the DHCP console. To regain the active leases for each scope, you must reconcile the server scopes as discussed in the next section.

5. To prevent conflicts with previously assigned leases, you should enable address conflict detection for the next few days, as discussed in "Avoiding IP Address Conflicts" earlier in this chapter.

Reconciling Leases and Reservations

Reconciling checks the client leases and reservations against the DHCP database on the server. If inconsistencies are found between what is registered in the Windows registry and what is recorded in the DHCP server database, you can select and reconcile any inconsistent entries. Once reconciled, DHCP either restores the IP address to the original owner or creates a temporary reservation for the IP address. When the lease time expires, the address is recovered for future use.

You can reconcile scopes individually, or you can reconcile all scopes on a server. To reconcile a scope individually, follow these steps:

1. In the DHCP console, right-click the scope you want to work with, and then click Reconcile.

2. In the Reconcile dialog box, click Verify.

3. Inconsistencies are reported in the status window. Select the displayed addresses, and then click Reconcile to repair inconsistencies.

4. If no inconsistencies are found, click OK.

To reconcile all scopes on a server, follow these steps:

1. In the DHCP console, expand the server entry, right-click the IPv4 node, and then click Reconcile All Scopes.

2. In the Reconcile All Scopes dialog box, click Verify.

3. Inconsistencies are reported in the status window. Select the displayed addresses, and then click Reconcile to repair inconsistencies.

4. If no inconsistencies are found, click OK.

Optimizing DNS

This chapter discusses the techniques you use to set up and manage Domain Name System (DNS) on a network. DNS is a name-resolution service that resolves computer names to IP addresses. When you use DNS, a fully qualified host name, omega.microsoft.com, for example, can be resolved to an IP address, which enables computers to find one another. DNS operates over the TCP/IP protocol stack and can be integrated with Windows Internet Name Service (WINS), Dynamic Host Configuration Protocol (DHCP), and Active Directory. Fully integrating DNS with these Windows networking features allows you to optimize DNS for Windows Server 2008 R2 domains.

Understanding DNS

DNS organizes groups of computers into domains. These domains are organized into a hierarchical structure that can be defined on an Internet-wide basis for public networks or on an enterprise-wide basis for private networks (also known as *intranets* and *extranets*). The various levels within the hierarchy identify individual computers, organizational domains, and top-level domains. For the fully qualified host name omega.microsoft.com, *omega* represents the host name for an individual computer, *microsoft* is the organizational domain, and *com* is the top-level domain.

Top-level domains are at the root of the DNS hierarchy and are also called *root domains*. These domains are organized geographically, by organization type, and by function. Normal domains, such as microsoft.com, are also referred to as *parent domains* because they're the parents of an organizational structure. You can divide parent domains into subdomains that you can use for groups or departments within your organization.

Subdomains are often referred to as *child domains*. For example, the fully qualified domain name (FQDN) for a computer within a human resources group could be designated as jacob.hr.microsoft.com. Here, *jacob* is the host name, *hr* is the child domain, and *microsoft.com* is the parent domain.

Integrating Active Directory and DNS

As stated in Chapter 7, "Using Active Directory," Active Directory domains use DNS to implement their naming structure and hierarchy. Active Directory and DNS are tightly integrated, so much so that you should install DNS on the network before you can install Active Directory Domain Services (AD DS).

During installation of the first domain controller on an Active Directory network, you have the opportunity to automatically install DNS if a DNS server can't be found on the network. You can also specify whether DNS and Active Directory should be integrated fully. In most cases you should respond affirmatively to both requests. With full integration, DNS information is stored directly in Active Directory, which allows you to take advantage of Active Directory's capabilities.

Understanding the difference between partial integration and full integration is very important:

- **Partial integration** With partial integration, the domain uses standard file storage. DNS information is stored in text-based files that end with the .dns extension. The default location of these files is %SystemRoot%\System32\ Dns. Updates to DNS are handled through a single authoritative DNS server. This server is designated as the primary DNS server for the particular domain or an area within a domain called a *zone*. Clients that use dynamic DNS updates through DHCP must be configured to use the primary DNS server in the zone. If they aren't, their DNS information won't be updated. Likewise, dynamic updates through DHCP can't be made if the primary DNS server is offline.

- **Full integration** With full integration, the domain uses directory-integrated storage. DNS information is stored directly in Active Directory and is available through the container for the dnsZone object. Because the information is part of Active Directory, any domain controller can access the data, and you can use a multimaster approach for dynamic updates through DHCP. This allows any domain controller running the DNS Server service to handle dynamic updates. Furthermore, clients that use dynamic DNS updates through DHCP can use any DNS server within the zone. An added benefit of directory integration is the ability to use directory security to control access to DNS information.

If you look at the way DNS information is replicated throughout the network, you will see more advantages to full integration with Active Directory. With partial integration, DNS information is stored and replicated separately from Active Directory. By having two separate structures, you reduce the effectiveness of both DNS and Active Directory and make administration more complex. Because DNS is less efficient than Active Directory at replicating changes, you might also increase network traffic and the amount of time required to replicate DNS changes throughout the network.

In earlier releases of DNS server for Windows Server, restarting a DNS server could take an hour or more in very large organizations with extremely large AD DS–integrated zones. The operation took this much time because the zone data was loaded in the foreground while the server was starting the DNS service. To ensure that DNS servers can be responsive after a restart, the DNS Server service for Windows Server 2008 R2 has been enhanced to load zone data from AD DS in the background while the service restarts. This ensures that the DNS server is responsive and can handle requests for data from other zones.

At startup, DNS servers running Windows Server 2008 R2 perform the following tasks:

- Enumerate all zones to be loaded
- Load root hints from files or AD DS storage
- Load all zones that are stored in files rather than in AD DS
- Begin responding to queries and remote procedure calls (RPCs)
- Create one or more threads to load the zones that are stored in AD DS

Because separate threads load zone data, the DNS server is able to respond to queries while zone loading is in progress. If a DNS client performs a query for a host in a zone that has already been loaded, the DNS server responds appropriately. If the query is for a host that has not yet been loaded into memory, the DNS server reads the host's data from AD DS and updates its record list accordingly.

Enabling DNS on the Network

To enable DNS on the network, you need to configure DNS clients and servers. When you configure DNS clients, you tell the clients the IP addresses of DNS servers on the network. Using these addresses, clients can communicate with DNS servers anywhere on the network, even if the servers are on different subnets.

NOTE Configuring a DNS client is explained in Chapter 17, "Managing TCP/IP Networking." Configuring a DNS server is explained in the next section of this chapter.

The DNS client built into computers running Windows 7 and Windows Server 2008 R2 supports DNS traffic over IPv4 and IPv6. By default, IPv6 configures the well-known site-local addresses of DNS servers at FEC0:0:0:FFFF::1, FEC0:0:0:FFFF::2, and FEC0:0:0:FFFF::3. To add the IPv6 addresses of your DNS servers, use the properties of the Internet Protocol Version 6 (TCP/IPv6) component in Network Connections or the following command:

```
netsh interface IPV6 ADD DNS
```

DNS servers running Windows Server 2008 R2 now support IPv6 addresses as fully as they support IPv4 addresses. In the DNS Manager console, host addresses are displayed as IPv4 or IPv6 addresses. The Dnscmd command-line tool also accepts addresses in either format. Additionally, DNS servers can now send recursive queries to IPv6-only servers, and the server forwarder list can contain both IPv4 and IPv6 addresses. Finally, DNS servers now support the *ip6.arpa* domain namespace for reverse lookups.

When the network uses DHCP, you should configure DHCP to work with DNS. DHCP clients can register IPv6 addresses along with or instead of IPv4 addresses. To ensure proper integration of DHCP and DNS, you need to set the DHCP scope options as specified in "Setting Scope Options" in Chapter 19. For IPv4, you should set the 006 DNS Servers and 015 DNS Domain Name scope options. For IPv6, you should set the 00023 DNS Recursive Name Server IPV6 Address List and 00024 Domain Search List scope options. Additionally, if computers on the network need to be accessible from other Active Directory domains, you need to create records for them in DNS. DNS records are organized into zones, where a zone is simply an area within a domain.

DNS client computers running Windows 7 or Windows Server 2008 R2 can use Link-Local Multicast Name Resolution (LLMNR) to resolve names on a local network segment when a DNS server is not available. They also periodically search for a domain controller in the domain to which they belong. This functionality helps avoid performance problems that might occur if a network or server failure causes a DNS client to create an association with a distant domain controller located on a slow link rather than a local domain controller. Previously, this association continued until the client was forced to seek a new domain controller, such as when the client computer was disconnected from the network for a long period of time. By periodically renewing its association with a domain controller, a DNS client can reduce the probability that it will be associated with an inappropriate domain controller.

NOTE You can configure a DNS client computer running Windows 7 or Windows Server 2008 R2 to locate the nearest domain controller instead of searching randomly. This can improve performance in networks containing domains that exist across slow links. However, because of the network traffic this process generates, locating the nearest domain controller can have a negative impact on network performance.

Both Windows Server 2008 and Windows Server 2008 R2 support read-only primary zones and the GlobalName zone. To support read-only domain controllers (RODCs), the primary read-only zone is created automatically. When a computer becomes an RODC, it replicates a full read-only copy of all the application directory partitions that DNS uses, including the domain partition, ForestDNSZones, and

DomainDNSZones. This ensures that the DNS server running on the RODC has a full read-only copy of any DNS zones. As an administrator of an RODC, you can view the contents of a primary read-only zone. You cannot, however, change the contents of a zone on the RODC. You can only change the contents of the zone on a standard domain controller.

To support all DNS environments and single-label name resolution, you can create a zone named *GlobalNames*. For optimal performance and cross-forest support, you should integrate this zone with AD DS and configure each authoritative DNS server with a local copy. When you use Service Location (SRV) resource records to publish the location of the GlobalNames zone, this zone provides unique, single-label computer names across the forest. Unlike WINS, the GlobalNames zone is intended to provide single-label name resolution for a subset of host names, typically the CNAME resource records for your corporate servers. The GlobalNames zone is not intended to be used for peer-to-peer name resolution, such as name resolution for workstations. This is what LLMNR is for.

When the GlobalNames zone is configured appropriately, single-label name resolution works as follows:

1. The client's primary DNS suffix is appended to the single-label name that the client is looking up, and the query is submitted to the DNS server.

2. If that computer's full name is not resolved, the client requests resolution using its DNS suffix search lists, if any.

3. If none of those names can be resolved, the client requests resolution using the single-label name.

4. If the single-label name appears in the GlobalNames zone, the DNS server hosting the zone resolves the name. Otherwise, the query fails over to WINS.

The GlobalNames zone provides single-label name resolution only when all authoritative DNS servers are running Windows Server 2008 R2. However, other DNS servers that are not authoritative for any zone can be running other operating systems. Dynamic updates in the GlobalNames zone are not supported.

Understanding DNSSEC

Windows 7 and Windows Server 2008 R2 support DNS Security Extensions (DNSSEC). DNSSEC is defined in several RFCs, including RFCs 4033, 4034, and 4035. These RFCs add origin authority, data integrity, and authenticated denial of existence to DNS. DNSSEC introduces four new resource records:

- DNSKEY (Domain Name System Key)
- RRSIG (Resource Record Signature)
- NSEC (NextSECure)
- DS (Domain Services)

The DNS client running on these operating systems can send queries that indicate support for DNSSEC, process related records, and determine whether a DNS server has validated records on its behalf. On Windows servers, DNSSEC allows your DNS servers to securely sign zones, to host DNSSEC-signed zones, to process related records, and to perform both validation and authentication. The way a DNS client works with DNSSEC is configured through the Name Resolution Policy Table (NRPT), which stores settings that define the DNS client's behavior. Normally, you manage the NRPT through Group Policy.

When a DNS server hosting a signed zone receives a query, the server returns the digital signatures in addition to the requested records. A resolver or another server configured with a trust anchor for a signed zone or for a parent of a signed zone can obtain the public key of the public/private key pair and validate that the responses are authentic and have not been tampered with.

Because of the way DNSSEC works, it may not be the best solution for your organization. Deploying DNSSEC is a multiple-step process that requires the following:

1. Upgrading DNS servers to Windows Server 2008 R2

2. Deploying DNSSEC on your DNS servers

3. Configuring and distributing trust anchors

If you want to use DNSSEC with IP security (IPSec), you also need to configure IPSec policy on your DNS servers and then configure IPSec and DNSSEC on DNS clients.

As part of your predeployment planning, you need to identify the DNS zones to secure with digital signatures. However, because a signed zone will no longer be able to receive dynamic updates, Microsoft does not recommend signing an Active Directory domain zone. If you sign an Active Directory domain zone, you need to manually update all SRV records and other resource records. Keep the following in mind:

- For file-backed zones, the primary server and all secondary servers hosting the zone must be a Windows Server 2008 R2 DNS server or a DNSSEC-aware server that is running an operating system other than Windows.

- For Active Directory–integrated zones, every domain controller that is a DNS server in the domain must be running Windows Server 2008 R2 if the signed zone is set to replicate to all DNS servers in the domain. Every domain controller that is a DNS server in the forest must be running Windows Server 2008 R2 if the signed zone is set to replicate to all DNS servers in the forest.

- For mixed environments, all servers that are authoritative for a DNSSEC-signed zone must be DNSSEC-aware servers. DNSSEC-aware Windows clients that request DNSSEC data and validation must be configured to issue DNS queries to a DNSSEC-aware server. Non-DNSSEC-aware Windows clients can be configured to issue DNS queries to DNSSEC-aware servers. DNSSEC-aware servers can be configured to recursively send queries to a non-DNSSEC-aware DNS server.

Configuring Name Resolution on DNS Clients

The best way to configure name resolution for DNS clients depends on the configuration of your network. If computers use DHCP, you probably want to configure DNS through settings on the DHCP server. If computers use static IP addresses or you want to configure DNS specifically for an individual system, you should configure DNS manually.

You can configure DNS settings on the DNS tab of the Advanced TCP/IP Settings dialog box. To access this dialog box, follow these steps:

1. Open Network And Sharing Center. For computers running Windows 7 or Windows Server 2008 R2, click Change Adapter Settings. For computers running Windows Vista or Windows Server 2008, click Manage Network Connections.

2. In Network Connections, right-click the connection you want to work with, and then click Properties.

3. Double-click Internet Protocol Version 6 (TCP/IPv6) or Internet Protocol Version 4 (TCP/IPv4) depending on the type of IP address you are configuring.

4. If the computer is using DHCP and you want DHCP to specify the DNS server address, select Obtain DNS Server Address Automatically. Otherwise, select Use The Following DNS Server Addresses, and then type primary and alternate DNS server addresses in the text boxes provided.

5. Click Advanced to display the Advanced TCP/IP Settings dialog box. In this dialog box, click the DNS tab.

You use the fields of the DNS tab as follows:

- **DNS Server Addresses, In Order Of Use**   Use this area to specify the IP address of each DNS server that is used for domain name resolution. Click Add if you want to add a server IP address to the list. Click Remove to remove a selected server address from the list. Click Edit to edit the selected entry. You can specify multiple servers for DNS resolution. Their priority is determined by the order. If the first server isn't available to respond to a host name resolution request, the next DNS server in the list is accessed, and so on. To change the position of a server in the list box, select it, and then use the up or down arrow button.

- **Append Primary And Connection Specific DNS Suffixes**   Normally, this option is selected by default. Select this option to resolve unqualified computer names in the primary domain. For example, if the computer name Gandolf is used and the parent domain is microsoft.com, the computer name would resolve to gandolf.microsoft.com. If the fully qualified computer name doesn't exist in the parent domain, the query fails. The parent domain used is the one set on the Computer Name tab in the System Properties dialog box. (Click System And Security\System in Control Panel, click Change Settings, and then display the Computer Name tab to check the settings.)

- **Append Parent Suffixes Of The Primary DNS Suffix** This option is selected by default. Select this option to resolve unqualified computer names using the parent/child domain hierarchy. If a query fails in the immediate parent domain, the suffix for the parent of the parent domain is used to try to resolve the query. This process continues until the top of the DNS domain hierarchy is reached. For example, if the computer name Gandolf is used in the dev.microsoft.com domain, DNS would attempt to resolve the computer name to gandolf.dev.microsoft.com. If this didn't work, DNS would attempt to resolve the computer name to gandolf.microsoft.com.

- **Append These DNS Suffixes (In Order)** Select this option to set specific DNS suffixes to use rather than resolving through the parent domain. Click Add if you want to add a domain suffix to the list. Click Remove to remove a selected domain suffix from the list. Click Edit to edit the selected entry. You can specify multiple domain suffixes, which are used in order. If the first suffix is not resolved properly, DNS attempts to use the next suffix in the list. If this fails, the next suffix is used, and so on. To change the order of the domain suffixes, select the suffix, and then use the up or down arrow button to change its position.

- **DNS Suffix For This Connection** This option sets a specific DNS suffix for the connection that overrides DNS names already configured for use on this connection. You usually set the DNS domain name on the Computer Name tab of the System Properties dialog box.

- **Register This Connection's Addresses In DNS** Select this option if you want all IP addresses for this connection to be registered in DNS under the computer's fully qualified domain name. This option is selected by default.

    NOTE Dynamic DNS updates are used in conjunction with DHCP to enable a client to update its A (Host Address) record if its IP address changes and to enable the DHCP server to update the PTR (Pointer) record for the client on the DNS server. You can also configure DHCP servers to update both the A and PTR records on the client's behalf. Dynamic DNS updates are supported by DNS servers with BIND 8.2.1 or higher as well as Windows 2000 Server, Windows Server 2003, and later server versions of Windows. Windows NT 4 doesn't support this feature.

- **Use This Connection's DNS Suffix In DNS Registration** Select this option if you want all IP addresses for this connection to be registered in DNS under the parent domain.

Installing DNS Servers

You can configure any Windows Server 2008 R2 system as a DNS server. Four types of DNS servers are available:

- **Active Directory–integrated primary server**   A DNS server that's fully integrated with Active Directory. All DNS data is stored directly in Active Directory.

- **Primary server**   The main DNS server for a domain that is partially integrated with Active Directory. This server stores a master copy of DNS records and the domain's configuration files. These files are stored as text files with the .dns extension.

- **Secondary server**   A DNS server that provides backup services for the domain. This server stores a copy of DNS records obtained from a primary server and relies on zone transfers for updates. Secondary servers obtain their DNS information from a primary server when they are started, and they maintain this information until the information is refreshed or expired.

- **Forwarding-only server**   A server that caches DNS information after lookups and always passes requests to other servers. These servers maintain DNS information until it's refreshed or expired or until the server is restarted. Unlike secondary servers, forwarding-only servers don't request full copies of a zone's database files. This means that when you start a forwarding-only server, its database contains no information.

Before you configure a DNS server, you must install the DNS Server service. Then you can configure the server to provide integrated, primary, secondary, or forwarding-only DNS services.

Installing and Configuring the DNS Server Service

All domain controllers can act as DNS servers, and you might be prompted to install and configure DNS during installation of the domain controller. If you respond affirmatively to the prompts, DNS is already installed, and the default configuration is set automatically. You don't need to reinstall.

If you're working with a member server instead of a domain controller, or if you haven't installed DNS, follow these steps to install DNS:

1. In Server Manager, select the Roles node in the left pane, and then click Add Roles. This starts the Add Roles Wizard. If the wizard displays the Before You Begin page, read the Welcome message, and then click Next.

2. On the Select Server Roles page, select DNS Server, and then click Next twice.

3. Click Install. The wizard installs DNS Server. From now on, the DNS Server service should start automatically each time you reboot the server. If it doesn't start, you need to start it manually. (See "Starting and Stopping a DNS Server" later in this chapter.)

4. Start the DNS Manager console. Click Start, point to Administrative Tools, and then click DNS. This displays the DNS Manager console shown in Figure 20-1.

FIGURE 20-1 Use the DNS Manager console to manage DNS servers on the network.

5. If the server you want to configure isn't listed in the tree view, you need to connect to the server. Right-click DNS in the tree view, and then click Connect To DNS Server. Now do one of the following:

- If you're trying to connect to a local server, select This Computer, and then click OK.

- If you're trying to connect to a remote server, select The Following Computer, type the server's name or IP address, and then click OK.

6. An entry for the DNS server should be listed in the tree view pane of the DNS Manager console. Right-click the server entry, and then click Configure A DNS Server. This starts the Configure A DNS Server Wizard. Click Next.

7. On the Select Configuration Action page, shown in Figure 20-2, select Configure Root Hints Only to specify that only the base DNS structures should be created at this time.

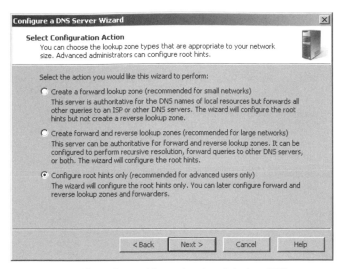

The figure shows a dialog titled:

Configure a DNS Server Wizard

Select Configuration Action
You can choose the lookup zone types that are appropriate to your network size. Advanced administrators can configure root hints.

Select the action you would like this wizard to perform:

○ Create a forward lookup zone (recommended for small networks)
This server is authoritative for the DNS names of local resources but forwards all other queries to an ISP or other DNS servers. The wizard will configure the root hints but not create a reverse lookup zone.

○ Create forward and reverse lookup zones (recommended for large networks)
This server can be authoritative for forward and reverse lookup zones. It can be configured to perform recursive resolution, forward queries to other DNS servers, or both. The wizard will configure the root hints.

● Configure root hints only (recommended for advanced users only)
The wizard will configure the root hints only. You can later configure forward and reverse lookup zones and forwarders.

[< Back] [Next >] [Cancel] [Help]

FIGURE 20-2 Configure the root hints only to install the base DNS structures.

8. Click Next. The wizard searches for existing DNS structures and modifies them as necessary.

9. Click Finish to complete the process.

Configuring a Primary DNS Server

Every domain should have a primary DNS server. You can integrate this server with Active Directory, or it can act as a standard primary server. Primary servers should have forward lookup zones and reverse lookup zones. You use forward lookups to resolve domain names to IP addresses. You need reverse lookups to authenticate DNS requests by resolving IP addresses to domain names or hosts.

After you install the DNS Server service on the server, you can configure a primary server by following these steps:

1. Start the DNS Manager console and connect to the server you want to configure, as described previously.

2. An entry for the DNS server should be listed in the tree view pane of the DNS Manager console. Right-click the server entry, and then click New Zone. This starts the New Zone Wizard. Click Next.

NOTE An alternative to using the DNS Manager console is to use the DNS Server node in Server Manager. Access this node, and then click DNS.

3. As Figure 20-3 shows, you can now select the zone type. If you're configuring a primary server integrated with Active Directory (a domain controller), select Primary Zone and be sure that the Store The Zone In Active Directory check box is selected. If you don't want to integrate DNS with Active Directory, select Primary Zone, and then clear the Store The Zone In Active Directory check box. Click Next.

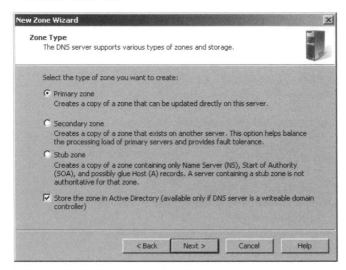

FIGURE 20-3 In the New Zone Wizard, select the zone type.

4. If you're integrating the zone with Active Directory, choose one of the following replication strategies; otherwise, proceed to step 6.

- **To All DNS Servers In This Forest**   Choose this strategy if you want the widest replication strategy. Remember, the Active Directory forest includes all domain trees that share the directory data with the current domain.

- **To All DNS Servers In This Domain**   Choose this strategy if you want to replicate DNS information within the current domain.

- **To All Domain Controllers In This Domain**   Choose this strategy if you want to replicate DNS information to all domain controllers within the current domain. Although this strategy gives wider replication for DNS information within the domain, not every domain controller is a DNS server as well (nor do you need to configure every domain controller as a DNS server).

5. Click Next. Select Forward Lookup Zone, and then click Next.

6. Type the full DNS name for the zone. The zone name should help determine how the server or zone fits into the DNS domain hierarchy. For example, if you're creating the primary server for the microsoft.com domain, you would type **microsoft.com** as the zone name. Click Next.

7. If you're configuring a primary zone that isn't integrated with Active Directory, you need to set the zone file name. A default name for the zone's DNS database file should be filled in for you. You can use this name or type a new file name. Click Next.

8. Specify whether dynamic updates are allowed. You have three options:

   - **Allow Only Secure Dynamic Updates** When the zone is integrated with Active Directory, you can use access control lists (ACLs) to restrict which clients can perform dynamic updates. With this option selected, only clients with authorized computer accounts and approved ACLs can dynamically update their resource records in DNS when changes occur.

   - **Allow Both Nonsecure And Secure Dynamic Updates** Choose this option to allow any client to update its resource records in DNS when changes occur. Clients can be secure or nonsecure.

   - **Do Not Allow Dynamic Updates** Choosing this option disables dynamic updates in DNS. You should use this option only when the zone isn't integrated with Active Directory.

9. Click Next, and then click Finish to complete the process. The new zone is added to the server, and basic DNS records are created automatically.

10. A single DNS server can provide services for multiple domains. If you have multiple parent domains, such as microsoft.com and msn.com, you can repeat this process to configure other forward lookup zones. You also need to configure reverse lookup zones. Follow the steps listed in "Configuring Reverse Lookups" on the next page.

11. You need to create additional records for any computers you want to make accessible to other DNS domains. To do this, follow the steps listed in "Managing DNS Records" later in this chapter.

REAL WORLD Most organizations have private and public areas of their network. The public network areas might be where Web, File Transfer Protocol (FTP), and external e-mail servers reside. Your organization's public network areas shouldn't allow unrestricted access. Instead, public network areas should be configured as part of perimeter networks (also known as *DMZs*, demilitarized zones, and *screened subnets;* these are areas protected by your organization's firewall that have restricted external access and no access to the internal network). Otherwise, public network areas should be in a completely separate and firewall-protected area.

The private network areas are where the organization's internal servers and workstations reside. On the public network areas, your DNS settings are in the public Internet space. Here, you might use a .com, .org, or .net DNS name that you've registered with an Internet registrar and public IP addresses that you've purchased or leased. On the private network areas, your DNS settings are in the private network space. Here, you might use adatum.com as your organization's DNS name and private IP addresses, as discussed in Chapter 17.

Configuring a Secondary DNS Server

Secondary servers provide backup DNS services on the network. If you're using full Active Directory integration, you don't really need to configure secondaries. Instead, you should configure multiple domain controllers to handle DNS services. Active Directory replication will then handle replicating DNS information to your domain controllers. On the other hand, if you're using partial integration, you might want to configure secondaries to lessen the load on the primary server. On a small or medium-size network, you might be able to use the name servers of your Internet service provider (ISP) as secondaries. In this case, you should contact your ISP to configure secondary DNS services for you.

Because secondary servers use forward lookup zones for most types of queries, you might not need reverse lookup zones. But reverse lookup zone files are essential for primary servers, and you must configure them for proper domain name resolution.

If you want to set up your own secondaries for backup services and load balancing, follow these steps:

1. Start the DNS Manager console and connect to the server you want to configure, as described previously.

2. Right-click the server entry, and then click New Zone. This starts the New Zone Wizard. Click Next.

3. For Zone Type, select Secondary Zone. Click Next.

4. Secondary servers can use both forward and reverse lookup zone files. You create the forward lookup zone first, so select Forward Lookup Zone, and then click Next.

5. Type the full DNS name for the zone, and then click Next.

6. Click in the Master Servers list, type the IP address of the primary server for the zone, and then press Enter. The wizard then attempts to validate the server. If an error occurs, be sure the server is connected to the network and that you've entered the correct IP address. If you want to copy zone data from other servers in case the first server isn't available, repeat this step.

7. Click Next, and then click Finish. On a busy or large network, you might need to configure reverse lookup zones on secondaries. If so, follow the steps listed in the next section.

Configuring Reverse Lookups

Forward lookups are used to resolve domain names to IP addresses. Reverse lookups are used to resolve IP addresses to domain names. Each segment on your network should have a reverse lookup zone. For example, if you have the subnets 192.168.10.0, 192.168.11.0, and 192.168.12.0, you should have three reverse lookup zones.

The standard naming convention for reverse lookup zones is to type the network ID in reverse order and then use the suffix in-addr.arpa. With the previous example, you'd have reverse lookup zones named 10.168.192.in-addr.arpa, 11.168.192.in-addr.arpa, and 12.168.192.in-addr.arpa. Records in the reverse lookup zone must be in sync with the forward lookup zone. If the zones get out of sync, authentication might fail for the domain.

You create reverse lookup zones by following these steps:

1. Start the DNS Manager console and connect to the server you want to configure as described previously.

2. Right-click the server entry, and then click New Zone. This starts the New Zone Wizard. Click Next.

3. If you're configuring a primary server integrated with Active Directory (a domain controller), select Primary Zone and be sure that Store The Zone In Active Directory is selected. If you don't want to integrate DNS with Active Directory, select Primary Zone and then clear the Store The Zone In Active Directory check box. Click Next.

4. If you're configuring a reverse lookup zone for a secondary server, select Secondary Zone, and then click Next.

5. If you're integrating the zone with Active Directory, choose one of the following replication strategies:

   - **To All DNS Servers In This Forest**   Choose this strategy if you want the widest replication strategy. Remember, the Active Directory forest includes all domain trees that share the directory data with the current domain.

   - **To All DNS Servers In This Domain**   Choose this strategy if you want to replicate DNS information within the current domain.

   - **To All Domain Controllers In This Domain**   Choose this strategy if you want to replicate DNS information to all domain controllers within the current domain. Although this strategy gives wider replication for DNS information within the domain, not every domain controller is a DNS server as well (and you don't need to configure every domain controller as a DNS server either).

6. Select Reverse Lookup Zone, and then click Next.

7. Choose whether you want to create a reverse lookup zone for IPv4 or IPv6 addresses, and then click Next. Do one of the following:

   - If you are configuring a reverse lookup zone for IPv4, type the network ID for the reverse lookup zone. The values you enter set the default name for the reverse lookup zone. Click Next.

     If you have multiple subnets on the same network, such as 192.168.10 and 192.168.11, you can enter only the network portion for the zone name. For example, in this case you'd use 168.192.in-addr.arpa and allow the DNS Manager console to create the necessary subnet zones when needed.

- If you are configuring a reverse lookup zone for IPv6, type the network prefix for the reverse lookup zone. The values you enter are used to automatically generate the related zone names. Depending on the prefix you enter, you can create up to eight zones. Click Next.

8. If you're configuring a primary or secondary server that isn't integrated with Active Directory, you need to set the zone file name. A default name for the zone's DNS database file should be filled in for you. You can use this name or type a new file name. Click Next.

9. Specify whether dynamic updates are allowed. You have three options:

- **Allow Only Secure Dynamic Updates**   When the zone is integrated with Active Directory, you can use ACLs to restrict which clients can perform dynamic updates. With this option selected, only clients with authorized computer accounts and approved ACLs can dynamically update their resource records in DNS when changes occur.

- **Allow Both Nonsecure And Secure Dynamic Updates**   Choose this option to allow any client to update its resource records in DNS when changes occur. Clients can be secure or nonsecure.

- **Do Not Allow Dynamic Updates**   Choosing this option disables dynamic updates in DNS. You should use this option only when the zone isn't integrated with Active Directory.

10. Click Next, and then click Finish. The new zone is added to the server, and basic DNS records are created automatically.

After you set up the reverse lookup zones, you need to ensure that delegation for the zones is handled properly. Contact your networking team or your ISP to ensure that the zones are registered with the parent domain.

Configuring Global Names

The GlobalNames zone is a specially named forward lookup zone that should be integrated with AD DS. When all the DNS servers for your zones are running Windows Server 2008 or later releases, deploying a GlobalNames zone creates static, global records with single-label names, without relying on WINS. This allows users to access hosts using single-label names rather than fully qualified domain names. You should use the GlobalNames zone when name resolution depends on DNS, such as when your organization is no longer using WINS and you are planning to deploy only IPv6. Because dynamic updates cannot be used to register updates in the GlobalNames zone, you should configure single-label name resolution only for your primary servers.

You can deploy a GlobalNames zone by completing the following steps:

1. In the DNS Manager console, right-click the Forward Lookup Zones node, and then click New Zone. In the New Zone Wizard, click Next to accept the defaults to create a primary zone integrated with AD DS. On the Active Directory Zone Replication Scope page, choose to replicate the zone throughout the forest, and then click Next. On the Zone Name page, enter **GlobalNames** as the zone name. Click Next twice, and then click Finish.

2. On every authoritative DNS server in the forest now and in the future, you need to type the following at an elevated command prompt: **dnscmd *ServerName* /enableglobalnamessupport 1**, where *ServerName* is the name of the DNS server that hosts the GlobalNames zone. To specify the local computer, use a period (.) instead of the server name, such as **dnscmd . /enableglobalnamessupport 1**.

3. For each server that you want users to be able to access using a single-label name, add an alias (CNAME) record to the GlobalNames zone. In the DNS Manager console, right-click the GlobalZones node, select New Alias (CNAME), and then use the dialog box provided to create the new resource record.

NOTE An authoritative DNS server tries to resolve queries in the following order: using local zone data, using the GlobalNames zone, using DNS suffixes, using WINS. For dynamic updates, an authoritative DNS server checks the GlobalNames zone before checking the local zone data.

TIP If you want DNS clients in another forest to use the GlobalNames zone for resolving names, you need to add an SRV resource record with the service name _globalnames._msdcs to that forest's forestwide DNS partition. The record must specify the FQDN of the DNS server that hosts the GlobalNames zone.

Managing DNS Servers

The DNS Manager console is the tool you use to manage local and remote DNS servers. As shown in Figure 20-4, the DNS Manager console's main window is divided into two panes. The left pane allows you to access DNS servers and their zones. The right pane shows the details for the currently selected item. You can work with the DNS Manager console in three ways:

-   Double-click an entry in the left pane to expand the list of files for the entry.
-   Select an entry in the left pane to display details such as zone status and domain records in the right pane.
-   Right-click an entry to display a context menu.

FIGURE 20-4 Manage local and remote DNS servers using the DNS Manager console.

The Forward Lookup Zones and Reverse Lookup Zones folders provide access to the domains and subnets configured for use on this server. When you select domain or subnet folders in the left pane, you can manage DNS records for the domain or subnet.

Adding Remote Servers to the DNS Manager Console

You can use the DNS Manager console to manage servers running DNS by following these steps:

1. Right-click DNS in the console tree, and then click Connect To DNS Server.

2. If you're trying to connect to the local computer, select This Computer. Otherwise, select The Following Computer, and then type the IP address or fully qualified host name of the remote computer you want to connect to.

3. Click OK. Windows Server 2008 R2 attempts to contact the server. If it does, it adds the server to the console.

NOTE If a server is offline or otherwise inaccessible because of security restrictions or problems with the Remote Procedure Call (RPC) service, the connection fails. You can still add the server to the console by clicking Yes when prompted.

Removing a Server from the DNS Manager Console

In the DNS Manager console, you can delete a server by selecting its entry and then pressing Delete. When prompted, click Yes to confirm the deletion. Deleting a server only removes it from the server list in the console tree. It doesn't actually delete the server.

Starting and Stopping a DNS Server

To manage DNS servers, you use the DNS Server service. You can start, stop, pause, resume, and restart the DNS Server service in the Services node of Server Manager or from the command line. You can also manage the DNS Server service in the DNS Manager console. Right-click the server you want to manage in the DNS Manager console, point to All Tasks, and then click Start, Stop, Pause, Resume, or Restart as appropriate.

NOTE In Server Manager, under the DNS Server node, expand the DNS node and then right-click the server you want to work with. On the shortcut menu, point to All Tasks, and then select Start, Stop, Pause, Resume, or Restart as appropriate.

Creating Child Domains Within Zones

Using the DNS Manager console, you can create child domains within a zone. For example, if you create the primary zone microsoft.com, you could create the subdomains hr.microsoft.com and mis.microsoft.com for the zone. You create child domains by following these steps:

1. In the DNS Manager console, expand the Forward Lookup Zones folder for the server you want to work with.
2. Right-click the parent domain entry, and then click New Domain.
3. Enter the name of the new domain, and then click OK. For hr.microsoft.com, you would enter **hr**. For mis.microsoft.com, you would enter **mis**.

Creating Child Domains in Separate Zones

As your organization grows, you might want to organize the DNS namespace into separate zones. At your corporate headquarters, you could have a zone for the parent domain microsoft.com. At branch offices, you could have zones for each office, such as memphis.microsoft.com, newyork.microsoft.com, and la.microsoft.com.

You create child domains in separate zones by following these steps:

1. Install a DNS server in each child domain, and then create the necessary forward and reverse lookup zones for the child domain as described earlier in "Installing DNS Servers."
2. On the authoritative DNS server for the parent domain, you delegate authority to each child domain. Delegating authority allows the child domain to resolve and respond to DNS queries from computers inside and outside the local subnet.

You delegate authority to a child domain by following these steps:

1. In the DNS Manager console, expand the Forward Lookup Zones folder for the server you want to work with.

2. Right-click the parent domain entry, and then click New Delegation. This starts the New Delegation Wizard. Click Next.

3. As shown in Figure 20-5, type the name of the delegated domain, such as **service**, and then click Next. The name you enter updates the value in the Fully Qualified Domain Name text box.

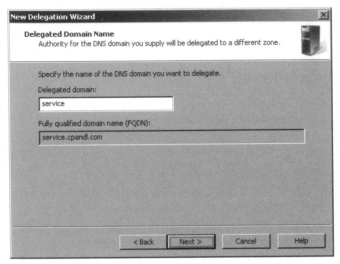

FIGURE 20-5 Entering the name of the delegated domain sets the fully qualified domain name (FQDN).

4. Click Add. This displays the New Name Server Record dialog box.

5. In the Server Fully Qualified Domain Name text box, type the fully qualified host name of a DNS server for the child domain, such as **corpserver01.memphis.adatum.com**, and then click Resolve. The server then performs a lookup query and adds the resolved IP address to the IP Address list.

6. Repeat step 5 to specify additional name servers. The order of the entries determines which IP address is used first. Change the order as necessary by using the Up and Down buttons. When you are ready to continue, click OK to close the New Name Server Record dialog box.

7. Click Next, and then click Finish.

Deleting a Domain or Subnet

Deleting a domain or subnet permanently removes it from the DNS server. To delete a domain or subnet, follow these steps:

1. In the DNS Manager console, right-click the domain or subnet entry.

2. On the shortcut menu, click Delete, and then confirm the action by clicking Yes.

3. If the domain or subnet is integrated with Active Directory, you'll see a warning prompt. Confirm that you want to delete the domain or subnet from Active Directory by clicking Yes.

NOTE Deleting a domain or subnet deletes all DNS records in a zone file but doesn't actually delete the zone file on a primary or secondary server that isn't integrated with Active Directory. The actual zone file remains in the %SystemRoot%\System32\Dns directory. You can delete this file after you have deleted the zones from the DNS Manager console.

Managing DNS Records

After you create the necessary zone files, you can add records to the zones. Computers that need to be accessed from Active Directory and DNS domains must have DNS records. Although there are many types of DNS records, most of these record types aren't commonly used. So rather than focus on record types you probably won't use, let's focus on the ones you will use:

- **A (IPv4 address)**   Maps a host name to an IPv4 address. When a computer has multiple adapter cards, IPv4 addresses, or both, it should have multiple address records.

- **AAAA (IPv6 address)**   Maps a host name to an IPv6 address. When a computer has multiple adapter cards, IPv6 addresses, or both, it should have multiple address records.

- **CNAME (canonical name)**   Sets an alias for a host name. For example, using this record, zeta.microsoft.com can have an alias of www.microsoft.com.

- **MX (mail exchanger)**   Specifies a mail exchange server for the domain, which allows e-mail messages to be delivered to the correct mail servers in the domain.

- **NS (name server)**   Specifies a name server for the domain, which allows DNS lookups within various zones. Each primary and secondary name server should be declared through this record.

- **PTR (pointer)**   Creates a pointer that maps an IP address to a host name for reverse lookups.

- **SOA (start of authority)**   Declares the host that's the most authoritative for the zone and, as such, is the best source of DNS information for the zone. Each zone file must have an SOA record (which is created automatically when you add a zone). Also declares other information about the zone, such as the responsible person, refresh interval, retry interval, and so on.

Adding Address and Pointer Records

You use the A and AAAA records to map a host name to an IP address, and the PTR record creates a pointer to the host for reverse lookups. You can create address and pointer records at the same time or separately.

You create a new host entry with address and pointer records by following these steps:

1. In the DNS Manager console, expand the Forward Lookup Zones folder for the server you want to work with.

2. Right-click the domain you want to update, and then click New Host (A Or AAAA). This opens the dialog box shown in Figure 20-6.

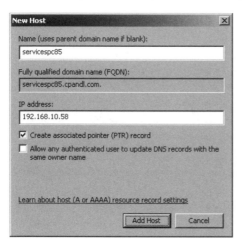

FIGURE 20-6 Create address records and pointer records simultaneously with the New Host dialog box.

3. Type the single-part computer name, such as **servicespc85**, and then the IP address, such as **192.168.10.58**.

4. Select the Create Associated Pointer (PTR) Record check box.

    NOTE You can create PTR records only if the corresponding reverse lookup zone is available. You can create this file by following the steps listed in "Configuring Reverse Lookups" earlier in this chapter. The Allow Any Authenticated User option is available only when a DNS server is configured on a domain controller.

5. Click Add Host, and then click OK. Repeat these steps as necessary to add other hosts.

6. Click Done when you have finished.

Adding a PTR Record Later

If you need to add a PTR record later, you can do so by following these steps:

1. In the DNS Manager console, expand the Reverse Lookup Zones folder for the server you want to work with.

2. Right-click the subnet you want to update, and then click New Pointer (PTR). This opens the dialog box shown in Figure 20-7.

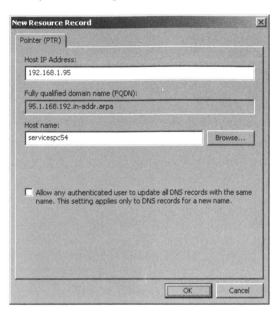

FIGURE 20-7 You can add a PTR record later if necessary with the New Resource Record dialog box.

3. Type the host IP address, such as **192.168.1.95**, and then type the host name, such as **servicespc54**. Click OK.

Adding DNS Aliases with CNAME

You specify host aliases using CNAME records. Aliases allow a single host computer to appear to be multiple host computers. For example, the host gamma.microsoft.com can be made to appear as www.microsoft.com and ftp.microsoft.com.

To create a CNAME record, follow these steps:

1. In the DNS Manager console, expand the Forward Lookup Zones folder for the server you want to work with.

2. Right-click the domain you want to update, and then click select New Alias (CNAME). This opens the dialog box shown in Figure 20-8.

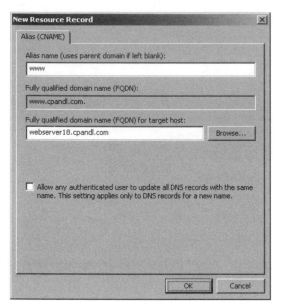

FIGURE 20-8 When you create the CNAME record, be sure to use the single-part host name and then the fully qualified host name.

3. In the Alias Name text box, type the alias. The alias is a single-part host name, such as www or ftp.

4. In the Fully Qualified Domain Name (FQDN) For Target Host text box, type the full host name of the computer for which the alias is to be used.

5. Click OK.

Adding Mail Exchange Servers

MX records identify mail exchange servers for the domain. These servers are responsible for processing or forwarding e-mail within the domain. When you create an MX record, you must specify a preference number for the mail server. A preference number is a value from 0 to 65,535 that denotes the mail server's priority within the domain. The mail server with the lowest preference number has the highest priority and is the first to receive mail. If mail delivery fails, the mail server with the next lowest preference number is tried.

You create an MX record by following these steps:

1. In the DNS Manager console, expand the Forward Lookup Zones folder for the server you want to work with.

2. Right-click the domain you want to update, and then click New Mail Exchanger (MX). This opens the dialog box shown in Figure 20-9.

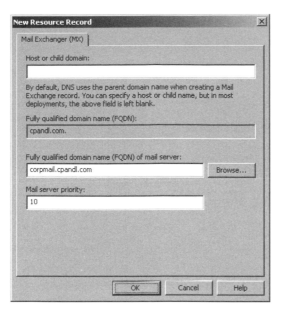

FIGURE 20-9 Mail servers with the lowest preference number have the highest priority.

3. You can now create a record for the mail server by filling in these text boxes:

- **Host Or Child Domain** Using a single-part name, enter the name of the subdomain for which the server specified in this record is responsible. In most cases you will leave this field blank, which specifies that there is no subdomain and the server is responsible for the domain in which this record is created.

- **Fully Qualified Domain Name (FQDN)** Enter the FQDN of the domain to which this mail exchange record should apply, such as **cpandl.com**.

- **Fully Qualified Domain Name (FQDN) Of Mail Server** Enter the FQDN of the mail server that should handle mail receipt and delivery, such as **corpmail.cpandl.com**. E-mail for the previously specified domain is routed to this mail server for delivery.

- **Mail Server Priority** Enter a preference number for the host from 0 to 65,535.

NOTE Assign preference numbers that leave room for growth. For example, use 10 for your highest priority mail server, 20 for the next, and 30 for the one after that.

REAL WORLD You can't enter a multipart name in the Host Or Child Domain text box. If you need to enter a multipart name, you are creating the MX record at the wrong level of the DNS hierarchy. Create or access the additional domain level, and then add an MX record at this level for the subdomain.

4. Click OK.

Adding Name Servers

NS records specify the name servers for the domain. Each primary and secondary name server should be declared through this record. If you obtain secondary name services from an ISP, be sure to insert the appropriate Name Server records.

You create an NS record by following these steps:

1. In the DNS Manager console, expand the Forward Lookup Zones folder for the server you want to work with.

2. Display the DNS records for the domain by selecting the domain folder in the tree view.

3. Right-click an existing Name Server record in the view pane, and then click Properties. This opens the Properties dialog box for the domain with the Name Servers tab selected, as shown in Figure 20-10.

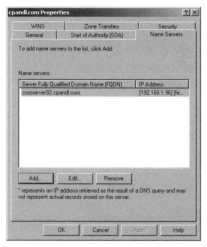

FIGURE 20-10 Configure name servers for the domain through the domain's Properties dialog box.

4. Click Add. This displays the New Name Server Record dialog box.

5. In the Server Fully Qualified Domain Name text box, type the name of a DNS server for the child domain, such as **corpserver01.cpandl.com**, and then click Resolve. The server then performs a lookup query and adds the resolved IP address to the IP Address list.

6. Repeat step 5 to specify additional name servers. The order of the entries determines which IP address is used first. Change the order as necessary using the Up and Down buttons. When you are ready to continue, click OK to close the New Name Server Record dialog box.

7. Click OK to save your changes.

Viewing and Updating DNS Records

To view or update DNS records, follow these steps:

1. Double-click the zone you want to work with. Records for the zone should be displayed in the right pane.

2. Double-click the DNS record you want to view or update. This opens the record's Properties dialog box. Make the necessary changes, and then click OK.

Updating Zone Properties and the SOA Record

Each zone has separate properties that you can configure. These properties set general zone parameters by using the SOA record, change notification, and WINS integration. In the DNS Manager console, you set zone properties by doing one of the following:

- Right-click the zone you want to update, and then click Properties.

- Select the zone, and then click Properties on the Action menu.

The Properties dialog boxes for forward and reverse lookup zones are identical except for the WINS and WINS-R tabs. In forward lookup zones, you use the WINS tab to configure lookups for NetBIOS computer names. In reverse lookup zones, you use the WINS-R tab to configure reverse lookups for NetBIOS computer names.

Modifying the SOA Record

An SOA record designates the authoritative name server for a zone and sets general zone properties, such as retry and refresh intervals. You can modify this information by following these steps:

1. In the DNS Manager console, right-click the zone you want to update, and then click Properties.

2. Click the Start Of Authority (SOA) tab, and then update the text boxes shown in Figure 20-11.

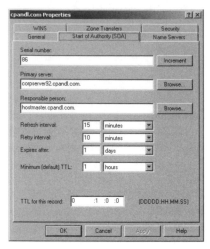

FIGURE 20-11 In the zone's Properties dialog box, set general properties for the zone and update the SOA record.

You use the text boxes on the Start Of Authority (SOA) tab as follows:

- **Serial Number** A serial number that indicates the version of the DNS database files. The number is updated automatically whenever you make changes to zone files. You can also update the number manually. Secondary servers use this number to determine whether the zone's DNS records have changed. If the primary server's serial number is larger than the secondary server's serial number, the records have changed, and the secondary server can request the DNS records for the zone. You can also configure DNS to notify secondary servers of changes (which might speed up the update process).

- **Primary Server** The FQDN for the name server followed by a period. The period is used to terminate the name and ensure that the domain information isn't appended to the entry.

- **Responsible Person** The e-mail address of the person in charge of the domain. The default entry is *hostmaster* followed by a period, meaning hostmaster@your_domain.com. If you change this entry, substitute a period in place of the @ symbol in the e-mail address and terminate the address with a period.

- **Refresh Interval** The interval at which a secondary server checks for zone updates. If the interval is set to 60 minutes, NS record changes might not be propagated to a secondary server for up to an hour. You reduce network traffic by increasing this value.

- **Retry Interval**   The time the secondary server waits after a failure to download the zone database. If the interval is set to 10 minutes and a zone database transfer fails, the secondary server waits 10 minutes before requesting the zone database once more.

- **Expires After**   The period of time for which zone information is valid on the secondary server. If the secondary server can't download data from a primary server within this period, the secondary server lets the data in its cache expire and stops responding to DNS queries. Setting Expires After to seven days allows the data on a secondary server to be valid for seven days.

- **Minimum (Default) TTL**   The minimum TTL value for cached records on a secondary server. The value can be set in days, hours, minutes, or seconds. When this value is reached, the secondary server causes the associated record to expire and discards it. The next request for the record needs to be sent to the primary server for resolution. Set the minimum TTL to a relatively high value, such as 24 hours, to reduce traffic on the network and increase efficiency. Keep in mind that a higher value slows down the propagation of updates through the Internet.

- **TTL For This Record**   The TTL value for this particular SOA record. The value is set in the format Days : Hours : Minutes : Seconds and generally should be the same as the minimum TTL for all records.

Allowing and Restricting Zone Transfers

Zone transfers send a copy of zone information to other DNS servers. These servers can be in the same domain or in other domains. For security reasons, both Windows Server 2008 and Windows Server 2008 R2 disable zone transfers. To enable zone transfers for secondaries you've configured internally or with ISPs, you need to permit zone transfers and then specify the types of server to which zone transfers can be made.

Although you can allow zone transfers with any server, this opens the server to possible security problems. Instead of opening the floodgates, you should restrict access to zone information so that only servers that you've identified can request updates from the zone's primary server. This allows you to funnel requests through a select group of secondary servers, such as your ISP's secondary name servers, and to hide the details of your internal network from the outside world.

To allow zone transfers and restrict access to the primary zone database, follow these steps:

1. In the DNS Manager console, right-click the domain or subnet you want to update, and then click Properties.

2. Click the Zone Transfers tab, as shown in Figure 20-12.

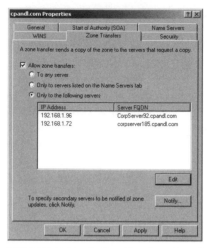

FIGURE 20-12 Use the Zone Transfers tab to allow zone transfers to any server or to designated servers.

3. To restrict transfers to name servers listed on the Name Servers tab, select the Allow Zone Transfers check box, and then choose Only To Servers Listed On The Name Servers Tab.

4. To restrict transfers to designated servers, select the Allow Zone Transfers check box, and then choose Only To The Following Servers. Then click Edit as appropriate to display the Allow Zone Transfers dialog box. Click in the IP Address list, type the IP address of the secondary server for the zone, and then press Enter. Windows then attempts to validate the server. If an error occurs, make sure the server is connected to the network and that you've entered the correct IP address. If you want to copy zone data from other servers in case the first server isn't available, you can add IP addresses for other servers as well. Click OK.

5. Click OK to save your changes.

Notifying Secondaries of Changes

You set properties for a zone with its SOA record. These properties control how DNS information is propagated on the network. You can also specify that the primary server should notify secondary name servers when changes are made to the zone database. To do this, follow these steps:

1. In the DNS Manager console, right-click the domain or subnet you want to update, and then click Properties.

2. On the Zone Transfers tab, click Notify. This displays the dialog box shown in Figure 20-13.

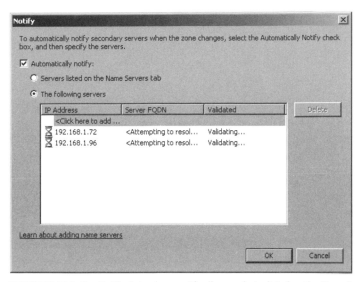

FIGURE 20-13 In the Notify dialog box, notify all secondaries listed on the Name Servers tab or specific servers that you designate.

3. To notify secondary servers listed on the Name Servers tab, select the Automatically Notify check box, and then choose Servers Listed On The Name Servers Tab.

4. If you want to designate specific servers to notify, select the Automatically Notify check box, and then choose The Following Servers. Click in the IP Address list, type the IP address of the secondary server for the zone, and then press Enter. Windows then attempts to validate the server. If an error occurs, make sure the server is connected to the network and that you entered the correct IP address. If you want to notify other servers, add IP addresses for those servers as well.

5. Click OK twice.

Setting the Zone Type

When you create zones, they're designated as having a specific zone type and an Active Directory integration mode. You can change the type and integration mode at any time by following these steps:

1. In the DNS Manager console, right-click the domain or subnet you want to update, and then click Properties.

2. Under Type on the General tab, click Change. In the Change Zone Type dialog box, select the new type for the zone.

3. To integrate the zone with Active Directory, select the Store The Zone In Active Directory check box.

4. To remove the zone from Active Directory, clear the Store The Zone In Active Directory check box.

5. Click OK twice.

Enabling and Disabling Dynamic Updates

Dynamic updates allow DNS clients to register and maintain their own address and pointer records. This is useful for computers dynamically configured through DHCP. By enabling dynamic updates, you make it easier for dynamically configured computers to locate one another on the network. When a zone is integrated with Active Directory, you have the option of requiring secure updates. With secure updates, you use ACLs to control which computers and users can dynamically update DNS.

You can enable and disable dynamic updates by following these steps:

1. In the DNS Manager console, right-click the domain or subnet you want to update, and then click Properties.

2. Use the following options in the Dynamic Updates list on the General tab to enable or disable dynamic updates:

   - **None**   Disable dynamic updates.

   - **Nonsecure And Secure**   Enable nonsecure and secure dynamic updates.

   - **Secure Only**   Enable dynamic updates with Active Directory security. This is available only with Active Directory integration.

3. Click OK.

NOTE   DNS integration settings must also be configured for DHCP. See "Integrating DHCP and DNS" in Chapter 19.

Managing DNS Server Configuration and Security

You use the Server Properties dialog box to manage the general configuration of DNS servers. Through it, you can enable and disable IP addresses for the server and control access to DNS servers outside the organization. You can also configure monitoring, logging, and advanced options.

Enabling and Disabling IP Addresses for a DNS Server

By default, multihomed DNS servers respond to DNS requests on all available network interfaces and the IP addresses they're configured to use.

Through the DNS Manager console, you can specify that the server can answer requests only on specific IP addresses. To do this, follow these steps:

1. In the DNS Manager console, right-click the server you want to configure, and then click Properties.

2. On the Interfaces tab, select Only The Following IP Addresses. Select an IP address that should respond to DNS requests, or clear an IP address that should not respond to DNS requests. Only the selected IP addresses will be used for DNS. All other IP addresses on the server will be disabled for DNS.

3. Click OK.

Controlling Access to DNS Servers Outside the Organization

Restricting access to zone information allows you to specify which internal and external servers can access the primary server. For external servers, this controls which servers can get in from the outside world. You can also control which DNS servers within your organization can access servers outside it. To do this, you need to set up DNS forwarding within the domain.

With DNS forwarding, you configure DNS servers within the domain as one of the following:

- **Nonforwarders** Servers that must pass DNS queries they can't resolve to designated forwarding servers. These servers essentially act like DNS clients to their forwarding servers.

- **Forwarding-only** Servers that can only cache responses and pass requests to forwarders. These are also known as *caching-only* DNS servers.

- **Forwarders** Servers that receive requests from nonforwarders and forwarding-only servers. Forwarders use normal DNS communication methods to resolve queries and to send responses back to other DNS servers.

- **Conditional forwarders** Servers that forward requests based on the DNS domain. Conditional forwarding is useful if your organization has multiple internal domains.

NOTE You can't configure the root server for a domain for forwarding (except for conditional forwarding used with internal name resolution). You can configure all other servers for forwarding.

Creating Nonforwarding and Forwarding-Only Servers

To create a nonforwarding DNS server, follow these steps:

1. In the DNS Manager console, right-click the server you want to configure, and then click Properties.

2. Click the Advanced tab. To configure the server as a nonforwarder, ensure that the Disable Recursion check box is cleared. To configure the server as a forwarding-only server, be sure that the Disable Recursion check box is selected.

3. On the Forwarders tab, click Edit. This displays the Edit Forwarders dialog box.

4. Click in the IP Address list, type the IP address of a forwarder for the network, and then press Enter. Windows then attempts to validate the server. If an error occurs, make sure the server is connected to the network and that you've entered the correct IP address. Repeat this process to specify the IP addresses of other forwarders.

5. Set the Forward Time Out. This value controls how long the nonforwarder tries to query the current forwarder if it gets no response. When the Forward Time Out interval passes, the nonforwarder tries the next forwarder on the list. The default is five seconds. Click OK.

Creating Forwarding Servers

Any DNS server that isn't designated as a nonforwarder or a forwarding-only server will act as a forwarder. Thus, on the network's designated forwarders you should be sure that the Disable Recursion option is not selected and that you haven't configured the server to forward requests to other DNS servers in the domain.

Configuring Conditional Forwarding

If you have multiple internal domains, you might want to consider configuring conditional forwarding, which allows you to direct requests for specific domains to specific DNS servers for resolution. Conditional forwarding is useful if your organization has multiple internal domains and you need to resolve requests between these domains.

To configure conditional forwarding, follow these steps:

1. In the DNS Manager console, select and then right-click the Conditional Forwarders folder for the server you want to work with. Click New Conditional Forwarder on the shortcut menu.

2. In the New Conditional Forwarder dialog box, enter the name of a domain to which queries should be forwarded, such as **adatum.com**.

3. Click in the IP Address list, type the IP address of an authoritative DNS server in the specified domain, and then press Enter. Repeat this process to specify additional IP addresses.

4. If you're integrating DNS with Active Directory, select the Store This Conditional Forwarder In Active Directory check box, and then choose one of the following replication strategies.

   - **All DNS Servers In This Forest** Choose this strategy if you want the widest replication strategy. Remember, the Active Directory forest includes all domain trees that share the directory data with the current domain.

   - **All DNS Servers In This Domain** Choose this strategy if you want to replicate forwarder information within the current domain and child domains of the current domain.

- **All Domain Controllers In This Domain** Choose this strategy if you want to replicate forwarder information to all domain controllers within the current domain and child domains of the current domain. Although this strategy gives wider replication for forwarder information within the domain, not every domain controller is a DNS server as well (nor do you need to configure every domain controller as a DNS server).

5. Set the Forward Time Out. This value controls how long the server tries to query the forwarder if it gets no response. When the Forward Time Out interval passes, the server tries the next authoritative server on the list. The default is five seconds. Click OK.

6. Repeat this procedure to configure conditional forwarding for other domains.

Enabling and Disabling Event Logging

By default, the DNS service tracks all events for DNS in the DNS Server event log. This log records all applicable DNS events and is accessible through the Event Viewer node in Computer Management. This means that all informational, warning, and error events are recorded. You can change the logging options by following these steps:

1. In the DNS Manager console, right-click the server you want to configure, and then click Properties.

2. Use the options on the Event Logging tab to configure DNS logging. To disable logging altogether, choose No Events.

3. Click OK.

Using Debug Logging to Track DNS Activity

You normally use the DNS Server event log to track DNS activity on a server. This log records all applicable DNS events and is accessible through the Event Viewer node in Computer Management. If you're trying to troubleshoot DNS problems, it's sometimes useful to configure a temporary debug log to track certain types of DNS events. However, don't forget to clear these events after you finish debugging.

To configure debugging, follow these steps:

1. In the DNS Manager console, right-click the server you want to configure, and then click Properties.

2. On the Debug Logging tab, shown in Figure 20-14, select the Log Packets For Debugging check box, and then select the check boxes for the events you want to track temporarily.

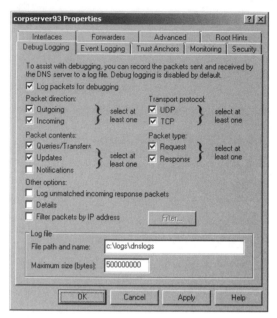

FIGURE 20-14 Use the Debug Logging tab to select the events you want to log.

3. In the File Path And Name text box, enter the name of the log file, such as **dns.logs**. Logs are stored in the %SystemRoot%\System32\Dns directory by default.

4. Click OK. When finished debugging, turn off logging by clearing the Log Packets For Debugging check box.

Monitoring a DNS Server

Windows Server 2008 R2 has built-in functionality for monitoring a DNS server. Monitoring is useful to ensure that DNS resolution is configured properly.

You can configure monitoring to occur manually or automatically by following these steps:

1. In the DNS Manager console, right-click the server you want to configure, and then click Properties.

2. Click the Monitoring tab, shown in Figure 20-15. You can perform two types of tests. To test DNS resolution on the current server, select the A Simple Query Against This DNS Server check box. To test DNS resolution in the domain, select the A Recursive Query To Other DNS Servers check box.

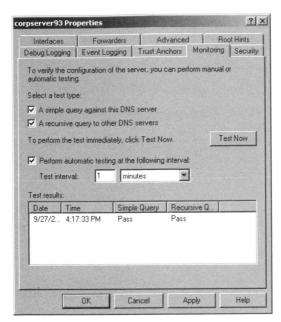

FIGURE 20-15 Configure a DNS server for manual or automatic monitoring on the Monitoring tab.

3. You can perform a manual test by clicking Test Now. You can schedule the server for automatic monitoring by selecting the Perform Automatic Testing At The Following Interval check box and then setting a time interval in seconds, minutes, or hours.

4. The Test Results panel shows the results of testing. You'll see a date and time stamp indicating when the test was performed and a result, such as Pass or Fail. Although a single failure might be the result of a temporary outage, multiple failures normally indicate a DNS resolution problem.

NOTE If all recursive query tests fail, the advanced server option Disable Recursion might be selected. Click the Advanced tab and check the server options.

REAL WORLD If you're actively troubleshooting a DNS problem, you might want to configure testing to occur every 10–15 seconds. This interval will provide a rapid succession of test results. If you're monitoring DNS for problems as part of your daily administrative duties, you'll want a longer time interval, such as two or three hours.

Index

Symbols and Numbers

32-bit operating systems, upgrading not allowed from, 47
64-bit systems only, no 32-bit option, 4, 44

A

access control entries (ACEs), 277
access permissions. *See* permissions
Account Lockout policy, 352
Account Operators group, 291–292
account policies. *See also* Group Policy
  changing with security templates, 192–193
  Default Domain Policy GPO management of, 146
  global user rights configuration, 307–309
  Kerberos policies, 305–307
  lockout policies, 304–305
  password policies, 302–304
  setting, 300–301
  user rights policies, configuring, 307
accounts
  Administrator account, 284–285, 293–294
  computer. *See* computer accounts
  domain. *See* domain user accounts
  group. *See* group accounts
  Guest accounts, 285
  importing and exporting, 346–347
  local. *See* local accounts
  LocalService account, 284
  LocalSystem account, 283–284
  lockout policy, GPO for, 146
  managed service accounts, 318–322
  managed virtual accounts, 318, 322

NetworkService account, 284
policies for. *See* account policies
user. *See* user accounts
ACEs (access control entries), 277
ACPI (Advanced Configuration and Power Interface), 7–10
Action Center, 519
activation, 45, 69, 76
active cooling mode, 7–8
Active Directory
  accessing data of, 227
  adding items with Dsadd, 239
  Adprep, 238–239
  ADSI Edit for maintenance, 231, 240, 269–270
  application directory partitions, 227
  audit policies, setting, 474–475, 478
  authentication mechanism assurance, 16, 214
  Certificate Services, 14–15, 33
  change tracking by, 273
  command-line tools, 238–239
  contact information, user, 323–325
  data stores, 14, 227–228
  dcpromo command, 212
  DHCP server authorization, 596
  directories. *See* data stores
  directory structure overview, 227
  displaying item properties, 239
  DNS integration, 19–20, 211–212, 630–631
  Domain Services. *See* AD DS (Active Directory Domain Services)
  domains, 14
  domains, relationships of, 215–216
  Dsadd, 239
  Dsget, 239
  Dsmod, 239
  Dsmove, 239
  Dsquery, 232, 239, 265, 352
  Dsrm, 239

exporting objects, 346–347
Federation Services. *See* AD FS (Active Directory Federation Services)
global catalogs, 222, 228–229
Group Policy, relationship to, 136–137
importing objects, 346–347
Installation Wizard, 221, 254–255
installing, 212
legacy server operating systems with, 221
Lightweight Directory Services, 15, 33
maintenance of, 269–272
managed service accounts, 16, 214
managed virtual accounts, 214
modifying item properties, 239
multimaster replication model, 222
new features for R2, 15–16, 213–214
non-server operating systems with, 221
Ntdsutil, 239, 523
offline domain join feature, 16, 214
overview of, 14–18
permissions, setting, 353–355
ports used by, 273
printer listings, 572
queries, saved, 242
recovery of, 523
Recycle Bin, 16, 213–214, 233–236
removing objects from, 239
replication. *See* replication of directory data
replication partitions, 227
Restartable Active Directory Domain Services, 16–18
restore mode, 18
Rights Management Services (AD RMS), 15, 33
schema data, 228
schema master role transfers, 257

About the Author

WILLIAM R. STANEK (*williamstanek.com*) has more than 20 years of hands-on experience with advanced programming and development. He is a leading technology expert, an award-winning author, and a pretty-darn-good instructional trainer. Over the years, his practical advice has helped millions of programmers, developers, and network engineers all over the world. He has written more than 100 books. Current books include *Active Directory Administrator's Pocket Consultant, Windows Group Policy Administrator's Pocket Consultant, Windows 7 Administrator's Pocket Consultant,* and *Windows Server 2008 Inside Out.*

William has been involved in the commercial Internet community since 1991. His core business and technology experience comes from more than 11 years of military service. He has substantial experience in developing server technology, encryption, and Internet solutions. He has written many technical white papers and training courses on a wide variety of topics. He frequently serves as a subject matter expert and consultant.

William has a BS in computer science, magna cum laude, and an MS with distinction in information systems. He is proud to have served in the Persian Gulf War as a combat crewmember on an electronic warfare aircraft. He flew on numerous combat missions into Iraq and was awarded nine medals for his wartime service, including one of the United States of America's highest flying honors, the Air Force Distinguished Flying Cross. Currently, he resides in the Pacific Northwest with his wife and children.

William recently rediscovered his love of the great outdoors. When he's not writing, teaching, or making presentations, he can be found hiking, biking, backpacking, traveling, or trekking in search of adventure.

Follow William on Twitter at *twitter.com/WilliamStanek.*

What do you think of this book?

We want to hear from you!
To participate in a brief online survey, please visit:

microsoft.com/learning/booksurvey

Tell us how well this book meets your needs—what works effectively, and what we can do better. Your feedback will help us continually improve our books and learning resources for you.

Thank you in advance for your input!

Microsoft®
Press

Stay in touch!

To subscribe to the *Microsoft Press*® *Book Connection Newsletter*—for news on upcoming books, events, and special offers—please visit:

microsoft.com/learning/books/newsletter